THE WEST

From the advent of Christendom to the eve
of Reformation

ARCHITECTURE IN CONTEXT is dedicated to my wife Juliet, without whose support – spiritual and material – it would never have been realized.
CT

THE WEST

From the advent of Christendom to the eve of Reformation

Christopher Tadgell

Routledge
Taylor & Francis Group

ARCHITECTURE IN CONTEXT IV

First published 2009 by Routledge
2 Park Square, Milton Park, Abingdon, Oxon, OX14 4RN

Simultaneously published in the USA and Canada by Routledge
270 Madison Avenue, New York, NY10016

Routledge is an imprint of the Taylor & Francis Group, an informa business

© 2009 Christopher Tadgell

Series design by Claudia Schenk
Image processing and drawings by Mark Wilson
pictures 1.174a, 1.174b by Daniel Mallo; picture 3.144a by Daniel Banks
Printed and bound by Replika Press Pvt Ltd, Sonipat, India

British Library Cataloguing in Publication Data
A catalogue record for this book is available from the British Library
Library of Congress Cataloging-in-Publication Data
A catalogue record for this book has been requested

ISBN13 978–0–415–40754–0

CONTENTS

In the text, AIC1 indicates a reference to *Antiquity: Origins, Classicism and the New Rome*, volume 1 in this series; AIC2 indicates a reference to volume 2, *The East: Buddhists, Hindus and the Sons of Heaven*; AIC3 indicates a reference to volume 3, *Islam: From Medina to the Maghreb and from the Indies to Istanbul*.

1.1

›ARCHITECTURE IN CONTEXT »RENOVATION OF GRAVITAS

PART 1 RENOVATION OF GRAVITAS

1.2

>**1.1 AUTUN, CATHEDRAL OF S. LAZARE,** from c. 1120: west portal with Christ in Judgement.

The portal, one of the most splendid in France and enhanced by its dramatic position in the open narthex at the head of a flight of steps, is attributed to Gisleber-tus, who worked at Cluny.

>**1.2 S. AUGUSTINE, DE CIVITATE DEI,** C. 1100: frontispiece (Florence, Laurentian Library, ms Canterbury).

Converting Platonic metaphysics – and the Pythagorean mysticism which lay at its heart – to Christianity, S. Augustine saw the City of God in terms of perfect number deduced from music. In his treatise on music, *De musica*, he defined the science of modulation in the arithmetical terms of ratio: the relationship between units of common measure or module in accordance with Pythagoras, especially the determination of the divine significance of the four numbers of the tetractys as 1:1, 1:2, 2:3, 3:4 (symmetry, octave, fifth and fourth). As the intervals of the monochord are marked off by divisions on a string, their ratios may be represented as linear proportions which, in turn, may readily be seen as applicable to the visual arts. Indeed, subscribing to the Pythagorean concept of cosmic order as based on these ratios – of beauty as God-given number – S. Augustine was bound to hear the eternal harmony of the divine in perfectly modulated music and to see it mirrored in architecture based on the same modulations: as music led reason towards the comprehension of God, so the church built in consonance with musical number must approximate God's City.

>**1.3 EPISCOPAL HIERARCHY AT THE EUCHARIST:** 10th-century Ottonian ivory book spine cover (Frankfurt, University Library).

PROLOGUE

The 'middle ages' were defined by 15th-century Italians to distinguish the essentially Christian period of European development between the destruction of Rome by northern barbarians and the rebirth of its humanist values in their time. Both positive and negative, the barbarian contribution was crucial, yet the basis for the political and spiritual life of that medieval era – and much beyond it – had been laid between the reigns of Diocletian (284–305) and Constantine the Great (306–337), nearly two centuries before the fall of the last emperor in the west (see AICI, pages 560, 665ff). Further, though the Christian imperative in art was contrary to Classical convention, early Christian architecture was still essentially Roman and in its emulation of empire, not least in symbolic architecture, the second half of the first Christian millennium was no less essentially Romanesque.

1.3

AUTHORITY IN EUROPE AFTER THE COLLAPSE OF ROME

Observing the terminal decline of Rome from a distance, S. Augustine (354–430) – bishop of Hippo in Tunisia – contrasted the vitality of Christianity with the mortality of paganism in terms of two cities, temporal and spiritual, in his great treatise *De civitate dei* (The City of God, 413–26).[1.2] He predicted that the order of Christ's city would prevail over the most eminent of earthly ones. Rome fell within 40 years of Augustine's death and the church found itself the sole instrument of supranational unity.

The disintegration of the empire under the onslaught of the barbarians naturally involved the disruption of the urban society on which it was based, and towns were in decline throughout Europe well before the abdication of Romulus Augustulus in 476. Vandal and Muslim pirates disrupted trade, the insecurity of government made land communications dangerous, the distribution and supply of goods and services could no longer be effected even on a provincial scale. Local self-sufficiency and barter replaced the urban interdependence of an international economy.

The basic unit of Roman provincial administration subsisted, though the town at its centre withered along with imperial authority as it became a rural district grouped with others under a 'duke' whose role combined those of Diocletian's diocesan vicar and the regional military commander (*dux*) – but now, of course, without effective control. On the other hand, the apostolic authority of the Catholic Church and the episcopal hierarchy of its dioceses and provinces, which had doubled the secular establishment, had emerged largely intact from the debacle – except in the peripheral reaches which had yet to be secured to the faith.[1.3]

Preserved too was much property, ecclesiastical and secular. The Church had been endowed lavishly since

Constantine promoted imperial faith in Christ. Sometimes church land was sequestered by the new rulers who had emerged from among the warrior leaders of the peripatetic German tribes and who, settled, needed land to sustain their pretensions – and endow their followers. More often land was appropriated from the declining or defunct estates of the old Roman nobility whose wealth and significance had grown at the expense of smallholders taxed out of existence in the pursuit of past imperial ambition. Powers to be reckoned with still, their scions had local experience which was invaluable to the intruders and their ancient tenure was often confirmed in return for service. The old and new elites merged soon enough: their descendants were the progenitors of the magnates whose power waxed in the recurrent ages of tenuous kingship.

MAGNATES AND FEUDALISM

Feudalism has many characteristics and feudal systems vary widely within and beyond Europe, but fragmented polity and economy are the norm. Within Europe feudal society evolved over many generations, ad hoc, and there were important regional differences. Yet at the risk of oversimplification – and of anachronism – it is convenient here to postulate the typical as it developed over the half-millennium from the disintegration of the western empire.

In early medieval Europe – as in the late empire and many other disintegrating polities – the failure of intra-urban economy led to local self-sufficiency on the subsistence level, with poor husbandry keeping most of the population on the land and commodity exchange limited to barter in the absence of a practicable transport system or any generally current coinage. And without state protection, dependence was on personal bond. The serf tied to the land was inherited from the destitution of the late empire, and the ever-present threat of reduction to serf-

›1.4 INVESTITURE AND HOMAGE: French 13th-century ms (London, British Library).

›1.5 THE MODEL MEDIEVAL MANOR (Bayeux, Tapestry Museum).
  The basic unit of feudal society: the manor with church and hall dominates the village community of the peasants who grow the crops and provide the soldiers. Owing allegiance to the overlord in his castle, the manor was defended against local trouble.

1.5

dom drove vulnerable freemen to accept the bond of a lord for protection as his vassal. Most paid in labour, but the more substantial – secular and ecclesiastical – surrendered land in return and often received it back as a benefice ('fief', Latin *feudum*, hence feudalism).[1.4] Beneath the secular magnates were the vassals entrusted with the manors on which power was based: they might be younger sons or lesser relatives but in general they were distinguished retainers in their liege's household rewarded for exceptional service – as their lord had been rewarded by the overlord. As lords of the manor, they attained a significant degree of freedom in its government from the manor house, with their household maintained from the proceeds of the manorial estate, ultimately supplemented by tolls on roads or rivers and licence fees for stalls at fairs.

  In the fragmented political and economic circumstances of the feudal age, the value of the manor lay primarily in the men whose services could be secured from it and only secondarily in the product of its inefficient agriculture. Its dependants were bound to it by varying degrees of obligation stemming from economic necessity, but if by the end of the 10th century most could still be called serfs, they were not actually slaves: it was the right to a man's services that the lord owned, not the man himself. The majority (villeins or poorer cottagers) were descended from the freemen of the Roman countryside, bound to remain on the land for tax purposes, or from free peasant cultivators of barbarian origin and from freed slaves.

  Farmers though they were, serfs and villeins lived life in communities for protection: the manor house and church were set in a walled compound which offered resort in time of trouble.[1.5] Agriculture was a communal activity too. In the most fertile parts of Europe the small enclosures of the Iron Age had given way to open fields in large blocks. These were cultivated by the cumbersome ox-drawn plough, which was difficult to manoeuvre and therefore impracticable on narrow plots. Crop rotation, in the lack of fertilizers, and drainage also demanded communal organization, and pasture, woodland and water resources were held in common.

Villeins had some sort of proprietary right over plots distinguished from the lord's personal holdings but were bonded to sow and reap the lord's crops and in principle all property reverted to him on its holder's death. They were subject to his will in all matters and he administered justice to them in place of the ancient county courts. But custom, ultimately proclaimed by the assembly of tenants in the lord's court, moderated this: his rights to their labour and property were fixed – with infinite variation, of course, immensely complicating the pattern of high-feudal relationships already complicated by the disparate rights and duties agreed between lord and overlord. The lord's power was also mitigated by close contact with his servants: there was little privacy in the communal hall of the manor, where many people of varied station ate and even slept together.

WARLORDS AND LAIRS

It was with the transformation of military duty into personal privilege, above all, that the Roman concept of public authority would be lost to feudal chaos. The finest professional army the world had seen maintained the Roman empire even for some time after it depended on the admission of men from the barbarian tribes it was principally dedicated to containing. But professional armies must be regularly paid and capable of rapid movement over long distances: both, of course, were impossible after the breakdown of Roman administration and the degradation of the Roman road system. Instead the barbarian kings deployed peasants conscripted from the land ceded to their magnates. The dual disadvantages are obvious: untrained

1.6

>1.6 CHINON, CHÂTEAU FORT: general view from the west.

>1.7 RHEINDIEBACH, FÜRSTENBERG, BURG-FRIED.

An early tower was renovated around 1220 and incorporated in a more extensive complex built by the archbishop of Cologne to protect his Bacharach estate.

1.7

and ill-equipped, the troops were available only for forty days per year, from late autumn to early spring when they could be spared from the fields; overweening, the power of the providers waxed at the expense of their benefactors who sapped their strength squabbling over the incessant division of their domains in accordance with tribal custom.

The four-square Roman camp, expansive of aspect, vanished with the legions which had kept much of Europe under control for so long – if it had not, in fact, become a depressed town – and in the 'Dark Ages' that followed the fall of the empire in the West those with means retreated to towers on inaccessible crags. The contrast in mentality behind these two types of military architecture is stark. The former is positive and aggressive, easy to enter and leave on its open site, and asserts confident authority. The latter is negative and defensive, providing for retreat through a succession of enclosures behind rings of walls and beyond a range of obstacles along a tortuous line of approach. But it is also vulnerable in its isolation and ultimately is at the mercy of outside forces – whether hostile ones demanding submission or friendly ones bringing relief.

In all civilizations from the earliest times this recourse has been obvious to those concerned with defence and a mean was developed between the two extremes – especially in Europe. The line descends from the great citadels of the Mycenaean age to the castle of Euryalus built to protect Syracuse on the east coast of Sicily, to Byzantine Saone in Syria and its European peers such as Chinon in western France.[1.6] As secure bases for defending territory, rather than retreats of last resort, these were certainly not without arrogance. More typical of the Dark Age norm, and descended from the ubiquitous watchtower, is the *burgfried* that crowns so many crags along the Rhine; not originally built of durable masonry, few survive in their primitive state.[1.7]

MONASTICISM AND CONVERSION

The expansion of the church depended on the monastery. Imported into Europe from Egypt before the end of the 4th century (AICI, page 672), monasticism was taken deep into Gaul in the wake of S. Denis (bishop of Paris, patron of France, martyred c. 250) by S. Martin, who established a community near Poitiers c. 365 and as bishop of Tours from 371 went on to found the monastery of Marmoutier-les-Tours. Another established near Cannes in the early 5th century by S. Honoratus, future archbishop of Arles, was a major centre of ecclesiastical education. Monks who graduated from there took the monastic ideal with them beyond Gaul as far as Ireland, where S. Patrick is believed to have introduced the faith in the mid-5th century.

The monastic communities of western Europe were largely unregulated until the 6th century when S. Benedict of Nursia (c. 480–547) – who was educated in, but retreated from, the decadence of post-imperial Rome – established his order at Monte Cassino in southern Italy (AICI, pages 672f).**1.8** Founded on earlier rules, but rejecting the extreme austerity of the first eastern communities, it is notable for its moderation and compassion in admitting basic human needs and acknowledging human weakness. It requires poverty, chastity, humility and communal harmony in complete commitment to the daily routine of four hours of study, five of labour, six of prayer, eight of sleep and absolute obedience to the authority of the abbot.

Discipline and benevolent authoritarianism recommended S. Benedict's rule to monasteries throughout Europe, dedicated to winning Rome's vanquishers. It was to the barbarian tribal leaders that Catholic monks went out to address themselves, knowing that to win the chief would win the tribe. Naturally, the task was easier in Romanized areas where Christianity was entrenched and the new rulers saw it as part of a superior culture.

1.8 S. BENEDICT CONVEYING HIS ORDER: 11th-century ms recension of 6th-century biography (Monte Cassino).

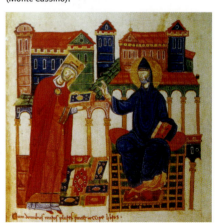

1.9a   1.9b

1.9 THE EARLY CHRISTIAN IRISH CROSS:
(a) Ahenny, South Cross (early 8th century); (b) Clon-
macnois, 'Cross of the Scriptures' (late-9th century).

S. Patrick had introduced the church to Ireland in
the 5th century. S. Columba probably founded the
monastery at Kells in 554 and planted his seminal community on Iona in 563; its Christian missionaries reinforced the faith among the northern Celts, though
monasticism had probably already reached Ireland.
With no tradition of government imposed by Romans
and no towns, the monasteries were the island's communal centres – spiritual and temporal, if the two may
be distinguished under the circumstances.

The potent focus of most monastic sites was a freestanding cross incised with icons of the faith in the context of fantastic curvilinear, asymmetrical abstract
motifs of abstruse symbolism. More than seventy
stone survivors date from the four centuries after c. 700
but they are generally believed to follow timber examples derived from the tradition of the processional
cross: of varied size and form – the most impressive are
identified as 'high crosses' – they are characteristically
endowed with a halo around the junction of post and
beam.

The early churches were simple timber structures,
though parabolic vaults rising from the ground in
corbelled masonry appear c. 700 – as at Gallarus in
County Dingle.

The most significant gain was the conversion of the
Frankish chief Clovis to the orthodox Catholicism of
Rome rather than to the Arianism favoured by other barbarian rulers (AICI, pages 676f).[1.10] That was c. 500. In 587
the Visigothic king in Iberia, Reccared I (586–601), also
converted from Arianism to Catholic Christianity. A generation later Gregory the Great sent Augustine to convert
the Anglo-Saxons, who seem to have eradicated whatever
gains the Christians had made against the strong tradition
of Celtic paganism under remote Roman rule. In the
meantime, the vigorous Irish monks of S. Columba's circle (c. 521–97) had gone forth to convert the Picts in Scotland and to take the faith into England from the north.
Many were to go much further and lead successful missions to central Europe – such as S. Columbanus (550–615)
and his followers, one of whom founded the great abbey
of S. Gall in Switzerland.[1.9, 1.27]

MEROVINGIA AND ITS CONTEMPORARIES

Tribes of Salian Franks settled on the lower Rhine in the
early 4th century and founded several principalities. Initially allied to Rome, Childeric I, son of Merovech, had led
the principality of Tournai to dominance. His son, Clovis
I (480–511), overawed his rivals and established a kingdom
based on Paris, which confronted the Burgundians and the
Visigoths of Aquitaine. The former eluded him, but the
latter fell c. 507 and Visigothic Provence was taken by the
Ostrogoths under their king, Theodoric (471–526).

The new Salian state, called Merovingian after Clovis's
grandfather, was recognized by the eastern emperor. Having embraced Catholicism, Clovis naturally advanced the
cause of the pope, though he asserted the right to appoint
the bishops in his realm. To contain both ecclesiastical and
secular magnates, he obviated the unrestricted beneficence

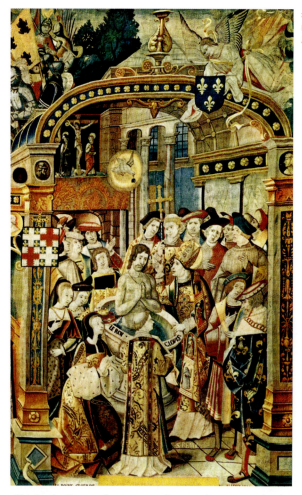

of his barbarian predecessors and granted estates and public offices to be held under contract only for the lifetime of
tenants – but, of course, effecting reversion to the crown
depended on the strength of its wearer.

On his death in 511, Clovis's kingdom was divided in
accordance with Frankish tradition between his four sons
– roughly equitably but not viably – and as brothers died
or were eliminated their lands were assimilated by the survivors. In alliance with Theodoric they overcame Bur-

gundy, and after the death of the great Ostrogoth in 526 Provence and Thuringia were acquired. A dependent duchy of Bavaria was established in 555. The extended kingdom was reunited under Clotaire I in 558 but divided again on his death three years later, and the resurgence of rivalry between the legatees fatally weakened them.

Gascons, pushed north from the Pyrenees by the Visigoths of Iberia, occupied the south-west. The Lombards, who had displaced the Ostrogoths in north Italy, raided the south-east. The Asiatic Avars, who crossed the Danube in the east about the time of Clotaire's triumph, were attacking Thuringia before the century was out and the Bavarians were asserting independence.

By the beginning of the 7th century the Merovingian domains were coalescing into two new states: Austrasia in western Germany and Neustria in northern Gaul. The two were reunited under Clotaire II in 613 but to secure support he ceded considerable power and fiscal privileges to the church and the secular magnates. After Dagobert I (629–39), the last effective Merovingian, a succession of weak rulers retained a fictional imperium but real power was wielded by the principal officers of state, the mayors of the palaces of Austrasia and Neustria.

In 687 the mayor of the palace of Austrasia, Pepin of Herstal, defeated his Neustrian peer and gained northern Gaul – still nominally under the Merovingian king. In 711, three years before Pepin's death, Muslim forces crossed from north-west Africa: led by the Umayyad prince who had escaped the massacre of his confrères at Damascus, they quickly overcame the Visigothic rulers of Rome's former provinces in the peninsula and established themselves at Córdoba. Within twenty years they had taken much of Aquitaine from the Neustrians. Meanwhile, Thuringia had been lost by Austrasia to the Avars and Provence was virtually independent.

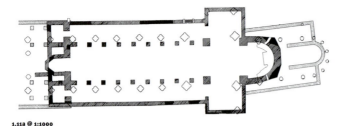

CHURCH BUILDING IN THE MEROVINGIAN ERA: GAUL

After the conversion of Clovis I, the Merovingians replaced temples with impressive churches on many of France's enduringly important sacred sites – not least on the northern approach to Paris, where Childeric I established the abbey of S. Denis c. 475 as the mausoleum of his father, the Merovingian progenitor. The widespread conversion of sites proliferated and despite the paucity of remains it is clear that antique buildings provided foundation and quarry for Christian ones.

Early Christian church planning north of the Alps, as south, typically followed the basilican formula. All the most important churches have been rebuilt many times,

1.11b

›1.11 EARLY CHRISTIAN REMAINS IN THE LANDS OF THE MEROVINGIANS AND THEIR PREDECESSORS: (a) S. Denis, plan of Merovingian foundations c. 475; (b) Tours, S. Martin, reconstruction of mid-5th-century basilica; (c) Poitiers, S. Jean, exterior (mid-4th-century base walls, 7th-century superstructure and apses, 11th-century porch).

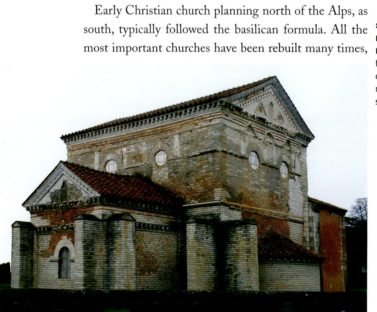

1.11c

of course. The oldest Christian building in France is the mid-4th-century baptistry of S. Jean, Poitiers, but the contemporary foundations of S. Bertrand de Comminges (in the foothills of the Pyrenees) represent the implanting of a great tradition. The abbey church of S. Denis (c. 475) and the contemporary S. Martin at Tours were its most prestigious representatives.[1.11a,b] The latter reveals that instead of the freestanding belfry common south of the Alps, towers were built over the crossing and on to the west end, not only to house the bells which advertised the times of mass, but also to provide the vertical aspiration which was so characteristic of northern architecture.[1.11c]

SPAIN

Little remains from the earliest years of Visigothic Spain, but there are several survivals – in whole or in part – from the period between the conversion of the nation under Reccared I in 587 and the triumph of the Muslims in 711. The crypt of Palencia cathedral is perhaps the most

1.12a

monumental of these. The most complete is the basilican church of S. Juan Bautista at Baños de Cerrato on the southern outskirts of Palencia. Other notable examples include the Greek-cross church of S. Comba de Bande (Ourense) and the Latin-cross variants of S. Pedro de la

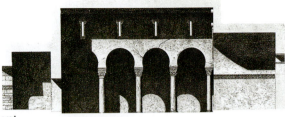

1.12d

1.12b

1.12c

>**1.12 VISIGOTHIC SURVIVALS IN SPAIN:**
(a) Palencia, cathedral of S. Antolín, crypt (c. 670); (b) funerary stele (2nd century, Burgos Museum); (c–g) Baños de Cerrato, S. Juan Bautista (built at the Roman spa by King Recceswinth in 661 in gratitude for a cure), east window detail, section, exterior from west, interior and plan; (h, i) Baños de Bande, S. Comba (672), plan and interior; (j, k) Quintanilla de las Viñas, S. María (late-7th century), exterior and detail of debased Classical interlace mouldings on external masonry bands.

1.12e

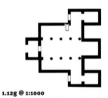
1.12g @ 1:1000   1.12h @ 1:1000

1.12f

1.12i

Nave (Zamora) and S. María at Quintanilla las Viñas (south-east of Burgos). The reuse of Roman materials, particularly columns, is characteristic. The crypt at Palencia has semicircular transverse arches, Roman in their gravitas. Barrel-vaulted or timber-roofed, the other examples are distinguished by varying degress of incurvature at the springing of the arches of doors, windows and arcades.

The 'horseshoe' form of arch may reflect divine symbolism or it may derive from the rough provincial building of the late-imperial period, but a seminal example is elusive. It made a precocious appearance in the early Christian architecture of Anatolia, where symbolic intent is not unlikely (AICI, pages 740f): this could have been known to the Ostrogoths and transmitted by them to the West but no obvious link is to be found where it might be expected, in the works of Theodoric at Ravenna (AICI, page 707). More plausibly, if the Visigoths were not simply dependent on the unrefined practice of their late imperial predecessors, they may have been inspired by the motifs of late-Roman funerary stelai in Iberia. Thus, potent symbolism may have promoted the evolution of similar forms coincidentally in the East and the West.[1.12]

1.12k

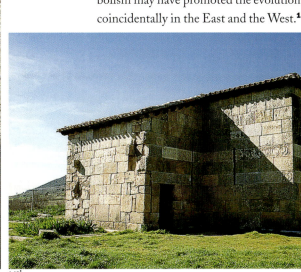

1.12j

BRITAIN

Little of substance remains of the very early Irish church, but chapel-shaped reliquaries – of imprecise date – offer some compensation. England has fared better though it is the word, not the wall, which represents the greatest legacy of the most important centres of Christianity implanted by missionaries from Ireland and Scotland – Lindisfarne, founded by S. Aidan of Iona c. 635, above all.**1.13a,b**

The conversion of pagan sites in the south began in the Canterbury of Pope Gregory's emissary, S. Augustine – though there were small Christian basilicas like the one at Silchester by the end of the 4th century. The builders in Augustine's train probably produced an aisled basilica of the type familiar to them in Rome for the first cathedral, which is known to have had a sanctuary raised over a crypt like S. Pietro in Vaticano. For the totally new church of S. Augustine's abbey, to the east of the cathedral, the aisles of the standard basilica ceded to compartments. This was not unique – there were compartments at S. Bertrand de Comminges – but was characteristic of the early English church.

In general, especially in the north, early Anglo-Saxon churches were simple halls and instead of an apse there would often only be a small chancel projecting from the end opposite the door: composition was an additive exercise often extending to a porch over which a tower might be built. Escomb in County Durham or the earliest remains at Jarrow – the refuge of the Venerable Bede, who wrote his history of the Church in England there c. 700 – are prime examples of this nave-and-chancel type from which many English churches descend. However, there was a more complex alternative which seems to have established itself in the aura of Canterbury: there are early traces above foundation level at Reculver in east Kent (c. 670) but the most substantial survivor is the late-7th-century church at Brixworth in Northamptonshire.**1.13c–g**

1.13a

1.13 EARLY CHRISTIAN SURVIVALS IN BRITAIN: (a) Irish reliquary shrine, (enamel on bronze over yew, 7th–9th centuries; Boston, Museum of Fine Arts); (b) English book illustration (Lindisfarne

1.13b

Gospels, c. 700; London, British Library); (c) Escomb (late-7th century), plan; (d) Reculver (c. 670), plan; (e–g) Brixworth, All Saints (founded late-7th century, much reworked in the 9th century and later), plan, exterior and interior.

Originally monastic, Brixworth was exceptionally large, its nave flanked with aisles or chapels: spur wall foundations between the nave arches make the latter the more probable and, therefore, of the type represented earlier at Reculver. Beyond a square presbytery, the chancel seems to have been apsidal from the outset – the ambulatory is later. The tower was originally of

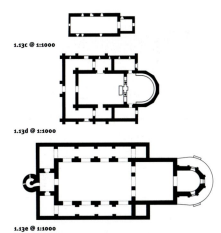

1.13c @ 1:1000

1.13d @ 1:1000

1.13e @ 1:1000

two storeys and probably gabled. The monastery was devastated by the Danes in the 9th century: when the church was restored for parish use in the 10th century the side spaces and ambulatory were abandoned but the western tower was raised and given a circular stair-turret. The apsidal chancel was replaced by a square one in the 15th century but was restored in 1865.

1.13f

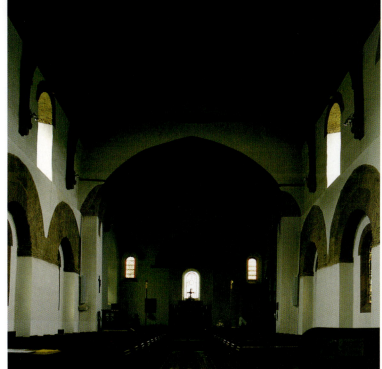

1.13g

1.14

1.1 EMPIRE REGAINED AND RELAPSED

1 CAROLINGIAN ACHIEVEMENT

PROGENITORS

By the early 8th century the monastic orders had built the
faith in western Europe into a bulwark against Muslim
iconoclastic fervour, from which a new force was able to
turn the tide of invasion. In 714 Charles Martel, Pepin of
Herstal's illegitimate son, had seized the initiative, soundly
defeating the Neustrians again, asserting his authority over
northern Gaul and restoring Frankish dominion in the
south. He then turned to confront the advancing Muslims
and repulsed them at Poitiers in 732. Charles reclaimed the
south-west and went on to frustrate Muslim designs on
Provence. He then reasserted Frankish authority over the
Germans east to Thuringia and south in Bavaria.

On his death in 741 his domain was divided between his
sons, Carloman and Pepin the Short. In 747, after widespread rebellion, Carloman resigned his inheritance to his
brother, who reasserted control, deposed the last of the
Merovingians and had himself elected king in their stead.
Pepin (751–68) then turned to Italy when the pope appealed
to him for help against the Lombards, who had extinguished the exarchate of Ravenna, and the Muslims in the
south. The Frankish forces intervened decisively in 754.

In return for halting the Lombards and furthering the
formation of a papal state, Pepin secured the pope's
endorsement of his *coup d'état*. In the process the Frankish monarchy was changed from a secular institution,
originally elective but made hereditary by Merovingian
pragmatism, to a quasi-sacred one held and inherited by
divine right. Binding the king to rule with Christian
virtue, the pope's confirmation of legitimacy and bestowal
of grace through coronation and anointment were seen by
the Church as substantiating its claim to the superiority
of the spiritual over temporal power.**1.14, 1.15**

›1.15 DONATION OF CONSTANTINE, early 13th-century fresco, Oratory of S. Sylvester in the Santi Quattro Coronati, Rome.

According to the *Constitutum Constantini*, to celebrate his conversion the emperor granted Pope Sylvester and his successors temporal and spiritual supremacy over Rome and the western empire. Since the end of the 10th century, but generally since the mid-15th century, the document has been recognized as a forgery: it was probably perpetrated in Rome, perhaps in the Frankish heartland, in the early Carolingian era when the threat of a revived empire must have alarmed the servants of the papacy.

Pepin sealed the unity of most of the land which would be France with the expulsion of the Muslims from their remaining holdings on the Mediterranean coast. In the lands which would be Germany, on the other hand, the Bavarians were independent of him again by 763, the Avars were still active in Thuringia and the Saxons remained unmollified. He died in 768 and was buried at S. Denis, where he had rebuilt the Merovingian abbey which became his tomb and was to become the French royal necropolis.

EMPEROR AND POPE

As usual the kingdom was divided between the late king's sons, Charles and Carloman. The latter renounced his rights and Charles proceeded to take the Franks to their apogee in his exceptionally long reign (768–814). He retook Bavaria and defeated the Avars. He succeeded in reducing the Saxons to vassalage, furthering their conversion to Christianity, and established a firm eastern front against the Slavs. He secured the north against the obstreperous Danes, but was less successful in the far south-west.

The Muslims had been driven back to the Pyrenees by Martel's immediate successors and beyond them after Charles's forces had liberated Navarre and Catalonia in the 770s. Thereafter, identified as Moors in virtue of their base in Rome's former north-west African province of Mauritania, they consolidated their hold on much of Iberia under the Umayyad caliphate of Córdoba. They were eluded by the small Suevi Christian kingdom of the Asturias in the mountains of Galicia. Alfonso the Catholic (739–57) began its southward expansion. His successors pressed on without external help but with faith in the aid of S. James the Great, whose tomb was identified in 813 at the place which thenceforth bore his name, Santiago de Compostela.

Charlemagne – as he was justly to be called – believed he had been preferred by God to protect and prosper Christ's church. He supported papal attempts to reform it, particularly to purge it of such venal practices as the sale of offices. He supported Pope Leo III (795–816) in Rome's running dispute with Byzantium over the perpetration of iconoclasm – indeed, this very issue persuaded the pope to welcome a new empire in the west. Charlemagne stamped on all deemed heretical by Rome and promoted the regularization of liturgy.

Entering Italy to confront the Lombards, taking their capital Pavia and their crown, Charlemagne expanded the papal state at their expense.**1.16** Leo III crowned him emperor on Christmas Day 800 and signalled the revival of the Roman empire not only on the basis of military might but also in virtue of the new faith acknowledged by most Europeans. The Church lent legitimacy to Charlemagne's rule and promoted its supranational triumph. Charlemagne lent efficacy to the papacy and promoted a truly Catholic church – as Constantine had done five hundred years earlier.**1.17**

Recalling the Constantinian caste system – or, rather, consolidating the feudalism which had developed from it ad hoc over the previous three centuries – and determined to enforce military service as the obligation of vassalage in all its ranks, Charlemagne saw the advantage of cementing all the echelons of his imperial society in a pyramid of bonds with his bond of protection at the apex. However, the position at the apex was ambiguous: claiming to inherit all the authority conferred on S. Peter by Christ, the pope saw the emperor as his servant and protector; asserting the authority of Caesar, acknowledged by Christ, the emperor saw the Church as his client. Charlemagne had the force of character to surmount the confusion but his successors succumbed.

>**1.16 THE IRON CROWN OF LOMBARDY,** late-6th century? (Monza, cathedral treasury).

Reputedly incorporating iron beaten from the nails of the Crucifixion, the circlet was made for Queen Theodelinda, widow of King Authari of the Lombards.

>**1.17 CHARLEMAGNE ENTHRONED:** from shrine of 1215 (Aachen, cathedral treasury).

Charlemagne was acknowledged by the eastern emperor, Michael I (811–13), as emperor of the Franks, but he clearly considered himself to have revived the empire of the Romans. He maintained the Frankish kingdom as a distinct entity and continued to wear the crown of Lombardy but guaranteed the autonomy of the papal state within an Italian kingdom conferred on his oldest son, Pepin. Meanwhile, he had fostered the rebirth of imperial grandeur in his seat at Aachen in Germany, emulating Rome but modelled on the chief glories of Ravenna. He revived the empire of Latin scholarship too.

Bent on fostering the revival of learning after the Dark Ages of its eclipse, Charlemagne ordered the establishment of schools in connection with every abbey in the empire. This was only partially realized but northern scholars played a prominent part in the project.**1.18** Beyond the north-west corner of the Carolingian empire the ways of the south, including facility with Latin, were foreign. The better to understand the Gospels, the monks there perceived that they must know Latin and taught it to themselves from books – religious and secular – free of the corruptions and colloquialisms of the speech of those brought up to it or of the various Romance languages developing from it. They were primarily interested not in scholarship, but in propagating a faith reinforced by an understanding of the scriptures. However, a key consequence was the appreciation of the literature, Christian and antique humanist, from which they worked – despite the perceived danger of exposure to pagan ideas.

In their quest for understanding, the northern scholars had uncovered the discrepancies and distortions inflicted by the many translators, copyists, commentators and interpreters of the Gospels. Convinced that there could be only one true account, Charlemagne entrusted the Anglo-Saxon Alcuin (c. 730–804) with the reconciliation of all the differences in a definitive catholic text. In acquitting the task, Alcuin and his school at Aachen brought the analytical interest in Latin developed by his earlier compatriots to the very heart of the empire and ensured that a considerable part of the Classical heritage was saved for all ages.

From reconciliation of differences between Christian authorities with the aid of Latin learned from the humanist masters of Rome, central to the so-called Carolingian renaissance, there grew a respect for those masters themselves and a will to reconcile their ideals with those of Christianity – to reconcile ancient philosophy with modern theology, godliness with secular learning. That renaissance was lost to chaos in the late-9th and 10th centuries but it prepared the way for the 12th-century progenitors of Gothic – as we shall see.

CAROLINGIAN BUILDING

Imperial revival north of the Alps and the emergence from the dark age which followed the dissolution of its model prompted a style of building which was essentially derivative – though the derivations were adapted to grand purpose new to northern Europe. Given the overwhelming cultural legacy of ancient Rome – not least the supreme skill of its engineers in spanning space with the semicircular arch and the vaulting derived from it – that style was inevitably Roman-like or 'Romanesque'. Substance was transformed but symbolism transposed to proclaim a political ideal as much as to glorify God and accommodate the faithful. These were perfectly consistent to a ruler like Charlemagne, whose cause in general was Romanesque.

With the progressive modernization of the great cult centres – and the complete disappearance of many of them – the basis for the reconstruction of the new imperial architecture is provided by the palatine chapel at

>1.19 S. RIQUIER ABBEY, consecrated 799: early 17th-century engraved view (after the Hariulf ms drawing of 1088).

The basilica, c. 76 metres long, had towers over the west entrance and the crossing, as in the original scheme for S. Martin, Tours. In the westwork, vaults of the outer and inner vestibules supported a high chapel dedicated to the Saviour: served by spiral stairs in twin turrets and surmounted by a triple-tiered spire, this aspiring space overlooked the nave through raised arcades. The account of the 11th-century chronicler

Hariulf makes it clear that a boys' choir sang from galleries in the chapel in response to men's choirs singing on either side of a special space (known as the choir) at the crossing, before the apsidal sanctuary. Over the crossing a second great tower matched the western one. Beyond the cloister, to the south, a polygonal chapel dedicated to the Virgin and the Apostles seems to have been modelled on S. Vitale, Ravenna.

Aachen, the tiny episcopal chapel at Germigny-des-Près and the foundations of the abbey church of S. Denis, the cathedrals of Autun and Clermont-Ferrand, and the churches of S. Martin at Tours, S. Germain at Auxerre and S. Riquier.

Well represented in an 11th-century image of S. Riquier, the most significant Carolingian innovations were the distinguishing features of the great Romanesque church.[1.19] Foremost is the 'westwork' for the reception of the emperor, incorporating the twin-towered portal which had been the symbol of ultimate power since its first appearance in Mesopotamia four millennia earlier (AIC1, pages 92f). The east end had multiple chapels for the celebration of numerous masses, its crucial transept separated from the sanctuary by a choir for the amplification of the chant – another great achievement of the age. Weighty walls and massive arcades sustained extensive galleries – and, above all, imperial scale. Little survives on that site but the more substantial remains at Lorsch compensate, at least for the ancillary buildings.[1.20]

1.19

>**1.20 LORSCH ABBEY:** gatehouse, c. 775.
    Presumably typical of its time, this *Torhalle* consists of an essentially northern hall for receiving the emperor over a triple triumphal arch meant to recall the imperial Roman type. It once led to the German empire's richest Benedictine monastery, which, like all its contemporaries, has disappeared under later rebuilding and destruction.

1.20

1.21b

1.21a @ 1:500

›1.21 GERMIGNY-DES-PRÈS, 806, extensively reconstructed 1867–76: (a) plan, (b) interior, (c) exterior.

The Greek cross in a square is defined by four central piers and an apse in the centre of each side – the western one pierced for the entrance. Framed with attached columns, the semidomical apses are linked by tunnel vaults to the central square and small domes cover the corner spaces. The central superstructure has been rebuilt to a level lower than the original but there seems always to have been a lantern tower, typical of the north, rather than a dome. Above the arches supporting the central superstructure are arcaded galleries which presumably reproduce in miniature those through which the Saviour Chapel overlooked the nave at S. Riquier.

The little Greek-cross church of Germigny-des-Près was built in 806. An adjunct to the palace of Bishop Theodulph of Orléans, a member of the emperor's circle, it betrays the influence of the east and, indeed, of the Visigothic – if not the Muslim – south. In plan it is a quincunx, as regular as any yet encountered in the Byzantine world, east or south. As in the Visigothic tradition of Spain – and the Moorish one subsequently developed there – its arches and most of its apses in plan are incurved like a horseshoe. But its central tower is northern in derivation and, despite its size, its monumentality is imperial.[1.21]

Outstanding by far, not only among the depleted remains from the time of Charlemagne but also from the early medieval period as a whole, is the octagonal palatine chapel of the palace complex at Aachen, now the cathedral. Emulating what they took to be antique, Charlemagne's servants modelled it on S. Vitale in formerly imperial Ravenna. Emblazoned with the image of imperial power in the splendid mosaics of Justinian and

1.21b

Theodora, S. Vitale was understandably significant to a patron with imperial pretensions. No less significant was the acknowledgement of the frontispiece of the palace attributed to the exarch of Ravenna as the archetype of the great palace, the symbol of a holy imperium.[1.22]

1.22a

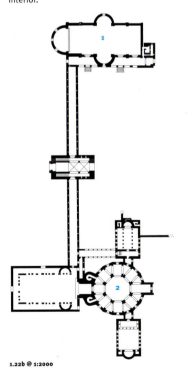

1.22b @ 1:2000

›1.22 AACHEN, PALACE COMPLEX, 792–805: (a) Charlemagne dedicating his palatine church to the Virgin with the Christ Child (early 13th-century gilded panel; Aachen cathedral treasury), (b) plan with (1) great hall of state, (2) palatine chapel (the arch zof appearance is on the chapel façade), (c, d) palatine chapel (dedicated 805) view from the south and interior.

Imperial revivals at Aachen

Replaced by the town hall in the 14th century, Charlemagne's two-storey triapsidal throne hall was inspired by both the great late-Roman basilicas attributed to Constantine (or Maxentius): the scale and the longitudinal orientation of the eastern entrance and the western throne apse recall the aula regia at Trier; development of the short cross axis with extra apses north and south clearly emulates the great work begun by Constantine's rival in Rome. Beside and beyond a rectangular court which was addressed by the imperial apartments and ancillary accommodation, an extended corridor linked this scene of high state ceremonial with the palatine chapel.

Like the structure identified with the palace of the Ravenna exarch (AIC1, page 776), the principal feature of the westwork is the central niche in which the emperor could appear before his subjects assembled in the atrium below – as in the arch of appearance of the ancient twin-towered palace portal and the Roman triumphal arch. Flanked by cylindrical stair turrets, the arch of appearance at Aachen opened off a throne room served by the first-floor gallery, which provided the imperial tribune overlooking the octagonal interior through arched colonnades. Over the throne room

1.22c

was a reliquary chapel and opposite it was a sanctuary for the emperor's worship above another opposite the entrance at ground-floor level. These disappeared with the addition of the choir in the 13th century. Separated by wedge-shaped spaces, the eight compartments of the ambulatory are

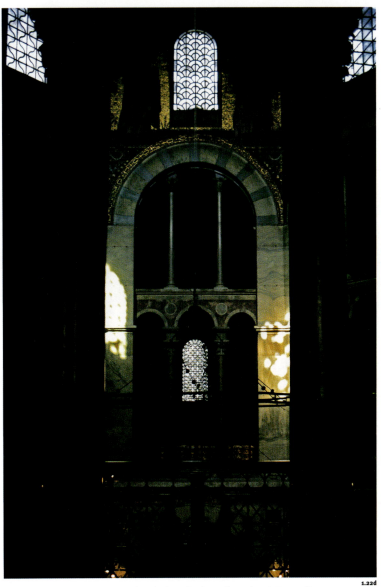

1.22d

groin-vaulted at base level and tunnel-vaulted at tribune level. Tower-like, the central space has an octagonal canopy vault. Rich marble revetment and mosaic ensured that the building made no less an impression than the masterpieces of Justinian.

2 POST-CAROLINGIAN DIVISION

Charlemagne was not long survived by his empire but his achievement was to be emulated for a millennium. He had planned a tripartite division between his sons, but on his death in 814 only the youngest, Louis of Aquitaine (814–40), survived him. Surnamed 'the Pious' and surrounded by clerics on whom the significance of the pope's presence at his father's coronation was not lost, Louis saw his office as a sacred charge for advancing the Catholic cause in a Christian commonwealth and had his coronation transformed into a sacerdotal ceremony centred on the anointment ritual.[1.23] He systematized the administration, to the advantage of prelates who were appointed to oversee the civil officials, and regulated the succession in favour solely of his oldest son, Lothair (died 855), to preserve the unity of western Christendom.

›1.24 CHARLES THE BALD AND MAGNATES,
including Count Vivien of Tours (right), whose domain
was to pass to Robert the Strong and, ultimately, to the
Capetian kings of France (Bible of Charles the Bald;
Paris, National Library).

In the event, Lothair's younger brothers, Louis and Charles, disputed their father's will with the connivance of the magnates. By the Treaty of Verdun (843) the empire was divided. The western section (much of modern France west of the Rhône and Meuse) went to Charles, 'the Bald' (died 877). The eastern section (much of modern Germany between the Rhine and the Elbe, plus most of Austria, Slovenia and Croatia) went to Louis, 'the German' (died 876). Lothair retained the imperial title and the middle section ('Lotharingia', stretching from Rome through Lombardy, Provence, Burgundy and Lorraine to the Netherlands).[1.24]

Beyond the turmoil caused by rival claimants to shifting realms, there was the terror wrought by new waves of barbarian invaders, the Slavs and Magyars in the east and the Norsemen. The mail-clad horseman – the precursor of the knight and the major offensive weapon of the high-feudal age – emerged to oppose them with some local success but they wreaked particular havoc on the Church, not only striking on exposed coasts but also along most of the major rivers of the north-west and east. They penetrated the lands which would be Russia from the Baltic to the Black Sea. They wintered periodically at the mouth of the Seine, forming a base there from which they threatened Paris in 845, and extended their rule over what was to be Normandy in fifty years. In the second half of the 9th century, too, they extended Danish rule over the rival kingdoms established by the Anglo-Saxons in eastern England. Their penetration of the Rhineland was the empire's undoing.[1.25]

Lothair's dominions, divided between his three sons on his death in 855, had been redistributed among the remaining two by 875. After the passing of many contenders over the next decade, the empire was again united when Louis the German's son, Charles the Fat, took the west from the infant heir of Charles the Bald. Preoccupied with the incursion of the Norsemen into northern France, the usurper failed adequately to defend the Rhineland and was deposed in 887. He was succeeded by his nephew, Arnulf, who fared no better against the Vikings in the north or Magyar tribes pressing from the east. In 899 the tottering realm passed to his son, Louis the Child, with whom the eastern Carolingian line died in 911. The magnates holding the office of duke had already seized the initiative.

PRINCIPALITIES AND POWERS

In their contentions with one another and with external invaders, Charlemagne's fractious successors bought support with counties, and great principalities were formed by the magnates of the west, as in the eastern part of the empire. Moreover, they often found it expedient to grant immunity to fief holders from state intervention in their lands: the private proprietor supplanted the county official as the arm of local government, particularly in the raising of feudal dues and the administration of justice.

Naturally, the chief beneficiaries were the major landowners, most of whom traced their lineage back to ancient Roman patrician families and/or to the elders of barbarian tribes who now substituted the title of their seats for the names of their ancestors. As their fortunes rose with the decline of the monarch, the magnates arrogated to themselves the hereditary right to the great offices of imperial state, the ducal military commands of central provinces or the marquisates of border lands, county civil governance and the endowment of abbots and bishops.

On the death of Charles the Bald in 877, several western principalities were as significant as the royal domain around Paris: Flanders, assigned by Charles to his brother-in-law, Baldwin Iron Arm, in 862; Burgundy, detached from Lotharingia for Charles in 869 and autonomous after the further divisions of the kingdom on his death;

>1.25 VIKING STELE, Gotland, 9th century? (Stockholm Historical Museum).

Brittany, a Celtish preserve never wholly part of the Carolingian empire, unified under its first duke in the mid-9th century; Touraine, Blois and Anjou, awarded to the magnate Robert the Strong by Charles in 861 to secure support against the Viking Norsemen; Aquitaine, disputed by the heirs of Louis the Pious and autonomous after 877; and Toulouse, carved from the south by the counts Fredelon and Raymond from c. 850. Provence passed to Lothair's son, Louis, and asserted its independence on his death in 875.

On the death of Charles the Fat in the year after his eastern deposition, a conclave of western magnates replaced him with Robert the Strong's son, Eudes of Anjou. His son, Hugh, secured the title Duke of the Franks after much contention with supporters of the Carolingians, who regained the initiative but lost it again to the Norsemen: the duchy of Normandy was ceded to them in the fateful year of 911.

On the death of Louis the Child in 911, the rump of Lotharingia acknowledged the Frankish king Charles the Simple. The German dukes who had seized the initiative reinstituted the principle of election to the monarchy and chose Conrad of Franconia – not without dissension. *Primus inter pares*, Conrad had to prove himself and failed. On his death in 918, power passed to the Saxons with the election of the Ottonian Duke Henry the Fowler (919–36). Opposition from Swabia and Bavaria was overcome and Henry's military prowess confirmed him in authority over all Germany.

Meanwhile, from his capital at Oviedo, Alfonso III of Asturias (died 914) had taken advantage of Cordoban disarray to extend his kingdom and to defend his eastern frontier with a chain of castles (after which a county established in the area was to be called Castile). His successor moved the capital south to León in 914, but a revival of

Cordoban fortunes and the emergence of a Basque kingdom in Navarra under Sancho I (905–26) were sorely to
challenge the Asturian ambition of restoring the Visigothic Christian kingdom in Iberia.

All three Christian states in the Iberian north – Asturias
(or León as it was now called), Navarra and Catalonia,
which had detached itself from the Carolingian empire as
an independent county – had been subjected to the brutal
rule of the Cordoban usurper al-Mansur by the end of the
10th century. After his death in 1002, however, the threat
of destruction receded. Instead, Sancho III of Navarra
took the other Christian states and willed them to his sons
as kingdoms on his death in 1035. United, León and Castile
emerged dominant and within fifty years Alfonso VI (1073–
1109) had expanded his dominion south to Toledo, the
ancient capital of the Visigothic kings – but provoked the
intervention of the fanatical Moroccan Almoravids, who
resecured the south and east (AIC3, pages 219ff).

THE IMPERIUM OF CLUNY

Monasticism was an essential element in the fragmented
polity of the feudal age – indeed, the survival of civilization depended on the diligence of the studious monk. By
the end of Charlemagne's reign the main Benedictine
stream was due for review. At a synod held in 817 at Aachen
under Louis the Pious, the Order was reorganized along
lines determined at Aniane in Languedoc by Abbot Benedict (c. 756–821) and the reformed rule was imposed on all
the monasteries of his empire. A contemporary document,
probably a copy of the blueprint for a reformed monastic
complex drawn up for Benedict and presented to the synod
at Aachen, has survived in the monastic library at S. Gall
in Switzerland: like the great new work undertaken from
802 at the monastery of Fulda, it was adapted to that site
as to many others in the empire.**1.26–1.28**

›1.26 MONK AT STUDY IN A MONASTERY: S.
Gregory the Theologian from a 12th-century manu-
script illumination (S. Catherine's Monastery, Mount
Sinai).

The monastic ideal

Modular, the ideal plan (460 by 640 Carolingian feet of 30.4 centimetres each) was conceived as a rectangle adaptable to level sites. The double-apsed basilican church (c. 91 metres long), comprehensively subdivided for multiple altars and maximum privacy for the monks celebrating mass, is towards the northern boundary and parallel to it, dominating the protected cloister (c. 30 square metres) to which its southern entrance is directly related. The main entrance to the site is from the west by a hostel for itinerants and a tethering ground for animals which also provide a barrier between the world at large and the enclosed world of the monk, centred on the cloister (as the name indicates). Further, the thin strip north of the church has other buildings related to the community served by the abbey, a guest house and school in particular; to the south is a cordon of workshops and service buildings. Framing the cloister are the main monastic living spaces, the dormitory and refectory, and beyond it to the east, furthest from the entrance, the rest of the monks' facilities – especially the infirmary and burial ground, which doubles as an orchard and vegetable garden in the economy of recycling.

›1.27 IDEAL MONASTIC PLAN AND THE BI-APSIDAL CHURCH: (a) redrawn document of c. 820 from the monastery of S. Gall (Switzerland) with (1) church, (2) entrance to monastic forecourt, (3) chapter house below, dormitories above, (4) abbot's palace, (5) cloister, (6) refectory, (7) novices' cloister, (8) infirmary, (9) guesthouse, (10) school, (11) workshops, (12) service buildings, (13) burial ground; (b) S. Gall, reconstruction of late-Carolingian monastery.

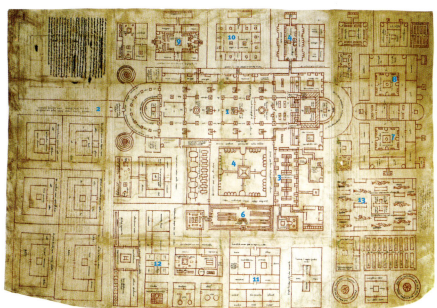

1.27a

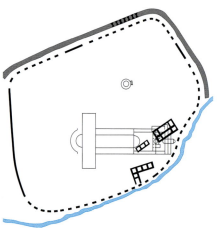

1.27b

1.28 @ 1:2000

›1.28 FULDA: plan of church as developed between 802 and 822.

The monastery was founded by S. Boniface in 744. After the return of his remains to his church, a new apsidal west end was projected to enshrine them. The Carolingian work, with later towers flanking the eastern apse and over the western crossing, was replaced in the early 18th century.

The plan of the church echoes recent developments at Fulda, where the new west end of c. 800 was inspired by the arrangements made for S. Peter in his great Roman basilica. The transept and high-altar apse there reversed the normal orientation but at Fulda the new work set an important bifocal precedent for northern Christian builders. It was reproduced closely by the formulator of the ideal preserved in the archives of S. Gall, though Abbot Gozbert (816–37), for whom the plan was annotated, did not follow it strictly in rebuilding the complex from 830.

In 910, the year before the cession of Normandy and the disappearance of the eastern Carolingians, the Duke of Aquitaine endowed the reformed Benedictine community of Abbot Berno of Baume-les-Moines and Gigny with a hunting estate at Cluny, in the Burgundian centre of Lotharingia. Dedicated to the revival of S. Benedict of Nursia's original spiritual ideal, lapsed again in the century since Benedict of Aniane, they converted the duke's villa and soon replaced it on a grand scale.

The reformed Cluniacs promoted corporate worship in

the splendour of sung mass as much to celebrate God with all the resources bestowed on man as to impress man with the fruits of temporal power. Contrary to S. Benedict's original rule, which envisaged the independence of each monastery, Berno asserted his authority as abbot of Cluny not only over affiliated priories but over abbeys to which his Cluniacs took reform. Monarchical in structure, in accordance with the authoritarianism of S. Benedict's concept of an abbacy, and bypassing episcopal and royal authority in its direct dependence on S. Pietro in Rome, Cluny was to extend a network of foundations across Europe which promoted its abbot to power hardly inferior to that of an emperor.

Though decadent at several reprises, the Benedictine order generated the prime spiritual force in Christendom. Poor, chaste and obedient – in principle, if not always in practice – its monks and nuns were dedicated to the spiritual and physical health of all God's servants. They housed the homeless, tended the sick and revived learning in many fields – medicine as much as theology, for instance – and imparted education to the poor as well as counsel to the rulers. They informed the beliefs of a society which, no matter how brutal, feared God.

God to the Romanesque Christian was the omnipotent, magnificent Pantokrator, the 'all-sovereign' vengeful judge rather than the sacrificed saviour. Celebrating him with all the resources bestowed on man naturally promoted great achievement in art: furthering the early Christian antihumanist iconic mode in translating the archtypical Graeco-Roman image of supreme divinity (AICI, page 404), the Romanesque painter elicited overwhelming awe of Christ's sovereignty in the Cluniac chancel apse and the sculptor reached an unsurpassed apogee in presenting him presiding in truly terrible majesty over the portals of Cluny's world.[1.1]

THE CHURCH IN THE DIVIDED EMPIRE

Spanning the territories ruled by Louis the Pious and his immediate successors, there are substantial representative remains in the three basilican churches on the island of Reichenau in Lake Constance, at S. Philbert de Grandlieu, at the cathedral of Auxerre and at Corvey on the Weser. The last is notable for its westwork, and also for the introduction of an ambulatory to the east end. Early developments catering for the passage of pilgrims through various curved and rectangular corridors are revealed in the crypts of S. Philbert de Grandlieu, Tournus, S. Germain at Auxerre and the cathedral at Chartres. The definitive solution to the problem, with apse and concentric ambulatory serving radial chapels, was achieved in the rebuilding of S. Martin, Tours, early in the 10th century.[1.29, 1.30]

>1.29 EVOLUTION OF THE AMBULATORY UNDER THE LATER CAROLINGIANS: (a, b) S. Philbert de Grandlieu c. 814–47, plans c. 839 of apse at ground level, below a raised apsidal sanctuary and revision of c. 847 with new east-end chapels *en échelon* (i.e. parallel to one another so that in plan their walls resemble the rungs of a ladder); (c) Chartres, mid-9th-century apse and ambulatory foundations, plan; (d) Tours, S. Martin (rebuilding dedicated 918), excavations of the chevet.

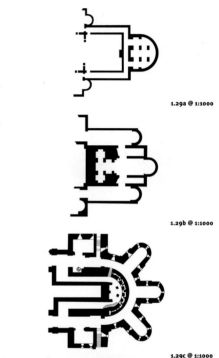

1.29a @ 1:1000

1.29b @ 1:1000

1.29c @ 1:1000

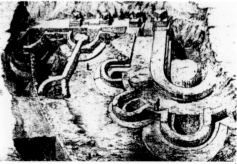

1.29d

Corvey and the evolution of the ambulatory

Novel in Germanic lands for its date, the apse at Corvey was surrounded by an ambulatory, though the aisles continued past it to terminate in rectangular chapels, and a larger cruciform chapel is added to the centre. This was anticipated at Brixworth and in French developments which may be traced to S. Philbert de Grandlieu. There, pilgrims to the relics of S. Philbert were first channelled through narrow aisle extensions to the sarcophagus in an apse at ground level,[1.29a] then through wider corridors on the three outer sides of the shrine below the apse, along and through parallel east end chapels.[1.29b] A similar arrangement on a clearer rectangular plan was adopted for the tomb of S. Germain below the sanctuary of his church at Auxerre. Shortly after that, in turn, a curved ambulatory around the apse at Chartres was screened from the sanctuary only by arcades so the pilgrims filing through the one could see the relics in the other without entering it.

The relics in the abbey church of S. Martin at Tours, taken to Auxerre in 872 to escape the raiding Norsemen, were returned to a new church after the removal of the Norse threat by the cession of Normandy in 911. The provision of corridors for pilgrims around three sides of a square shrine

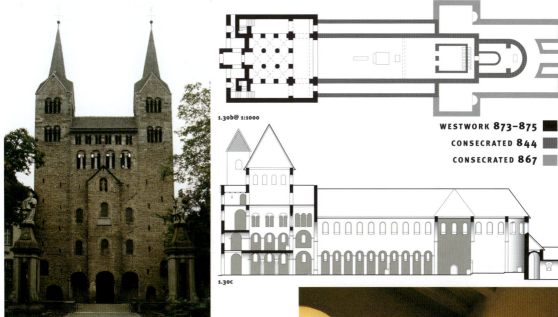

1.30a

1.30b@ 1:1000

1.30c

›1.30 CORVEY ABBEY, 873–85: (a) westwork, (b, c) plan and section, (d) interior.

Corvey was founded by monks from Corbie in Picardy in 822 as a centre for the further expansion of the faith to the east. They took with them the influence of S. Riquier,[1.19] which then must have been the dominant complex in the region of their parent house. The westwork is the most complete example of the type from the later Carolingian period, though the part between the side towers was raised later to obscure the original central tower. Before reconstruction in the late-17th century, the nave arcade was carried on simple rectangular piers, regularly repeated. Above the vaulted vestibule, as at S. Riquier, an elevated chapel overlooks the basilica through an arcaded gallery.

1.30d

area – as at Auxerre where the arrangement was known to S. Martin's entourage and presumably found less than felicitous by them – was replaced by a curve simply repeating that of the pierced apse – as at Chartres. There the relics were enshrined in the sanctuary at ground level, rather than in a crypt, and the water table imposed the same situation at Tours. There were chapels radiating from the corridor at Chartres and their similar arrangement around the circumference at Tours follows simple geometrical logic but its exact date is obscure as the church was rebuilt after a fire in 977.**1.29c,d**

ITALY

The Italians sustained the early Christian tradition throughout the Carolingian period, as they were largely to do for a long time thereafter. Absorbing the exarchate of Ravenna in the 8th century with awe for its architecture, the Lombards were responsible for considerable developments, particularly in masonry techniques, vaulting and the organization of masons into a regulated guild. This may have been initiated at Como: *magister comacini* became synonymous with 'master builder' and *lambardi* with 'mason' as their itinerant teams promoted technological advance and professional convention throughout Europe.

The Lombards are often credited with effecting the transition from the Carolingian 'renaissance' in architecture to a 'first Romanesque' – though the former might as well be seen as the latter. Apart from the improvement in masonry marked by the reintroduction of walls built entirely of regular bricks or dressed stone in small blocks, rather than Roman dressed concrete or rubble, the major characteristics of their work were the tauter integration of still-autonomous parts, masonry vaulting, nave arcades carried on piers articulated with pilasters rather than on columns, external pilaster strips for rhythmic articulation as well as buttressing, blind arcading – especially in corbel tables fringing eaves – and prominent bell towers.

›**1.31 CIVIDALE DEL FRIULE, S. MARIA IN VALLE:** interior detail of sactuary and nave vaulting with stucco embellishment over west door (c. 770).

>1.32 MILAN, EARLY ROMANESQUE SUR-
VIVALS: (a, b) S. Satiro, exterior as reformed in the
late-15th century and interior; (c) S. Vincenzo in Prato
(c. 830 and later), exterior from the east; (d) S. Ambrogio, apse interior.

The centralized planning incorporating a Greek
cross, perfected for S. Satiro, was certainly not uncommon for early Christian martyria and baptistries – as
we have seen – but was not yet the dominant characteristic of the church even in the east.

The origin of S. Vincenzo is dated to 833 but there
was much later rebuilding when the chancel was
raised in the early 11th century. In both phases of construction the exterior is assumed to have been articu-

1.32a   1.32b

1.32c

In their formulation of the bell tower the Lombards followed, and disseminated, the late-Roman square example
of the Milanese at S. Lorenzo and the mid-8th-century
eastern tower of S. Pietro, rather than the circular exarchate type. Ravenna, however, was the source for assertive
pilaster strips, blind arcading with colonettes and decorative miniature arcades supporting eaves. The construction
of tunnel, domical and groin vaults over timber centering
descended, of course, from the Romans (AICI, pages 723ff).

The major contribution of the Lombards to medieval
architecture was the development of the groin vault instead
of the wooden roof or masonry tunnel, especially over the
chancel where it simulated the canopy of the imperial
throne appropriated for the vicars of Christ. While the
tunnel vault admits light only from the ends and needs
thick walls to support it, the groin vault is carried by four
arches over a rectangular bay which may be lit from all sides
and buttressed in series by the counter-opposition of forces
rather than by dead weight. Unprecedentedly sophisticated in their command of the dynamics of structure, the
Romans made the transition from the one to the other on
a grand scale in the early 2nd century (AICI, pages 634ff).
Their Lombard heirs made a similar transition after the
Dark Ages had obliterated such sophistications. Paradox-
ically, one of the earliest-known examples, the 'Tempietto'
of S. Maria in Valle at Cividale, has a groin-vaulted nave
and tunnel vaults carried on columns in the sanctuary.[1.31]

Milan preserves little of Lombard work earlier than the
apse of S. Ambrogio – decorated in the mid-10th century.
Exceptional are the mid-9th-century church of S. Satiro
and the basilica of S. Vincenzo in Prato. From the limited
legacy elsewhere S. Pietro, Agliate, and S. Abbondio,
Como, are generally singled out to represent the development of the Lombard style, though they had been restored
or rebuilt conservatively by the early 11th century.[1.32, 1.33]

1.32d

There is some doubt about the dating of S. Vincenzo's chancel vaulting. The groin vaulting of S. Pietro's crypt is usually assigned to the late-9th century and so are the groin-vaulted chapels flanking the tunnel-vaulted chancel above. S. Abbondio preserves Italy's oldest-known groin-vaulted chancel, buttressed by twin belfries: the wooden-roofed nave is flanked by double aisles and a regular series of cylindrical piers.

The Lombards were to develop a rhythm from the pairing of the aisle bays within square nave compartments: inviting groin vaulting, the process was furthered by the

lated with pilasters and blind arcading in the exarchate manner but it is probable that the open arcading under the eaves of the main apse dates from the rebuilding. If so this developed the motif from S. Pietro at Agliate (founded c. 870), a more primitive survivor, though prophetic in its raised chancel over a groin-vaulted crypt. As pillaged materials were rarely available at the time these churches were founded, the elements of structure were increasingly specific: reused columns would have been obviated by masonry vaulting but – the crypt apart – both these works were vaulted only over the sanctuary and the builders of S. Pietro still managed to find old columns for their nave.

›**1.33 COMO, S. ABBONDIO,** founded in the 4th century, much rebuilt from c. 1030: (a, b) exterior from the east and west, (c) nave and chancel.

The doubling of the aisles is naturally rare in a relatively small church: here it followed the example of the great patriarchal basilicas of Rome, perhaps because the original dedication was to S. Peter and S. Paul. The half colonettes on the exterior of the chancel are somewhat precocious as supports for the now-familiar arched corbel tables. Austerity reigns elsewhere, except for sparing relief on the west front.

1.33a

1.33b

1.33c

1.34

introduction of the composite pier instead of the increasingly precious antique column. An early example, still roofed in timber, is S. Maria at Lomello (c. 1020). Differentiation of the major and minor supports was the obvious next step, taken at the end of the century, as in S. Sigismondo at Rivolta d'Adda.**1.34, 1.35**

SPAIN

The basilica was the western norm even beyond the orbit of empire, notably in Christian Asturias. Presumably inheriting a debased Roman style from the Visigoths, though there is little evidence for this, its formulators were not unaware of developments in the empire and confirm unsurprising contacts with the British Isles. The scant remains of their cathedral in Oviedo, the capital from the reign of Alfonso II (the Chaste; 791–842), reveal a little of their post-Roman origins but the palatine chapel of S. Julián de los Prados is exceptionally informative of remote regional eclecticism in the early 9th century, especially in its decoration. The Germanic component is at its most apparent in the main surviving work of Alfonso's successor, Ramiro I (843–50): this is a ceremonial hall at Naranco, with belvederes of appearance at each end, a portico to the north opposite a lost southern projection and a full crypt.**1.36**

>**1.34 LOMELLO, S. MARIA,** c. 1020.

Cruciform piers with a pilaster strip rising through the internal elevation to the clerestory, pilasters supporting the transverse arch between each aisle bay and lateral attached half columns supporting the aisle arcading were repeated down the length of the nave but every second one carried a diaphragm arch dividing the main space into roughly square compartments.

>**1.35 RIVOLTA D'ADDA, S. SIGISMONDO,** c. 1100: nave

The first bays, before the sanctuary, are tunnel-vaulted. The later bays are doubled between piers in the form of colossal pilasters which support primitive domical groin vaults.

1.35

1.36a

1.36b

1.36c

›1.36 OVIEDO: (a) Cámara Sancta (early 9th century, refurbished and embellished in the 12th century), nave and sanctuary; (b–d) S. Julián de los Prados (c. 830), longitudinal section, interior and exterior; (e–g) S. María de Naranco (c. 840), exterior from southeast and north-east, section; (h, i) S. Cristina de Lena (c. 850), exterior from south-west, screened sanctuary.

Of the cathedral founded in 802 by Alfonso the Chaste (791–842), under the direction of one Tioda, the principal surviving element is the reliquary chapel known as the Cámara Sancta. The tunnel vaulting in masonry (and the quality of the later sculpture) betray the influence of France.

A basilica with a dominant transept higher than nave or sanctuary, this was a palatine church linked with Alfonso's residence: presumably part of his apartment, the king's tribune overlooked the north transept through a large window framed by an even taller arch. The tunnel-vaulted sanctuary is flanked by parallel chapels (*en échelon*). The nave, screened from the transept with an arch matching the proscenium of the sanctuary, has three arched bays with simple rectangular piers surmounted by a clerestory. Nave and transept are painted with feigned aedicules in a highly unexpected re-evocation of the late-Pompeian style (AIC1, pages 543f). Except for the sanctuary, the roofs are wooden.

In the near-contemporary hall church of S. María, Naranco (consecrated 848), the longitudinal halls on

1.36d

1.36e

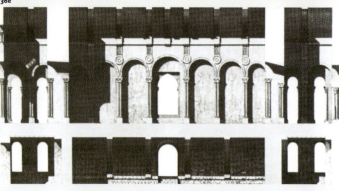

1.36g

1.36f

both levels are tunnel-vaulted over transverse arches but the taller and grander upper hall has blind buttressing arcades, slightly incurved. The lower chambers on the long axis are unvaulted but the upper ones are vaulted like the main hall. As at Aachen, the short axis is developed with buttressing extensions to the north and south (rectangular rather than apsidal): the former provides entrances at both levels; the southern arm is presumed to have contained a sanctuary which may or may not have been ancillary.

Stoutly buttressed, the main rectangular volume of S. Cristina is supplemented by near-square projections to both ends of each axis – for porch, sanctuary and putative transepts. The raised sanctuary is entered through a colonnaded screen which incorporates perforated Visigothic panels – the central one with miniature horseshoe- or keyhole-shaped arches.

›1.37 BERLANGA, S. BAUDELIO, c. 910: (a, b) interior details showing Visigothic arcading, central column and vault.

1.37a

1.37b

1.36h

1.36i

Several works from the 10th century elsewhere in northern Spain display the horseshoe arch characteristic of the so-called Mozarabic style which was developed from their experience of Moorish architecture by Christian refugees from the caliphate of Córdoba as much as from the Visigothic legacy.[1.12] From the early 10th century, there was considerable variation in the style on the Greek-cross plan of Germigny-des-Près – if not the Byzantine east – some even more elementary.[1.37] The outstanding basilican examples, S. Miguel de la Escalada near León, the abbey of S. María, Ripoll in Catalonia or S. Michel, Cuxa, on the

1.38a

1.38b

>**1.38 S. MIGUEL DE LA ESCALADA,** c. 912–13:
(a) exterior, (b) interior.

The wooden-roofed basilica, with its arcades of incurved arches, was built by monastic refugees from Córdoba. Beyond the chancel screen the vaulted apses are horseshoe-shaped in perimeter and elevation. The external gallery to the south was added c. 940.

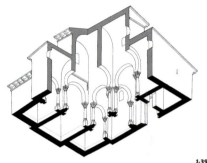

1.39

>**1.39 LEBEÑA, S. MARÍA,** 924: cutaway and
worm's-eye view axonometric.

A variation of the quincunx produces a square nave and sanctuary before and beyond an oblong crossing, smaller square transept arms, oblong chapels on either side of the sanctuary, square ones on either side of the nave and an oblong narthex flanked by square chapels. All the arches are incurved except for the profiles of the tunnel vaults that run longitudinally over an interpolated clerestory for the nave, crossing and sanctuary, laterally for the lower subsidiary spaces. Columns are attached to the piers as they were to the walls of S. María, Naranco, and, indeed, to the piers of Germigny-des-Près.

>**1.40 RIPOLL, ABBEY CHURCH OF S. MARÍA,**
rebuilt from c. 1020 and again from 1886: plan.

>**1.41 CUXA, S. MICHEL,** c. 955: (a) plan, (b) flank
of church and tower from cloister.

Founded in 878, the abbey prospered and was able to construct a substantial basilican church. A rectangular sanctuary continued the lines of the nave arcade beyond an extended transept with twin apsidal chapels to each arm. After 1010, a rectangular ambulatory with three apsidal chapels encapsulated the sanctuary, twin towers were built over the end transept bays and a narthex preceded by a quatrefoil Trinity Chapel was added to the west. Somewhat modified in the 11th century, the original style was Mozarabic as at S. María,

French side of the Pyrenees, span much of the century, but the form was widely approximated in churches and synagogues converted from mosques of the same style.**1.38–1.41**

The Mozarabic style was to be dominant in the south – especially in the articulation of brickwork – for long after the Christians took the key central city of Toledo in 1085. It was not an ingredient of the Asturian mix, however, and when the churches at Ripoll and Cuxa were rebuilt early in the 11th century the Mozarabic elements were suppressed: then the dominant influence, transmitted through southern France, was Lombard – in the design of

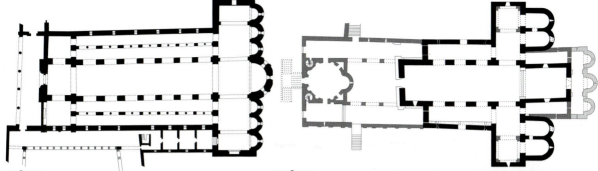

Ripoll, where an even grander vaulted basilica with apsidal sanctuary was begun c. 977. There was no ambulatory at Ripoll even after substantial enlargement from 1020, but in the smaller contemporary church of S. Pere de Roda near Gerona (consecrated 1022) the apse opened through arcades to a semicircular ambulatory.

›1.42 S. MARTIN-DU-CANIGOU, founded c. 1000, restored: (a) monastery overview, (b) nave interior.

The church is a tunnel-vaulted triapsidal basilica at both crypt and main floor levels: nave and aisles are separated by arcades carried on piers in the crypt but at the main level piers interrupt colonnades only in the middle. The tower is Lombard in its articulation with pilasters supporting blind arcading but the crenellation is Moorish.

›1.43 S. MARIA DEL MUR: apse frescoes from the second half of the 12th century (transposed from the foothills of the Catalan Pyrenees to the Museum of Fine Arts in Boston).

1.41b

towers and, especially, in vaulting. The tunnel vault appears in Catalonia about the middle of the 10th century and subsists well into the 12th century, together with the characteristically Lombard blind arcading and frescoes of metropolitan quality. The latter distinguished S. María del Mur in particular. Lombard articulation is well represented at S. Cecilia de Monserrat (c. 955) and, most substantially, at Ripoll. Back in the French Pyrenees, the most spectacularly sited example is S. Martin-du-Canigou. However, S. María del Mur and S. Martin-du-Canigou, begun early in the 11th century, bring us into a new imperial era of great developments.**1.42, 1.43**

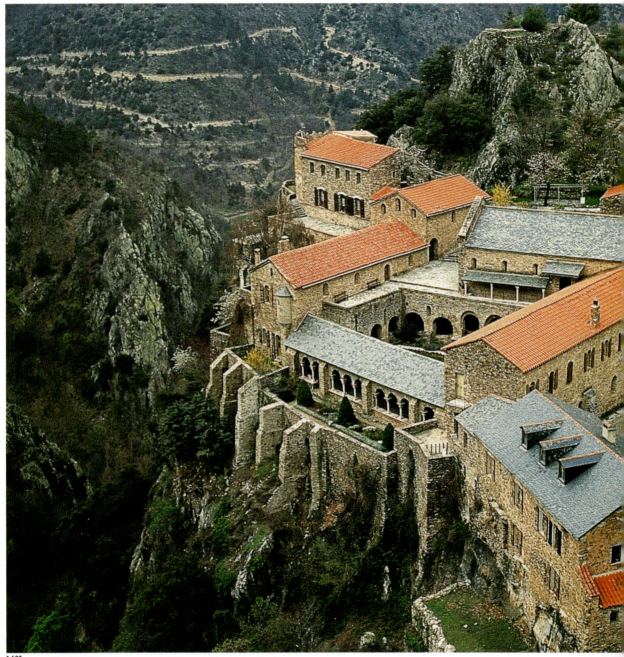

1.42a

›ARCHITECTURE IN CONTEXT »RENOVATION OF GRAVITAS

1.42b

1.43

›ARCHITECTURE IN CONTEXT »RENOVATION OF GRAVITAS

1.2 THE CENTRE: HOLY ROMAN EMPIRE

1.44a

1.44b

3 THE KINGDOM OF THE GERMANS

OTTONIAN SUPREMACY

The Ottonian Duke Henry the Fowler (919–36), elected German king in place of Conrad of Franconia, succeeded where his predecessor had failed. His personality alone checked the autonomy of the secular magnates and he promoted ecclesiastical ones to the principal officers of state. He laid the foundations for Saxon ascendancy in the west with the reacquisition of Lotharingia. He gained the initiative in the east by turning back the Hungarians. To protect the realm from barbarian incursion – and internal opposition – Henry revived Roman fortification where possible and constructed innumerable forts and a series of fortress towns, which usually consisted of a citadel on high ground overlooking the surrounding terrain and protecting a ward for the rehoused local population – after the pattern long-adopted on the much smaller scale of the individual landholder.

On the basis of his father's achievement, Otto I, the Great (936–73) re-established the empire. He defeated the dukes of Franconia, Swabia and Bavaria who had united against him, kept the Franconian counties under direct control, as in Saxony, and delegated those of the other two duchies to relatives. As counties fell vacant elsewhere, he retained or bestowed them on the Church to counter secular power. He crushed the Magyars in 955 but failed permanently to extend Saxon authority – and Christianity – to the Slavs. He gained Lombardy by marriage in 951.

Returning to Italy in 962 to be crowned emperor by Pope John XII (955–64), Otto confirmed imperial protection of the papal state. However, the papacy having descended to venality at the behest of the Roman aristocracy, the next year he deposed the teenaged pope for treachery, asserted the right to ratify papal elections and chose the next two popes – Leo VIII (963–65) and Benedict V (964–66). He reached an accord with the eastern emperor Romanus II (959–63) whose daughter, Theophano, married his son in 972. That son acceded as Otto II the following year.[1.44]

Otto II, Otto III (983–1002) and Henry II (1002–24) travelled incessantly to check the local authorities and furthered the policy of disrupting the duchies by transferring power from the hereditary secular aristocracy to ecclesiastical magnates whose celibacy was meant to prevent its permanent arrogation. If only in virtue of this interdependence of church and state against the secular magnates, Otto's domain was not irrelevantly called the 'Holy Roman Empire'. And the Saxon kings, especially the theocratic Otto III, acknowledged that interdependence at the highest level in partnership with the pontiff.

Asserting the sole right of the German king to be crowned emperor in Rome, Otto I sustained the principle of election in deference to papal opposition to its inheritance through primogeniture. Yet, like Charlemagne,

1.44c

›1.44 IMPERIAL IMAGERY: (a) Henry II and Empress Kunigunde (relief from the Imperial Tomb, Bamburger Dom); (b) crown of the Holy Roman Empire, made for Otto I but given the arched band and enlarged cross later (Vienna, Schatzkammer); (c) Otto II c. 983, manuscript illumination by the master of the Registrum Gregorii, Trier (Chantilly, Condé Museum); (d) cover of

1.44d

the *Codex Aureus* from Echternach, presented to the abbey by Otto III and his mother, Theaphano (wood, ivory, gold leaf, cloisoné and precious stones).

›1.45 GOSLAR, PFALZ, PALACE OF HENRY III, 1050, rebuilt in part 1132, restored 1873.

One of several similar palaces, but reputedly the peripatetic emperor's favourite base, the main building consists of a great hall over service rooms. It is attached to the south to the Chapel of Our Lady built by Conrad II c. 1035. The throne was probably always placed in the great hall's wider central bay, but Henry III's building seems to have been unbroken by a central transept, at least at roof level: stressed in the 19th-century reconstruction, this may have originated in the rebuilding of 1132. Probably at that time, too, imperial apartments and the centralized Chapel of S. Ulrich were added to the north of the great hall and joined to it by a gallery.

1.45

Otto I and his immediate successors had the strength of character to surmount the ambiguities inherent in the relationship between pope and emperor.

SALIAN ACCESSION AND THE 'INVESTITURE DISPUTE'

On the death of Henry II, the imperium passed to the Rhenish Salian Franks with the election of Conrad II of Speyer (1024–39). After overcoming various challenges he was crowned King of Italy in Milan in 1026 and emperor in Rome the next year. His major territorial gain was Burgundy, left to him on the death of its childless duke in 1032, but he also won back lands lost to the Poles. His son, Henry III (died 1056), concentrated on further increasing the independence of the crown at the expense of the nobility and the profit of a dependent church. This provoked reaction from both sides: ecclesiastical reformers who disclaimed lay authority over the church; and the nobility, disenchanted not only with the rich endowment of churchmen but also with the preferment to the imperial entourage of a knightly class from below its own ranks. Opposition asserted itself as the emperor's powers began to fade with illness and his judgement in bestowing fiefs faltered. At its height, however, those powers were impressively displayed in the great palace complex which the emperor developed as his principal residence at Goslar.**1.45**

Henry III sought to extend his control of ecclesiastical affairs from the appointment of bishops to the election of popes. Descending on Italy for his imperial coronation in 1046, he found it deplorably degraded once more. He dismissed the dissolute, thrice-elected Benedict IX (1032–44, 1045, 1047–48) and two anti-popes in favour of his German nominee, demanded the decisive vote in future conclaves, ensured the accession of three more German popes and excited a reform movement within the Church –

inspired by the reformed Cluniacs – which was to react against him.

The reforming emperor chose a reforming pope in Leo IX (1049–54), who immediately denounced the sale of ecclesiastical offices and condemned lay interference in the appointment of bishops. To eliminate abuse and regularize church practice in accordance with a canon of ecclesiastical law, Leo asserted papal primacy unequivocally and led the church to its great schism primarily over the wording of the creed – the Byzantines maintaining that the Holy Ghost proceeds from the Father, the Romans from the Father and the Son.

Leo's successors continued the reform process with vigour, limiting papal election to the college of cardinals and proscribing lay investiture of bishops. Then in 1075 Gregory VII (1073–85), believing that secular intrusion had corrupted the Church and that healing would flow only from the spiritual authority of the pontiff, declared papal infallibility. The implications for the relationship between Church and state were far-reaching, of course, but the immediate result was the so-called 'Investiture Dispute'.

The edicts of Pope Leo IX and his successors against temporal involvement in church affairs inhibited the emperor's efforts to counter the secular magnates. As legates, moreover, bishops were the mainstays of imperial authority in towns and the emperor was bound to defend his right to invest them. Henry IV (1056–1106), who succeeded his father when a small boy, was able to do so on attaining his majority: he declared Gregory VII deposed in early 1076. The pope responded by excommunicating the emperor, absolving his subjects of their oaths to him. Dethronement threatened.**1.46**

In penance the emperor went barefoot in the snow to the pope at Canossa and was readmitted to the Church. But this lost him the confidence of the major German mag-

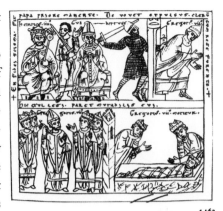

1.46a

›1.46 EMPEROR HENRY IV AND POPE GREGORY VII AT THE HEIGHT OF THE INVESTITURE DISPUTE: (a) the emperor with his anti-pope Clement III and the expulsion of Pope Gregory, top; Gregory in rival conclave and death, bottom (contemporary engraving from the imperial perspective); (b) the emperor at the gates of Canossa (from *Foxe's Book of Martyrs*, 1563).

1.46b

1.47

›**1.47 HERZBURG,** c. 1073: model (waiting room of Herzburg cable car).

The irregular enclosure was dominated by a stout cylindrical watchtower, but the imperial accommodation was in a rectangular block behind. The power of the Ottonian and early Salian emperors had ensured that castle building was much rarer in Germany than elsewhere in feudal Europe, until the investiture crisis in the second half of the 11th century. The earlier watchtowers were usually square in plan, but cylindrical stair turrets were common in ecclesiastical westworks.

›**1.48 SALZBURG, FESTUNG HOHEN-SALZBURG.**

One of a chain of fortresses dominating the passes through the Alps, the original tower at the heart of the complex was founded in the papal cause in 1077, the year of Emperor Henry IV's submission to Pope Gregory VII at Canossa. As usual, the rest of the site was developed over several centuries. The civil strife provoked by the Investiture Dispute, furthering the feudal decentralization of power, naturally led to the proliferation of castles which had been strictly controlled by Henry's predecessors.

nates – especially the Saxons – who proceeded with the dethronement. The Rhineland remained loyal, so too did most bishops and several important southern vassals and Henry forged an alliance with the common people. He survived on this basis and with a staunch chain of castles in the Herz mountains of Saxony – though the enemy countered with fortresses guarding the passes to Italy.[1.47, 1.48]

The twenty-year struggle between emperor and pope exhausted the resources of both sides and divided the Ger-

1.48

man Church whose lands were widely pillaged for recompense. There was a truce when Henry's son, who had turned against him in alliance with the magnates, succeeded as Henry V (1106–25). The crown had gained strength from its alliance with the people against the nobles, but lost it in the opposition of father and son.

Resuming the struggle with the papacy and the princes, Henry V overawed the pope (Paschal II, 1099–1119) and forced his own coronation, but was unable to regain fully effective supremacy over either papacy or princes. The latter gained as arbiters in the recurrent investiture struggle and brokered a compromise that conceded the canonical election of bishops in return for the ruler's right of endowment. Henry left a weakened monarchy to which his principal Saxon opponent, Lothair of Supplinburg (1125–37), was elected in his stead.

THE IMPERIAL CHURCH

In line with the aims of the Saxon dynasty to restore coherence to their domains through military might and to sustain it in the catholicity of the Church, the imperial will promoted a relatively homogeneous style of ecclesiastical architecture across the lands which now constitute Germany. Fundamental to this was a tauter integration of the parts of the church which had emerged as standard from the Carolingian achievement: the wooden-roofed basilica with many towers, westwork and extra sanctuaries for more masses, as at Corvey.[1.30]

Composition was still additive, but the semicircular geometry of the ambulatory occasionally disciplined the process – though the full implications of this were not to be realized in Germany – and a framework of pilasters or attached columns, anticipated at Germigny-des-Près, bound all the parts into a whole greater than their sum.[1.21] Apart from improved vaulting, the Lombards contributed the agents of enhanced external articulation which they, in turn, had derived from Ravenna. Beyond western imperial inspiration, moreover, Byzantium proffered the richness of varied rhythm in internal elevations.

The Saxon emperors asserted authority with grand new cathedrals throughout their domain, but their particular concern was to build bastions of the faith as bridgeheads to the pagan east. The lost 10th-century cathedral at Halberstadt was an early example, which closely followed Corvey except for the putative rhythm introduced by varying

1.49a

>1.49 MAGDEBURG, UNSER LIEBEN FRAUEN
MONASTERY CHURCH, 1015: (a) cloister, (b) westwork.

The Augustinian monastery was founded as a Germanic outpost and base for further expansion into
Slavic lands. The nave was vaulted in the early 13th century; the church was extensively restored after World
War II. The original cloister is outstanding.

1.49b

the size of its arcade piers. The greatest example was Otto
the Great's cathedral at Magdeburg, but – like the contemporary cathedrals at Mainz and Worms in the Rhenish west
of his empire – that disappeared in subsequent rebuilding.
However, the church of the Unser Lieben Frauen
monastery, built less than a century later on the neighbouring site to its north, offers admirable compensation.**1.49**

1.50a

1.50b

The grandest extant representative of the Ottonian type is the convent church of S. Cyriakus at Gernrode.**1.50** There the influence of works like S. Demetrios, Thessaloniki (AICI, pages 735ff) is discernible in the development of the alternating rhythm of columns and piers in the nave arcade and the introduction of triforium galleries. Formal descent from S. Riquier is not hard to see but the original

>1.50 GERNRODE, S. CYRIAKUS, founded c. 960: (a) exterior from the west, (b) general view from the south, (c) interior looking east.

The convent and its great church were founded under the patronage of Empress Theophano by the margrave Gero as a bastion against the Slavs – like imperial Magdeburg and probably in similar form. Aisled basilicas with transepts were the Ottonian norm, inherited from Fulda and Corvey, but there were exceptions – like the contemporary S. Pantaleon, Cologne (966–80). The triforium galleries at S. Cyriakus are the earliest significant examples in Germany and the form was not subsequently popular there: Greek in origin, like the richly varied capitals of the nave arcade, it is possible that they were introduced here as secluded

1.50c

accommodation for the inmates of the convent at the instigation of the patroness, Otto II's Byzantine wife – though galleried basilicas were long out of date in her father's capital. The ambulatory, which made a putative appearance at Corvey to discipline the additive composition of the east end, was not repeated here and it was largely undeveloped in Germany.

Over a reduced narthex, eliminated with the addition of the western apse, the westwork is less massive than at S. Riquier or Corvey, dispensing with the central tower and upper chapel, and substituting cylindrical stair turrets for the square-sided tower.

unbroken transept recalls S. Pietro, Rome, and external articulation in terms of pilaster strips and blind arcading derives from Lombardy. Pilasters and a valence of miniature arcades under stringcourses and eaves appear too in the westwork of the near contemporary church of S. Pantaleon at Cologne – its towering form asserting itself over the squat nave as the most potent Ottonian derivative

from the imperial Carolingian tradition. Still Lombard in articulation, the formula persisted in the mid-12th-century rebuilding of Trier cathedral – for example.[1.51, 1.52]

The later addition of a western apse at S. Cyriakus, conforming to the Aniane blueprint for church planning adopted at Fulda,[1.28] was subsequently far from uncommon: the westworks of the cathedral at Trier is a prominent example. The second apse could accommodate an additional choir and, hence, provide for polyphony.

In the generation after the completion of S. Cyriakus, the biapsidal form recurs often in imperial churches, notably S. Michael's in Hildesheim and the great cathe-

›1.52 TRIER, CATHEDRAL OF S. PETER, from c. 1040 in rebuilding work on the early Christian site.

The double cathedral, developed by Constantine and augmented in the second half of the 4th century with a square choir (*Quadratbau*) for the northern church, was destroyed by the Franks in the 5th century, rebuilt and destroyed again by the Norse in the 9th century. Rebuilding across the following century began with the refection of the square north-eastern *Quadratbau* – transforming its original columns into piers – but was not to approach its definitive form until the accession of Archbishop Poppo (1016–47). Under him, work proceeded beyond the reformed *Quadratbau* to a new apsidal westwork: the twin-towered structure, with stair turrets and precocious external galleries flanking the apse projection, was well advanced on the archbishop's demise and completed under his successors.

drals of Mainz and Worms – though much of the latter is later. The twin-towered crossings with their twin turrets and galleries, the alternating rhythm of the nave arcade, the regular geometry and the Doric logic of the 'Order' – as at Hildesheim – mark the achievement of the Ottonian ideal just as power passed to the Salians. The builders of the new dynasty were to pursue the ideal on an even grander scale in their Rhenish homeland and more modestly elsewhere – at Quedlinburg, for instance. Meanwhile, Benedictine reform initiated in 10th-century Cluny prompted a return to early Christian simplicity manifested architecturally in the colonnaded basilica without rhythmic alternation.**1.53**

1.53a

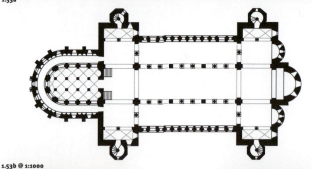

1.53b @ 1:1000

1.53c

›1.53 HILDESHEIM, S. MICHAEL, begun 1010, dedicated 1015, completed 1033: (a) general view from the south-east, (b) plan, (c, d) interior, looking east and detail of west end.

In the external massing, towers proliferated in accordance with the early Romanesque additive approach to composition, but their disposition integrated the parts. There is an apse beyond a transept at each end and the nave colonnade is divided by the interpolated piers into three triads, defining compartments commensurate with the squares of the crossings: tectonic blocks, consistently undercut from semicircles to all four faces but unembellished with foliage, were preferred to sub-Corinthian variations for the capitals as work progressed. However, symmetry of massing is disrupted by the extended western sanctuary bay and the ambulatory passage serving the crypt on which it is raised. There is no crypt to the east. As the two apses were original, the church was entered through the south aisle as in the blueprint for the abbey church devised for Benedict of Aniane where access was directly from the cloister. There are no galleries except at the ends of the transepts where they could accommodate choirs for enhanced polyphony.

1.53d

1.54a

1.54b

›1.54 THE TWIN-TOWERED WEST FRONT: (a) Strasbourg, cathedral of Notre-Dame (begun c. 1015), reconstruction; (b) Marmoutier abbey church (c. 1150).

The westwork has ceased to be a self-contained block: the triple arcade in the centre led through a porch directly to the nave. The towers flanked the porch and the twin doors at their base led through square chambers to the aisles.

›1.55 SPEYER, CATHEDRAL OF SS. MARIE AND STEPHAN, begun in its present form c. 1030, vaulted from 1082, ruined in the 17th century, rebuilt in the 18th and 19th centuries: (a) plan, (b) general view, (c) crypt, (d) nave to east.

The twin-towered westwork of Trier is prophetic – quite different to S. Cyriakus, S. Pantaleon and their extraordinary successors at Paderborn or Soest. The immediate precedent was the original westwork of the cathedral at Strasbourg, begun under Henry II around 1015. Like the near-contemporary west end of Cluny II, this dispenses with the typical Carolingian central tower block flanked by a pair of stair turrets in favour of twin towers: it has disappeared under later work but the type, amplified with a splendid central belfry, is well represented much later at Marmoutier.[1.54]

The original plan of S. Cyriakus, with a transept before the sanctuary raised over a crypt in the apse, recalls S. Pietro in the Vatican at least after its high altar was raised c. 600. Imperial pretension recommended the Constantinian church as the pre-eminent model for the great metropolitan churches of the revived empire – as at Fulda. The Salians were to amplify it on a spectacular scale. Of course, Charlemagne's palatine chapel at Aachen – and its Justinian model at Ravenna – were also often emulated. At Essen (c. 980), for example, a semihexagonal derivative rises to the full octagon in association with a square tower flanked by cylindrical stair turrets. Among several simpler but more complete examples of such homage, the convent church of Ottmarsheim in Alsace may be taken as representative.

With Conrad of Speyer's accession the centre of architectural gravity was definitely the Rhineland, despite important work at far-off Hersfeld. Limburg an der Haardt apart, that centre was at Speyer, where a great church was projected as a shrine befitting the pretensions of a new imperial dynasty from Franconia. Descent from S. Riquier is clear in the constituent elements but the imperial model for the nave, in scale as in much else, was the late-Roman basilica at nearby Trier.[1.55]

Speyer

Without chapels *en échelon* or ambulatory, the apsidal east end is conservative. On the precedent set in Rome at S. Pietro, followed in Germany at Hildesheim, it is raised over a crypt. So too is the transept. The most magnificent of its period, the crypt was produced in the first campaign of work under Conrad II as a dynastic mausoleum: each of the three compartments under the transepts is divided by four columns into nine groin-vaulted bays, and an extension of the system supports the sanctuary.

The central square bay of the crossing is crowned by a great octagonal tower: paying homage to Aachen, that was to be much emulated by later imperial builders. The westwork is Carolingian too: dispensing with a projecting choir, it retains the central tower characteristic of earlier imperial works but the twin rectangular stair turrets are displaced from the ends to the eastern side where they terminate the aisles. Blind arcading and recessed portals emphasize the thickness of the wall and the various parts of the vast structure are bound together by Lombard galleries.

In the nave (c. 72 by 14 metres and c. 27 metres high), originally roofed in timber but flanked by groin-vaulted aisles, the Ottonian alternating rhythm of piers and columns is abandoned in favour of the regular succession of massive piers. These are articulated with attenuated half-columns – the precedent for which may be found in the crypt of the now-ruined abbey church at Limburg an der Haadt – and from them blind arches soar up over the aisle arcade to frame the clerestory and unify the fenestration. The exercise is a powerful restatement of the exterior of the basilica at Trier: as there, moreover, the superimposition of arches recalls the typical Roman aqueduct.

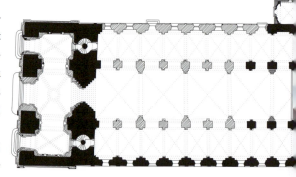

1.55a @ 1:1000

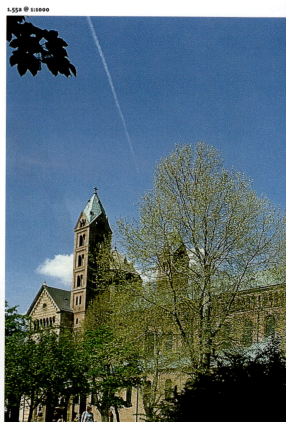

1.55c

1.55b

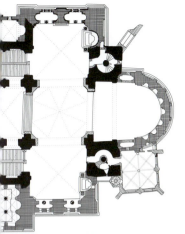

With obvious didactic intent, Henry IV transformed the interior after 1082 – at the height of the Investiture Dispute – by replacing the original timber roof with groin vaults over paired bays. Hardly precedented in scale since antiquity – at least north of the Alps – these required the strengthening of alternate piers: transverse arches, separating the paired bays, are supported by two tiers of superimposed columns, sturdier than the originals and attached to pilaster-like projections. The lateral arches enclose a second clerestory. Though there were antique groin vaults in the Rhineland that could have provided models for the Salian architects, the idea probably came from Italy. Pilaster strips and a gallery under the eaves suggest a northern Lombard influence that may well have been found first hand at, for example, S. Pietro, Agliate, or S. Abbondio, Como.

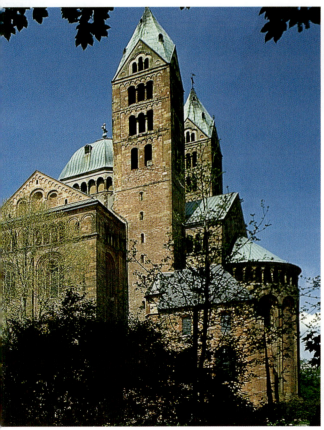

1.55d

1.56a

1.56b

>**1.56 WORMS, CATHEDRAL OF S. PETER,**
rebuilt from c. 1000 over Merovingian and Carolingian
foundations, and again from c. 1125, restored from
1846 and again after World War II: (a, b) west end exterior and interior, (c, d) nave and eastern crossing, (e)
model of complex with S. John's church left.

Hitherto dated to the half-century from c. 1170, work
on the extant cathedral has recently been moved back
half a century on the strength of the dendrochronology
of timberwork above the springing of the east-end
vaults. Similarly, the nave clerestory has been dated to
c. 1170 and the west choir to shortly after consecration
in 1181.

Both choirs project between circular stair turrets,

1.56c

1.56d

Completed after some fifty years, the greatest of Salian buildings is an imperfect record of their achievement. The other major Rhenish cathedrals of Worms and Mainz have also had chequered histories. The former, once thought to be wholly Hohenstaufen, is now seen to have been begun c. 1125, over early 11th-century biapsidal foundations, and consecrated in 1181 with only the towers and the west front incomplete.[1.56] Mainz cathedral is usually ranked among the greatest German Romanesque compositions.[1.57] It was

the rectangular east slightly, the polygonal west end, with its superimposed roses, boldly: the articulation is essentially Lombard but the upper galleries are at their most assertive. The octagonal crossing tower closely follows the one at Speyer. The doubled bays of the nave are separated by piers with pilasters and attached shafts: only the north elevation has pilasters over the intermediate piers and on both sides there is considerablr variation in the blind arcading at clerestory level. The domical bays are rib-vaulted throughout.

To the south-east of the magnificent 14th-century south portal, the late-12th-century octagonal church of S. John – which presumably once accommodated baptism – was demolished in 1802.

1.56e

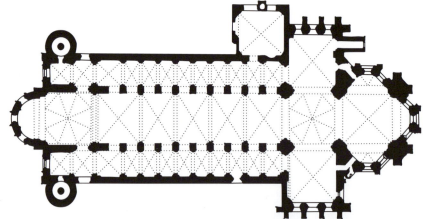

1.57a @ 1:1000

1.57c

>1.57 MAINZ, CATHEDRAL OF S. MARTIN, founded 978, rebuilt 11th century and later, west tower heightened 1480 and rebuilt 1767 and 1879, the whole much restored in the 19th and 20th centuries: (a, b) late-12th-century plan and reconstruction, (c) east end, (d–f) west crossing, south aisle and nave to west.

First rebuilt on a grand scale under Otto II from 978, burnt at its dedication in 1009, rebuilt and reconsecrated by 1036, rebuilt again 1060–1137 and yet again 1181–1239, the cathedral has been much developed since but on the Ottonian basis. Like S. Pietro, Rome, the high altar was at the western rather than the eastern end, but there was no crypt. Like that great model, too, there was one apse beyond one great transept, here endowed with an octagonal lantern tower at the crossing, which was later heightened. As at S. Pietro, again, a funerary chapel was later attached to the end of the main transept (by Archbishop Adalbert c. 1130): to the north the double-height Gottardkapelle, rising to an octagon from a square, like the Palatine chapel at Aachen, marked the advent of the type known as *Doppelkapelle*.

After the manner of S. Cyriakus, Gernrode, the church was biapsidal before 1036. A western transept may date from that time, in inception at least, but it was with the construction of additional apses to the sides of the sanctuary bay in a trefoil form and the insertion of another grand crossing with an octagonal tower, that the west end came to eclipse the east in the early 13th century. All the apses have open galleries and the whole is articulated in the Lombard manner.

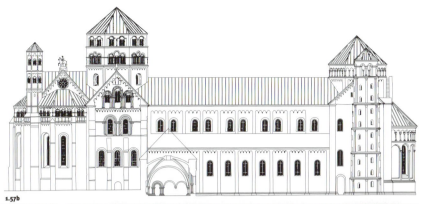

1.57b

1.57d

1.57e

1.57f

founded in 978, destroyed on the day of its consecration in 1009, rebuilt from 1136 with apses at each end and amplified under the late Hohenstaufens (c. 1200–39) with a trefoil western sanctuary. This followed the example set c. 1060 for basilican S. Maria im Kapitol, Cologne, and its variations in the second half of the 12th century for the same city's Gross S. Martin and S. Aposteln churches. The semi-

›1.58 **1.58 THE TREFOIL SANCTUARY IN COLOGNE:** (a–c) S. Maria im Kapitol (begun c. 1040, reworked c. 1200), plan, exterior from north-east and interior of crossing; (d) S. Aposteln (begun c. 1190), exterior from north; (e, f) Gross S. Martin (consecrated 1172), exterior from south-east and interior to east.

The trefoil sanctuary of S. Maria has ambulatories curving the system of the aisles right round its perimeter to bind the parts together as effectively as the external articulation of alternating pilasters and

1.58b

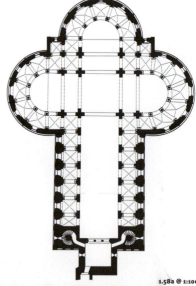

1.58a @ 1:1000

attenuated columns below, miniature blind arcading above: the ambulatory had been groin-vaulted by the end of the 12th century; the nave remained unvaulted until 1219 but the high vaulting of sanctuary and transept was completed soon after 1200 and the exterior endowed with Lombard articulating detail.

S. Martin and the S. Aposteln have simpler plans without ambulatories but are similarly rich in Lombard unifying detail: S. Martin has one enormous square tower over the crossing but a single tower projects boldly from the west end of the other two churches in the Aachen manner: the inclined lozenge-shaped roof planes between the assertive gables of the S. Aposteln's tower were to be enduringly popular in Germany. The thickness of the wall is emphasized by blind arcading, outside and in, and the Salian will to unity distinguishes the consistent articulation of the exterior.

1.58c

1.58d

centralized work of the Kapitol was developed from a square crossing; the S. Aposteln's crossing recalled the octagon of imperial Aachen and beyond that the Milanese S. Lorenzo as well as S. Vitale in Ravenna.[1.58]

Like the major Rhenish cathedrals, most of the great imperial churches have changed over time. The purest image of Salian Romanesque is provided by the abbey of Maria Laach and, in so far as its silhouette is concerned, by the cathedral at Tournai – though that is outside the Salian field and has additional importance in its four-storeyed interior.[1.59, 1.60]

1.58e

1.58f

1.59a

›ARCHITECTURE IN CONTEXT »RENOVATION OF GRAVITAS

1.59b

1.59c

The scale and monumentality of Conrad's work, inspired by the remains of Roman imperial greatness, are matched by an austerity springing certainly not from paucity of resource. The impulsion, rather, was the force of a conviction rooted in the concept of the church as the scene of man's encounter with transcendant majesty as much as with the threshold of the supernatural. For the Salians that threshold was still a westwork of the Carolingian type and the original one at Speyer is certainly not atypical in incorporating a triple portal. That recalls the imperial Roman triumphal arch form retained by Constantine and that, in turn, derived from the ancient Mesopotamian twin-towered portal of epiphany (AICI, pages 92f). Already in late-Ottonian Strasbourg the towers, reduced to pylons by the Romans, had reasserted themselves as essential elements in the entrance to the City of God.

>**1.59 MARIA LAACH, ABBEY CHURCH,** 1093–1156: (a) exterior from west, (b) interior to sanctuary, (c) atrium.

In a long but conservative building campaign, the formula achieved at S. Michael, Hildesheim – with two apses, two transepts and six towers – is perfected with the addition of an atrium and the vaulting of the interior over a regular succession of piers with attached shafts.

>**1.60 TOURNAI, CATHEDRAL OF NOTRE-DAME,** 1110 and later: (a) exterior from south, (b) south transept and twin towers, (c) nave (c. 1135).

The nave elevation is a prime example of arcade surmounted by gallery, triforium and clerestory: piers relieved with shafts of blue stone and an external gallery at clerestory level recall Lombardy. A trefoil east end was added from 1165. Twin towers flanked each apse, as at S. Riquier and S. Cyriakus, Gernrode, but here they are square. The eastern ones disappeared when the sanctuary was extended in the 13th century, but the northern and southern ones, associated with the crossing lantern, provide the most spectacular witness to imperial Romanesque aspiration.

1.60a

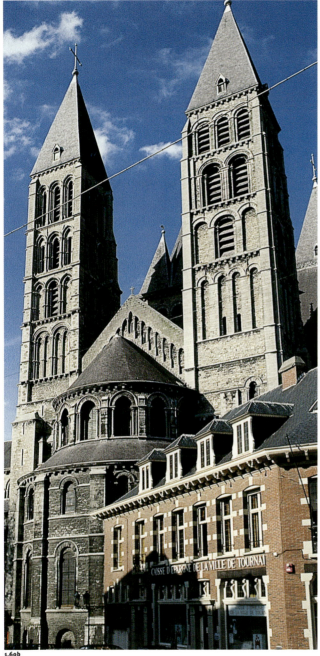

1.60b

1.60c

›ARCHITECTURE IN CONTEXT »RENOVATION OF GRAVITAS

begun c. 1060: (a) façade, (b) nave towards the sanctuary apse.

A church enshrining the 3rd-century martyr S. Miniato was posssibly a Carolingian foundation, certainly an Ottonian one: rebuilding from the mid-11th century sustained the Roman basilican formula without transepts. The columns are modelled on Roman ones – if they are not actually antique survivors – but they are grouped into triads between composite piers of the Lombard type supporting diaphragm arches.

The crypt is entered through three central arches and the chancel raised over it is served by steps at the ends of the aisles: the sanctuary apse was decorated in mosaic from 1297 by the great Florentine artist Cimabue. The geometrical patterning of the two-toned marble revetment, realized over several generations from the early 12th century, was to remain popular in the area beyond the medieval era. The Badia at Fiesole is perhaps the most prominent early follower.

›1.62 AQUILEIA, CATHEDRAL, founded 313, rebuilt from 1021: apse with fresco of the Madonna and Child flanked by Emperor Conrad II, Empress Gisela of Swabia and their son, the future Emperor Henry III. Patriarch Poppo holds a model of the church whose rebuilding he initiated.

1.61a

4 DISPUTED ITALY

Italy sustained early Christian traditions well beyond the opening of the second millennium. Greek-cross – or near-centralized – plans with domed crossings of eastern resonance were not unfamiliar in coastal areas, east and west of the peninsula from Portofino in Liguria to Portonovo on the Adriatic, and the quincunx was the norm in the south until the second half of the 11th century, as we shall see. Elsewhere works carried out then – such as the cathedrals at Torcello and Aquileia, and Florentine S. Miniato al Monte – reveal little change in the standard western type of basilica over the last half of the first millennium (AICI, pages 693f).**1.61, 1.62**

1.61b

1.62

1.63a

›1.63 **EARLY CHRISTIAN REVISION IN MEDIEVAL ROME:** (a) S. Clemente (founded c. 380, restored c. 900, rebuilt from 1108), interior; (b, c) S. Maria in Cosmedin (founded on a Flavian hall in the 6th century, enlarged in the 8th, renovated in the early 12th century, tower c. 1200), exterior and interior.

ROME

Similarly, the venerable tradition is respected in contemporay renovations in Rome, at S. Maria in Cosmedin, S. Maria in Trastevere or S. Clemente most notably. Apart from 'Cosmatesque' decorative inlay work on pavements and furniture – grand marble baldachinos above all – the major new elements were the pier interpolated in the aisle colonnade to provide rhythm or adopted throughout due to the scarcity of antique columns, the raised sanctuary on a partially revealed crypt and the bell tower.[1.63]

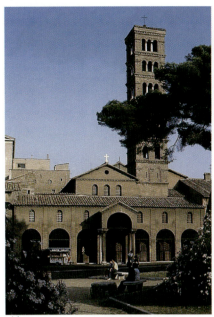

1.63b

1.63c

Archaizing renovation in Rome

S. Clement was rebuilt from 1108 with much reuse of original materials and furniture but on a reduced basilican plan and with piers in the central bay of the colonnade. The baldachino and the great mosaic in the apse also date from the 12th century. This is the case with the mosaics of S. Maria in Trastevere but the baldachino there is a 19th-century reproduction.

At least from the 8th century, S. Maria in Cosmedin was distinguished from the standard type by the inclusion of galleries – after the example of S. Lorenzo fuori le Mura. These were eliminated in the rebuilding, presumably returning the nave to its original form in conception, if not elevation: as at S. Clemente, the piers date from a rebuilding phase strengthening support for the upper walls. The arcaded and gabled portico projecting over columns from the narthex represents a type which recurs in Rome. The tower at the west end of the south aisle, with its seven storeys graded in weight, is a splendid representative of the form which proliferated in Rome in the later 12th and 13th centuries: like the somewhat less elevated tower of S. Maria in Trastevere, it dates from c. 1200.

The redecoration of these churches is most notable for the introduction of elaborate mosaic pavements of coloured marble tiles and gold tesserae within a white marble armature of rectangular and circular lines: as in the contemporary embellishment of S. Clemente's furniture, this was due to the brothers Lorenzo and Jacopo Cosmati who gave their name to the style of ornament which flourished widely in the 13th century. In contrast to the 'neo-Classical' example at S. Clemente, with its rich *pavonazzetto* columns but no typically Cosmatesque embellishment, the baldachino of S. Maria in Cosmedin is due to a late-13th-century member of the Cosmati dynasty.

The tower was inherited through early Christian Syria from remotest antiquity where it was associated with epiphany as much as with surveillance (AICI, pages 92f and 742f). With bells to announce prayer, the Romanesque type derives from developments at S. Pietro in Rome. So too does the raised sanctuary. As in Germany, the specific influence of the prime patriarchal basilica was potent at the highest level of patronage in Italy: examples are numerous, unsurprisingly, but they were evidently nowhere better represented than in the lost rebuilding of the venerable abbey of Montecassino by the abbot Desiderius from 1066.

LOMBARDY AND ITS NEIGHBOURS

The highest level of patronage in Italy was not located at the peak of a single hierarchical pyramid. The failure of both emperor and pope conclusively to counter the power of local magnates or civic authorities throughout the peninsula ensured marked diversity in developments there – and a dearth of decisive documents for dating. If there was a pervasive theme, echoed across the Alps, it was the reinforcing of the venerable Constantinian Christian tradition on the strength of the overwhelmingly impressive ancient imperial structural legacy – and the example of the Exarchate in articulation – at the hands of the Lombards.

The Lombards continued to pay particular attention to developing the tower: the 10th-century one to the south of S. Ambrogio's narthex is a putative example; Pomposa's nine-storey belfry of c. 1060 asserts early maturity.[**1.64**] In place of the typical early Christian revealed roof truss, most significantly, the Lombards also continued the develop-

›1.64 **POMPOSA, BENEDICTINE ABBEY CHURCH,** founded in the 8th century and given its belfry c. 1060.

The extraordinarily elevated nine-storey tower is articulated with pilaster strips and blind miniature arcades to the stringcourses and eaves in the manner evolved by the Lombards under the inspiration of Ravenna.

The church was an early Christian foundation, but
the apse, crypt and subsidiary eastern sanctuaries are
of the mid-10th century. Limited records and analysis of
the fabric suggest that the old nave survived until 1067
and a new one was in use by 1093, though the western
bay was still incomplete when the atrium was begun in
1098 and even when the north tower was begun in 1123.
Meanwhile, major damage was inflicted by an earthquake in 1117 and the nave vaults were repaired thereafter: that they were embraced by the original
conception of the new nave is implied by the incidence
of the composite piers but some analysts maintain that
they were realized only after 1117. The fourth bay collapsed under the weight of its superstructure in 1196
and rebuilding extended well into the 13th century.

ment of masonry, the vaulting that impressed Henry IV
and the rhythmic articulation of the internal elevation.
Their achievement of the latter together with the introduction of the rib to the groin vault is marked by the nave
of S. Ambrogio, Milan.**1.65**

The Lombards and the rib vault

The Lombards were doubtless aware of the ribbing of the great dome of H.
Sofia in Constantinople and of later Muslim practice in all those parts of the
Mediterranean littoral to which ships took many Italians. More particularly
familiar with the brick skeleton of Roman concrete vaults, they would have
found that the construction of a permanent centring across the diagonals of
square bays facilitated the laying of groin vaults and they may well have
believed that ribs provided necessary reinforcement where two membranes

1.65a

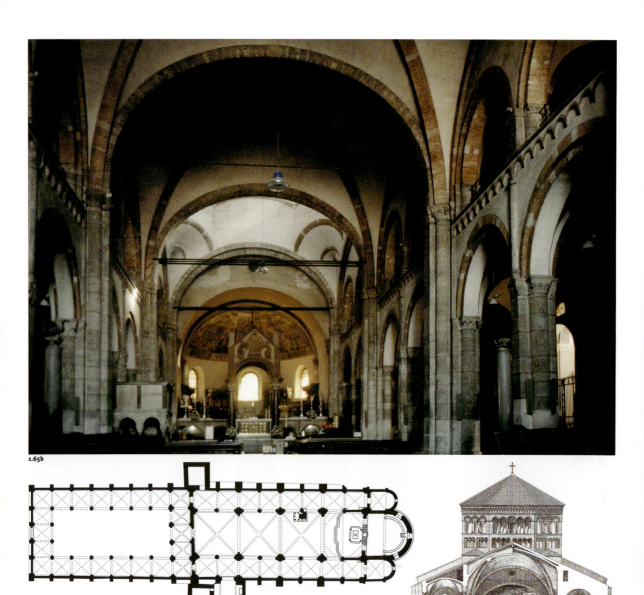

1.65b

1.65c @ 1:1000

1.65d

of vaulting met in large-scale constructions. But their purpose was at least as much aesthetic: they revealed the ribs to articulate structure at the salient line of intersection of each segment of vaulting and to bind the lateral arches of each bay into a completely integrated skeletal frame.

The vaults of S. Nazaro Maggiore, Milan (formerly the church of the Holy Apostles, begun 382) may be earlier than those of S. Ambrogio, even if the latter are assigned to the building campaign begun c. 1067, but it is probable that primacy belonged to some other work destroyed by the earthquake of 1117. The ribbed groins of S. Sigismondo, Rivolta d'Adda – primitive in execution – are generally dated to the last decade of the 11th century. And around that time there was an early incidence of rib vaulting at S. Nazzaro Sesia, near Novara. Slightly later, S. Michele at Pavia is comparable to S. Ambrogio in its internal articulation and vaulting.

The enrichment of articulation, inside and out, by enhancing the third dimension of the traditional blind arcading to produce a colonnaded gallery is a phenomenon hardly unrelated to the articulation of the stresses implicit in vaulting. The octagonal tower over the crossing of S. Ambrogio is a prominent example, echoed by many semi-octagonal or circular apses. In this and in its vaulting the example of S. Ambrogio – and/or its lost predecessors – was followed across northern Italy from Pavia to Parma.**1.66, 1.67**

>**1.66 COMO, S. FEDELE,** 12th century: (a, b) polygonal sanctuary, exterior and interior.

Unusual in Italy for its date, the trefoil sanctuary is possibly inspired by S. Maria in Kapitol, Cologne. The external arcading is among the earliest surviving examples.

1.66a   1.66b

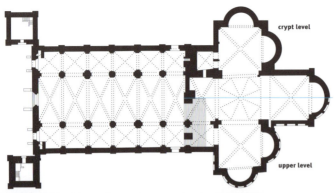

crypt level

upper level

1.67a @ 1:1000

›1.67 **PARMA, CATHEDRAL AND BAPTISTRY,** hall crypt dedicated in 1106, substantially rebuilt after an earthquake in 1117, vaulted after 1162; baptistry 1196: (a) plan of crossing and part of six-bay nave, (b) view from north-west, (c) baptistry vault, (d) view of baptistry and bell tower (e) nave to east .

The façade of the cathedral represents an enrichment of the Lombard formula primarily in stone rather than brick: the broad gable and its stepped gallery rise from a massive wall pierced by two horizontal galleries and a portico still recalling the central motif (at least) of the Palace of the Exarch, Ravenna – and the Carolingian westwork. The columns of the main portal are characteristically carried on the backs of lions. Inside, the alternating rhythm of the nave's major and minor piers is sustained through triforium and clerestory but the implied division of the nave into roughly square bays is not expressed in the vaulting. Beyond the sixth bay of the nave, broad steps lead up over the extensive crypt to the square crossing from which the transept arms and sanctuary project as roughly equal squares: each has an apsidal end and the transept arms have eastern apses as well. The colonnaded galleries which distinguish the exterior of the octagonal baptistry recur inside in support of the spectacular 13th-century rib vault.

1.67b

The basilica at Parma was consecrated in 1106 but rebuilt after the earthquake of 1117 and rib-vaulted over regularly repeated rectangular bays in 1162. The façade is of the

1.67c

unified wide-span galleried gable type established with somewhat military severity for S. Michele in Pavia and developed in Piacenza among other Lombard sites. This was to be complemented by a pair of bell towers, freestanding in the Lombard tradition, of which only the southern one reached full height. Beside the latter, the final element is an unexcelled octagonal baptistry with five tiered galleries completed in the 13th century.

The Parmesan cathedral complex, not unique, was rivalled perhaps only at Florence and Pisa. The baptistry

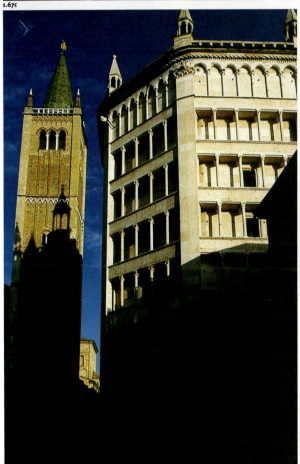

1.67d

1.67e

1.68b

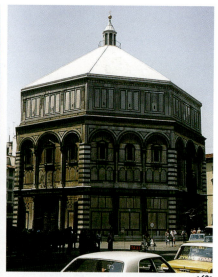

1.68a

›1.68 **FLORENCE, BAPTISTRY OF S. GIO-VANNI,** dated variously between the 6th and 11th centuries: (a, b) exterior and interior.

On the site of an early Christian baptistry, converted from a Roman temple, an octagonal replacement seems to have been built in the late-9th century: this followed the removal of the cathedral from S. Lorenzo to the 6th-century church of S. Reparata (replaced by the existing great church of S. Maria del Fiore from 1296). The baptistry's consecration in 1059 is thought to have followed its reconstruction to a larger scale: it served as the cathedral while S. Reparata was enlarged.

An inner structure incorporating an arcaded gallery over freestanding columns was inserted at the end of the following century to support a conical vault with its splendid mosaic cycle: essentially foreign to Florence, the Byzantine medium was introduced by a Greek master called Apollonius c. 1225 initiating a campaign of work which was to last for a century. The original sanctuary apse was replaced on a rectangular plan at this time. The exterior revetement, Classicizing like the definitive interior articulation – though uncanonical in accordance with the late-imperial and early Christian practice of raising arches over columns – also probably dates from c. 1200, except for the later quoins strengthening the corners.

›1.69 PISA, CATHEDRAL COMPLEX WITH BAPTISTRY AND BELL TOWER, 1063–1118, nave extended by five bays in 1261–72: (a) general view from south-west, (b–d) cathedral from east, plan and interior.

Begun in celebration of naval triumph over the Saracens in 1062, the cathedral was consecrated in 1118. The nave is flanked by doubled aisles, the inner ones surmounted by galleries: the colonnaded arcades and pilastered galleries are unbroken in their regularity but continue across the transepts beyond composite piers. The apsidal transepts are hardly less than additional single-aisled basilicas perpendicular to the main east–west one: their conjunction recalls the great cruciform shrine of S. Simeon at Qal'at Si'man in Syria (AIC1, pages 744f) – not necessarily coincidentally, as the Pisans transported Crusaders to the Holy Land from the end of the 11th century. The crossing is covered by an unusual oval dome carried on squinches and basilican spaces are roofed in timber.

alone remains from the early Christian context at Florence: its dating is obscure but the revetment from a late stage is clearly related to the work at S. Miniato, with its applied Order and geometric patterning in contrasting marbles, and the resplendent interior marks a new departure for Florence later reflected in S. Miniato's apse.**1.68**

The splendid triad at Pisa is marred only by the tilt to its tower. The basilica is exceptionally grand and varicoloured in its internal revetment, like many Italian works, but continuation of the nave arcading across the transepts is more common in the Byzantine east (AIC1, pages 735f).**1.69** The striated alternation of light and dark marbles, as in the galleries, is distinctly Pisan in sharp contrast to the geometric approach of the Florentines.

1.69a

1.69b

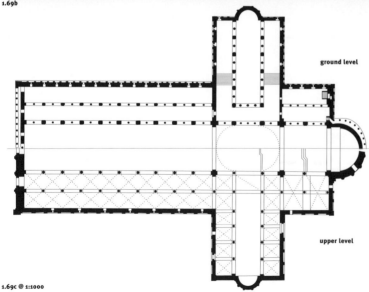

ground level

upper level

1.69c @ 1:1000

The whole is clad in marble and the façade, a direct expression of the basilican volume with tiers of elegant arcades, was probably anticipated before the 13th-century extension of the nave. The arcading of the tower – circular in plan like the belfries of Ravenna rather than rectangular as in Lombardy but badly founded – is consistent in style and date, and was continued (with pragmatic adjustment) even after subsidence initiated the lean. Consistent in style before its remodelling of the upper storeys in the mid-13th century, the baptistry recalls the Constantinian Anastasis rotunda in Jerusalem (AIC1, pages 700f). That seminal work seems variously to have been covered both by a conical roof and a dome: the former was originally adopted here, the domical element is later.

1.69d

However, the most obvious feature of the Pisan style is the superimposition of façade colonnades doubtless elaborated from the open galleries of Lombardy. Not without affiliation in Genoa and its network of trading partners – especially in striated revetment – the school was respected

for its elegant approach to the lightening of mass as far **>1.70 GENOA, CATHEDRAL OF S. LORENZO,** consecrated incomplete in 1118: nave to west.
inland as Arezzo, probably informed the baptistry at
Parma and had particularly close adherents at Lucca in
the face of Florentine pretensions.[1.70–1.72]

In S. Miniato al Monte, apart from the raised chancel,
the principal structural novelty we have detected is the
interpolation of diaphragm arches carried on piers of four
addorsed half-columns which divide the nave into compartments spanning three aisle bays.[1.61] Diaphragm

1.71

>**1.71 AREZZO, PIEVE DI S. MARIA,** c. 1200: apse.
Works of this kind may be seen to have a common
source in Lombardy, of course, but the degree of superimposition seems Pisan.

>**1.72 LUCCA:** (a) S. Michele in Foro, exterior (begun c.
1140); (b) cathedral of S. Martino, façade (begun c. 1200).

1.72a

1.72b

arches, originally supporting a wooden roof, an alternating rhythm and raised chancel are all features of the cathedral at Modena, but apart from inserting a transept to the width of the aisles, the builders added a floorless gallery to the interior and an inaccessible one to the exterior in exceptional preference of form over function. Without gallery or diaphragm arches, the alternating rhythm recurs most impressively – if somewhat irregularly – in S. Zeno Maggiore, Verona.**1.73, 1.74**

1.73a

>**1.73** VERONA, S. ZENO MAGGIORE, founded c. 1030, mainly built over several decades from 1123: (a) west front, (b) nave to sanctuary raised over the crypt.

The absence of galleries below the clerestory is common in Italy, as is the sanctuary raised over an extensive crypt; the trefoil profile of the wooden roof recurs elsewhere in the north-east, notably at Padua. The façade prefers conventional expression of the basilican profile to contrived unity in the Lombard manner but retains Lombard articulation with particular refinement.

1.73b

**›1.74 MODENA, CATHEDRAL OF S. GEMINI-
ANO,** 1099–1162 with 15th-century vaulting: (a) plan
(with later vaulting shown on upper half), (b) façade
detail, (c) nave to sanctuary.

The unusually decisive documentation of this work
extends even to the identity of the architect, Lanfranco.
The foundation stone was laid in 1099 at the behest of
Matilda of Canossa who was also a patron of S. Miniato
al Monte.

1.74b

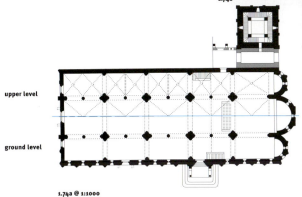

upper level

ground level

1.74a @ 1:1000

1.74c

1.75b

1.75a

APULIA AND SICILY

Towards the end of the 11th century the Normans played a major part in the crusades against the Muslims in the Holy Land. First, however, they liberated Sicily which had been taken from Byzantium for Islam by Aghlabid forces in the 9th century and ruled under the suzerainty of the Fatimids from early in the 10th century (A1C3, page 95).

Marauding from c. 1030 in southern Italy – where the hold of Byzantium was fast failing after its reassertion by the Macedonian dynasty from c. 970 – the Normans had hired themselves as mercenaries to the pope and others interested in expansion in the area. Their success frustrated the ambitions of their employers and their leader Robert Guiscard (c. 1015–85), son of Tancred de Hauteville, was recognized by Pope Nicholas II as Duke of Apulia and Calabria in 1059. The pope also endowed the Normans with Sicily, though it was still claimed by Byzantium and reconquest was far from complete. As Robert concentrated on Apulia and died in 1085, his brother Roger led the final phase of the expedition in Sicily to completion in 1091. Roger II (1130-54) was accorded the title of king in 1140.

The Normans were to make a major contribution to the development of medieval architecture but the first signs of their specific talents appeared in their homeland after the expeditionary forces had departed. Thus the great new

›**1.75 OTRANTO, S. PIETRO,** 9th century: (a) exterior, (b) interior.

The building is reputed to have been the primitive cathedral. There was a plethora of such works in southern Italy after the revival of Byzantium under the Macedonians extended to the reassertion of power there from c. 970 – though their affiliation is primarily with the translation of the quincunx into the vernacular of southern Greece and the Aegean islands.

›**1.76 BARI, S. NICOLÒ,** begun c. 1088, dedicated 1196: (a) plan, (b) portal, (c) nave to east.

The remains of S. Nicholas arrived in Bari from Anatolian Myra in 1087 and the great church which was to enshrine them was begun immediately: designed to receive pilgrims, the essential feature for the accommodation of the tomb under the apsidal sanctuary and transept of the basilican church was a large colonnaded crypt of the north-Italian type but served by stairs from the aisles – rather than an ambulatory around the apse at ground level which would distinguish the mature works of Normandy. The 1:3 relationship of nave to aisle bays – repeated to reduced scale in the transept screen – specifically recalls S. Miniato al Monte, even to the profile of the intermediate pier, but the diaphragm arches integral there were echoed at Bari only as interpolated remedial bracing. Triforium galleries echo those of Pisa in their depth and rhythm and external galleries, common in Lombardy, are especially characteristic of the style developed between Pisa and Lucca.

The east end has minor apses projecting from the transepts to either side of the sanctuary apse, in a rectangular enclosure. The unmatched, incomplete western towers – the northern one distinctly Lombard like the articulation elsewhere on the external fabric –

which provide extraordinary extension to the unrelated façade, may well have resulted from afterthought inspired by such works as S. Ambrogio in Milan, but smaller towers to the east of the crossing are integrated in the manner of S. Abbondio, Como.

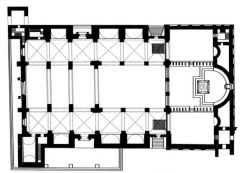

1.76a @ 1:1000

cathedrals of the period opened by their advent in southern Italy, radically different from the type of the domed quincunx hitherto dominant there,[1.75] are best explained by the wresting of the area from its tired Byzantine rulers and the transfer of its ecclesiastical affairs from the Orthodox to the Roman Church hierarchy: they must be considered in the context of contemporary Italy. So too should the major works of the Normans in Sicily, though they are altogether more eclectic.

A great series of cathedrals was built along the coast of Apulia – a trade and pilgrimage route from the north to ports serving the Holy Land. One of the earliest works, S. Nicolò at Bari, is fully in accord with the north Italian

1.76b

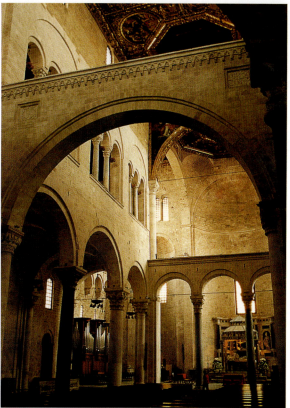

1.76c

1.77a

1.77b

tradition in its basilican plan with doubled nave bays and sanctuary raised over a colonnaded crypt. Lombard in its external articulation and in the disposition of its towers, it is specifically indebted to Modena for its arcaded galleries, inside and out. On the other hand, Bari may have originated the motif of the portal flanked by columns carried on the backs of heraldic animals which was to be universally popular in Romanesque Italy.[1.76]

The motif is ubiquitous in Apulia, as is fine, light grey ashlar. And the inspiration of S. Nicolò is manifest in most of the cathedrals erected in the region for well over

1.77c

›1.77 APULIAN VARIANTS: (a) Ruvo, cathedral of S. Maria Assunta (early 13th century), nave to east; (b, c) Bitonto, cathedral of S. Valentino (begun 1175), nave to west, exterior from south-west.

1.78b

1.78c

1.78a

›1.78 TRANI, CATHEDRAL OF S. NICOLÒ,
begun 1098: (a) exterior from west, (b) interior to east,
(c) crypt.

a century, sometimes with the 1:3 relationship of nave to aisle bays, as at Bitonto, often with an uninterrupted arcade, as at Ruvo.**1.77** However, the cathedral at Trani – one of the earliest works in the series after S. Nicolò – is a distinct masterpiece: Lombard in detail too, it has a full crypt, uninterrupted aisle arcades, unscreened transept, one integrated western tower and revealed eastern apses.**1.78**

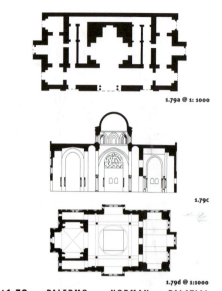

1.79c

1.79b

1.79d @ 1:1000

›1.79 PALERMO, NORMAN PALATIAL RETREATS, c. 1180: (a, b) La Ziza (al-'aziza, 'the magnificent'), plan and entrance front; (c, d) La Cuba, section and plan.

The Normans in Sicily established new Latin episcopal sees, providing them with cathedrals and themselves with palaces. In these works, both religious and secular, they promoted a spectacularly eclectic style of architecture in which northern Romanesque grandeur was grafted on to the hybrid Byzantine-Arabic stock already flourishing there: semicircular arches, overlaid with one another in syncopated semitones, join the Muslim pointed arch; intricate Muslim muqarnas applied to the flat surface of ceilings in the artesonado style, join resplendent Byzantine mosaics.

The Muslim palaces, catering for a cultivated court, excelled anything the Normans knew at home. The best-preserved of them are several agricultural estate houses which provided for summer retreat in a vast park surrounding Palermo, especially La Ziza and La Cuba.**1.79** They are symmetrical in rectangular plan and elevation in drastic reduction of the plan type represented by the palace of a Fatimid vassal at Ashir in Algeria. However, La Cuba

The formidable walls of La Cuba, projecting in the centre of each front, are relieved throughout by doubled blind arcades rising to full height from a substantial socle and enclosing minimal fenestration: the central cube is flanked by a hall on each side, all to full height.

La Ziza, also articulated with blind arcading but on three distinct levels, is better lit and more complex spatially: the double-height nucleus is T-shaped with a lateral vestibule serving a faceted square chamber with a deep recession opposite the iwan-like entrance; labyrinthine corridors separate this ceremonial core from the triads of living rooms to each side on each level. The main spaces of both buildings were enlivened by muqarnas embellished in mosaic.

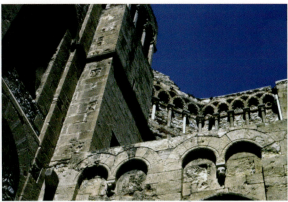

1.80a

1.80b

>**1.80 CEFALÙ CATHEDRAL,** begun 1131, embellishment from 1148, façade 1240: (a) exterior detail showing interlaced arches, (b) sanctuary.

is named for its domed central square nucleus which – *en bloc* – recalls the Qasr al-Manar at Banu Hammad, also in Algeria. The latter was unfenestrated and La Cuba was essentially introverted, unlike La Ziza with its triad of arches on the ground floor and large windows on the upper two storeys (AIC3, pages 119, 216).

The cubical palace block was a specific import from North Africa. Of more general relevance is the pointed arch: the Fatimid governors of Sicily would certainly have been familiar with it and it had been transmitted to southern Italy before the reconstruction of Montecassino abbey in the 1060s. However, its comprehensive application in the Norman kingdom awaited the reign of Roger II when the palace in the centre of Palermo was adapted organically from the Arab complex. The principal surviving elements are a massive side tower with an annex containing the 'Sala di Re Ruggero' and that king's gorgeous Cappella Palatina, both completed c. 1140.

A small triapsidal basilica with narthex and raised sanctuary, the Palermitan palace chapel conforms in miniature to the great cathedrals at Cefalù and Monreale, founded by Roger II in 1131 and William II in 1174 respectively.**1.80–1.82** All are aisled basilicas of the Latin early Christian type – with transepts at Cefalù and Monreale –

1.81b

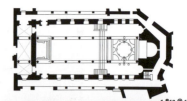

1.81a @ 1:1000

1.81c

›1.81 PALERMO, PALATINE CHAPEL OF ROGER **II,** built between 1132 and 1143, embellished over the following two decades: (a) plan, (b–d) interior details.

Behind marble colonnades supporting the pointed arches which separate nave from aisles, the walls are embellished with mosaics over a marble dado, the nave ceiling is an unexcelled artesanado work of scintillating muqarnas executed by North African craftsmen and the sanctuary vaults have no-less-celebrated mosaics executed by Byzantine craftsmen.

but the east ends are triapsidal like Cluny II. Classical columns carry Muslim pointed arches in support of the revealed polychrome timber trusses over the nave – the scale was too large for an artesonado ceiling. The massive walls of the sanctuaries carry groin vaults. The towers which flank the loggia and interlaced blind arcading of the west front at Cefalù recall the Aghlabid minaret type represented at Sfax (AIC3, page 96). Monreale displays the full flowering of the essentially decorative, hybrid Sicilian-Norman style, with its resplendent interior revetment of Byzantine mosaics over marble dado, characteristically Norman exterior articulation of interlaced pointed arches on two levels and four-square Muslim paradise garden (*chahar bagh*) in the richly arcaded cloister.**1.82d**

1.81d

1.82a

›ARCHITECTURE IN CONTEXT »RENOVATION OF GRAVITAS

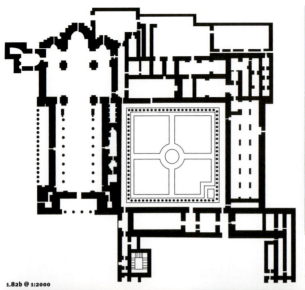

1.82b @ 1:2000

1.82c

›**1.82 MONREALE, CATHEDRAL OF S. MARIA NUOVA,** 1174: (a) nave to west, (b) plan, (c) east apse exterior detail showing interlaced arches, (d) cloister.

1.82d

1.83a

1.83b

1.83c

›**1.83 PALERMO:** (a, b) S. Cataldo (built from c. 1150 by Maio of Bari, chancellor of William I), exterior showing bell tower of La Martorana (left) and interior; (c) S. Maria del Ammiraglio (or La Martorana, built 1143–51 by George of Antioch, Roger II's admiral), quincunx interior.

Three small churches in Palermo, built during the reign of Roger II but not by the crown, are based on variations of the domed quincunx rather than basilicas. The Martorana conforms to the Byzantine canon with a dome over the central square beyond atrium and narthex. S. Giovanni degli Eremiti and S. Cataldo, on the other hand, are rectangular blocks articulated with blind arcading in the style of La Cuba and crowned by three semicircular domes rising from drums without impost mouldings. An essentially Byzantine succession of domed spaces is not uncommon in post-conquest Apulia too: Molfetta cathedral is a notable example, though the articulation is Lombard.**1.83**

Byzantine mosaicists were retained by widespread patrons in medieval Italy – and their contribution to the development of western painting is generally recognized as fundamental. However, nowhere there – or, indeed, in the Byzantine world at large – is the empyrean more persuasively evoked than in the mosaics of La Martorana in Palermo, except in the north-east where the Venetians were building S. Marco.

VENICE

Early Venice followed Byzantine models in both the religious and secular fields. The remains – and restoration – of several palatial merchant houses there recall the arcaded palatine ideal of late-imperial Ravenna, itself reflecting something of Constantinople's lost secular splendour.[1.84]

The standard basilica was retained for the most important churches built in various parts of the lagoon at the head of the Adriatic: not least for its mosaics, the cathedral at Torcello, reconstructed at the beginning of the 11th century, is the most splendid example.[1.85] In contrast, the supreme achievement of Justinian's centralizing masters inspired the great metropolitan church of S. Marco, undertaken by the Venetians in emulation of their unfailingly

1.84

>1.84 VENICE, PALAZZO FARSETTI, 13th century or earlier in origin, heavily restored in the 19th century.

1.85a

prestigious Eastern trading partner and rival to enshrine the relics of its dedicatee stolen from Alexandria (AICI, pages 780f).**1.86**

Like H. Sofia in Constantinople, S. Marco was designed as both cathedral and a palatine church: in it the doge met the patriarch. Basilica and Greek cross are again combined but here the central domed space is repeated for the nave and the other three arms of the cross have full domes too. The complex is transformed by a complete set of mosaics within and celebrated in a mosaic self-portrait over the portal: nowhere are the physical realities of this world more triumphantly denied, the image of the church as the image of the City of God – the *porta coeli* – more gloriously conveyed.

1.85b

>1.85 TORCELLO, CATHEDRAL OF THE ASSUMPTION, founded 639, reconstructed from 1008, mosaics, 11th century: (a) interior, nave to sanctuary, (b) detail of the apsidal mosaic of Madonna and Child, (c) west-end mosaic of the Last Judgement.

1.85c

1.86a

›1.86 VENICE, S. MARCO, built from 1063 over 9th- and 10th-century foundations: (a) west front as depicted in 12th-century mosaic on the north-west door and with later embellishment, (b) plan, (c) façade from Piazza S. Marco, (d, e) transept, sanctuary vaults.

The portrait of the west front, the earliest mosaic to survive there, postdates 1204 since the four horses pillaged then from Constantinople are shown in place over the central portal. As here too, the narthex was extended, the baptistry installed in the south-west corner and the exterior remodelled, to celebrate the Venetian victory and to incorporate stolen marble. Originally expressed directly on the outside, the domes were covered by timber cupolas in the 13th century and these too seem to be represented here – rather oriental in profile like some of the additional narthex arcading.

The gables have yet to undergo their final transformation in accordance with the florid taste of the later Middle Ages. The ogee profiles were introduced in the campaign of marble revetment which began in the 1380s.

S. Marco

Reputedly responsible for converting the northern shore of the Adriatic to Christianity, S. Mark was also credited with the foundation of the see of Alexandria, whence his remains were taken by the Venetians early in 828. The original church built shortly thereafter to enshrine his relics seems to have followed the Greek-cross precedent set by Justinian's rebuilding of the church of the Holy Apostles in Constantinople which was later modified by raising the domes over drums. Restored after a fire in 976, the church was rebuilt over little more than a decade from 1063 on the renovated Justinian model with a degree of magnificence – long in the process of realization – reflecting the republic's conception of its standing as a maritime power especially *vis-à-vis* Constantinople.

Retaining some of the original structure, the 11th-century rebuilding expanded and developed the initial conception, carefully following the prototype even in such detail as the design of the capitals. Fine relief on friezes and cornices acknowledges the more recent achievements of Macedonian and Comnene workers in Constantinople and where brickwork remains unconcealed by external marble revetment it is patterned in the contemporary eastern manner. Contemporary western practice is reflected in the raising of the chancel over a crypt and with limited

1.86c

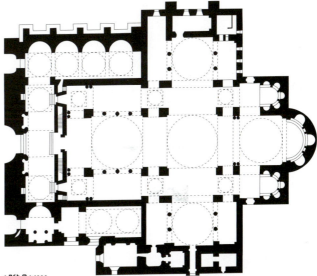

1.86b @ 1:1000

deference to the basilican tradition the nave was enlarged to exceed the dimensions of the other arms in virtual duplication of the crossing. Whether there were originally masonry vaults throughout is unknown though the precedent of five domes separated and flanked by tunnel vaults was well established. Much of the structure hidden by the rich revetment is of poorly laid brick-encased rubble. The domes are of brick laid in concentric rings rather than radially as in the east.

The vault mosaics were begun soon after the structure was completed at the end of the 11th century, though work continued on them until the cycle was finished in the 18th century. The elimination of galleries over the aisles, allowing light in through the lateral tunnel vaults, as in the renovation of the church of H. Irene in Constantinople, and the piercing of the drums of the five main domes with windows, after the example set by the renovators of the church of the Holy Apostles in the same city, enhanced the effect of these mosaics immeasurably: bathed in light, they extend a diaphanous veil over the upper fabric of the building, dissolving its mass and dissipating any sense of physical constraint interposed between the Christian soul and heaven. In marked contrast, the lower zone, earthbound and reveted in marble (largely from the second half of the 12th century) remains dark.

1.86d

1.86e

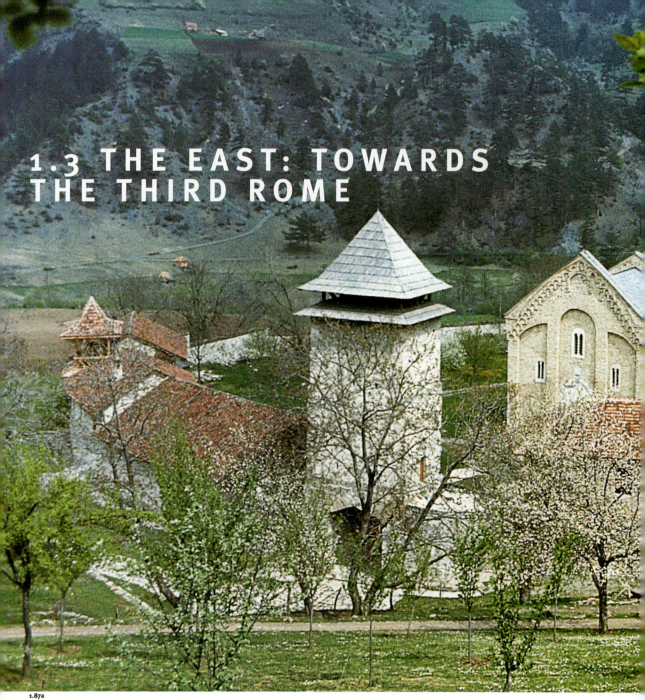

1.3 THE EAST: TOWARDS THE THIRD ROME

1.87a

›ARCHITECTURE IN CONTEXT »RENOVATION OF GRAVITAS

›**1.87** STUDENICA, MONASTERY WITH THE CHURCH OF THE VIRGIN, c. 1190: (a) general view, (b) church exterior, (c) interior.

›**1.88** TROGIR (DALMATIA), CATHEDRAL OF SVETI LOVRO (S. Lawrence), begun 1213: (a) interior to east, (b) portal.

The portal, of the Apulian type popular in Lombardy but executed by the Croatian master-mason Radovan c. 1240, is celebrated for its integration of worldly and biblical imagery. The Romanesque pulpit and ciborium were also produced in the 13th century.

1.87c

5 THE MEETING OF EAST AND WEST

Byzantium ruled much of the Balkans in various reprises, as we have seen, and the Bulgar or Serb nations ultimately established in former imperial domains were always cultural provinces of Byzantium – though exposed to varying degrees of influence from the Romanesque west as the eastern empire waned. The Byzantine style subsisted, naturally, in the parts of Italy regained by the Macedonian emperors but the western centre of gravity – political and cultural – had shifted across the Alps to the new Frankish empire in the north. In the east another new empire was emerging in Russia: never subject to Byzantine emperors but allied to them, trading with their subjects and converted to Orthodox Christianity, the rulers of Kiev were overawed by Byzantine culture and established a splendid affiliated tradition.

1.88a

1.88b

Christianity had long been advancing into the Balkans on two fronts, north-western and south-eastern: with it came the styles of the Lombards, well established in Dalmatia by the end of the 10th century, and the Greeks – as we have seen (AIC1, page 835). The initial encounter of the two traditions is nowhere better represented than at Serbian Studenica just before the end of the 12th century: the integration of the longitudinal and centralized is not uncharacteristic of Serb – or Bulgarian – foundations, the profile of the dome and the interior fresco cycles are Byzantine but the pilasters and blind eaves arcading came from Lombardy through Dalmatia.[1.87, 1.88]

Such cross-fertilization of the two main strands of early medieval Christian architecture is natural to the border area between the Catholic and Orthodox worlds. However, the Romanesque was arrested before penetrating

1.90a

1.90b

›**1.89 PRAGUE (HRADCANI), BASILICA OF S. JIŘÍ,** 1142: (a) interior to sanctuary, (b) crypt under raised sanctuary.

1.90a

>**1.90 BORGUND, STAVE CHURCH,** C. 1150: (a) exterior, (b) reconstructed cut-away interior.

Constantly raiding Christian settlements, the Vikings knew the power of the faith but they did not espouse it officially until the baptism of the Danish king Harald Blue-Tooth (950–86) and his Norwegian follower Olaf Tryggvason (995–1000). Of about a thousand timber churches built in the first two centuries thereafter, some thirty still stand. The type name derives from the general use of upright timbers rather the horizontal logs common elsewhere. At first the 'scissor trusses' of the characteristically high pitched shingle roof were carried by a 'box' frame of pine posts sunk in the ground: as these deteriorated, a masonry base was introduced and the timbers were preserved with tar. Diaphragm bracing to all parts of the frame imitates semicircular arches, perhaps after the style of Romanesque masonry. There are rare centralized structures but, as in early Britain, the norm is either basilican – with impressively tiered roofs – or a simple combination of nave and chancel.

1.90b

much further into the Balkans than Studenica by the native style of the missionaries from Greece who succeeded, where the Latins had failed, in giving an alphabet to the southern Slavs. In the north after the triumph of the Ottonians, on the other hand, German Romanesque was exported with Catholicism to the Magyars of Hungary and to the Slavs of future Bohemia, Moravia and Poland from whence it penetrated the Orthodox Russias.[1.89]

RUS

The Slavic tribes, who had emerged as an agricultural nation in the basins of the Vistula and Upper Dnieper towards the end of the 1st millennium CE, grouped themselves into kin communities governed in accord with elementary democratic principles: they rarely benefitted from supratribal leadership. Harried by the Huns, Avars and various Turkish tribes, they accepted protection from Vikings, called Rus, who founded numerous forts, most notably Novgorod on the Volkhov in the north, near Lake Ilmen, and in the south at Kiev which dominated the lower Dnieper valley. Trade – in fur, above all – along the great river system which linked the Black Sea with the Baltic – Byzantium with the Norse homelands – was their chief interest and to develop it they extended protection over a steadily increasing area, leaving the tribesmen autonomous provided they acknowledged their suzerainty and paid tribute.

Oleg of Novgorod took the trading settlement of Kiev in 882 and entered into a commercial treaty with Byzantium in 911 – when Normandy was conceded to his distant cousins. The imperial power of Byzantium might wax and wane but the city of Constantine stood on its ancient Greek foundations at the crossroads of trade: east–west by sea to Italy and Spain or by the Danube to Central Europe, and north–south across Russia to Scandinavia. To the barbarians of the north and east, with trade went Christianity and with Christianity went culture.

Following the trade routes across Russia, Christianity first claimed a princess of Kiev, Olga, the widow of Oleg's son Igor. Oleg's successors took Slav names and there was a pagan resurgence under Igor's son Svyatoslav. However, in 988 the Orthodox faith was adopted as the official religion of Rus by Svyatoslav's son Vladimir the Saint.

Vladimir achieved the extraordinary coup of a marriage alliance with the sister of the emperor Basil II. He doubtless saw the new faith – and the alliance – as an instrument of unity effective against the disparate localized pagan cults in his drive for imperial dominion and his most immediate impression of it was conveyed by his traders and envoys from magnificent Byzantium. Thereafter the cathedral church was the focal point of Russian town life, the liturgical centre of political authority, and the monastery dominated the countryside – not merely as a place of retreat but as the local centre of commerce, of craft and education, and even as a stronghold of state.

Striving to represent the perfection of God's House, like the contemporary Byzantine quincunx, metropolitan and monastic churches seem from the outset to have risen to predominance in pyramidal gradations over Greek-cross plans – the former more complex than the latter as befitted their ceremonial pre-eminence. They were first built of logs like everything else and, hence, the imported domical ideal was expressed in the folk vernacular with the degree of elaboration warranted by the importance of the commission and the availability of materials: 11th-century chronicles referring to octagonal, tent-roofed and thirteen-domed edifices indicate virtuosity comparable to the most spectacular surviving permutations of the perennial tradition. The result is in clear contrast with the stave tradition of the Rus's Norse relatives.**1.90–1.92**

1.91a

›ARCHITECTURE IN CONTEXT »RENOVATION OF GRAVITAS

1.91b

1.91c

The timber vernacular tradition

At its simplest, the timber church derives from the log hut of the north-Slav peasant: the logs were laid horizontally and, instead of shingle over inclined joists, a steep-pitched 'tent' roof was often formed by continuing

1.91d

›1.92 CHURCH OF THE NATIVITY OF THE VIR-GIN, c. 1530, from Perdki, Borovichy district (Novgorod, Vitoslavlitsy Museum of Wooden Architecture).

to lay logs horizontally in rectangles or octagons of diminishing dimensions. The basic unit had two rooms (for living and storage) linked by a vestibule but there was usually also an upper room, over the store above the snow line, accessed by an external staircase. In the typical tricellular church, the main room accommodated the congregation, the storeroom beyond became the sanctuary but the vestibule was displaced from its linking position to the entrace. Like the house, the church could be extended by simple cellular accretion – horizontally or vertically, symmetrically or otherwise. The basic approach to elaboration, naturally, was to project cells from the sides of the central space: further elaboration prompted the addition of cells to all sides of a central octagon to provide chapels buttressing increasingly high tent roofs and, of course, there was no end to the addition of cell to cell in principle, if not in practice.

The Novgorod chronicles refer to the first S. Sofia there, commissioned by Prince Vladimir's emissary, as a wooden structure of thirteen domes: a commission by Vladimir himself in Kiev is hardly likely to have been less well endowed. The 'onion' form of dome, so well represented in multiplicity at Kizhi and so characteristic of the Russian tradition, is sometimes thought to have been contributed by the Tatars who invaded from the east in the 13th century, but it had doubtless recommended itself before the sophistication of the timber style in the 11th century for its efficiency in shedding water: the pointed crest obviates the tendency for water to remain and solidify on, seep from and rot the faintly inclined segment at the top of a semicircular dome.

Immediately after the official adoption of Christianity, Vladimir called on his brother-in-law for experts to initiate monumental masonry building in Kiev with the quincunx church of the Tythe of the Most Holy Mother of God.[1.93a] After the invocation of the Byzantine ideal, Russian ecclesiastical architecture may be seen primarily in terms of varying the imported theme within the constraints of a tight form: the variations embraced the number and configuration of ambulatories, narthexes, apses and domes within or above an envelope which remained roughly rectilinear, at least on three sides, and which might or might not be articulated with pilasters, arcades, gables and stringcourses which might or might not relate to structural reality. Running in counterpoint was the folk theme which invited richer development: the native timber tradition continued to assert itself in organic accretion of major and minor motifs in a hierarchy of clearly differentiated masses expressing the distinction between primary and ancillary space – formally or freely disposed. We have seen the result in wood: we shall see it also in masonry.

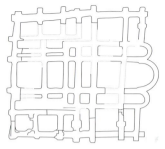

1.93a @ 1:1000

›1.93 KIEV: (a) Tythe of the Most Holy Mother of God (Desyatina Presvyatoy Bogoroditsi; begun 989, consecrated 996, reconstructed after a fire in 1017, destroyed in 1240), plan; (b) 'The Great Gate' (remains of one of three gates of the walls of 1036); (c–g) S. Sofia (Sobor Sofii; 1037–46, much reconstructed and redecorated in the 17th century), exterior from south-east, section, plan, south aisle, crossing and sanctuary.

Modern excavation at the site of the Tythe church has revealed a quincunx plan, with transepts equal in length to the radius of the nave dome, three apses (for the sanctuary flanked by pastophoria) and narthex.

1.93c

1.93b
There are also the remains of walls built of alternating courses of stone and brick: as in the earliest churches elsewhere – sometimes of *opus mixtum*, as here, sometimes wholly of brick bonded with mortar of varied thickness – there was no plaster revetment.

After Vladimir's death in 1015 rivalry among his sons – in which two of them, Boris and Gleb, became Russia's first Christian martyrs at the hands of a neo-pagan pretender – was terminated by the triumph of Prince Yaroslav, governor of Novgorod, over the rival tribe of the Pechenegs. In his long reign (1019–54) he extended control to the north-east, fortifying the main settlements of Suzdalia, and united all the Rus domains under Kiev. His domain was recognized as a grand-duchy in 1037, when the patriarch of Constantinople asserted his authority over it, but he entered into a network of marriage alliances extending to western powers as well as Byzantium – his daughters were queens of France, Denmark and Norway. Western influence supplemented eastern from his reign but his primary objective was to cloak his regime in Byzantine splendour – the perpetuation of Roman glory.

Kiev was given new defences from 1036.**1.93b** The metropolitan who exercised the Byzantine patriarch's authority was given a cathedral dedicated to S. Sofia and built in emulation – but not imitation – of Justinian's stupendous work in Constantinople to serve similar liturgical purposes, above all the ceremonies of the Little and Great Entries (AICI, pages 796ff). However, on a complex expansion of the post-iconoclastic Byzantine quincunx, it rises to a pyramid of domed towers after the example of its greatest wooden predecessors.**1.93c–g**

Kiev, S. Sofia

The cathedral of the Holy Wisdom, founded by Yaroslav on on the site of his final victory, remains one of the glories of the Orthodox world despite many vicissitudes – especially at the hands of the Mongols in 1204 and, ultimately, its late-17th-century restorers. With the great height of its central dome (29 metres) and twelve lesser domes at the junctions of its doubled aisles, it is far grander than its Kievan predecessors.

Enveloping the nave, the preserve of the clergy under the high dome representing heaven, the outer bays of the core quincunx – restricted to half the width of the nave – are doubled to form an inner and outer ambulatory with tribune galleries. Linked to the palace, the latter would have accommodated the ruler and his entourage in the observation of the performance on the central stage. The aisles accommodated the laity and their doubling provided for the separation of the congregation from the processing clergy without denying the one a view of the other: congestion, obviated by the vast width of the aisles in Justinian's great work, would otherwise have been an acute problem on this scale. Moreover, there is a third ambulatory range for access, initially built without tribune galleries, and beyond that buttressing was provided by flying arches which were later incorporated in double-height parekklesia: for access to the upper galleries, domed spiral-staircase towers were interposed between these side wings and the generous exonarthex.

The sanctuary and all six aisles terminate in apses. The piers at their junctions are cruciform but the intermediate ones supporting galleries across the arms of nave and transepts are octagonal. In addition to the great dome over the central bay of the nave, there are domes over the corner bays of the inner core and the first enveloping range – thirteen in all, the only source of direct light as the aisle galleries mask the side windows, their profiles are early 18th century.

Built in irregular courses of brick-faced rubble and stone, brick supplanting stone towards the top, the exterior is relieved with a series of arcaded niches: the banded masonry, apparently not deemed aesthetically satisfactory, was plastered and frescoed at some stage but probably not from the outset. The interior decoration is novel in its combination of fresco and mosaic in a unified scheme: the areas of mosaic damaged over the centuries and most of the faded frescoes succumbed to oil paint in the 19th century from which the latter have only partially been recovered. The splendid Pantokrator, one of his flanking archangels and the Virgin Orans in their canonical places in the dome and apse respectively, are the only major ones to have survived from early Kiev: they mark the triumph of a new faith and the advent of a new imperium.

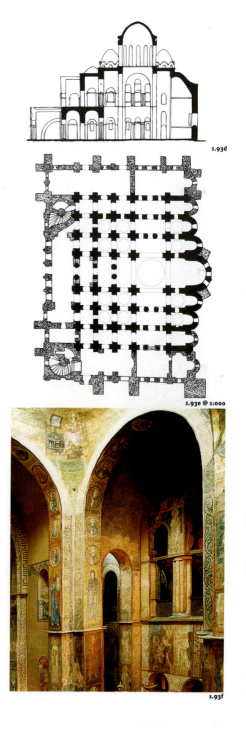

1.93d

1.93e @ 1:000

1.93f

1.938

›ARCHITECTURE IN CONTEXT »RENOVATION OF GRAVITAS

1.94a

1.94b

›1.94 **NOVGOROD, CATHEDRAL OF S. SOFIA** (Sobor Sofii), 1045–52, restored in the 19th century, repaired and reformed after World War II: (a, b) exterior from the south-east and north-west, (c) interior, (d) section, (e) plan, (f) 'Korsun' portal (c. 1150).

The Novgorod quincunx has doubled aisles over which a gallery was inserted: thus there is one less aisle than at Kiev and the second one here has no apse. There is also a U-shaped conjunction of parekklesia and exonarthex equalling the nave in width: arcades (originally open, later walled) are subdivided into burial chapels and surmounted by galleries with sloping roofs which avoided concealing the semicircular and triangular gables of the central nucleus. The narthex is curtailed by a single massive circular staircase tower to the south of the entrance. Only this tower, the central bay and the four corner bays of the core quincunx are domed. The roofline reflects the arcaded interior in the manner known as *zakomari*.

1.94d

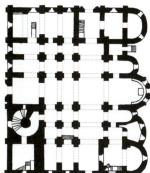

1.94e @ 1:10000

1.94c

The structure is of undressed limestone, irregularly laid but not originally plastered. The compact, elevated interior was lit from above and the aisles remained in shadow. Little of the original mid-12th-century fresco scheme survived repainting in the 19th century: exceptional are the portraits of Constantine and S. Helena in the south vestibule. The major element of 12th-century embellishment (sometimes dated to a century earlier) is the pair of bronze doors made in Magdeburg for Varengian Sigtuna and stolen by the Novgorodniks in 1187 (or 1117 according to the earlier chronology): the biblical scenes and saints in most of the relief panels rank among the greatest masterpieces of early medieval bronze casting.

Imperial in motive, the metropolitan of Kiev's new seat set the standard for works founded by viceroys and client rulers in other major centres of power. Of the type representing the grandeur of state authority, the cathedral of S. Sofia at Novgorod was initiated in 1045 by Yaroslav's son Vladimir, the governor of the northern province: this was four years before fire destroyed the thirteen-domed timber cathedral, built c. 989.[1.94]

1.94f

A regular domed quincunx without ambulatory but with lateral extensions, the relatively small cathedral of the Transfiguration in Chernigov – a provincial centre on the Dneiper north of Kiev – was begun a decade earlier by its governor, Yaroslav's brother Mstislav who was interred there before the work was finished.**1.95** Elsewhere – particularly at Smolensk, further up the Dneiper, and at Polotsk to the west – these works had several important contemporaries, now lost.

As the seat of a metropolitan subject to the patriarch of Constantinople, the prototype of the state cathedral provoked local opposition – in policy and typology. Initially the centre of that opposition was Kiev's Pecherskaya (cave) monastery, founded by humble hermits and dedicated to serving the populace at large. Fostering the ideal of independence from Byzantine authority, that institution promoted the veneration of national saints and produced the first Russian metropolitan, Hilarion, who was appointed by Yaroslav the Wise in 1051.

As the prime candidates for national sainthood were Prince Vladimir Sviatoslavovich and his martyred sons Boris and Gleg, the ideal naturally inspired princely patrons to support the popular cause: Prince Sviatoslav Yaroslavovich built the Pecherskaya cathedral of the Dormition in 1073 for common service in which the priest approached the sanctuary directly through the congregation: that purpose was served by the simple quincunx without ambulatories, articulated largly in accord with structural reality, and the example was widely followed – first in Kiev.**1.96**

From these works, the monastic cathedrals at least as much as the metropolitan ones, the great tradition of Russian orthodox architecture was to develop along distinct regional lines after the disintegration of the first Kievan 'empire' in the late-12th century. Essentially Byzantine,

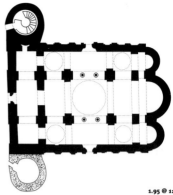

1.95 @ 1:2000

›1.95 CHERNIGOV, CATHEDRAL OF THE TRANSFIGURATION (Spasopreobrazhenski sobor), 1031, damaged by the Mongols in 1240, restored: plan.

The simple triapsidal quincunx of its main predecessor, the Tythe church of Kiev, is closely followed – including the lateral access passage between the sanctuary and the pastophories – but the screening of the side arms with arcades supporting galleries introduces a quasi-basilican accent. The five-domed mass, articulated with blind arches responding to the internal bays – at least on the entrance front – presumably also recalls the earlier work. There seems, however, to have been an outer range, as later at S. Sofia: the royal burial chapels, parallel with the pastopheries at the eastern end, may have terminated parekklesia extending along the northern and southern flanks. Access to the galleries over aisles and narthex was provided by a spiral staircase in a projecting round tower at the northern junction of the parekklesia range and the narthex: this was raised in height and a similar tower added in an extensive campaign of restoration in the 18th century.

›1.96 KIEV, THE MONASTIC CATHEDRAL TYPE: (a) the Dormition, Pecherskaya (built between 1073 and 1089, rebuilt after devastation by the Mongols in 1240, restored in the 15th and 17th centuries, destroyed 1941) plan; (b, c) the Saviour (Tserkov Spasa), Berestovo (the monastery was founded before 1072; the church was commissioned by Vladimir Monomakh early in the 12th century for dynastic burial; it needed extensive rebuilding in the mid-17th century and restoration in the early 20th century), plan and view from south-east; (d) S. Mikhail, Mikhaylovski (the monastery, also known as Dmitriyevski or Vydubetski, was founded

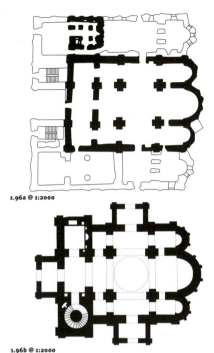

1.96a @ 1:2000

1.96b @ 1:2000

1.96d

by Prince Izyaslav Yaroslavovich after 1050; the church, variously dated between 1080 to 1108, was partially destroyed in the 1930s), view from the south.

1.96c

and therefore Romanesque in the Greek sense, that development was not unimpressed by the Romanesque of the west but the process of transmission was inevitably slow. It was initiated, perhaps, by Grand Duke Yaroslav's western marriage alliances but the first tentative signs have been traced on the exterior of the cathedral of SS. Boris and Gleb at Chernigov, whose foundation has been variously dated to c. 1120 and at least a generation later: groin vaults are introduced and miniature blind arcading cuts across the otherwise resolutely Byzantine gables in the somewhat controversial rebuilding after World War II.

The unity imposed by Yaroslav did not long outlast the reign of his effective grandson, Vladimir Monomakh (1113–25): divided succession in Kiev a nd the development of trade between north Rus and western Europe were major factors. The citizens of Novgorod, enriched through the colonization of the north, rejected the ascendancy of the Kievan prince in 1136, expelled his vice-regal relative and established a primitive republic under the suzerainty of the archbishop. To assert his authority in the commercial quarter known as Yaroslav's Court, opposite the citadel (kremlin) on the left bank of the river, the prince had founded the cathedral of S. Nikolai but his plans for a work

1.97a

on the grand establishment scale were curtailed by his opponents: the result was a quincunx as simple but as impressive as the Kievan monastic nationalist type. Also founded before the prince was discomforted, the cathedral of the Yuriev monastery, to the south of the city, was conceived along those lines from the outset. As soldier-in-chief forced to recognize the superiority of the archbishop and his council in the kremlin, the prince resorted to a new palace facing the Yuriev complex from the opposite bank of the river.[1.97, 1.98]

In the north-east, where Vladimir had been founded by Monomakh in 1108 as a fortress to supplement Suzdal but had emerged dominant, the Kievan princely governor, Andrei Bogoliubski, asserted his independence in 1157. In 1181 the Kievan ruler acknowledged the establishment of a second grand principality in Smolensk. Not surprisingly, more definite signs of western influence than those of rebuilt Chernigov have been traced in the north – especially in Novgorod, the major junction of the western trade route with the north–south Dnieper system, and at Pskov where the Novgorod prince settled after the republicans banished him in 1136.

>1.97 NOVGOROD: (a) the Nikolai cathedral in Yaroslav's Court, founded by Prince Mstislav Vladimirovich in 1113: view from south-east; (b–d) the cathedral of the Yuriev monastery, (1119, inaccurately restored in the 19th century but reformed in the 1930s), plan, view from north-west and interior; (e–g) S. Paraskeva Piatnitsa in Yaroslav's Court (c. 1207), general view of restored remains, plan and reconstruction.

Like the Kievan Pecherskaya cathedral and, ultimately, the Tythe church, the plan of this work is a simple triapsidal quincunx with the western arm slightly longer than the others. The walls are thick enough to accommodate the stairs, obviating a tower: within them the superficial area seems more restricted than hitherto, enhancing the impression of elevation.

Built of plastered brick and stone in alternating courses, the system of bays is expressed on the exterior with blind arcading over pier buttresses. Domes on tall drums originally covered all five square compartments but they remain only over the central square and the end bays of the narthex. The cornice line has been changed and the 'helmet' form of dome supplants the original hemispheres.

Like the Nikolai cathedral, the Yuriev monastery cathedral was commissioned by Mstislav, son and viceroy of Grand Prince Vladimir Monomakh, who also supported the near-contemporary foundation of the Antoniev complex by one Anthony the Roman – a convert to Orthodoxy from the west. Over a quincunx plan extended to a narthex, west, and a deep apsidal sanctuary flanked by apsidal pastopheries, east, there are domes (originally hemispherical) on tall drums only over the central square and the end bays of the narthex (as also at Anthony's church). While that disposition follows Thessalonikan practice the Yuriev work also distantly recalls the German westwork despite the displacement of its northern dome to a square stair tower beyond the perimeter. The simple but bold articulation integrates the tower with the main body of the building despite the asymmetrical distribution of the domes. Little of the original fresco cycles has survived time and 19th-century repainting.

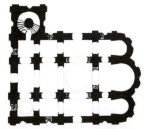

1.97b @ 1:2000   1.97c

Lombard miniature blind arcading appears in Novgorod in the second decade of the 12th century, probably first on the Nikolai cathedral in Yaroslav's Court, certainly in both the Antoniev and Yuriev monasteries. In the Antoniev church of the Nativity of the Virgin, it supports the eaves of the main volume and the domes. In the Yuriev cathedral, as on the restoration of S. Nikolai, it fringes only the domes as the original eaves line followed the contours of the arcading (zakomari). However, rather than thick piers as hitherto, the Yuriev's structural bays are expressed on the exterior walls in terms of blind arches carried on slender pilasters in the Lombard manner – as on the external flanks of S. Cyriakus at Gernrode,[1.50] and perhaps Ottonian Magdeburg,[1.49] but rising from the ground as in the interior of the cathedral at Speyer.[1.55] Similar articulation relieves the much smaller mass of Pskov's Mirozhski monastery church: probably founded by the ousted prince of Novgorod just before his death in 1138 and completed to a contracted quincunx plan by his resolutely Orthodox successor, it is an early representative of the single-domed type common to smaller monastic foundations.

1.97d

1.97e

1.97f

After the departure of the prince, Novgorod was endowed by its merchant rulers and monastic orders with few large-scale works. Typical of the late-12th century is the contracted, single-domed quincunx without narthex which may be represented by the monastery church of SS. Pyotr i Pavel on Sinichia Hill: the original eaves have been lost but they are presumed to have followed the usual zakomari lines. The church of S. Paraskeva Piatnitsa in the marketplace is a notable variant with a colonnaded quincunx, originally of great height relative to its width, an extended sanctuary flanked by apsed pastophories to the east, galleried porches protruding from the other three sides and colonnettes clustered about the corners instead of pilasters. The original roof has been long lost here too but it probably conformed to the trefoil type which had replaced the zakomari form on tall, narrow works by the beginning of the 13th century, such as the church of the Nativity of the Virgin at Peryn.

The earliest example of a tall slender quincunx with a trefoil eaves line and stepped gables, acknowledging the native timber additive tradition, is thought to be the cathedral of the Transfiguration (c. 1150) in the S. Euphrosyne monastery at Polotsk. The form was popular thereafter at

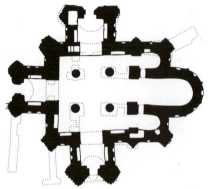

1.97g @ 1:500

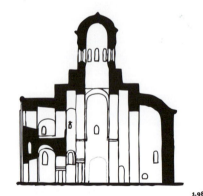

1.98

›**1.98** POLOTSK, TRANSFIGURATION CATHE-DRAL, monastery of the Saviour and S. Euphrosyne, c. 1150, altered in the 19th century: section.

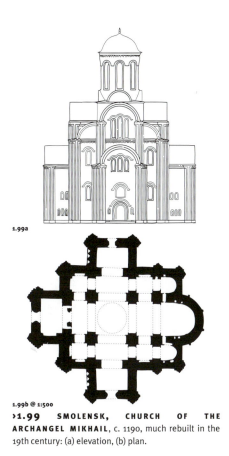

1.99a

1.99b @ 1:500

›1.99 SMOLENSK, CHURCH OF THE ARCHANGEL MIKHAIL, c. 1190, much rebuilt in the 19th century: (a) elevation, (b) plan.

›1.100 CHERNIGOV, THE CHURCH OF PIAT-NITSA, late-12th century, rebuilt in the 17th century and restored to its supposed original form after severe damage in World War II: exterior of unplastered brick relieved with colonnettes, niches in frames of varied profile, blind arcading of Lombard type and lattice or zig-zag patterns.

Smolensk where slender verticality, extended porches and corner colonnettes were characteristic – indeed, the recurrence of these features has prompted the attribution of Novgorod's Paraskeva Piatnitsa to an architect from Smolensk. The late-12th-century church of Piatnitsa at Chernigov is an elaborate example, celebrated for its patterned brickwork.**1.99, 1.100**

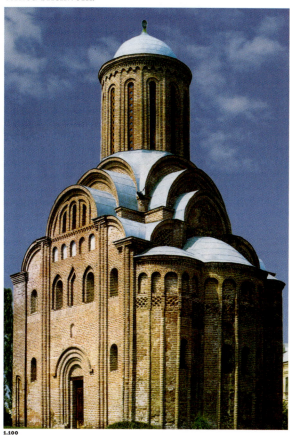

1.100

While Kiev was wracked by dynastic rivalry and Novgorod was in the hands of merchants more interested in investment in trade than grand building, the ruler of Suzdalia succeeded in locating the centre of architectural gravity in his domain. The foundations were laid in Vladimir by Monomakh's son, Yuri Dolgoruki, before his final triumph in the long struggle with his brothers for the succession to the grand duchy in 1157 – the year of his death and the assertion of Vladimir's independence by his son Andrei Bogoliubski. Most of Dolgoruki's works have been lost or reworked: the remains reveal conservative planning.[1.101] However, the innovative use of finely dressed limestone relates to near-contemporary work further west, at Halich, and beyond that in Poland. Elaborated on this basis, Bogoliubski's legacy is magnificent.

Dedicated to expanding his rule at the expense of the older northern and southern states, unlike that of his predecessors, Bogoliubski's ambition was not to occupy Kiev but to eclipse it by his own power base: this was achieved in 1169 when his forces sacked Kiev and imposed his client on the merchants of Novgorod as their ruler. The year after his accession he had inaugurated his reign by founding the palace and cathedral of a pretentious new seat, Bogoliubovo, to the east of Vladimir. In the same year he began work on the refortification of Vladimir and founded a new cathedral there too. The ceremonial 'Golden Gate' of Vladimir clearly emulated the chapel-crowned 'Great Gate' of Kiev and the Golden Gate of Constantinople beyond that.[1.102] However, his churches seem to turn west, away from the Kievan tradition, at least in their masonry and embellishment.

The cathedral of the new seat, linked to the palace by a raised gallery, represents an elaboration of the late Dolgoruki single-domed quincunx type: it collapsed in the early 18th century but its close follower, the nearby church of the Intercession on the River Nerl, survives largely in fine state. The new cathedral in Vladimir was initially an imposing but simple five-domed quincunx with narthex, like the merchant's cathedral of S. Nikolai at Novgorod. However, superior in its masonry, it would

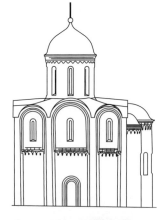

1.101a

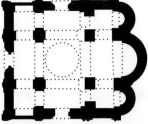

1.10b @ 1:500

›1.101 SUZDAL (KIDEKSHA), CHURCH OF SS. BORIS I GLEB, c. 1150, rebuilt in the 16th century: (a) reconstruction, (b) plan.

The foundation was the palatine church of Dolgoruski's new seat on the prestigious site of a camp of the martyred princes. Rather than alternating courses of brick and stone, as usual in Kiev and Novgorod, the walls are rubble sheathed with finely dressed limestone inside and out: the exterior was relieved with a stringcourse of miniature blind arcades. The compartments of the simple, single-domed quincunx were originally expressed with blind zakomari arcading carried on pilasters – recessed through the slight changes of the wall's plane between the storeys – but the eastern bays are now truncated and the remaining mass is subjected to flattened eaves throughout. The reconstruction is guided by the surviving contemporary work at Pereslavl-Zalesski.

be one aisle short of emulating the great northern city's kremlin cathedral of S. Sofia when its ambulatory was added from 1185.**1.103, 1.104**

Andrei Bogoliubski of Suzdal and the church

Both the palatine cathedral – of which the foundations have been traced beneath its 18th-century replacement – and the church on the Nerl – raised on a mound over the floodplain – were built of rubble between skins of ashlar limestone over a simple quincunx plan without narthex. In all this they recall the church of SS. Boris i Gleb at Kideksha and the cathedral of the Transfiguration at Pereslavl-Zalesski. However, the western bays of Bogoliubski's works are slightly wider than those to the east of the crossing, to compensate for the absence of a narthex. The proportions of the church on the Nerl, at least, are lighter as its main vertical lines exceeded the horizontals and were slightly tapered to obviate any impression of splaying. Moreover, the central supports in the cathedral were columns rather than the usual cruciform piers retained in the later work, and both exteriors were much more elaborately relieved.

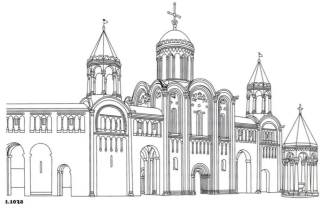

1.103a

Most notable at Nerl and in the remains of the palatine staircase tower is the blind arcading of the stringcourse rising from colonnettes supported on corbel blocks over the roof of an ambulatory (now traceable only in foundations along the north, west and south sides of the later work). Either way, the motif may be seen as a shallow version of the one derived by the Ottonians and their successors from the external galleries of the Lombards: a related motif appears soon after at Chernigov. The three-arched windows of the palace tower and the recessed portal of the church on the Nerl are distinctly western too.

In the Nerl church moreover, as presumably in its model, the upper storey is richly embellished with reliefs, the planar variation between the storeys is enhanced and the recessed pilasters separating the bays have acquired attached shafts – like those of the nave at Speyer and, later, the exterior of Chernigov's Piatnitsa. The sculptural detail – unprecedented in Rus except, presumably, at Bogoliubovo itself – distantly reflects western Romanesque practice too: the main relief panels, representing the biblical warrior King David – scion of the Virgin's house, conqueror and seminal monarch emulated by Bogoliubski – flanked by the lion and bird of prey which traditionally symbolize royal might, are located in the tympana on each side; the boldly recessed arches of the portal jambs, rising from Corinthianesque capitals, are variously plain, scalloped or foliate and the corbels supporting the blind colonnade are variously anthropomorphic and more or less fantastically zoomorphic. The original dome was hemispherical, like those of its predecessors in ancient Rus: below a serrated valence suspended from its rim, a colonnaded arcade rings the cupola drum in complement to the articulation of the main volume below. This

1.103b

›1.103 BOGOLIUBOVO: (a, b) perspective and axonometric reconstructions of original cathedral (begun in 1158, collapsed during refenestration in the mid-18th century), (c) general view showing remains of the north tower and gallery linking the palace to the rebuilt cathedral of the Nativity of the Virgin (Rozhdestvenski Sobor; c. 1160, the tower was given an extra storey and a new tent-roofed belfry in the 17th century).

1.103c

1.104a

›1.104 CHURCH OF THE INTERCESSION ON THE NERL (Tserkov Pokrova), founded in 1165 in a monastic context now lost: (a) exterior, (b) interior.

1.104b

form of cupola had achieved its grandest proportions in the twelve-bay work over the crossing of the cathedral in Vladimir.

The Dormition cathedral was buit over the traditional regular quincunx with three-bay narthex, central dome (rising to the same height as that of S. Sofia in Kiev) and apsidal sanctuary flanked by apsidal pastopheries. Like the dome, the masonry and façade embellishment were executed in parallel to the work in and near the ruler's new seat. Much of that embellishment, but not the original structure's zakomari, was obscured by the projection of the three new eastern apses and the enveloping of the other three sides in the double-height, domed ambulatory. In general the articulation of the envelope's exterior, including the four new domes over the end bays of the side aisles, follows the original formula but without the sculptural reliefs. Colonnettes still rise from corbels to support the arcaded stringcourse on the west front but on the sides they are based on the outer plane of the lower wall and are therefore even truer to the distant Italianate prototype. A novel feature is the projection of the corner of the cuboid mass between the end colonnettes of the zakomari system of the north, west and south façades. Within that system, echoed over the higher mass of the original structure, concentric semicircles had never been more assertive in the articulation of the churches of Rus.

The refection of Vladimir's cathedral of the Dormition was achieved by Bogoliubski's successor, his half-brother Vsevolod Yurevich (1177–1212). The elimination of sculptural detail from the exterior, in deference to Byzantine rather than western Romanesque practice, is generally seen in the light of the new prince's long exile in the eastern imperial capital. Be that as it may, the second extant major work of the new reign, the Vladimir palatine church of S. Dmitri – a simple, single-domed quincunx without narthex or ambulatory – is even more profuse in its sculptural embellishment than any of its predecessors. With its simple Byzantine quincunx, Romanesque articulation and native embellishment, the work as a whole may be read as an eclectic statement of expansive ambition.**1.105, 1.106**

1.105a

1.105b

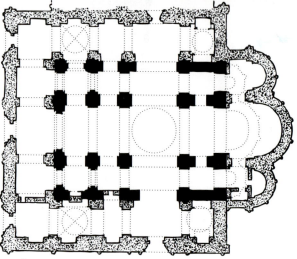

1.105c @ 1:2000

>1.105 VLADIMIR, CATHEDRAL OF THE DOR-
MITION (Upenski Sobor), founded 1158, apses
extended and ambulatory with mortuary chapels
added from 1185 after fire damage, further damage
inflicted by the Tatars was not repaired until the 15th
century when an important fresco cycle was executed
which now survives only in small part: (a) exterior from
north-east, (b) entrance façade, (c) plan.

While the articulating colonnettes and recessd portals may be seen as genetically Romanesque, the sheltering of iconic statues in blind arcades specifically so,
there is little Germanic or Italianate in the motifs which
ramp in low relief from the upper walls to the tympana
of the zakomari: on the contrary, apart from the biblical, Christian, Classical and contemporary Russian
images of divine and earthly authority slotted in above
the windows, there is something of the Caucasian car-
pet about the naïve native celebration of the natural
world in many of the lower reliefs.

>1.106 VLADIMIR, CATHEDRAL OF S. DMITRI,
founded 1194 in the palatine complex now lost, embellished with fresco cycles in the early 13th century of
which little survives, shorn of galleries to the north and
south in the 19th century: (a) exterior, (b) detail.

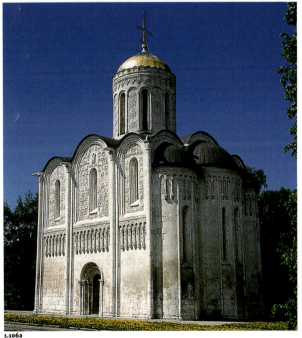

1.106a

Rampant reliefs were not unique to Vladimir, but they
were rare and their most notable later incidence, on the
cathedral of S. Giorgi at Iurev-Polskoi (c. 1230), subsists
only in partial and jumbled re-evocation. The motif of the
blind arcade was to distinguish all the works of Bogoliubski's line for several generations: one of its later manifestations survives on the lower storey of the cathedral of
the Nativity, under later rebuilding. That dates from 1225,
the year Russia was first subjected to the scourge of the
Mongols – or 'Tatars' as Russians know them.

Bent on the extirpation of urban life – as elsewhere
within their wide range across Asia and Europe – the
hordes assaulted Vladimir in 1237–38: their impact was
devastating, especially on palatine Bogoliubovo; they
extinguished Prince Vsevolod's heir, his son Yuri, and his
domain's dominance. Two years later they extended their
carnage to Kiev. Novgorod escaped the worst but architecture was at a low ebb everywhere in Rus for at least a
century – though the Tatars remained much longer.

A dozen or so rival principalities emerged as clients of
the Tatar khans. Novgorod was potentially the most powerful but it was Moscow, where a kremlin was founded
about 1147, which ultimately won. The late-Byzantine-
Romanesque hybrid provided the basis for the ultimate
revival of architecture there and the wide-ranging ambition symbolized in works like S. Dmitri at Vladimir
would be channelled in the revival to the achievement of
the Third Rome.

1.106b

1.4 THE WEST: POST-CAROLINGIAN DIVERSITY

6 LATE GAUL: EARLY FRANCE

ADVENT OF THE CAPETIANS

The first Capetian king, Hugh Capet (987–96), freed his succession from the ancient Frankish tradition of election and the crown passed through an unbroken male line for well over three centuries. It was nearly half that time before the dynasty freed itself from the reality of its feudal origin.

Count of Paris, Hugh was elected to replace the last of the Carolingians because he was seen as the weakest contender and his domain was encircled by its greater feudatories – as its name, Île-de-France, implies. Chief of those nominal feudatories was the duke of Normandy, arguably the greatest power in Europe after he had taken the crown of England in 1066: Normandy's support had been crucial in Hugh's elevation but the duke's successors were determined to keep the Capetians in place.

Hugh's descendants fought incessantly to extend the royal domain beyond the Île-de-France and to reassert central control by exploiting divisions among the magnates. They succeeded in Champagne but their ambition naturally turned supporters into opponents and the Normans effectively frustrated it for two centuries. The details of French feudal rivalry are beyond us here, except in so far as they prompted the transformation of the castle and ensured that within the overall unity of the massive round-arched Romanesque style there was much greater diversity of approach to the planning and detailing of the church than in the German empire. And there was regional diversity in the structure of feudal society too. There was, however, one major – if indirect and far-reaching – consequence of feudal rivalry which we should notice here.

PILGRIMAGE AND CRUSADE

Christ was represented as the terrible judge over the Romanesque church portal but his mission was beneficent to the worthy and he was believed to be responsive to the intercession of his mother and the host of saints who had suffered for his Church. Consequently, holy and saintly relics were highly prized. And pilgrimage to their shrines, particularly to the burial places of S. Peter in Rome and S. James the Great at Compostela, was the chief motive for medieval travel – other than war.**1.107**

The tributaries of the pilgrimage route to Santiago de Compostela rose in all the regions of France: with the pilgrims and their ecclesiastical guides came soldiers of fortune as Crusaders to swell the ranks of the Asturians as they pushed the Moors back through the Iberian peninsula. The ground had been long prepared by Alfonso VI (1065–1109), who reunited the kingdoms of Navarra, Aragón, Castile and León and took the key central city of Toledo in 1065. He assumed the patronage of Compostela and assigned the neighbouring county of Oporto, secured in the previous generation, to his daughter and her Burgundian husband: their son Alfonso Henriques – and his Crusaders – had taken all of Portugal by 1143 and asserted his independence.

The ultimate goal of pilgrimage was, of course, the scene of Christ's Passion in Jerusalem but that was virtu-

›**1.107 PILGRIMS TO SANTIAGO:** (a) en route (14th-century stained glass, León cathedral); (b) destination – the enshrined relics of S. James the Great.

›**1.108 POPE URBAN II AT THE COUNCIL OF CLERMONT,** 1095 (later medieval engraving).

1.108

1.109a

>1.109 CRUSADERS: (a) departure for the Holy Land (14th-century French ms; Paris, National Library); (b) captors of Jerusalem (13th-century Venetian ms; Padua, Seminary Library).

1.109b

ally unattainable under Muslim occupation. In November 1095, at Clermont in south-central France, the reforming French pope Urban II called for the energies of militant feudalism to be directed to the penance of a crusade to recover the Holy Land.**1.108** Cleansing the Church of licentiousness and venality, defending it from lay interference, stamping out heresy, asserting infallibility, the successors of Leo IX were bound to turn their attention to reclaiming jurisdiction over the holiest of Christian places, lost to Christendom by the incompetent Byzantines whose heretical church Rome had finally rejected.

This was a God-fearing age but the spiritual mission had material purpose too: the population – including the ranks of lordly younger sons looking for opportunity – was expanding and economic growth in much of western Europe was unprecedented since the fall of the Roman empire, releasing great energy despite the dissipation of a feudal age. Castles were still rude but the Church was increasingly sumptuous – especially in Cluniac domains – and Italian merchants in particular wanted to recover access to the luxuries of the east, lost to the Muslims.

The emperor was in no mood to support the further advance of papal power and prestige, but the French and Normans were enthusiastic. The problems of organization and transport, of leadership and coordination with the eastern emperor were far from fully resolved when the first of four contingents, led by the brother of the Capetian king Philip I (1060–1108), set off in August 1096. Some went overland, others by sea on ships provided by Italian maritime republics. After great vicissitude Jerusalem fell in July 1099 and a Latin kingdom was established in Palestine. There were to be many more crusades to sustain it – and many more landless younger sons of feudal magnates joining them in the hope of finding fortune in the east.**1.109**

›1.110 CHINON, COUDRAY WARD: model (Castle Museum).

The middle ward replaces a Roman fort. There and in the western sector, the Château du Coudray, is some 10th-century masonry, but most of the walls were rebuilt in the second half of the 12th century and augmented over at least two hundred years.

THE CASTLE

In response to the Viking incursions which decisively weakened central power under the later Carolingians, French magnates built the greatest concentration of castles in western Europe in the 10th century, but there are few remains earlier than the 11th century.

As ever everywhere, an elevated site was obviously ideal and an extensive tract of water – or marsh – was a time-honoured defence. However, the security of the inaccessible which characterized the lair of the Dark Ages – and remained dominant in Germany – was renounced in favour of ease of access and egress by the typically arrogant lord of high-French feudalism: constantly on the offensive to extend his manorial holdings as well as to protect them and keep the population in subjection, he relied primarily on an entourage of knights capable of rapid sorties.

Perched on a crag cut off from a chain of hills at the confluence of the Cher and Loire, Chinon is a textbook example of the defensive castle as it developed in the early Capetian era: across the ravine separating the crag from the neighbouring outcrop of rock, three wards are isolated by deep trenches traversable only by a drawbridge. Saone in Syria is exemplary of the defensive type too: the basic disposition is Byzantine but the great square stone keep

The walls around the extensive plateau, on which the rectangular citadel was originally centred, are Byzantine in origin and it is probable that Byzantine engineers excavated the great trench that cuts the plateau off from the neighbouring high ground, leaving a slender pinnacle to support the extended draw-bridge. The castle was taken by Latin Crusaders in the early 11th century; they added the square tower which controls the approach over the drawbridge probably in the early 12th century. From that time at the latest, the main line of approach was a circuitous path at the base of the southern ramparts and the entrance was through a square tower near the centre of the range.

guarding the transition from the outer to the inner ward is due to the early Crusaders.[1.110, 1.111]

The more aggressive approach depended on a mound (motte) – natural or artificial – supporting the command post in a palisaded compound (bailey) on a relatively open site: as we shall see, the type was perfected by the Normans. Protected by the River Loire on only one side, Fulk Nera's Langeais is the prime example from a century earlier – not least for the rectangular stone keep on its motte. Loches is among the most impressive early followers of Langeais – as indeed, is the keep at Saone.[1.112, 1.113]

›1.112 **LANGEAIS CASTLE,** late-10th century: keep.

Dominated by the earliest significant example of a rectangular stone keep enclosing a great hall, as distinct from a tower with strictly limited accommodation, the first castle at Langeais was built by 995. The keep was c. 16 by 7 metres; the masonry of its surviving east and north sides is rough, but regularly coursed. The hall, raised over service quarters and entered from a stair turret, had a timber floor and roof.

The castle's lord was Fulk Nera, who succeeded to the county of Anjou in 987 and pursued a notoriously brutal career until his death in 1040, and its main purpose was to overawe Tours and keep at bay Nera's principal rivals, the counts of Blois. Both counties had belonged to Robert the Strong, ancestor of the Capetians, but with the elevation of his descendant, Hugh, to the duchy of the Franks they were entrusted to viscounts who soon assumed the title of count in nominal vassalage to the king.

›1.113 **LOCHES, KEEP.**

The site was fortified in Merovingian times, but its surviving stone keep (c. 24 by 14 metres and originally c. 40 metres) was begun late in the career of Nera and finished, with its shorter rectangular projection to the north for access, in the late-11th century. If not the rectangular form of the main volume and its adjunct, the splendid ashlar masonry, relieved with semicylindrical shafts, demonstrates considerable advance over the work at Langeais. Over service rooms at ground level, halls with wooden floors and roofs were superimposed on three storeys. The ring walls with their towers built over a semiparabolic plan were begun in the late-12th century.

The perimeter at Loches, like the Château du Coudray at Chinon, was transformed after the mid-12th century when circular multifoil and polygonal forms were preferred for keeps and for the towers set at intervals around the enceinte: they provided lateral lines of fire (flanking) but less cover for the enemy than the protruding corners of rectangles and their greater cohesiveness made it more difficult for sappers and miners to bring them down, especially if splayed at the base for enhanced structural security in accordance with age-old practice.

1.113

›ARCHITECTURE IN CONTEXT »RENOVATION OF GRAVITAS

1.114

The advantage of circular forms seems initially to have been realized – or reappreciated – by Europeans in Spain after Christians forces acquired Muslim strongholds built in accordance with a tradition which goes back at least to the Umayyad qasr (AIC3, pages 60f).**1.114** The rectangular keep appears first, perhaps, on the edge of Castile – at

›**1.114 MONTEALEGRE,** 11th century, but restored on earlier foundations: alcázar.

The plan is trapezoidal rather than rectangular as is more usual in the Arabic tradition, but the regular disposition of the towers to each side is typical of the form brought to Spain from Syria by the Umayyads in the 8th century – though semicircular projections were the norm there.

1.116

›1.115 COVARRUBIAS, TOWER OF DOÑA URACCA, c. 950.

The masonry style recalls Muslim work. The corbels, which once carried a wallwalk, are later.

›1.116 ÁVILA, 1088–91: view from the west.

The walls average 10 metres in height and are punctuated by 88 of the earliest round towers in medieval Europe. Though attributed to a Roman named Cassandra, who presumably was familiar with ancient imperial precedents, the influence of the Muslims – themselves dependent on Roman precedent – is inescapable.

Covarrubias c. 950, for instance – and many captured qasrs were endowed with one. Towards the end of the next century, cylindrical towers punctuate the stone walls of Ávila: built to protect a base for the troops of Castile in the aftermath of the conquest of Toledo and therefore far more extensive than a castle, the exercise was unprecedented in Europe – if not the Middle East – since Roman antiquity (AICI, page 559).[1.115, 1.116]

Ávila's walls are crenellated with the time-honoured purpose of providing marksmen with unrestricted shelter. The earliest European crenellations were rectangular, in the straightforward Roman manner, and they were usually to remain so. However, those of Ávila derive from the Ummayad merlon whose ancient Middle Eastern ancestry had admitted the elaboration of the profile. Projecting wallwalks (hoardings), on the other hand, seem to have been a later European invention: they were timber long after stone had become the normal material for defences by the mid-12th century.

Ávila stands at the head of a great line of walled cities

1.117

which developed with the revival of the urban economy from the late-12th century. Meanwhile the square stone tower continued to dominate the feudal stronghold in most of Europe. Henry IV's Herzburg[1.47] marks the culmination of a great spate of such building in the imperial domain and its marches but the efforts of the magnates scarcely flagged for centuries.[1.117, 1.118]

>1.117 LAKE GENEVA, CHILLON CASTLE, from late-10th century: view with Tour d'Alinge centre.

The Tour d'Alinge, probably begun about the same time as Langeais, was more than a watchtower. The extensive range of subsidiary towers is later.

>1.118 MARKSBURG, view from south-west.

The *burgfried* was rebuilt in the 13th century by vassals of the Elector Palatine. The wings around the court retain 12th-century work. The complex was renovated in the 19th century.

1.118

›ARCHITECTURE IN CONTEXT »RENOVATION OF GRAVITAS

THE CHURCH: INTRODUCTION

Feudalism naturally promoted the development of distinct schools of Romanesque architecture within the diversified realms of Europe, especially in the West. Use of materials, conceptions of mass and volume, articulation and embellishment all differ but behind the diversity lay community of aim: to reflect God's ordered creation – and also to assert a political ideal. Above all, the great church was an enduring structure: this meant that it was of stone and sophistication in the handling of stone – particularly the transition from rubble to small dressed blocks (*petit appareil*) to monumental ashlar (*grand appareil*) – was acquired through reference to Roman antiquity.

The regular colonnade, clerestory and revealed timber roof truss of the early Christian basilica were long to survive, particularly in Italy. However, northern builders were most impressed by the superimposed arcades of the ancient aqueducts or arenas as models for their main interior elevations. They enhanced monumentality and security by remastering Roman vaulting techniques – tunnel, groin, domical (AICI, page 553) – and, replacing columns with piers as eastern church builders had long done, they varied the rhythm of the main arcades.

Antiquity also provided a repertory of decorative detail and its literal translation in areas with prominent Roman remains was a principal characteristic of the Romanesque. Beyond that, more usually and more abundantly when the mastery of masonry took the style to its apogee, the abstract order of antique humanism is eclipsed by the didactic representationalism of Christianity.

Apart from building types, techniques and ornament, the Romans also provided the principal motifs of Christian architecture: above all the vault of heaven, before all the triumphal arch. Dedicated to the apotheosis of emperor or hero, the form of the latter was abstracted from the twin-

›1.119 CLUNY ABBEY, SECOND PHASE OF DEVELOPMENT, c. 1050: plan with (1) church, (2) entrance to monastic forecourt, (3) chapter house, (4) abbot's palace, (5) cloister, (6) dormitories, (7) refectory, (8) novices' cloister, (9) infirmary, (10) guest house, (11) workshops, (12) service buildings, (13) burial ground, (14) lady chapel.

First installed in a villa, augmented with a church by 927, the monks of Cluny began systematic rebuilding in 955. The new basilican church, tunnel vaulted to provide the optimum acoustic for choral chant, was dedicated in 981. The complex is roughly square (c. 90 metres), but comparison with the S. Gall plan[1.27] is striking: the main differences are the designation of the chapter house (where those responsible for running the community deliberated) before a chapel dedicated to Our Lady to the east of the central cloister, the provision of a second cloister for novices to the south of the refectory (rather than by the infirmary) and the extension of the dormitory range along the east side of both cloisters. The completion of the scheme to accommodate 100 monks took a century.

towered portal of the ancient Mesopotamian palace, the place of epiphany of the divine ruler – as we have already noted (page 26). Of obvious symbolic relevance to a faith centred on the concept of resurrection, the triumphal arch as the church door presided over by Christ the Judge was the most powerful theme of Romanesque art: we have foreseen the role of the Cluniacs in the achievement.

Beyond the triumphal arch, palace imagery always pervaded the Christian concept of the church – as a building apart, the institution of God's elect, above all as the image of God's heavenly mansion to which it was the door. And the concept of Heaven as a palace prefigured here on Earth by the church was sustained throughout the Middle Ages: with it went the idea of God as the supreme architect and the dedication of the church builder to emulate the perfection of his work.

CLUNIAC OPULENCE

Though feudal regionalism was manifest in distinct schools of Romanesque architecture in the lands which would be France, the extended arteries of the pilgrimage routes and the extensive network of relationships between the monasteries – especially the imperial system of the Benedictines ruled from Cluny – ensured that no single approach was long confined to a particular region. And after the settlement of the Normans, relief released great reconstructive energy.**1.119**

Cluny was well placed to effect a synthesis of the main strands of Romanesque architecture for its quasi-imperial network of monasteries: in the heart of Burgundy, it was at the crossroads of communication with the Loire valley (where there was innovative

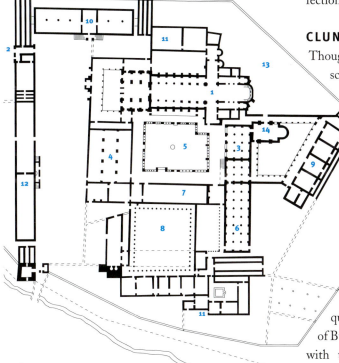

1.119 @ 1:2000

1.20a

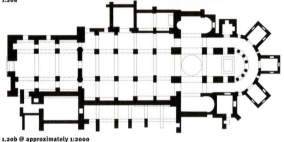

1.20b @ approximately 1:2000

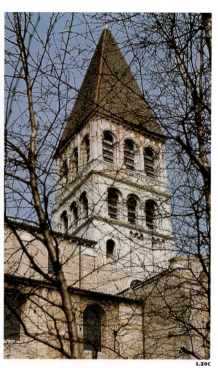

1.20c

planning), with the Rhône and Lombard Italy (where there was technological development) and with the empire to the east (where munificent patronage had produced the truly imperial church). There were two main phases in the development of its great church.

Cluny II, begun c. 950 after Hungarian raids had devastated the area, was completed in the early 11th century. As the order's magnificence reached its apogee in the last quarter of that century, it was superseded by the entirely new Cluny III built to its north. The sanctuary of the earlier work was retained as the chapter house and its narthex was incorporated in the abbot's palace to either side of the enlarged cloister but most of the complex was destroyed in the early 19th century.

S. Philibert, Tournus goes some way to compensate for the loss of Cluny II. Fleeing Deas in 856, where they had

›1.120 TOURNUS, S. PHILIBERT DE GRAND LIEU: (a) sanctuary dedicated 1019, nave vaulting begun 1066, (b) plan, (c) tower.

›1.121 S. BENOÎT SUR LOIRE, c. 1080–1130: (a) plan (b) nave, (c) view from the west.

Founded c. 673 to enshrine the bones of S. Benedict, brought to the Loire valley after the desecration of Monte Cassino by the Lombards, the abbey church was rebuilt to cater for the growth of pilgrimage to the site in the last quarter of the 11th century. A dedication ceremony was held in 1108, but construction is thought to have continued for another generation.

Over the narthex, the westwork is a development of the form of tower attached to the west end of the original church of S. Martin, Tours, rather than of the arrangement at S. Riquier.[1.19] The westwork contains a Chapel of S. Michael, but it lost its upper stages in the 16th century. Flanked by groin-vaulted aisles, the nave originally had a wooden roof over a clerestory but no triforium. The arcades are carried on piers with attached columns (the main ones cut off from the base). The lines of nave and aisles are continued

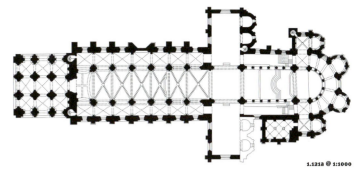

1.121a @ 1:1000

1.121b
beyond the transept to form the tunnel-vaulted sanctuary, but the piers are replaced by columns. The crossing has a lantern after the precedent set for S. Martin, Tours. A second transept separates the sanctuary from the apse and the ambulatory with its radiating chapels.

1/121c

sought to escape the Normans and developed an ambulatory in their new church, the monks of Grandlieu settled in 875 by the River Saône just north of Cluny's future site. Devastated again in 937 by the Hungarians, they rebuilt after 950 and this time planned for stone vaults. As at Cluny, the nave at the new site joined a long transept with a central tower and a twin-towered westwork with a chapel over a narthex. A generation earlier, Cluny II retained parallel apses at its east end but the relics of S. Philibert were enshrined in a crypt with a semicircular ambulatory and radiating chapels which were repeated at ground level beyond the sanctuary apse. That followed the prime example set for S. Martin, Tours, whose influence is also apparent in both the chevet and the westwork of the church at S. Benoît sur Loire, begun c. 1080.**1.120, 1.121**

The nave at Cluny had its regular tunnel vault by 1010 but originally there was a wooden ceiling at S. Benoît and probably at Tournus. S. Benoît waited well over a century for its rib vault but S. Philibert's vaulting began early in the 11th century with groins in the aisles and narthex, and regular tunnels over the sanctuary, transept and westwork chapel – the latter with pilaster strips in the Lombard manner and transverse arches. However, from c. 1066 each nave bay was given a transverse tunnel, admitting more light through larger clerestory windows than the normal form at Cluny.

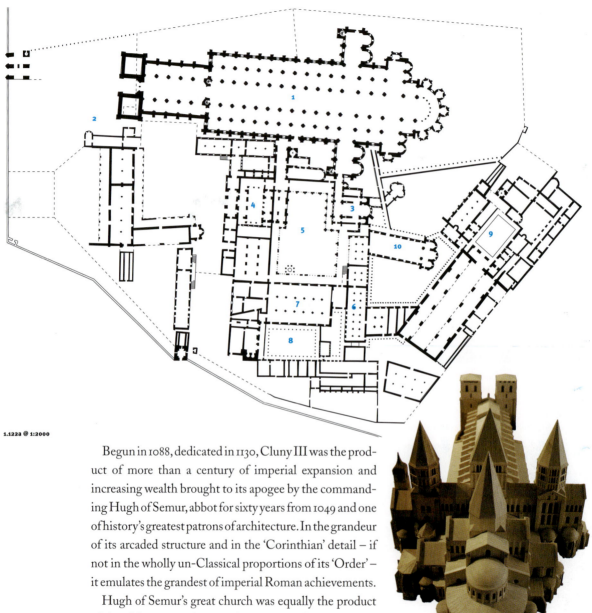

1.122a @ 1:2000

Begun in 1088, dedicated in 1130, Cluny III was the product of more than a century of imperial expansion and increasing wealth brought to its apogee by the commanding Hugh of Semur, abbot for sixty years from 1049 and one of history's greatest patrons of architecture. In the grandeur of its arcaded structure and in the 'Corinthian' detail – if not in the wholly un-Classical proportions of its 'Order' – it emulates the grandest of imperial Roman achievements.

Hugh of Semur's great church was equally the product of the elaboration of music, the mastery of stone carving and the development of the basilica with chevet, towered transepts, tunnel-vaulted naves with transverse arches,

1.122b

1.122c

1.122e

>1.122 CLUNY ABBEY, THIRD PHASE OF DEVELOPMENT, begun c. 1088: (a) plan with (1) new church, (2) entrance to monastic forecourt, (3) sanctuary of Cluny II adapted as the scene of special conclaves adjacent to chapter house, (4) narthex of Cluny II adapted as the court of the abbot's palace, (5) cloister, (6) dormitories, (7) refectory, (8) novices' cloister, (9) infirmary, (10) lady chapel, (b) block model (Cluny Abbey Museum), (c) consecration by Pope Urban II in 1095 (12th-century ms), (d) remaining south transept from the west, (e) model, (f) transverse section through church, (g) reconstruction of nave.

complex piers, galleries and clerestories, groin-vaulted aisles, and twin-towered westworks. The influence of S. Martin, Tours, fundamental here as elsewhere, was channelled most directly through S. Benoît sur Loire with its substantial narthex and two aisleless transepts.[1.115, 1.122]

The third abbey church of Cluny

Under Abbot Hugh, elected in 1049, the number of monks at Cluny grew from around 70 to 200 by 1085, and much extra accommodation was needed. To house the whole brotherhood of the order, the scale of the new church was unprecedented. It was built with impressive speed over a plan defined in harmony with a modular system inspired by Vitruvian concepts of symmetry, and also celebrated for its acoustics.

Preceded by a westwork rising over a narthex longer than its predecessor's nave, the main body of the church was c. 160 metres long: it extended to eleven bays before the first of two transepts, and two more before the second transept, sanctuary and apse. The ambulatory was screened from the apse by a semicircle of columns, but throughout the rest of the church the main arcade was carried on recessed piers with attached columns. The aisles were doubled, as at Tours (at least after 1050). Except in the apse, there were both triforium and clerestory throughout and an additional zone

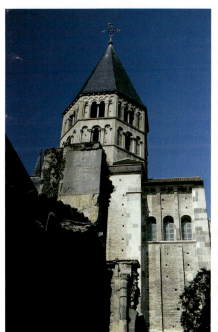

1.122d

1.122f

of clerestory lighting above the inner aisles produced a four-storey elevation to the narthex (c. 1122): the main body rose to c. 30 metres.

The tunnel vaults over the nave and the transverse arches between the groin-vaulted bays of the aisles were pointed in profile to reduce the thrust – at least in so far as the one daringly thrown over the nave was concerned. Nevertheless, part of the vault fell in 1125 and heavy quadrant arches – putative flying buttresses – were projected out from the clerestory to transmit the thrust of the vault over the inner aisle to the intermediate piers. The first of these buttresses may have been inserted in the early 1130s when the construction of the narthex was begun, but dating is obscure in both exercises as they continued into the next century.

Appearing north of the Alps for the first time on such a scale, the pointed arch seems to have come via Monte Cassino from Sicily – where the Islamic tradition was sustained by the Christians, as we have seen (pages 102ff). Much else of oriental derivation was manifest in the decorative detail, not least the cusped arches of the triforium – the arcade masking the pitched roofs of the inner aisles which takes the place of a gallery. Yet the capitals of the pilasters and half columns which articulated the great piers of the nave re-evoked the Classical Corinthian. Elsewhere, particularly on the columns screening the sanctuary from the ambulatory, Classical stylization was superseded by Christian didacticism.

1.122g

The largest of medieval churches, in its turn it succumbed to early 19th-century vandalism, except for a transept and fragments of its westwork, but the plan has been reconstructed from the foundations, internal and external elevations from descriptions, documents and the surviving elements.

›1.123 PARAY-LE-MONIAL, NOTRE-DAME, c. 1110: exterior from the north-west.

The church is one of the closest reduced versions of the model provided by Cluny III, though far less complex in plan and mass.

›1.124 NEVERS, S. ÉTIENNE, after 1083: east end with ambulatory.

Lucid in plan, meticulous in its masonry, S. Étienne marks the maturity of the Cluniac style on the reduced scale of a dependent abbey. Single aisles flank the barrel-vaulted nave; there is a single barrel-vaulted transept before the sanctuary and ambulatory, but there are galleries and a clerestory throughout. The three original towers were reduced after the French Revolution.

Derived from Tours, the accumulation of chapels around the chevet was French but the accumulation of towers was positively imperial, as was the repetition of transepts. However, the combination of all these with the discipline of consistent modules and semi-centralized, essentially centrifugal, planning about the eastern crossing tower generated a mass not equal in majesty to H. Sofia, Constantinople (AIC1, pages 787ff). As in Byzantium, the Pantokrator dominated the interior, but from the main apse rather than a central dome.

Apart from the surviving transept, an idea of the greatness of Cluny III's loss is conveyed by S. Eutrope at Saintes, S. Étienne at Nevers (begun just before Abbot Hugh's great church), Notre-Dame at Paray-le-Monial and the cathedral of S. Lazare at Autun. Disparate in style, the abbey church of S. Madeleine, Vézelay, marks the further development of substituting groin vaults for the tunnel over the nave and ribbing them in the narthex. Ribbed vaults in combination with the pointed arches and flying buttresses of Cluny III provided the key to the future. And entrance to the celestial future is announced in the splendid portals of these last two churches which, with Moissac, best compensate us for the loss of Cluny's own portal.**1.123–1.128**

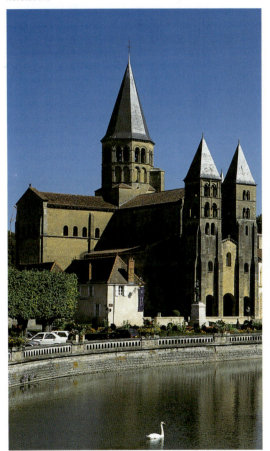

1.123

1.124

1.125a

1.125b

1.125c

›1.125 SAINTES, S. EUTROPE, 1081–96: (a) crypt, (b) monk's choir (now nave) to west, (c) section.

The aisles of the nave (destroyed in the aftermath of the French Revolution) were originally connected via short flights of steps with the crypt over which the monks' choir was raised: pilgrims to the saint's relics could thus circulate without prejudice to the discretion of the monks. The crypt, overwhelming in its monumentality, is distinguished by its splendid didactic sculpture and precocious rib vaulting.

›1.126 MOISSAC PRIORY CHURCH: south portal, c. 1115.

Possibly originally intended for the west front of the church founded c. 1065 by Abbot Hugh of Cluny (rebuilt), the portal was moved to the south side of a chapel tower (of the type represented at S. Riquier) where it provided an important precedent for Spanish builders in particular.

1.126

1.127a

>**1.127 AUTUN, CATHEDRAL OF S. LAZAR,** C. 1120: (a) capital illustrating the Flight into Egypt, (b) nave.

The nave is a close follower of Cluny III but above the three-bay triforium each clerestory bay has only a single light and instead of shaft-like half columns the piers are articulated with pseudo-Classical pilasters with superb didactic capitals rather than Corinthian acanthus foliage. In the absence of an ambulatory, three tiers of windows light the apse.

1.127b

1.128a

›1.128 VÉZELAY, S. MADELEINE, 1096–1137: (a) narthex, (b) nave.

An essential element in the S. Benoît sur Loire formula, the narthex was begun before the one on Cluny III. It shelters a portal which, opening to the nave under the Redeemer as the *porta coeli*, is one of the chief glories of medieval France: like the comparable work at Cluny and Autun, it is attributed to one Gislebertus.

Built in place of its burnt Carolingian predecessor, the nave does not conform to the Cluniac formula: there is no triforium, except in the apse – later enclosed in an ambulatory – and the groin-vaulted bays are separated by bold transverse arches of varicoloured masonry. There is, however, a Classicizing tendency in the proportions and detail of the attached columns from which the nave arcade springs.

1.128b

CISTERCIAN AUSTERITY

The spiritual revival of the late-11th century – the age of zealous popes and humiliated emperors – promoted wide-ranging reform within the Christian establishment which certainly did not fail to affect Cluny's empire. Several new orders emerged from dissatisfaction with manifest luxury and perceived laxity within the Benedictine world in the contrary conviction that the best way to God was through humility and self-denial.

1.129

One band of monks dedicated anew to S. Benedict's original ideal left the abbey of Molesme in 1098 to establish a severely ascetic rule at Cîteaux: manual labour was reintroduced for all, feudal endowments were rejected and absolute simplicity of liturgy was reflected in the uncompromising austerity of building. This Cistercian order spread particularly rapidly after the young brother Bernard was sent out from Cîteaux to found a new house at Clairvaux in 1115.[1.129] Under his direction, the process was repeated many times, but the central ideal was not diluted: each new house was dependent on the one from which it was founded, all were to subscribe to precisely the same rule, each was to be visited annually by the abbot of its founding house and all the abbots were to meet annually at Cîteaux.

S. Bernard (1090–1153) was profoundly influenced by S. Augustine, his theology of number and his discovery of the key to the City of God in musical harmony. In the consonance of music S. Bernard heard ultimate truth and his notorious puritanism was bent to the moulding of a context in which no other sensory delight would interfere with the apprehension of that truth through sound – except the inner eye of the soul attuned to harmony which would see the translation of those aural consonances into the perfect proportions and pure geometry of the church.

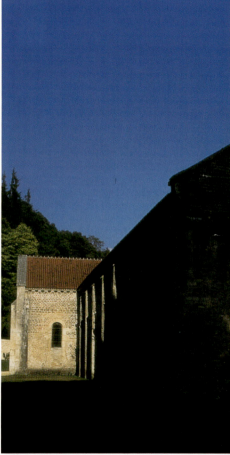

1.130a

1.129 S. BERNARD OF CLAIRVAUX: initial letter from a 13th-century ms (Canterbury, S. Augustine's Abbey).

›**1.130 FONTENAY ABBEY,** 1139–47: (a) exterior, (b) plan with (1) church, (2) chapter house, (3) dormitory, (4) refectory, (5) fountain, (6) workshops, (c) interior of church to east, (d) chapter house, (e) dormitory, (f) cloister.

Facilities for outsiders were strictly limited and were confined to the west gate. In the design and construction of their abbeys, as in all else, the Cistercians aimed at self-sufficiency.

S. Bernard rejected the grand scale and sumptuous ornament of Cluny as inconsistent with the humility proper to the monk but the representationalism of Cluniac sculpture was not condemned out of hand. Except perhaps for the expense, it was admissible to resort to material imagery for the instruction of the laity, but it was a

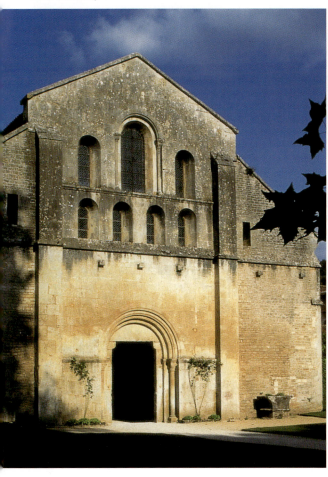

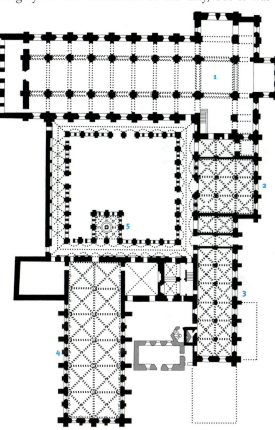

1.130b @ 1:1000

1.130c

The main ratios are 1:1 for the façade and the essentially cubical bays of nave and aisles below the springing of the vaults; 1:2 for the width of aisles to nave, for the length of transept to nave, for the width and length of the transept and for the height of the aisle arcade to the internal elevation of the nave wall; 2:3 for the width of the sanctuary to its total length including the crossing; 3:4 for the width of the nave plus aisles to the length of the transept.

1.130d

›ARCHITECTURE IN CONTEXT »RENOVATION OF GRAVITAS

1.130e

1.130f

distracting irrelevance to a monk aspiring to the vision of God's City revealed in the perfect ratios translated by S. Augustine from the Pythagorean *tetractys*.

In contrast with Benedictine display, Cistercian austerity is nowhere better represented than at Fontenay, though it was common to all the houses of the uniformitarian order. It was imposed by standardized planning derived from Benedict of Aniane's blueprint[1.27] – though secluded remoteness of site was preferred and topography often dictated deviation. Without a towered façade, ambulatory or crypt, generally rectangular in plan, and devoid of sculpture, the church relied for aesthetic effect solely on the regular repetition of arches – but these were

1.131a

invariably pointed like those of Cluny III and Autun. Certainly no less austere were the main buildings around the cloister – south or north of the church, as the site determined – the vaulted chapter house, the dormitory accessible directly from the church, the refectory perpendicular to the furthest cloister range and the nave of the church.**1.130, 1.131**

1.131b

›1.131 SÉNANQUE ABBEY, founded 1148: (a) overview, (b) dormitory.

›1.132 S. GILLES DU GARD, PRIORY CHURCH, mid-12th century: west front.

›1.133 ARLES, S. TROPHÎME, c. 1180: (a) façade, (b) nave, (c, d) cloister range and details of capitals (pages 142–143).

In the synthesis of triumphal arch and temple front, no less than in the proportions of the columns, Classicism is honoured in the breach rather than in full faith – despite the abundance of models in close proximity.

The stout corner piers, providing support for the quadrant vaults, have fluted pilasters and figures in high relief. The arches of the intermediate bays spring from a variety of circular and octagonal shafts with a spectacular set of didactic and Corinthianesque capitals.

1.132

REGIONAL VARIETY

Re-evoked Classicism was not confined to Burgundy. Certainly it was at its richest where the abbots of Cluny maintained that all the resources of art should be employed for the glory of God, but it was hardly less rich in Provence, itself exceptionally rich in Roman remains. Insecurity of dating has left ultimate responsibility for the revival of Roman ornament unclear. Because of its heritage, Provence seems the most obvious source, but the most obvious examples are generally thought to postdate the conception of Cluny III.

The triumphal portal of S. Trophîme, Arles, for example, has been placed in the 1170s at the earliest, when the nave was rebuilt, and the even more sumptuous three-arched version at S. Gilles du Gard is possibly a generation earlier – at least in inception. On the other hand, the relatively austere portal of Notre-Dame des Domes, Avig-non, has been dated to c. 1200 though the aisleless nave is earlier. In Provence, as elsewhere, Classicism was

1.133a

1.133b

transformed with didactic decorative detail: portals apart, this is especially striking in the wide variety of capitals in cloister colonnades which typically present immediately appreciable images of the wages of sin.[1.132, 1.133]

Beyond varied approaches to ornament, French Romanesque admitted no less variety of plan, space and mass, and though distinct regional preferences may be discerned, they are far from absolute. S. Trophîme, Arles, and the church at S. Gilles du Gard are basilican. However, many Provencal churches are aisleless like Notre-Dame des Domes, Avignon, or the fortified church at Les SS. Maries de la Mer: the form derives from the unobstructed space of the antique council chamber – the basic basilica (AICI, pages 530ff).[1.134] The two types, the single volume and the composite, were developed in parallel – even cross-fertilized – elsewhere, most notably in western France.

The aisled basilica is certainly the most common form throughout France, as almost everywhere else, with or

1.133c

›**1.134 LES SS. MARIES DE LA MER,** 12th century: (a, b) exterior and interior.
The main volume is a hall with lateral chapels.

1.134a

1.134b

without stone vaulting. The ambulatory with radiating chapels predominates after Cluny III but does not entirely supplant parallel apses. Some form of westwork is normal, usually with twin towers as at Cluny III, often with one, occasionally with three. Internal elevations vary too, but not in accordance with any regional pattern: the aisles may be lower than the nave, permitting a two-storey elevation with clerestory as in the early Christian form – and as at S. Benoît sur Loire or S. Madeleine, Vézelay.[1.121, 1.128] There may be a gallery, as at S. Martin of Tours (at least after its early 11th-century rebuilding),[1.154] or both gallery and clerestory, as at Cluny III[1.122] and in the great churches of the Capetian domain where aspiration in building matched imperial pretension – though, as yet, technology did not.

The stone vault had obvious advantages of durability but limitations of scale, as structural technology in the period of its inception restricted the height, width and lightness of naves. Thus, until well into the 11th century the wooden roof was usually preferred because it was easier and cheaper to construct and because it allowed a lighter structure to the body of the church and wider spans to the main spaces – especially in the north where light was at a premium and where the danger of raids was less

›1.135 REIMS, S. REMI, begun 1005, 13th-century vaults reconstructed in the 20th century: nave.

The first church enshrining the tomb of S. Remigius, the baptist of Clovis I, was consecrated in 852. A grander new one was built between 1005 and 1034 in response to the great popularity of pilgrimage to the site. Its three-storey internal elevation, with wide, light arches to aisles and galleries, supported a flat wooden roof over the exceptionally broad nave. Narrow aisles around the transepts led to a sanctuary with parallel apses, and later in the century an ambulatory with radiating chapels was built around the main sanctuary apse, completing the church's concordance with the pilgrimage type defined for S. Martin, Tours.[1.154] Later still, the wooden roof was replaced with rib vaults, despite the great width of the main spaces, and the substantial mass of wall above the triforium was relieved with blind pointed arches.

acute in great centres remote from coasts, like Chartres or Reims. Both these considerations – the vulnerability of timber, the limitation of space – ensured that most of the greatest mature Romanesque churches of the French monarchy's heartland have disappeared. S. Remi is perhaps the main exception.[1.128]

Vaulting on the scale of Cluny III was exceptional at the end of the 11th century, of course. However, in general the influence of that great work was as widespread as its network of priories, but its formula was used, or varied, more widely still at various scales. Nowhere is this better illustrated, perhaps, than in neighbouring Auvergne – though the influence of the Loire, which helped mould Cluny III, had already affected the mid-10th-century architects of the cathedral at Clermont-

1.136

early 12th century: nave towards the sanctuary.

Flanked by aisles and triforium gallery but no clerestory, like S. Martin, Tours, the four-bay, tunnel-vaulted nave is exceptionally dark. On the other hand, light enters through and above the ambulatory around the apse and the raising of the transept bays adjacent to the crossing tower for the insertion of clerestory windows is exceptionally dramatic in its effect. The cusped arches of the gallery echo the oriental influence detected earlier at Cluny III or the direct impact of the Mozarabic style transmitted by pilgrims returning from Santiago de Compostela. The crypt under the apse and ambulatory follows the precedent set nearly two centuries earlier in the nearby cathedral, which also followed the precedent set for S. Martin.

›1.137 ORCIVAL, S. AUSTREMOINE, early 12th century: exterior from the east.

Typical of the Auvergnat churches related to Notre-Dame-du-Port, Clermont-Ferrand, the effect on the external massing of raising the transept bays next to the crossing tower is hardly less dramatic than its admission of clerestory light to the interior.

1.137

Ferrand. That work has long been obscured, but its influence – and local idiosyncrasy – are all well represented by Notre-Dame-du-Port at Clermont-Ferrand and many churches in smaller settlements around the metropolis, like S. Austremoine, Orcival.**1.136, 1.137**

In a cross between our two types of basilica, aisles and nave may match in height though not usually in width or vaulting technique: the subdivision of a volumetric entity is preferred to the accretion of distinct elements. Thus east ends may be triapsidal but more usually the sanctuary apse may be surrounded by an ambulatory for circulation around a reliquary. The elimination of clerestory and gallery and the substitution of comparatively light colonnades for much weighty masonry was popular in north Aquitanian Poitou where architects seem to have been interested in spatial integrity but not necessarily in preserving it absolutely – as in Provence. Alternative structural styles are represented by the abbey church at S. Savin sur Gartempe, with its great colonnades and splendidly frescoed tunnel vault over the nave (completed c. 1115), and at Notre-Dame la Grande, Poitiers (c. 1140), with its articulated piers and pointed arches.**1.138, 1.139**

1.138

>**1.138 S. SAVIN SUR GARTEMPE,** begun mid-11th century: nave (completed c. 1115).

>**1.139 POITIERS, NOTRE-DAME LA GRANDE,** first half of 12th century: (a, b) interior looking east and west, (c) plan, (d) exterior from south-west, (e) detail.
Rather than a freestanding commemorative arch, the façade's superimposed arcades recall a Roman triumphal city gate like the Porta dei Borsari, Verona (AIC1, page 604) or its many northern equivalents, but it is inhabited by an even richer panoply of figures – despite the absence of the tympanum usual in the main portal – and pointed arches join semicircular ones. The clustered colonnettes of the turrets and the fish-scale masonry of their conical tops are typical of the region. Inside, except in the ambulatory, the monumental cylindrical columns of S. Savin sur Gartempe are supplanted by clustered piers.

1.139a

Notre-Dame la Grande well represents the Poitevan predilection for the rich decoration of façades, Classical in inspiration if not in effect. Elaboration of form in the region is well represented by the contemporary crossing towers of S. Jean de Montierneuf, Poitiers – unfortunately ruined.[1.140]

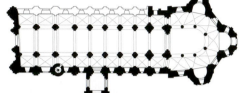
1.139c @ 1:1000

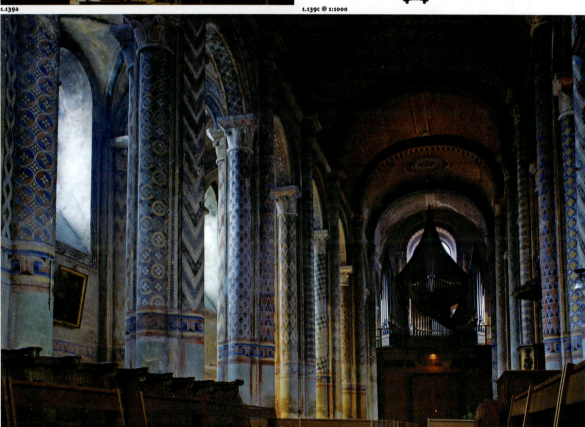
1.139b

›ARCHITECTURE IN CONTEXT »RENOVATION OF GRAVITAS

1.139d

1.140

1.139e

>1.140 POITIERS, S. JEAN DE MONTIER NEUF,
consecrated 1096: detail of chevet and crossing tower.

›ARCHITECTURE IN CONTEXT »RENOVATION OF GRAVITAS

1.141

In the neighbouring Saintonge region, many churches are almost equally as rich in ornament as their Poitevan contemporaries and there is similar elaboration of form. However, though a circuit for pilgrims was introduced well before the end of the 11th century in S. Eutrope at Saintes, the survival of the triapsidal east end of the standard aisled basilica is frequent: exemplary are S. Marie des Dames at Saintes, S. Pierre, Aulnay and, at least in so far as external embellishment is concerned, S. Hilaire, Melle, or Notre-Dame of Rioux. **1.141–1.143**

>**1.141 RIOUX, NOTRE-DAME,** 12th century: polygonal apse.

>**1.142 MELLE, S. HILAIRE,** 12th century, west front.

>**1.143 AULNAY, S. PIERRE**, 12th century: general view from south-east.

1.142

1.143

1.144a

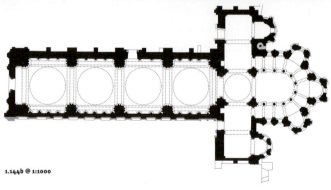

1.144b @ 1:1000

>**1.144 FONTEVRAUD,** c. 1120: (a–c) church, nave towards the sanctuary, plan, choir, (d, e) kitchen, exterior and interior.

The abbey was founded c. 1100 and, as the sanctuary was dedicated in 1119, the church must have been begun little more than a decade later. The nave followed over the next decade. In the vicinity of Angers, capital of Anjou, the church attracted royal patronage and was adopted by Henry II Plantagenet as the Angevin dynastic necropolis.

The four domed bays of the nave (c. 84 metres long) were revaulted in the early 20th century. Earlier than the nave, the tunnel-vaulted transept has five square

1.144c

bays smaller than those of the nave, but commensurate with the width of the sanctuary.

The splendid abbey kitchen – extensively restored but perhaps the best surviving early medieval domestic building in Europe – presents a conical variant of the dome on squinches. The octagonal cluster of major and minor cone-vaulted spaces may be likened to a centralized sanctuary with ambulatory and radiating chapels to all sides. Aligned, two such forms provide the nave of the church of S. Ours, Loches (before 1168).

1.144d

1.144e

From Fontevraud (well to the north near the Loire) to Agen (well to the south on the Garonne), the most distinctive Aquitanian solution to the problem of preserving uninterrupted space depends on the pendentive dome.[1.144] A single dome over the shrine of S. Front, Périgueux, seems to have initiated the development not only of the great church there but also of an extended process in which domed spaces were aligned longitudinally or combined to form Greek and Latin crosses – with or without knowledge of the main masterpieces of the Byzantine tradition but certainly in the recognition of the self-buttressing potential of a series of domes. S. Marco, Venice,[1.86] was doubtless well enough known even in Aquitaine, so too perhaps Sicily where the Byzantine tradition was well established, and although S. Front's first dome is generally dated to a generation before the First Crusade, the process of accumulation may well have stemmed from first-hand familiarity with Byzantine practice gained on the passage to Palestine (AICI, page 800).[1.145]

1.145a

A 10th-century basilica enshrining the remains of S. Front was apparently given a dome before the mid-11th century, but it was burnt c. 1120. The nave walls were retained for the atrium of a vast new church begun soon after the fire, and the base of its crossing tower, raised through three stages of superimposed arcades, formed the porch. The domed sanctuary containing the saint's tomb was rebuilt on a grander scale. The main axis was continued with two similar domed chambers to the east (forming an exceptionally oriented nave as the sanctuary was retained in its original position) and two more domes were added on the cross axis.

If the longitudinal alignment of domes is not uncommon in the naves of western France, the Greek-cross plan of S. Front is unique in the degree of its homage to the east – in particular to the church of the Holy Apostles, Constantinople (c. 536–50), built by Constantine, rebuilt by Justinian, which provided the model for S. Marco, Venice. The position of the high altar has been moved from west to east and back again several times. The 'restorations' perpetrated by Paul Abadie in the 19th century are generally regretted, especially in so far as they interpreted the exterior.

Developed over at least half a century from 1070, S. Front is the most spectacular example of a cruciform arrangement of domed spaces. At much the same time, the

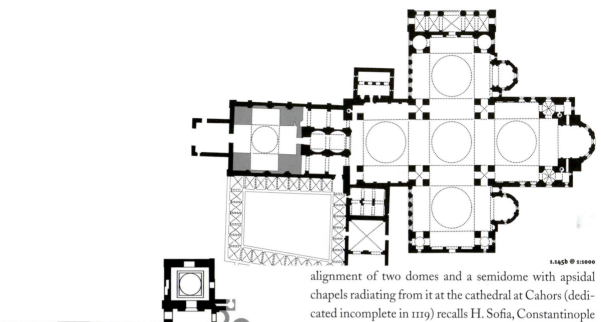

1.145b @ 1:1000

alignment of two domes and a semidome with apsidal chapels radiating from it at the cathedral at Cahors (dedicated incomplete in 1119) recalls H. Sofia, Constantinople (AICI, pages 787ff) in a primitive way, but the principle is more representatively extended at Angoulême or Fontevraud – the latter with ambulatory, the former with semicircular chapels dependent directly on the great central apse and transepts.**1.146, 1.144**

1.146a @ 1:1000

>**1.146** ANGOULÊME, CATHEDRAL OF S. PIERRE, first quarter of the 12th century: (a) plan, (b) interior towards sanctuary.

1.146b

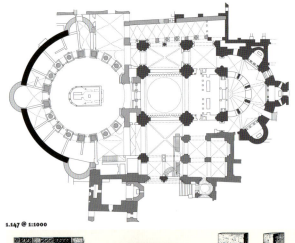

1.147 @ 1:1000

>1.147 JERUSALEM, CHURCH OF THE HOLY SEPULCHRE ON GOLGOTHA, 4th–12th century: plan.

The complex built under Constantine incorporated a basilica, an irregular trapezoidal court to the west and the Anastasis rotunda, enshrining the holy sepulchre, further west. During restorations carried out in the mid-11th century, the Byzantine emperor Constantine Monomachos projected chapels from an ambulatory around the rotunda. The Crusaders demolished the eastern apsidal chapel and filled the court with a new sanctuary extending to the east from the domed crossing of a transept – transept, crossing, sanctuary, apse and ambulatory in fact reproducing the arrangements developed in Europe to cater for pilgrims. A new chapel south of the new sanctuary enshrined Golgotha, the site of crucifixion. The original basilica survived in part as the chapel of S. Helena, who is reputed to have discovered the remains of the cross on the site.

1.148a

>1.148 CAMBRIDGE, CHURCH OF THE HOLY SEPULCHRE (THE ROUND CHURCH), c. 1130: (a) plan, section and details, (b) exterior.

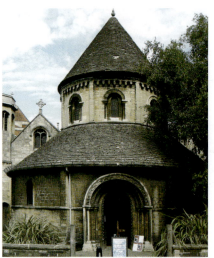

1.148b

The domed church was ubiquitous. If not in Aquitaine, its Latin culmination was in Palestine in the mid-12th century with the addition of an ambulatory and the domed crossing of a transept to one of the most important rotundas in all Christendom, Constantine's archetypal church of the Holy Sepulchre, Jerusalem. Protected by the Knights Templar, and reflected in their many foundations elsewhere, that was the principal goal of pilgrims, whose security was ostensibly a main motive of the Crusades (AICI, pages 700–701, and see pages 218ff below). If there was a truly international Romanesque, it was that of the pilgrimage church whose essential element was not the dome but the ambulatory – the main new form introduced by the Latins to Jerusalem.**1.147, 1.148**

THE ROAD TO COMPOSTELA AND THE PILGRIMAGE CHURCH

Because the Alps presented a more formidable obstacle than the Pyrenees, northern European pilgrims favoured the route to Compostela, the reputed burial place of S. James the Great in north-west Spain, over Rome, the seat of S. Peter and the centre of Christendom after the loss of the Holy Land to the Muslims. With the pilgrims – and the soldiers of fortune – Cluniacs, Cistercians, a host of lesser monastic orders, engineers and architects poured into it from its tributaries. As these rose in all the regions of France, it is hardly surprising that the diversity in planning and elevation which we have seen in those regions is well represented in the Christian domains of northern Spain. And there the newcomers occasionally worked in a Visigothic context or beside native Mozarabacists, whose style retained its dominance in the south, as we have noted (pages 16, 17, and 47ff).**1.149, 1.150**

The Burgundian – as distinct from the Mozarabic – pointed arch makes occasional appearances in Castilian

>1.149 SAHAGUN, S. TIRSO, 12th century: east end and tower.

The work well illustrates the eclecticism of pilgrimage route exercises: the triapsidal east end is ubiquitous, if perennially popular in the regions of south-west France through which the pilgrims passed before entering Spain; Lombard influence is apparent in the multi-storey tower and the blind arcading but the horseshoe profile of the latter – and the brickwork – sustain the native Mudéjar tradition. In the background is the tower which dominates the scanty remains of the great Benedictine abbey.

1.149

1.150a

1.150b

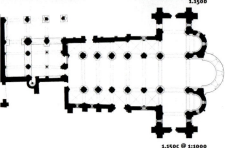

1.150c @ 1:1000

territory from the early 12th century and by then sculpture approximates Cluniac splendour (pages 160ff). **1.150a** Even along their sectors of the route to Compostela, however, the Castilians and their neighbours rarely adopted the ambulatory despite the prestige won for the form at Cluny and its wide promotion in France specifically to cater for pilgrims. They remained conservatively attached to the multi-apsidal basilica inherited from Lombardy through Catalonia – later from Aquitaine through Navarra – and

1.151

>**1.150 LEÓN, S. ISIDORO,** mid-11th–mid-12th century: (a) basilica interior, (b) pantheon interior, (c) plan of basilica and Pantheon de los Reyes.

The portico, developed under Alfonso VI as the royal pantheon after the example set by the Carolingians at S. Denis, is a six-bay groin-vaulted narthex flanked by galleries to the north and west. It originally served a basilica of commensurate width which was rebuilt over a greatly widened plan with tunnel-vaulted nave, aisles and transept – the latter is divided from the nave by Mozarabic cusped arches rising through the zone of the clerestory.

>**1.151 S. DOMINGO DE SILOS:** cloister (late-11th century), general view.

The original church has gone but the quality of ecclesiastical embellishment on the pilgrimage route is nowhere better illustrated than in the northern and eastern ranges of the cloister.

1.152b

1.152a

>**1.152 SANTILLANA DEL MAR,** 12th century: (a) exterior from the south, (b) interior.

The south porch, with its precedents in Aquitainian works like the one at Cluniac Moissac, is far from uncharacteristic of 12th-century Spanish Romanesque. Its embellishment and that of the cloister sustain the achievement of the masters of S. Domingo.

>**1.153 FROMISTA, S. MARTIN,** second half of the 11th century: exterior from the south-east.

The monastery was founded by the widow of Sancho II in 1066 but the accomplished sculpture has been dated to the last decade of the century. Poitevan influence extends to the elevation of tunnel-vaulted aisles nearly matching that of the tunnel-vaulted nave.

that conservatism extended from Catalonia along the Mediterranean coast ultimately as far as Valencia. It also extended to Portugal although the builders of the new kingdom there were mainly Burgundians well acquainted with the ambulatory – and the pointed arch – of Cluny III.[1.151–1.153]

Beside the clearly defined routes which channelled pilgrims through France to Compostela – punctuated with

1.153

hostels and hospices set c. 32 kilometres apart – there were of course secondary pilgrimage destinations with churches enshrining the remains of saints who had died in the cause of Christ or had been distinguished by the marks of divine favour. In all these, obsession with the veneration of relics prompted the full realization of the High Romanesque ideal in the specifically pilgrimage type of church. Restrained in its exterior articulation, enhancing the direct expression of the interior, this is distinguished by its continuous aisles and ambulatory. The process may be traced from S. Martin at Tours to S. Sernin at Toulouse, S. Foi at Conques and Santiago de Compostela, all begun in the 1070s, the last with considerable assistance from Alfonso VI, one of Cluny's greatest patrons.**1.154–1.157**

>**1.154 TOURS, S. MARTIN,** early 11th century: (a) plan, (b) section, (c) detail of tower chamber with rib vault.

Begun in the late-9th century, completed in the mid-11th century, the nave had doubled aisles (like S. Bénigne, Dijon, 1001–18), but only one range continued around the transepts to the ambulatory. It had triforium galleries, a clerestory and five towers, one at the crossing, one on each end of the transept and a pair flanking the western portal with rib-vaulted chambers. The east end was rebuilt from 1202. The church was destroyed after the French Revolution.

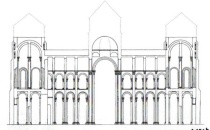

1.154b

1.154c

1.154a @ 1:1000

Towards Santiago

Venerable remains had usually been interred in the crypt under the sanctuary of the great church – as at Speyer**1.55** and Santiago de Compostela – but the inevitably restricted confines of that situation were inadequate to cope with the influx of ever-increasing numbers of pilgrims. The sanctuary or

1.155a

1.155b

›1.155 TOULOUSE, S. SERNIN, c. 1080: (a) nave, (b) exterior of crossing.

The sanctuary was consecrated in 1096 but the ambulatory was not completed until a couple of years later. The nave was substantially complete by 1120, but not yet vaulted.

choir was endowed with a ceremonial sarcophagus or statue of the saint, ultimately in a rich shrine, and the east end was reformed around it. After the example of S. Martin, Tours, rebuilt following a fire in 997 (see page 40), the aisles were extended from the twin-towered westwork into an unbroken circuit along the nave, skirting the transepts, around the sanctuary through an ambulatory with radial chapels so that the pilgrims could make a complete tour without interrupting the mass being celebrated. In elevation, the serried ranks of the bays were defined by composite piers, the groin-vaulted aisles were surmounted by quadrant-vaulted galleries but not clerestories and tunnel vaults replaced the original wooden roofs of nave and transepts c. 1050.

Conque represents the ideal in miniature. The unscreened ten-bay nave of S. Sernin, flanked by doubled aisles like S. Martin, is the grandest of the whole pilgrimage series except for Santiago de Compostela where the aisles are not doubled but there is an extra bay beyond the tenth bay screen. At S. Sernin nothing now interrupts the splendid sequence of nave and sanctuary bays. Beyond the vast transept (of six bays to each side of the square crossing), Santiago's sanctuary is raised over the crypt containing the tomb recognized in 813 as that of the apostle: above this, most of the east end within the ambulatory is filled with a Baroque reliquary shrine, with stairs down to the crypt and up to a bridged gallery behind an effigy of the saint.

As at Conques and S. Sernin, nave and transepts are tunnel vaulted throughout the great church at Santiago. The ribbed vaulting over the crossings is invariably domical in profile: conforming to the French example, the architect dispensed with the intricacy of the great Iberian Muslim tradition represented in the chapter house of the Old Cathedral of

1.156b

1.156a

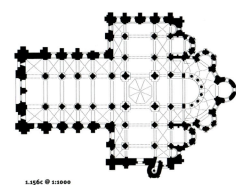

1.156c @ 1:1000

Salamanca – where the crossing tower took the domical rib vault to a specifically Spanish apotheosis (c. 1174), as we shall see.

The west front of S. Sernin was never completed according to the original plan and Conques needed much restoration. However, the west portal of Santiago – one of the most glorious achievements of medieval Europe – survives intact: raised over a high basement corresponding to the crypt, since the 18th century it has been protected by a spectacular Baroque façade. The great sculpted tympanum, related to the Cluniac work at Vézelay,**1.128** was executed between 1168 and 1188: it replaced an earlier Transfiguration scene, which was relocated to the south portal.

1.156d

›1.156 CONQUES, S. FOI, c. 1050?: (a) overview, (b) crossing, (c) plan, (d) reliquary of S. Foi.

Construction seems to have begun with the nave, the east end followed after 1080 and the work was completed with the crossing tower c. 1130. Twin western towers were added in the 19th century on either side of the magnificent Christ in Judgement portal of c. 1125.

›1.157 SANTIAGO DE COMPOSTELA, begun c. 1075, mainly complete 1125: (a) worm's-eye axonometric, (b) nave from the west, (c) crypt, (d) main hall of the palace of Archbishop Gelmirez (c. 1125 and later), (e) portal.

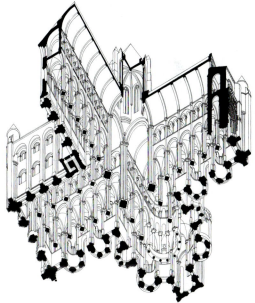

1.157a

Given Cluny's international standing, its presence in many priories tending pilgrims along the road, its responsibility for two of the principal pilgrimage churches and its indebtedness to the patron of another, it is hardly surprising that the Cluniac formula for church planning, derived from old S. Martin at Tours and applied internationally, differs from the pilgrimage church type only in its unaisled transepts. It was, however, the extension of the aisle

1.157b

1.157c

arcades around the whole perimeter of the pilgrimage church which took the Romanesque to the perfection of a fully integrated skeleton of lateral and transverse arches in which pillars, columns, colonnettes, capitals and moulded voussoirs were systematically applied to all apertures from the triumphal entrance, symbolizing the threshold of Heaven, to the great bays of the nave and, ultimately, across those bays to the vaults symbolizing Heaven itself.

1.157d

1.157e

›ARCHITECTURE IN CONTEXT »RENOVATION OF GRAVITAS

FV GA VER :TIT: RED ...NES HIC MILITES WILLELMI DVCIS: PVG...NANT:CONTR

7 THE NORMANS AND ENGLAND

That Anglo-Saxon England had not entirely succumbed to the Danes in the late-9th century was due to Alfred the Great (871–99) of Wessex: repulsing them and taking London, he rallied the English to the offensive before he died and thus ensured that England, unlike France, emerged from the period of Viking incursions as a centralized power. His son, Edward the Elder (899–924), received the submission of most of the Danes in the east and north in twenty years of relentless combat, but it was not until his son Athelstan (924–39) finally took Northumbria in 927 that England was united under one king for the first time: the achievement was exceptional in post-imperial Europe.

Converted to Christianity in a revival of the Church reformed along lines inspired by Cluny, the Danes were accorded autonomy but Ethelred II (978–1016) massacred many of them in face of a renewed Viking threat at the end of the century and attracted vengeance. He fled to his brother-in-law, the Duke of Normandy, in 1013 and England's crown fell to the Danish king Canute II (1016–35).

Canute married Ethelred's widow, Emma of Normandy, and when his son by a previous marriage died without issue in 1042, her son by Ethelred succeeded. Known as Edward the Confessor (1042–66), he too died without issue, reputedly having promised the succession to his cousin,

>1.158 BAYEUX TAPESTRY, between late-11th and mid-12th centuries, detail with a motte-and-bailey castle (Bayeux, Tapestry Museum).

A visual chronicle of the Norman conquest of England in wool on linen, this great work is associated with the circle of William the Conqueror's consort, Queen Matilda.

Traces of mound-and-ward (motte-and-bailey) castles in Normandy are rare, suggesting that the conquerors developed the form – which, as we have seen, is an age-old product of pragmatism – as they advanced into England. The rapidity and cost of that advance obviated the use of stone even for the tower which surmounted the motte – timber remained the norm until well into the 12th century – except for the most important works. As elsewhere, site rather than foresight determined which of the two elements came first.

William, Duke of Normandy (1027–87). This was disputed by magnates, descended from the pre-Danish Anglo-Saxon kingdoms, whose power waxed under Edward's weak rule. One of the most powerful, Godwin, Earl of Wessex, was exiled for insubordination but returned in force to promote the ambition of his son, Harold (c. 1020–66). In Normandy in 1064, Harold swore to support Duke William's claim, according to the Normans, but Edward named Harold as his successor on his deathbed in January 1066. With papal blessing for the punishment of broken oaths, William invaded and Harold was slain at the Battle of Hastings in September.**1.158**

The Norsemen had consolidated their hold on Normandy, expanded it with the ruthless extirpation of local opposition and established a rigorous feudal system in which local power was delegated to viscounts based on castles. Castle-based power could be used against the centre when it was weak, as in late-Carolingian France, but Normandy was ruled by a succession of strong dukes and vassalage was strictly controlled. The system was exported to England and the Anglo-Saxons, largely undefended on their land, found themselves subjected to a conqueror who had forged an aggressive weapon from the motte-and-bailey type of fort. That, in principle, we encountered in Henry the Fowler's fortified towns and their precedent in the fortified farmstead of the Dark Ages (see page 54).

William brought feudalism but developed the most effectively unified state in Europe on Anglo-Saxon foundations. Norman magnates replaced Anglo-Saxons as military governors but on reduced estates and stationed in castles built under royal licence, as in Normandy. They held their lands in return for supplying a specified number of knights and troops to the king's army and were allowed only garrisons. Beneath them were the manorial lords – lesser Normans or even Anglo-Saxons.

>**1.159 LEWES CASTLE, SUSSEX,** c. 1240: model (Castle Museum).

Granted as a barony by the Conqueror to William of Warenne for service in the conquest, Lewis was quickly fortified as an administative centre and strategic port on the mid-Sussex coast. The castle conforms to the motte-and-bailey type widely implanted by the early Normans to keep their conquests under control and augmented with hall and ancillary chambers by their Plantagenet successors. Unusually, the hilly site prompted the development of two mottes from natural mounds flanking the oval bailey – the first (north-east) controlling the river route inland, the other (south-west) providing surveillance of the coast. The latter was predominant after its timber palisade was replaced by a flint curtain when William II was in contention with his brother, the Duke of Normandy. The replacement of timber with stone continued under Henry I and Henry II.

Though his successors had to compromise, William refused to recognize the claims of the reformed papacy to supremacy in England. He appointed Normans to the bishoprics and endowed them with estates on terms similar to those imposed on the secular lords. He and his successors also endowed them with a set of new cathedrals which constituted the most magnificent building exercise of its age. In England as in Normandy, moreover, abbeys were seen as keys to pacification and the Benedictines were also magnificently endowed.

The principal officers of state were drawn from the Norman magnates, ecclesiastical and secular, but on Anglo-Saxon precedent they were summoned to regular conclave in a putative parliament and court of justice dominated by the king – and most of the Norman kings were exceptionally forceful. William was succeeded in 1085 by his oldest son, Robert, in Normandy and by his second surviving son, William in England. Killed while hunting, the latter was succeeded by his younger brother Henry, who ultimately also acquired Normandy.

Having lost his only son, Henry I (1100–35, surnamed 'Beauclerc' because he was unusually lettered for a prince of the era) forced the English magnates to swear allegiance to his daughter, Matilda (1102–67), widow of the emperor Henry v and soon to be married to Geoffrey, Count of Anjou (1113–51). In the event her cousin, Stephen of Blois (1135–54), stole the throne but her son, Henry II Plantagenet (1154–89), recovered it after a protracted conflict settled by his adoption as Stephen's heir. His was an empire in all but name: apart from England, he inherited Normandy from his mother and the usurper, Anjou and Touraine from his father and Brittany from his brother, Geoffrey. Aquitaine was added when he married its divorced heiress, Eleanor, after her repudiation by the Capetian king Louis VII (1137–80).

1.160a

>**1.160 THE NORMAN MOTTE-AND-BAILEY CASTLE PETRIFIED:** (a) Restormel (c. 1100 with 13th-century masonry), overview; (b) Arundel (original motte 1068, stone ring walls after 1135).

The so-called shell keep replaced the timber palisade on the motte in the early 12th century at strategically important sites like Restormel which was built to command the Fowey valley. Other prominent examples include Launceston and Windsor.

NORMAN CASTLES

By the time the Normans crossed the Channel, the castle had proliferated through fragmented France as the base for feudal power, but it was hardly known in unified England, except as a royal preserve. The type imported by the Normans had originated in the defensive establishment of the Dark Ages, but the aggressive feudatories of France had led in transforming it into a base for the advance of power, rather than of retreat.

Not regular like the Roman camp but sited in open country, the Conqueror's motte-and-bailey castle was conceived to fulfil the same function of holding down the conquered. Several examples are illustrated in the Bayeux tapestry.[1.158] A natural eminence was usually chosen or a mound (motte) constructed for surveillance beside a tract of ground expansive enough to accommodate the garrison (bailey). A timber tower and palisade crowned the motte, and the bailey was protected by rings of wooden posts on ramparts of impacted earth excavated from a surrounding ditch.[1.159] Gradually the wooden palisades were replaced by stone walls – as at Launceston in Cornwall or Restormel.[1.160] This, of course, is not to be mistaken as betraying a negative, defensive mentality: the walls were for protection, like the walls of a Roman camp, as hostile installations attract hostility and must be able to withstand it.

William had come over the sea and his first concern was to protect his rear: a chain of fortresses was built from Dover, the nearest point to France, and at strategic points along the route from there to London. Then the major lines of communication to the principal bases of power within the kingdom were similarly controlled. The Tower of London, the hub of the network, is essentially a motte-and-bailey castle: in the absence of a natural eminence at the crossing of the Thames where the Roman Londinium was sited, but using at the outset part of the old Roman

1.160b

1.161a

1.162

›1.161 THE NORMAN STRATEGIC CASTLE: (a) London, White Tower (1078), model (Bayeux, Tapestry Museum); (b) Rochester (begun 1087).

The Conqueror's castle at Winchester, his main seat, was taken over from the Saxons. Like it, the roughly rectangular stone keep of London belongs to the type represented by Fulk Nera's Langeais,[1.112] but was probably modelled on the palace built at Rouen by Nera's Norman contemporary, Duke Richard I (942–96). Square stone towers reinforce the corners except to the south-east where the apse of the staunch Palatine Chapel imposes a prophetic curve. The tower was entered at first-floor level from steps to the south – the basement strongrooms for stores (and occasional prisoners) were not accessible from the ground. The upper storeys are divided by a massive cross wall which provides internal support as well as diversification of space. The outer walls, of Kentish rag, are c. 27 metres high and c. 4.5 metres at base, decreasing to c. 3.4 metres at the top.

Built shortly after the conquest by the engineer who built the White Tower, but slightly larger, the keep at Rochester was rebuilt in stone early in the reign of Henry I and improved under Henry II.

›1.162 CASTLE RISING, NORFOLK, c. 1150: keep from earthworks to the south.

The earthworks are among the most substantial surviving from the Norman period. Archaelogical evidence suggests that they are in the main contemporary with the stone keep built by William d'Aubigny soon after 1138 when he married Henry I's widow. Closely related to the keep at Norwich, built by the crown a decade earlier but refaced in the 19th century, it is exceptional in the richness of its articulation: piers with colonettes on the corners, thinner pilasters regularly spaced between them, the blind arcading of the forebuilding containing the monumental staircase. This led to a vestibule before a great hall raised over a basement of service rooms, as at Langeais. There was also a chapel, chamber and ancillary rooms, including a kitchen, at that level rather than several storeys of accommodation, as at Rochester for instance. In the centre of the hall's south wall is a recess like a fireplace but without a flue: it seems probable that it framed the lord at table. In accordance with practice common in lofty halls with stone floors throughout the Middle Ages, there was either a central hearth or a series of metal braziers and a louvered opening in the vault to evacuate the smoke. There is a great flue in the corner tower serving the kitchen.

1.161b

city wall, a massive square tower stands for the motte in the centre of the bailey.[1.161a]

To ensure all-round protection and provide for the expanding needs of the court as the Norman monarchy increased its hold on England, the original single palisade was doubled. Exceptional because it was to be a seat of the king, though Winchester remained the capital, the Tower itself was built of stone from the outset. Norwich, Canterbury and Rochester, among others, followed its example in the reign of Henry I.[1.161b, 1.162]

NORMAN CHURCHES

The Norman dukes began building – or rebuilding – churches within a generation of the establishment of their realm, and if the scale was modest at first, the ambition was not. Architecturally, that ambition was fed from as many sources as the long ships had reached with their Viking ancestors. The twin-towered westwork of the Rhine and the galleried internal elevation of the Loire distinguished their earliest efforts for S. Pierre, Jumièges, which was well advanced by 950.

Monastic reformers came from the orbit of Cluny at the beginning of the new century. Several of their new abbey churches built early in the 11th century retained the parallel apses of Cluny II: Bernay is a prominent example.[1.163] However, the form *en échelon* was already superseded by the chevet – the ambulatory with radiating chapels developed by the banks of the Loire for S. Martin, Tours, which was being rebuilt at the same time.[1.154] That form was adopted for the cathedral at Rouen, the Norman capital, where it surrounded a sanctuary raised over a crypt. That, in turn, was the model for the abbey church of Notre-Dame which overawed the earlier S. Pierre at Jumièges, but there complex piers alternate with columns in the doubled bays of the nave.[1.164]

1.163a

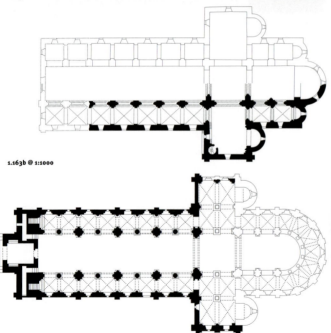

1.163b @ 1:1000

1.164a @ 1:1000

1.164b

›1.163 BERNAY ABBEY, CHURCH OF NOTRE-DAME, 1017–55: (a) view from the east, (b) plan.

Related in plan to Cluny II,[1.27a] but larger and more elaborate in such details as the half columns applied to the sides of the rectangular piers, Bernay introduces the distinguished line of churches built both in Normandy and England with triapsidal ends and three-storey elevations to nave and transepts – though the gallery lacks depth in the manner of a triforium.

›1.164 JUMIÈGES, NOTRE-DAME, 1037–67: (a) plan, (b) west front, (c) ruins from the ambulatory.

Founded under ducal auspices, the plan followed that of the cathedral in Rouen (begun before 1037), but the ambulatory lacked radiating chapels. There are piers with thin pilasters and attached columns to each face. Those on the nave elevation rise through the gallery to support the diaphragm arches which carried the wooden roof over the square compartments formed from doubled bays: the intermediate supports are cylindrical. The alternation between column and rectangular pier – popular in Norman England – was probably introduced to Ottonian Germany from Greece in the early 10th century, and imperial pretensions were certainly not foreign to Norman ducal patrons. The aisles were groin-vaulted and the galleries above continued over the transepts (as often in Greece) and around the ambulatory. The Corinthianesque capitals are another possible connection with Germany and remote Greece.

Like a Carolingian westwork, the west end is a powerful mass with superimposed spaces of its own rather than as an adjunct to nave and aisles. Its example was not forgotten in England, at Lincoln (1073), for example, or Winchester[1.170] – though the latter remained unrealized – but a much more integrated pair of towers already distinguished the abbey at Westminster (c. 1050–65) before the conquest.

›**1.165 MONT S. MICHEL,** fortified abbey: detail of nave (from 1122).

The elevation of the gallery, with twin arches each with interpolated twins, may be seen as a contraction of the double-bay system at Jumièges in contrast to the single arches of S. Étienne at Caen – or the multiple miniature arches of the triforium of Sainte Trinité. Unlike those of the latter churches, the attenuated colonettes which define the bays here lack overt structural purpose in the absence of diaphragm arches supporting the stone vault which may have been intended to replace the extant timber tunnel.

1.164c

1.165

Bernay's parallel apses and the alternating rhythm of Jumièges were imported into England by Edward the Confessor for his new abbey at Westminster, which was evidently meant to set the standard for replacing the inadequate stock of Anglo-Saxon cathedrals. The parallel apses, if not the alternating rhythm, were retained for many prestigious Norman works in the second half of the century, most notably the churches of Sainte Trinité and S. Étienne at Caen – the Abbaye aux Dames and the Abbaye aux Hommes. Mont S. Michel retained the ambulatory of Jumièges but not the alternating supports.[1.165, 1.166]

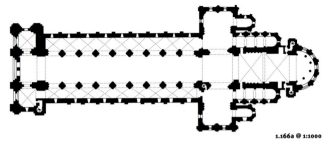

1.166a @ 1:1000

Caen: royal abbeys

Built *ex voto* by William the Conqueror and his wife Matilda, the two great abbeys of Caen mark considerable advance over Bernay or even Jumièges: the twin-towered west front is integral; the articulation of the internal elevations is rigorously logical, every element of the complex piers bearing a specific load in the almost-equally generous arcades of aisles and galleries; a wall passage throughout the clerestory level sustains visual depth. And the sanctuary of Sainte Trinité had a groin vault.

Sainte Trinité was built in emulation of Edward the Confessor's abbey at Westminster. The nave has the great length of its English predecessor, but the piers are uniform. There are five parallel apses at the east end: the main one, with a freestanding arcade on two levels, received the body of Queen Matilda in 1083 and may have been given its groin-vaulting in consequence. Groins were added soon after to the transepts; the nave had a wooden roof until c. 1115 or even later. The gallery throughout has the restricted dimensions of a triforium, but the clerestory has the depth of a considerable wall passage: the weight of the triforium and the depth of the clerestory are, of course, manifestations of the great mass represented by the multifaceted piers on which the Anglo-Norman church depends – structurally and aesthetically.

The east end of S. Étienne, with an ambulatory from the outset, was rebuilt in the early 13th century. The grand nave survives from the original campaign of work. The decorative triforium of Sainte Trinité cedes here to an arcade virtually matching the one below it in scale – a true triforium appears above the great arches of the central crossing in the first storey of the tower. Both aisles and galleries were vaulted – with groins and quadrants respectively. The piers are repeated with the slight variation of an added pilaster rising to the stringcourse below the clerestory between

1.166b

1.166c

>1.166 CAEN: (a–c) Abbaye aux Dames, Sainte Trinité (begun 1062), plan, west front, choir to the east; (d, e) Abbaye aux Hommes, S. Étienne (begun c. 1068), west front, nave to the west.

The integrated western towers of S. Étienne were heightened in the 13th century. The twin western towers of the Sainte Trinité were unfortunately reworked in the 19th century.

the paired bays, possibly for aesthetic reasons, possibly to buttress the gallery vaulting, probably because vaulting was envisaged from early in the project. Perhaps from the second decade of the century, the wooden roof was replaced with ribbed groins over doubled bays, and the symmetry of the clerestory bays was distorted by the loss of a side window in each bay to accommodate the intermediate transverse ribs of a sexpartite (six-membrane) scheme. The vaults of Sainte Trinité, in contrast, are essentially quadripartite (four-membrane), but a diaphragm arch inserted between the clerestory windows divides the side zones into pairs of asymmetrical sub-bays. The result has been termed 'pseudo-sexpartite'.

1.166d

1.166e

1.167

›1.167 BRADFORD-ON-AVON, S. LAWRENCE,
8th century, possibly rebuilt in the late-10th century:
view from the south.

Recorded in the 12th century as having been built by
S. Aldhelm in the early 8th century (but restored c. 975,
to a degree over which there is some controversy), the
chapel at Bradford originally consisted of a small, tall
nave (c. 7.6 by 4 metres c. 7.6 metres high) with projecting porches and an even smaller chancel, separated by
narrow doors and lit by slit windows placed high in the
walls. Inside, austerity is relieved only by a pair of
angels in relatively high relief above the slender chancel arch. The exterior is much richer, with pilaster strips
at the corners and, in the centre of each side, an
arcaded frieze below the eaves and pilasters in the
eastern gable. Having been converted for secular use
after the dissolution of the monastery in the 16th century, the church was restored and reconsecrated in 1871
with only the south porch missing.

›1.168 BARFRESTON, S. NICHOLAS, late-11th
century: (a) chancel arch, (b) view from north-east.

The anti-architectonic embellishment, especially
the vigorous chevron moulding which relieves the
arches, is foreign to Normandy but fully in accord with
English whim – if not with a precise surviving Anglo-
Saxon precedent. It was to be ubiquitous in Norman
England, even on the grandest scale, as at Durham.[1.174]

›1.169 EARL'S BARTON, ALL SAINTS, second
half of the 10th century: tower from south-west.

Apart from the 'nave-and-chancel' type, well represented by S. Lawrence, the Anglo-Saxons occasionally
built churches in which the tower was the main element. This seems to have been the case at Earl's Barton: the present aisled church is much later than the
tower but the latter's quoins are complete on all four
corners, suggesting that the original nave or chancel
attached to the east side was narrower – as at Barton-
on-Humber. And as there, a network of stringcourses
and slim pilaster strips, incorporating semicircular and
triangular elements, manages to be both rich and
naïve. In contrast to the blind arcading, the door and
most of the windows are framed with weighty arches,
several with stocky columns and intrados carved from
lintel blocks rather than constructed with voussoirs.

As we have noted, the Norman conquerors annexed the
most effectively unified state in Europe – other than
Normandy. If the Anglo-Saxon polity was an essentially
insular creation, the architecture developed to match the
prestige of its establishment owed much to Normandy
but it was resolutely English on the provincial level. And
on that level the parish church was its most significant
legacy. Under the new dispensation, the manorial lords –
lesser Normans and even Anglo-Saxons – were not slow
to increase the stock. The majority of their works are of
the nave and chancel type, with or without compartments to each side and often with attached towers like
Brixworth. At the most elementary level, the transition
from late-Saxon S. Lawrence at Bradford-on-Avon to
early Norman Barfreston in Kent – for example – could
hardly be more direct.[1.167, 1.168]

Viking invasions destroyed the cultural life promoted by
the first monasteries and little of English building remains
for the two hundred years after Brixworth. During that
time, however, the insular Saxons developed idiosyncrasies

1.168a

1.168b

1.169

which were to mark English architecture throughout its history. These appear in the churches built after Dunstan of Glastonbury promoted monastic revival and reform in the mid-10th century, under the inspiration of contemporary developments on the Continent. Again, little is left from the period but it is assumed to have been conservative except for its wayward, anti-architectonic decoration. The web spun of attenuated structural forms and applied irregularly out of context to the tower of All Saints at Earl's Barton, Northamptonshire, is characteristic.[1.169] And columns bulge as if made of some soft plastic substance: those of Earl's Barton are typical but at its most extreme in the crypt at Repton the bulges need to be contained with spiral binding.

When the Normans fulfilled the objective of effacing the essentially provincial Anglo-Saxon church with a metropolitan majesty matching their new royal status, the form of Bernay – and the abbey at Westminster – persisted in plan but was transformed in elevation in emulation of Caen: Winchester is a prime example. Edward the Confessor's Westminster had ceded nothing in grandeur to its

1.170

›1.170 WINCHESTER, CATHEDRAL OF THE HOLY TRINITY, S. PETER, S. PAUL AND S. SWITHUN, begun 1079: model (Bayeux, Tapestry Museum).

In the first campaign of great church building under the Conqueror, affinity with Normandy was close, as Winchester demonstrates, though the Norman work survives only in the crypt and transepts as the rest was rebuilt from 1189. The extreme length was to be characteristic of the English church: its steady increase may be traced from Canterbury (1070), via Lincoln (1072) and S. Albans (1077), to its culmination at Winchester, asserting the conquest in the old Saxon capital with the longest building of its time – except for Cluny III. Bishop Walkelyn, the patron and last Anglo-Saxon bishop of the see, 1070), retained the raised chancel and ambulatory of the cathedral at Rouen (dedicated 1063), but with orientated chapels like remote Corvey.[1.30] He kept Sainte Trinité's clerestory passage and the grand gallery of S. Étienne, virtually repeating the scale of the aisle arcade as there but here subdivided with two interpolated arches, and he maintained the essentially Norman logical articulation of pilasters and half columns, each carrying a segment of the arcading or rising to provide visual support for the timber ceiling. Foreign to Normandy, however, is the cushion-shaped capital popular in Germany. This had made its most prominent English appearance to date at Canterbury where the gallery of S. Étienne had also been introduced and the raised chancel of Rouen retained in a triapsidal sanctuary. In contrast and in direct competition nearby, the even longer abbey of S. Augustine, Canterbury (1073), reproduced the chevet.

›1.171 GLOUCESTER, CATHEDRAL OF S. PETER AND THE HOLY TRINITY, begun 1087: nave to choir.

The cylindrical piers which line the naves of Gloucester and the abbey at Tewkesbury (c. 1090) recall those of S. Philibert de Grandlieu, Tournus,[1.29] but, screening aisles two-thirds the height of the original Norman nave, they are far more massive. Over a reduced triforium, the clerestory was changed when the vault was inserted from 1242. It seems that the choirs of both buildings had galleries butting into the shafts of the great piers, producing putative four-storey elevations.

›1.172 SOUTHWELL, MINSTER, begun 1108: nave towards the crossing.

contemporaries in Normandy – indeed, the grandeur of the British Romanesque style surpassed its Norman model and was itself unsurpassed anywhere, except at Cluny. It was developed in the series of abbeys and cathedrals begun in England under William the Conqueror – Battle Abbey near Hastings (1067), the year after the conquest, Canterbury and Bury (1070), Lincoln (1072), Old Sarum (1076), Rochester and S. Albans (1077), Winchester (1079), Worcester (1084), Gloucester (1087).[1.170, 1.171]

The dimensions were exceptionally grand, especially the length of the nave, but monumentality was produced by the regular repetition of pure circular forms in precise masonry. Arcades were occasionally still supported by unarticulated rectangular blocks of Anglo-Saxon type, as at S. Albans. In the west, particularly, they were sometimes simply massive cylinders, but elsewhere, as at Winchester, the great thick walls produced piers. The westwork is no

1.171

1.172

longer a self-contained entity: the towers are integrated with the main mass of the building, though there are distinct chambers at the bases, and the central portico leads to a narthex unscreened from the nave. The disposition recalls the ancient twin-towered palace portal (AICI, pages 92f), place of epiphany, ancestor of the Roman triumphal arch, threshold of apotheosis: the *porta coeli* relieved with pilasters and semicylindrical shafts dividing the bays and supporting the intrados of arch within arch. The generous curves of those arches echoed, from storey to storey, those of the gallery subdivided internally into two, the clerestories admitting ample light from triads through the depth of a wall passage. Unusually, there were three towers, but Winchester was planned for five.

In a second great campaign under the Conqueror's successors, planning was conservative but the rigorous logic imported from Normandy for the first phase was relaxed and overlaid by a somewhat wayward approach to decoration, which has been identified as characteristically English. Inconsistency reigned. Noble simplicity might run to the prophetic elimination of the verticals altogether: this was anticipated stupendously at Gloucester, fully realized at the minster at Southwell – where the three original towers survive – and essential to the English Cistercian aesthetic in the context of the pointed arch.**1.172**

On the other hand, there was much experimentation with varying the form of the pier and developing alternating rhythm – anticipated at Notre-Dame, Jumièges, and Westminster, indeed in Ottonian Germany and Byzantine Greece – between rectangular piers with pilasters and half columns and cylindrical ones with or without attached shafts. The composite mode is generally more finely tuned, if not strictly logical any more, and is represented nowhere better than at the cathedral at Peterborough where the purpose of the vertical shafts

1.173

›ARCHITECTURE IN CONTEXT »RENOVATION OF GRAVITAS

›1.173 PETERBOROUGH, CATHEDRAL OF S. PETER, S. PAUL AND S. ANDREW, begun 1118, nave towards the sanctuary.

A monastery was founded on the site in 655, destroyed by the Danes in 870, refounded in 970 and destroyed by fire in 1116. The present church was consecrated in 1238 but Norman work has been replaced significantly only at the east end. Like Ely (begun 1083, nave mainly from twenty years later) and Norwich (begun 1096), the arcades of the two main storeys have a third plane of arcading, each with roll mouldings. The alternation of rectilinear and cylindrical piers distinguishes these works too, but the logic of Norman articulation cedes to English pragmatism: about the cylindrical piers individual support is denied to the inner recessions at Ely and the intermediate ones at Peterborough where, consequently, the ribs of the aisle vaults float free.

is clearly aesthetic – providing visual support for the wooden roof rather than the structure for missing groins.[1.173] The alternation of rectangular and cylindrical forms, the latter with a variety of unarchitectonic spiral and chevron incisions, had reached its apogee earlier in the cathedral at Durham.

Perhaps the major contribution of the Normans to medieval architecture was the development of the rib vault. A permutation of the form appeared in the tower chambers of S. Martin, Tours, as rebuilt c. 1050[1.154] and passed to Normandy with the rest of the legacy of that seminal work, appearing first in the chamber at the base of the north-west tower of the cathedral at Bayeux c. 1077. Doubtless in the knowledge of contemporary Lombard developments, probably brought by itinerant masons, ribs thereafter were applied consistently to the groin vault though they were of stone rather than of brick, were more richly moulded and were set much higher than their earliest Italian counterparts. Their diagonals completed the articulation of the skeleton of arches upon which the High Romanesque church depends.

In Normandy the rib vault appears in the second decade of the 12th century at Lessay, in place of groin vaults originally projected at the beginning of the century, and at Sainte Trinité and S. Étienne, Caen, in place of the original timber over the naves. These all depend on doubled nave bays forming roughly square compartments divided by a diaphragm arch across the centre but, as semicircular diagonals over squares will rise higher than the sides and the diaphragm, consistency of height could only be achieved by distorting the geometry or by springing the arches from different heights (stilting). Both methods were tried in these pioneering Norman works and found to be wanting, both visually and structurally. Much of this was anticipated at Durham.[1.174]

1.174a

Durham

The plan of Bernay survived at Durham until the ambulatory of the Chapel of the Nine Altars was added to the east end from 1242. The alternation of rectilinear and cylindrical piers is simplified by the elimination of shafts from the latter, the arcading rising directly from the broad capitals. On the other hand, it was complicated by the projection of much more assertive shafts between them. The aisles rise higher than those of the other major cathedrals of eastern England, if not as high as Gloucester or the abbey at Tewkesbury, and the gallery is reduced almost to a triforium: neither the grand gallery of S. Étienne nor Sainte Trinité's regular repitition of four shallow arches, this consists of two pairs of arches framed by blind arcades carried on piers with attached columns, as at Mont S. Michel,[1.165] but here echoing the basic division of the main arcade into paired bays.

The shafts of the cylindrical piers are incised with a bizarre variety of chevron and interlaced motifs in addition to oddly Classical fluting. There are two main planes to each of the arches, but they tend to coalesce into one rich form with a variety of profiles leading to a roll moulding in the centre. The chevron motif, in deep relief rather than incised, plays a promi-

1.174b

›1.174 DURHAM CATHEDRAL (CATHEDRAL OF CHRIST, MARY AND S. CUTHBERT), begun 1093: (a) view from south, (b) west end, (c) section through nave and aisles, (d) plan, (e) nave towards sanctuary, (f) chevron mouldings and arches in nave, (g) detail of southern exterior, (h) Galilee Chapel.

nent part in this context – as it did already in the new choir of Canterbury built from the early 12th century on the double-transept scheme of Cluny III. And if a structural member is overlaid with a non-structural one, as the chevron on the arch, the arch is reduced to the purely decorative interlace along on the side walls of Durham's aisles. This complete departure from Norman logic was to prove particularly popular in England too.

The building seems to have been designed for vaulting at the outset in 1093: as elsewhere, it was introduced c. 1099 over the sanctuary: the choir was completed c. 1104, the north transept a decade later and the nave vault by 1133 when defective construction led to the renovation of the sanctuary. The rib vaults were based on double bays as in the two great churches of Caen, Sainte Trinité and S. Étienne, but they are separated by pointed transverse arches rising from the boldly projecting shafts. Rather than sexpartite or pseudo-sexpartite, the vaulting of each doubled-bay compartment has seven zones due to the elimination of the intermediate transverse arch. The sexpartite system of S. Étienne was adopted in early Gothic France, but the reintroduction of the transverse arch to the system of Durham provided the key to the much more rational quadripartite type of vaulting over single bays which was universally adopted in the High Gothic period. In England, as in Normandy, the earliest groin and rib vaults were usually of rendered rubble.

1.174c

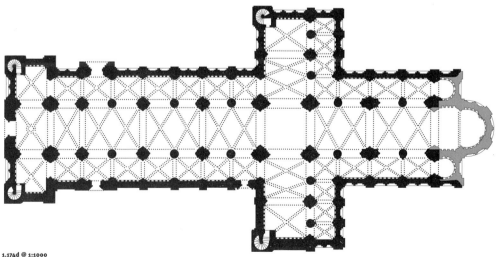

1.174d @ 1:1000

1.174e

1.174f

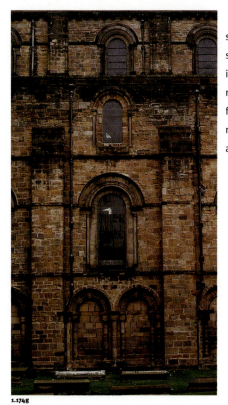

1.174g

The integration of pointed arches with semicircular ones achieved consistent height in a way that was aesthetically and structurally far more satisfactory than stilting. The pointed arch was prominent at Cluny III, but in the context of the tunnel vault where its potential was only partially realized and the thrust of the tunnel was ultimately met with interpolated flying buttresses. Durham has quadrant arches hidden under the aisle roofs which anticipate these buttresses, but their primary role was probably to support the gallery roofs rather than the clerestory wall.

The use of the rib vault with the pointed arch and the putative flying buttress marked the way ahead. In place of the thick walls and piers needed to meet the pressure of heavy tunnel vaults, the groin vault and its ribbed variety are carried at its corners and one buttresses another in a series — until the end where extraneous support is required. This realization led to the revival of an antique structural principle admitting the free flow of space and light around slender pillars: the counter-opposition of forces in a fully integrated network of lateral and diagonal arches. Thus the rib in the tower of S. Martin, Tours, may be seen to have provided the key to an entirely new style: the Gothic, which was invented in the Île-de-France within a decade of the completion of the vaulting at Durham.

1.174h

2.56e

PART 2
REFRACTION
OF LIGHT

2.1

›ARCHITECTURE IN CONTEXT »REFRACTION OF LIGHT

2.0 INTRODUCTIONS TO THE GOTHIC AGE

I THE POLITICAL MAP OF GOTHIC EUROPE

It may well be said that the Romanesque era belonged to the abbey, the Gothic to the cathedral – apart from the castle. Abbots continued to provide great patronage throughout the Middle Ages, but from the early 12th century bishops come to the fore and the greatest buildings of the age – among the greatest of any age – are undoubtedly their cathedrals. The abbey was as much a product of the political chaos of rural feudal Europe as the castle. The cathedral rose with the resurrection of the town.**2.1**

Despite the withering of trade, the disruption of the distribution of goods and services, the self-sufficiency of the manor, towns survived five centuries after the fall of Rome and the rise of feudalism. Of course they were gravely reduced and depopulated. Even the Eternal City, which had a million people at the empire's height, had shrunk to about fifty thousand. But the age of devastating invaders seemed past and trade was reviving within Europe and across the Mediterranean.

With the advance of trade, pivoted on Italy, towns revived all over Europe. Many were Roman in origin, others developed around fairs held under the auspices of an abbey. As we shall see, they prospered with the improvement of agriculture in the 12th century and the consequent growth of population: many manorial tenants commuted feudal obligations for money to seek their fortunes in commerce or industry under a charter of urban freedom sealed by an effective authority. This was usually an expansive monarch and, profound in its impact on the development of all major building types – within and without the town – the process of recentralizing power must be traced as an introduction to the architecture of Gothic Europe.

PAPACY AND EMPIRE

By the early 12th century the papacy was the principal power in Europe though the Holy Roman Emperor, the overlord of Germans and Italians, refused to recognize this and the King of England, Duke of Normandy, controlled the strongest single realm. After the Investiture Dispute, in which the emperor was humiliated and the pope asserted infallibility (pages 57ff), a measure of moderation emanated from Rome but zeal was sustained.

Urban II (1088–99) pressed ahead with reform and in the crusade to recover the Holy Land he found an external cause for the assertion of leadership, not only over the combined material forces of kings and princes, but also over the combined spiritual forces of the eastern and western Churches riven by schism under Leo IX (1049–54). Church reform, notably the assertion of the jurisdiction of papal courts over diocesan ones, and the prestige won for the pope by the capture of Jerusalem strengthened the authority of Rome and the pope's position approximated that of a secular monarch.

A consequence of papal assertiveness, which weakened episcopal authority over towns, was the advance of the communal movement in Italy: except in the great trading cities, which were led in the assertion of independence by Venice (pages 108ff), ecclesiastical and county authority proved effective against civic autonomy until the Investiture Dispute. Then emperors bought support, but sowed dissent, in Italy by granting privileges to towns which rivals emulated. The Florentines asserted independence in 1115 and others followed, establishing communal government in which land-owners, merchants and plebeians vied for pre-eminence.

Threatened by the communes, papal pretensions were again challenged by an emperor less than a century after Gregory's triumph. Frederick I Barbarossa (1152–90)**2.2**

›2.1 SEGOVIA: from the north.

Ancient Iberian Segobriga was taken by the Romans in 80 BCE and developed into a prosperous city. It was a Visigothic bishopric in the 6th century and a centre of the cloth industry under the Moors in the 9th century. It fell to the Christian reconquerors in 1085, became a royal seat and was endowed with a new cathedral in the 12th century and another in the 16th century. The latter is typical in its dominance over the secular world. Equally characteristically, the castle is the next most prominent element and it is symptomatic of urban revival in the Gothic period that it is incorporated into the town defences.

›2.2 FREDERICK I BARBAROSSA and his two oldest sons, the future emperor Henry VI to his right (Weingarten Chronicles, 1179; Fulda, National Library).

Barbarossa was the son of Frederick of Hohenstaufen, Duke of Swabia, and Judith, daughter of Henry IX Welf, Duke of Bavaria. His election as German king on the death of his uncle, Conrad III, in 1152 united two of the most important rival factions. He was elected emperor in 1155.

He had distinguished himself on crusade in the Holy Land with his uncle in 1147 – though the expedition was

2.2

disastrous. On his accession he set about restoring order in Germany, initially by mollifying the nobles, as a necessary condition for the reassertion of imperial authority in Italy. While there, his German settlement unravelled. This time he rearranged ducal authority: in particular, he gave the Palatinate to his half-brother Conrad and transferred Bavaria from the Austrian margrave to the Saxon duke Henry the Lion. Several campaigns in Italy were designed to reduce papal pretension and restore the rights of its king – as confirmed by experts from Bologna. Imperial officers (*podestas*) assisted in reclaiming revolted cities but their exertions in the enforcement of the regalian rights provoked a league of communes – and the vigorous opposition of the pope. After many vicissitudes – not least due to plague, more trouble in Germany and, ultimately, the treachery of Henry the Lion – the league was victorious at Legnano in 1176. Accord was reached with the Lombards in 1183 but dispute with the papacy – especially over the marriage of Frederick's son Henry to the heiress of Sicily – subsisted for another five years. After that was settled by arms – and Henry's coronation as King of Italy confirmed – the emperor mollified the pope by embarking on another crusade but he was drowned on campaign in Cilicia.

›2.3 'THE CHURCH MILITANT': Andrea di Bonaiuto's fresco of 1366 on the east wall of the Spanish Chapel, S. Maria Novella, Florence.

'Ecclesia' is represented by the Florentine cathedral as projected, but far from completed, c. 1360. Enthroned before the church are the pope (identified as Urban V or Innocent VI) and emperor (Charles IV) supported by the hierarchies of church and state – with the former asserted as primary. The sheep represent Christ's flock, of course.

acceded without the say of Pope Eugenius III (1145–53) and the latter's need for help against opposition from the commune of Rome, bent on re-establishing a republic, gave the emperor the upper hand. Support turned to subjugation but the emperor was forced to retreat from an alliance of the papacy and a league of Lombard communes by treachery in Germany in 1176: he held Tuscany but the Lombards reclaimed their communal rights and the pope's supremacy was reasserted.**2.3**

2.3

The papacy resolved its communal problem in Rome by conceding the legality of the popular assembly in return for recognition of the pope's superiority over the senate. Beyond Rome, however, the pope was faced with growing opposition to the centralization of power at the expense of the bishops. Even the monastic clergy was alarmed: the saintly Bernard of Clairvaux (1090–1153), a major supporter of centralization so long as it was directed to cleansing the Church, was the most revered of those who turned against the Roman establishment as promoting venality. Propelled by signs of new decadence, if not simply by the fire of faith, mendicant ascetics took the spirit of S. Bernard from the cloister out into the street and ministered to the sick and destitute in poverty and humility: first was Francis of Assisi (1182–1226). Poverty and humility in renunciation of seclusion for ministry to the suffering in the world at large were the most primitive of the Christian ideals and, despite the problems attendant on acceptance of official patronage as an order, the Franciscans and their 'poor sisters' of S. Claire prospered in their mission to bring the alien world of urban man back to the God their patron had found in nature.**2.4**

2.4

›2.4 S. FRANCIS GIVING HIS CLOAK TO A BEGGAR: fresco c. 1300 attributed not without controversy to Giotto (Assisi, upper church of S. Francesco).

It was under the light of S. Francis's naturalistic and humanistic vision that Italy developed a national school of painting, distinct from the Byzantine, first in the great basilica at Assisi at the hands of the elusive Master of S. Francis and, more particularly, Cimabue and his followers who may have included the young Giotto. The new school, like the old, served a Christian ideal and would proceed to explore every facet of nature as a manifestation of the glory of God.

The most recent precedent for devotion to poverty is to be found in the Waldensian movement, which originated in the 12th century under the organization of Peter Waldo, a wealthy Lyons merchant. His followers, who stressed poverty and austerity, were blessed by Pope Alexander III but forbidden to preach without authorization. As they ignored this and challenged the dogma of apostolic succession in the light of their study of the Bible in the vernacular, they were declared heretical in 1184.

In the face of papal pretension to infallibility, heresy proliferated: foremost in the late-12th century were the Albigensians in Languedoc who, resentful of the worldly wealth of the Church, disclaimed the corporeal nature of Christ. A band of mendicant missionaries was formed by a Castilian friar named Dominic of Calaroga (1170–1221) to preach the error of their ways to the Albigensians: his Dominican order went on to provide the 13th century with its main intellectual and anti-heretical force with fervour which ultimately became fanatical.**2.5**

Threatening to undermine the papal edifice, heresy provided the occasion for its most impressive consolidation under Innocent III (1198–1216). A great jurist, he used the pre-eminence won by the papal courts to make himself the arbiter of Europe and his decisions formed the basis of canon law amplified by his successors. He joined the forces of church and state in a bloody crusade against the obdurate Albigensians but, more characteristically, he confronted heresy with the establishment of a tribunal which came to be known – infamously – as the Inquisition. He faced the evil within too, renewing reform in the cause of the spiritual welfare of the church. Moreover, obviating a potential threat to the establishment, he extended his patronage to the mendicant Franciscans and Dominicans – the former dedicated to the poor, the latter principally to teaching and the Inquisition.

›**2.5 S. DOMINIC DISPUTING WITH HERETICS:** detail from Andrea di Bonaiuto's fresco of 1366, The Church as the Path to Salvation, on the east wall of the Spanish Chapel, S. Maria Novella, Florence.

As elsewhere in the fresco, the dogs represent the Dominicans.

2.5

2.6

›**2.6 INNOCENT III** (1198–1216): fresco (Subiaco, S. Speco).

At the beginning of the new century Innocent III projected another crusade to secure the Holy Land, but it was deflected by the Venetians to the sack of their rival, Constantinople, in 1203.**2.6** The pope also inspired the crusade against the Muslims in Iberia. Under his auspices the main Christian powers, Castilla (divided from León in 1157),

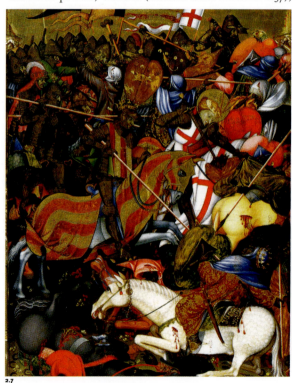

2.7

›**2.7 JAMES I OF ARAGÓN** (1208–76), known as the Conqueror, overcoming the Moors of Valencia at Puig in 1237 (early 15th-century Spanish re-evocation; London Victoria & Albert Museum).

Aragón (united with the Catalonian county of Barcelona in 1162), Navarra (separated from Aragón in 1134) and Portugal (independent since 1139), combined forces and defeated the Almohad ruler of Morocco, champion of the Muslims in Spain, at Las Navas de Tolosa in 1212 (AIC3, page 223). Reunited with León under Ferdinand III (1230–56), Castilla led the reconquest to Seville and had eliminated the sultanate there by 1282. Meanwhile the Aragonese were sweeping the east coast. By the end of the century only the Algarve and Granada were left to the Muslims.[2.7]

Innocent III was guardian to Frederick of Hohenstaufen, the infant heir of Emperor Henry VI (1056–1106) who had acquired Sicily and southern Italy through his marriage to Constance, daughter of the last Norman king. With the pope's support, Frederick regained his dynastic domains in Germany and reasserted his authority in his southern Italian kingdom. He was crowned emperor in 1220 but in his successful conflict with the Lombard communes he was opposed by Innocent III's successors and was on the point of entering Rome when he died in 1250. His preoccupation with Italy left the German magnates – and many towns founded by imperial rescript on imperial land beyond the aristocratic feudal structure – relatively free and the empire disintegrated in their rivalry.

POST-HOHENSTAUFEN ITALY

As Frederick's heirs fought for their inheritance in Italy, they fell to the papal nominee Charles of Anjou, brother of King Louis IX (1226–70) of France. Sicily, but not Naples, rejected the Angevins in favour of an Aragonese prince and the Norman kingdom succumbed to the division. As in Germany indeed, division was the lot of post-Hohenstaufen Italy as a whole: either the vicars to whom imperial authority had been delegated or the communes triumphed in the north.

The commimes had been dominant in Tuscany since the demise of Frederick I. Pisa had replaced Lucca as the principal rival to Florence by the end of the 12th century and locked itself in rivalry with Genoa for dominance over Tyrrhenian trade, to which Sardinia was seen as the key. Genoa triumphed in 1284 but was also locked in struggle with Venice for much wider dominance of Mediterranean trade. Venice gained the upper hand in the east after its shameful deflection of the Fourth Crusade to the sack of Constantinople but Genoa continued to prosper from western Mediterranean trade.

Pisa's worsting by Genoa left the way open for Florence to emerge as the principal Tuscan power by the end of the 13th century – though Pisa was a recurrent problem. The ascendancy of Florence exacerbated the long-festering enmity of Siena. While their rivalry was to have major

2.8b

2.8a

›2.8 CIVIL STRIFE AND ITS MANIFESTATIONS: (a) unrestrained in Mantua's Piazza Sordello, with the seat of secular power (right) and the cathedral (centre) (late-15th-century painting by Domenico Morone; Mantua, Palazzo Ducale); (b) channelled in Siena into the Corsa del Palio, the horse race between representatives of the city's wards whose colours are displayed individually at their boundaries and flown together as flags on major buildings (as here on the Palazzo Chigi-Saraceni).

›**2.9 MONUMENT TO BERNABO VISCONTI**
(Bonino da Campione, before 1363; Milan, Castello
Sforzesco).

The most relevant precedent for the equestrian
statue was set by Visconti's rival, Cangrande della
Scala (died 1359) in the precinct of S. Maria Antica,
Verona. The origin of the motif has been traced to a
Romanesque image in S. Zeno in the same city.

architectural consequences, cultural rivalry was by no
means unique to them.

The constant communal bickering provided the context
for Frederick II's advance in Italy. Thereafter, between and
within them the conflict of those who had supported the
emperor – Ghibellines – with those who supported the
pope – Guelfs – grew increasingly violent despite the reality of imperial and papal impotence. The constitutional
consequences were disastrous. Some polities managed to
channel the violence under a semblance of communal control.**2.8** Well before the end of the 13th century, however,
many disorderly republican regimes in northern Italy had
given way to *signorie*: despots either called in from outside
or promoted from the civic guard to check one sectional
interest on behalf of another. They usually extended their
own power until it was virtually absolute and hereditary –
at first, at least, to the relief of traumatized citizenry.

By the end of the second decade of the new century, the
emperor had confirmed Visconti as lord of Milan,**2.9** the
Scaliger ruled Verona, the Carrara Padua, the Este Ferrara and the Bonacolsi Mantua – the last surviving only
until 1328 when they were superseded by the Gonzaga.
The Castracci tyrant of Pisa – who had taken Lucca in
1316 – defeated the Florentines in 1325. Their republic, sustained by the mercantile guilds to the exclusion of the
nobility, was reformed but after the plague of 1348 it succumbed to the tyranny of the Guelf nobility in the face of
an alliance between their Ghibelline rivals and the
Milanese Visconti: a generation later, popular revolt promoted the renewed reform of the republican constitution.
Meanwhile, a succession of short-lived popes had seen the
papal monarchy undermined by the emergence of despots
in many of its domains – Bologna, Rimini, Ravenna,
Urbino, among others – and finally eclipsed by the power
of France.

FRANCE AND ENGLAND

Throughout the 11th century and beyond, the dukes of Normandy had succeeded in keeping the Capetian kings in their place – the encircled domain known as the Île-de-France (page 143). But that place was rich in grain-growing land and it was central, and when the Norman regime succumbed to anarchy, after Stephen of Blois (1135–54) usurped the English throne of Henry I's daughter Matilda (1102–67), France was ready to benefit.

Louis VI 'the Fat' (1108–37) had reached out from Paris to assert authority over the main towns on the periphery of his domains: Orléans in the south-west, Amiens in the north, Laon in the east. He was served by an exceptionally able minister, Suger, whom he raised to the abbacy of S. Denis, at the heart of the French monarchy. He joined the papacy in its struggle with the emperor over investiture and secured recognition of the king's 'domination' of the French bishoprics: the bishops in turn supporting the king against the secular nobility. So well had the work of consolidation been done that when the emperor, Henry V, threatened invasion in 1124, the vassals of France met him united under the banner of S. Denis enshrined in the great church entrusted to Abbot Suger.**2.10**

Suger was retained by Louis VII (1137–80) but his demise in 1151 was followed by a great reverse. Louis had married Eleanor, heiress of William X of Aquitaine in 1152. Her lands – five times the size of his – took France to the ocean, cutting the great duchies of the north, Normandy and Brittany, from the rulers of the south, the counts of Toulouse and kings in Provence. But France divorced Aquitaine soon after Suger's death and the formidable duchess immediately married Louis's principal rival, Henry Plantagenet, Count of Anjou, Duke of Normandy, son of Henry I's daughter Matilda and Stephen's adoptive heir.**2.11**

›2.10 S. DENIS, BASILICA: reconstruction of the westwork as rebuilt by Abbot Suger from 1135.

The imperial pretensions of the patron – and victory – are implicit in the elements of the westwork. The precedent for division into three bays by buttresses related to the twin towers was set by the rival Normans but unlike the front of S. Étienne, Caen, for instance,**1.166** the fenestration has a hierarchy of its own, culminating in the rose window in the third level of the central bay. Derived from Romanesque Italian works such as Modena cathedral,**1.74** and designed primarily for external display, the location of the rose responds to the rhythm of the tripartite Roman triumphal arch adopted for the main portals. The central door is presided over by Christ at the Last Judgement – as in many Romanesque churches – but the towers are set back beyond a crenellated parapet to reinforce its impact in the self-contained façade: the *porta coeli*, the entrance to the stronghold of God – and the shrine of the French monarchy.

2.10

2.11a

2.11 HENRY II AND THOMAS Á BECKET: (a) the tomb of the king and his wife, Eleanor of Aquitaine (late-12th-century effigies, Fontevraud abbey church); (b) the murder of the archbishop (Becket window, c. 1320, Christ Church cathedral, Oxford).

2.11b

Henry II (1154–89) brought extraordinary ability to bear on restoring the prerogatives surrendered by Stephen in his attempts to buy support, restoring the sound government of his Norman forebears. In this, inevitably perhaps, he clashed with the Church, particularly with the Archbishop of Canterbury, Thomas à Becket (1120–70), his trusted minister who had been elevated to the primacy of England specifically to counter papal pretensions. The details of Henry's dispute with Becket are beyond us here, but the latter's murder in Canterbury cathedral and the development of a major pilgrimage to his shrine – soon to be amplified with great splendour in the burgeoning French style later to be known as Gothic – had great consequence, political and architectural.

The dismemberment of royal justice by irresponsible lords of the manor – pernicious under Stephen as under the weak successors of Charlemagne – led to endless ambiguity which reassertive central authority generally sought to eradicate. Henry was well on the way to recovering the unity of the realm from the magnates and reconstructing a centralized government, based on the king's court, but his penance for Becket's murder before Canterbury cathedral implied the moral superiority of the Church and lost him the authority to deny autonomy to the ecclesiastical courts in England.

Despite his reverses, Henry II was the most effective power of the middle decades of the 12th century and he held his diverse realms together with a strictly ordered exchequer and a professional army whose constitution was independent of the feudal levy. He refrained from patronizing particularism by delegating provinces to his sons. After his humiliation at Canterbury, they rebelled in 1174 with the connivance of France and Scotland and, though they failed, they sapped his strength and undermined the realm to the advantage of the Capetians.

Louis VII's heir, Philip II (1180–1223), earned the title of Augustus in an amazing reign that began when he was hardly 15 and completely reversed the balance of power with England. He took advantage of the long absence of Henry II's heir, Richard I the Lionheart (1189–99) – on crusade and in detention by the Duke of Austria – to advance on Normandy. Unexpectedly returning, Richard checked this but he was killed in the conflict and his lax successor, John (1199–1216), had lost Normandy within a decade. Despite England's retention of Aquitaine, France was now the greatest power in Europe and that power was further extended with the annexation of Languedoc after the suppression of the Albigensians in the 1220s.

The early Capetians had been peripatetic, in the manner of kings everywhere since time immemorial, but Philip Augustus established Paris as his permanent capital and reformed its defences, incorporating into their western range a tower which came to be known as the Louvre. South of the river, clerics connected with the basilica of S. Geneviève (patron of Paris) and their students formed the nucleus of the university whose formation may be dated to 1200 when the king recognized their association.

>**2.12 MAGNA CARTA** (rescension of 1297).

Humiliation apart, the tax burden of unsuccessful war – let alone the loss of the resources of Normandy – caused widespread disaffection in King John's England. The barons seized their chance to rebel against the centralization re-instituted by Henry II. In 1215 they forced the king to sign the Magna Carta: reforming his government to constrain arbitrary rule and to guarantee the barons' conception of their rights as well as the security of ordinary free men, this seminal document laid the foundations for the development of a regular national parliament from the feudal council called at the king's will.**2.12** John died the following year: his heir, Henry III (1216–72), sustained losses in Guienne during his minority and was never

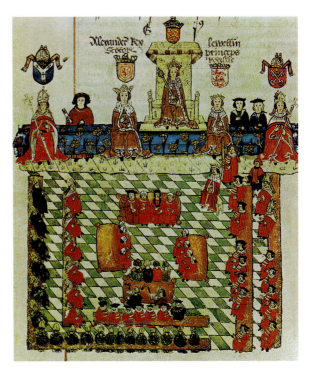

strong enough to regain the initiative from the barons but he was a great patron of the arts – devoted to the French style of architecture in particular.

Henry III's successor, Edward I (1272–1307), was a strong-willed ruler determined to restore the dignity of the crown while respecting the rights of its subjects, if the two were consistent. He saw necessity and advantage in securing the active cooperation not only of the magnates but also of the free men in government and convened councils composed of both which came to be called parliaments.**2.13** These were still irregular and dependent on his initiative but the delegates came with full representative powers to agree tax levies. And much money was needed by the king for his conquest of Wales in the first decade of the reign, the attempted conquest of Scotland in the last two decades and the continuous conflict with France over Gascony.

Henry III's French contemporary, Louis IX (1226–70), had succeeded to the throne as a minor but instead of chaos an unusually successful period of regency ensued under his clever mother, Blanche of Castilla, who instilled a high sense of moral responsibility in her son. The Count of Toulouse submitted and the young king was married to Provence. Moral authority won over feudal violence as the king's peace embraced the magnates in the triumph of general respect for Louis's justice: the aspiration of that authority has never been more gloriously represented than in the Sainte-Chapelle added to the Parisian palace. Yet, though saintly – and ultimately canonized – Louis was a warrior and he won more territory in the south and south-west in wars with rebels and with England – whose king acknowledged his suzerainty for all Aquitaine. Saintliness and soldiering took him to his death on a final crusade.**2.14**

2.14a

>**2.14 LOUIS IX, THE SAINTLY WARRIOR:** (a) with his mother as regent, Blanche of Castilla, (*Bible abrege* c. 1250; New York, Morgan Library); (b) departing for the Seventh Crusade in 1348 (14th-century French ms; London, British Library); (c) Paris, the royal palace on the Île-de-la-Citè with the Sainte-Chapelle, right (*Trés Riches Heures du Duc de Berry* by the Limbourg brothers, c. 1415; Chantilly, Condée Museum).

The Sainte-Chapelle was built in the 1250s to enshrine the relics of Christ's Passion which the king acquired from Constantinople.

2.14c

2.14b

The high moral tone of the French monarchy was not sustained for long after the death of S. Louis. His astute and ambitious grandson, Philip IV the Fair (1285–1314), was far more concerned with money and the process of law. The details are again beyond us here – indeed they were beyond most of Philip's contemporaries – but his money bought much territory in the east, including Lyon, and his legalism was turned against the Church and its servants to provide it. The Templars of Palestine, whose order had developed with the crusades and lost its role with the loss of the Holy Land, were tried, condemned and expropriated in the name of morality, but in fact for siding with the pope against the king. The king then turned against the pope.

The monarchical power bequeathed to his successors by Innocent III had alienated both secular and episcopal authorities. When Boniface VIII (1294–1303) reasserted temporal as well as spiritual sovereignty in forbidding the laity to tax the clergy, he was dragged before Philip IV, went mad and died. The king secured the election of a French pope, Clement V (1305–14), who chose to reside with Dominicans in Avignon and never went to Rome. After protracted election disputes, his successors established the papal court in the formidable palace which dominates the town from its elevated site beside the cathedral but the papal monarchy had been abrogated and once again the papacy itself descended into disrepute.

2.15a

›2.15 EPISODES IN THE HUNDRED YEARS' WAR: (a) the battle of Sluys, 1340; (b) the battle of Crécy, 1346 (both from the late-14th-century Chronicles of Jean Froissart; Paris, National Library).

Froissart (c. 1337–c. 1405) was the leading chronicler of the first phase of the Hundred Years' War and parallel events in the second half of the 14th century.

THE HUNDRED YEARS' WAR: THE FIRST PHASE

Meanwhile, stagnation and truce in the Anglo-French conflict led to an alliance, Edward I marrying Philip IV's sister and Edward's heir marrying Philip's daughter. On the failure of the male line with Philip's sons, the ancient law of the Salian Franks was invoked to debar females from succession and the crown passed to the Count of Valois. The validity of this was denied by Edward III (1327–77),

2.16b

son of Edward II and Philip IV's daughter Isabella: the result was more than a century of intermittent conflict.

Honours in the so-called Hundred Years' War went first to the English: their king was on the offensive and rich from trade in wool; the battles raged over the fields of agricultural France and the Valois king, on the defensive, lacked the resources properly to equip his forces. After thirty years of ruinous fighting and the nightmare of the Black Death (the plague that raged between 1347 and 1351), Edward III regained considerable territory in return for the renunciation of his claim to the French crown. However, the able Charles V, 'the Wise' (1364–80), recouped much that France had lost, reordered his kingdom, extended the defences of his capital, rebuilt the Louvre in conjunction with them and took French medieval secular art to its apogee with his brother, the Duc de Berry.**2.15, 2.16**

›**2.16 FRENCH COURTS IN THE AGE OF CHARLES V:** (a) the king's new seat at the Louvre; (b) the Duc de Berry depicted in his *Trés Riches Heures* (the Limbourg brothers, c. 1415; Chantilly, Condée Museum).

2.17b

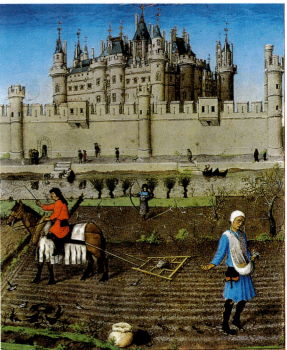

2.17a

Edward III and Charles V were both succeeded by minors, Richard II (1377–99) and Charles VI (1380–1422) respectively, at a time of steep economic decline. The obvious immediate reason for depression was the appalling loss of life in the mid-century outbreak of the plague and its periodic recurrence throughout Europe.[2.17] However, some analysts have detected the signs of economic recession much earlier: the reasons are disputed but at base it seems probable that, failing radical technological development, advancing prosperity and its attendant population growth had reached the limits of sustainability by the end of the 13th century.

From 1377 and 1380 respectively, there was a divided regency in both England and France and popular unrest responded to a general sense of malaise in government, secular and ecclesiastical. The most celebrated manifestation of discontent, in England at least, is the peasants' revolt of 1381 which was occasioned by parliament's attempt to impose a universal poll-tax. It was reinforced by a religious fundamentalism articulated by the radical Oxford cleric William Wycliffe (died 1384): revolted by the degeneration of the papacy, he maintained that legitimate lordship depended on divine grace, that disreputable clergy should be dispossessed and that papal claims to authority had no basis in scripture. Even more fundamentally, the leaders of the Kentish peasants reputedly retorted to the lords and commons assembled in the king's name: 'When Adam delved and Eve span, who was then the gentleman?'

The young King Richard distinguished himself before the peasants but neither he nor his mentally unstable French peer proved worthy of the challenge facing them on their assumption of personal rule in 1388–89. The English resumed armed conflict in pressing their claim to France: they campaigned in Flanders on behalf of the pope in Rome; thus excited, the French formed an alliance with the Scots for a projected – but abortive – invasion of England. Mismanagement on both sides resulted in stalemate until 1396: tacit truce was converted into reconciliation and Charles gave his daughter to Richard – who had lost his first wife, the daughter of Emperor Charles IV.**2.18**

>**2.18 MARRIAGE OF RICHARD II OF ENGLAND AND ISABELLE OF FRANCE** (late-14th-century ms illumination after Froissart; Paris, National Library).

ITALY: THE EMERGENCE OF GREAT POWERS

With the empire lost to dynastic rivalry after the annihilation of the Hohenstaufen and the papacy at the low ebb of captivity in Avignon, there was a political vacuum in Italy just as its major cities reached a peak of prosperity in the first decades of the 14th century. That was boosted by the indebtedness of the principal belligerents in the Hundred Years' War to Italian bankers. However, in 1339 Edward III of England renounced his vast debts to the Bardi and Peruzzi banking houses and their consequent collapse ruined Florentine credit everywhere.

Within a decade the Great Plague of 1348 reduced the population by as much as 60 per cent in many cities and the weakened survivors were further decimated by return bouts every ten to fifteen years. Declining demand and profits, increased labour costs and business failure – especially in international commerce where Italy led – entailed depression. The economic difficulties intensified internal struggles, of course, further disrupting town life and dramatizing the need for more effective government to subject competing special interests to the commonweal.

Consolidation of power through the control of centralizing bureaucracy was backed by armed force: distrusting communal armies, oligarchic rulers even in republics preferred foreign mercenary forces led by *condottieri* and these were now answerable to the *signorie* – at least nominally.**2.19** Proliferating in the later 14th century, especially with military unemployment at a time of truce in the Hundred Years' War, they were notoriously unreliable – indeed, several seized the states they served or prevailed over the citizens to make them *signorie*.

Despotism may have been the norm but it was not universal at the dawn of the 15th century in Italy. In Florence, Lucca, Siena and Venice, for example, variously consti-

›2.19 SIR JOHN HAWKWOOD ('Giovanni Acuto', died 1394): fresco by Paolo Uccello, 1436 (Florence Cathedral).

Hawkwood was a mercenary general who was employed – by no means exclusively – by the papal legate in Bologna against the Florentines in 1393–94 and by the Florentines against the Milanese twenty years later.

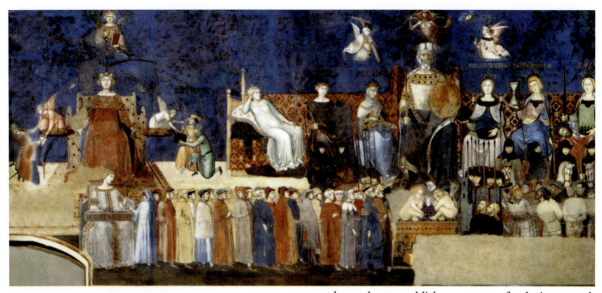

**›2.20 SIENA: ALLEGORY OF GOOD GOVERN-
MENT:** fresco of c. 1340 by Ambrogio Lorenzetti
(Siena, Palazzo Publico).

The Council of Nine, the governing body constituted
from the nobility, commissioned Lorenzetti to embellish their chamber with a cycle of frescoes demonstrating the benefits of their rule in stark contrast to the
corruption of tyranny. In the main image, in opposition
to bound malefactors, the orderly populace processes
between Justice, enthroned with Concord at her feet,
and the personification of Siena surrounded by the
Virtues: the model was the perennially familiar one of
the Last Judgement.

tuted merchant establishments were firmly in control:
their regimes were oligarchic in practice but in principal
they respected the republican ideal of sovereignty residing
with the people rather than with a monarch – as in Naples
and much of the rest of western Europe – let alone the
despotic rule of force.**2.20** Yet republics and tyrannies alike
pressed their neighbours into expanding states – by conquest, marriage, purchase – until the innumerable petty
polities of the early 14th century had given way a century
later to five great powers: Milan, Florence, Venice, the
Papal States and Naples.

The Guelf-dominated Florentine republic had survived
confrontation with Giovanni Visconti after he had
acquired Bologna in 1350 and presented himself as the
champion of the Ghibellines. Within a generation they
were allied with Bernardo Visconti in the face of a perceived threat of annexation by the Holy See. The Guelfs,
eclipsed during this episode, attempted to reassert themselves on its conclusion in 1378 but their previous excesses
had excited popular unrest. Anarchy supervened until 1382

when the guild companies regained control, issued a new constitution guaranteeing their power and paving the way for the reassertion of Guelf dominance.

Weakened by internal division, Milan recovered the initiative after the advent of Giangaleazzo Visconti (1378–1402), whose triumph over the Veronese della Scala in the 1380s alarmed the Venetians and Florentines. Having won the title of duke from the emperor, a marriage alliance with the French royal house of Orléans and all the road to Bologna, Giangaleazzo was poised to take Florence in 1402 when he died unexpectedly. With the Visconti in disarray, Florence reconsolidated its hold over Tuscany and extended its rule to Pisa in 1406, finally gaining access to the sea.

Venice was the principal legatee of Milanese reverse in the north. Having eliminated a major threat to her maritime empire on the defeat of Genoa in 1381, prosperous and stable at home, 'La Serenissima' turned on the threat posed by potentially hostile neighbours to the free passage of its goods along the overland trade routes to the Alpine passes. Recognizing the potential catastrophe to a non-food-producing maritime state of blockade, moreover, it was even more alarmed by the advance of the Ottomans

2.21a

2.21b

in the east: they had defeated the forces of Christendom at Nicopolis on the lower Danube in 1396, opening the road to their domination of the Balkans and isolating Constantinople. Looking for land-based dominion in the west for both these reasons, Venice took Verona and Padua in 1405.**2.21**

Meanwhile, with the popes domiciled in Avignon at the behest of the French, Rome was in full decline and chaos reigned in the Papal States – an ambiguous collection of feudal or communal Emilian, Umbrian and March territories. The rump of the Roman ecclesiastical establishment saw the pressing need to reassert its authority and their cause was attractive to the emperor and his allies who were naturally alienated by the French bias of the Avignonese regime. Papal elections, responding to the shifting balance among those powers – as well as to the pressure of Italian magnates and Roman mobs – culminated in schism: pope (Urban VI, 1378-89) and anti-pope (Clement VII, 1378-94) resided in Rome and Avignon respectively.

Urban VI's successor, Boniface IX (1389–1404), found an unexpected ally in Naples where the last of the direct line of the French Angevin rulers was replaced by the energetic king Ladislaus (1386–1414). With his support, papal authority was restored in Rome and, with Florence embroiled with Milan and threatened by Naples, the pope was able to regain a measure of his temporal power in central Italy. The cost was perpetuated schism, France maintaining the anti-papacy in Avignon.

THE HUNDRED YEARS' WAR RESUMED

A pro-French policy, which extended to collaboration over the healing of the papal schism, was unpopular in England and the highly cultivated but inept Richard was deposed by his cousin Henry of Lancaster. As Henry IV (1399–1413), he exploited anti-French sentiment and regained lost ground in England and France where feudal strife had also supervened with the intermittent insanity of Charles VI. After a succession of brilliant victories in opening the second phase of the Hundred Years' War, Henry V (1413–22) was adopted as heir to France on his marriage to Charles's youngest daughter. Fortune turned after the accession of their son to both thrones as a minor: Henry VI (1422–61, 1470–71) was prey not only to dissension in England but also to his French grandfather's mental instability and to the mystique of Joan of Arc, the 'Maid of Orléans'. He had lost most of France by 1453.

Fought for feudal rights but ultimately with standing armies funded by loans from wealthy merchants and promoting a sense of patriotism inimical to feudalism, the Hundred Years' War ruined England and France. Henry VI's failure provoked his cousin of York to challenge his Lancastrian claim to the English throne and the ensuing internecine strife, recalling the worst excesses of feudalism, is known as the Wars of the Roses.**2.22**

Not until York seized the crown in 1461 as Edward IV was order tentatively restored: the barons, whose private forces had threatened a return to feudalism, had been decimated and the merchants, whose towns emerged largely unscathed but whose business interests were in disarray, readily cooperated with a regime willing to respect them in parliament and back them in trade while rebuilding centralized authority on fiscal and administrative reform. A resurgence of trouble during the brief reign of Edward's brother Richard III (1483–85) was ter-

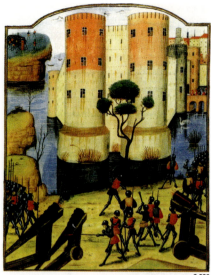

2.22a

›2.22 WAR AND POST-WAR ORDER: (a) artillery siege in the last phase of the Hundred Years' War; (b) the Wars of the Roses, Battle of Barnet; (c) London and the restitution of order and trade under Edward IV; (d) Henry VII Tudor (Michael Sittow); (e) Charles VII Valois (Jean Fouquet); (f) Louis XI instituting the Order of S. Michael (after Jean Fouquet).

2.22b

2.22c

2.22d

2.22e

2.22f

minated by the triumph of Henry VII Tudor, who reinforced his flimsy Lancastrian claim to the throne, and put paid to internecine strife, by marrying the sister of the eliminated Yorkist heir.

Parliament, on whose acclamation Henry's accession depended, enforced laws against feudal retainers – long-standing but ignored – and defined the jurisdiction of the king's privy council by statute. On the other hand, the king constituted an inner council of men chosen for ability rather than birth and obviated unpopular parliamentary taxation by reclaiming all the royal estates alienated in the period of internecine strife. Revenue was increased not only through extortion from the magnates but through the much more constructive encouragement of trade and industry. Further, allied through marriage with both Scotland and the newly unified power of Spain, the regime turned England's attention from the ruinous continental preoccupations of the Plantagenets out into the Atlantic in pursuit of commercial wealth. Within five years royal authority was re-established in cooperation with parliament and the king was lending rather than borrowing.

The Plantagenets and their catastrophic ambitions in France retarded the centralized development of the Valois state which their strongest rulers furthered in England. The annihilation of the English armies in the decisive battles of Formigny and Castillon, ensuring the conquest of Normandy and Gascony, at last provided the French with the foundation on which to begin constructing a modern centralized state – though Brittany and Burgundy remained beyond them, as yet.

The heir of victory, if not its architect, was Charles VII (1429–61). The new king had pretensions to autocracy but his able advisers enrolled the bourgeoisie in the cause of constructing the edifice of state from the rubble of the Hundred Years' War. The essential was sound defence, with Europe's first professional army paid for by a permanent tax and stronger than its potential opponents in the artillery which won at Formigny. Obviously crucial too were sound finances based on the central coordination of statutory taxation – though magnates were mollified only by the conversion of wartime tax rights to permanent prerogative. The promise of new prosperity was underwritten by sound administration through a bureaucracy whose development extended well into the next reign.

With the acquiescence of a devastated nation, prepared to renounce the luxury of liberty for the protection of established order against the threat of resurgent feudal chaos, Charles's able, avaricious and devious son, Louis XI (1461–83), freed the royal council from supervision by the States General, preparing the way for absolutism. The bourgeoisie were courted by the king's affectation of thrift – and an international web of trade treaties. They were heavily taxed but saw noble privileges curtailed: indeed, several magnates were expropriated in the cause of repossessing royal patrimony lost to war and much else was gained – notably Anjou and Provence on the death of King René.

Louis XI survived several coalitions of magnates determined to frustrate him. These were often engineered by the dukes of Burgundy who, bent on forging a kingdom from disparate holdings which ran like a fissure through Europe from Flanders to the western edge of Switzerland, were responsible for relocating the major theatre of conflict in western Europe from the marches of England and France to those of France and Germany.

BURGUNDY

Following the division of the Carolingian empire, Burgundy was subdivided into a duchy owing allegiance to France, and a county owing allegiance to the emperor. The last count, Otto IV (1279–1303) married his daughter,

2.23a

›2.23 BURGUNDIAN EMINENCE: (a) Philip III the Good (1419–67), receiving the 'The Rule of Princes' from Giles of Rome (frontispiece illumination; Brussels, Royal Library); (b) The Arnolfini Marriage (Jan van Eyck, oil on panel 1434; London, National Gallery).

Despite his modernizing administrative reforms and the establishment of an Estates-General, like the parliament revivified by his cousin Charles VII in France, Philip's court conformed to the most elaborate conventions of medieval chivalry. It was financed by the profits from the wool trade and promoted an exceptionally rich bourgeois culture. In turn, its patronage enhanced prosperity, not least by promoting Burgundian artefacts and arts to the height of fashion in many of the courts of northern Europe.

Giovanni di Niccolò Arnolfini was a merchant from Lucca, resident at Bruges and one of the financiers to the ducal court. His fortune was based on exporting woollen goods to his family enterprise in Lucca and importing silk and cloth of gold for the court. His wife was Costanza Trenta whose family, also from Lucca, was connected by marriage to the Medici: she is reported to have died in 1433. A second wife is not recorded except indirectly by the painter who, present in the mirror, inscribed his work as a witness to the union in 1434: however, as only the husband is observing the witness, the possibility remains that the work was commemorative.

The range of artistic endeavour at the service of the Burgundian hierarchy, from illuminated manuscript to penetrating portrait in oil on panel, will not have failed to impress.

2.23b

Jeanne, to Philip v of France. Their daughters, Jeanne and Margaret, were married respectively to Eudes IV, Duke of Burgundy, and Louis II, Count of Flanders and Artois. Duke Eudes was succeeded by his grandson Philip who had married Margaret, grandaughter of Louis and Margaret of Flanders. Philip died in 1361 without issue: the county of Burgundy, known as Franche-Comte, remained with his widow Margaret who had also inherited the reversion of Brabant from her mother; the duchy of Burgundy reverted to the French crown and John II bestowed it in 1363 on his fourth son Philip, known as the Bold. Philip married his predecessor's widow Margaret in 1369, reuniting much of old Lotharingia and setting it on the ascent to political and cultural eminence.**2.23a**

Appointed to the council which governed France during the incapacity of his nephew Charles VI, Philip II of Burgundy aroused the enmity of his other nephew, Louis Duke of Orléans. Enmity turned to bitter hostility when Orléans was murdered at the instigation of Burgundy's heir, John the Fearless (1404–19). John's murder in revenge turned his heir, Philip III, the Good (1419–67), into an ally of England in the second phase of the Hundred Years' War. Economics supported politics: the duke's wealth came primarily from the Flemish textile industry and that, in turn, depended on supplies of wool from England. Burgundy prospered not least at the expense of devastated France.

Phillip, who moved his court from Dijon to Bruges and Ghent in 1420, asserted his right to Brabant as well as Flanders and extended his power to the north-Netherlandish provinces of Zeeland, Holland and Utrecht. His realm – the most densely urbanized in Europe outside Italy – achieved the apogee of splendour and the patronage of court, church and merchants promoted Flemish culture to an eminence matched only by that of Florence.**2.23b**

>**2.24 THE EMPEROR CHARLES IV AND THE GOLDEN BULL:** (a) the imperial seal; (b) the emperor enthroned with the seven electors – from left to right the archbishops of Mainz, Trier and Cologne, the King of Bohemia, the Count Palatine, the Duke of Saxony and the Margrave of Brandenburg (ms illumination of c. 1375; Brussels, Royal National Library).

2.24a

THE EMPIRE RESTORED

The fortunes of the empire revived in the brilliant reign of
Charles IV (King of Bohemia from 1346, German king
1347, emperor 1355) to whom Prague is greatly
indebted.**2.24, 2.25** His 'Golden Bull' of 1356 defined the
imperial electors (dominant since the collapse of the
Hohenstaufen) as the archbishops of Mainz, Cologne and
Trier, the king of Bohemia, the count Palatine of the Rhine,
the duke of Saxony and the margrave of Brandenburg. The
electors remained sovereign in their domains and there
were many imperial free towns. To preserve their freedom,
these had banded together in leagues and there were so
many by 1356 that Charles IV proscribed them in a decree
known as the Golden Bull – unsuccessfully.

2.24b

2.25

Charles IV's son Sigismund (1368–1437), who married the heiress of Hungary in 1385 and led an unsuccessful crusade against the Ottomans to free that kingdom, was elected German king in 1411, succeeded to the throne of Bohemia in 1419 and was elected emperor in 1433. With France embroiled to its initial cost in the opening rounds of the second phase of the Hundred Years' War, he seized the initiative and brokered an ecumenical council dedicated to the healing of the 'Great Schism' – in which the antipapal Avignonese succession continued to draw its main support from France in opposition to the Roman papal line supported by the Empire, England and princes of the Italian Church. However, in promoting church unity the emperor was faced with an intractable problem: to understand it we must digress to religious fundamentalism via scholarship and popular education – on completing our outline of political developments.

HABSBURG SUCCESSION AND THE SPANISH CONNECTION

The emperor Sigismund's daughter Elizabeth, heiress of Bohemia and Hungary, married Albert of Habsburg, Duke of Austria (1404–39). He was elected to succeed his father-in-law in 1438. Thereafter emperors were almost always Habsburgs ruling from Vienna.**2.26**

In his long reign, the feckless Frederick III (1440–93) lost the prestige his office had inherited from the great Charles IV in acquiescence to magnates and papacy. His able son, Maximilian I (1493–1519), attempted to reverse the situation with centralizing reforms in emulation of Louis XI of France and Henry VII of England. His ultimate aim was to substitute hereditary succession in his Habsburg line for the elective system regulated by the Golden Bull of Charles IV. He invented an imperial council to circumvent the imperial diet, whose complex con-

›2.25 PRAGUE, HRADČANY AND THE CATHE- DRAL OF S. VITUS: view from the Charles Bridge.

The eminence on the right bank of the River Vltava was the seat of a prince from the late-9th century and of a bishop from 973. A settlement on the opposite bank had been founded in the early 6th century and had prospered as a commercial centre by the late-12th century when it was granted privileges by royal charter and was connected to the settlement at the base of the citadel (Mala Strana) by a stone bridge. The citadel palace and both settlements were extended, the cathedral and the bridge rebuilt magnificently, under Charles IV.

›2.26 VIENNA, CATHEDRAL OF S. STEPHAN: model.

Built on the site of a Romanesque church and its mid-13th-century successor, the choir of the present church was commissioned in 1304 by Albert I, the second Habsburg to occupy the imperial throne (reigned as king of the Romans but uncrowned as emperor, 1298–1308), and consecrated in 1340 by Albert's grandson, Rudolph IV, Duke of Austria. The southern tower was built between 1368 and 1433. Work on the northern tower began in 1450 but ceased in 1511 at midheight.

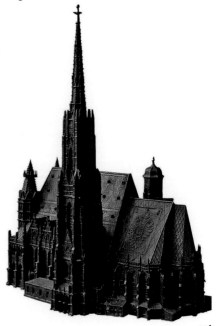

2.26

The roof of the choir is emblazoned with the arms of Austria on the double-headed eagle. The supporter of the arms of the Holy Roman and Austrian emperors, the device was adopted definitively by the emperor Sigismund, but its origin is obscure. It may represent the division of the Roman empire into two by the emperor Theodosius in 395: it was sustained by the tsars of Russia, heirs to the east, as by the Habsburgs in the west.

›**2.27** **THE HANSEATIC PORT OF HAMBURG** (15th-century ms; Hamburg, National Archives).

The origins of the Hanseatic League may be traced to the granting of trading privileges to Lübeck after its acquisition from Holstein by Duke Henry the Lion in 1158. Access to the Baltic and North Sea fishing grounds prompted the Lübeck merchants to enter an alliance in 1241 with Hamburg, which controlled access to salt-trade routes: together they gained control over the salt-fish trade and Cologne joined them in 1260.

With the lapse of security for trade in the post-Hohenstaufen empire, the Hansa expanded with formal agreements for confederation with free cities – or aspirants to freedom from feudal control – throughout the empire. Of prime importance was the treaty of affiliation with the Scandinavians, ending opposition to Lübeck's activities in the Baltic and opening the way to trade with Russia. Ultimately extending to some 160 towns, the network had affiliates in England, the Netherlands and Poland as well as Scandinavia and Russia.

The League was never a formal organization but diets were convened irregularly from its members, first in Lübeck in 1356. By then it was virtually unassailable politically: indeed, at the height of its power it used its ships and their armed escorts to influence imperial policy. The economic crises of the late-14th century did not spare the Hanseatic League but its decline was ultimately due to the rise of the nation state.

stitution favoured the Electors but failed to provide effective means of enforcing its decisions, but the development of an independent administration with general tax-raising powers eluded him.

If the magnates had the power of money and men to keep the emperor at bay, none of them was strong enough to harness nationalist sentiment and master the others – of which the traditional division of inheritance had made many – and, antipathetic to the freedom of the imperial cities, none was interested in manipulating popular discontent. If the magnates countered one another, the cities gained strength from unity in leagues despite imperial prescription: the most notable were the Hanseatic in the north and the Swabian in the south.**2.27**

In face of Frederick III's ineptitude, the Swabian affiliates prospered from 1488 by enrolling princes in the imposition of the order essential to commerce: its effectiveness

2.27

was demonstrated by the rise of Augsburg to financial pre-eminence largely on the initiative of the Fuggers to whom Maximilian and his successors were heavily indebted in the absence of adequate tax revenue. The Hanseatic League dominated northern European commerce throughout the 15th century: it flourished on the growth of trade in luxuries with the improvement of sea links to the Mediterranean and it monopolized the Baltic trade in timber, metal, naval stores, grain from Poland and Prussia and wool from England. Crucial to its success was the zoning of its members' operations. But the gains of expansion encouraged defection, first from the Netherlands, and decline had set in by the end of the century.

The complexity of the empire's ramshackle structure may have defeated Maximilian's attempts to consolidate imperial power but he vastly expanded the power of his dynasty. In addition to his personal qualities, he retained his father's sole talent: the arranging of advantageous marriages. In 1477 he married Mary, heiress of Burgundy; she died five years later and in 1494 he married Bianca Maria Sforza, niece of Ludovico il Moro, Duke of Milan. There was no issue from that second marriage but it gave the Habsburgs ground in Italy which provoked extended conflict with the Valois kings of France, who had a rival claim to the Milanese duchy. On the other hand, the future of Europe was to be shaped by the issue of the emperor's first marriage to Burgundy: Philip the Fair who married Joanna, daughter of Ferdinand of Aragón and Isabella of Castilla whose own marriage had unified most of Spain.**2.28**

IBERIA AND ITS NEW WORLD

In the land that would be Spain, the two kingdoms retained their different constitutions. Aragón, including the county of Barcelona, was a relatively small Mediter-

2.28a

›2.28 IMPERIAL MARRIAGES AND THEIR ISSUE: (a) Maximilian I with Mary of Burgundy and Bianca Maria Sforza; (b) Maximilian and Mary with their son Philip the Handsome (top right) and grandsons, the future emperors Charles V and Ferdinand I (B. Strigel; Vienna, Art-Historical Museum); (c) Ferdinand and Isabella (portal detail, University of Salamanca); (d) the fall of Grenada (Toledo, choir-stall relief); (e) the 'Catholic Kings' with their lost heir, Juan, and heiress, Juana, backed by their Dominican confessors (M. Sittow; Madrid, Prado Museum).

2.28b

2.28c

2.28d

2.28e

ranean trading polity (with a population of about one million c. 1469), long involved with Sicily and Naples. Castilla was an arid agricultural land, good mainly for sheep but also centred on a rich manufactory of weapons: through marriage and conquest, most notably of Andalucía, it had acquired a large population (about five million c. 1469) and northern and southern ports facing the Atlantic.

Both realms had representative institutions convened by royal summons – but the need was rarely felt by the joint monarchs. On the other hand, like the contemporary Tudor and Valois rulers, they did much to lay the foundations of a centralized state and begin the construction of the edifice. The army was reinforced with an infantry of long-pikemen, making it the most formidable fighting force in Europe for more than a century. The main executive council was reconstituted with a majority of lawyers instead of feudal magnates and set about tax reform, first with measures to increase the yield from commerce.

National identity derived above all from the ideal of crusade in the struggle of the Christians to regain the peninsula from the Moors. As we have seen, that had largely been achieved by 1266 – except for Granada which held out until 1492 – and both sides had settled with one another in an atmosphere of tolerance, cross-fertilizing their cultures. Nobles and even commons enjoyed liberties incompatible with ascendant monarchy but after the marriage of Castilla and Aragón it was in the personage of the *Reis Católicos* that Spain found its legal identity. That identity might have been defined in traditional terms either of fanaticism or tolerance: tragically, the former prevailed with the enforcement of orthodoxy through the Inquisition.

Queen Isabella's advisers – in particular her sinister confessor, Tomas de Torquemada, Grand Inquisitor from 1483 until his death in 1498 – soured her native piety. This consumed the traditional communal peace and engulfed the

2.29a

non-Christian communities. The Jews were given the alternative of baptism or expulsion in 1492: most chose to emigrate with disastrous consequences for Spanish trade and industry. In 1502 it was the turn of the Moors of Granada, though they had been guaranteed religious freedom on the annexation of their sultanate in 1492: most chose baptism but peaceful coexistence was defunct.

In the year of the conquest of Granada, which closed the frontier of Christian reconquest, a vastly wider new frontier was opened by Iberian navigators. Seeking to circumvent the hostile Ottomans – as well as hostile Asian terrain or the pirates of Arabian seas – for their traders in all the luxuries of the east, the Portuguese played the leading role. Inspired by the direction of their prince, Henry the Navigator (died 1459), who promoted the development of caravel, compass and astrolabe, they mapped West Africa, rounded the Cape of Good Hope in 1486 and entered the Indian Ocean. And Henry's navigators had also opened the possibility of penetration westward into the Atlantic: from Europe the winds and currents were unfavourable but the reverse prevailed from West Africa.**2.29**

Christopher Columbus, who may have been Genoese, presented the Portuguese king with a grand plan of sailing west from Cape Verde to reach east Asia: it had been surmised that China lay across the Atlantic but the geography of Asia was still far from clear to the European mind, despite the epic land journeys of the Venetian Polos in the 14th century. Portugal unimpressed, Columbus went to the Spanish monarchs and, though financially drained by the Granada campaign, they equipped him for his epic conquest of the Atlantic.

On the first of three voyages, Columbus reached the Bahamas and several Caribbean islands which he mistook for off-shore Asia and called the 'Indies'. Not lost to the significance of the achievement, the Catholic monarchs

›2.29 **PORTUGUESE EXPLORATION:** (a) Henry the Navigator (1394–1460: detail from the São Vicente polyptych of Nuno Gonçalves, c. 1460; Lisbon, National Museum of Art); (b) caravel of the type used by Bartolomeu Dias; (c) *nau* of the type used by Vasco da Gama (Lisbon, Belém, Maritime Museum).

2.29b

2.29c

›2.30 **THE COSA CHART OF THE OLD AND NEW WORLDS,** c. 1500.
    Based on the tradition of the *portolan* – the 'pilotbook' chart, first recorded c. 1300 – this is the oldest surviving complete record of the mid-Atlantic and both its peripheries.

›2.31 **OUR LADY OF THE SEAFARERS** (Virgen de los Navigantes): retable of c. 1510 by Alejo Fernández (1475–1545; Seville, Royal Palace).

2.30

2.31

saw the need for international recognition of their claim to the new lands discovered – and to be discovered – in their name by a succession of epic navigators.**2.30** The Spanish pope Alexander VI responded with a proposal to divide the extra-European world longitudinally between Spain and Portugal and the line was drawn 270 leagues west of the Azores in the Treaty of Tordesillas in 1494 – Spain gaining the west.**2.31** Four years later, the Portuguese Vasco da Gama finally conquered the Indian Ocean and reached the real India for King Manuel I (1495–1521). In the same year – the year after the Cabots had landed on Labrador for England – Columbus found the coast of modern Venezuala and the continent soon to be named America after Amerigo Vespucci, the Italian sailor who began to chart it. Before his Spanish patrons had time to build an empire there, they married the ancient European one but by then the humanists of the Italian renaissance had opened a new era and closed the one they called medieval.

II SCHOLARSHIP, EDUCATION AND DISSENT

Several of the Avignonese popes may have been unfairly tainted by association but the luxury of the secularized court at Avignon naturally furthered corruption. And way beyond Avignon, disillusion with the Church establishment was widespread: the college of cardinals, unrepresentative of all the provinces of the Church, was mainly concerned with protecting its power against the pope. If cardinals were venal, the majority of bishops appointed by popes and princes were men of the world who resigned their duties to deputies and lapsed into luxury sustained, in part, by the sale of justice in the ecclesiastical courts – as in secular ones. The curial clergy, dependent financially on collection of church taxes and forced by declining revenues in the economic recession of the later 14th century to the accumulation of livings and absenteeism, were also increasingly seen as predominantly mercenary. And their obligation to celibacy was a key problem: naturally it led to immoral liaisons and, deplorably, that led to the episcopal sale of licences for concubinage.

The popular equation of Avignon with the iniquities of ancient Babylon (as perceived by biblical writers) had furthered the development of national churches. John Wycliffe was in the van. However, Marsilius of Padua (c. 1270–1342) and William of Ockham (c. 1287–1347) had already pointed to the Bible as the supreme authority in Christendom and promoted the council of the whole Church as the supreme repository of Christian power.

Wycliffe castigated the worship of saints, promoted the translation of the Bible into the vernacular and denounced the doctrine of transubstantiation. Condemned by Pope Gregory XI (1370–78), he retired from Oxford under aristocratic protection but his followers went underground. Lollardy, the biblical fundamentalism emanating from his teaching, survived repression to merge with the continental Protestantism of the early 16th century – as we shall see.

Wycliffe's voice of dissent was not the only one to be heard in post-Plague Europe. The tide of humanism, on the flow in Italy in the age of Petrarch and Boccaccio (pages 650, 664ff), was threatening to wash away superstition and erode Christian obsession with the supernatural – in principle, if not wholly in practice except at the most elevated intellectual and the most basic popular levels. As we shall see in due course, 13th-century popular culture was earthily naturalistic and popular education was inculcating anti-clerical – if certainly not anti-Christian – ideals. At all levels, the locus was then the town. Well over two centuries earlier, the tide of humanism had turned in the orbit of the monastery where the guidance of Alcuin and his followers had not been forgotten.

RETREAT INTO THE ABSTRUSE AND ADVANCE TO EMPIRICISM

High medieval endeavour in the liberal arts, identified as scholasticism, comprehended the *trivium* of grammar, dialectic and rhetoric, and the *quadrivium* of arithmetic, geometry, music and astronomy. The importance of grammar to the Carolingians has been noted when we encountered the putative 'renaissance' of humanism in the school of Aachen – and suggested that it would not prove to have been abortive. Rhetoric was the main tool of the didactic mendicants who operated primarily in the secular world. Mastery of dialectic was crucial to the contemplative majority of scholastics concerned with the reconciliation of differences between Christian authorities and between Christians and humanists.**2.32**

Outside the school of Chartres, whose contribution to the development of Christian humanism informed the inventors of Gothic – as we shall see in that context – the

›2.32 SCHOLASTIC MATHEMATICS AND ASTROLOGY (early 13th-century French ms).

range of scholastic endeavour is beyond us here. At the risk of distortion in simplification, however, it may be said that in the main it bent reason to predetermined purpose contrary to the Classical ideal. But what if scepticism surfaced and the means became the end?

Orthodoxy insisted that the subordination of reason to faith was propitious but Bernard of Clairvaux characteristically rejected any application of dialectic to the realm of faith as impious. He clashed famously with Peter Abelard (1079–c. 1142), whose *Sic et Non* (Thus and Otherwise, c. 1123) took scholasticism to its peak in the formal counter-opposition of articles of dogma, theological and philosophical: restricting himself to interpretation in pitting one authority against another, he perfected the dialectical means but renounced the end of determining validity.

Several generations after the confrontational Abelard, Thomas Aquinas (c. 1225–74) was credited with restoring harmony between philosophy and theology by preserving the integrity of reason and faith on the premise that they both come from the sole source of all truth, God, and achieve the same object by different means. Yet he recognized that faith, remaining open where reason is closed, is transcendent and his followers came to see that an increasing number of doctrines had to be withdrawn from the sphere of the one and left to the other. The extent of these withdrawals ultimately amounted to a confession that scholasticism had failed in its objective – though abstruse abstraction was characteristically preferred by scholastics to confession.**2.33**

Aristotelian dialectic was long disdained as the source of the abstractions with which the last scholastics masked their failure: the full dividend of Aristotle's legacy was long to be realized generally in Europe. Yet the medieval world was certainly aware that, apart from his status as a logician, he taught empiricism and promoted scientific

›**2.33 THE TRIUMPH OF S. THOMAS AQUINAS:** Andrea di Bonaiuto's fresco of 1366 on the west wall of the Spanish Chapel, S. Maria Novella, Florence.

The saint, enthroned under the cardinal virtues as Sapienta holding the Book of Wisdom, is flanked to his left (and from left to right) by Solomon, Isaiah, Moses, S. Luke and S. Matthew, and to his right by Job, David, S. Paul, S. Mark and S. John. At his feet are prominent

2.33

heretics including Averroes and Arius. Enthroned below are the personifications of the liberal arts (Grammar, Rhetoric, Logic, Astronomy, Geometry, Arithmetic) and to the left personifications of the theological 'sciences' (according to Vasari but not without dispute in the absence of most of their labels). The theme of reconciliation between antique and Christian scholarship could hardly be more graphically conveyed.

enquiry as an essential alternative to the rationalism of his master, Plato (AIC1, pages 441ff).

After Constantinople fell to the Crusaders in 1204, Latin scholars had direct access to Greek learning and sound texts from which to survey the whole range of Aristotle's work. Rescensions had previously been generally available – though usually corrupt: Muslim scholars from Persia to Spain were indebted to them for their advances in science and mathematics and these were transmitted to western Europe from Córdoba. Not of least significance in this regard, empiricism had been implanted in England with Mozarabic science by Pedro Alfonso, the converted Spanish Jew who was physician to Henry I ('Beauclerc') at the outset of the 12th century: scholastic rationalism, as it developed in France, could hardly have been more remote – and the philosophic bent of the two nations was ever to be essentially different.

FROM LATIN TO THE VERNACULAR

By the mid-12th century the main thrust of intellectual training had moved from abbey to town, to the cathedral school or cosmopolitan university which made education more widely available. Latin was the language of learning and the clergy long retained domination of teaching. Their particular vocation led mendicant Dominicans to outnumber other clerics in teaching but by the 13th century the majority of clergy entered only minor orders, permitting them to live a largely secular life organized under a variety of canons dedicated to teaching and associating with their pupils to a degree of formality from which the 'university' emerged. The Parisian one was the first of these to be recognized officially – by Philip II Augustus c. 1200. It attracted scholars from all over Europe and was divided into faculties according to the subjects they professed. Offering instruction in Latin, essential for the dominant

›2.34 TUTOR AND STUDENTS AT THE UNIVER-
SITY OF PARIS: 14th-century French ms illumination
(London, British Library).

disciplines of theology and law, the faculty of arts was the
largest.**2.34** The model was followed in Italy, France, England and Spain and by the emperor Charles IV, who
founded his in Prague in 1347. By 1500 there were nineteen
universities in the empire and one each in Switzerland,
Denmark, Sweden and Poland.

Ever the language of learning, Latin guaranteed the survival of a considerable measure of universality in the intellectual life of Europe but the proliferation of institutions
entailed significant vernacular diversification. If that was
true at the tertiary level, it was naturally even more so in
the primary and secondary fields.

Far from the abstruse abstractions of late-scholasticism,
popular education was being promoted by charitable orga-
nizations on the basis of vernacular Bible reading – especially in the north. The Brothers and Sisters of the
Common Life, for example, constituted a congregation of
clerks and laymen not belonging to an order but linked in
common devotional life within secular society. Dedicated
to charity and particularly concerned with the religious life
of laymen, they had emerged from the Netherlands under
the guidance of the ex-Carthusian monk Gerard Groote
(1340–84), who taught that true spiritual communion must
be combined with moral action, after the example of

Christ. They prompted debate over whether religious life could be sustained in secular society – outside an Order – and were certainly not alone in maintaining that it should. They were the prime instigators of the new secular, individual, piety. Not least under their inspiration, a suspicion of clerical institutions, a tendency to supplement, even supplant, corporate worship with personal contemplation, and the proliferation of books and preachers on popular piety became common phenomena in 15th-century Europe.

Mysticism – yearning for direct contact with God – had always been an important strand in Christianity: hermitical in origin, it was projected into lay society by the Franciscans and the radical Dominicans. Of the vast output of mystical writing for lay readers in the later Middle Ages, most influential was *The Imitation of Christ* by Thomas à Kempis (c. 1380–1471). A guide for the individual Christian mystically to accompany the Saviour in his secular mission, it recommended fervent study of holy scripture and much private contemplation. It also sought lay communion at the eucharist: this had been common in the early Church but was contrary to the policy of the medieval hierarchy, especially after the promulgation in 1215 of the doctrine of transubstantiation – that the substance of bread and wine was transformed into the substance of Christ's body and blood in the mystery of the eucharist.

With religion tending to the personal rather than the institutional, especially with the promotion of the mystical in direct experience of the divine spirit, emphasis was shifting to service, not office. The idea that office – in church or state – should be awarded on merit and that merit could be judged even by the laity was certainly not countered by the manifest venality and luxury in high Church places. Abuse in practice apart, the stand was one of principle: that it was the responsibility of the clergy to minister to the faithful, not distract themselves with secular powers and wealth. As we have noted, the secular corollary was clearly enunciated at the same time as disenchantment with the Church establishment was at its most acute: 'When Adam delved and Eve span, who was then the gentleman?' (page 235).

IMPERIAL PRAGUE AND HUSS

Promoting Church reform at home and abroad – particularly keen to winkle the anti-pope out of Avignon – and bent on attracting leading scholars, Emperor Charles IV opened his university in Prague to a wide range of thought. Following the marriage of his daughter to Richard II of England, there was considerable interchange between the kingdoms and the imperial zeal did nothing to discourage transmission of Wycliff's ideas to Czech scholars: Jan Huss (c. 1372–1415), lecturer in philosophy at the Caroline university from 1398, was to prove the most influential.

Charles IV also encouraged popular piety and in the last decades of the 14th century preachers in the vernacular, urging private devotion, made much headway in attacking the rapacity and corruption of the clergy at a time when the Church owned one-third of the land and Germans held most of the important ecclesiastical offices in Bohemia. In elaborating his opposition to the imposition of episcopal hierarchy, for which – like Wycliffe – he could find no scriptural justification, Huss emerged as the leading preacher. His appeal gained a nationalist dimension from the opposition of the Germans. Subjected to inquisition by the archbishop for heretical views and inciting discord between Germans and Bohemians, he was forbidden to teach. Defying the interdiction, he was supported by King Wenceslas IV (1378–1419). The Germans left to found the university of Leipzig in 1409. Huss was rector of the Caroline university the following year.

Denouncing the development of religion into priestly

ritual, deploring the sale of indulgences and despising obsession with relics and image worship, Huss followed the main line of late medieval dissent in seeking to restore the centrality of the Gospels. Excommunicated, he retreated to sanctuary and elaborated his radical views until summoned abroad to account for them – and to his death.**2.35**

KONSTANZ AND THE ABORTIVE CONCILIAR MOVEMENT

Disillusion and questioning sounded within the Church itself in the era of papal schismatism which issued from the Avignonese captivity. That, in turn, led to the attempt to consitute a higher authority than the pope through the Conciliar Movement which had its origin in a body convened to address the need for reform by Innocent III in 1215. Relaunched with the objective of healing the schism, this represented a double challenge to the traditional Church order: it confronted papal absolutism with representative elements and it increased opportunities for the involvement of laymen. As many of these came from universities, particularly schools of law, it was no coincidence that it looked to antiquity – to the primitive Church as the community of the faithful – to redress medieval failings. These were most clearly manifest in the arrogation of corporate responsibilities exclusively to the conclave of cardinals whose corrupt deliberations resulted in the election, not only of inadequate popes, but of anti-popes.

Following an irregular synod which met at Pisa in 1409 and failure to resolve the papal schism, a general council was at last convened under the sponsorship of the Bohemian king Sigismund at Konstanz in 1414. Far broader than its predecessor, its members were admitted on educational qualification as well as ecclesiastical office.

›2.35 THE IMMOLATION OF HUSS AT KON-STANZ: from the near-contemporary Jena Codex (Prague, National Museum).

In 1415 they decreed their own supremacy as representatives of the whole Church, deriving authority immediately from Christ and owed obedience in matters of faith by all, of whatever dignity, even the pope: uncanonical in establishment eyes, of course, this was justifiable on Ochamian, Wycliffian and Hussite grounds. It deposed the anti-pope (John XXIII) – with the aid of King Ladislaus of Naples – and prevailed upon the legitimate claimant (Gregory XII) to resign. Martin V (of the Roman Colonna clan), elected in the stead of both pope and anti-pope in 1417, returned to Rome to begin the restoration of its degraded fabric. The restoration of the moral authority of the Church was another matter.

Despite the enfranchisement of lay members, the clerical establishment prevailed at Konstanz. The reforms sought by the emperor and many of the councillors at Konstanz – Hussite and otherwise – were blocked. Indeed, offered safe conduct to the Council of Konstanz to account for his mission, Huss was condemned for heresy and executed. Czech nationalism was the immediate beneficiary: Church reform was not.

Beyond the ending of the schism, little other than the blueprint for a new church constitution was achieved at Konstanz. To deliberate on this, and on healing the breach with the Orthodox east, the council met again at Basel (1431–49) under the auspices of Eugenius IV (1431–47). Unsurpassed in length, range of attendance, topics and exchange of ideas, its attempts to meet the underlying need for comprehensive constitutional change were stillborn in the face of resistance to its pretensions by the Church establishment and the pope had the support of the new Aragonese regime in Naples – whose accession he had endorsed. His successor, Nicholas V (1447–55), was elected unchallenged and proceeded with the restoration of the papal monarchy.

Roman revival, including reconsolidation of papal secular authority at the expense of the despots who had gained control of large parts of the papal domain during the Avignonese period, was furthered under Pius II Piccolomini (1458–64). However, the revival of papal monarchical pretensions in Italy carried little weight beyond the Alps where the spirit of conflict between secular and ecclesiastical authority had been reinforced by the challenge of the Conciliar Movement. Pius II was able to declare any appeal to a general council heretical but had to concede a variety of liberties to foreign rulers and their national churches in *concordats*. The wonder remains that an outstanding humanist, as Aeneas Piccolomini had been before his elevation, did not foresee the consequence of resistance to the force of critical opinion within and beyond the Conciliar Movement.

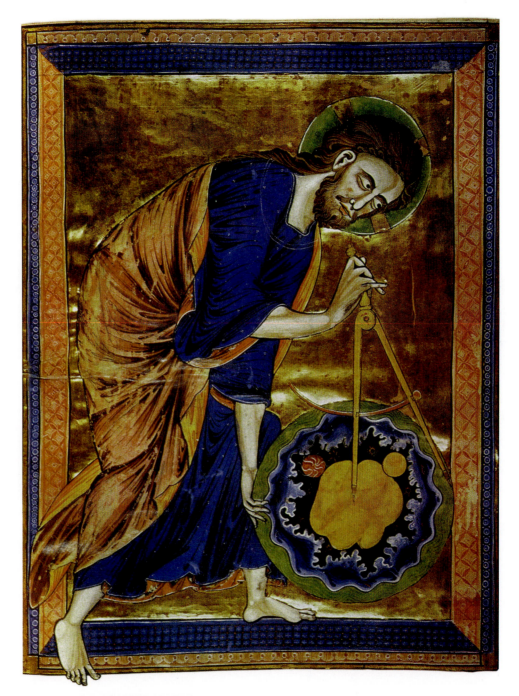

2.1 LIGHT INTO STONE: THE GOTHIC CATHEDRAL

Bright is the noble work; but, being nobly bright, the work
Should brighten the minds, so that they may travel, through the true lights,
To the True Light where Christ is the true door.
In what manner it be inherent in this world the golden door defines:
The dull mind rises to truth through that which is material
And, in seeing this light, is resurrected from its former submersion.
(Abbot Suger, translated by Erwin Panofsky)

›2.36 GOD THE OMNISCIENT ARCHITECT: 13th-century French Bible *moralisée* (Vienna, Austrian National Library).

2.37a

›2.37 CHARTRES, CATHEDRAL OF NOTRE-DAME, c. 1145–c. 1225: (a) west front, 'Door of the Virgin' tympanum, (b) statues of Old Testament kings and a queen flanking the central door of the portal, (c) statues of Christian saints in the east door of the portal.

In the portal dedicated to her, the Mother of God is enthroned over reliefs devoted to the major events in her life and surrounded by representations of the seven liberal arts – *trivium* and *quadrivrium* – in the voussoir's band: Aristotle representing dialectic (outer band base left), Cicero for rhetoric, Euclid and Boethius for geometry and arithmetic (either side of the apex), Ptolemy for astronomy, Pythagoras and Donatius for music and grammar respectively (inner and outer band base right).

›2.38 PISA, BAPTISTRY, c. 1260: Adoration of the Magi, relief by Nicola Pisano (1205–80).

Evidently employed by Emperor Frederick II, whose Classicizing endeavours in the arts reinforced his determination to assert imperial power on the antique model, Pisano showed the way back to the humanist ideal in place of iconic Gothic form through the imitation of antique sarcophagi.

THEOLOGICAL CONTEXT

Until the 12th century, the divinity of Christ tended to eclipse his humanity. Rather than his suffering in crucifixion for man's salvation, it was his triumph over death in resurrection that most impressed the early Christians. As the final judge of mortal man, the Pantokrator was a terrible presence at the door of the dark, heavy, awe-inspiring church. By the early 12th century, however, certain monasteries were fostering a reawakened humanism: Christ's Passion and compassion moved them and love ameliorated terror among the faithful. In particular, the Marianism associated with the monastic school of Chartres – on the southern edge of the Île-de-France – was symptomatic and formative of this development in promising the intercession of the immaculate Virgin for the salvation of suffering humanity.

Inevitably, obsession with the soul and its progress from this world was supplemented by the Chartres scholars with concern for man's suffering body and the physical context of his painful existence in this world. Essential to the process was a re-evaluation of humanistic naturalism

2.37b

2.38c

2.38

in art and this may best be monitored in the development of the sculpture at Chartres from the mid-12th-century ideographic figures of the west front – pillars of the Church – to the personalities inhabiting the south porch from c. 1225. Shortly after the middle of the 13th century in Italy Nicola Pisano was able to order spatial depth for three-dimensional figures in bas relief, under the inspiration of antique sarcophagi. By the middle of the next century, Cimabue and Giotto had given corporeal substance and real space even to the most sacred iconic figure of the crucified Christ in planar painting.**2.37–2.39** And, of course, comprehension of space and mass requires light.

THE SCHOLARS OF CHARTRES AND THE THEOLOGY OF LIGHT

Dedicated to the Mother of God, whose perfect wisdom is implicit in her perfect purity, the scholars of Chartres wrestled with the reconciliation of Christianity and Platonic metaphysics – of the ancient humanist ideal with their patroness's perfection – in the belief that admirable ancient learning and Christian dogma could not be contradictory. The *quadrivium* was bent to their purpose.

Like S. Augustine, subscribing to the teaching of Pythagoras which underlay Plato's cosmology, and like S. Bernard, the scholars of Chartres found divine order in number (page 166, AICI, pages 378, 442f). In the *Timaeus*, known to Chartres in a fragment, Plato applies the ratios of the first tetractys (i.e. 1:1, 1:2, 2:3, 3:4) to the constitution of the World Soul. Identifying the World Soul with the Holy Ghost as the orderer of precreated chaotic matter, the Chartres school comprehended divine order as perfect musical harmony which, through the consistent application of the ratios of the first tetractys, was commensurate with perfect visual beauty. In this they followed S. Augustine's pupil Boethius, who maintained that 'the ear is affected by sounds just as the eye is by optical impressions'. To order was to adorn. The order imposed on chaos was the beautiful: the city of the archetypical architect, God.**2.36**

To the scholars of Chartres and their contemporaries beauty is truth – or, rather, it is the radiance of truth. The order of God's City is the consonance of music and its substance is light. Spiritual, yet apprehended by the senses and to that extent approximating the material, light is the manifestation of the divine: through it we know God. Nowhere is this more clearly revealed than in the iconography of the Annunciation, which was henceforth to become one of the most popular subjects in Christian art: the Holy Ghost penetrating the Virgin is light.**2.40**

The light of the Good in Plato's *Republic* is not only the author of visibility in all things, but also generation, nourishment and growth. The late-antique Neoplatonists saw it as the creative principle of the universe, the revealer of divine truth – the very word 'enlightenment' enshrines an intellectual idea. S. Augustine appropriated the concept for Christ, the Light of the World. S. John had already illuminated the way in the resplendent opening of his Gospel:

> In the beginning was the Word, and the Word was with God, and the Word was God. The same was in the beginning with God … In him was life; and the life was the light of men. And the light shineth in darkness; and the darkness comprehended it not.

›2.40 ANNUNCIATION, with the Expulsion from the Garden of Eden in the background: by Fra Angelico (Guido di Pietro; c. 1387–1455), tempera on panel (Madrid, Prado).

Theologies of light are not rare but the most significant from our point of view was formulated in the light of John's Word by a 5th-century Syrian, schooled by the Neo-platonists but determined to convert their ideas to Christianity: he is known as Dionysius the pseudo-Areopagite because he pretended to be a 1st-century Greek disciple of S. Paul. The deception, devised to lend authenticity to the revelation, worked in the west at least. Sent there by the eastern emperor Michael II in 827 with an embassy to Louis of Aquitaine 'the Pious' (814–40), a rescension of his thesis was entrusted to the monks of S. Denis perhaps because the author had already been identified with their patron saint, the first bishop of Paris, 3rd-century apostle and martyr (in Greek, Denis is Dionysius). Their abbot undertook to compile a biography proving this but it was nearly twenty years before the scholar Erigen reduced the mystifying text to the comprehensible.

The details of Dionysius's theological and epistemological constructs on this basis – the indivisibility of light and the unifying motive of God's self-revelation in creation – are beyond us here (and doubtless beyond many in the 9th-century western empire). However, the essence as distilled by Erigen and his French scholastic followers through the mesh of Augustinian rationalism must be taken for the understanding of the specifically Gothic conception of the Church as the City of God: God shows himself indivisible in light above all else; God's order, deducible in the harmony of musical consonance (and revealed in the design of the temple entrusted to Solomon), is manifest in the ineffability of his light.

1 ADVENT TO APOGEE IN FRANCE

Towards the late-1140s a novel revision of antique building technology transformed the Christian church with a new style, later to be derided by Renaissance Classicists as 'Gothic'. But that style may certainly not adequately be defined solely in terms of technology: it was the most spiritual style ever attained in the West – or anywhere other than India, perhaps. The ingredients of the innovative technology had long been familiar, but the invention of the new style may be attributed to the determination of one man: Abbot Suger of S. Denis, inspired by a revision of theology also long prepared.

Some scholars – notably Erwin Panofsky, whose analysis of scholastic method is exemplary – see a parallel between the mode of scholastic thought and the design process of Gothic architects. Others – notably Otto von Simson, whose comprehension of Chartrain metaphysics is fully matched by his penetration of Dionysian theology – persuasively assert that the evidence for the influence on Gothic architects of the school of Chartres in particular, if only circumstantial, is strong: time and place, eminent teachers of mathematics and distinguished architect-pupils, Platonism and applied geometry. On the other hand, as Simson demonstrates, the evidence that the Gothic was created under the inspiration of the pseudo-S. Denis's theology of light could hardly be more direct.

SUGER AND HIS SEMINAL WORK

The inspiration of his supposed patron saint's theology of light infuses the account provided by S. Denis's Abbot Suger of his work on his church from c. 1135.**2.41** Founded by its dedicatee, the first bishop of Paris, and rebuilt by Charlemagne as the burial place for French rulers, S. Denis was unrivalled in its prestige: it was the repository of the crown, as well as the royal necropolis, and in reaffirming

›**2.41** **THE CONCEPTION OF THE GREAT CHURCH:** Benedictine monks blessing the construction of an abbey church, by Jan II van Coninxlo, from S. Benedict triptych, c. 1530 (Brussels, Royal Fine Arts Museum).

S. Denis as the patron saint of France, Louis VI had declared it the national shrine in gratitude for the protection he had invoked in meeting the imperial invasion of 1124. As the king's chief minister and architect of change in the fortunes of the French monarchy, Suger celebrated the achievement as the architect of transformation at S. Denis. Apparently conceived immediately after the triumph of 1124, this was of patent political significance. Vested with the radical theological significance of Dionysian light on the assumed identification of the pseudo-Areopagite with the apostle of France – challenged by Peter Abelard – its impact was overwhelming.

Undertaking the first major building campaign for generations in the area around Paris, Suger called on experts from several centres of architectural activity to forge a style that would at once serve the pretensions of the dynasty and the theology of light – practical men able to execute his spiritual conception, his aides are unknown but the mobility of ideas in the age of pilgrimage and of itinerant masons is not to be underestimated. Their definitive achievement was the combination of the rib vault, the pointed arch and the flying buttress to form an essentially new skeletal structural system relying primarily not on the dead weight of mass but on the fact that the forces set up by one arch in a series are counteracted by those of its neighbours.

The counter-opposition of forces was the key to the achievement of the Romans not only in their great aqueducts, but also in groin-vaulted halls such as those of the imperial baths or the Basilica of Maxentius (AICI, pages 66of) which stand at the head of the western tradition of spatial form. Slowly regained at the instigation of Italians studying their inheritance, comprehension of the technique was the outcome of the Romanesque quest for a fully integrated system of arches but it was first fully demonstrated in serving Suger's purpose – forging a casket of light.

›**2.42 BEAUVAIS, S. ÉTIENNE**, c. 1130: aisle and nave from the crossing.
The vaulting of the aisles began with the easternmost bay where the ribs, square in section, contrast sharply with the rounded forms of the succeeding bays.

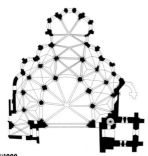

2.43a @ 1:1000

›2.43 PARIS, S. MARTIN-DES-CHAMPS, CHEVET, after 1130: (a) plan, (b) exterior (after Lenoir, 1867), (c) interior.

The choir was rebuilt under Prior Hugues (1130–42): the first phase of the work, the quadrant bays, retained groin vaults; rib vaults were adopted to solve the more complex vaulting problems presented by the somewhat irregular development of the central axis in the final phase. The double ambulatory actually consists of a series of radial bays opening out to contiguous and interconnected radial chapels. Radial chapels were certainly not uncommon in the late-Romanesque, as at S.-Benoît-sur-Loire or its follower, Fontgombault (1120s), which provides the immediate precedent for extending the first bays of the chevet beyond the sides of the nave: unlike the chapels there, some were contiguous but originally not open-sided.

2.43b

The deification of number apart, the full integration of all the parts depended on the pointed arch. With the semicircular arch, width dictates height and vaults will be domical and bays autonomous unless their diagonals are distorted. The pointed arch, on the other hand, can be freely adjusted to produce straight-ridged vaults of uniform height even over oblong nave bays, repeating the divisions of the aisles, and the bays will be links in a chain.

As we have seen, the diffusion of the pointed arch is one of the general developments of later Romanesque: the Cistercians used it consistently wherever they built. The Cluniacs were familiar with it and it appears in the Île-de-France c. 1130 in the aisles of S. Étienne, Beauvais, the ambulatory of Morienval and the chevet of S. Martin des Champs in Paris.**2.42, 2.43** The rib vault, descended from Durham and Caen, appears with it and the Cistercians,

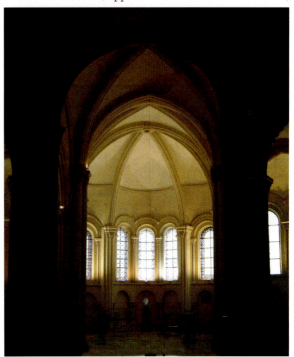

2.43c

rigorously rational in their planning, were among the first to equate their aesthetic and structural advantages.

As in the pilgrimage church above all, the typical Romanesque approach to composition was additive, respecting the integrity of autonomous parts in a more-or-less coherent context. Inspired by the Augustinian – ultimately Pythagorean – geometry of the Cistercians, Gothic architects generally conceived unified wholes divided and subdivided along structural lines into interrelated polygons. In this lies the importance of the chevet of Prior Hugues at S. Martin des Champs: instead of a single series of compartments, autonomous but ranged around a hemicycle to provide a distinct corridor, the transition to a network of assimilated bays began with doubling the ambulatory with radial chapels; rather than containment, the planning principle – yet to be fully realized with the aid of pointed rib vaults – was spatial expansion laterally and longitudinally.

Hardly had S. Martin's chevet been completed c. 1140 when work began on Suger's choir at S. Denis. The Dionysian light which the seminal synthetic approach was to admit is invoked at the outset, in an inscription on the Golden Door to the new narthex, to illuminate the mind and draw it 'to the true light to which Christ is the portal'.**2.44**

›2.44 S. DENIS, ABBEY CHURCH, c. 1135–44: (a) plan with (1) Merovingian church, (2) Carolingian church, (3) Suger's narthex, (4) Suger's chevet, (5) Suger's projected nave, (6) 13th-century completion, (b) interior of the narthex, (c) project for the west front, (d, e) exterior and interior of the chevet.

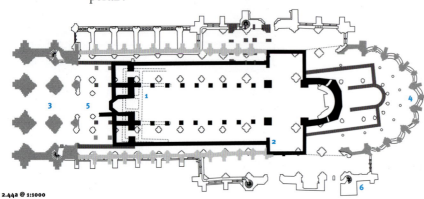

2.44a @ 1:1000

2.44c

2.44d

2.44e

Suger's S. Denis

Suger began work on the reconstruction of the Carolingian basilica c. 1135 with the western end. Replacing the dilapidated westwork of c. 775, he had a three-bay narthex, with chapels above, built considerably further west, the central bay wider than the side ones over which the towers were constructed with venerable symbolic effect.**2.44c** All the bays were given rib vaults springing from shafts related to each element of the load: the tripartite rib mouldings are an advance over the simple convex ones in the aisles of S. Étienne, Beauvais.**2.42** However, the use of rib vaulting in the context of heavy retaining walls is not yet persuasively Gothic: a structural frame encases the massive piers which carry the towers, but it is the dead weight of the mass, not the counter-opposition of forces, which matters. Despite the buttresses, on the other hand, the triumphal arrangement of doors and windows in the centralized composition of the façade is already in marked contrast to the former Romanesque agglomeration of autonomous parts.

Early in the 1140s Suger turned his attention to the sanctuary and its ambulatory. Built over the Carolingian crypt, enlarged and revaulted at a higher level, the new work was directly related to the slightly earlier chevet at S. Martin des Champs – though that was obscured by the replacement of the clerestory to a much larger scale in the 13th century. Crisp and precise, Suger's articulation is much more regular, his sanctuary and ambulatory are differentiated in height and the segmental chapels, which he describes as *circuitous oratoriorum*, are much more clearly detached than the earlier work. Massive piers and walls were replaced by a skeleton of arches except between the outer windows. With far more void than solid and emphasis on slender verticals, the result was light as distinct from both heavy and dark, as in Romanesque.

The columns ringing the sanctuary – enlarged when the clerestory was altered – were doubtless designed to match the arcades of the Carolingian nave which Suger intended to respect in his rebuilding: hemicycles of columns around the apses of basilicas were certainly not rare in Romanesque France – in the domain of Cluny and, especially, in the pilgrimage church. Above the columns, the articulation of the skeletal frame depends on the consistent use of tubular forms for the imposts of the arches and the ribs of the vaults.

Work on the nave was superseded in the 13th century. Excavations uncovered mid-12th-century foundations which indicated that the perimeter was to be unbroken by projecting transepts, as at Sens and Paris in the next generation. The aisles were to be doubled to match the width of the chevet but the intercolumniations of the nave arcade were narrower than those of the ambulatory due to the preservation of the Carolingian work.

The pointed arch, rib vault and putative flying buttress had already been combined in England, but Durham cathedral is not Gothic – unlike Suger's synthesis. With their thick walls, often expressed in doubled planes, Norman structures were safe and the installation of stone vaulting was not adventurous. Impressed by the prestige of such spacious, light, elegant buildings as S. Remi, Reims,[2.55] early 12th-century northern French builders retained the thinner walls of timber-roofed structures and the problem of imposing heavy vaults on them provoked experimentation in building technology. The first response was to thicken piers with engaged columns and pilasters, as in S. Étienne, Beauvais,[2.42] until it was realized that the counter-opposition of forces in a fully integrated system of pointed arches allowed even the piers to be lightened.

Suger's chevet at S. Denis clearly announces the new approach: the slender columns, aligned on axes radiating from the centre of the choir, carrying fully pointed arcades and ribbed vaults, built of finely dressed stone half as thick and heavy as Norman rubble, oppose as little mass as possible to the penetration of light. Presenting his sanctuary as the visual equivalent of music, Suger's insistence in his booklet on unity and harmony is as obsessive as his preoccupation with light and all implicitly derives from the theology attributed to S. Denis guided by the essentially Augustinian practice of the Cistercians. The point is made in the portal inscription specifically referring to the physical reality of the new structure and to the spiritual ideal enshrined in it (page 263). And in penetrating the stained glass of exceptionally large windows, God's light illuminates the representation of his word in images as it illuminates the representation of his City in the building itself.

THE SCOPE OF DEVELOPMENT

Once formulated, the Gothic synthesis was continuously modified. The prelates who held the sees of the heartland of the French monarchy – principally Sens, Noyon, Laon, Paris and Chartres – most of whom were at the consecration of Suger's great church in 1144, gave the new style its initial impetus: Sens while Suger was still active, Noyon from c. 1150, Laon and Paris in the next decade. The stupendous series continued with Soissons, begun in the

1170s and transformed from the late-1190s when a classical standard was being realized at Bourges and Chartres. Ever greater height was pursued at Reims from 1210, Amiens from 1218, and Beauvais in the 1230s: the apogee was there surpassed with disastrous consequence and relative moderation governed the conception of the new nave of S. Denis in the same decade. Meanwhile, the transformation of Rouen cathedral from the start of the 13th century celebrated the French conquest of Normandy and the resurgence of the monarchy for which Suger had laid the foundations.

TOWARDS THE CLASSICAL CANON

The first great project to be executed generally in accordance with the Gothic system was the cathedral at Sens (from c. 1145).**2.45** Spacious in width and length, but not yet in height, it provides the most tangible image of Suger's ecclesiastical ideal, unrealized at S. Denis until the 1230s. To ensure consistency of measure, early medieval architects – the Cistercians in particular, as we have seen – composed their plans of squares and the procedure was respected here in the pairing of the nave bays. Alternating with paired columns, the main support piers have clusters of shafts rising from the ground to the springing of the main arches bearing the vaults: these are sexpartite, unlike those of Suger's sanctuary. The alternating rhythm and heavy transverse arches accord with common Romanesque practice – Jumièges and Durham in particular – and the triforium, in place of the gallery which was such a prominent feature of Caen's S. Étienne, is also Norman. Nevertheless, further advanced than the narthex at S. Denis – if not the chevet – Sens marks the transition from Norman Romanesque to Gothic, from massiveness to the counter-opposition of forces within relatively thin walling, from dark to light.

2.45

›**2.45 SENS, CATHEDRAL OF S. ÉTIENNE,** probably begun c. 1130, changed after 1142: interior to the east.

The essentially Romanesque foundation scheme, with the great width permitted by a timber roof as at S. Remi, Reims,**2.55** was transformed after 1142 in accordance with developments at S. Denis, but the aisles were not doubled.

In the triforium, as at Durham, two pairs of arches framed by a blind arcade are carried on piers with attached columns but here they reduce and double the basic division of the original clerestory, which itself reduced and doubled the paired bays of the main arcade.

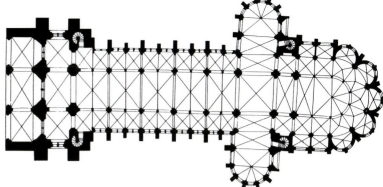

›2.46 NOYON, CATHEDRAL OF NOTRE-DAME, founded c. 1150: (a) plan, (b) west front, (c) chevet, (d) nave (from c. 1170) interior to the east.

Construction began with the choir and sanctuary. The first oblong bay of the choir is clearly differentiated with compound piers to all four corners supporting quadripartite vaults. The other bays, with semicircular arches to the sides and pointed ones around the apse, are all carried on columns. Shafts are attached to the intermediate columns of the aisle arcade and there is also some ambiguity in the echoing of the gallery arcade mouldings, which articulate structure, as purely decorative surface relief to the wall above.

The vaulting system changes but the four-storey elevation was redeployed for the nave from c. 1170 with consistently pointed arches on alternating compound piers and columns. The clerestory windows are doubled in each bay but the four arches of the triforium form a single sequence. The rhythm of voids in the elevation is thus in the ratio 2:4:8 or 1:2:4 (within the first Pythagorean tetractys).

The gallery had reappeared already at Senlis in the early 1150s, but without the triforium. The four-storeyed elevation recalls Tournai (c. 1135).[1.60] The apsidal transept derives from the trefoil Romanesque form of the Rhineland and Tournai: the idea probably

2.46a @ 1:1000

By c. 1170 the influence of Sens had extended beyond France to Lausanne on Lake Geneva and to Canterbury in south-east England – as we shall see. In the intervening decades nearer home, at Noyon, there was already advance towards the High Gothic arrangement of tripartite nave and quinquepartite sanctuary separated by a transept – though the latter is apsidal at both ends.[2.46] The internal elevation, too, is a more advanced expression of

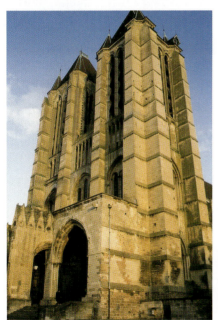

2.46b

2.46c

2.46d

the Gothic ideal of integrating piers and shafts, longitudinal, diagonal and transverse pointed arches, into a skeleton whose visual significance matched its structural role in
the negation of the wall. Gothic aspiration through greater
height is first represented here with the reintroduction of
a gallery – which provided buttressing – and the retention
of a triforium to mask the zone of the gallery roof in a four-
storey elevation. The triforium was blind at first, as at
Caen's Sainte Trinité, but when work progressed on the
transept and nave it was given the depth of a wall passage.
The recession of the clerestory to the depth of that passage behind an arcade effects scenographic screening
rather than revealing the weight of mass – indeed wall
cedes to skeletal structure. A decade later scenography was

passed from Flanders to the Île-de-France via Cambrai,
which also had an apsidal transept (but certainty about
that destroyed building runs only to its unusual height
for the time).

›**2.47 SOISSONS, CATHEDRAL OF S. GERVAIS AND S. PROTAIS,** 1177: interior of the south transept.

›**2.48 BRAINE, S. YVED,** from 1190: interior to east.

The plan is distinguished by the insertion of paired chapels on the diagonals between the commensurate bays of transept and choir. As c. 1174 at S. Vincent, Laon, the internal elevation dispenses with a gallery, but retains the triforium passage of the nearby cathedrals of Noyon, Laon and Soissons.

enhanced in the apsidal south transept of Soissons cathedral with the addition of an ambulatory with a substantial chapel projecting from it but the four-storey elevation had already been revised elsewhere.**2.47, 2.48**

The sexpartite vault, inherited by Sens from Normandy, is retained for the nave at Noyon: the doubled bays are again defined by alternating piers and columns which fail to match the complexity of the rib system arising from them. However, clarification of structure and assertion of horizontal continuity had already been enhanced in the sanctuary and transepts by quadripartite vaulting, presumably inherited from S. Denis. Apart from this, the sequence of circular piers at Laon (from c. 1160) represents the first significant departure from the late-Romanesque

2.49a

accretion of paired bay units towards the High Gothic continuous sweep of identical piers. The sexpartite vault continued to imply the pairing of the bays: the selective application of shafts to the later piers of the series, asserting the verticals of those supporting the transverse arches which divide the vault into compartments, was an incompletely satisfactory attempt at obviating discrepancy.**2.49**

Seven towers were projected for Laon, two each on the west front and the prominent twin-aisled transepts, one

›**2.49** LAON, CATHEDRAL OF NOTRE-DAME, c. 1165–90: (a) interior to the east, (b) plan, (c) view from north-east, (d) west front.

The four-storey elevation of Noyon is combined with the relatively great length of Sens, but it is cut in the middle by the particularly prominent aisled transept. Distantly recalling the old Romanesque *echélon* plan, the original apsidal sanctuary was echoed in the small-scale chapels projecting to the east at both ends of the transept. The choir was lengthened early in the 13th century and given a rectangular east end. In the absence of compound piers, the shafts that rise from the columns – five on a square abacus for each lateral

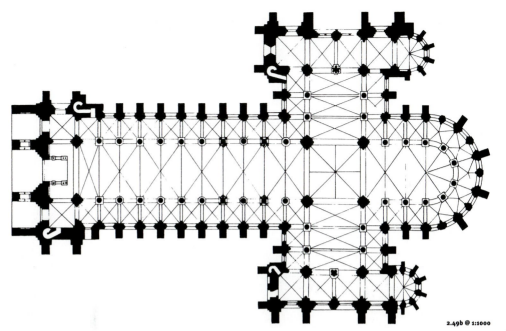

2.49b @ 1:1000

arch, transverse arch and diagonal rib of the vault, three on an octagonal abacus for each lateral arch and intermediate spur rib – are bolder, giving the impression of greater plasticity. The depth of the wall revealed by the triforium is sustained in the central tower where both the triforium and the clerestory are repeated.

Expanded in scale from the precedent set at S. Denis and completely eclipsing the windows below, the rose has become the dominant element in the composition of all four fronts. The process began on the north transept front but the most dramatic use of recession through the development of the double-wall system was reserved for the west front: transmitted from the bold portico via gables sharply delineated against a triforium-like frieze of windows to the deeply hooded rose and its companion windows and stepping on up through a full triforium, it culminates in the animal-inhabited diagonal projections of the towers. It is the predominance of near-round arches in this virile context that recalls the mature Romanesque but the projection and recession are even bolder.

over the crossing: the scheme would have surpassed its model, Tournai, but only five were realized. In the composition of the west front, completed late in the 12th century, the divisive verticals of the buttresses are obscured by the vigorous projection and recession of the storeys. This produces a much more dramatic contrast between solid and void than in the otherwise-related transept façades.

2.49c

2.49d

›ARCHITECTURE IN CONTEXT »REFRACTION OF LIGHT

2.50b

There were important developments occuring in parallel in France – particularly in Anjou and Poitou. Several Poitevan churches – Romanesque in origin – were given multi-ribbed vaults in the mid-12th century: these were usually domical in section, as in the cathedral of Angers where they are carried on the perimeter wall of the simple aisleless volume.**2.50** In the traditional local hall churches, with nave and aisles assimilated in height, these were soon to cover the autonomous compartments defined by composite piers which are more clearly related to those of the pilgrimage church than to the synthetic system elaborated for Suger's S. Denis: Poitiers cathedral (c. 1162) is a prime example.**2.51**

>2.50 ANGERS, CATHEDRAL OF S. MAURICE, from 1149: (a) nave to sanctuary, (b) southern rose window.

The typical Angevin Romanesque sequence of square domed bays, inherited from Aquitaine, is 'Gothicized' by the application of sexpartite rib vaults. The new technique admitted greater breadth – and height – of space but the autonomy of the bays is not prejudiced. This remained the case even though ribs were added when the choir of Romanesque S. Martin was vaulted in the third quarter of the century and S. Serge was built with them on slender columns from 1215. The vaulting of the nave of Le Mans cathedral (from c. 1145) is comparable to its Angevin near-contemporary, though the system is quadripartite and the structure basilican.

A late French Romanesque precedent for the rib-vaulting of square domical bays has been detected in the nave at S. Loup-de-Naud, south-east of Paris. Lombard influence there may be attributed to a faction of Suger's advisors – though Lombard masons were ubiquitous. For the Lombard precedents, see pages 89f.

2.50a

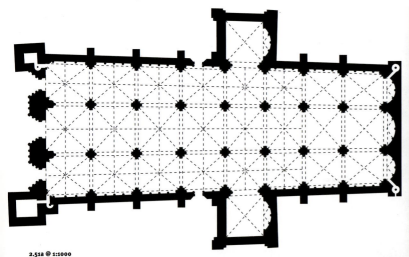

2.51a @ 1:1000

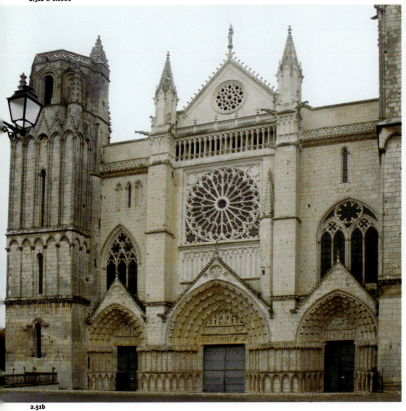

2.51b

2.51c

›2.51 POITIERS, CATHEDRAL OF S. PIERRE,
from 1162: (a) plan, (b) north-west front, (c) central
sanctuary window, (d) nave to sanctuary.

Transformation in the next generation of the Poitevan hall type with its nave and aisles rising to similar
height is comparable to the application of rib vaulting
to the domical bays of the Angevin aisleless type of hall
church. The discretion of each bay is preferred to the
tunnel-vaulted continuity of Notre-Dame-la-Grande,
for immediate example. However, the inherent light-

2.51d

ness of the Gothic system, admitting slender piers of clustered shafts to support the canopy of pointed arches and ribs, ensured an exceptional measure of spatial unity.

>**2.52** **CANDES-S.-MARTIN, COLLEGIAL CHURCH,** later 12th century: (a) porch, (b) detail of vaulting.

2.52a

2.52b

2.53a

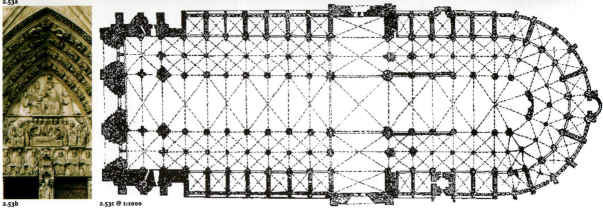

2.53b

2.53c @ 1:1000

›ARCHITECTURE IN CONTEXT »REFRACTION OF LIGHT

2.53d

›2.53 PARIS, CATHEDRAL OF NOTRE-DAME, c. 1210: (a) nave to east, (b) west front, Portal of the Virgin, detail, (c) plan, (d) exterior from the west.

The largest work of the late-12th century in the Île-de-France, in height (c. 35 metres) and width (37 metres to outer aisles), the perimeter of the double-aisle, double-ambulatory plan is unbroken but a transept asserts itself internally. There were originally four storeys but the blind oculii at triforium level, masking the gallery roof, were replaced early in the 13th century when the clerestory was enlarged (the present ones beside the crossing were restored in the 19th century by E.E. Viollet-le-Duc, restressing the mural quality of the original conception).

Back in the Île-de-France, harmony was the overriding concern of the architect responsible for Notre-Dame in Paris: the plan is compact and the light structure is lightly etched on the flat plane of walls unrelieved by triforium or recessed clerestory.**2.53** In the choir (c. 1163), as later in the nave, the inherent incompatibility of the sexpartite vault and the regular repetition of identical piers was admitted: alternation was abandoned and no distinction made in the expression of support below the springing of the vault arches – except at the western extremity.

2.54a

2.54b

To receive the thrust of the vault over doubled aisles – usually transmitted by the transverse arches of a single gallery directly to an external buttress – the intermediate piers of the sanctuary bays and ambulatory, together with the enclosing fabric, were strengthened at the expense of light. As an alternative, the flying buttress was used in a fully Gothic context for perhaps the first time in the construction of the nave from c. 1175. The earliest examples were superseded in the 1230s but their mark was left and the profile is matched by the buttresses of the church at S.-Leu d'Esserant which was being constructed over a unified plan from c. 1180.**2.54**

The basic pattern established for the west front at Laon is retained in Paris but the bold virility has been modified: the flat plane of the wall is lightly relieved by the frieze of niched kings above the portals and the filigree arcade above the windows but deep recession is reserved for the monumental portals which far surpass human scale – solid and void, the heavy and the light, the vertical and the horizontal are as near to equilibrium as Gothic designers were ever to want.**2.53d**

›2.54 S.-LEU-D'ESSERENT, CHURCH, c. 1180: (a) exterior from the south-east, (b) interior to east.

The quadrant profile of the flying buttresses matches that of a relieving arch in the south-west buttress of the south transept of the Parisian cathedral, which was retained from the original structure of the late-1170s in the new work of the 1230s. At Paris quadrant arches to every second choir bay originally transmitted the thrust of the sexpartite vaults over the galleries to the columns between the aisles and over the aisles to the outer piers. When the nave was projected c. 1175 this concealed system was superseded by flying buttresses, also apparently in two registers. As at S.-Leu, they were applied at the point of greatest stress where the radius of the vault is at 30 degrees to the horizontal.

APOGEE

The flying buttress was quickly adopted for new work and adapted to work in progress – as at Noyon, Laon, the south transept at Soissons and the new chevet of S. Remi at Reims.**2.55** The architects of Chartres and Bourges c. 1194–95 realized the logical conclusion of its application: the gallery, obviated for buttressing, could be eliminated and the enclosing wall lightened as at S. Vincent, Laon, and S. Yved, Braine. Superimposed in tiers and multiplied in depth by the beginning of the new century, flying buttresses sail out over doubled aisles and ambulatories. The wall ceded to the structural frame in designs of great organic vitality and much play was made with the manipulation of plane to modulate the subsisting mass.**2.56, 2.57**

>**2.55 REIMS, S. REMI** c. 1170–80, interior of the choir.

The great width of the Romanesque nave, originally roofed in timber, is sustained in the new choir added from c. 1170 and with stone vaults projected throughout it is hardly surprising that the building was among the earliest to be equipped with flying buttresses. The four-storey elevation and quadripartite vaulting adopted for Noyon are retained but with the relationship of solid to void greatly lightened and enhanced by a second colonnade in the ambulatory, framing the chapels. The Laon form of gallery is repeated, but a novel three-light clerestory is prophetically integrated with a six-arched triforium through the extension of exceptionally slender mullions.

Chartres and Bourges

The compact plan type, initiated at S. Denis, approximated at Sens, furthered at Paris, perfected at S.-Leu-d'Esserent, produces a volume nowhere more resplendent than at Bourges. The double ambulatory of S. Denis is continued throughout, as in Paris, but whereas the cross is expressed there in elevation and section, if hardly in plan, here the envelope is unbroken: integrity and consistency of form are as complete as the differentiation of sanctuary from entrance admits. On the other hand, the architect of Chartres achieved the definitive High Gothic plan of single-aisled nave and double-aisled sanctuary separated by a transept: this appeared at Noyon but now the transepts are also tripartite and, no longer apsidal, they project one bay further than the outer choir aisle. At Bourges

›2.56 BOURGES, CATHEDRAL OF S. ÉTIENNE, 1195–1255: (a) exterior from south-east, (b) plan, (c) transverse section, (d, e) interior to east and detail of stained glass (pages 214–215), (f) west front.

At 14.3 by 37.5 metres, the nave was the greatest of the 12th century. With double flying buttresses in serried ranks throughout instead of the internal structural partitioning of a gallery, the central space opens fully to the light of the windows through the main arcade carried on columns 65 metres high.

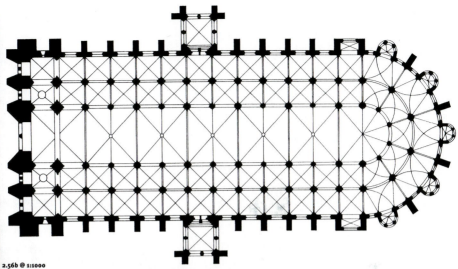

2.56b @ 1:1000

2.56a

organic growth seems to cede to rationalist determinism except, perhaps, for the niche-like ambulatory chapels: perched on corbels supported by the pier buttresses rising from the crypt, these seem to have been clamped on as an afterthought. In contrast, the radial chapels of Chartres, pressing through the outer ring of pier buttresses, evolve dynamically from segments of the apse.

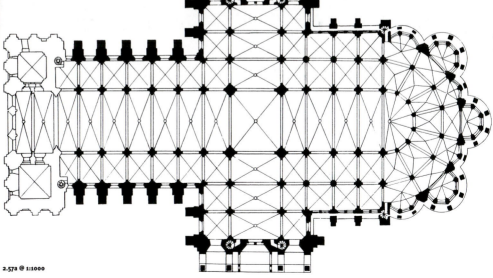

2.57a @ 1:1000

2.56d

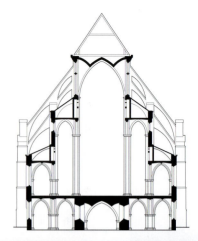

2.56c

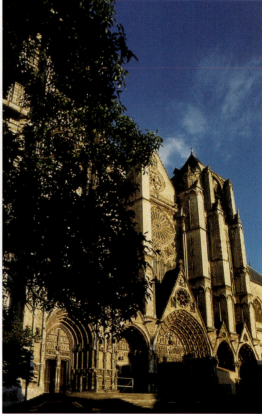

2.56f

From the square bays of Sens and Noyon, with sexpartite vaulting over alternating supports, transition to a regular succession of oblong ones progresses from Laon to Paris to Bourges and Chartres. Bourges retained sexpartite vaulting and with it minor discrepancy in the expression of support at the upper and lower levels of the internal elevation: eight shafts attached to the soaring columns relate to the superstructural arcades and vaults but above the imposts of the arches the number of shafts rising

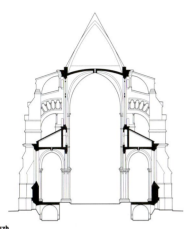

2.57b

›**2.57 CHARTRES, CATHEDRAL OF NOTRE-DAME,** early 13th century: (a) plan, (b) transverse section, (c) interior to the east, (d) north transept rose window from within, (e) south elevation (after Dehio and von Bezold).

The Romanesque cathedral was burnt in June 1194. Rebuilding on the old foundations began with the nave, which was finished by 1210. The choir was largely complete c. 1220, the transepts by 1230. Influenced by the Romanesque remains, especially the venerable crypt enshrining the tunic of the Virgin Mary, the articulated plan is subjected to the contraction of the transepts and expansion of the sanctuary ambulatory to produce a clearly ascending hierarchy of parts from west to east. At 34.5 metres high, the vault is slightly lower than at Bourges.

At Sens, Noyon, Laon and Paris the crossing bay is square (at least in principle) like the double nave bays. At Chartres the nave retains its Romanesque predecessor's width (16.4 metres) but the transept is narrower (c. 14 metres), hence the crossing is not square. A pentagon with sides of 16.4 metres will be described by a circle c. 14 metres in radius and the ratio approximates that of the Golden Section. The ratios 1:1 and 1:2 remain important at Chartres but the Golden Section has been found throughout the plan and elevation.

2.57c

through the full elevation alternates in accordance with the number of ribs in the major and minor sections of the sexpartite vault. The definitive solution to that problem was achieved in the contemporary work at Chartres: quadripartite vaults permit the regular repetition of single-nave bay compartments matching the aisles and defined by identical piers. The latter are octagonal with heavy shafts to each axis, the ones to the sides carrying the aisle arcades, those projecting into the nave rising through the capitals to support the transverse arches and slenderer ones rising from the capitals to support the diagonal and lateral ribs of the vault.

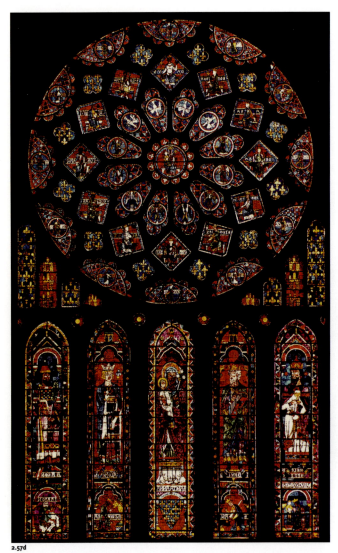

2.57d

Comparison of the internal elevations of Sens, Noyon, Paris, Bourges and Chartres shows progression to ever greater height and lightness, with the steadily increasing dominance of void over solid and of vertical over horizontal. At Bourges the nave arcade soars to a great height, permitting light to flood in through the upper level of the inner aisles, and triple windows fill the clerestory above the triforium. Exceptionally tall, the triforium screens most of the remaining wall and is echoed between the aisles. At Chartres, the internal elevation is reduced virtually to two storeys as the arcades of the single aisles and the brilliant clerestory are separated only by a much-reduced triforium: the dominant clerestory, comparable in height with the lower storey thanks to the daring deployment of the flying buttresses, leaves minimal wall though the twin lancets and oculii may still be read as having been punched from a curtain of masonry.

After the example of Laon, the rose in each façade at Chartres was expanded beyond the scale of the one at S. Denis: the western one of c. 1200 is a self-contained composition of autonomous oculii, but the northern and southern ones of a generation later are elements in a greater arched whole incorporating a centripetal filigree over slender lancets. The flying buttresses incorporate radial arches like those of the western rose.

The Romanesque cathedral of Chartres had been built to enshrine the tunic believed to have been worn by the Holy Mother at Christ's birth: the church was destroyed by fire in 1194 but the tunic miraculously survived – and that was not the first miracle of salvation ascribed in Chartres to the compassionate intercession of the Queen of Heaven. Under these auspices, the rebuilding of the cathedral was to prove the pivotal event in the development of the new Gothic style.

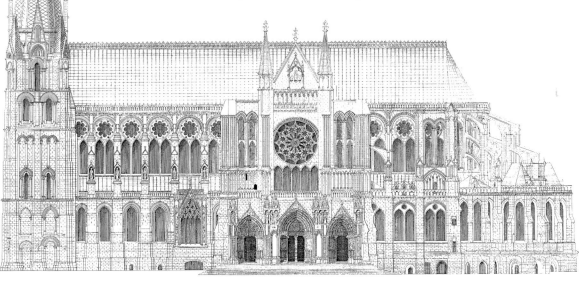

2.57e

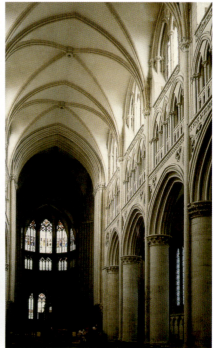

2.58

2.59

2.60

The influence of Chartres was intermittent throughout provincial France. In its light, the plans for Rouen were altered in the course of execution (c. 1200) to suppress the gallery with which the nave had been equipped when work began from the west c. 1190 and shafts were aligned on the diagonal faces of diamond-shaped piers. Elsewhere in Normandy – and even the Île-de-France – the gallery survived or the triforium was given comparable expression at least until the 1240s when the choir of Coutances was re-designed in the light of Bourges without gallery and with the triforium reduced to little more than a balustrade.**2.58–2.61**

High Gothic architects were obsessed with the expression of the continuity of the main structural elements from the base of the piers to the apex of the vaults. Their experiments at Chartres and Bourges, based on the application

›**2.58 ROUEN, CATHEDRAL OF NOTRE-DAME,** (begun late in the 1190s): nave to sanctuary.

›**2.59 CAEN, S. ÉTIENNE,** c. 1200–15, sanctuary.
Rebuilt to a late-12th-century plan, the chevet was completed with a light screen before a wall passage at clerestory level, a heavily recessed gallery and an aisle arcade with rosette-punctured spandrels further asserting the weight of the wall. This rosette motif was to be popular in early Gothic England and Normandy and the revelation of several planes, as in the screened clerestory, was to prove an extremely fertile derivation from the original 11th-century clerestory schemes of both the great abbeys at Caen.

›**2.60 SÉES, CATHEDRAL OF NOTRE-DAME,** from 1235: nave to sanctuary.

›**2.61 COUTANCES, CATHEDRAL OF NOTRE-DAME,** 1220–55: (a) exterior, (b, c) interior to east and west, (d) tower vault.

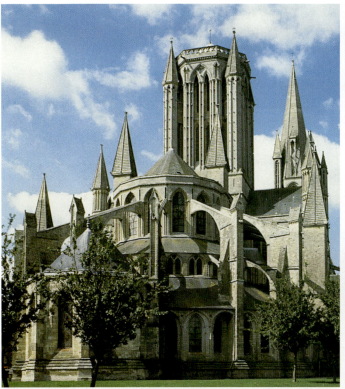

2.61a

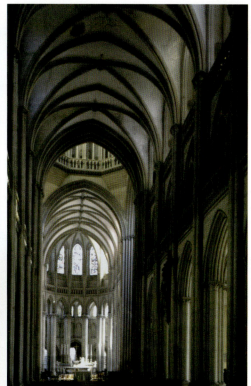

2.61b

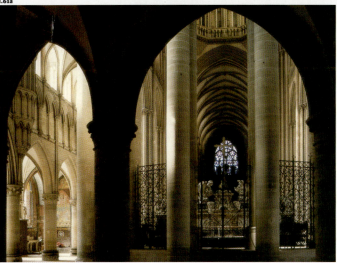

2.61c

2.61d

of slender shafts to circular or octagonal piers to support the ribs of the vault and soaring into the light with the aid of the free-flying buttress, were furthered at Soissons (c. 1210 to an earlier design) and Le Mans (c. 1217) respectively. At Soissons, proportions were lightened by the raising of the height of the aisle arcade relative to the already elevated clerestory, and at Le Mans the triforium was eliminated from the main volume in a two-storey scheme. The cage of autonomous flying buttresses enclosing the sanctuary there takes an essentially structural, yet formal, aesthetic to an apogee hardly approached since the days of high-Doric Classicism.**2.62**

›**2.62 LE MANS, CATHEDRAL OF S. JULIEN,** from c. 1217: chevet from the east.

The enlargement of the mid-12th-century transitional cathedral with a new choir and sanctuary to be built beyond the city walls was authorized in 1217. The work was completed in 1254. Through the astonishing cage of buttresses – heightened, bifurcated and multiplied beyond precedent – the projection of the chapels from the piers is revealed as even more assertive than at Chartres.

2.67a

2 EARLY GOTHIC ABROAD

The essentially structural, ultimately rational, Gothic style of the Île-de-France was imperfectly understood elsewhere – except where its emissaries were directly involved, as at Canterbury. In many permutations which are beyond us here, it was soon grafted on to the Romanesque legacy – or transformed in accordance with local traditions – throughout France and abroad, but it was certainly not to be the preserve of France alone.

BEYOND THE RHINE

In distinction from 'Romanesque', the term 'Gothic' was one of abuse associated in the minds of the south with Germanic barbarians. Not surprisingly, thus, while the Italians were long to make little of the style – other than a new cloak for their still early Christian forms – the Germans claimed it as their own. In fact, however, it gained ground overawed by Carolingians, Ottonians and Salians only slowly: largely derivative, it clothed forms sustained from the powerful Romanesque tradition for several generations.

2.67b

2.63a

›2.63 **EBERBACH, ABBEY,** founded 1135: (a) church nave (begun 1145), (b) chapter house (1186, vaulted 1345).

Foundation by monks from Clairvaux as a sister establishment predated the demise of S. Bernard: the austere basilica is archetypical. The chapter house vault, from the height of the Gothic era, is the earliest in western Germany to be expanded on a broad scale over stout central piers – except for those in the chapter house at Maulbronn (c. 1335).

As elsewhere, the Cistercians promoted their native Burgundian approach. Early works, such as Eberbach, sustained the round-arch tradition with great austerity.**2.63** However, well before the end of the 12th century they may be credited with introducing an integrated system of pointed arches – if not yet as the bones of a skeletal structure. At Maulbronn, for example, the abbey church recalled the pointed style of Autun in its unvaulted mass but as work progressed there in the 1220s a skeletal frame is sketched somewhat irrationally in the round-arched, rib-vaulted porch.**2.64**

›**2.64** **MAULBRONN, ABBEY CHURCH,** begun 1147, church consecrated 1178: view from the west.

The foundation is one of the earliest by the Cistercians in Germany. The rectangular sanctuary is framed by a transverse proscenium arch: the nave, in which monks and laity were separated by the surviving median rood screen, was vaulted in the 15th century. At the other end, the typically Cistercian porch has the earliest vaulting (early 13th century): an irregular transitional exercise, it is carried on arches springing from different levels.

2.63b

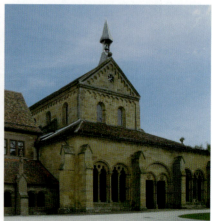

2.64

2.65b

2.65a

The pointed arch is first used consistently in conjunction with the rib vault in the magnificent cathedral which dominates the river at Limburg-an-der-Lahn (c. 1220). However, the massive structure and the external articulation are still Romanesque and the work may thus best be categorized as proto-Gothic, if more advanced towards French achievement of two generations earlier than the Cistercians had yet produced at Maulbronn.[2.65]

>2.65 LIMBURG-AN-DER-LAHN, CATHEDRAL OF S. GEORG, early 13th century: (a, b) exterior from north-west and detail of west front, (c, d) interior to east and detail of sanctuary, (e) plan, (f) exterior from south.

Doubtless emulating Laon and ultimately Tournai with its seven towers,[1.60] the forms are resolutely Rhenish Romanesque even to the point of acknowledging that style's Lombard antecedents – in the outside gallery to which the French flying buttresses are awkwardly abutted. Inside, the four-storey elevation recalls Tournai at least as much as Noyon.[2.46] The alternating rhythm, with major cruciform piers and minor rectangular ones, is characteristic of German Romanesque, but the sexpartite vaulting is supported by colonnettes rising from the base of the former and from corbels at gallery base level above the latter. Passages and recessed windows at each level assert the thickness of the wall in the Norman manner, but there is incomplete consistency in the rhythm of the gallery and triforium arcading.

2.65c

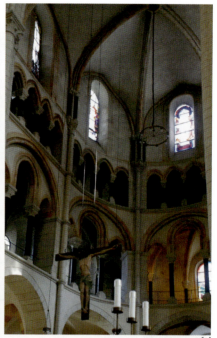

2.65d

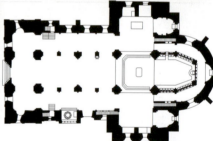

2.65e @ 1:1000

2.65f

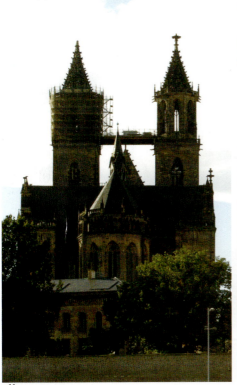

2.66a

2.66b

›2.66 MAGDEBURG CATHEDRAL: (a, b) apsidal east end, exterior and interior.

The new work was under way by c. 1210. Its patron, Archbishop Albrecht, was inspired by his first-hand experience of contemporary Parisian architecture but, not surprisingly, he was unable at first to find local masons capable of freeing themselves entirely from the weighty tradition of the great building they were commissioned to replace – even though the 10th-century foundations were rendered obsolete by revised orientation. The model for the polygonal apse, at least, was Laon but despite the applied shafts, it is the weight of the piers which prevails in the basic arcade and the groin-vaulted bays of the ambulatory beyond are still Romanesque.

Several stages further were reached over the first six decades of the century as work advanced from apse to nave in the rebuilding of the great Ottonian cathedral at Magdeburg which was destroyed by fire in 1207: from the outset and within three years of the catastrophe the pointed arch was used throughout the external articulation – though void is overwhelmed by mass at the east end except at the level of the parapet which recalls a Lombard gallery.**2.66** Solid and void are more equally matched in the west choir at Bamberg of c. 1230: progression to that pure early Gothic exercise from the Romanesque eastern choir, through the proto-Gothic nave, encapsulates the history of the advent of Gothic to the empire in the age of the Hohenstaufen.**2.67**

2.67c

2.67d

›**2.67 BAMBERG, CATHEDRAL OF S. PETER AND S. GEORG:** (a, b, page 299) north portal and 'Ritter', (c) exterior from north-west, (d) nave to east.

A double-choir basilican cathedral was consecrated in 1012, damaged by fire in 1081, and destroyed by fire in 1181. The new cathedral was begun in 1211 and consecrated in 1237. The expanded plan retained both the eastern and western choirs but twin towers were incorporated at both ends, the eastern ones rectilinear and relatively massive, the western ones with open arcaded turrets on each corner after the style of Laon. Otherwise the articulation is conservative, with round-headed windows, blind arcading and dwarf galleries in the manner derived from Lombardy.

›**2.68 COLOGNE, CHURCH OF S. GEREON:** (a) plan, (b, c) exterior and interior of decagon (c. 1220).

The Gothic decagon envelops the niched perimeter of the 4th-century ovoid rotunda which needed renovation and had been overshadowed by the addition of the sanctuary.

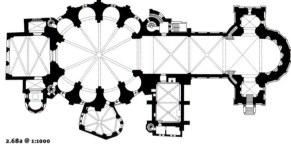

2.68a @ 1:1000

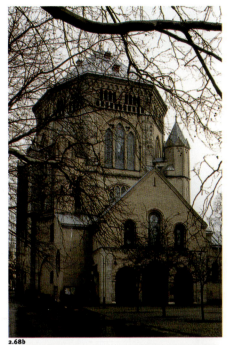

2.68b

2.68c

The evolution of Magdeburg cathedral is apparent in the inconsistency of its parts. Similar inconsistency marks the contemporary proto-Gothic work in Cologne on the elevation of S. Gereon's early Christian octagon, which had been overshadowed by Romanesque extension: there, however, the motive was antiquarian.[2.68] Similarly at Trier, a centralized Gothic structure was elevated over venerable foundations in a Romanesque context. In place of the earlier chapter house there, the self-contained new work, the Liebfrauenkirche, begun c. 1235, was juxtaposed to the old cathedral over a Greek-cross plan – extruded for the choir – with pairs of polygonal chapels in the quadrants. Despite the large tracts of blind wall which mask the roofs of these chapels in the lower zone of the tall clerestory, the building is essentially and consistently skeletal: the quadrant chapels buttress the arcades of the cross arms whose elevation does not require flying buttresses; in the absence of an ambulatory, stout piers rise from the ground to buttress the apsidal ends.[2.69, 1.52]

Contemporary with the Liebfrauenkirche, S. Elisabeth at Marburg is of clearer French derivation though, like the Trier work, it did not aspire to the height of its French contemporaries and, therefore, needed no elegant flying buttresses to supplement its relatively massive conventional ones. Around the polygonal sanctuary apse there is, in any case, no ambulatory to be bridged and the nave is of the Poitevan hall-church type with the aisle vaults countering

2.69a

2.69b

2.69c

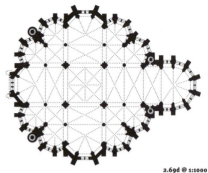

2.69d @ 1:1000

›**2.69** TRIER, LIEBFRAUENKIRCHE, after 1235: (a) general view with cathedral, (b) interior, (c) exterior from the south-west, (d) plan.

Replacing a dilapidated parish church developed from the Constantinian double cathedral (AIC1, page 696), the new structure dedicated to Our Lady was destined for the chapter. The near-square sanctuary of the old structure promoted a centralized solution under the influence of Champagne with which the see of Trier was contiguous: the specific model was the church of S. Yved at Blaine: the choir and transept of the latter, with paired chapels on the diagonals, were simply doubled (except for the apsidal extension of the sanctuary). Departures from the model include the reduction of the clerestory, elimination of the triforium passage and the subdivision of the apse windows with tracery derived from Reims.

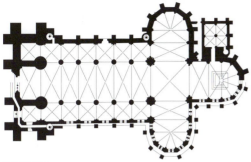

2.70a @ 1:1000

›2.70 MARBURG, S. ELISABETH, from 1235: (a) plan, (b) nave to sanctuary, (c) Visitation altar panel (late-14th century).

The westwork, with porch sandwiched between towers, revises a familiar German Romanesque formula. There are, too, important Rhenish precedents for the triconch plan of the east end and less prominent ones even for the hall-type of church but well-lit Noyon is more persuasively recalled by the former, Poitiers by the latter and pilgrimage doubtless informed Marburgers of both. The internal elevations of the triconch, with Reimsian window tracery, resemble the sanctuary apses of the contemporary Liebfrauenkirche at Trier. The two-storey system is sustained for the perimeter elevations.

S. Elisabeth is buried in the northern apsidal transept, her husband and his successors as the Count of Thuringia are entombed in the southern one.

2.70b

2.70c

much of the thrust from the nave – though the cylindrical piers with colonettes attached axially are nearer to Bourges or even Chartres than to the compound forms of half a century earlier in Poitiers cathedral. The transept ends echo the apsidal sanctuary, as in the great churches of Romanesque Cologne and as at Noyon – except for the absence of an ambulatory. However, here each lobe has a specific dedication: the central one to the main service, of course; the southern one to the enshrining of S. Elisabeth; the northern one to the accommodation of the tombs of the Counts of Thuringia into whose house the princely saint had married.**2.70**

2.71a

2.71b

OVER THE PYRENEES

Pilgrims and Cistercians first brought Gothic forms to Spain in the age of the reconquest: the new style then confronted the strength of the venerable native Romanesque, the old style of the first Christian kingdom of Asturias. The apogee of that style was the pilgrimage church at Santiago de Compostela and there the Portico de la Gloria, itself clearly related to the greatest of Burgundian achievements, was covered by a rib vault in the second half of the 12th century.

The replacement of the tunnel vault – requiring great mass in its support and, therefore, obviating clerestory light – was the way forward to the new style in the sanctuaries and naves of Normandy, the Île-de-France and the domains of the Angevins. The portico of Compostela is far more Norman than Gothic, though at the time of its construction inspiration might more readily have been drawn from the works of Angers or Poitiers at the head of one tributary to the pilgrimage route. Back beyond the infiltration of French influence from whatever region, however, Iberian Muslims had long delighted in the play of ribs in vaulting. Among the many Mudéjar works of the

›**2.71 ZAMORA CATHEDRAL,** founded 1152: (a, b) crossing dome, exterior and interior.

Characteristic of the Zamora region of north-west central Spain, the ribbed dome here achieves its apogee in the context of massive walls, proto-Gothic pointed arcades and domical ribbed vaults. The exterior, with its corner turrets, distantly recalls Montierneuf (page 190).

›**2.72 SALAMANCA, OLD CATHEDRAL,** founded c. 1150: (a) nave, (b) domed crossing tower c. 1200, (c) sacristy dome from within.

2.72b

2.72a

2.72c

proto-Gothic era, their ingenuity is sustained in the sacristy of the Old Cathedral at Salamanca: in contrast there, as at Zamora and Toro on the upper reaches of the Duero, the ribs of the crossing dome are radial.**2.71, 2.72**

The cathedrals of Zamora and Salamanca, founded in the 1150s, are traditional in their triapsidal plans and essentially Romanesque in their massing. Not without Mudéjar detail, their external articulation is also Romanesque,

2.73b

2.73c

2.73d

2.73e

2.73f

2.73a @ 1:1000

2.73g

indeed Poitevan in the turrets attached to their extraordinary domes. However, throughout their naves the rib vault was used consistently in conjunction with the pointed arch. The latter was the hallmark of Cistercian architecture in Iberia, as elsewhere: the supreme surviving example is Alcobaça in Portugal.**2.73**

›**2.73 ALCOBAÇA, ABBEY OF S. MARIA,** founded 1153: (a) plan with (1) church, (2), chapter house, (3) dormitory, (4) refectory, (5) cloister and fountain, (b) chapter house, (c) dormitory, (d) refectory, (e, f) cloister fountain, exterior and interior, (g–i) church exterior with flying buttresses, interior to east and detail of ambulatory.

The abbey was founded by the founder of the Portuguese monarchy, Alfonso I Henriques, in the year of the death of his relative S. Bernard of Clairvaux and in strict accordance with his principles. The original church was replaced from 1178 with greater aspiration furthered by flying buttresses attenuated in their proportions: nave and aisles soar to similar heights over closely aligned piers and the effect is not without Burgundian Cistercian austerity except in the Poitevan domical rib vaulting of the subsidiary spaces. A consecration, presumably of the choir, was recorded in 1223. A second consecration in 1252 doubtless marked the completion of the work.

The main elements of the monastic quarters were developed in the later 12th and 13th centuries with increasing concession to the essential lightness of Gothic – as elsewhere in the Cistercian world.

2.73i

2.73h

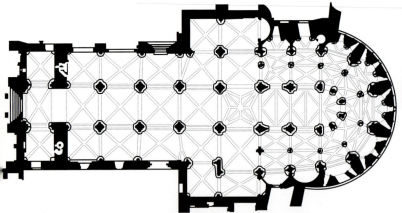

2.74a @ 1:1000

2.74c

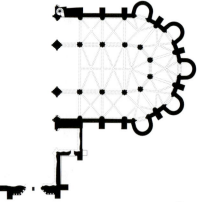

2.74b

>**2.74** ÁVILA, CATHEDRAL OF S. TERESA, c. 1180: (a) plan, (b) apse, (c) choir from the south transept.

The choir of Ávila was built over a double-ambulatory plan derived from S. Denis but the thickness of the wall is Burgundian. The retention of sexpartite vaulting over single-aisle bays involves splitting the gallery and clerestory while the diaphragm supports above the apices of the main arcade echo work in Burgundy – like the choir of Vézelay, though that may have been slightly later.

>**2.75** BURGOS, CATHEDRAL OF S. MARÍA, begun 1221: plan of original east end.

2.75 @ 1:1000

Beyond projecting transepts – prominent like those of Le Mans – the plan is an adaptation of the chevet of Bourges. The cylindrical piers with eight attached shafts and the design of the triforium derive from the same source but the vaulting is quadrapartite – as at Le Mans again – and there is only a single ambulatory. The building was heavily reworked in the 15th and 16th centuries.

>**2.76 TOLEDO, CATHEDRAL OF S. MARÍA,** 1227: (a) plan, (b) ambulatory, (c) detail of choir.

The choir was built from 1227 on a plan derived from Notre-Dame in Paris and Bourges: the contained transept of the former and the semicircular radial chapels of the latter, and the doubled aisles and ambulatory of both. The cylindrical piers with eight colonnettes recall Bourges, rather than Paris, but they are heavier and the arcading lower than in the model. The relatively straightforward sexpartite radial geometry of Bourges is rejected for a more complex, but incompletely rationalized, transition from the six columns of the inner apse, through ten intermediate supports to the fifteen radial chapels. Work continued on the nave and transept until the late-14th century.

Pointed arches and rib vaults were also of course major motifs of the Muslim tradition imported from North Africa into Spain and into Sicily from where it passed to Benedictine Cluny and Autun through Montecassino – as we have noted (see pages 102f and 160). As at Autun, the wall remained pervasive: thus, as at Angers, the pointed arch and the rib vault extruded from it were supported by dead weight. They were applied in a coherent Gothic context in Spain c. 1180 at Ávila – then the seat of Alfonso VIII (1157–1214).**2.74**

Thereafter, to celebrate their success, the Spanish *conquistadors* wholeheartedly espoused the prestigious French style – of Paris, Bourges and Chartres in particular – to supplant the Mudéjar legacy. It was manifest in their northern bases such as Burgos, at whose gate Alfonso VIII had established his Cistercian retreat and where, little more than a decade later, Ferdinand III founded a new cathedral on the plan of Chartres: the sanctuary was ready by 1230 but the huge complex was expanded and embellished over several centuries – as we shall see.**2.75** It reigned

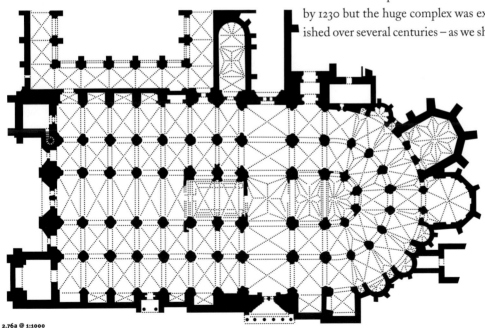

2.76a @ 1:1000

2.76b

2.76c

above all at Toledo, the seat of the archiepiscopal primate of Spain where their ascendancy had been sealed: the plan of the Parisian cathedral was adopted c. 1220 as the basis for asserting the superiority of an essentially Christian style; the Mudéjar subsists in subjection. **2.76**

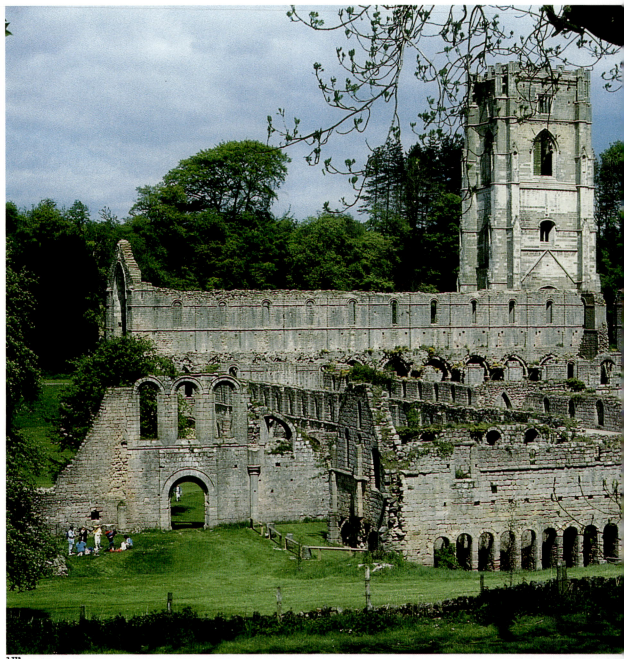

2.77a

2.77b

ACROSS THE CHANNEL

The ribbed vault had first been raised to the monumental scale of a great nave at Durham in northern England. It even appeared there in conjunction with spur arches over the aisles which, if not yet true flying buttresses, pointed the way to free-sailing lateral bracing.[1.174] That was at the very beginning of the 12th century and it was followed by

2.77c

2.77d

›2.77 CISTERCIANS IN THE NORTH: (a, b) Fountains Abbey (after 1135), general view and detail of nave elevation; (c, d) Rievaulx Abbey (from 1132), general view and detail of nave arcading; (e, f) Roche Abbey (founded 1147), general view and detail of transept vaulting; (g) Byland Abbey (from 1147), west front.

As elsewhere, the prime English Cistercian works are included here not with the implication that they are Gothic: they represent the peculiarly Burgundian austere transitional style – derived from the deployment of a system of pointed arches in a weighty Romanesque context – with which contemporary developments in the Île-de-France may readily be contrasted. On the other hand, the first Cistercian builders rejected the Anglo-Norman Romanesque, with its elaborate ornament, and paved the way for the elegant simplicity of early Gothic which was readily espoused by their successors.

At the outset, Fountains was lighter – in both senses – than Clairvaux because of the incorporation of a clerestory under a timber roof and its cylindrical piers are Anglo-Norman (so too, incidentally, was the central tower). Hardly more than a decade later, at Kirkstall, compound piers support rib vaults in the choir. A decade further on at Roche, the whole volume was vaulted over a three-storey elevation – incorporating a triforium and articulated with shafts rising from the ground – as in late French Romanesque works like the nave of Le Mans cathedral, though with the sense

2.77f

2.77e

of mural mass enhanced by the blind triforium and restricted clerestory. Yet another decade on and the builders of Byland erected screens of superimposed arches in bays defined by shafts in the Gothic manner but roofed the structure in timber: the latter, ignoring the significance of the French structural skeleton, betrays the motive of the former as decorative.

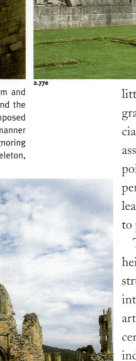

2.77g

little more than two generations of perfecting a fully integrated system of articulated structure. To this the Cistercians made a crucial contribution with the consistent assertion of the structural and aesthetic advantage of the pointed arch.**2.77** Thus it is not surprising that an independent school of Gothic developed in England and – not least when overlaid with whimsical decoration – it was also to prove seminal.

The French were obsessed with clarity, simplicity and height: logical, economical, they quickly realized the structural potential of counter-opposing forces in a fully integrated system of arches and the aesthetic advantage of articulating them to the annihilation of the wall. Though certainly not inimical to Norman rationalism in planning, indeed promoting consistently rectilinear lines, the English had other interests. They delighted in extensive scenographic vistas, projected along sustained horizontal lines through volumes of relatively modest elevation. They devoted their imagination to decorative relief which at once revealed and concealed the persistent weight of their perimeter walls – usually in counterpoint to the characteristically Norman passage revealing the depth of the mass at clerestory level in the typical basilican interior elevation.

The introduction of the ribbed vault, in the context of Romanesque mass rather than as integral to a system of interacting arches, was one major pointer to the Anglo-Gothic future. Blind arcading was another. Indeed, the delight of the English in pressing structural elements into decorative service, which has already been observed at Anglo-Saxon Earl's Barton,[1.169] ensured that their early Gothic style was literally skin deep.[2.78] Well before the 12th century was out, a Frenchman showed them how the synthesis of pointed arch, rib vault and flying buttress – all long familiar in England – had transformed building technology in his homeland but native sentiment and Norman substance long subsisted as the mental and physical context for Gothic building in the Plantagenet realm.

The choir and sanctuary of the great Romanesque cathedral built at Canterbury by Archbishops Lanfranc (1070–89) and Anselm (1093–1109) burnt down in 1174 – four years after the murder of Thomas à Becket, when a major pilgrimage cult was developing around his remains. The rebuilding to accommodate the martyr's shrine was entrusted to William of Sens – where the first complete Gothic cathedral was an object lesson of unrivalled significance. As much as possible of the old fabric was to be retained: this dictated the plan of the choir, but a shrine for Becket was projected further east, beyond a second transept, in an organic process which was to be characteristic of England but which contrasted sharply with the rationalism displayed at Sens.[2.79, 2.45]

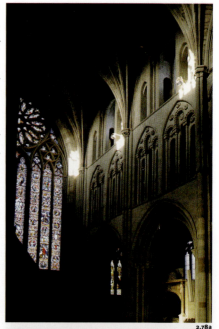

2.78a

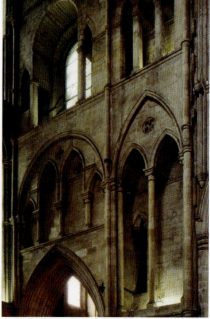

2.78b

›2.78 **TRANSITION FROM NORMAN TO GOTHIC IN ENGLAND:** (a) Worcester, cathedral of Christ and the Blessed Virgin Mary (from c. 1165), western bays of the nave; (b) Ripon, cathedral of S. Peter and S. Wilfred (c. 1175), detail of north-west nave bays.

A Norman cathedral was built at Worcester from 1084. The triforium and clerestory of the two most westerly bays mark the transition to Gothic: the wall shaft and rib vault were introduced, but the thick Norman wall still prevailed. In the north a similar and contemporary process, initiated at Byland Abbey, was followed at Ripon. Aisleless originally, the nave walls of the latter were deeply recessed within pointed arcading of an unstructural, decorative nature. The surviving elements in the western bays evidently echo the articulation of the lost nave of Byland.

Gothic in Engand: the primacy of Canterbury

The monk Gervase kept a record of work on the reconstruction of the choir at Canterbury. Beginning with the choir, the French architect had advanced a three-storey basilican elevation of the Sens type: it had been completed between the transepts before he fell from scaffolding in 1179. He transmitted Suger's inspiration to William the Englishman – whether directly or indirectly is not known – who completed the work of enshrining Becket in the Trinity Chapel by 1184.

Though eliminating compound piers, the Frenchman began the articulation of a skeletal system with the systematic relationship of shafts and ribs – of load and main support rising from the ground – but it was not consistently developed further east. One bay of quadripartite vaulting, before the radial system of the apse, is surrounded by a regular sequence of paired columns. Elsewhere the sexpartite vaults of Sens – and the Norman tradition in England – dictated doubled bays but, instead of the alternation of piers and twin columns as at Sens, cylindrical and octagonal columns succeed one another in the aisle arcades flanking the choir and Becket's Trinity Chapel.

Colonnettes are applied to the octagonal columns which mediate between the two pairs of doubled bays flanking the choir and three shafts rise over them to support the central branch of vault ribs. However, no colonnettes relieve the columns between the choir and the Trinity Chapel, though the transition from sexpartite to quadripartite vaulting did not

›2.79 **CANTERBURY, CATHEDRAL OF S. PETER,** from 1174: (a) plan with (1) nave, (2) choir, (3) Trinity Chapel, (4) corona, (b) interior of choir from the east towards the Trinity Chapel, (c) detail of crossing.

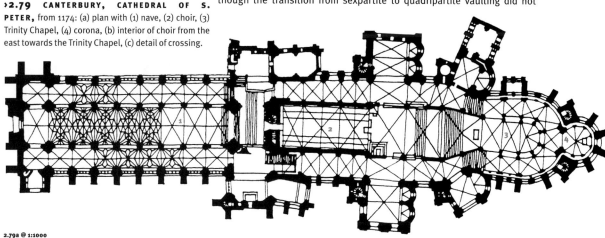

2.79a @ 1:1000

affect the number of ribs there, and single shafts rise through the chapel's triforium to support the ribs of quadripartite or radial vaults. In Becket's shrine marble columns, doubled as at Sens, rise to marble shafts from a marble floor.

2.79b

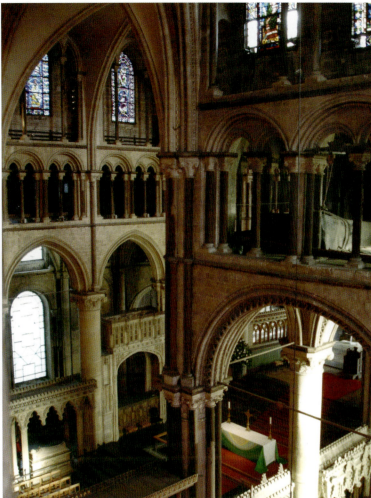

2.79c

Throughout, the insubstantial verticals are traced in black Purbeck marble over white Caen stone, doubtless in deference to English taste for the decorative, though the precedent is provided at Tournai, near Valenciennes, where William of Sens was working before being invited to England. At the instigation of the Englishman, presumably, the linear French system is countered with the Norman tradition of the thick wall revealed in the depth of the triforium and the recession of the clerestory windows – as in the great abbeys at Caen.[1.166]

2.80a

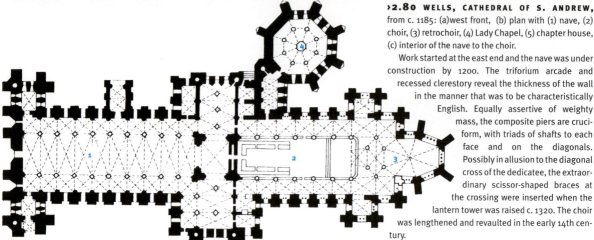

2.80b @ 1:1000

›2.80 WELLS, CATHEDRAL OF S. ANDREW, from c. 1185: (a)west front, (b) plan with (1) nave, (2) choir, (3) retrochoir, (4) Lady Chapel, (5) chapter house, (c) interior of the nave to the choir.

Work started at the east end and the nave was under construction by 1200. The triforium arcade and recessed clerestory reveal the thickness of the wall in the manner that was to be characteristically English. Equally assertive of weighty mass, the composite piers are cruciform, with triads of shafts to each face and on the diagonals. Possibly in allusion to the diagonal cross of the dedicatee, the extraordinary scissor-shaped braces at the crossing were inserted when the lantern tower was raised c. 1320. The choir was lengthened and revaulted in the early 14th century.

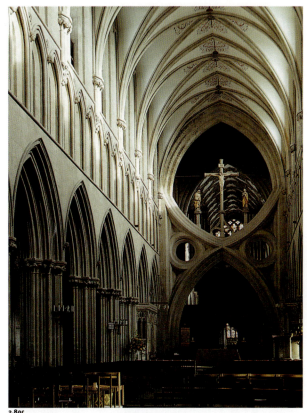

2.80c

>2.81 UFFINGTON, PARISH CHURCH OF S. MARY, 13th century: view into sanctuary.

2.81

The prestige of the work at Canterbury established Gothic in England and its synthesis between weighty mass and counter-opposed forces, the essence of the English style, was to endure in Normandy too. That was hardly surprising, but it even echoed through Flanders to Champagne and far-off Burgundy where the great Romanesque tradition inhibited the penetration of Gothic until the rebuilding of the choir at Vézelay in 1185. Yet, direct influence from Canterbury is hard to detect in the first major English cathedral constructed consistently in the new style.

The synthesis between weighty mass and counter-opposed force is first demonstrated on the scale of a complete cathedral at Wells. The thick Norman wall subsisted there but the counter-opposition of forces prevails. Though the rhythm of the triforium arcade changes from double to single beats between nave, transept and choir, an extended campaign of work kept persistent faith with the original conception of c. 1180. And horizontal continuity was then established as the hallmark of the English style: the aisle arcade marches to an insistently regular beat below a sustained stringcourse from which the shafts providing visual support for the vault rise through the triforium. On a double-transept plan, the internal scenographic vista is complemented by the juxtaposition of blocky volumes outside but squat towers hardly disturb the long, low silhouette. **2.80, 2.81**

In 1185 an earthquake dilapidated the Norman cathedral at Lincoln, except for the west front. That was to be retained, but a fresh start was made for rebuilding the rest within the remains. Constrained as at Canterbury by inherited mass and, therefore, not by the logic of skeletal structure, the result reveals the English attitude to the legacy of Sens. Rather than unified, as at Sens or at Notre-Dame, Paris, the plan is diversified in the English manner, with two transepts as at Canterbury and Wells. Much in the elevation conforms to precedent but, most significantly, as the skeletal frame was deployed for the articulation of structure – rather than as its armature – the architect was free to further the English fashion for the weaving of decorative patterns with its elements: introducing extra ribs of visual rather than structural significance – tiercerons – to the vaulting of S. Hugh's Choir, he pointed to the anti-architectonic way Gothic was to follow in the late Middle Ages.[2.82]

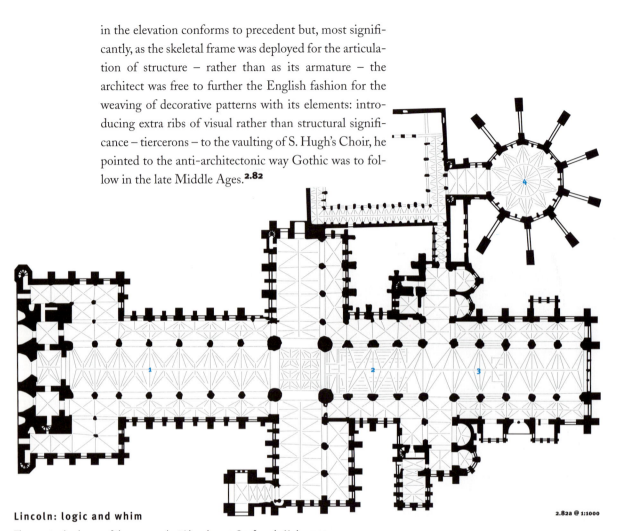

2.82a @ 1:1000

Lincoln: logic and whim

The master in charge of the new work at Lincoln was Geofrey de Noier, possibly of Norman descent but certainly well attuned to the English mode of design. He began with the eastern transepts and S. Hugh's Choir.

The choir recalls Canterbury in its three-storey elevation – standard in early Gothic England – and so does the use of Purbeck marble to enhance the relief provided by the shafts, but that was taken further than at Canterbury. The wall is still thick enough for a passage at clerestory level, screened with an arcade carried on bundles of shafts: unlike Canterbury

2.82b

›2.82 LINCOLN, CATHEDRAL OF S. MARY: (a) plan with (1) nave, (2) S. Hugh's Choir, (3) Angel Choir, (4) chapter house, (b) exterior from the south-west, (c, d) S. Hugh's Choir (from 1192), dado arcading and interior of the vault, (e) nave (from c. 1220), interior to the east, (f) chapter house (from c. 1220), interior.

A stunning decorative display of twenty ribs fans out from the central cone to frame the ten sides of the chapter house. The late-12th-century octagonal work at Worcester provides a precedent for the centralized alternative to the rectangular norm.

2.82c

or Wells, these rise from the spandrels. Unlike either Canterbury or its model, but as at Wells, the complex piers, with shafts to the diagonals as well as on the orthogonals, are repeated without alternation: they are not as massive as their predecessors but the span of the main arcade is among the widest in England. Flying buttresses were used to sustain this lighter structure but on a much smaller scale than in France as there was no aspiration to great height.

As usual in England, the triforium and recessed clerestory assert the depth of the wall. Further, the convention of the double-skin wall was given a purely decorative dimension in the syncopated superimposition of two strands of blind arcading below the windows of the choir aisles: the contrast between the Purbeck marble shafts of the front range and the stone of the inner range gives the illusion of greater depth.

Master Geofrey, presumably, was responsible above all for the incomparable vaulting. The earliest phase, in the east transept, is orthodox sexpartite except for its novel ridge rib. Thereafter, the irrational supervenes to revolutionary effect in S. Hugh's Choir: along the ridge rib, asserting

2.82d

horizontal continuity, are strung the bosses at which the diagonals should join; rather than crossing through a central boss to articulate structure, as in the quadripartite norm of the orthodox arcuate system, the diagonal ribs of each bay are disrupted, deflected to alternate bosses and tied to the opposite side by an interpolated third rib (hence tierceron) traced across the surface of a single membrane of vaulting.

In the vaulting of the nave, the ridge rib is sustained, but now there are five bosses per bay for the coordination of the lateral, diagonal and divergent tierceron ribs which all spring like fronds from the tripartite shaft clusters which rises from the spandrels of the main arcade. The confection is wholly symmetrical but quadripartite logic is obscured by the interpolation of the tiercerons and completely denied by the intervention of extra diagonal ribs which, meeting at detached bosses, are joined to the main system only through the agency of liernes.

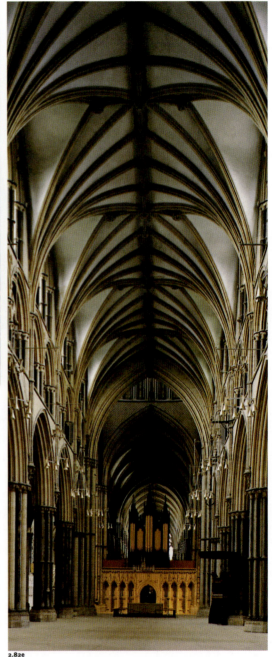

2.82e

2.82f

As we have seen, apart from the cross-ribbed domical vaults of Muslim Spain, taken over by the Christians, precedents for the multiplication of ribs in vaulting may be found in the works of the Angevins – with whom Plantagenet England was closely linked. The cathedral at Poitiers, for example, has ribs on the orthogonals as well as on the diagonals of each compartment, but as the vaulting is semidomical there is no horizontal continuity and each rib in fact articulates the conjunction of different membranes in a perfectly rational manner. Looking for reason in the bizarre asymmetry of the vault of S. Hugh's Choir is futile, especially as Lincoln's builders extracted the irrational tierceron from the heterodox arrangement and deployed it regularly in the longitudinal nave from the mid-1220s. The procedure was followed over the choir at Ely within a decade. Well before either of these works was complete, the full implications of the tierceron's regular deployment were realized in the fountain of ribs springing from the conical core of Lincoln's centralized chapter house: a dodeconal exercise of considerable complexity, unprecedented in France, this has been seen as the culmination of the first phase of English Gothic.

A screen of arcades was extruded from the Norman west front at Lincoln to accommodate statues. Bands of contiguous niches were conventional in England, as in France, but the small scale of the elements composing Lincoln's screen is at odds with the original mass as, of course, is the projection of the screen itself from the physical reality of the volume behind that mass. Peterborough's builders took the opposite approach and superimposed a screen of giant arches, unprecedented in their monumentality even by the portals of the Île-de-France, over the whole of the original Romanesque west end, diminutive towers included. The architects of Wells effected something of a synthesis between these two

2.83

approaches: their screen extends beyond the basilican volume to embrace towers but small-scale niches are superimposed in continuous bands throughout and the three
portals are insignificant compared with those of France –
or Peterborough.[2.83]

Lincoln exerted wide influence: it is first apparent c.
1224 in the ridge ribs of the vaults and the contrapuntal
arches of the triforium in the choir at Worcester;[2.84] a
decade later, even the extra diagonals and liernes are

>**2.83** **PETERBOROUGH, CATHEDRAL OF S.
PETER, S. PAUL AND S. ANDREW,** from 1195:
west front.

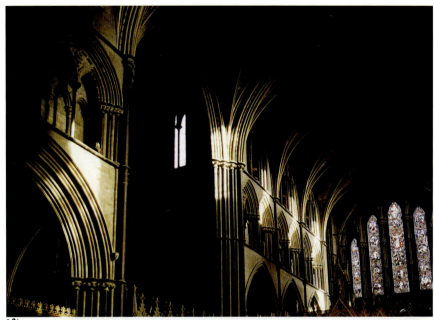

2.84

>**2.84 WORCESTER, CATHEDRAL OF CHRIST AND THE VIRGIN MARY**, from c. 1224: choir.

Fire damage to the Norman choir in 1202 prompted reconstruction, but the main incentive for the new work was the internment of King John in 1216.

>**2.85 SALISBURY, CATHEDRAL OF S. MARY**, from 1220: (a) exterior from the north-east, (b) plan with (1) nave; (2) choir, (3) Lady Chapel, (4) chapter house, (c) nave to east.

In 1219 Bishop Richard Poore obtained papal permission to abandon the inhospitable pre-Conquest site of Old Sarum and to construct a new cathedral on virgin ground by the river a little way to the south. The plan is long and complex with the crisp, rectilinear projection of the Lady Chapel beyond the sanctuary and two transepts: the former is typologically related to the Poitevan hall church, the latter follows Wells and Lincoln. The regular repetition of lancets brings the mechanical order of the plan to the multifaceted elevation. This is ameliorated by the splendid tower and spire (1320) which is, at c. 123 metres, the highest in England. The western façade (c. 1258) was inspired by the screen at Wells, but it lacks the crucial reinforcement of the towers there.

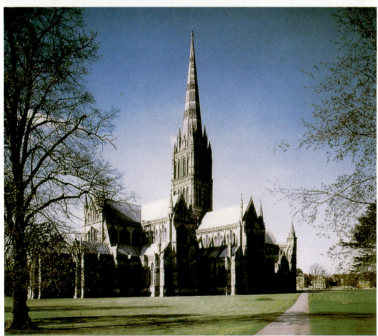

2.85a

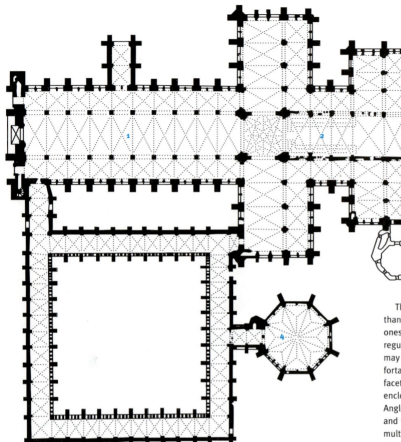

2.85b @ 1:1000

The internal articulation is generally less elaborate than Lincoln. The piers are derived from the mediate ones of William of Sens at Canterbury,[2.79] but they are regularly repeated in the English manner. The triforium may be seen to descend from Sens but it is an uncomfortable compromise with a gallery: the stilted multifaceted arch, which frames the paired blind arcades enclosing twin open ones in each bay, sustains the Anglo-Norman insistence on the thickness of the wall and the whole is greatly enriched by the insertion of multifoils in the spandrels at both levels. The clerestory too is deeply recessed and even more delicately screened with inner arcades carried on bundles of four slender shafts, as at Lincoln. As at Wells, horizontal continuity is undisturbed: above an assertive string-course, the triple shafts which articulate support for the ribs of the vault rise only from the outer arches of the triforium.

echoed in the vault of the eastward extension of the choir at Ely. Compared with Lincoln, however, the cathedral at Salisbury (begun 1220) was conservative especially in its mechanically rectilinear plan, repetitive lancets, quadripartite vaults, double-skin clerestory, triforium gallery and insistent Purbeck marble shafts reinforcing the horizontality of the three-storey elevation: however, its wholly coherent purity and elegance, achieved over an extended campaign in consistent faith with the original conception, are exceptional.[2.85]

2.85c

3 FRENCH 'RAYONNANT'

FROM REIMS TO BEAUVAIS: CHALLENGING PHYSICS

Well within the Capetian domain and its tributaries, Reims (1210) took the Chartres precedent to spectacular heights. Apart from the clear coordination of the exterior and interior elevations, there was a major innovation there: instead of the grouped windows of the Chartres clerestory, there were huge single ones subdivided by thin bands of masonry. The decorative potential of this 'bar tracery' was to prove enormous – not least in extension beyond fenestration. In the realization of the Gothic ecclesiastical ideal, however, the replacement of wall with tracery enhanced illumination of the divine manifest in the geometrical principles of planning drawn from the Augustinian canon of musical proportions adopted by S. Bernard: this, certainly, was not lost on Villard de Honnecourt, a contemporary architect who compiled a guide to design from personal knowledge of all the great cathedrals of the Île-de-France and dependent areas.[2.87]

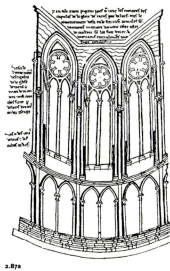

2.87a

2.87b

›ARCHITECTURE IN CONTEXT »REFRACTION OF LIGHT

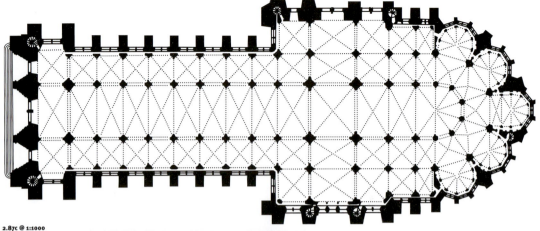

2.87c @ 1:1000

2.87d

Developments at Reims were soon acknowledged, notably at Tours, and furthered at Amiens (1220). Even higher and narrower, the main volume is the supreme masterpiece of High Gothic space. The triforium is glazed and continuous mullions unite it with the clerestory throughout, anticipating the final reduction of the internal elevation to two storeys later in the century. And at the crossing, the culmination of High Gothic is superseded as the revealed logic of structure cedes to the tierceron brought in from England.**2.88**

>**2.87 REIMS, CATHEDRAL OF NOTRE-DAME,** from 1210: (a) Villard de Honnecourt's drawing of tracery, (b) interior to the east, (c) plan, (d) view from south-east.

Begun in 1210, work was interrupted in 1223, taken up again 1241 and was still under way early in the 14th century. There seem to have been four architects, the first possibly being Jean d'Orbais, who based his choir on the new Gothic one of nearby S. Remi.**2.55** His partially articulated plan depends on the reduction of the doubled aisles of the Paris type to the basilican single norm, the reduction of the Chartres type of transept to one bay and the retraction of the radial chapels of the chevet to the zone of the outer ambulatory so that the general effect is one of compression rather than dynamic expansion.

The virile piers of Chartres are retained throughout except where the apse is ringed with unarticulated columns. The proportions of height to width (c. 38 by 14.5 metres) achieve a greater sense of aspiration for the nave than at Chartres and the aisle arcade is higher, relative to the clerestory. Mural mass is reduced to the minimum in the upper storeys but the Anglo-Norman layering of planes is recalled in the aisle elevations. In the apse the lines of the clerestory mullions continue down into the triforium, as they had done at S. Remi.

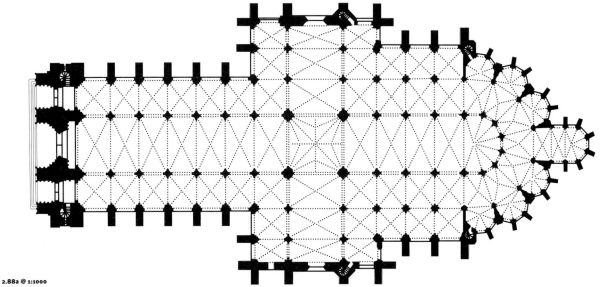

›**2.88 AMIENS, CATHEDRAL OF NOTRE-DAME,** from 1220: (a) plan, (b) west front, (c) nave to the east.

Amiens and the proliferation of tracery

At Amiens the more expansive plan formula of Chartres is retained in preference to the contraction of Reims. The nave (14.6 by 42.3 metres, a ratio of 1:3) was built first, under the master Robert de Luzarches, the choir from 1236 to 1269. The aisle arcade now rises through half the elevation and, hence, the piers appear lighter than those of Chartres, though they are of the same type. The twin lancets and single oculus of the clerestory at Reims are repeated, but subdivision reproduces the whole to a smaller scale within each lancet, further removing the system from its loadbearing origins. The outer roll moulding of the central mullion descends through the triforium where, instead of four arches differentiated only by a stouter column in the centre, each bay has a pair of arches framing a triple arcade and a trefoil. The introduction of the tierceron to the crossing is dated to 1260.

The clarity and uninhibited verticality of the interior contrast starkly with the west front: concordance between exterior and interior seems to have been the objective, as at Reims, but the great height of the whole and the parts made this difficult to achieve on the same terms. The multiple planes suggest weight, especially in the lower storey, but the superimposition of a filigree band of niches for statues of kings over a complex arcaded frieze obviates the repose of the Paris composition. The elevation

2.88b

2.88c

of the aisle arcades and the insertion of windows above the ambulatory chapels dictated the inner arches rising over the gabled portico, and the tall slenderness of the nave required the doubling of the triforium if the rose was to be set free of an arched window filling the clerestory; elevated and constricted in accordance with the dimensions of the nave, however, the rose in isolation seems too small.

2.89

2.90

›2.89 TROYES, CATHEDRAL OF S. PIERRE
AND S. PAUL: from nave to choir, rebuilt after 1227.

›2.90 STRASBOURG, CATHEDRAL OF
NOTRE-DAME, from c. 1240–75: nave.
  Strasbourg follows the formula of S. Denis and
Troyes but on Ottonian foundations, hence the greater
width of the main volume and proportions considerably less elevated than the French High Gothic ideal –
though not so low as to obviate flying buttresses. The
three storeys include a glazed triforium. The shafts of
the compound piers vary in thickness according to their
load.

›2.91 S. DENIS, ABBEY CHURCH: nave and
heightened sanctuary (1230s).
  Suger's plans for the rebuilding of the nave at S.

2.91

Denis, never realized, were superseded from 1231 by the master Pierre de Montreuil (referred to in this connection in a document of 1247) and at least two others, and the original Gothic chevet was transformed to match. The boundary of the new and the old may be detected in the west bays of the sanctuary where compound piers replace columns. Combined, triforium and clerestory were subtly differentiated: there are two skins to the triforium, the recessed one glazed, the forward one incorporating the clerestory mullions in a delicate arcade screening the wall passage. The transept façades have detached towers, linked at ground level.

›2.92 BEAUVAIS, CATHEDRAL OF S. PIERRE, from 1225: (a) exterior from the south-east, (b) interior.

Work began on the choir in 1225 and had reached the base of the triforium by 1240. It continued after 1247 to a revised design that was lighter in detail, if not in proportions: aspiration to great height was combined with will to consummate insubstantiality. The choir vaults collapsed in 1284 and were rebuilt over a revised clerestory and a reinforced nave arcade. This involved the insertion of intermediate piers, splitting the original arches into two at the expense of concordance with the aisle bays, and sexpartite vaulting. The transept and the adjacent bay of the nave were completed in the 16th century.

In plan the surviving choir and transept bay conform to the pattern established at Chartres and perfected at Amiens, and the ambulatory chapels project to much the same extent. The extreme lightness of elevation had been anticipated at S. Denis, the extreme height (48.2 metres compared with 42.3 metres at Amiens) furthered the tendency already exaggerated in the choir of the cathedral at S. Quentin (1220–57). The ambulatory rises above the vaults of the apsidal chapels but the clerestory is much taller still and its height is further enhanced by integration with the glazed triforium.

At Reims the three storeys of the internal elevation are expressed on the exterior: on piers to the height of the aisles, plinths to the height of the triforium and pinnacles to the height of the clerestory. Here the assimilation of triforium and clerestory is expressed in the continuity of the flying buttresses, extremely attenuated even before the superimposition of a second tier.

The extension of tracery from windows to walls and its convoluted elaboration either to hold glass or to relieve masonry are the distinguishing characteristics of the style known as 'Rayonnant' after the centripetal patterns of rose windows. Developed in surface detail rather than structure – linear and insubstantial, responding to the new lightness of structural form – the style was created by leaders of the new professional class of architects, above all Hugues Libergier (who worked in Reims), Robert de Luzarches (who began Amiens), and Jean de Chelles and Pierre Montreuil (who worked in Paris).

If not in the reconstruction of the upper storeys of the choir of Troyes cathedral after storm damage in 1227, the first major manifestation of the Rayonnant after its inception at Reims and Amiens was in the transformation of the abbey at S. Denis in the 1230s. Articulation, though linear and insubstantial, web-like rather than skeletal, is systematized with strict logic: columns with colonnettes cede to diamond-shaped compound piers with shafts all supporting ribs of the vault or facets of the aisle arcade and subtly graded in accordance with their structural significance; integration of clerestory and triforium was fully achieved. Aspiration to great height was renounced but at Beauvais the builders soon overreached themselves.**2.89–2.91**

At Beauvais, as at S. Denis, the linear network of tracery shafts contrasts with the still-vigorous main framework of articulation. However, the slender verticals of the tracery began to penetrate the dado below the windows of the north nave aisle in the Parisian cathedral and the device was used widely over the following decades to integrate the main storeys, as in the choirs at Sees and Troyes. From there it was taken to the peripheries of future France, notably Strasbourg and Metz. Beyond that, indeed, the cage-like fabric was to be characteristic of the last phase of Gothic architecture – especially in England.

2.92a

2.92b

CASKETS OF LIGHT

Meanwhile, the High Gothic ideal of the church as a casket of light, an empyrean of glass, had achieved its supreme
expression in the Sainte-Chapelle: a reliquary casket
amplified, it was built from 1243 in the Parisian royal palace
to enshrine the relics of the Passion acquired by S.
Louis.**2.94, 2.86** Related to the ambulatory chapels of
Amiens, but with jagged gables instead of horizontal
balustrades, the parapet profile of this ethereal work set the
pattern – first influencing the completion of the chevet at
Amiens. At the same time, the Cistercians and other
orders dedicated to austerity, like the Augustinians,
offered an alternative: the simplicity of form, purity of line
and sobriety of detail typical of their works from the days
of S. Bernard, are very well represented in the Augustinian priory chapel of S. Martin-aux-Bois.**2.93, 2.95–2.97**

›**2.93 AMIENS, CATHEDRAL OF NOTRE-
DAME,** 1236–69, chevet.

The ambulatory chapels, recalled in the exterior
elevation of the Sainte-Chapelle, were built between
1236 and 1245, but the clerestory was completed
from 1254 to a revised design that equally clearly
takes note of the royal chapel's achievement. Apart
from the filigree parapet of gables and pinnacles,
derived from Paris, the resplendent new style runs to
multiform buttresses with multiple finials and multi-
sectioned flying buttresses with intricate tracery con-
tradicting the radial lines of the voussoirs.

2.94a

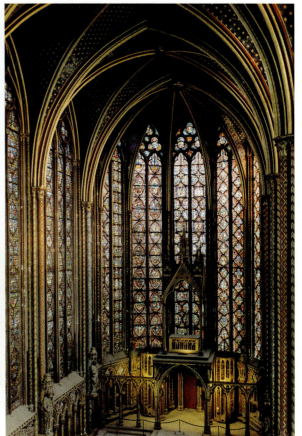

2.94b

›**2.94 PARIS, SAINTE-CHAPELLE,** 1242–48:
(a) exterior, (b, c) interior of upper and lower chapels.

The curtain of glass that forms the upper chapel, sustained by slender but assertive buttresses, is suspended over a substantial podium enclosing the crypt-like lower chapel. If constraint rules outside – at least below cornice level – inside, the physical realities of this world pale into insignificance.

The immediate precedent was the royal chapel of S. Germain-en-Laye (late-1230s). Of several distinguished followers, the most notable are S. Stephen's Chapel added c. 1290 to the Palace of Westminster, London, and the choir added to the cathedral in Aachen to enshrine the remains of Charlemagne between 1355 and 1414.

2.94c

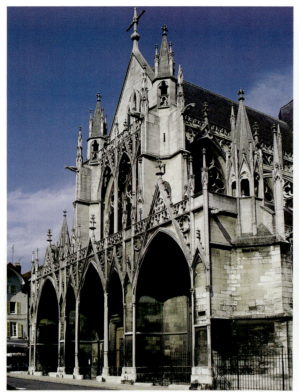
2.95a

2.95b

The glazing of the triforium in the Amiens chevet was the essential premise for its complete elimination. The example was set in the 1260s by S. Urbain, Troyes: the main arcade cedes to fenestration in the apse where it is distinguished from the clerestory only by a thin transom and a change of plane. The delicate screen of tracery there extends over plain surfaces elsewhere, and the façade is a many-planed confection of insubstantial elements repeated to varying scales.**2.95**

With mass masked by lace-like filigrees of tracery, the course was set for yet another evocation of the City of God in terms hardly less diaphanous than Byzantine mosaic. Inside and out, examples are many but the process of development may be traced most effectively

>**2.95 TROYES, S. URBAIN,** founded 1262: (a) west front, (b) choir.

A two-storey elevation of the old basilican type flanks nave and choir but in the apse the conjunction of the lower storey and clerestory simulates a complete curtain of glass – though the lower window is recessed beyond a screen of tracery. As already in England (in the cellars at Fountains), the arcades of the south portico rise from floor to apex unbroken by capital mouldings.

>**2.96 NARBONNE, CATHEDRAL OF S. JUST,** begun 1272, unfinished: (a) exterior, (b) interior.

The architect, Jean de Champs, emulated Amiens in height but preferred the austere simplicity promoted by the mendicant orders – even setting his windows in plain walling.

>**2.97 S. MARTIN-AUX-BOIS,** begun c. 1250: (a) exterior, (b) interior.

2.96b

2.96a

2.97b

2.97a

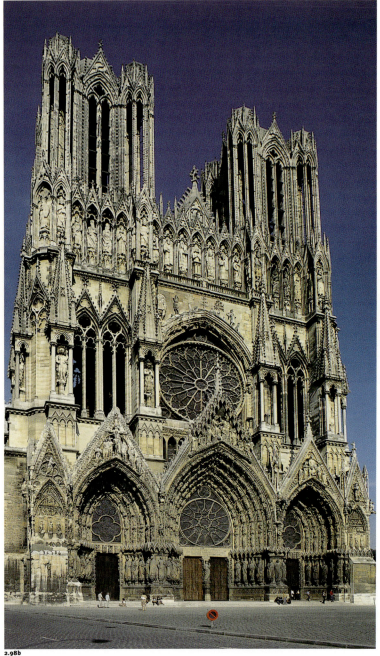

2.98a

›**2.98 REIMS:** (a) S. Niçaise, façade (1230s); (b) cathedral of Notre-Dame (after 1250), west front.

Reviewing the expression of the section on the façade – as most recently on the transepts of S. Denis – Hugues Libergier opted for freer, more open composition at S. Niçaise, relatively unconstrained by horizontal divisions: in particular, the portals, in a novel sequence of seven arch-and-gable canopies, are lower than usual, leaving a great vertical void to express the nave and smaller widows for the aisles. The arch-and gable-motif recurs on many funerary monuments, notably that of Libergier himself in the cathedral.

The concordance between exterior and interior, sustained across the transepts of the cathedral c. 1220, was masked on the west front by luxurious detail in later-13th-century remodelling which effaced the triforium to accommodate larger porticoes. Nevertheless, the clerestory window motif is carried into the towers and the central rose is knit into the great arch in which the clerestory culminates. The raising of the gallery of kings to fringe the top with its pinnacled niches removed one of the elements of restraint – at Paris, for instance[2.100] – and echoed the clerestory zone further to enhance the sense of vertical aspiration.

2.98b

2.99a

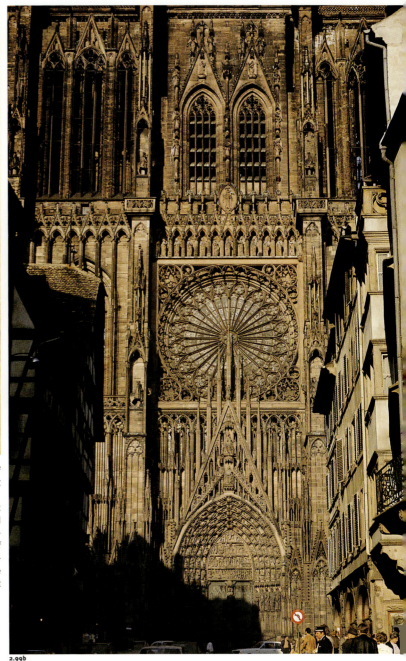

›**2.99 STRASBOURG, CATHEDRAL OF NOTRE-DAME, WEST FRONT:** (a) project drawing of c. 1277, (b) as completed after 1298.

Strasbourg's west front was designed c. 1277, but the screen of slender tracery shafts was incorporated after the work was interrupted by a fire in 1298: the layering of the tracery over both solid wall and the void of windows – over the whole, not merely the parts – represents the climax of the double-skin approach which we have traced at least from the clerestories of the great Norman ducal abbeys at Caen.[1.166]

2.99b

from the west front of Reims (c. 1250) to the west front of Strasbourg (c. 1275): already in the earlier work, the penetration of elements from one horizontal zone up into the next denied the stratification still so clearly asserted in the west front of Paris. In sharp contrast to the latter, moreover, the transept at Paris – which projects from the volume only in its upper zones – was transformed on the S. Denis model in the 1260s: the Rayonnant style triumphs in the intricate tracery of the rose, filling a complete square though only the circle is glazed, and in the repetition of essentially structural motifs to diminishing scale out of context, especially filigree gables flanked by pinnacles. **2.98–2.100**

›2.100 PARIS, CATHEDRAL OF NOTRE-DAME, c. 1163–95: view from the south-east.

On both façades (the north from c. 1240, the south from 1258) the four-storey internal elevation is reduced to three by the masters Jean de Chelles and Pierre de Montreuil: the portico corresponding to the outer aisles rises through the zone of the gallery over the inner aisle; the triforium continues in blind tracery into the gallery zone; the huge rose eclipses the clerestory.

In the decade before work began on the north transept front, the original nave buttresses were amplified and augmented where it was originally thought that the diaphragm arches of the sexpartite vault did not need them – the work was heavily restored in the 19th century by Viollet-le-Duc. Also in the 1230s, the east end was equipped with flying buttresses to match those of the nave when the clerestory windows were enlarged.

2.101a

2.101b

MENDICANTS AND THE SOUTH

While there was somewhat more weight of masonry in the Augustinian priory chapel of S. Martin-aux-Bois c. 1250 than the Gothic ideal, the interior was bathed in light from opalescent windows which were far from unusual in taking the place of stained glass by the mid-13th century.**2.74** Panels of masonry, fields for didactic painting, frame clerestory windows in many works of the later 13th century, especially those of the new mendicant orders whose vows of poverty entailed even more austerity than the Cistercians by then allowed. Moreover, the didactic Dominicans, the ministering Franciscans and their relatives dispensed with the hierarchical division of choir from nave, seeking to accommodate large congregations in utilitarian halls.

In the south of France, where the Albigensian crusade interrupted building and the Dominicans first set themselves against heresy, the hall church was a major Romanesque type and the mendicants adapted it to their purposes with or without internal columns. Toulouse has several splendid examples of the former. The masterpiece of the genre without columns is undoubtedly the militant brick cathedral at Albi. **2.201, 2.102**

2.102

›**2.101 ALBI, CATHEDRAL OF S. CÉCILE,** founded 1282: (a) exterior from the south-west, (b) interior.

Founded by the Dominican bishop Bernard de Castanet, head of the Inquisition in Languedoc, the fortress-like mass splayed at the base like a castle could hardly be bettered as a symbol of Dominican militancy in defence of the orthodox faith. The great hall of the nave is ringed by buttressing chapels to full height. Apart from the later choir screen, only the tracery in the relatively small windows betrays awareness of the Rayonnant.

›**2.102 TOULOUSE, CHURCH OF THE JACOBINS,** 1275–92: interior.

Built for a fraternity of Dominicans, the integrity of the great hall is not compromised by the division of nave from choir or the insertion of a transept, but bifurcation was entailed by the need for internal columns to support a brick vault at the height of 21 metres. Rather than filling the whole arch of each side bay, as in the Gothic ideal, the windows are again cut from wall.

›**2.103 BRUSSELS:** (a) cathedral of S. Michel and S. Gudula (mid-13th–late-15th centuries, west front completed 1490); (b) Notre-Dame-de-Sablon (mid-14th–mid-15th centuries), nave to sanctuary .

2.103a

2.103b

4 RAYONNANT ABROAD

As we have seen, the rational structuralism that led the builders of the Île-de-France to Chartres had been imperfectly understood and only intermittently imitated elsewhere – with the exception of England which developed its own approach. Backed by the prestige of S. Louis, the essentially non-structuralist Rayonnant, on the other hand, was an immediate success among France's continental neighbours, south-west and east. In the north, it was taken directly from Picardy to Cologne on the lower Rhine but was soon filtering through Flanders and the Netherlands.**2.103-2.105** Over the upper Rhine it passed from Strasbourg to Freiburg, east to Regensburg and beyond through Germany to the domains of the western Slavs. And, of course, it was carried to Spain along the pilgrimage route. This time the essential principles and spiritual essence of particular French models went too.

2.104

> **2.104 UTRECHT, CATHEDRAL OF S. MAARTEN,** begun 1254, completed 1520: general view from the south-west.

The nave collapsed from storm damage in 1674, leaving the great tower isolated.

> **2.105 S'HERTOGENBOSCH, CATHEDRAL OF S. JAN,** founded c. 1220, rebuilt from 1340, choir completed c. 1450: choir from south-east.

2.105

2.106a

2.106b

BEYOND THE RHINE

The great flowering of Gothic in the Empire and its free towns in the second half of the 13th century is at the heart of the German claim to the patrimony of the style – no less acute for flying in the face of the French. In fact, of course, emulation of the French is apparent at all the great sites in all the quarters of Germany: in addition to those which we have already visited, these range from from Freiburg in the Swabian south-west – where the style arrived from Strasbourg – to Regensburg (1275) in the Bavarian south-east, from Cologne in the Rhenish north-west to Halberstadt (c. 1260) in the Saxon north-east and, beyond Magdeburg, far north to Lübeck (1173–1335) – though floridity was somewhat inhibited in brick-building areas. And while the collapse of the Beau-

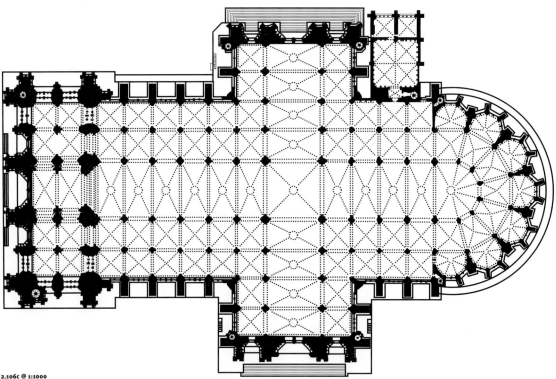

2.106c @ 1:1000

vais vaults may have checked the aspiration to record height of builders in the Île-de-France, it did not discourage emulation by their contemporaries elsewhere – Cologne above all. **2.106**

Unfinished, Cologne was seen to improve on its French model – indeed, to perfect the French High Gothic system which had failed at Beauvais. As a huge and highly complex entity it proved unsurpassable in the main though several of its facets were reflected in buildings throughout the many quasi-autonomous states of the decentralized Empire where, otherwise, much derived from the various native traditions. Ambulatories with radiating chapels – and the oversailing elegance of radial flying buttresses – are not usual in German-speaking domains and nor are grand tripartite western portals. Not

›2.106 COLOGNE, CATHEDRAL OF S. PETER AND S. MARIA, begun 1248: (a, b) general view and detail from south-east, (c) plan, (d) detail of gallery, (e) choir looking east.

Work began with the choir on the model of Amiens' chevet plan but with a regular sequence of radial chapels and double aisles projected throughout. It had reached the vault, 43 metres above the pavement, by 1304 and was dedicated in 1322. Meanwhile, work on the gigantic west front – projected to take the twin-towered formula with spires to its apogee – had begun in 1300 with the tripartite division corresponding to nave and doubled aisles and with the three storeys of the interior elevation imprinted on the towers. The south-west tower was begun c. 1355 and had reached c. 55 metres when construction stopped in 1410. Work on the south aisle of the nave had also begun in the mid-14th century but stopped in 1560. The completion of the cathedral was undertaken in the full flood of German Romantic nationalism between 1842 and 1880.

2.106d

2.106e

›ARCHITECTURE IN CONTEXT »REFRACTION OF LIGHT

unusual, on the contrary, is subsistence of the Romanesque double-choir plan and sustained reverence for the specifically imperial Romanesque gravitas drawn from the weight of monumental masonry inside and out: piers and buttresses tend to be bulky, tracts of plain wall are not uncommon in nave elevations, especially where the French would have had a triforium, and, while interiors may be rich in sculptured embellishment, exteriors are relatively austere.

Cologne is exceptional in general but not least in the majesty of the twin-spired west end with its multiple por-

>2.107 HALBERSTADT, CATHEDRAL OF S. STEPHANUS, founded 1220s, nave completed from c. 1260: (a) nave from west, (b) west front.

Halberstadt cathedral, like Ulm, well represents the many basilicas in which the venerable imperial tradition was transformed along French Gothic lines, but without the relief of a triforium the overall impression is of greater weight and simplicity. The pier design adopted for the westward extension of the early Gothic nave of Halberstadt follows the precedent set at Cologne.

2.107a

2.107b

tals. However, before the age of late-Gothic prolixity, Freiburg, Halberstadt and Magdeburg, at the western and eastern extremities of the imperial heartland, should also be cited – Freiburg for its innovative filigree tower, begun before 1280, and the last two for their assertive early 14th-century western portals, at least. The influence of Laon – which we have already observed in the central motif of the Limburg façade and the western towers of Bamberg – subsisted well into the 13th century but when the west front of Magdeburg was conceived the model was clearly Strasbourg.**2.107–2.109**

>**2.108 FREIBURG IM BREISGAU, MINSTER:** tower (begun 1250, spire after 1280).

The void-revealing filigree tracery of the spire, erected over the solid earlier tower, was inspired by the designs for the west front of Cologne cathedral, as yet unexecuted: its influence reached as far as Burgos in northern Spain.

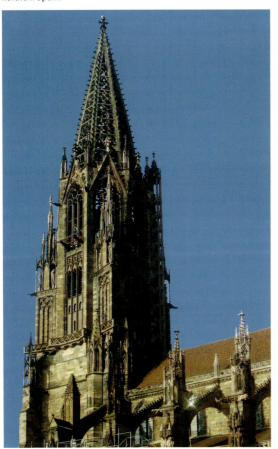

2.108

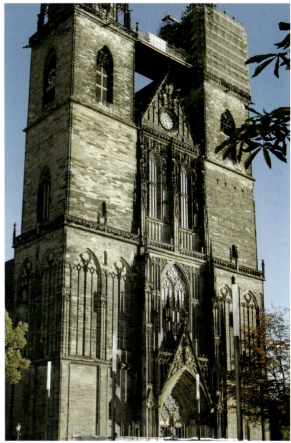

2.109a

2.109b

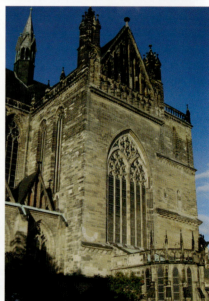

2.109c

2.109d

2.109e

2.110

As we have seen, Magdeburg's builder adopted a French plan with ambulatory as early as 1209 but Romanesque structural procedure was not entirely superseded until the 1260s when the apse clerestory was under construction. The contemporary nave is also typical of early German Gothic but after the mid-1270s there is minimal tracery in the clerestory lancets and Rayonnant elaboration in the great windows of the transepts where the lancet is lost to French expansiveness – though the ratio of solid to void in the façade composition as a whole is far from French, unlike the contemporary work at Regensburg (begun c. 1273). Half a century later Magdeburg was no longer behind the times: while the west front was being embellished in the filigree Strasbourgeois manner c. 1335, flying tracery vaulted over the so-called 'Tonsure' hemicycle which projects from the north cloister range.**2.109, 2.110**

As the phases of development from Romanesque to early Gothic may be monitored at Bamberg, so the transition from early Gothic to Rayonnant is clearly articulated as building progressed over the traditional twin-choir plan at Naumburg. The replacement of the Romanesque nave from c. 1210 – contemporary with the first phase of work

2.111a

2.111b

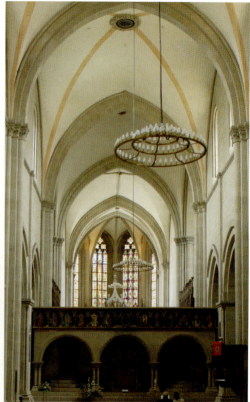

2.111c

at Magdeburg – is resolutely early Gothic. The west choir of c. 1250 marks the advent of proto-Rayonnant tracery in the manner of early Reims: the sculptural embellishment of its screen and choir stalls is exceptional but most celebrated are the statues of its founders which mark a key stage in the development of the north European humanist ideal. Finally, c. 1330, the polygonal apse of the eastern choir is semi-centralized on a boss displaced from the main transverse arch and it introduces an axial pier in the heterodox manner common in the last phase of Gothic in German-speaking lands. Meanwhile, triangulation and virtuoso elaboration of tracery are nowhere better represented than in mid-13th-century Erfurt.**2.111, 2.112**

2.111d

2.111e

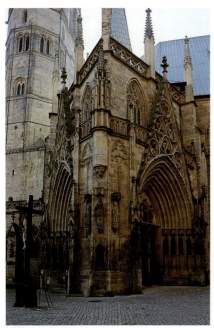

2.112a

2.112b

2.112c

›**2.112 ERFURT, CATHEDRAL OF S. MARIE,**
Romanesque basilica begun 1154, Gothic choir and
north porch from c. 1330, nave replaced in the mid-15th
century with aisles to comparable height: (a) north
porch, (b) view from the east, (c) chancel.

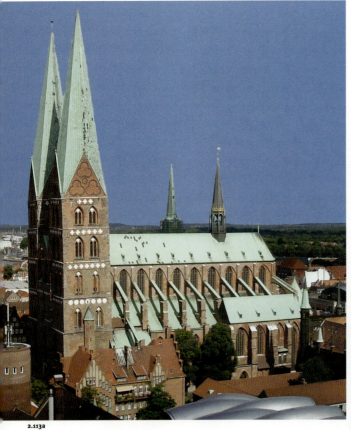

2.113a

2.113b

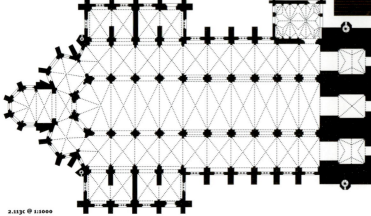

2.113c @ 1:1000

›2.113 LÜBECK, MARIENKIRCHE, 1277–1337:
(a) overview, (b) nave to chancel, (c) plan.

The aisles lead to an ambulatory composed of a series of polygons, pentagons (or truncated hexagons) at first, hexagons incorporating passage and chapel on the diagonals, and finally a pentagon expanded into a hexagon for the axial chapel. Between aisle arcade and clerestory is an unvaulted gallery passage in place of a triforium.

2.114a

2.114b

Of the regional styles, most distinctive are those developed in the context of a brick vernacular – especially in
the Hanseatic north. The material typically prompts un-
Gallic bulk in the mass, especially of towers, but the greatest works in the rich trading cities of the Baltic periphery
may be French in plan and cede little to the French in clarity of form. The prime inspiration for the latter was the
Lübeck Marienkirche, built from 1277 in rendered brick
with limestone detailing especially in fenestration
expanded well beyond the early Gothic lancet.[2.113] The
cathedral in the same city, founded a century earlier, is
naturally weightier and darker. The influence of the former may be traced – with diminishing returns – from the
Marienkirche of Stralsund c. 1384 at least as far as S. Peter
in Riga early in the 15th century. S. James in the latter city
is typical of the earlier mode and even as late as 1343 the
nave of S. Maria's church at Gdańsk is lit mainly through
lancet-like windows.[2.114, 2.115]

2.115

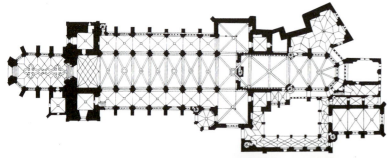

2.116a @ 1:1000

2.116b

›2.117 HEILIGENKREUZ, a hall-type chancel replaced a late Romanesque structure c. 1280–95: (a) chancel, (b) plan.

›2.118 VIENNA, CATHEDRAL OF S. STEPHAN, Romanesque foundation rebuilt from the mid-13th century, choir c. 1310–40, nave built again from 1359: (a) nave from the west, (b) sanctuary from crossing.

2.117a

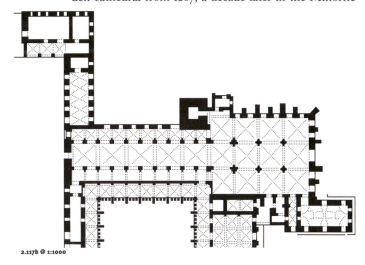

2.117b @ 1:1000

The lands of the Empire and the parts of east-central Europe to which Christianity was extended from Saxony are particularly rich in transeptless hall churches – in which, as we have seen, the high elevations and flying buttresses so characteristic of the French style were obviated. Though Poitevan in precedent, the type might indeed pass as national despite its wide promotion by the international mendicant orders to meet their didactic purposes in consolidating that expansion of the faith.

Not for mendicants alone, two alternative approaches were developed to varying degrees in German-speaking lands as the 13th century progressed: a wide nave, flanked by a pair of relatively narrow aisles beyond thick piers, assertive of the east–west axis in the traditional way except for the height of the aisles; lateral expansion into wide side bays defined by relatively slender piers, countering traditional longitudinal orientation. Following the sober example of S. Elisabeth at Marburg,[2.70] the former is well represented by Halle and Meissen cathedrals (begun c. 1280 and c. 1290 respectively).[2.116] The expansive mode, ambivalent of axis, is represented with three aisles at Minden cathedral from 1267, a decade later in the Minorite

2.118a

›ARCHITECTURE IN CONTEXT »REFRACTION OF LIGHT

2.118b

church at Soest and the choir at Verden an der Aller, or twenty years later in the nine-square choir of Cistercian Heiligenkreuz (from 1288).[2.117] S. Severus at Erfurt (under construction c. 1280) has five aisles but there is no grander representative of the type than the Viennese cathedral of S. Stephan as expanded in the 14th century.[2.118]

2.119a

2.119b

OVER THE PYRENEES

The great Romanesque tradition in Spain had given way to imported French forms in the early 13th century and the greatest age of Spanish Gothic cathedral building was to advance with the consolidation of the centralized monarchy in the 15th century. Two-hundred years earlier full comprehension of the French High Gothic achievement and its Rayonnant permutation is apparent in the

›**2.119** LEON, CATHEDRAL OF S. MARÍA, c. 1258–1303: (a, b) exterior from south-east and west front, (c, d) details of south and west portals, (e) interior at crossing.

The models for this most completely French of Spanish cathedrals were Reims for the plan (especially the chevet) and S. Denis for the fenestration and the façade with detached towers; the piers are those of Reims but with the shaft clusters rising to the vault from the ground, as at S. Denis.

continued work on the cathedral of Toledo (initiated in 1227), in extensions to the cathedral at Burgos and, above all, in the new cathedral at Leon.**2.119**

The adoption of the French Rayonnant architectural model for Leon responded to the ambitions of Alfonso X (1253–84) to replicate the French model of the centralized state: failure of the latter countered the prestige of the former. Elsewhere in the central Christian kingdom,

2.120a

2.120b

2.120c

›2.120 TOLEDO: (a) S. María la Blanca (a synagogue of c. 1250 converted for Christianity in 1405),
interior detail; (b) S. Roman (1221) interior detail; (c) El
Tránsito synagogue (1366).

A North African and Cordoban mosque building type
derived from the basilica, with a pair of aisles either
side of a wider nave, is the origin of both S. María la
Blanca and S. Roman. The incurved arch, characteristic
of the Moorish style and its Mozarabic derivative,
descends from the earliest phase of Abbasid architecture – mid-8th century at least (AIC3, pages 7off). The
basilican model was irrelevant to Jewish practice in
which full exposure to the Torah wall is of prime importance.

Romanesque planning was not to be forgotten and nor was
Mudéjar intricacy in weaving patterns from structural
motifs in and out of context: apart from the mid-13th-
century synagogue, later converted to the church of S.
María la Blanca, and the mid-14th-century work known
as El Tránsito in Toledo, prominent Castillian examples
include the early 13th-century churches of S. Roman or
Santiago de Arrabal and the Puerta del Sol in the same city,
the chapels of the Asssumption and Santiago at Las Huel-
gas near Burgos and the several spaces inherited by the
convent of S. Clara from the palace of Pedro the Cruel at
Tordesillas.**2.120, 2.121**

With economic instability partly due to the rebellion
of the magnates against Alfonso X, partly to the cost of

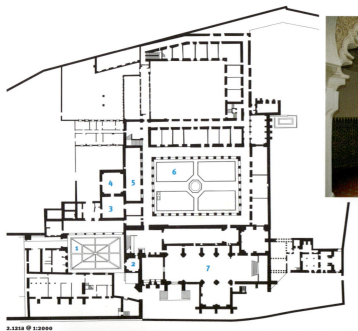

2.121a @ 1:2000

2.121b

›2.121 **TORDESILLAS, CONVENT OF S. CLARA**, founded 1363 in a palace of c. 1340: (a) plan with outer court (1), palace portal and vestibule (2), inner patio of S. Pedro (3), antichamber or oratory adapted as the Capilla Dorada (4), late-16th-century refectory (5), 17th-century cloister (6), chapel developed over several generations from 1373 (7), (b) inner patio, (c) Capilla Dorada, (d) palace portal, (e) presbytery ceiling.

The palace built by Alfonso XI (1311–50) was ceded by Pedro the Cruel (1350–69) to his daughter as a retreat for the Poor Clares: several important elements of the palace were retained for the convent, including the portal and vestibule, inner patio and antechamber. Outshining even these – and the Gothic work in the church – is the extraordinary artesonado ceiling of the presbytery attributed to Master Diego Lopez Arenas and dated to c. 1450.

2.121c

2.121d

2.121e

2.122a

obsession with reconquest, building flagged in northern Spain in the last quarter of the 13th century and was not fully revived until the 1390s – as we shall see. In Andalucía, meanwhile, the Muslim seat at Seville had fallen to the Christians in the middle of the 13th century but there and elsewhere the conversion of mosques served the provisional purposes of the church until the beginning of the 15th century – as we shall also see in due course.

As the 13th century progressed, the most dynamic area was Aragón, especially Catalonia, where the mendicants were responsible for a formidable chain of works descending from Albi to Barcelona, Gerona and on out

>**2.122 BARCELONA:** (a) cathedral of S. Eulalia (La Seu), choir interior (1298–1329) from the nave (vaulted by 1420); (b, c) S. María del Mar (1328–83), plan and interior to the east.

Strongly influenced by the southern French approach, like Albi in particular in perimeter plan, the scheme of Barcelona cathedral hovers ambiguously between basilica and hall church due to the interpolation of an aisle arcade rising beyond the springing of the vaults to blind arcading below a restricted clerestory. Beyond the aisle, a continuous circuit of chapels is formed by the spur walls which provide internal buttresses. Lit through tall windows above the ambulatory chapels and a clerestory, the choir seems disparate from the nave, which is lit only from the clerestory. Square with quadripartite vaults, the nave bays are exceptionally wide (14 metres).

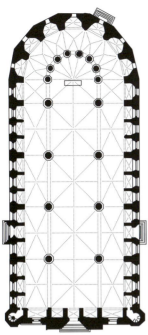

2.12b @ 1:1000

A revision of the cathedral scheme, avoiding the disparity between nave and choir, the main internal elevation of S. María del Mar is reduced to a single arcade and clerestory. The intercolumniations are narrowed around the apse and simple octagonal columns replace the complex piers of the cathedral. There are windows in and above the chapels throughout. Beyond the spur wall buttresses which frame the chapels the perimeter wall is unbroken even by a transept.

›2.123 GERONA, CATHEDRAL, 1312–1598: interior.

With a high aisle arcade and two-tiered clerestory (the lower one in place of a triforium but without passage), the choir recalls that of Narbonne cathedral (begun 1272) but its basilican form is cut short by a diaphragm wall to the west of which is the huge hall of the Albi-like nave. Begun in 1417, but not finished until the late 16th century, at c. 23 metres wide and c. 24 metres high, this overawes the choir.

2.122C

to Palma de Mallorca. Though occasionally masked with extraneous detail borrowed from the north, volumes were monumental in their interpretation of one or other of the hall-church types. The first such work of note in Barcelona is the Dominican church of S. Catalina of c. 1200. The grandest permutation is the Barcelona cathedral, founded in 1298. The latest example, the sailors' parish church of S. María del Mar, takes us well into the 14th century when radical developments were already underway as the outcome of England's particular permutation of Rayonnant. **2.122, 2.123**

2.123

›ARCHITECTURE IN CONTEXT »REFRACTION OF LIGHT

›2.124 CANTERBURY, CATHEDRAL OF S. PETER, 12th–15th centuries: exterior from the north-west.

The Norman nave which survived the intervention of the Gothic architects late in the 12th century was replaced from 1379. The south-west Norman tower was remodelled c. 1430, the north-western one was made to match four centuries later. The central tower (c. 72 metres), called Bell Harry, was begun in 1433 but not completed until c. 1500: the final form seems to have been established c. 1494 by the master mason John Wastell.

ACROSS THE CHANNEL: THE ENGLISH DECORATED STYLE

The light, elegant, aspiring, dissolving forms of Rayonnant respond to diffused light: though Spaniards and other southern builders were to be seduced by them, they are very northern in stark contrast to the crisp, clear-cut rational forms of the Mediterranean littoral – the ancient Greek Doric for supreme example. Nowhere is this more apparent than in misty England with its sustained tradition of organic planning, diversified massing and ingenious dissolution of structural forms.**2.124**

In England, in an era of new wealth generated primarily by the wool trade, the High Gothic Rayonnant style is uniquely identified as 'Decorated'. As its name implies, it depended upon painted and sculptural embellishment, primarily of iconographic significance, of course, but often also whimsical. However, its unique distinction derives from the native realization of the decorative potential of tracery. The immediate effect was decorative and had its secular appeal but, at its highest, the motive was ethereal: to evoke a supraphysical environment for the multitude of intercessionary saints – the Virgin Mary above all – whose images populated the grand refurbishment or extension of cathedrals and abbeys and the more modest additions to an unrivalled corpus of parish churches. Most of the images fell to successive waves of Protestant reform: many of their environments survive.**2.125–2.127**

>**2.125 THORNHAM PARVA, S. MARY'S CHURCH:** central panels of retable (c. 1330).

>**2.126 WINCHESTER CATHEDRAL:** altar screen (c. 1480, Protestant mutilation repaired in the 19th century).

2.126

2.127

>**2.127 DORCHESTER ABBEY,** Jesse window detail.

2.128a

›2.128 LONDON, WESTMINSTER ABBEY,
from 1245: (a) pilgrims at S. Edward's shrine (13th-
century ms illumination; Cambridge University
Library); (b) north transept front, (c) nave to choir,
(d) choir from crossing, (e) detail of crossing, (f) plan.

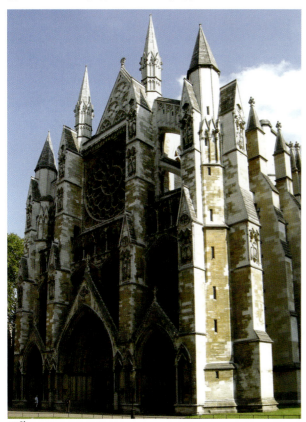

2.128b

The first major promotion of 'Decorated' architecture was at Westminster: there the venerable foundation of S. Edward the Confessor, the coronation church of English kings, was rebuilt from 1245 for Henry III: he intended it for his interment in the enhanced aura of the founder's shrine and lent it immense further prestige with the endowment of a phial of the Holy Blood in 1247. Superseding a scheme for a Lady Chapel – the most important adjunct to the great churches of the age – the comprehensive new work at Westminster is attributed to Henry of Reynes, who is not uncontroversially identified with Reims. Be that as it may, the king could retain international talent, unlike most episcopal patrons of the insular early English style.

The king's new church was French, at least in principle, in its ambulatory plan and its tall, slender interior elevation with shafts rising from ground level through an elongated clerestory unrelieved by a wall passage. Specifically, the crucial advance from wall to window, from lancets to tracery subdividing most of the void within the external arches, follow the seminal work on the great churches at Reims and S. Denis – respectively dedicated to the coronation and burial of French kings. After the advent of the Holy Blood, moreover, the reliquary nature of the exercise also prompted emulation of the Sainte-Chapelle currently under construction in Paris to enshrine Louis IX's fragments of the True Cross and Crown of Thorns in intricate splendour. Yet, contrary to French logic, a ridge rib is joined by tiercerons in the nave and a gallery subsists where Reims has a triforium. Avoiding the consistency of the French High Gothic, moreover, the builder promoted lavish surface ornament – in addition to the host of high-relief icons which emulate those of S. Louis's reliquary – and stressed detail, most obviously in picking out colonnettes in different coloured stone like his predecessor at Salisbury.**2.128**

Henry III began a new Lady Chapel in 1220. It was roofed in 1234 but was superseded by the total rebuilding of Edward the Confessor's church within a decade. An equilateral triangle, based on the aisled transept, projects into the sanctuary where the head of S. Edward in his sarcophagus was located at its apex. An ambulatory, unusual by its date in England, is described from that point, but the retention of the new Lady Chapel slightly distorted the alignment of the radial chapels. The columns of polished marble are English, as is the ridge rib and, in general, the richness of texture – in particular the diaper pattern on the spandrels of choir and transept. The incorporation of tiercerons in the nave vaulting furthers the process of enrichment begun at Lincoln. Flying buttresses obviate thick walls at the expense of the English wall passage, as in the French Gothic ideal, though they are not revealed to dramatic effect. Tracery seems to have been introduced via Binham Priory, Norfolk (c. 1240).

Among the abbey's many monuments, the influential canopy tomb of Edmund Crouchback, Earl of Lancaster (c. 1297), is visible lower left. England was at the forefront of canopy tomb design: Edward I commissioned this one for his younger brother from the principal royal architect, Michael of Canterbury.

2.128c

2.128d

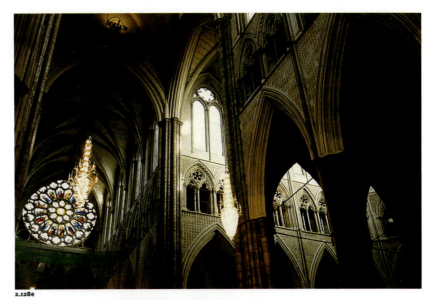

2.128e

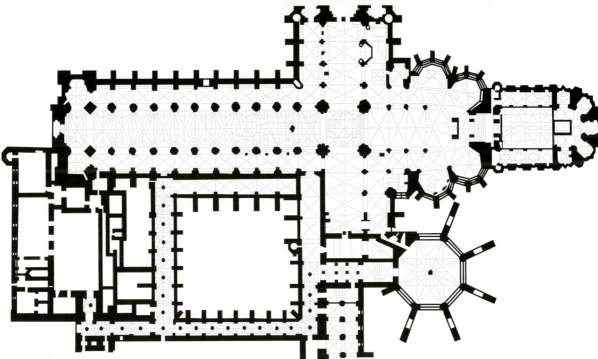

2.128f @ 1:1000

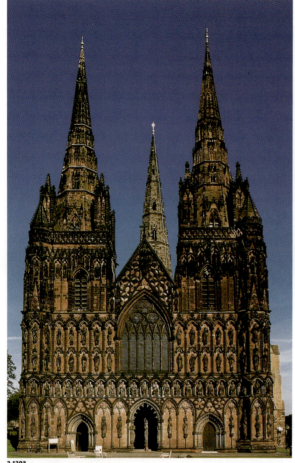

2.129a

2.129b

›**2.129 LICHFIELD, CATHEDRAL OF S. CHAD AND S. MARY,** begun c. 1200, substantial rebuilding from c. 1260: (a) exterior (c. 1300, restored in the 19th century), (b) nave to choir (nave from c. 1260, choir of c. 1220 extended early in the 14th century to the Lady Chapel, begun 1320).

›**2.130 LINCOLN, CATHEDRAL OF S. MARY, ANGEL CHOIR,** begun 1256: interior.

The choir extension conceived to enshrine the tomb of S. Hugh of Avalon (bishop of Lincoln from 1186 to 1200 and patron of the rebuilding of the cathedral after the catastrophe of 1185), follows Westminster but in the development of themes first stated in work undertaken at Lincoln itself – the anti-architectonic use of the tierceron and the wide intercolumniation in particular. Contrary to the French form of Westminster, moreover, the English rectangular plan is retained and the thickness of the wall is reasserted with passages at the level of the clerestory, behind an elegant screen of tracery, as well as the deeply recessed triforium. The tracery follows Westminster but it ultimately derives from Amiens.**2.88, 2.93** The name comes from the angels in the spandrels of the triforium arcade: these also follow Westminster (where angels embellish the transepts) but ultimately they derive from the Sainte-Chapelle in Paris.**2.94**

The influence of Westminster may be traced in particular details of widely dispersed buildings: in Lichfield cathedral, for instance, the shafts expressing support for the vault rise through the entire elevation and the clerestory has no passage.**2.129** In general, however, the spinning of webs of structure-concealing decoration was the principal preoccupation of later 13th-century English architects. The ribs of vaults were the prime elements to hand but the introduction of Rayonnant tracery led to coordination in the treatment of ceiling, window and

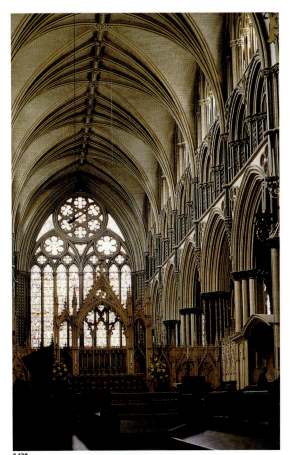

2.130

residual wall. The objective was approached at Lincoln in the late-1250s, when the richly embellished Angel Choir was projected with free-standing tracery inboard of the clerestory passage.**2.130** It was elusive when work began on the nave of Westminster at the end of Henry III's reign and still c. 1310 when England's most assertive tiercerons were arrayed over the nave of Exeter cathedral: as Rayonnant proceeded by multiplication, so the ribs of the vault were multiplied but the main fields of tracery in the clerestory, recessed beyond an unscreened passage though surmounting a screened triforium, were obscured by the extra ribs and there was no organic relationship between them.**2.131**

›2.131 EXETER, CATHEDRAL OF S. PETER, c. 1280: interior of the choir to nave.

The nave was finished c. 1300 and from then most of the choir was rebuilt (until c. 1335). The two transepts, rectangular sanctuary and definitive three-storey elevation conform to English practice. So too does the double-wall structure, the depth of which is asserted by the triforium and clerestory passages, the mass by the accumulation of shafts on the diamond-shaped piers. The palm-like ribs of the vaulting (eleven rather than seven as at Lincoln) rise at the base of the clerestory from shafts stemming from corbels in the spandrels of the aisle arcade. The east and west windows – the latter with rose (background) – fill the whole void in the structural section. The influential bishop's throne (left) was executed in bravura carpentry c. 1313.

2.131

At the east end of the Angel Choir the vault was juxtaposed with a huge window in which lancets and oculii, conjoined as at Westminster after the pattern of Reims, were multiplied and enlarged in the manner typical of Rayonnant France but on a scale unrealizable in the context of the French chevet. In Exeter's west front (complicated by the retention of the Early English façade screen) the oculus has been amplified into a veritable rose over the tracery lancets. Thereafter, the window reigned supreme as the main field of decorative invention in England. And from the coincidence of the arcs of arch and oculus holding the glass, the English extracted a new tracery motif: the ogee which was crucial in the weaving of unconstrained webs.

Departing from the contrapuntal blind arcading along the aisles at Lincoln and leading to the scalloped niches of Bristol, the cusped arch was the prime ingredient of the 'Decorated' style. Cusping is, of course, not uncommon – the Christians doubtless borrowed it from the Muslims – nor is it necessarily anti-structural – as it may be seen to derive from corbelling – but it is hard to reconcile it with the voussoir upon which Gothic structure actually depended. Beyond that, the motif of the ogee arch is a further elaboration essential to the style.

Extrapolated from a framework of support, but essentially non-structural itself, the ogee motif first appears in England in low-relief on the bases of several crosses erected to mark the resting places of the coffin of Queen Eleanor of Castile, wife of Edward I, on its route south from Nottinghamshire where she died in November 1290.**2.132** Next it was being used on the base of the vigorously cusped Pecham canopy tomb in Canterbury cathedral. It was further elaborated c. 1320 for the Alard tombs at Winchelsea, c. 1325 for Aymer de Valence in Westminster Abbey and for the knights de la Beches at Aldworth in the following decade.**2.133** Then too it was introduced

›**2.132 GEDDINGTON, ELEANOR CROSS:** one of three surviving crosses from the series of twelve erected by Edward I between 1291 and 1294 after the precedent set for Phillipe-Augustus in France.

2.133a

›**2.133 INFUSION OF THE OGEE:** (a) tomb of Archbishop Pecham (c. 1295), Canterbury cathedral; (b) tombs of the knights de la Beches (c. 1335), S. Mary's church, Aldworth.

2.133b

2.132

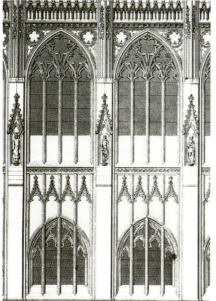

›2.134 LONDON, WESTMINSTER PALACE, S. STEPHEN'S PALATINE CHAPEL, 1292–1348: (a) exterior bay (engraving by F. Mackenzie, 1844), (b) undercroft chapel (restored after the destruction of Westminster Palace in the fire of 1834).

2.134a

2.134b

to the tomb of Edward II and, most significantly perhaps, to the fenestration of the lost Chapel of S. Stephen, Westminster: there, on the basis of work begun in the previous generation, its context was an equally innovative net of tracery extended over the structure to conceal, rather than elucidate, its lines.**2.134**

Tracing proliferation

Implied in the interlaced patterns of window tracery, where only glass was to be supported, the attenuated 'c' curve between impost and apex of the pointed arch is broken into two where it touches the circle, turned against itself to form an 's' on either side, and extruded into a spike at the top which denies any loadbearing capacity. Its unique assumption of monumentality to support the tower of Wells cathedral is, thus, wholly ironic. The evocation of its true potential in the flowing, fluid line of window tracery patterns was rich indeed – not only for ingenious diversity, but also, ultimately, for homogeneity in the enclosing fabric of wall, window and vault. The trajectory of the latter may be traced from S. Stephen's Chapel in the Palace of Westminster.

S. Stephen's Chapel seems to have been conceived under the inspiration of the Sainte-Chapelle in Paris. It was part of a programme of refurbishment at Westminster by the recently widowed Edward I before his strategic remarriage to the sister of Phillip IV. It is attributed to Michael of Canterbury, author of the Eleanor Cross erected in London's Cheapside. Construction was halted by lack of funds in 1297 but was taken up again at various reprises, most notably under Thomas of Canterbury from 1320 to 1336, and finished in 1348 evidently in accordance with the original conception. Of two storeys, the upper one for the royal family, as in Paris, it was lost in the fire which destroyed Westminster Palace in 1834 – except for the inaccurately restored ground floor.

As in the Parisian model, prominent vertical buttresses punctuate the exterior. As in the clerestory and triforium at Amiens – indeed throughout the near-contemporary three-storey elevation of S. Thibault-en-Auxois (c. 1290) – extended mullions integrate the two levels. Unlike either of these lucidly logical French works, however, this produces confrontation rather

2.135

than conformity in the lower zone: in each bay the deeply recessed window is a distinct entity embraced by a single arch rather than a quartet of lancets defined by the tracery descending from above. There is a string-course between the two levels but, even if it coincided with the floor, its junction with the upper tracery ignores the actual void. The ogee arch – and its polyfoil elaboration – are rampant in the fenestration tracery at both levels and in the niches on the buttresses which define the bays.

Thomas of Canterbury was appointed to complete S. Stephen's Chapel at Westminster by Edward II. Before the decade was out he seems to have received the commission for the tomb of that unfortunate monarch – murdered at Berkeley Castle in September 1327 and interred in the abbey church of S. Peter, Gloucester, now the cathedral.**2.135** The canopy tomb, of which this is a consummate example, was one of the most characteristically elaborate forms of later Gothic England, and was certainly more highly developed there than elsewhere. The arch-and-gable canopies of earlier works, like Michael of Canterbury's Crouchback Tomb in Westminster Abbey (c. 1297), had been spun from architectural elements extracted from the fabric of the buildings around them – at Westminster fainéant gables derived from the parapet of the Parisian Sainte-Chapelle and ultimately from Reims or even the pinnacles of Chartres. In the royal tomb at Gloucester, however, there is an obsessive accumulation of tabernacles, each a complete miniature structure. Depth still comes and goes with the nodding ogee but the airiness of the framework, ironically plausible as structure once more, is the essential characteristic.

›**2.135 GLOUCESTER, CATHEDRAL OF S. PETER AND THE HOLY TRINITY:** tomb of Edward II (1330–35).

›**2.136 WELLS, CATHEDRAL OF S. ANDREW,** c. 1293: interior of the chapter house.

Unlike the chapter houses of Westminster and Salisbury, where the window dominated, vaulting clearly takes precedence here over fenestration with the overwhelming cone of thirty-two ribs echoing all round.

›**2.137 SALISBURY, CATHEDRAL OF S. MARY,** c. 1280: interior of the chapter house.

Unlike Lincoln, but as at Westminster (which was rebuilt in the 19th century) the traceried windows predominate: they fill the whole void and push the cone of ribs up higher to spring from the imposts rather than from halfway up the lancets. As there are eight rather than ten sides, moreover, there are less fronds to the pine: light is preferred to density of surface pattern.

›**2.138 ELY, CATHEDRAL OF THE HOLY TRINITY,** 1322: interior of the octagonal crossing lantern.

The crossing tower of the Norman cathedral collapsed in 1322 and damaged adjoining bays. In the reconstruction immediately undertaken, these bays were not rebuilt. Instead the corners were cut on the diagonal to produce an irregular octagonal space. Precedents are elusive but the form suggests a chapter house with a lantern instead of a cone or a kitchen with an open oculus.

2.136

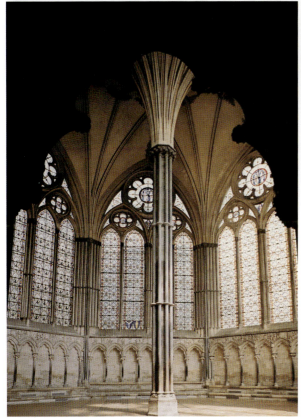

2.137

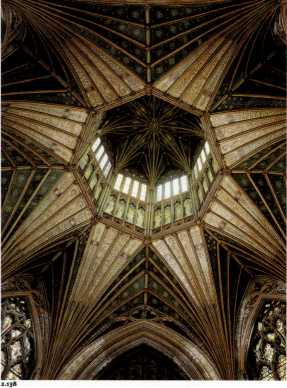

2.138

A measure of homogeneity in the enclosing fabric was achieved in the context of the centralized chapter house, with its network of arches stemming from the slender central column like the fronds of a palm, which Westminster inherited from Lincoln and transmitted to Salisbury. Owing to a master from Exeter furthering the experiments there, the most spectacular concordance yet achieved between vaulting and fenestration was displayed c. 1293 in the Wells chapter house: the virile central fountain of ribs seems to rain down and dissolve in the ogee-arched tracery of the windows on the periphery. Even more spectacular is the star vault and octagonal lantern built of timber over the crossing at Ely after the Norman central tower collapsed in 1322.**2.136–2.138**

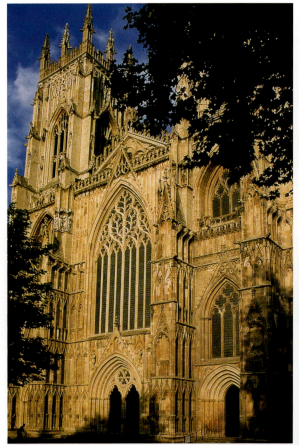

2.139a

The lyrical freedom achieved in English tracery design by the mid-14th century – well before the flamboyant last phase of French Gothic – is nowhere better displayed than in the hearts, drops and flame-like patterns woven with ogees in the upper zone of York Minster's great west window (c. 1335). The lower zone, in contrast, is conventionally perpendicular in its tracery. Unusually in the articulation of English nave elevations, rectilinear tracery is extruded on one plane to unify clerestory and triforium, as in France, and traditional Anglo-Norman bulk cedes to skeletal elegance.**2.139**

2.139b

2.139C

›**2.139 YORK MINSTER,** rebuilt on Norman foundations, transepts from 1220, nave from 1291, choir from 1360, towers completed 1480): (a) west front, (b) nave to west, (c) choir to east.

›**2.140 PERSHORE ABBEY,** from 1288: detail of choir vault.

Exceptional width, not height, was the York architect's ambition but he failed to solve the problem of vaulting in stone. The carpenter took over and structural logic ceded to innovative visual effect: bosses at regular intervals along the ridge rib were linked to both the transverse and diagonal arches with short sections of wholly non-structural ribbing known as liernes. The earliest exercise of the type, with its characteristically polygonal patterning, is generally thought to be the choir vault of Pershore Abbey where homogeneity is furthered, in a two-storey elevation, by the screening of the deeply inset clerestory with an arcade hardly more substantial than a network of ribs.**2.140**

2.140

Simplicity of structure prompted contrary elaboration of decorative detail but the English taste for scenography was certainly not essentially superficial – even if the feigning of masonry in immaculate carpentry may fairly be dismissed as such. It prompted great spatial inventiveness. A prime example is in the complex of the extended rectangular choir, hexagonal retrochoir and semi-elliptical Lady Chapel added at Wells from c. 1320. Another is the choir at Bristol begun shortly thereafter. This was devised as a hall church of the Poitevan type, with the

2.141a

2.141b

main space and aisles rising to the same height. Transmitting the thrust of the central vault to the external buttresses, transverse arches define each aisle bay but together constitute a scenography far richer than the central space: most amazingly, they are reinforced with girders which carry the rib cones produced by the capricious bifurcation of the aisle vaults.**2.141, 2.142**

With crocketed tiercerons and liernes, the architects of both Bristol and Wells wove rib patterns from the tracery of the windows but the latter went further in repeating the hexagons and diagonally disposed squares of the one in the other. The reduction of ribs to tracery in this way was the solution to the problem of developing an organic relationship between piers, vaults and windows. It was the key to the final, 'Perpendicular', achievement of English

›2.141 WELLS, CATHEDRAL OF S. ANDREW:
(a) interior of choir, (b) retrochoir link to the Lady
Chapel (1320s).

The choir extension retained the thick wall of the
original but the three new bays vary the three-storey
scheme first imposed on the old: the mullions of the
enlarged clerestory continue down through the triforium to terminate in the extrados of the aisle arcades;
the rectilinear mesh incorporates niches and is
deflected to the diagonal beside the windows.

Work on the retrochoir seems to have followed the
completion of the Lady Chapel with its stunning star
vault c. 1326. English pragmatism disrupts regularity in
the geometry, even varying the size of corresponding
piers (the eastern ones of the choir are larger than the
western ones of the Lady Chapel but the vault of the
retrochoir springs from both). The result is marked disparity between the plan and the innumerable compartments of the vaulting: there are more ribs than logic
requires but logic is clearly irrelevant.

›2.142 BRISTOL, ABBEY OF S. AUGUSTINE
(now the cathedral), c. 1315: (a) interior of the choir, (b)
south choir aisle with burial niches, (c) vault of passage
to Berkeley Chapel.

The rebuilding of the late-Romanesque choir may
have been projected at the very beginning of the 14th
century but the scheme as realized seems to date from
no earlier than 1315. The fantasy of the vaulting
extends from the scalloped burial niches in the aisle
walls.

›2.243 TEWKESBURY ABBEY, 1330s: choir
vault.

2.143

Gothic. Still in the 'Decorated' mode, however, the implications were nowhere better traced than in the choir vault
at Tewkesbury where the stellar outshines the merely
polygonal.**2.243**

As we have noted, the distinction of the English Decorated style derives from the ingenious variety of anti-
architectonic devices which we have seen variously
displayed at Westminster, Pershore, York, Wells, Bristol

and Tewkesbury. Many games were played with the elements of structure, extracting them from their context and forging them into homogeneous decorative patterns which denied a sense of physical substance. A prime example is the three-dimensional development of the ogee, the 'nodding' ogee arch, which seems to derive from the fantastic timber joinery of the bishop of Exeter's throne (c. 1313). It was dazzlingly deployed in stone in the Lady Chapel at Ely, c. 1322, but possibly appeared a little earlier on the north portal at S. Mary Redcliffe, Bristol. These techniques were, of course, new ways of satisfying the old Christian purpose of denying the realities of this world in opening the door to the next.**2.144, 2.145**

2.144a

>2.144 ELY, CATHEDRAL OF THE HOLY TRINITY: (a, b) Lady Chapel (1321–53), interior and niche detail.

2.144b

2.145b

›2.145 BRISTOL, S. MARY REDCLIFFE, c. 1320: (a–c) north portal, general view and details.

Separate from Bristol in the Middle Ages and wealthy from trade – not least in wine from Portugal – Redcliffe boasted a parish church of cathedral stature. The original church of c. 1200 was replaced in the second half of the 14th century with the present great vaulted work. First, however, the early 13th-century north porch had become the popular shrine of an image of the Virgin Mary and a new porch was needed as a vestibule both to shrine and church. This seems to have been begun c. 1320. The precedent for its rare hexagonal plan is elusive but there is obviously no coincidence in the use of the same form for the probably contemporary retrochoir at Wells, which was also a vestibule to a Marian shrine. The encrustation of the exterior with images in nodding ogee-arched niches was clearly a demonstration of unearthly splendour – the denial of physical realities in the anti-architectonic manipulation of form has rarely been more complete.

2.145c

S. Mary Redcliffe's contorted thicket of once-structural elements, entwined with highly naturalistic foliage, provides shelter for numerous exquisitely observed little birds and animals. Such extreme sensitivity to nature was, in fact, characteristic of the 'International Gothic' of the period. It may seem ironic that denial of the structural realities of this world is accompanied by minute and loving attention to its flora and fauna – but, of course, they are symbols of Christ's Passion as the church portal itself is the symbol of entry to Heaven for the faithful through the intercession of Christ's Mother.

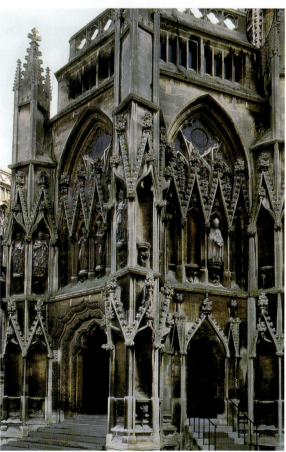

2.145a

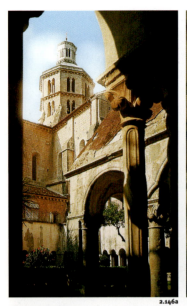

2.146a   2.146b

5 ITALY

The rib vault had appeared early in Italy but not as an essential element in a skeletal system depending on the counter-opposition of forces: the fashion from France was overlaid on the native Romanesque and the antique gravitas of the latter was rarely eclipsed by the exotic grace of the former. The Cistercians led the way to a semblance of Gothic with their austere hybrid, as at late-12th-century Fossanova, where the presence of a French architect is not hard to detect or unusual in the Italian works of the order.[2.142]

In the 13th century, an age of economic boom and experiment in all the arts, the expanding orders of mendicants achieved a still more elementary hybrid than the Cistercians in promoting the development of a form which satisfied their didactic purpose. Essentially simple in plan and restrained in plastic embellishment, often utilitarian and essentially cost-effective, the structures were usually impressive in scale but vertical ascendancy is characteristically checked by basic horizontality and solid

Begun a couple of years after his death, at the time of S. Francis's canonization, the church was projected to cater for the pilgrims who were already flooding to Assisi. The lower hall is dark antespace, the upper one tall, commodious and relatively light despite the expansive surfaces for frescoes below and beside the slender lancets of the nave – those of the sanctuary apse fill their bays. The vaults spring from clustered colonnettes but the ribs are rectangular or pentagonal in section – curved surfaces are kept to the minimum.

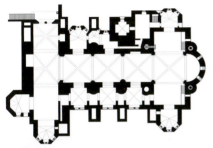

2.147a @ 1:1500

prevails over void. Thus the dress may be Gothic in line but the virile skeletal frame of shafts and ribs and flying buttresses, which the builders of Suger's France had invented to enlighten structure, is secondary to the flat plane of the wall, delineated to define unified space in which optimum clarity of sight and sound of the priest is denied to no member of the congregation. The ideal is at its purest in the mother foundation of the Franciscans at Assisi (begun 1228), where the upper and lower churches are single-volume vaulted halls – except for elementary transepts – and didactic purpose achieves the highest plane in the expansive mural frescoes preferred to the glass curtains of the north.**2.147**

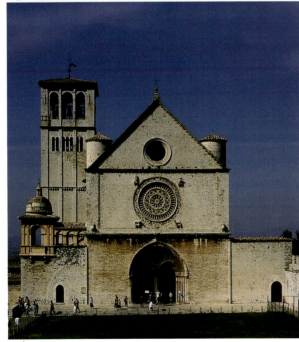

2.147b

2.147c

2.148a

2.148b

›**2.148 PADUA, SANT'ANTONIO** ('Il Santo'),
begun 1231: (a) exterior from the north-west, (b) detail
of domical vaulting.

In distinction from the Greek-cross formula perfected for S. Marco, Venice, a Latin-cross arrangement
of seven domed spaces was provided to cope with the
volume of pilgrims to the extremely popular shrine of S.
Anthony.

2.149a

2.149b

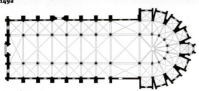

2.5149c @ 1:1500

›2.149 BOLOGNA, S. FRANCISCO, begun 1236, consecrated 1250: (a) nave to sanctuary, (b) west front, (c) plan.

The material throughout is the brick of the Emilian vernacular. The screen façade is of the Emilian Romanesque type which was popular also in Lombardy where it was taken to an extreme at Crema. However, the basilican plan with sunken transepts and chevet is rather more French than is usual with the Franciscans – and not specifically Cistercian. So too the height of the nave relative to its width, but not the ratio of solid to void, takes the French example beyond the Italian mendicant norm and there are rib vaults throughout. Consequently, the elevation has atypically prominent flying buttresses: these are much bulkier than their French contemporaries and at the east end they rise between stolid rectangular radiating chapels which are quite unlike their French counterparts. Semicircular shafts are confined to the sanctuary – the nave has attenuated pilasters and faceted ribs.

The antique legacy and its early Christian investment remained pervasive. The influence of the domical Byzantine tradition, transmitted through S. Marco in Venice, subsists in the neighbouring *terra firma* at Padua.[2.148] Elsewhere the basilica remained the norm. The mendicants usually recalled it in flanking cavernous naves, timber-roofed or groin-vaulted, with aisle arcades: in profile these were Gothic, like the slender windows that punctuated the pervasive wall, but little else transformed the ancient prototype. S. Fortunato at Todi is a variant of the hall type with aisles rising to the same height as the nave – as in Poitiers cathedral and its many German derivatives. However, far more prevalent in Italy is the ancient type with clerestory: prime examples are the Franciscan Frari and Dominican Ss. Giovani e Paolo, Venice, S. Francesco, Bologna (founded 1236) and the Dominican S. Maria Novella and Franciscan S. Croce of later 13th-century Florence. The last, built against the protest that its complexity ill-accorded with the austere ideals of the order's founder, is attributed to the sculptor Arnolfo di Cambio who also worked on the Florentine cathedral and in Rome.[2.149–2.153]

2.150a

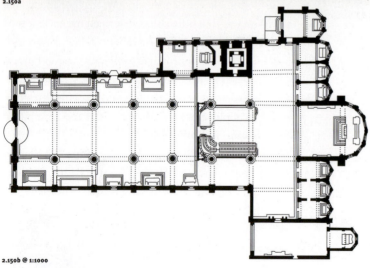

2.150b @ 1:1000

›2.150 VENICE, FRARI, 1250–1338: (a) interior, (b) plan.

Franciscan S. Maria Gloriosa dei Frari was built in place of an earlier church. Like it, Dominican Ss. Giovanni e Paolo – the burial church of many doges – was rebuilt from c. 1333 in expansion of a mid-13th-century foundation but not consecrated for nearly a century.

Both are cruciform basilicas of the early Christian type, the bays of the nave – square in the Dominican work – are broad but light is restricted to a shallow clerestory below the quadripartite vaulting except in the great apses – the last part to be completed by the Dominicans, the first of the Franciscans (rebuilt in the 15th century). The ratio of height to width and the reduction in the superficial area of clerestory wall surpass those of the great mendicant Florentine works and, naturally, the effect is lighter: the contrast with S. Maria Nuova is most significant as both are vaulted.

Contrary to Tuscan or Umbrian preference, but as in several 13th-century mendicant churches of the western Veneto (Vicenza in particular), semicircular or near-circular polygonal forms complement the rigorously rectangular wall planes inherited from the Cistercians: the piers are cylindrical or trefoil, the sanctuary apse is a heptagonal polygon flanked by ranges of near semicircular or polygonal chapel apses and the tradition of the Byzantine dome is sustained by the Dominicans over their square crossing. But the corollary of tall slender piers carrying broad arches is intrusive bracing.

›2.151 FLORENCE: (a, b) S. Maria Novella (begun 1279) interior, plan; (c, d) S. Croce (begun c. 1295 in expansion of earlier 13th-century foundations), interior and drawing for tramezzo chapel attributed to Arnolfo di Cambio.

The Florentine mendicants followed the Cistercians in planning for simple basilicas with a two-storeyed internal elevation. The east end of S. Maria Novella – whose apparent distance from the entrance is enhanced in perspective by the diminution of the last two nave bays – is rectangular, as in S. Bernard's formula, but a ratio of void over solid foreign to that formula results from exceptionally wide aisle arcades rising through two-thirds of the height from slender composite piers: the polychrome arcading enhances the lucidity of the structural frame but much has been lost with the fresco cycles which originally obviated any oppressiveness of plain surface.

The quadripartite vaulting of S. Maria Novella is foreign to S. Bernard's norm. It contrasts sharply with the extended timber roofs of aisles and nave in the later Franciscan church of S. Croce where, in consequence, the spaces are broader and the arches defining them wider and higher at the expense of residual wall. The building, begun in the last decade of the century to plans evolved from c. 1285, is traditionally attributed to Arnolfo di Cambio. However, substantive verification is elusive as little survives of his known work at the cathedral or elsewhere and nothing beyond the sanctuary chapels had been completed by his death in 1302. Beyond the high transept arches, which echo the central motif of the sanctuary screen, the nave progressed slowly from c. 1315 to the end of the century without significant changes. The elevated sanctuary bays were once screened from the nave whose unity is asserted by the regular repetition of all the members below and above the gallery – unbroken throughout except where it ramps up to clear the crossing arches beyond the lost screen – and of the roof trusses which quadrangulate the volume. And, despite the lightness of the structure, that obviates any sense of a virile skeletal organism.

2.151a

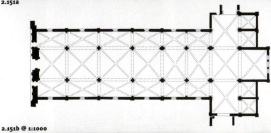

2.151b @ 1:1000

2.151c

2.151d   2.152

The canopies of Arnolfo and his followers

An early 14th-century measured drawing associated with the choir screen of S. Croce – one of the earliest such documents in the history of European architecture – is clearly related in detail to several ciboria in Rome, notably the one over the high altar of S. Paolo fuori le Mure completed in 1285 and attributed to Arnolfo di Cambio in its inscription. Despite crocketing to the pediments and, especially, trefoil relief to the spandrels of the arches, the conception is essentially architectural. And the incorporation of sculpture does nothing to diminish this in the realization of the rationally planned Roman work: the figures are accommodated, not applied *hors d'œuvre*.

The tomb of Clement IV in S. Francesco, Viterbo, attributed to Pietro Oderisi, is closely related to the S. Croce drawing – at least in its canopy.

2.153

2.153 SIENA, CATHEDRAL OF S. MARIA ASSUNTA: tomb of Cardinal Petroni (c. 1318).

Tino had first referred to the canopy precedent set by Arnolfo di Cambio at Orvieto for the Pisan tomb of the emperor Henry VII who died on his way to challenge Robert of Anjou's rule in Naples (begun c. 1315, that work has been dismembered). His work for Petroni demonstrates his indebtedness to Giovanni Pisano in the main figures as much, probably, as to the morphology of Nicola Pisano's lost Arco di S. Domenico in Bologna.

2.154 SIENA: S. DOMENICO, begun c. 1310: interior.

Spatial complexity runs only to a transept and that is an uninterrupted, timber-roofed space just screened from the single volume of the timber-roofed nave.

>**2.155 NAPLES:** (a) S. Maria donna Regina, tomb of the founder, Queen Mary of Hungary (wife of Charles II of Anjou, 1285–1309); (b) S. Chiara (1310), interior to east with tombs of the founder, Queen Sancia di Maiorca, and her husband, King Robert of Anjou (1309–43); (c) S. Giovanni ai Carbonnara, tomb of King Ladislaus (1399–1414).

A supporter of the Florentine Guelfs, allied to the Neapolitan Angevins, Tino di Camaino (c. 1280–c. 1337) fled from Siena to Naples when the Ghibellines triumphed in Tuscany early in the next decade. There he collaborated with Gagliardo Primario – to whom S. Chiara has been attributed – on the tomb of Mary of Hungary in S. Maria donna Regina in accordance with her will of 1323: the queen's bier, relieved with portraits of her sons, is supported by the cardinal Christian virtues and surmounted by angels drawing the curtains back to reveal saintly example.

2.154

2.155a

2.155b

2.155c

The type represented here evolved from the protective elevation of the ubiquitous church floorslab tomb over short legs, heraldic animals or, ultimately, a tomb chest (derived from the antique sarcophagus): the canopy (symbolizing the heaven into which the deceased was to ascend) was added for greater distinction – as the ciborium over the altar, particularly in Arnolfo's style.

Pietro Oderisi, who may be identified with the Italian artist of similar name who worked on the shrine of Edward the Confessor in Westminster Abbey for Henry III c. 1270, seems to have collaborated with Arnolfo on the S. Paolo ciborium. Assigned to Arnolfo and datable to the early 1280s, the

Tino worked with his studio on the tombs of Charles of Calabria and Mary of Valois in S. Chiara in the 1330s. His example was followed there several times before the century was out, most notably by Giovanni and Pacio da Firenze for the centrally placed tomb of Robert of Anjou (c. 1343). That four-tier work was exceeded by the tomb of King Ladislaus in S. Giovanni Carbonara which is surmounted by the equestrian statue of the deceased – a motif of Romanesque origin which, as we have seen, was popular with the despots of the north.

›2.156 MILAN, S. EUSTORGIO: Arco di S. Pietro Martire (1339).

The bier of Nicola Pisano's Arco di S. Domenica, with its splendid relief panels, was apparently supported by six virtues: here Giovanni di Balduccio has eight which prompt the tripartite elevation of a profile like that of a standard basilica (with nave flanked by lower aisles). Perhaps also derived from Nicola's composition, the trapezoidal coffer lid and crowning tabernacle have their counterparts in Tino's Sienese work for Pertoni but here the undrawn curtain is a minor motif: in general the morphology most clearly recalls Tino's Neopolitan work (within the baldachino) for Mary of Hungary.

2.156

tomb of Cardinal de Braye in the Dominican church at Orvieto, may be reconstructed with the same canopy motif. That is French in origin but Arnolfo seems to have invented the main surviving motif of Braye's tomb: acolytes drawing curtains to shroud the recumbent effigy on its bier.

The canopy tomb was to have a prolific career: the Scaliger tombs in Verona well represent various stages in its elaboration, culminating in the work of Bonino da Campione. The idea of the retractable canopy curtain was also of wide appeal. Among the first to develop it was Tino di Camaino, the Sienese master from the circle of Giovanni Pisano who also transmitted the influence of Nicola Pisano and Arnolfo di Cambio to his followers. His earliest surviving essay of the type is the tomb of Cardinal Petroni in Siena cathedral (c. 1318): he developed the theme in Naples. Giovanni di Balduccio is prominent among those who adopted the motif in the north.

2.157 VERONA, MONUMENT TO CANSIGNO-RIO DELLA SCALA: tomb (Bonino da Campione, before 1375, S. Maria Antica precinct, Verona).

Bonino da Campione, taking the adjacent tombs of Cangrande and Mastino II della Scala (died 1351) as his precedent (authors unknown), evolved his formula for the type surmounted by an equestrian statue in works for the Visconti in Milan.

Within a decade of his death, Cansignorio's heirs had lost their Veronese heartland to the Visconti.

2.157

The ascetic ideals of S. Francis may have fallen from view in the Venetian Frari and the Florentine S. Croce but simplicity on a grand scale is the order of many early 14th-entury mendicant churches, notably the aisleless brick halls of S. Francesco and S. Domenico in Siena.**2.154** There are numerous other examples, varied in plan and, indeed, in scale: to name the works of but one order in the south – to complement our northern and central examples – S. Chiara (1310) in Naples is a great hall with the bays in the place of aisles partitioned to form chapels; its slightly earlier sister, S. Maria donna Regina (1307) is a small hall with a choir for nuns oversailing most of the main floor plane. Tino di Camaino provided canopy tombs for the patrons of both these churches and his work was emulated in Naples for more than a century.**2.155**

Ambitious scale matched the success of the mendicants in popular appeal but, of course, it was not their sole preserve. Italy had inherited a vast corpus of Romanesque cathedrals but the newly prosperous burghers of the 13th century and their descendants vied with one another in the replacement of them – until the nightmare of the Black

Death. Their builders – masons and sculptors turned architects, like Arnolfo di Cambio, still in collaboration with priests - were often hardly less austere than the mendicants in their conceptions. In scale, characteristically, the most ambitious were determined to surpass one another in the assertion of civic pretension inflated by mercantile wealth. The Sienese and Florentines, for instance, took rivalry to the extreme. With S. Maria del Fiori the Florentines projected the most monumental cathedral of the age but their ambitions exceeded their medieval resources – of patronage and essentially Romanesque technology. The Sienese responded with an extension to their cathedral of unrealizable megalomania (1339) yet managed an awesome space within the essentially Romanesque hulk left towering over their city.**2.158, 2.159**

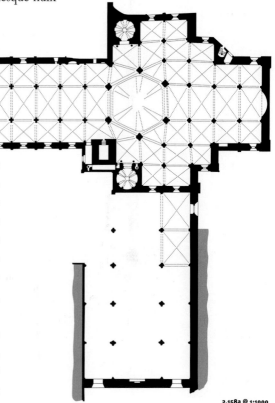

2.158a @ 1:1000

Florence and Siena: pretension, genius and folly in competitive cathedral building

The replacement of the old Florentine cathedral of S. Reparata – rather than its renovation – seems to have been decided upon by 1295 and entrusted to Arnolfo di Cambio. A timber-roofed basilica of the S. Croce type, but with an octagonal crossing in a triapsidal composition to the east, was apparently planned from the outset: there were northern precedents on a smaller scale – notably in Cologne – but if domical vaulting in masonry was envisaged by Arnolfo, it was beyond the technology of his time at the projected diameter. Arnolfo died c. 1302 when construction, which seems to have begun at the west end, had reached no higher than the three portals of the projected west front. Progress is elusive from then until the late-1350s but the austerity of the executed building, derived not least from purely rectilinear articulating members, perpetuates Arnolfo's architectonic aesthetic.

At Siena, the early 13th-century basilica sustained the Romanesque tradition of semicircular arches and – possibly – even of tunnel vaulting, but departed from it mainly in the extraordinary hexagonal crossing with its feigned domical vault. The influence of the baptistry at Pisa has been

2.158b

2.158c

detected in the latter – the bizarre plan apart – as in the monumental weight of the arcading in the basilica. And Pisa's contribution ran to the greatest sculptors of successive generations – first for the main item of furniture, subsequently for the external embellishment.

The pulpit executed in three years from 1265 by Nicola Pisano and workshop, including the presumably young Arnolfo di Cambio, is of the polygonal type produced by the master for the Pisa baptistry five years earlier: the earlier work is hexagonal rather than octagonal and somewhat more architectonic in articulation, but common is a parapet, with didactic reliefs on each panelled side, carried on trefoil arches and raised over central and peripheral columns, the former with figured base, the latter alternately resting on lions. The inspiration of antique Roman sarcophagus relief sculpture is clear. Instead of striving for a transcendant ideal, either of Classsic corporeality or Christian spirituality, Pisano is generally credited with primacy – after the sculptors of the south portal at Chartres – in advancing naturalism in both the distinct personalities of his human figures and the space they inhabit. Celebrated variants, decreasingly

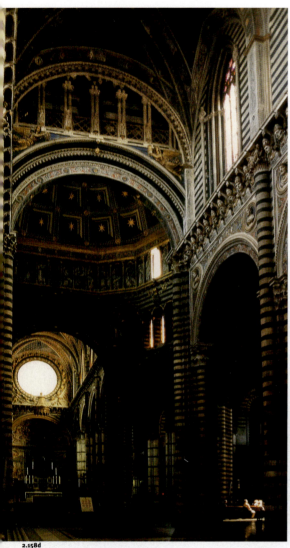

2.158d

2.158e

architectonic, were produced by Nicola's son Giovanni for S. Andrea at Pistoia and Pisa cathedral in the first decade of the new century.

Giovanni Pisano seems to have been responsible for work on Siena's western façade from c. 1290. Possibly based on earlier work, it had risen no higher than the portal arcades within several decades of Giovanni's disappearance from the scene c. 1297: the rest followed after c. 1370 when

›2.158 SIENA, CATHEDRAL OF S. MARIA ASSUNTA, work had begun by c. 1225, unfinished expansion was begun in 1339: (a) plan, (b) general view from north-east, (c) pulpit, (d) interior of crossing, (e) west front, (f) project for baptistry façade c. 1399 (Siena, Cathedral Museum).

2.158f

the original nave had been heightened. Yet the upper level, in which the main verticals are unaligned with those below, more clearly recalls the highly charged sculptural morphology of Giovanni's late work: unlike Arnolfo's scheme for Florence, where the architecture contains the sculpture, the lavishly detailed Sienese architecture seems to provide a backdrop against which the figures sculpted in full relief assert themselves on projecting ledges.

In 1316, following the development of the grandiose scheme for Florence, excavation began at the base of the Siena site's steep eastern slope to provide a baptistry in the basement of an extension to a heightened choir: a commission appointed in 1322 advised against further work on both aesthetic and structural grounds but this was ignored until mid-century when the Black Death supervened. By then the eastern façade of baptistry and choir had reached two-thirds of its projected height pending completion of the new choir vaults. Meanwhile (c. 1339), a vast new nave – double the height and nearly double the width of the old one but without piers of comparably increased mass – was projected at right angles to the existing building: this was to be retained with heightened vaults as the transept, sanctuary and crossing. Though the structure was exceptionally light, with wide intercolumniations like the Florentine S. Croce, vaulting was envisaged throughout, as in the Florentine cathedral, but stability must have been a grave concern for any objective observer: commissioners called in from Florence condemned the scheme in 1358 – and, humiliatingly, the folly was suspended. Nevertheless, the vaulting of the old nave at a higher level, to accord with work in progress on heightening the choir, was furthered after the disaster of the Black Death had abated.

In Florence, meanwhile, a design for the freestanding campanile to the south of the nave was produced, not by another sculptor-master mason, but by the greatest painter of the day, Giotto: begun in 1334, its execution reached only to the stringcourse which – contrary to the idea recorded in a drawing dated to the beginning of the decade – divides the socle into two registers. The completion of the tower after the Black Death – without attenuated pinnacles, octagonal cupola or graded progression in lightening the ratio of solid to void in five main stages – was entrusted to Francesco Talenti.

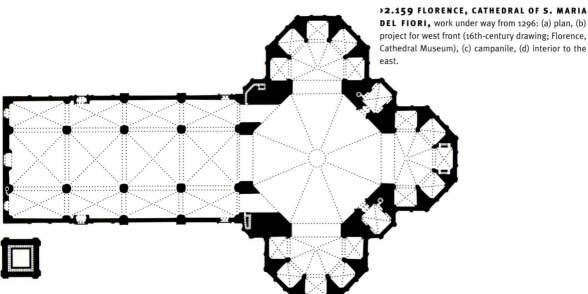

2.159a @ 1:1000

Talenti's revisions were also followed from 1357 in furthering the basilican structure, with its massive nave arcade and domical quadripartite vault. The nave arcades were well advanced seven years later, when Talenti's responsibility was diminished, and by 1366 it had been decided that there was to be an extra bay. It is not clear when the semi-centralized – trefoil – crossing was adopted definitively but it had been projected at least as early as 1360: the dimensions of the great octagon had been determined by then but the means of achieving its vaulting were elusive until the intervention of Filippo Brunelleschi at the dawn of the Renaissance in the early 15th century.

A new scheme for the façade was also produced in 1357, presumably with the involvement of Talenti. A 16th-century drawing in the cathedral archives may record revision of Arnolfo's work furthered subsequently: the record clearly subordinates sculpture to architecture in the articulation of the registers flanking the portals, as in Arnolfo's Roman ciborium – though in an infinitely more complex context – and indeed the ciborium motif itself is applied in pure elevation to frame the side portals. The façade awaited its realization until the 19th century – despite many earlier attempts at finding consensus in its design.

2.159b

2.159c

2.159d

›ARCHITECTURE IN CONTEXT »REFRACTION OF LIGHT

2.160a

2.160b

The body of the building – essentially Romanesque, except in its height and the width of its timber-roofed nave – was begun in 1290: the sanctuary was enlarged and transepts projected beyond the remarkable sequence of the lateral chapel exedrae from c. 1330. In 1310 the Siennese master Lorenzo Maitani was called in to supervise the daring vaulting of the high crossing and the rich polychrome façade was then begun under his direction. The central portal remains Romanesque, the flanking ones are pointed like the elongated lancet of the sanctuary and, as the construction seems to have been supervised by the one master in one campaign (of about twenty years), there is no problem of disjointed verticals like that entailed by the erratic evolution of the project at Siena. Craftsmen from many other centres of artistic activity in Italy and beyond were consulted or employed – notably the sculptor Andrea Pisano, who was paid for work in 1347, and the mosaicist Piero di Puccio, who negotiated a new fee in 1386.

›**2.161 BOLOGNA, S. PETRONIO,** 1390: nave (with 16th-century ciborium by G.B da Vignola).

Conceived as a vaulted Latin-cross basilica by Anto-

The challenge to Siena and Florence had originally been issued by Orvieto where the superb cathedral was founded c. 1290.**2.160** In that work, as in most of its Italian contemporaries, early Christian and Romanesque forms subsisted beneath Gothic raiment, which was at its most

2.161

nio di Vicenzo, construction had reached the first two bays of the nave when he died in 1401. His scheme was taken up again after a forty-year lapse: four more bays were added to the nave and chapels flanked the aisles throughout but the crossing and sanctuary were never to be built: their projected form is unknown.

The commission of a large-scale model (1:12) early in 1390 implies that the projected work of some 182.5 by 136.8 metres would greatly exceed the cathedral then being planned by the Milanese – which Antonio went to study. Antonio also planned to exceed the Florentine cathedral: from his studies there he obviously carried away a clear impression of the fenestration and articulation – though, disclaiming strict rectilinearity in the latter, he admits semicircular shafts to supplement his chamfered pilasters. He had no taste for the northern gloom of Milan and his lightening of the Florentine proportions is enhanced by the absence of a cornice gallery – as at S. Francesco 150 years earlier though with much-reduced residual wall.

lavish on western façades, in the chapels of benefactors and sometimes in the sanctuary. And in this respect, too, the façade of the cathedral at Orvieto set a standard of embellishment in marble and mosaic which was never to be surpassed in the Middle Ages – though the Sienese tried.

With work at Orvieto admirably complete and the Sienese *hors de combat* at the end of the 14th century, it was left to the Bolognese to challenge the Florentines with their S. Petronio (from 1390).[2.161] Meanwhile, c. 1385 the Milanese had embarked on an expansive double-aisled basilican exercise which, drawing on the expertise of late-Gothic architects from the north, knew no equal in the prolixity of its ornament – except perhaps in Spain, as we shall see.

6 LATE GOTHIC

PERPENDICULAR ENGLAND

The mesmerizing intention of the Decorated style was furthered in 14th-century England not through the penetrating depth of works like the north porch of S. Mary Redcliffe, Bristol[2.145] – ambiguous as it was due to the shifting planes of the nodding ogee – but with the filigree network of insubstantial arches and ribs spun over everything: the example was set at S. Stephen's Chapel, Westminster,[2.134] and followed in such works as the extended choir at Wells.[2.136] Based on the rectilinear geometry of the Rayonnant extension of clerestory tracery into triforia, and hence called 'Perpendicular', this was the final phase of English medieval architecture.

In the absence of S. Stephen's Chapel, the seminal Perpendicular work is generally seen to be the masking of the Romanesque choir at Gloucester to enshrine the remains of Edward II from 1330 with a cage of slender vertical and horizontal ribs, crossing to form panels relieved only by a fringe of flattened multifoil arches. The grid extends over the east window, the largest of its era, and over much of the exterior, including the Lady Chapel and tower: in the cloisters it is even – perhaps most characteristically – squeezed into a fan to express support for vaulting.[2.162]

2.162a

>**2.162 GLOUCESTER, CATHEDRAL OF S. PETER,** as transformed between 1327 and 1377: (a) overview from the east, (b) choir, (c) cloister.

Assertion of the perpendicular

There were three main campaigns of work on the transformation of Romanesque Gloucester: the south transept from 1331 to 1336, the crossing from 1337 to 1351 and, after the interruption of the Black Death, the presbytery from 1351 to 1377. It is attributed to London architects familiar with the progress of S. Stephen's Chapel. The transept retained its original height but the clerestory of the choir was raised considerably and verticality was stressed by keeping the horizontals to a minimum. The Norman apse was demolished to make way for a rectangular extension to the sanctuary and

2.162c

2.162b

›ARCHITECTURE IN CONTEXT »REFRACTION OF LIGHT

the subsisting line of the crypt ambulatory dictated the most astonishing feature of the new work: the bowed east window, which seems to hang like a curtain and, potentially, float free of constraint.

Surprisingly, perhaps, the rectilinear net was not extruded across the vault of Gloucester's new choir: this was treated to a different pattern, derived from the new choir at Wells. Disparate in scale and sustaining the substance of ribs, it eliminated the main structural diagonals. At much the same time in the consistently panelled cloisters, however, a similar network was projected on to the conical sprouting of the vaults as a three-dimensional fan. An organic relationship between the structure – or its masking – and the curtain extended over the void was achieved at last – ironically in the formal, rather inorganic terms of the extrusion and compression of the grid.

2.163

The fan vault and perpendicular tracery-like screen were to be a persistent theme of English ecclesiastical architecture for the 150 years from the mid-14th century to the advent of the Renaissance – often overlaying earlier work, as at Gloucester.[2.162] Much of this period was unprolific in royal building because of the Hundred Years' War and the Wars of the Roses but there were, of course, many monastic patrons. Foreign war made many rich and there was considerable affluence in countryside and town, particularly

>**2.163 NORWICH CATHEDRAL CHOIR:** detail of early 16th-century Perpendicular insertion at the expense of the original Norman structure.

>**2.164 BRISTOL, S. MARY REDCLIFFE,** c. 1320–75: (a) exterior from south, (b) interior.

Separate from Bristol in the Middle Ages and wealthy from trade – not least in wine from Portugal – Redcliffe boasted a parish church of cathedral stature. The original church of c. 1200 was replaced in the second half of the 14th century with the present great vaulted work. First, however, the early 13th-century north porch had become the popular shrine of an image of the Virgin Mary and a new porch was needed as a vestibule both to shrine and church.[2.144] This seems to have been begun c. 1320. The precedent for its rare hexagonal plan is elusive but there is obviously no coincidence in the use of the same form for the probably contemporary retrochoir at Wells, which was also a vestibule to a Marian shrine. The encrustation of the exterior with images in nodding ogee-arched niches was clearly a demonstration of unearthly splendour – the denial of physical realities in the anti-architectonic manipulation of form has rarely been more complete.

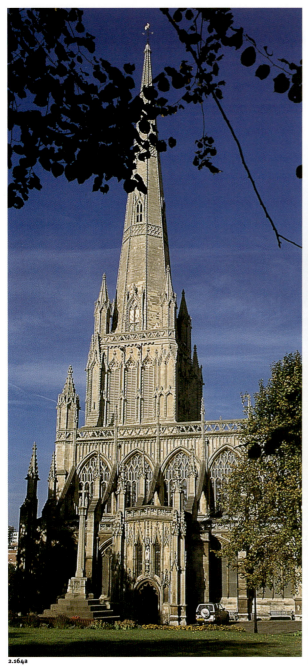

among wool growers and traders. The great expansion of England's unrivalled collection of parish churches is one manifestation of this affluence. The peculiarly English phenomenon of the chantry chapel, endowed by the affluent for the eternal invocation of grace in the afterlife and distinguishable from the tomb only in virtue of the space defined by its filigree screen, is another. **2.163–2.171**

2.164a   2.164b

2.165

2.166

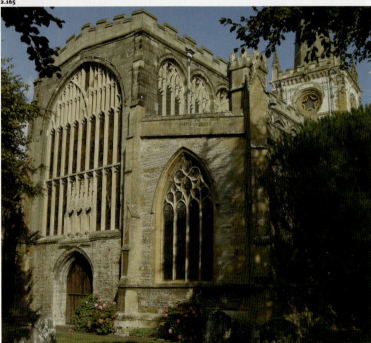

2.167a

2.167b

2.168

Denying the substance of arched ribs, the fan vault was considered too insubstantial for the main spaces of the great church and reserved at first for subsidiary elements, chapels and chantries, the square ceilings of crossing towers or, later and extensively, ambulatories such as the one built around the Norman sanctuary at Peterborough c. 1500 or, again, the vestibule of the Oxford Divinity School. In the vaults of naves and choirs, Perpendicular articulation was to issue in a variety of geometric patterns. The replacement of the Norman nave at Canterbury by Henry Yeveley from c. 1400, the contemporary transformation of the exceptionally long one at Winchester by William Wynford and the later vault over the Norman choir of Christ Church cathedral in Oxford provide splendid examples of tiercerons and liernes woven into geometric patterns in coordination with Perpendicular articulation.**2.172, 2.173**

2.165 LAVENHAM, CHURCH OF S. PETER AND S. PAUL, completed c. 1530: general view from the south-east.

A prime example of the so-called 'wool churches'.

2.166 BLYTHBURGH, MOST HOLY TRINITY CHURCH, 15th century on earlier foundations: nave with 'angel roof' and rood screen.

2.167 STRATFORD-UPON-AVON, HOLY TRINITY CHURCH, 13th–15th centuries: (a) exterior from south-west, (b) nave to chancel.

2.168 TEWKESBURY ABBEY, CHANTRY CHAPELS: Beauchamp or Warwick (1430, left) and Fitzhamon or Founder (1397) with Hugh Despenser's tomb (1348) to the right.

2.169 OXFORD, DIVINITY SCHOOL, 1427–83: interior.

Adjacent to the Bodleian Library, this is the university's oldest surviving hall built specifically for lectures and discussions on theology.

2.169

›2.170 CANTERBURY, CATHEDRAL OF S. PETER: (a) nave (from c. 1400), (b) vault of crossing tower (1500).

›2.171 PETERBOROUGH, CATHEDRAL OF S. PETER AND S. PAUL: fan vaulting in the ambulatory (c. 1500).

The full fan-vaulting of space, primary and secondary, was the main theme of the last phase of English medieval architecture, when significant royal patronage resumed after the Wars of the Roses. Henry VII was responsible for

2.172

›2.172 OXFORD, CHRIST CHURCH CATHE-
DRAL, late-12th century: choir.

›2.173 WINCHESTER, CATHEDRAL OF THE
HOLY TRINITY, S. PETER, S. PAUL AND S.
SWITHUN, nave begun c. 1360, completed 1394–
1410: bays of the nave before the crossing and choir.

The first campaign of work on the rebuilding of the
nave ended c. 1366 following the death of the patron,
Bishop Edington: the second campaign was begun c.
1394 by Bishop William of Wykeham. The architect was
constrained to incorporate as much of the Norman
masonry as possible, hence the piers lack the slenderness of Canterbury where Yeveley had a freer hand.
'Panelled' in the Perpendicular manner first developed
at Gloucester, the original massive structure was cut
back considerably and impressed with shafts but still
imposed a marked shift of plane in the clerestory.

2.173

realizing the major projects of his predecessors, Edward
IV's chapel dedicated to S. George at Windsor and the
chapel of Henry VI's college at Cambridge but, of course,
there were many monastic patrons as well.

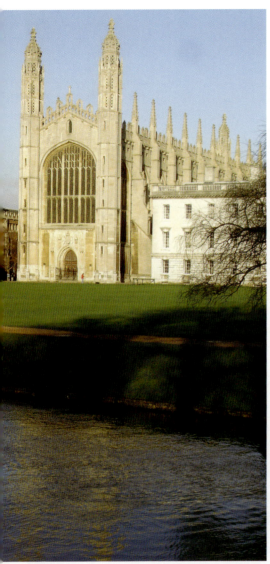

Liernes and tiercerons survive in S. George's Chapel at Windsor, with fan vaulting over the crossing, but the apogee of the homogeneous fan-vaulted Perpendicular style was certainly achieved in the lightbox of King's College Chapel in Cambridge.[2.174] Thereafter, the transverse

2.55b

›2.174 CAMBRIDGE, KING'S COLLEGE CHAPEL, 1446–1515: (a) exterior from west, (b) interior, (c) exterior from south-west with neo-Gothic gatehouse in the foreground.

The first campaign of work, undertaken by the college's unfortunate but scholarly patron, Henry VI, lasted from 1446 to 1461. It was taken up again under Edward IV from 1477 but was stopped in 1485 by the troubles faced by his successor, Richard III. The chapel was completed under Henry VII from 1508 with the fan vaulting of John Wastell based on strong transverse arches. It was modelled on the Gloucester Lady Chapel, which developed the theme of the choir on an unconstrained site. Wastell, called in from Peterborough where he had vaulted the ambulatory, pursued homogeneity further than his predecessors at Gloucester and achieved perfect accord between windows, panelling and fan vaults of unprecedented scale.

›2.175 WESTMINSTER, ABBEY, CHAPEL OF HENRY VII, 1503–19.

Robert and William Vertue undertook the work to accommodate the king at private worship in place of Henry III's Lady Chapel. The complex geometry of the plan, the density of ornament and, above all, the introduction of pendants, partly revealing a skeleton of flying arches, deny the clarity of the contemporary work of Wastell.

2.175

arches, which seemed at once to support and be supported by the semi-cones welling from the peripheries, were to sprout full stalactite-like pendants to either side of their flattened apexes. This final denial of structural pretension in the whimsically tectonic context of the Perpendicular, inspired by carpentry, first appeared in the Divinity School at Oxford but achieved its greatest excess in Henry VII's Chapel at Westminster where it was accompanied by the first signs of the Renaissance of antique rationalism in England.**2.175**

FLAMBOYANTE FRANCE

›**2.176 S. MACLOU,** 1436–1521: (a) west front detail, (b) nave towards choir.

The extension of tracery in lace-like patterns was an obsession not of the English alone. It greatly appealed to the 14th-century French too and they accelerated the transition from the structural to the decorative – but in the detail of the parts rather than in the conception of the whole. Unlike the Perpendicular English, however, they spun their webs in immaterial flame-like forms elaborated from the ogee arch – hence their latest medieval mode is called 'Flamboyant'. However, the flickering, fragmented, fire-like movement of the tracery was complemented in the

2.177a
›2.177 ÉVREUX, CATHEDRAL OF NOTRE-DAME: (a) choir interior (from c. 1270), (b) north transept front (from 1506).

2.177b

dynamic of the period by the smooth continuity of shafts rising unbroken from base to vault: the essential simplicity of the frame contrasts with the extreme complexity of the framed.**2.176**

The great age of building on the scale of the three-storey basilican cathedral or abbey did not end with S. Denis but such buildings were rare: the cathedral of S. Croix at Orléans (from 1287 but largely rebuilt in the 17th century) and the abbey church of S. Ouen at Rouen (from 1318), with its high glazed triforium, are outstanding examples; notable too are the choir at Évreux (from c. 1300), also with

2.178a

an exceptionally high glazed triforium, and the nave at Auxerre (from c. 1320), where the early 13th-century choir was determinant in height.[2.177] In the prosperity which followed the conclusion of the Hundred Years' War, great height was again pursued through three storeys, notably at Tours, where transepts and nave were added to the 13th-century choir over much of the 15th century, and at Nantes, where the nave of a new cathedral was begun in 1434 but not completed until the 17th century. Otherwise the two-storey precedent of S. Urbain, Troyes, was widely followed: examples range from the lost priory church of S. Louis at

2.178b

›2.178 TOURS, CATHEDRAL OF S. GRATIEN: (a) west front (c. 1430–1537), (b) choir from nave (begun c. 1240 and early 14th century respectively).

›2.179 POISSY, ABBEY CHURCH OF S. LOUIS, begun 1298, destroyed: side elevation (early 18th-century survey drawing by R. de Cotte; Paris, National Library).

›2.180 VENDÔME, ABBEY CHURCH OF LA TRINITÉ: (a) nave to west, (b) west front (late-15th, early 16th centuries).

2.179

Poissy (from 1297) to the Trinité at Vendôme (from c. 1350), S. Maclou in Rouen (from 1436) to the new choir of S. Étienne, Beauvais (from 1502) or the abbey church of Brou at Bourg-en-Bresse (after 1512). **2.178–2.180**

2.180a

2.180b

2.181

›2.181 BEAUVAIS, S. ÉTIENNE: choir (1506).

The ambulatory contains some of the most remarkable early 16th-century coloured glass to be seen in France. The tracery containing it is typical of the Flamboyant in contrast to the relatively pure geometry of the clerestory windows.

›2.182 ROUEN, S. MACLOU, 1436–1521: (a) west front detail, (b) interior.

Recalling the west front of S. Urbain at Troyes, the bowed front with its five filigree gables is attributed to Pierre Robin.

›2.183 ALENÇON, NOTRE-DAME: west front (c. 1510).

2.182a

2.183

2.182b

To either scale, the tend was to eliminate imposts or stringcourses to avoid breaking the verticals of the clustered piers, whether curved into the aisle arcades or soaring to carry the main vault. As at Troyes, too, the resolution of the skeletal frame in the quadripartite vault – perfected at S. Denis with minimal residual wall – remained the norm, unelaborated with tiercerons or liernes except occasionally over crossings. However, rich screens were woven to mask exteriors, old and new, in the new style when *chantiers* were reinfused with vigour after the end of the protracted war with England: Rouen offers prime examples on the cathedral and the church of S. Maclou, so too do Alençon and Évreux; elsewhere, Sens, Toul, Tours and Troyes offer splendid examples. Above all, of course, the aspiring, dissolving style recommended itself for towers, western, central or lateral.**2.181–2.183**

2.184

>**2.184 ALBI, CATHEDRAL OF S. CÉCILE,** begun 1282: south porch, added late-14th century.

>**2.185 BOURG-EN-BRESSE, BROU ABBEY CHURCH,** 1516–31: (a) exterior from west, (b) interior looking west, (c) tombs of Margaret of Austria (foreground) and Margaret of Bourbon flanking the choir.

The church was built by Margaret of Austria to commemorate her husband, Duke Philibert of Savoy (died 1504), in fulfilment of a vow of his mother, Margaret of Bourbon, on the recovery of her husband from a hunting accident. The form, with the image of the deceased lying on a sarcophagus under a canopy, is traditional, but the exuberance of the canopy is unexcelled in a prolix genre. The design was provided by Jean of Brussels in 1516 and executed from 1526 by Conrad Meyt.

Even at their most prolix early in the 16th century, in such works as the canopy over the south porch at Albi, the French indulged in the Flamboyant for the denial of weight to mass rather than the consumption of the structural frame.**2.184** Only occasionally does indulgence run to the flagrantly anti-architectonic, as in the abbey church of Brou, where the Habsburg ruler of the Netherlands employed the Flemish architect Loys van Boghem to provide an ethereal context for the most elaborate of late-medieval dynastic tombs.**2.185**

2.185a

2.185c

2.185b

2.186a

Enriched by the war between England and France –
especially from the wool trade – the Flemish at home produced an Anglo-French hybrid: filigree façades were
extruded from vast windows etched with Flamboyant tracery and Perpendicular arcading veiled the residual basilican mass but neither denied the logic of structure even in
the vaulting – except, occasionally, over distinguished space
or in the elevated zone of a crossing tower.**2.186**

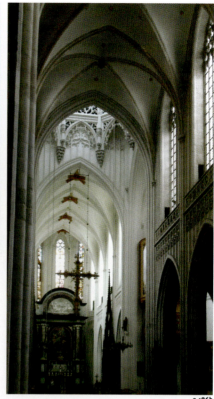

2.186b

>**2.186 ANTWERP:** (a, b) Liebfrauenkirche (begun
c. 1350, tower from c. 1500), exterior from south and
nave to choir; (c) church of S. Paul (from c. 1570 with
later furnishing), nave to choir.

2.186c

The chapel was built for Bishop Berthold von Bucheck (1328–53) by Johannes Gerlach who was then working on the western towers. His star vaults, influential in Germany and Bohemia, were reconstructed in the mid-16th century.

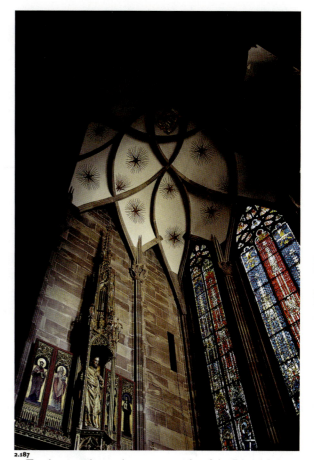

2.187

Further south, on the western side of the Rhenish border between the Frankish sphere and the Germanic, daring knew few bounds – and that was to be typical in the heart of the Empire. Most significant in the gravity-defying mode, dependent on virtuoso masons, was the canopy vault which seems to float unsupported, as at Strasbourg.**2.187** Again, the point is the denial of physical reality yet, as in England, concern with this world of suffering humanity promoted increasingly naturalistic carved decoration in place of the monumental ideograms of Romanesque fresco and sculpture.

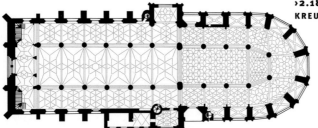

2.188 @ 1:1000

PROLIXITY UNBOUNDED: BEYOND THE RHINE

If late-medieval architecture is characterized by exuberance and ingenuity, late-medieval central Europeans demand special note. After the development of the hall church, especially the type with expansive aisles like the Viennese cathedral, 14th-century builders declared a new freedom in planning: the correlation of inner and outer ambulatory bays in accordance with French logic, as at Verden, was often abandoned and sometimes a pier-buttress closed the main axis in the centre of the outer range – as in the western choir at Naumburg.[2.111] If not the Cistercian abbey church at Zwettl in Lower Austria, the primary example of discordance is usually taken to be the choir of the Heilig-Kreuz Minster at Schwäbisch Gmünd (1351); that is attributed to Heinrich, the progenitor of the Parler dynasty of architectural adventurers from Cologne, or to his more celebrated son Peter.[2.188]

The polygonal apse was the late-medieval German norm, by no means always with ambulatory.[2.189] However, variations on the Schwäbische formula are legion after it was developed within a decade for S. Sebaldus in Nuremberg – where Peter Parler is supposed to have worked on the Frauenkirche (begun 1351), at the instigation of Emperor Charles IV, before being translated to the imperial capital at Prague.[2.190] Notable examples include several in which the main axis is closed with a central pier

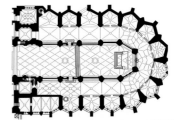

2.189a @ 1:1000

2.189b @ 1:1000

›2.189 CLOSING THE MAIN AXIS: (a) Freiburg minster: choir plan (begun 1354, interrupted c. 1375 for about a century); (b) Landshut, Heilig-Kreuz church (begun 1407), plan.

The precedent for closing the sanctuary axis with a column was provided by Peter Parler in the church of S. Bartholomäus, Kolin-an-der-Elbe (begun 1360): S. Barbara at Kutna Hora in Bohemia, attributed to Parler's son Johannes, omits the column but has a pier in the centre of the ambulatory perimeter – as do several later German churches. The work of Johannes von Gmund at Freiburg is notable in the sealing of the main axis with columns behind the altar and a pier buttress between the two easternmost chapels.

2.190a

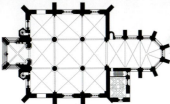

2.190b @ 1:1000

> **2.190 NUREMBERG:** (a, b) Frauenkirche, view from market square and plan; (c–e) S. Sebaldus, exterior from south-east, plan, interior of choir and detail of the saint's reliquary.

2.190f

2.190c

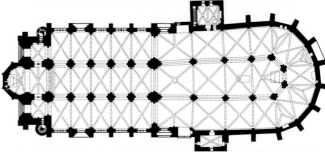

2.190d @ 1:1000

2.190e

2.191a

2.191b

›2.191 PRAGUE, CATHEDRAL OF S. VITUS, from 1348: (a) nave to choir, (b) the royal gallery.

Founded c. 925, the cathedral from 973, the first church on the site was rebuilt in basilican form in 1060. The great new Rayonnant cathedral that dominates Prague from the Hradčany was projected in 1348 on the elevation of the see to an archbishopric by the future emperor Charles IV, king of Bohemia since 1346. The French plan of Mattias of Arras seems to have been transmitted via Cologne but after Peter Parler took over in 1356 the awareness of English and German developments becomes apparent in the undulating clerestory, generated by the canting of the side panels, as in the choir at Wells,[2.80] and the decorative, rather than structural, vaulting. Parler completed the choir and began the nave: his sons continued his work after his death in 1399 but it was interrupted by the Hussites in 1421. Work began again under Benedikt Reid in the reign of Vladislav II (1471–1516). The royal gallery with its bizarre rustic detail dates from the early 1480.

Rather than crossing from corner to corner through a central boss, as usual, the diagonal ribs intersect with one another, cross through alternate bosses at the apex of the vault and join in the truncation of the transverse arch which would normally have defined each bay. The definition of the bays is asserted by the unbroken outer shafts of the first three composite piers of the choir but thereafter vertical continuity is overwhelmed by the zig-zag horizontal motion effected by splaying the triforium arcading – and corresponding fragments of the clerestory tracery – to mask the piers.

either in the outer or inner range of the ambulatory – like the choirs of Freiburg or the Heilig-Kreuz at Landshut in Bavaria (1407). In contrast, the greatest work of the Parlers, the cathedral of S. Vitus which crowns Prague, is conventionally French in plan – if in little else beyond its three-storey internal elevation.

The expansive vaults of multi-aisled halls, adopted by cathedral builders and Benedictines as well as mendicants, provided a particularly fertile field for rampant growth but the basilica offered special opportunities. The Parler school led the way in central Europe to the development of complex networks in tracery and in vaulting, ignoring or even denying structure. The prime example is the choir of Prague's cathedral. The zany arrangement of S. Hugh's Choir at Lincoln is reviewed in the light of quadripartite logic but – hardly less wilfully – an intricate lattice is woven instead to deny the definition of the bays. Ambiguity is preferred to resolution of the inherent conflict between horizontals and verticals.**2.191, 2.60d**

The game initiated at Prague was played by many of Peter Parler's lesser followers, usually with less *éclat*. Parlers called Heinrich and Michael followed the school example in the choir of the great church at Ulm which was later raised to cathedral status: the hall format, originally projected throughout, survives in the choir, where the vaulting is worthy of the master, but Ulrich von Ensingen's later development of a basilican nave avoided any ambiguity in the relationship of the vault to clearly defined bays, unrelieved by a triforium. However, producing the highest of cathedral towers – and one of the most intricate – at his new west end, Ensigen eclipsed the towers founded by Peter Parler in Prague but unfortunately never carried up beyond the height of their adjoining transepts.

Though the diagonal ribs converge on twin bosses, displaced to either side of the longitudinal axis by lateral liernes, the vault format at Ulm is essentially quadripartite.[2.192] On the other hand, in the contemporary hall church of S. Martin at Landshut – also distinguished by an exceptionally tall tower – a simplified variation on the Parler lattice argues against the insistent definition of bays by the soaring octagonal columns.[2.193] Myriad other variants were displayed throughout the 15th and well into the 16th century: some retained transverse arches, as in the Munich Frauenkirche (from 1468) where they frame

2.192a

›2.192 ULM, CATHEDRAL, begun 1377: (a) general view from the south, (b) nave.

The Protestant cathedral was begun on the plans of Heinrich Parler the Elder and continued by Ulrich von Ensingen, who had worked at Strasbourg cathedral.[2.187] He began the spire c. 1390 but most of it was built a century later, and it reached its apogee, the highest of any Gothic cathedral, in 1890.

2.192b

2.193a

2.193b

>**2.193 LANDSHUT, CHURCH OF S. MARTIN,** 1385–1460: (a) overview (tower completed c. 1500), (b) interior to east.

>**2.194 MUNICH, FRAUENKIRCHE,** 1468–88: (a) overview, (b) aisle, asymmetrical star vaulting.

2.194b

2.194a

2.195

2.196

symmetrical patterns over the nave but asymmetrical ones over the aisles;**2.194** some added a second tierceron to double the lattice, as in Bremen cathedral (c. 1500); others multiplied the liernes to effect semicentralized domical patterns, as in S. Ulrich's, Augsburg, or, on the contrary, to establish longitudinal continuity between semiautonomous bay patterns as in the Marktkirche at Halle.**2.195, 2.196** The most virtuoso variations on net vaulting drew enhanced fluidity from swirling florid curves throughout, sometimes in virtually complete detachment from the canopy membrane, as in the central boss of the Marktkirche, Halle, the Ingolstadt Frauenkirche and the Heiligenkreuz Chapel of the Willibrordidom, Wesel.**2.198**

›**2.195 HALLE, MARKTKIRCHE UNSER LIEBEN FRAUEN,** 1529–54: nave to west.

The church was formed from the unification of the 11th-century salt-workers' S. Gertruden to the west and the 12th-century S. Marien of the upper market shopkeepers to the east: above the foundations, virtually only the twin towers of each remain to either end of the spectacular new hall church.

›**2.196 AUGSBURG, S. ULRICH AND S. AFRA,** 1474–1500: nave to sanctuary.

The Benedictine basilican church with high clerestory respected the type of the monastery church burnt in 1474 – but the net vaulting followed the latest fashion.

2.197a

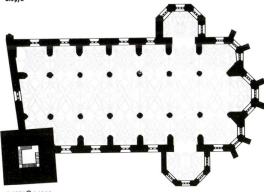

2.197c @ 1:1000

›**2.197 ANNABERG, S. ANN,** begun 1499: (a) detail
of aisle vaulting, (b) general view of hall, (c) plan.

2.197b

Beyond mere prolixity – and they were certainly in danger of self-immolation in the Flamboyant – the Germans delighted in treating the anti-architectonic network of ribs like a living vine, pruning it and leaving the severed ends exposed in brutal denial of the continuity upon which stability depends. This is a feature of the exceptionally beautiful web spun over the central volume of the hall church of S. Ann at Annaburg – which remains attached, if only physically. Though in the same plane, the aisle vaults are generated from branch ribs which grow only from their side of the great hexagonal column trunks except on the periphery where they are brutally invaded by the buttresses dragged inside to frame chapels and support a gallery. This stunning exercise is associated with the Bavarian master Benedikt Reid who worked for Vladislav IV in his palace at Prague – as we shall see – as well as on the Bohemian churches of Kutna Hora and Louny.**2.199**

2.198

›**2.198 WESEL, WILLIBRORDIDOM:** detail of Kreuzkapelle vault (c. 1525).

2.199a

2.199b

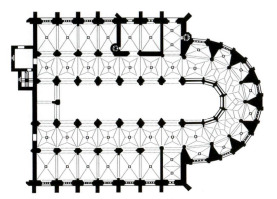

2.199c @ 1:1000

2.199d

›**2.199 BENEDIKT REID IN BOHEMIA:** (a, b)
Louny (Laun), S. Nicholas (1520–38), detail of vault,
exterior from north-east; (c–e) Kutna Hora (Kutten-
berg), S. Barbara (work had begun by 1420, ceased
until 1481, achieved the completion of the choir in 1499
and proceeded with the nave thereafter), plan, choir
exterior detail and interior to east.

The first phase of work at Kutna Hora seems to have
been directed by Peter Parler's son Johannes. Reid
transformed the original basilican conception – in part
with interconnected chapels beyond the aisle chapels –
into a hall church by raising a clerestory gallery to the
full height over dimly lit side chapels.

›**2.200 MEISSEN, CATHEDRAL OF S. JOHN
THE BAPTIST AND S. DONATUS,** 12th-century
structure replaced from 1298, west front begun c. 1315,
Chapel of the Magi (Prince's Chapel, 1423–46): (a)
model of west end (Meissen, Albrechtsburg), (b, c)
Chapel of the Magi interior details.

The Chapel of the Magi – forming a west choir – was
begun in front of the early 14th-century bases of the
towers to provide the Wettin dynasty with a mausoleum to commemorate the conferring of an elect-
orate on the margrave, Friedrich der Streitbare. Over
these same bases, Arnold von Westfalen began construction of twin towers in 1471 but only the first openwork storey was complete when work stopped ten
years later: the upper storey and spires were added in
accordance with an early 20th-century interpretation of
his intentions.

2.199e

2.200a

2.200b

2.200c

Needless to say, virtuosity in the manipulation of structural form for decorative effect in apparent disdain for physics was not confined to vaulting: of course it affected main supporting members too – for example, the twisted columns of Brunswick cathedral. After Freiburg, Strasbourg and Cologne, the filigree work of towers grows in dazzling complexity from Ulm to Regensburg to Vienna but a sense of stability must obviously prevail in such iconic structures. **2.200–2.202** This is not so with the towering altar retable or pulpit in which flight of fantasy could soar in

›2.201 REGENSBURG, CATHEDRAL OF S. PETER, choir replaced from 1273 after a fire destroyed its predecessor, nave from 1325, west front begun c. 1345: view from south-west (19th-century engraving, Franz Habutschek).

›2.202 VIENNA, CATHEDRAL OF S. STEPHAN: south tower.

The foundations were laid c. 1360 with those of the nave, completed in 1450, matching the north tower. The last was left incomplete in 1511 and capped in 1578.

2.201

2.202

2.203a

2.203c

2.203d

2.203b

2.203e

2.203f

2.203g

2.203h

>2.203 GERMAN LATE-GOTHIC VIRTUOSO MASONRY AND WOODWORK: (a, b) Annaberg, S. Ann, gallery and north aisle portal (early 16th century); (c) Prague, S. Vitus, Wladislav oratory gallery (Benedikt Reid, 1490; (d, e) Augsburg, S. Ulrich, S. Simpert Chapel vault and pentagonal portal (from 1481); (f) Vienna, S. Stephan, pulpit (Anton Pilgram, c. 1510); (g) Transylvanian altarpiece (Kisszeben, c. 1515); (h) Rothenburg ob der Tauber, Tilman Reimenschneider's Holy Blood altar (1501–04)

timber – though it may triumph even over stone, as in portals. Timber also served daring in the projection of the lateral gallery, a common feature of the hall churches of Saxony in particular. However, on the limited scale of provision for minstrels, the challenge of denying the logic of masonry construction was irresistible to late-medieval German craftsmen: S. Vitus in Prague and S. Ulrich in Augsburg offer outstanding examples.**2.203**

The elaboration of complex decorative patterns from once-structural elements on widely disparate scales is admirably represented by Benedikt Reid's Bohemian vaulting of c. 1500, as by Anton Pilgram's Viennese pulpit of 1510. But by then this was happening all over Europe. Typical of the application of the intricate to the monumental is the lacy masonry of Milan in northern Italy, where flamboyance exceeds apotheosis.**2.204**

2.204a

Milanese display

In the conception of their cathedral the Milanese were not to be outdone by any other Italian city but their case is special: no less grandiose than its southern predecessors, theirs was a truly Gothic work and Gothic masters from the north were consulted. The French recommended their Rayonnante formula, the Germans promoted height in emulation of Cologne, the Bolognese recommended the more Classical proportions they were adopting at the time for the equally ambitious church of S. Petronio. The double-aisle plan was derived from Cologne,**2.106** the proportions were broader, the piers heavier, the windows narrower. The exterior, unrivalled for its lace-like intricacy, was not completed until the 19th century.

>**2.204 MILAN, CATHEDRAL,** begun 1387: (a) exterior from the south-west, (b) interior from the west.

2.204b

2.205a

2.205b

›**2.205 PAVIA, CHARTERHOUSE,** from 1396: (a) nave to choir, (b) detail of vaulting.

Activity ceased until Filippo Maria consolidated his power. By 1429, the first of the Solari dynasty of master masons/architects, Giovanni (born c. 1410), had risen to prominence at the site but progress continued to be slow as Filippo's fortunes waxed and waned. Under Francesco Sforza, Giovanni Solari was still in place but he was assisted by his son, Guiniforte (1429–81), from 1459. The structure of the church – but not its façade, tower or internal embellishment — was finished in 1472.

›**2.206 CHAMPMOL (DIJON), CHARTER-HOUSE:** (a) church portal, (b) Moses fountain, (c) tomb of Philippe the Bold (design and socle by Jean de Marville, main figures by Claus Sluter of Haarlem and his workshop, 1391–1404, moved from the choir of the church to Dijon, Fine Art Museum).

The programme of the portal, unorthodox for a sculptural scheme in that context if not in an easel picture, has S. John the Baptist and S. Catherine of Alexandria presenting the duke and duchess to the Madonna and Child for intercession: apart from the inclusion of mortal patrons among the holy images in a church portal, the scale of the fully corporeal, emotionally charged sculpted figures breaks the bounds of convention in overwhelming the architecture. Similar attributes distinguish the figures of prophets standing forth from the pedestal of the fountain which, before its

Giangaleazzo Visconti (1378–1402), who initiated the rebuilding of the cathedrals of Milan, Como and Monza, founded the charterhouse of Pavia to celebrate the union of that province with Milan in 1385. Work began the next year on the monastic quarters and the great Gothic church: the latter was to enshrine the dynastic tombs after the sumptuous example recently set by the duke of Burgundy at the charterhouse of Champmol.**2.205, 2.206**

2.206a

2.206b

2.206c

mutilation, represented the salving mission of Christ intimated in prophecy and initiated in baptism. Again, intense psychological insight enlivens the markedly individualistic images of the mourners who process through the arcades of the sarcophagus socle: the ducal effigy was irredeemably defaced by the Revolutionary vandals.

The Charterhouse of Champmol, near Dijon, was founded by Philippe II (the Bold), Duke of Burgundy, in 1385 and the church – a hall without transepts terminating in a polygonal apse – was dedicated in 1388. Apart from the sumptuous ducal tombs – removed to Dijon – the project's claims to current fame are Claus Sluter's superb sculptures of the donors and intercessionary saints on the portal and the cloister fountain: these are the sole substantial survivals of Revolutionary depredation in 1792.

OVER THE PYRENEES

The Milanese apart, no late-medieval school exceeded the Iberians in prolixity. The Spanish, schooled by their Mozarabic masters, outdid even the Germans at expanding exquisite detail across stupendous surfaces in their vast and cavernous late-medieval cathedrals and funerary chapels.**2.207, 2.208** They too – or their Flemish servants

Founded by Ferdinand III in 1221, consecrated in 1260, the design was essentially French Rayonnante. Between 1442 and 1458 the west front was endowed with spires in a fretted style by Juan de Colonna. Between 1482 and 1494, his son Simon added the octagonal Capilla del Condestabile to the east for Pedro Hernandez de Velasco, Constable of Castile, who died in 1492 (the retable, the work of Diego de Siloe, was added in 1532). Simon's son Francesco designed the prodigous lantern over the crossing, but it was not completed until 1568 under the supervision of Juan de Vallejo.

2.207a

2.207c

2.207b

2.207d

2.208a

2.208b

›ARCHITECTURE IN CONTEXT »REFRACTION OF LIGHT

›2.208 TOLEDO, CATHEDRAL OF S. MARÍA,
13th–15th centuries: (a) retable (by a team of Flemish and
Spanish artists under the direction of Enrique de Egas
and Pedro Gumiel, 1497–1504), (b) silver-gilt monstrance
(Enrique de Arfe, 1517–24), (c) west front tower (begun
1380) and Puerta del Perdon (Portal of Mercy, begun
1415), (d) Capilla Mayor and screen (enlarged 1504,
screen of Villalpando, 1549), (e) Capilla de Santiago (mid-
15th century), (f, g) artesonado ceilings in the chapter
house and vestibule.

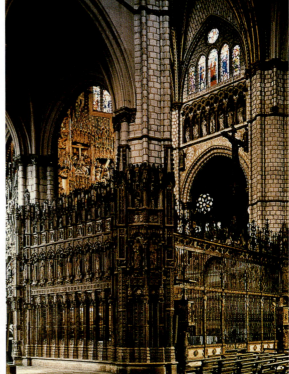

2.208d

2.208c

who came in the train of wool traders – delighted in spinning webs of ribs in vaulting, particularly in stellar form,
but usually to provide selective emphasis rather than to
promote mannered ambiguity. They indulged the Mudéjar taste for cusped arches and fringing with lace-like
valences – indeed, for intricate repetition in general. On
their invariably composite piers, further, they might
extrude filigree detail from capitals and stringcourses or
niche heads in a manner worthy of the Flemish. Beyond
that and in addition to the real weight of cover – which, of
course, the ribbing web was conceived to deny in the manner familiar since the high noon of the Cordoban caliphate
– their piers may bear three-dimensional figure sculpture,
as in Flanders.

As we know, Flanders belonged to the dukes of Burgundy in the 15th century and the late-medieval Flemish tradition is at its most prolix in the ducal tombs of Bourg-en-Bresse. As we will also recall, Flanders was linked with Castile through trade in wool – in particular – and artists came too, especially under King Juan II (1406–25), who devoted himself to lavish patronage of the arts and left government to the constable, Don Álvaro de Luna. The latter, nephew of the archbishop of Toledo, chose the ambulatory there for his burial chapel: Hanequin of Brussels was accorded the commission and Flamenco efflorescence in Spain may be seen to follow his introduction of the Flamboyant style to the project. Hans of Cologne and his son Simon were most prominent in the later 16th century: the father produced the towers of Burgos cathedral, the son added the Capilla del Condestabile. They were followed by Gil de Siloe (probably from Antwerp, died 1501), who produced the retable of S. Ana for the same cathedral (c. 1487) and the burial chapel of Juan II and his wife Isabella in the Cartuja de Miraflores (c. 1490) near Burgos.**2.209**

2.208f

2.208e

2.208g

foundation of Juan II, 1441, church from 1454 by Juan and Simon de Colonia, completed from 1488 by Isabella the Catholic to entomb her parents and brother: (a, b) retable (Gil de Siloe, 1496–99) beyond the tombs of Juan II and Isabella of Portugal, (c) tomb of the Infante Alfonso.

2.209a

2.209c

2.209b

The efflorescence of Flamenco notwithstanding, the Mudéjar tradition remained vital in distinguishing the Hispano-Christian hybrid style from its Flamboyant contemporaries elsewhere in Europe. We need look no further than Toledo for major Mudéjar examples from the waning Middle Ages – as we did for their predecessors. Such works apart, examples of Flamboyant Gothic prolixity – in which the Mudéjar mentality is rarely indiscernible – multiply prodigiously after the early 15th century when the building industry revived as Castile emerged from its era of dissent. In the centre and all four quarters of the expanded realm of the Catholic Kings, none surpasses the latest confections at Toledo, Burgos, Zaragoza and Palencia or the new basilican exercises at Plascencia, Salamanca, Segovia and Seville – of which the last, expanded in the early 15th century from the converted great mosque, acknowledges no superior cathedral in superficial area. On the relatively small scale, the funerary chapels of Juan II in the Cartuja de Miroflores and of the Catholic Kings at Toledo and Granada must be included.**2.210–2.213**

The most characteristic feature of the late-medieval Spanish church interior, perhaps, is the retable: inhabited by the major Christian icons in their hierarchically ordered ranks, this is essentially a tiered structure in gilded timber but, hedged in fecund flora, the framework is dematerialized as inconsistent with the ethereal ethos. Virtually all altars are backed with one – many postdating the waning of the Middle Ages – but obviously the greatest examples will distinguish the high altar in the Capilla Mayor, which is usually an enclosed zone at the head of the nave, and/or the sanctuary apse. Not all the complexes listed above retain a major late-medieval example but the genre certainly achieved its apotheosis in the stupendous Flemish exercises at Toledo and in the royal funerary chapel of Miraflores.

2.210a

›**2.210 TOLEDO, S. JUAN DE LOS REYES,** from 1476: (a) cloister detail, (b, c) church crossing details.

2.210b

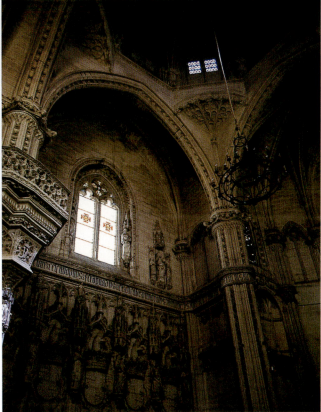

2.210c

2.211a

2.211b

2.211c

›2.211 PALENCIA, CATHEDRAL OF S. ANTOLIN, begun on earlier foundations 1321: (a) nave (c. 1450–1510), (b) apse vault (1424), (c) crossing.

2.212a

›**2.212 ZARAGOZA, CATHEDRAL OF S. SAL-VADOR** (La Seo), reworking from c. 1120 to c. 1550 of a mosque built over a Visigothic church: (a) south aisle (added c. 1500 to the original twin-aisled basilica), (b) Capilla Mayor and lantern (built from 1498 in place of collapsed Mudéjar structure of 1346), (c) south front, Mudéjar brickwork.

2.212b

2.212c

2.213a

2.213c

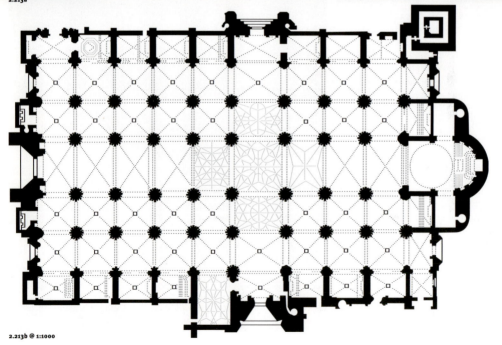

2.213b @ 1:1000

›ARCHITECTURE IN CONTEXT »REFRACTION OF LIGHT

›2.213 SEVILLE, CATHEDRAL OF S. MARÍA DE LA SEDE, 1401–1519: (a) exterior from south, (b) plan, (c) nave interior.

Built on the site of one of Spain's most extensive mosques (and incorporating the Giralda minaret as its bell tower), Seville cathedral is the largest of all medieval churches in area. The nave is flanked by doubled aisles, almost reaching its height, and the choir inserted into the central zone is itself as big as many cathedrals. The retable is Flemish.

The apotheosis of Hispano-Flamenco Gothic as the quintessentially Christian style is the prodigious elaboration of the retable: it was projected on to façades in celebration of the triumph of the Catholic Kings in the late realm of Islam. The procedure, naturally, was best suited to the single-volume hall church: the most prominent examples include Gils de Siloe's heraldic exercise at the entrance to the Colegio de S. Gregorio at Valadolid and the west front of S. Pablo there. The heraldic form was sustained well into the era of the Renaissance – despite the ideological import of its original style.**2.214**

›2.214 VALLADOLID, CONVENT OF S. PABLO, 1492: (a) portal, (b) cloister, (c) façade.

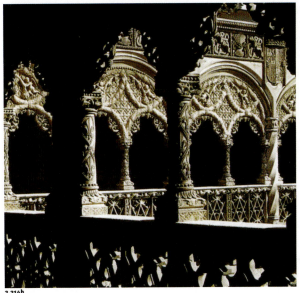

2.214b

2.214a

2.214C

›ARCHITECTURE IN CONTEXT »REFRACTION OF LIGHT

›2.215 LISBON, CATHEDRAL OF S. MARIA MAIOR: ambulatory (projected mid-14th century, executed after 1400).

PORTUGAL

Portugal has comparatively little to represent the early Gothic era. At Évora there are the cathedral cloisters, which retain massive supports for a conventional quadripartite vault as late as 1350, and the single-volume church of S. Francisco which still eludes the enlightenment of Gothic more than a century later. There is the putative exercise of adding an ambulatory to Lisbon's Romanesque cathedral at the behest of Alphonso IV but that was not completed until well into the 15th century.**2.215**

Development accelerated. Well before the 14th century was out the first phase of work on the royal funerary church of S. Maria de Vitoria at Batalha incorporates Rayonnant elements: the two-storey nave elevation is divided into bays by the outer shafts of composite piers; these rise unbroken to the residual impost blocks bearing the transverse arches of the later quadripartite vault, and both the storeys of the sanctuary apse are lit. Within a generation an idiosyncratic Decorated style was developed for the square mausoleum of the founder at the west end (1436) and for the even more splendid – if unfinished – polygonal one destined for his successor to the east (1435).**2.216**

Mozarabic notes sound through the funerary chapels of Batalha: in the founder's chapel the elements of the cusped arches may be Gothic but their application is exotic – if certainly not alien to the Iberian Moorish tradition. In the later chapel there are also echoes of the bizarre notes which distinguish the Decorated style of Bristol – a regular destination of Portuguese traders – and the articulation of the basilica's exposed flanks even struck a Perpendicular chord: it is attributed to a master who may have been English though identified as Huguet. By the end of the century the cloisters combine the Perpendicular and the Flamboyant with the secular emblems of navigation which, supplemented by heraldic devices responding to those of

2.216a

2.216b

>**2.216** BATALHA, S. MARIA DA VITÓRIA,
1388, unfinished: (a) mortuary chapel of Manuel I
(1495–1521), (b) west façade, (c) cloister, (d) fountain,
(e) plan with church (1), Capelo do Fundador with tomb
of King João I (2), Capelas Imperfeitas (3), cloister (4)
and fountain (5), (f) interior of church, (g) cupola, (h)
chapel interior with tomb of Manuel I, (i) tomb of João I,
(j, k) Capelas Imperfeitas.

A Dominican establishment, it was founded to commemorate the battle of Aljubarrota in 1385 with which
the Avis dynasty asserted its claims against its rival
from Castile after the extinction of the previous line of
rulers. It was endowed c. 1430 with the most sumptuous array of cloisters in Iberia. A series of royal mortuary chapels was developed from these cloisters,
starting with that of the founder of the dynasty, João I,
in 1434. The unfinished Manueline chapel, the last of
the series, dates from the late-15th century.

Long-established contacts between Portugal and
England, particularly Bristol and Oporto, fostered the
final flowering of the Redcliffe organism transplanted
in Portugal.

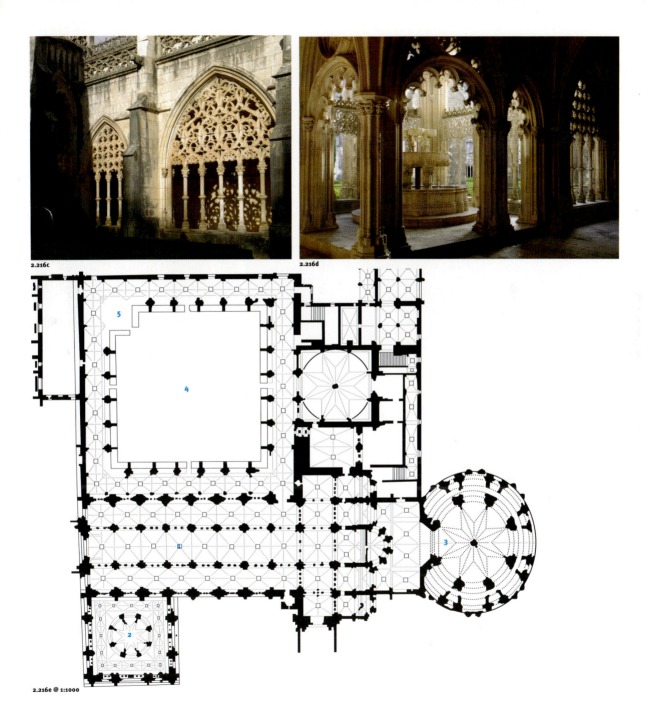

2.216c

2.216d

2.216e @ 1:1000

2.216f

2.216g

2.216h

2.216i

›ARCHITECTURE IN CONTEXT »REFRACTION OF LIGHT

2.216j

contemporary Spain, were to be the most characteristic features of the ultimate Portuguese late-Gothic style known as Manueline – after King Manuel I (1495–1521), whose sailors navigated Portugal to world power under the cross of the chivalric Order of Christ and with the aid of the armillary sphere. Apart from the portal with which Huguet's Portuguese successor provides access between the Capelas Imperfitas and the basilica at Batalha – and in which reminiscence of Bristol is at its strongest – the major Manueline masterpieces are the Monastery of the

2.216k

2.217a

2.217b

›2.217 BELÉM (LISBON), MONASTERY OF THE JERÓNIMOS, 1502–72: (a) portal, (b) cloister, (c) nave.

Jerónimos (Hieronymites) at Belem and the sanctuary of the knights of Christ at Tomar.**2.217, 2.218**

Thoroughly medieval in its conception as a hall church, with slender piers supporting a net of ribs in the high

Before completing his work at Batalha, Manuel I abandoned it for Belém where he founded a vast monastic complex dependent on a tripartite hall church, notable for its convoluted columns and star vaulting. The two-storey cloisters are typical of Iberia

in their scale and sumptuous embellishment: celebrating the discovery of the sea route to India, the filigree arches flying between the piers recall the richest of Hindu traditions (AIC2, pages 98ff).

2.217C

pointed vault, the Jerónimos complex admitted motifs from the primitive repertory of renaissante Classicism. Like Flamboyant vegetation – or the seaweed, rocaille and ropes of Tomar – they were used to embellish already

2.218a

articulated structural elements but their intrusion into the hybrid Manueline style announces transition to the new way of thinking about architecture which a century of Italians had been developing from antique humanist precept and which the current French were attempting to reconcile with Gothic ideals – as we shall see.

›2.218 TOMAR, CONVENT OF THE ORDER OF CHRIST: (a) castle entrance and keep (from mid-12th century), (b) chapel with 12th-century rotunda (Charola) centre, (c, d) Cloister of the Cemetery (mid-15th century), (e) chapel plan, (f, g) rotunda (late-12th-century arcade with early 16th-century superstructure and embellishment), (h–j) Manueline additions, chapterhouse window, nave vault detail, main portal.

2.218b

2.218c

2.218d

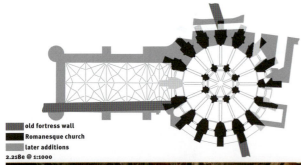

old fortress wall
Romanesque church
later additions

2.218e @ 1:1000

The seat of the Knights Templar in Portugal was established in the castle of Tomar, one of a chain of defences constructed by the victorious Crusaders from the mid-12th century. The church rotunda (late-12th century) was inspired by the church of the Holy Sepulchre in Jerusalem – and the Dome of the Rock which the Knights Templar associated with the Temple of Solomon (AIC1, page 700, AIC3, pages 48f).

The Cloister of the Cemetery was built under Henry the Navigator, who was master of the order from 1417 until his death in 1460. King Manuel I (1495–1521), who had been master of the order from 1484, heightened the rotunda, lavishly embellishing its new vault, and added a rectangular nave with a sacristy in its basement from 1499.

2.218f

2.218g

2.218h

2.218i

2.218j

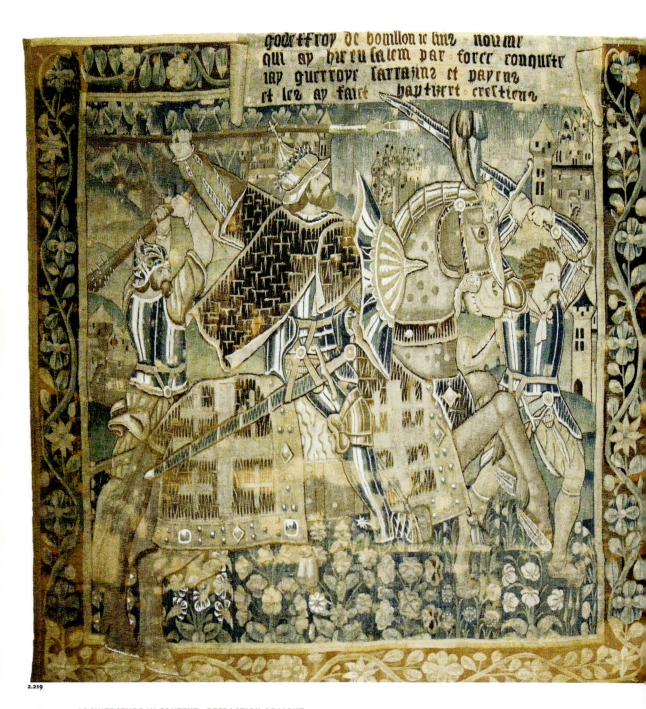

godefroy de bouillon ie suis nommr
qui ap hirrusalem par force conqurstr
iap guerrope sarrasins et papens
et les ap fait baptisrt crestiens

2.219

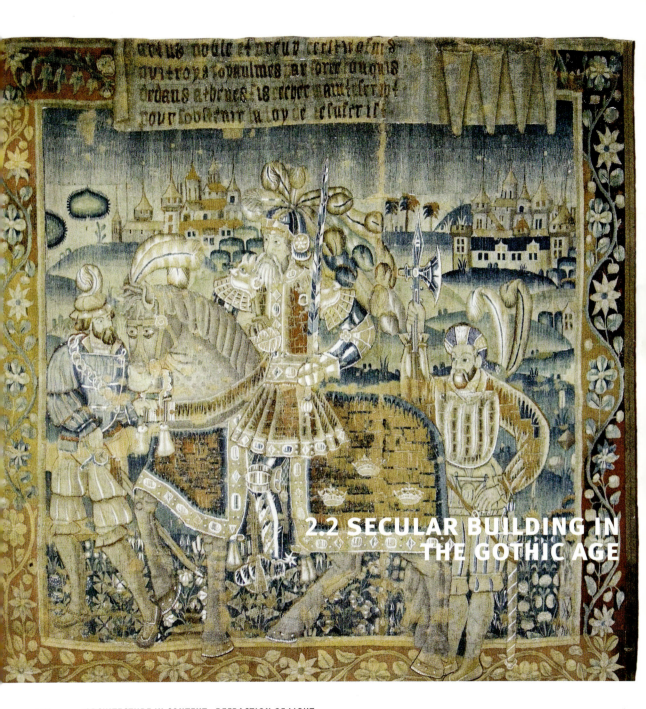

2.2 SECULAR BUILDING IN THE GOTHIC AGE

INTRODUCTION: I FROM FEUDALISM TO CENTRALISM

KINGS AND MAGNATES

As we have seen, the chief beneficiaries of the weakness of the later Carolingian emperors were the magnates – the great landowners who converted the public duty to defend imperial interests into personal rights over territory and, ultimately, arrogated to themselves the hereditary title to the great offices of imperial state. For some three hundred years from the middle of the 9th century – the high age of feudalism – their sovereign ambitions were limited by the stagnation of the fragmented economy and the degradation of the means of transport, which the very circumstances of their emergence entailed. They were, of course, also limited by the strength of their neighbours and there was a two-way struggle between them and traditional or putative centralizing powers on the one hand, residual county or radical communal authorities on the other.

The magnates won in Germany where the authority of the emperor had been undermined by papal triumph in the Investiture Dispute and the Hohenstaufen attempts to restore it were abortive (pages 55ff). Magnates also retained powerful duchies or marquisates in northern Italy but had to contend with both the monarchical ambitions of the papacy and the anti-monarchical urban communes which had emerged following the weakening of episcopal authority as a consequence of the Investiture Dispute. The county authorities remained effective in the great duchies of Aquitaine and Burgundy, well after their peers had been mastered elsewhere. In Iberia, in southern Italy, in England and ultimately in France, however, the most determined warlords welded the lands of their weaker rival magnates into kingdoms and reconstituted public authority on national bases – but with major differences.

On the one hand, substituting the relationship of subject and sovereign for that of vassal and lord, the new kingdoms were built on the revival of Roman ideas of sovereignty and commonweal. On the other hand, the king's position took on a biblical dimension. The early barbarian kings were chosen by their followers who settled in their conquests and they ruled in virtue of their acclamation. As we have noted, however, the first of the Carolingian kings, Pepin the Short, was consecrated in a ceremony drawn from the Old Testament (page 22). Thereafter, his security sanctified, his power moderated by moral responsibility, his elevation subject to the prerogative of the pope rather than merely the national will, the Lord's Anointed began his ascent to divine ordination.

The will of God in regard to kingship was deemed manifest in male primogeniture. By the end of the 12th century this was seen in the light of the success of the Norman line in Sicily and England, where the Conqueror's mastery of feudalism was furthered by his son Henry I and re-consummated by his Plantagenet great-grandson Henry II. It was also seen in the unbroken succession of Capetian kings through the male line from 978 to Suger's glorification of the monarchy under Louis VI and the impressive advent of Philip Augustus (page 228).

ROYAL GOVERNMENT

As the manorial establishment was the lord's entourage, royal government in embryo was the king's household. Four departments – the origin of the departments of state – were responsible for the quarters of the palace: the hall, where the king sat in state and presided over his court of justice, as over banqueting; the chamber, the most secure room, where the king slept and therefore also the repository of the royal treasure; the chapel, which provided clerks as secretaries, accountants and archivists; and the court-

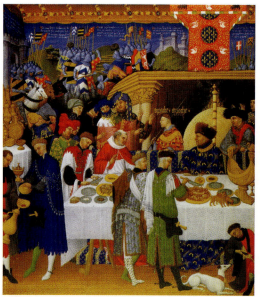

2.220a

2.220b

yard, where the stables provided for the peripatetic king's movements and promoted improvements in communications which inevitably undermined feudal localism.**2.220**

The hereditary principle, essential to the very concept of the king's divine right to rule, was naturally applied to these offices. The magnates endowed with them delegated their prerogatives to increasing numbers of specialized surrogates as the king's business expanded – but they jealously guarded the right to take regular part in the king's council of advisers in return for surrendering any feudal pretensions to sovereignty. More sophisticated but more cumbersome, the royal administration was less mobile and the concept of a settled royal capital emerged – even if the king failed to settle himself solely in any one place.

MONARCHS AND MONEY

The clumsy complexity of tenurial obligations made them increasingly inadequate for magnates on the move to monarchy. The king might be the greatest of feudal

›**2.220 OFFICERS OF STATE**: (a) the high profile of the steward; (b) the discretion of the chamberlain; (c) the dictate of the chancellor; (d) the opulence of the constable (Limburg brothers, *Les Belles Heures*, *Les Petit Heures* and *Les Très Riches Heures du Duc de Berry*, c. 1380–1416).

The nuclear hall was governed by the steward who also bore overall responsibility. The chamber was the province of the chamberlain who, as guardian of the treasure, also bore responsibility for revenue collection. The chaplain was assisted by clerks who had taken minor orders and who were often alone educated enough to draft documents, record decrees, keep financial accounts, collect and organize information: after the example set by episcopal administration, the clerks were supervised by a 'chancellor', who was responsible for the authentication of royal acts as keeper of the king's seal and held the key to the practicability of central government. The principal officers of the courtyard were the constable (count of the stable) and the marshal of the royal horse: responsible for transport, they naturally assumed control of the armed forces with which the king confronted his feudal rivals.

2.220c

2.220d

landowners but far-flung feudal levies of ill-trained and ill-equipped peasants, strictly limited in availability, were totally inadequate for ambitious imperial rulers like Henry II Plantagenet or Frederick I Barbarossa. Centralized power entailed the constitution of royal authority on the sovereign rights of the Lord's Anointed, rather than on personal claims to the service of vassals: the corollary was payment for services, first in kind and then the commutation of obligation for money.

If there was a prime agent in the decline of feudalism it was money. Before all, of course, the money had to be made anew. The old imperial monetary system was long defunct but the agricultural economy of many counties benefited from early Carolingian unity and flourishing market centres provided the basis for the ultimate revival of urban life and a monetary economy. However, the silver coinage instituted by Charlemagne had been corrupted under his weak successors. The resurrection of a sound imperial basis waited until 1231 when Emperor Frederick II issued the first gold coins of commercial viability since their ancient Roman exemplars had failed in the Dark Ages.

Economic advance, especially the revival of trade, was favoured by various developments over two centuries from the crucial year 911 (page 35): the settlement of the Vikings from Normandy to Kiev; the defeat of the Magyars and the penetration of German settlers east into Slav territory, spreading Christianity; the advance of the Christians in Iberia; the Norman expulsion of the Muslims from Sicily and the eclipse of Byzantium in southern Italy; the growth of agriculture with land clearance and its improvement with more efficient tools, drainage and transport. The population rose and so too did the proportion of free men: their number increased as free tenancies were granted widely to encourage clearing and settlement of new lands.

The scourges of the 14th century, the Hundred Years' War and the plague of 1347–50 – the Black Death – reversed the situation: the population fell to about half, villages disappeared and the value of labour took on a new dimension. The traditional pattern of manorial agriculture was obscured but the need for common action persisted and an assertive tenant could now claim the initiative. Paternalism died hard in the conservative countryside but the logic of the situation was manifest in peasant revolts – notably in France in 1358 and England in 1381 – and many villeins were able to bargain for their freedom with their labour or commute their servile obligations altogether for money.

By 1400 the ranks of the free outnumbered those still in bondage – both in the depressed countryside and in the towns. Many of these had continued to prosper despite the plague but were not to recover their pre-plague levels for two-hundred years or more. An overwhelming preponderance of free men had in fact been achieved two centuries earlier in Italy, for that is where the new money was first made on the revival of trade.

›2.221 TRADE AND THE TOWN: the Byzantine emperor John Paleologus leaving for Venice (attributed to Fra Angelico, c. 1440).

In the artist's eye, the typical town of his period is walled and many-towered.

TOWNS AND TRADE

As we have noted, Roman urban society was not lost entirely to the destruction of the empire. As the Church based its administration on the imperial system, many towns survived as the seats of bishops and some prospered as market centres. Moreover, despite the conquest of the Levant by Islam and the consequent disruption of traditional patterns of east–west Mediterranean trade by Muslim navies and pirates, commercial activity subsisted in Italian ports. Nominally ruled by Byzantium, several of these were granted preferential treatment in trade in the rump of the eastern empire. And Levantine Muslim potentates were not long to remain inimical to the profits of trade with Christians.

Ravenna, Salerno, Amalfi, and Naples were among the most important Italian trading towns but Venice led, winning self-government in the 9th century and successfully challenging the Byzantine monopoly of Levantine trade by the end of the 11th century.**2.221** By then north European wool producers offered, at last, a commodity in short supply in Constantinople to supplement the slaves and metals upon which exchange had hitherto depended. By then, too, Normans and Venetians had made significant gains against eastern pirates.

By the middle of the 12th century, Venetian domination was being challenged by other Italian ports, notably Genoa and Pisa. Their naval power was developed in action against piracy in the western Mediterranean. Their navigators pioneered the sea route to Flanders and England. Their merchants capitalized on the direct access to eastern trade offered by Crusaders transported by their fleets. In 1203 the Venetians countered by deflecting the Fourth Crusade against Constantinople: looting its treasures, they seized its mantle as queen of the Mediterranean.

North of the Alps, as in the south, an ancient forum was the natural site for a market. So too was the lea of an abbey or castle by a harbour, river, ford or road junctions and several of the major church foundations attracted annual great fairs.**2.222** From the early 12th century, the growth of settlement around markets was a direct consequence of the rise in commercial activity, north and south, the consequent amelioration of communications and expansion of the mechanism of exchange. It was an indirect consequence of improvements in agriculture: on the one hand, subsistence was supplanted by specialization of produce with a view to exchange in the town market or fair; on the other hand, the population increased beyond the means of the manorial system to support it, many were reduced to menial labour but the more fortunate – doubtless those who profited from the improved husbandry of their personal plots and found their lords ready enough to commute their obligations for money at a time of surplus labour – were freed to seek employment with townsmen dedicated to exchange or manufacture.

›**2.222 THE BISHOP OF PARIS BLESSING THE FAIR (LENDIT)** held each June between Paris and S. Denis (French ms c. 1400).

Rhenish towns, which had emerged from the Investiture Dispute in the early 12th century as quasi-independent political entities under the patronage of the emperor, were developing trade in northern products – timber, pine oil, wax, amber, furs and corn in particular – and acting as entrepots for exchange with southerners bringing the luxuries of the east – sumptuous brocades, plate and spices – to meet a growing demand from secular as well as ecclesiastical magnates. By the mid-13th century the network of exchange extended deep into Germany as emperors increased their revenues and diminished the power of the magnates by granting charters of urban liberty from the feudal system.**2.223** By then too, numerous ports along the Elbe and around the German fringes of the Baltic promoted the expansion of trade with colonization further

2.223

›2.223 NUREMBERG: general view over market square to imperial castle (19th-century engraving showing the density of housing before the destruction of the city in World War II).

The burgfried was founded in the 10th century and was augmented with hall and ancillary chambers over several hundred years. The town which grew under its protection was granted permission to establish a mint and a market by Henry III, c. 1050. Though assigned to the duke of Bavaria by the emperor Lothair in 1127, Frederick I appointed an imperial officer (*Burgraf*) to oversee its council of patricians.

east through the corn-growing Slav lands of future Prussia and Poland. To pursue common interests, moreover, many linked themselves in leagues. As we know, the most important was the Hanseatic association of Elbe and Baltic ports led by Lübeck and Hamburg (pages 247f).

Italy's central position obviously put her merchants at an advantage in the maritime exchange of goods from the east with those of the north but the continental centre was Champagne, Troyes in particular, where the greatest of annual great fairs was held at the crossroads north–south, east–west. The counts of Champagne were particularly enlightened in encouraging the development of commerce in their lands with favourable fiscal arrangements, improved roads and treaties granting merchants safe conduct through neighbouring lands. Bruges similarly benefitted from the enlightenment of the counts of Flanders as regulators of commerce and became the principal entrepot for the collection of northern goods brought by sea for despatch south by road and river. As there, entrepots naturally thrived wherever goods were transferred from one form of transport to another – drays to river barges, barges to ships, ships back to drays or barges, etc. Lübeck and Hamburg are special cases in point: river ports serving important sea lanes but linked by the road circumventing the Jutland peninsula.

In conjunction with the expansion of commerce, naturally, went the development of industry. In an age of constant warfare, leatherwork, metalwork and armoury were obviously significant. However, second only to agriculture in the employment of labour was the production of textiles in its multiple aspects – growing the wool, carding it, weaving it into cloth, finishing the textiles with softeners and dyes, shipping and marketing them. Based on wool grown in England (and Spain, to a lesser extent), it was the generator of urban prosperity from the 12th century in Flanders and north-central Italy above all. Bruges specialized in the gathering and processing of the raw wool, Ypres, Ghent, Arras and many others in the weaving, but not necessarily the finishing, of the fabrics. That was the speciality of Italian towns sited by fast-flowing rivers which supplied suitable fresh water, like Florence on the Arno. And in Italy the textile industry provided a sound basis for banking: long experienced at moving merchandise across continents, between branches of family trading firms, the Italians proved themselves particularly adroit at moving money – and at making money from money.

Prevented from owning land, but not subject to the Church's proscription of usury, the Jews were the normal source of early medieval credit, first as pawnbrokers or moneychangers in the market place. By the mid-13th century, however, Christians had found ways into money exchange that circumvented – or ignored – the anti-usury laws and, above all, the Knights Templar had began banking on the huge resources of the estates with which they had been endowed to succour the Crusaders: their fortunes were reversed early in the 14th century by King Philip IV of France, as we have seen (page 231). By then the great Florentine merchant-banking houses – the Bardi, Alberti and Peruzzi, supplanted in the 15th century by the Medici, Strozzi and Pitti – were profiting enormously from the transfer of funds internationally and the contracting of loans to princes secured by the right to collect customs dues. The Sienese, too, were building banks and fortunes on their experience of collecting papal revenues and transmitting them to Rome from all over Europe. The Lombards took Christian banking beyond the Alps but the Flemish soon proved themselves avid merchant bankers on the profits made from the liberalization of trade.**2.224**

>2.224 ANTWERP IN THE EARLY 16TH CENTURY (Antwerp, National Maritime Museum).

Philip the Good of Burgundy encouraged his Flemish merchants to break out of the trading zone allotted to them as members of the Hanseatic League and compete in the Baltic. The English, whose commercial economy was developing under the encouragement of Edward IV and his successors, were also keen to free their trade from Hanseatic control and to develop their own weaving industry. The conservative merchants of Bruges were alarmed but their more speculative rivals from Antwerp were amenable to the idea of importing English fabric – cheaper and coarser than the Flemish product – finishing it and selling it on to developing markets such as those around the Baltic. The profits were considerable: forging ahead of Bruges by the end of the century, Antwerp went on to unbounded prosperity in collaboration with Portugal's Atlantic traders who, on opening the sea route to India, had seized

dominance in the spice trade from the Venetians at the end of the traditional caravan route. And Antwerp's bankers served the cause of the emperor Maximilian who ruled Flanders through his marriage to the Burgundian heiress Mary.

International commerce and banking gave merchants great power, of course, but power was not the monopoly of the most affluent: the claims of the broader burgher community were furthered by the development of guilds. Originally fraternities dedicated to religious observance, these seem to have been initiated in response to the institution of the feast of Corpus Christi by Pope Urban IV around 1264. There were to be many other dedicatees. Beyond prayer, it was natural that people of a common calling should form such fraternities, especially in towns, and by the middle of the 14th century most involved in commerce and industry – south and north of the Alps – belonged to a guild for concerted action in the struggle with competitors or suppliers, for insurance, for the regulation of business or craft, for charitable and public works. And through the power of association, the guilds aspired to control the constitution of town councils.

GUILDS AND CIVIC GOVERNANCE

Guilds were largely successful in asserting power and fostering stability in the major trading towns of northern Europe. This was not the norm in Italy, as we have seen (page 225). In the ideal there, clan and class rivalry ceded to compromise between two authorities in the 'well-governed city' – patrician and civic, executive and council. The executive might be a college of *signori* or a duke, the council might be appointed by the chief executive or, owing more or less deference, it might be elected to represent social groups, guilds and/or districts, or it might be hybrid. **2.225, 2.226** In reality, social unrest – due to clan and class rivalry, especially the exploitation of workers by guild masters and their exclusion from council – led many civic governments to subversion by tyrannies: a *podestà*, captain or military leader would capitalize on factionalism to consolidate his personal power in centralized control over all

2.225

2.226

›ARCHITECTURE IN CONTEXT »REFRACTION OF LIGHT

Prosperity, fostered by peace and delivered by merchants, smiles on the ideal, manifest in the preponderance of open-fronted houses over castellated towers but elusive in Italy.

›2.226 S. GIMIGNANO: overview of cathedral and main square.
Unlike the rest of Europe, where the nobility was essentially rural, Italy had an urban aristocracy – descended in the main from the retainers of the ecclesiastical lords ruling from the cathedral or from landowners forced to live within a town whose growth embraced their estates. They – or their sons – were usually unruly and flamboyant and they built towers of exaggerated height ostensibly to protect themselves but obviously to assert their rival pretensions. As they had little option but to engage in commerce, their rivalry extended to the self-made merchant and the proletarian labourer. And long after the demise of the Hohenstaufen, the class struggle was complicated by the feuding of the supporters of pope and emperor – Guelfs and Ghibellines.

organs of government and acquire the title of duke from the emperor. As we have noted, this was by no means universal: among the great powers, Florence maintained republican governments in principle, though in practice they were oligarchic and Venice was exceptional in the stability of its oligarchic constitution.

KINGS AND BURGHERS

In the new monarchies beyond the Alps, the magnates might be mollified with great offices of state and places in the royal council but they were the natural enemies of kings reclaiming public authority. The natural allies of kings opposing privatized power were the commoners, even those whose commerce and industry paid him crucial tax dividends. Indeed, though the independence of town councils was naturally limited by the advance of royal government, the burghers were increasingly significant supporters of centralized monarchy precisely because a powerful king could best maintain fiscal stability and win commercial privileges abroad. And centralization of power was seen as conducive to furthering the main specific objectives of town and guild councils which included reduction of tolls, marketing licences and custom duties, release from the complex web of overlapping feudal jurisdictions, harmonization of commercial policy and improvement of international routes. Crucial was freedom from the magnates' courts of justice and the establishment of the juridical concept of the town as a corporate person equivalent to a magnate. Financial power won them the day.

Wise monarchs entered into regular dialogue with their subjects in general assemblies. Spain and England led the way – the inevitably attenuated way – to representative government, from different directions. An assembly summoned to Leon in 1188 included representatives of the towns and set the precedent for the composition of the Spanish *Cortes* with the three estates of clergy, nobles and merchants. In England in the minority of Henry III, assemblies of the notables were called in the king's name to coincide with the sittings of his courts of justice and finance committees which were attended by multiple interested parties from the shires: by the end of the 13th century coincidental meetings had crystallized into 'parliaments' and by the middle of the next century these were being held relatively regularly with the knights, shire commoners and burgesses meeting separately from the magnates, lay and ecclesiastical.

There were limited moves towards representative government elsewhere in the 14th century. The estates of the extensive French kingdom bequeathed by Louis IX were gathering in assemblies – north (Languedoil) and south (Languedoc) – and the principle of division by estate was applied at the provincial level but the king was by no means bound to heed them. The imperial *Reichstag* had long been the supreme assembly of the German magnates and the representatives of the imperial free cities but it was no more effective than the emperor: far more significant were the assemblies of the provincial estates in that world of contending magnates anxious to avoid trouble at home.

The most hotly contested issue in parliaments – always – was the raising of revenue. Revenue, of course, was the key to the king's effectiveness and changes in its conception were essential to the abrogation of feudalism. Rents or the commuting of complex webs of obligation altogether for cash largely prevailed by the 14th century in most of western Europe. However, the escalating cost of increasingly sophisticated government from the late-12th century entailed the supplementing of dues or rents with taxes not necessarily related to land ownership. Income tax – anticipated by church tithes and introduced to finance

2.227

›2.227 **JACOB FUGGER 'THE RICH' OF
AUGSBURG,** imperial banker, with his chief account-
ant (German ms, 1519).

Italian and Flemish bankers were a long-tapped
source of royal subvention – not always to their advantage as defaulting kings, like Edward I of England,
could cause widespread bankruptcy – but by the 15th
century the rulers of the north were also heavily
endebted to native merchants like Jacques Cœur in
France, or the Fuggers of Augsburg.

›2.228 **YPRES, CLOTH HALL,** begun 1202,
rebuilt since destruction in World War I.

the Crusades – was common by the 13th century and, naturally, those called on to pay wanted a say – where they had
a voice in a parliament. In return for customs dues, in particular, the merchants demanded participation in the formulation of commercial policy and they were not derisible
as they were creditors to kings and magnates who usually
needed to raise money more urgently than cumbersome
revenue-collection mechanisms allowed.**2.227**

In the assertion of the pride of the self-made man, cred-
itor to kings, town and trade hall rivalled cathedral and
palace in magnificence – especially in Flanders, where the
counts found it to their financial advantage to rule that
cloth be marketed in central halls rather than in private
establishments.**2.228** And the pride of the self-made man
is manifest in more than his material legacy: it promoted
a burgeoning enfranchisement of the mind from the allegorical mysticism which had engulfed the increasingly
abstruse scholastic attempts to reconcile Classical wisdom
with Christian dogma – as we shall see.

2.228

II CHANGES IN WARFARE

The emergence of the town as the base of power and centralization under kings in their capital cities – above all –
changed the nature of warfare. Hardly less important, the
substitution of cash for service in the constitution of royal
revenues changed the nature of the armed forces. The feudal levy of all men of military age, as cumbersome in its
complexity as the whole system of feudal dues, was largely
outmoded by the end of the 12th century – except for garrison duties in particular castles and, in general, in the
Italian republics. Instead, mercenary troops in large numbers were fielded by monarchs bent on suppressing feudalism – or one another – though it was not until early in
the 14th century that laws were issued limiting the number of liveried feudal retainers.**2.229**

By the beginning of the 13th century, in any case, the age
of specialization had dawned. In war, certainly, this had
been anticipated by the knight but he was cripplingly
expensive after the introduction of plate armour to supplement chainmail and the consequent need for heavier
horses – and he was characteristically flamboyant in individuality inimical to discipline. Moreover, the number of
knights due to be provided by the king's vassals to form his
cavalry was never enough – except, perhaps, in England

›2.230 **EXPIRY OF THE KNIGHT:** effigy of recumbent but virile figure drawing his sword, possibly Sir John Holcombe who died in 1270 (Dorchester Abbey, Oxfordshire).

›**2.231 OPEN-FIELD BATTLE BETWEEN ENG-LISH LONGBOWMEN AND FRENCH KNIGHTS** (15th-century Chartier ms; Paris, National Library).

where all men were required to bear the arms appropriate to their rank and commissioners chose them for payment in the king's service.

The days of the knight were numbered by the long-bowmen recruited by the English in the first phase of the Hundred Years' War: they demonstrated unequivocally the importance of specialized infantry training in 1346 at Crécy where they felled the flower of French cavalry. Thus served, English commanders preferred open-field fighting to siege warfare and decimated another genera-tion of French knights in the early stages of the second phase of the Hundred Years' War, particularly at Agin-court in 1415.**2.230, 2.231**

2.231

Swiss pikemen were no less effective. Armed with weapons longer than those normally wielded by a mounted horseman, they first made their mark when the Bernese defeated a coalition led by the Habsburgs at Lau-pen in 1339: thereafter, the mercenary pikemen of impov-erished Swiss cantons were to the fore in demonstrating the advantage of a professional army of well-trained infantrymen – costly as they were – and in promoting the obsolescence of the cumbersome, expensive and egotistical knight. Artillery finished him off: changing the nature of war, it also had a fatal effect on stone walls.

Gunpowder had been introduced into Europe – ultimately from China – in the early 14th century but the inefficiency of firearms greatly restricted their use. A century after the introduction of the cannon, ballistae, trebuchets and mangonels still hurled comparable missiles but the relatively light small-calibre handgun was beginning to replace the heavy, awkward crossbow – though that remained lethal in the exceptionally skilled hands of the Genoese. Handguns incorporated metal tubes but early cannon were constructed of hooped rods. By about 1450, the Florentines were casting barrels in metal and stone balls ceded to cast-iron shot which required smaller calibre bores and, hence, lighter cannon for greater efficiency.

Not matched by the English, who mounted guns at Crécy in 1346 but found them foreign to open-field fighting, these advances were crucial in sieges, as the French demonstrated in their triumph at Orléans in 1428 and often elsewhere in their campaign for the recovery of Normandy. In 1450 at Formigny, moreover, the French artillery triumphed over the English longbowman. The French crown emerged from the struggle with England with Europe's first professional standing army: it was composed of infantrymen whose release into civil unemployment could well have destabilized the kingdom either through vagrant marauding or in the service of the opponents of centralized power. There was no such problem of unemployed soldiers in England where the Wars of the Roses, largely fought in the open field, had supervened over disputed claims to the throne.

2.232a

**›2.232 THE CHANGING IMPACT OF WAR-
FARE:** (a) the castle and artillery showing spherical
and barbed canisters for demolishing buildings and
shattering against personnel respectively (late-
medieval artillery manual; London, National Army
Museum); (b) the knight and the chivalric contest of the
tournament (15th-century English illumination).

Artillery and open-field warfare with professional
armies of infantrymen, which together put paid to the
career of the knight, were equally decisive in promoting
the obsolesence of the castle as fortress-residence. In 1453
Constantinople fell when its walls were breached by
Ottoman cannon (AIC3, pages 326f): they were the most
prestigious walls in Europe, the very symbols of imperial
power, and if they failed before artillery, the average castle
obviously stood little chance.**2.232a** It had, in fact, long
been eclipsed by the town as the principal object of contention and the consolidation of centralized power naturally required the curbing of private fortifications by
punitive demolition in conjunction with limited licensing
to crenellate. As we shall see, the outcome was either a
barely-habitable royal gun emplacement or a private country house. And the fall of knight and castle from their significance in the high feudal chess-field of war coincided
with – indeed determined – the age of high chivalry: the
substance of power gone, the trappings of form and ritual
were infinitely and intricately elaborated to essentially
decorative effect.**2.232b**

2.232b

III SECULAR SENTIMENT

While ecclesiastical authority reigned supreme in the realm of the mind, it may well be true that the majority of medieval Europeans saw this world of the flesh as the mere prelude to the infinitely better or worse and, lost to the devil, not worthy of amelioration. Yet medieval man was certainly not lost entirely to meditation on God, the soul and the life beyond the grave, to hallucination, mystic vision and superstition.

Beyond the shadow of abbey or cathedral, in the hall of castle or manor at least as early as the late-11th century, the feudal lord and his servants were entertained by itinerant French *jongleurs* – later imitated by Italians – who sang vernacular epics celebrating the traditional histories of worldly heroes: these were probably Carolingians at first, then also Greeks and Trojans, and the inventive elaboration of romances from the legend of King Arthur in particular were certainly not devoid of natural human sentiment. The early historical chronicles, in verse, were related to these *chansons de geste*, and they had a measure of the fabulous in their constitution. With vernacular prose came pragmatism and by the mid-13th century there were histories focused on a lay conception of the real world.**2.219**

Sentimentality was the main preserve of the *chanson-nières* whose lyrics extolled courtly love – especially Provençal troubadours popular in Italy.**2.233** The genre had its parodists in the 13th century and its greatest product, embracing the sentimental and the satirical, was the extended miscellany known as the *Roman de la Rose* which traces the course of love in quasi-scholastic allegory, frequently resorting to the mystical but also digressing to the empirical in observation of the mundane. This too was not lost on the Italians, particularly the Tuscans, who had found their own voice by the third quarter of the century,

›2.233 TROUBADOURS ENTERTAINING AN EARLY 14TH-CENTURY GERMAN MAGNATE: the leader of the troupe is identified as Heinrich von Meissen.

to express not only deep feeling but to dramatize vivid fantasy and political reality – especially in reformative Florence. On this basis, Dante Alighieri (1265–1321) took medieval Italian poetry to its apogee.

At the most popular level, the 13th century relished the unprecedented *fabliaux*, the usually comic, sometimes satirical verse recital of ordinary human affairs in which moral ceded to incident and sensuality was all the more enticing scantily veiled in conventional allegory. The effects were vital and diversified. The typical *fabliaux* irreverence for authority signalled the rise of the lower orders and turned bitter with the exposition of their wrongs in the related, wider-ranging, more overtly satirical collection of ballads known as the *Roman de Renart*.

The wandering students called *goliardi* translated *fabliaux* material into Latin but dispensed with convention in the overtly carnal content of the collection of ballards known as the *Carmina Burana*. Raising it to high art, Boccaccio polished away the genre's extreme crudeness the better to reveal sensitivity to character: his achievement was not lost on Chaucer. And, by the mid-13th century, stock figures from the *fabliaux* began to appear in the profane plays on mundane subjects mounted to supplement the popular mystery and miracle dramatizations of scripture or the lives and deaths of the saints which, over the previous century, had developed naturally from the clergy's quasi-theatrical performance of the Church's mystical offices.

If the halls of the great rang with music which might not be much beyond the tavern, grace was lent to them by the so-called 'International' style of painting – and tapestry design – which delighted in observing nature in prolix detail as the context for both secular and religious subjects. Beyond embellishment, in literature and painting the mode inspired the garden – as we shall see.

The main weapons of attack on castles were various missile throwers designed to breach the walls from a distance: the ballista, responding to tension like a giant bow, the mangonel responding to torsion, and the trebuchet to leverage – all familiar to Vitruvius. Close encounter involved battering rams, scaling ladders and – where practicable – siege towers to provide cover and height for assault parties and protective sheds for sappers and miners whose job was to undermine the walls.

7 PERFECTION OF THE CASTLE

Residence and military installation, the castle long remained a rude establishment, overbearing in its impressiveness but with little time for art. Offensive or defensive, it was naturally designed to withstand attack from projectiles, battering rams, scalers, sappers and miners. Beyond a moat and living rock for foundation – and the massive walls themselves, of course – it is inevitably the sophisticated range of protective devices which characterized them in the latter day of their redundancy when the vitality of their aggressive forces had long been spent.

An elevated site was obviously ideal and an extensive tract of water – or marsh – was a time-honoured defence. However, the security of the inaccessible, which characterized the lair of the Dark Ages and remained dominant in Germany,[1.118] was renounced by the typically arrogant lord of high French feudalism in favour of the mobility of his forces and the practicability of their supply. And open sites, easy of access and egress were, of course, favoured by the most aggressive – the Normans in particular.[1.161] Their deployment of the motte-and-bailey type of castle as an instrument of conquest was of lasting significance.

Thrusting into subjugated territory and dominating the manorial countryside, the stone-walled ward and elevated keep were characteristic of established feudalism in general. With accommodation for its lord in the keep and a communal hall in a ward expansive enough for a garrison of knights and their horses, it was certainly the instrument of advance of a great magnate on the offensive. From it devolved a chain of observation posts, depots, consolidation points, garrison bases and courts of administration entrusted to a faithful vassal. And, of course, the base of the vassal was also a link in the network of the overlord's defences designed to dislocate the thrust of an invading army. As it would control an artery of passage – pass, river, ford, road – the hostile commander would need to neutralize it to protect his lines of communication from the rear and this would involve the division of his forces in the stultifying cause of investing it with the cumbersome siege machinery whose transport would have imposed a drag on his advance.[2.234]

French – initially Norman – developments were followed in southern Italy and England, the English furthering them in rivalry with the French. In Iberia, where feudalism was not entrenched and most castles were built to consolidate the gains of Christian reconquerors rather than as seats of privatized power, Muslim precedents were at least as important – as at Ávila, as we have seen.[1.116]

The lesson of Ávila was not immediately appreciated in the rest of western Europe. The keep, rather than the enceinte with regularly spaced towers, was still the main concern for another century and it remained rectangular, like Fulk Nera's precocious stone one at Langeais.[1.112] It naturally suited magnates who required an impressive hall, as at the Gravensteen in Flanders c. 1180 or, a generation earlier, at Castle Rising in Norfolk.[1.162]

From the early 12th century the French and their opponents experimented with circular, multifoil and polygonal forms for keeps as well as mural towers. At Houdin c. 1130, for example, a large central cylindrical tower has four smaller cylinders projecting in the cardinal directions.[2.235a] The 'Tour César' at Provins followed this precedent c. 1160, but with an octagon as its main body. Between these works, the multifoil 'Tour de Guinette' at Étampes (c. 1150) is based on the cruciform disposition and

2.235a @ 1:500

›2.235 VARIATIONS ON KEEP PLANNING IN THE DOMAINS OF HENRY II: (a) Houdin, donjon, plan of basement (c. 1140); (b, c) Étampes, 'Tour de Guinette' (c. 1150), plan of basement and general view; (d) Niort (c. 1180, the twin keeps were linked in the 15th

2.235b @ 1:500

2.235d

2.235c

century), view from south-west; (e) Orford Castle, keep (c. 1170); (f, g) Conisborough (c. 1180), model and view from south-east.

In both the French and English examples there are superimposed chambers, varied in height. Entrance is at the ill-lit lowest level.

intersection of four tangential circles.[2.235b,c] The twin keeps at Niort varied the Houdin precedent but with square plans for the main body (c. 1160–80). Built under Henry II c. 1185, Conisborough in Yorkshire also follows Houdin but approximates a polygon with its six rectangular towers projecting from the central cylinder.[2.235f,g] Orford, one of Henry II's main works in East Anglia, has a central polygon with three rectangular projections.[2.235e]

2.235f

2.235e

2.235g

2.236a

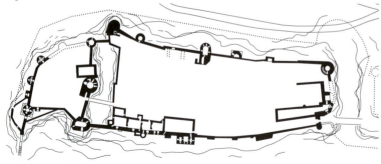

2.236b @ approximately 1:3000

›2.236 CHINON, CHÂTEAU, 10th century and later: (a) general view, (b) plan.

Founded by the Counts of Blois towards the end of the 10th century on the site of a Roman fort, Chinon passed with their inheritance to Henry Plantagenet but was lost by his son King John to Philip Augustus in 1204. Set on a spur at a bend in the Vienne, the complex is separated into three wards – virtually three independent strongholds – by two ravines. The western-most retains 10th-century masonry in its enceinte walls and the base of the Tour du Moulin (left), the slender original keep at the south-western extremity. It was eclipsed under Henry II by the cylindrical Tour de

Coudray, dominating the bridge from the middle ward, and the still more formidable mid-13th-century Tour de Boissy, at the south-east corner of the Coudray enceinte (left centre). The middle ward, built over the Roman remains, was transformed, like most of the rest of the complex, in the second half of the 12th century.

The king's palatial apartments, overlooking the Vienne to the south (centre left), and the gatehouse which dominates the bridge over the eastern ravine, were renovated and the latter heightened in the 14th century.

As the base from which to control his Angevin possessions, Henry II preferred Chinon on its elevated outcrop of rock at the confluence of the Vienne and Loire rivers: he undertook the perfection of its venerable succession of wards by incorporating massive circular towers on splayed bases.[2.236] In England, he established Windsor as a principal royal residence and give it a roughly eliptical stone shell keep in place of the original palisade on the motte between its two baileys.[2.237]

In Henry II's principal northern English castles, at Richmond, Scarborough and Newcastle (all begun c. 1174), and at Dover (1181), the landfall of the shortest crossing between England and France, the royal engineers retained the multistorey rectangular type of keep well represented in the castles of William II and Henry I at Canterbury and Rochester on the road to London – and, of course, by the Tower of London itself. The precinct of the last was greatly extended and the semicircular form was adopted for the fourteen towers which punctuate the new doubled enceinte for the first time on such a scale in western Europe since Ávila.**2.238, 2.239**

>**2.237 WINDSOR CASTLE**: aerial view.

A Saxon palace on the site was superseded by the motte-and-bailey castle built on a small neighbouring mound for William the Conqueror c. 1075: unusually, there was a bailey to both the east and the west of the motte. There must have been some palatial accommodation as early as 1114, as Henry I held court at Windsor then and was married there seven years later. Henry II inserted a suite of rooms (mainly of timber) around a lightwell in the keep c. 1175 and built a hall and a range of ancillary accommodation (partly of stone) on the north side of the eastern bailey. In the middle of the 14th century the royal apartments were extended around the eastern bailey with offices for retainers.

›2.238 DOVER CASTLE, 1179–81: overview.

Superseding a motte-and-bailey complex developed by William the Conqueror from a Saxon predecessor, itself built over a Roman fort, the four-square keep (c. 30 by 29 metres by 29 metres high to the top of the turrets, with a chapel above the stairs in a forebuilding) descends from the pioneering work of Henry's Angevin ancestor, Fulk Nera, at Langeais:[1.112] the outer curtain (completed under John) has fared far less well than the inner one (begun 1185) though the towers of the latter were reduced in the 18th century for the mounting of cannon.

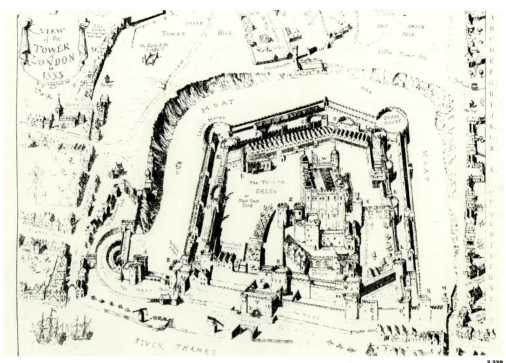

The provision of concentric ring walls, protecting one another and tiered to provide marksmen with different ranges of fire, was a major innovation at Dover and elsewhere under Henry II: it set the pattern for the reinforcement of the defences of the Tower of London and most other important royal bases in the next century. The inspiration came from the walls of Constantinople, which Crusaders to the Holy Land knew well, but it was certainly a permutation of the age-old principle of defence in depth (AICI, pages 156ff). Henry II's son, Richard Coeur de Lion, effected a stupendous synthesis of the two approaches for Château-Gaillard which dominates the Seine from a naturally defensible site at Les Andelys. Its fall early in the reign of King John, well within a decade of its conception, demonstrated that no system of defence is proof against the demoralization of the defenders.**2.240**

›**2.239 LONDON, TOWER:** aerial view of concentric development (after a drawing of 1597).

The construction of ring walls began under Henry II: the inner bailey range had reached its full extent with thirteen towers by the middle of the 13th century; the outer bailey range with eight towers, surrounded by a moat, was completed under Edward I in the 1280s.

›**2.240 LES ANDELEYS, CHÂTEAU-GAIL-LARD,** 1196–98: (a) view from west, (b) plan with (1) outer ward, (2) middle ward with (3) chapel, (4) inner ward with (5) keep, (c) overview.

2.240a

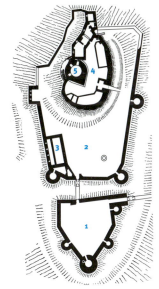

2.240b @ 1:20,000

Château-Gaillard

Château-Gaillard was built in compensation for the cession of the powerful fortress of Gisors (built by Henry I and reinforced by Henry II) under the terms of the Treaty of Issoudun (1195) between Richard of England, Duke of Normandy, and Philip-Augustus, King of France: it was on the border between their domains.

Inviting a longitudinal approach to defence, the site hardly permitted the builders to expand on the bold innovative example of Dover but the enceinte enclosing the keep is doubled in part and the outer ward, protecting the entrance to the middle one, is a putative barbican. Between the latter and the massive curved bastion on the cliff edge (c. 100 metres high), there are three wards, each with its own moat, oblique entrance and curtain. Timber hoardings for the protection of the sentries patrolling the walls from an advanced position were replaced by overhanging galleries with holes in the pavement through which missiles could be dropped (machicolation).

2.240C

The curtain of the inner ward is formed extraordinarily of compacted towers giving a scalloped profile over a battered base. Also on a steeply battered base, the keep is semicylindrical on the cliff front, semirectangu-

lar within the ward for the deflection of missiles and its projecting wall-walk, with the precocious machicolation, may have been carried by arches supported on the tapering piers which survive to the level of imposts.

CRUSADERS AND THE DECENTRALIZATION OF MASS

The renewed emphasis on the enceinte and the introduction of the concentric principle in Europe followed closely on developments in the Holy Land. Shortage of Crusader manpower and enhanced difficulties of relief and supply obviated lengthy sieges, encouraging concerted attack and promoting decentralized defence to meet any eventuality with uniformly distributed strength – except, of course, at the gatehouse where the greatest vulnerability required the stoutest mass.

A magnificent chain of castles defended the Levantine coast of later Syria and Lebanon. Many had rectangular keeps like the castles at home. To the Byzantine context at Saone, however, the great keep-like block tower was added to protect the main entrance and its extraordinary bridge.[1.111] Even more significantly, the new site at Belvoir was developed after the example of the Roman *castrum* with concentric square enceintes entered through doubled gates to the east and a formidable gatehouse to the west. The last contained a hall but there was no keep.[2.241]

The Crusaders rarely developed a coherent strategy backed by these castles and their defence was less than resolute until the advent of the knightly orders of Hospitalers and Templars: the former was founded in 1131 and dedicated to tending wounded Crusaders in a hospital established in Jerusalem; the latter was founded in 1136 to protect pilgrims and defend the site of the Temple in Jerusalem. They transformed many castles, notably Belvoir from 1168, Margat and Krak des Chevaliers from 1147.[2.242, 2.243]

The Crusader castle at its apogee

Margat was the most southerly of the formidable string of fortresses built on or near the coast for the protection of the Crusader principality of Antioch and the County of Tripoli. In the hands of the Hospitalers it played an

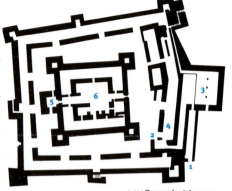

›**2.241 BELVOIR, SYRIA,** 1198: plan with (1) main entrance, (2) inner gate, (3) east tower, (4) stores and stables, (5) entrance to inner stronghold, (6) inner courtyard.

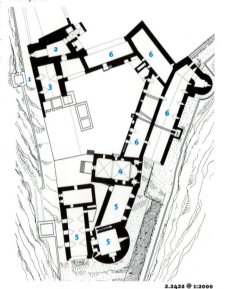

›**2.242 MARGAT (MARKAB), CRUSADER CASTLE,** mid-12th century and later: (a) plan with (1) main entrance to outer ward, (2) entrance to inner ward, (3) chapter house basement, (4) chapel, (5) main halls and chamber, (6) barracks and magazine chambers, (b) general view from south with keep foreground.

An extensive outer bailey is enclosed in large part by doubled walls punctuated with semicircular and rectangular towers at irregular intervals: a recessed tower guards the main gate in the western range. To its south, beyond a wide ditch, the roughly triangular inner bailey is also enclosed with doubled walls within the completed circuit of the outer bailey walls: the main strength is the massive tower at the southern apex where the main accommodation is concentrated in a triangular complex not expansive enough to frame an additional ward.

increasingly important role after the two states were united in 1174. It held out against Salah al-Din's invasion of 1187 and the Hospitalers moved their headquarters to it when Jerusalem fell to the great Kurdish general (AIC3, page 167). As augmented thereafter, a massive square tower protects its entrance and an even more massive cylindrical one reinforces the walls of the extended polygonal enceinte at their most vulnerable southern apex.

The majestic eminence of Krak, which dominates the main route from Damascus to the sea through the anti-Lebanon range, was under the control of the Knights Hospitaler by the 1140s. They first built the central D-shaped enceinte with its stupendous glacis. Extensive further building was undertaken after the union of Tripoli with Antioch in 1174 and again after the fall of Jerusalem in 1187.

2.242c

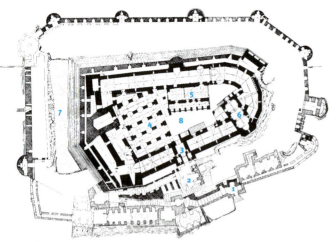

2.243a @ 1:2000

The reinforcement was decentralized: an outer enceinte largely doubles the inner one on the concentric principle and the tiered ramparts were overawed by a complex of linked towers at the north-east corner to protect the main entrance.

At Margat the accommodation was largely arranged between the doubled walls of the enceinte – except for the laterally disposed chapel. At Krak too, the accommodation was initially mural – except for the chapel – but developments in the first half of the 13th century encroached on the roughly trapezoidal court: in particular a new great hall was graced with a

2.243b

2.243c

>2.243 KRAK DES CHEVALIERS: Crusader castle (founded 1031 by a Kurdish chief, captured by the Christian forces of Antioch in 1109): (a) plan with (1–3) lower, upper and inner main gates at the beginning and end of acute-angled ramp, (4) vaulted magazines supporting terraces, (5) great hall and loggia, (6) chapel, (7) reservoir ditch, (8) court, (b) south-west view, (c) court.

The complex, on its ridge beyond a ditch, is first

defended from galleries in the southern sector of the outer enceinte: this was the main area of development under the Mamluks who repaired the damage they had inflicted and added the massive square tower. Upper defensive galleries link the massive circular towers of the inner enceinte's southern flank: each tower has stacked apartments, the south-western one accommodating the commandant.

loggia in a precocious exercise of embellishing a military establishment in the Gothic style.

Krak was among the last Crusader holdings to fall to Sultan Baybars in 1271: apart from repairing the damage caused by his breach of the outer walls, the Muslim conqueror commissioned the great square southern tower.

2.244a

Before the embarcation of the First Crusade at the end of the 11th century, the European castle was by no means invariably dominated by an isolated keep: the *seigneur's* accommodation was usually and most conveniently stacked in a tower but it was sometimes distributed informally around the ward enclosed by the ramparts – as at Chinon, for example, or at Angevin Angers on the Loire well before the enormous renovations of Louis IX.**2.236, 2.244** However, Krak and Margat anticipate the most significant trend in French castle planning after the rise of Dover and the fall of Gaillard: abandoning the disposition of wards before or around an isolated tower but retaining concentric walls, this promoted a more aggressive concentration of strength all round the perimeter and deployed the greatest weight at the principal gate rather than in a central keep.

›2.244 ANGERS, CHÂTEAU, 10th–13th centuries: (a) view from south-east, (b, c) models showing phases of development, notably the decapitation of the towers.

Dominating the River Maine from a ledge of rock fortified by the Romans, the castle at Angers was the seat of the Counts of Anjou from the middle of the 9th century. The river and the rock escarpment largely provide for defence from the north-west. Around the other sides, a moat doubles the ramparts with their formidable succession of seventeen cylindrical mural towers due largely to Louis IX. Within, in lieu of a keep, there was a comtal hall dating at least from the time of Henry II and an earlier chapel. The existing palatial buildings are largely 15th century. The towers were reduced to the height of the walls under Henry III in 1585.

2.245
›**2.245 COUDRAY-SALBERT** (Deux-Sèvres), c. 1220.
Built by the Seigneur de Parthenay, a roughly rectangular enceinte protected by the Sarthe river is punctuated with six round towers, those at the outer corners slightly pointed in profile the better to deflect missiles.

A massive gatehouse offered ample accommodation for the *seigneur* and the complementary tendency was to build the hall and ancillary facilities either between the doubled walls framing a courtyard or against the inner range. Dourdan, built for Philip Augustus c. 1222 with a near square enceinte and regularly spaced cylindrical mural towers of which that on the northern corner has the larger proportions of a keep, is one example. Another is the castle of Carcassonne, which dominates the main line of approach from Toulouse to the north-west and protects the main gate in the town walls. Coudray-Salbert (1220) is one of the most impressive representatives of the type.**2.245**

PERSISTENCE OF THE KEEP IN FRANCE

Great keeps with three or more halls superimposed over storage cellars persisted throughout the 13th century and later. Rectangular forms remained common, especially in Italy, and there were even triangular ones, as at Beaucaire on the Rhône where Provence meets Languedoc. Cylinders were more usual in France than elsewhere: the Louvre of Philip Augustus and the main towers of Châteaudun, both isolated within the enceinte, Falaise and Coucy, integrated with the enceinte like Dourdan, rank with the most formidable examples.

The keep at Coucy, clearly recalling Margat in its form, as its apartments recall Krak in their Gothic elegance, dominated a roughly trapezoidal ward from the side of a ravine protecting the approach.**2.246** As there, by the middle of the century barbicans were regularly projected for the advanced protection of entrances, bartizans extended the range of vision and overhanging galleries with machicolation were carried solely on corbels to the exclusion of piers which might interfere with surveillance of the perimeter of the walls below. In the absence of Coucy,

2.246a

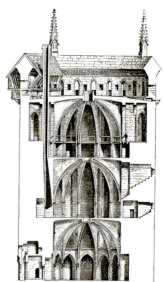

2.246b

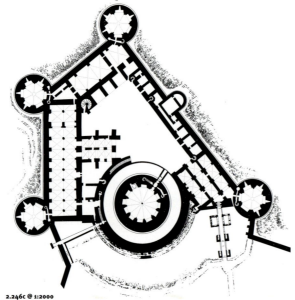

2.246c @ 1:2000

destroyed by German artillery in World War I – but imaginatively reconstructed in the previous century by Viollet-le-Duc on the basis of survey drawings and romantic watercolours – Vitré in Brittany may be taken to represent the cylindrical keep and its repertory of defensive devices.**2.247**

›**2.246 COUCY-LE-CHÂTEAU,** 1225–45: (a, b) reconstruction and section (after Viollet-le-Duc), (c) plan.

The château of Enguerrard III de Coucy was built from 1225 over 10th-century foundations on a spur beyond the enceinte of its small town. The massive cylindrical keep was 55 metres high and 31 metres in diameter. The ward was surrounded by walls rising almost to the height of the four subsidiary cylindrical towers at the corners (40 metres). Apart from the three vaulted chambers superimposed in the keep, the main accommodation was built against the three outer ranges of wall.

›**2.247 VITRÉ, CHÂTEAU,** 11th–14th centuries: view from south-west.

The vast triangular enceinte is protected by cylindrical towers at the corners and puntuated by square ones in between, all on battered bases. The entrance, in the centre of the eastern range, is flanked by twin round towers – in the time-honoured way. Apart from the largest tower at the southern apex, the gatehouse and its north-easterly extension provided the main accommodation. The Margat formula, varied here, was often to be followed.

2.247

2.248

The original castle built by Henry I's chancellor Geoffrey de Clinton, of earthwork and timber, was replaced in stone after the property passed to the crown c. 1180, the enceinte keeping to the original roughly circular line and the massive keep conforming to the rectangular formula employed so impressively elsewhere in the latter part of Henry II's reign. The outer curtain was begun under King John.

DEVELOPMENTS IN ENGLAND AND WALES

In England Henry III imported a new standard of civilization from France to ameliorate the roughness of castle life – at least for the royal circle – but new castle building was not prolific. Circular and multifoil keeps were built at Pontefract and York.**2.248** However, the devolution of strength to the enceinte had begun to counter concentration on the keep: the mural towers were reinforced as autonomous units, each a key to a section of wall so that the fall of the whole could only be accomplished by diversified action, and gatehouses were augmented in mass.

The walls of Dover were strengthened and divided into sectors and the Tower of London was ringed with a double concentric system between 1250 and 1280.**2.239** The gatehouse at Newcastle was greatly augmented in 1247. At Kenilworth the early 13th-century outer curtain, protecting the 12th-century bailey, was reinforced with great towers at the salient points and a succession of formidable twin-towered gatehouses sealed the entrance causeway with which the stream-fed moat had been extended into a great lake.**2.249**

2.249a

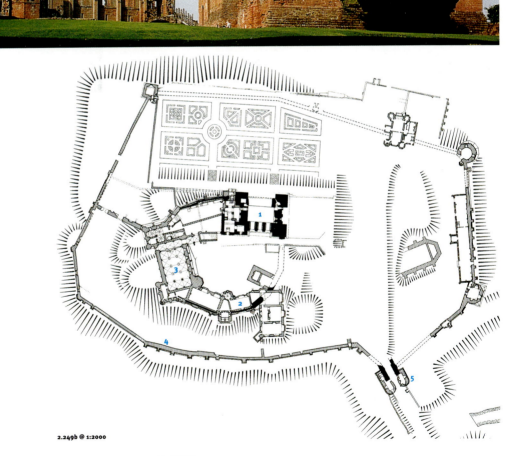

2.249b @ 1:2000

›ARCHITECTURE IN CONTEXT »REFRACTION OF LIGHT

2.250a

The culmination of these developments was in Wales. Kidwelly and lake-engulfed, concentric Caerphilly (from 1268) had massive gatehouses instead of keeps, five at Caerphilly placed virtually on the east–west axis of an almost symmetrical complex: organic unity had supplanted the ad-hoc disposition of disparate units to pronounced aesthetic effect.**2.250** On this basis, perfection was pursued towards the end of the 13th century for Edward I of England: the Savoyard master James of S. George d'Esperanches was in charge of the royal works but the king

›2.250 CAERPHILLY CASTLE, from 1268: (a) main complex from eastern gatehouse, (b) great hall (c. 1326).

Built to protect Cardiff by Gilbert de Clare, Earl of Gloucester, lord of Glamorgan, the complex is set on an island in an artificial lake – as at Kenilworth where Earl Gilbert had taken part in the siege of 1266. The monumental barrage exceeds the causeway at Kenilworth and, though there is a heavily defended gate at its southern extremity, the main access cuts across its line from the formidable eastern gatehouse – the first of the five on the main axis. The outer curtain is low with curved projections to the four corners, concentric to the drums of the four inner curtain corner towers, and

2.250b

minor twin-towered gates before the major ones flanking the central courtyard. The dominant eastern one, defensible from outside and in, had two storeys of accommodation for the patron and his constable – the former in a large, well-lit hall on the second level. This proved inadequate, however, and was superseded early in the 14th century.

The screen at the entrance end of the hall is modern but reproduces an important feature of the 14th-century hall, acting as a draught break and masking the doors to storerooms behind the end wall. The present roof dates from the restoration of the castle undertaken by the Marquess of Bute in the 1870s.

himself had unrivalled knowledge of castle design gained on crusade to and in the Holy Land and in fighting for his inheritance in France.

Master James was commissioned to construct castles beyond the Scottish border in the attempt to consolidate Edward's conquests there towards the end of the 13th century but the projected series was not significantly extended beyond Kildrummy and Bothwell. For the protection of his flank while confronting the Scots, the king needed to deal with the Welsh whose prince, Llywelyn, refused to acknowledge his suzerainty. He fought three campaigns (1277, 1282–83, 1294) and built ten castles to secure the principality: work began in 1277 with rebuilding at Flint, Aberystwyth, Rhuddlan and Builth and progressed to the new masterpieces at Conway, Caernarvon, Harlech and Beaumaris after Llywelyn's death in 1282. The last two are particularly confident, coherent, symmetrical exercises, their principal mass displaced from the centre to form imposing axial gatehouses. A great hall and lesser accommodation adheres to the walls in all four of the later works but it is in the formal context of Harlech and Beaumaris that the secular quadrangle seems first to emerge.[2.251]

2.251a

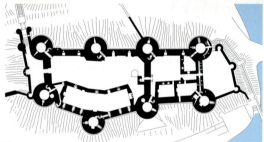

The achievement of Edward I

Edward I's Welsh castles were built primarily with the military purpose of sheltering garrisons committed to the subjection of a conquered population and, apart from the centre of provincial administration at Caernarvon and its contemporary at Conway – to a lesser extent – their residential purpose was limited. Design was sometimes constrained by existing work but siting with access from the sea for provisioning and relief was crucial to the strategy of containing the Welsh in a virtual siege. The earliest in the series, incorporating earlier town defences, were varied in perimeter and at least partially concentric. One round tower usually dominated: at Flint, for example, a keep recalling the one at Coucy is detached from the south-west corner of a roughly square enceinte.

>**2.251 THE LATE WELSH CASTLES OF EDWARD I:** (a, b) Conway (1283–87), general view from north-west and plan; (c, d) Caernarvon (1283), view from south and plan; (e, f) Harlech, view from south-west and detail of east front gatehouse; (g, h) Beaumaris, aerial view and detail of main gate.

Built without a dominant gatehouse keep, without concentric walls, the curtain at Conway follows the irregular edge of a narrow, elevated rock ledge at the confluence and estuary of the Conway and Gyffin Rivers to its east and south. The north flank, adjoining the garrison town, is protected by a moat and there are barbicans at both the eastern and western ends. Eight massive cylindrical towers, the size of many earlier keeps, project well beyond the walls and the wallwalk continues round them: the pair at each end frame the gates in the manner of the twin-towered portal, of course, but the main body of a gatehouse keep is lacking. The east and west ends are machicolated but there are support holes for timber hoardings on the towers. A cross-wall slightly to the east of centre divides the quarters of the garrison (with the great hall for general assembly) from the royal apartments. Posterns open from the inner bailey to the river (south) and the estuary (east).

2.251c

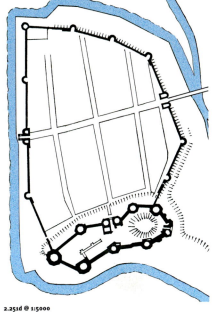

2.251d @ 1:5000

In the four late Welsh masterpieces and in his Scottish exercises, decentralization was a variable formula for Master James. A pragmatic response to site – and existing work – was naturally the foremost determinant and prompted an elastic irregularity, with the perimeter advancing and recessing about partial pentagons at Conway and Caernarvon.

The enceinte of Caernarvon, projected to incorporate an existing motte on a level site by the River Saint, was integrated with the defences of a new town, as at Conway. Master James was responsible until 1295 when Walter of Hereford began work on the north face and the King's Gate. The latter has some of the characteristics of a gatehouse keep and its dependencies once divided the compound into two wards, the outer one for the garrison served by the secondary Queen's Gate, the inner for the royal entourage. The Eagle Tower at the junction of the royal ward with the town acts as keep (as at Flint). The coloristic banded masonry and polygonal towers recall the Theodosian walls of Constantinople in an unequivocal demonstration of imperial power(AIC1, page 704). Edward I's heir was born there in 1284 and later invested with the principality of Wales.

2.251e

Harlech commands the coastal plain from a magnificent elevated site, Begun in 1282, substantially finished in 1285, it is related to Caerphilly but is more regular: it marks the apogee of 13th-century castle design for its lucidity and functional efficiency. As at Caerphilly, there is a massive gate-house and a low outer curtain which bends round the four great corner towers of the main enceinte to follow the line of the walls: there is room for a moat on the south flank and before the eastern barbican but the security of the posterns opening on to the precipitous north and west faces of the spur is reinforced by a meandering outer wall bounding the path which descends to a water gate in the floodplain below. The massive strength of the gatehouse keep was, of course, presented to the most accessible east front: beyond it is a smaller gate in the outer curtain defending a drawbridge across the moat, as at Caerphilly. As there too, the constable could be accommodated in the gatehouse but there was a great hall and ancillary accommodation around the perimeter of the trapezoidal inner bailey. As at Conway, the wallwalk carried by the immensely thick curtain continues around the inner faces of the angle towers (12 metres high) but not through them, preserving their integrity.

2.251f

2.251g

2.251h

Faced with another Welsh rebellion in 1294, Edward I commissioned Beaumaris – the last of his great series of castles – to protect the sea lanes supplying Caernarvon. It is set low on the shore to provide a bridgehead from the sea: the flat plain between land and water is the key to the perfection of the exercise – the perfection of the Caerphilly formula of two axial gatehouse keeps controlling a concentric compound. The compound, square in octagon, is perfectly symmetrical, and the identical masses of the main gatehouses are aligned virtually north–south but the gates in the outer curtain are deflected off axis to the north-east and south-west with the time-honoured purpose of denying assailants a direct line of approach. The sea to the south is admitted through a dock to feed the moat which protects the outer curtain all round: the south-western entrance is a water gate, the north-eastern one is served by a drawbridge. The outer curtain was finished after 1320, the corner towers of the inner curtain were never to reach full height and the accommodation around the ward was always to remain provisional. Nevertheless, the concentric form achieved its apogee in the rational formalism of Beaumaris – if not at Harlech.

2.256a

8 FROM CASTLE TO HOUSE IN ENGLAND

Complementing the process of consolidation in the design of the castle for efficacy of fortification, its domestic aspect was extracted from the military context and relaxed, opened to light and air. This is first widely apparent in insular England where there was an idiosyncratic degree of security under the Normans and Plantagenets. The process – symptomatic of the decline of feudalism under effective monarchy – was given impetus under Henry II by the demolition of many unlicensed castles built in the anarchy of his predecessor's reign and strict limitation of licences for new ones.

The evolution of the domestic establishment in the 13th century, especially for redundant knights paid off by their overlords or enriched in the French wars, entailed the diversification and decentralization of space. This led in the 14th century to the production of ever larger houses, increasingly ordered in design and pretentiously emblazoned with once-defensive elements – moat, gatehouse, machicolation, crenellation – out of serious military context as badges of former feudal power reclaimed by the monarch.

2.252a

2.252b

›2.252 OAKHAM CASTLE, RUTLAND, c. 1185: (a) exterior, (b) interior of hall.

The aisled hall (c. 20 by 13 metres) was built within an existing motte-and-bailey castle by Walkelin de Ferrars who was lord of the manor of Oakham between 1166 and his death in 1201. Internal columns, separating aisles and nave as in a church, are characteristic of secular buildings with wide-span roofs but the sculpture, closely related to the contemporary early Gothic work in the choir of Canterbury cathedral, is exceptional. Filled-in windows and doors on two levels at the east end indicate that there was once a solar block.

THE GREAT HALL

Following Saxon precedents and perhaps aware of the imperial *Pfalz* (pages 596ff), Williams I and II led the way from keep to hall at Winchester and Westminster respectively. Emulating the king, from the middle of the 12th century at least, great lords built well-lit, easily accesible halls in the baileys of their castles: the most prominent early examples, both from c. 1150, are in Leicester and at the Farnham seat of King Stephen's brother, Henry of Blois, Bishop of Winchester. The hall of Henry II's Clarendon (c. 1174) is lost but the splendid one built a generation later in Oakham Castle, Rutland, doubtless gives some indication of its appearance.**2.252**

The grandest surviving 13th-century example is the aisled hall of Henry III's castle at Winchester. Its descent from the ancient Roman basilica ('the place of the king') is obvious but the scale and complexity of its carpentry link it with the greatest of tithe barns in the construction of which the technology for spanning truly monumental space was advanced.**2.253, 2.254**

Royal Winchester

The Saxon capital, maintained in conjunction with London by the Normans and several of their Plantagenet successors, Winchester was the birthplace and favoured residence of Henry III who enlarged and reroofed the hall originally built by William the Conqueror. Measuring c. 34 by 18 metres, it is divided by clustered marble columns with gilded capitals into nave and two aisles. The roofs over the aisles, steeply pitched in line with the trussed rafters of the nave and pierced with dormers, was raised to the present level and the dormers eliminated during the reign of Richard II.

Traceried windows assert the influence of French ecclesiastical Gothic, which the king was to promote on a major scale in the rebuilding of Westminster Abbey. Yet the palace was still essentially Norman in the irregular arrangement of buildings of various sizes within the castle bailey. The king's chamber (c. 24 by 8 metres and 9 metres high) was the most important room, apart from the great hall, and its comfort was enhanced with wainscotting, painting and glazing (completed by 1236). The hall was restored and reroofed in 1874.

›2.253 WINCHESTER, GREAT HALL OF HENRY III, 1222–36: interior.

›2.254 GREAT COXWELL, BARN, c. 1300: (a) exterior from south-west, (b) interior from south-east.

Built on the manor of Faringdon, with which King John endowed the Cistercian community later established at Beaulieu, the barn (c. 44 by c. 12 metres) served one of the five manor farms for the storage of grain and wool. The walls are of roughly dressed Cotswold stone, except for the ashlar quoins and buttresses. There were originally only two doors, in the eastern and western walls – the latter with a large porch (the doors in the gable walls date from the 18th century). Aisled, the hall's intermediate posts rise from stone plinths, are tied back to the side walls and are double-braced to the main purlins and the cross-beams spanning the central space. The roof rises steeply in one plane: subsidiary purlins in the section over the aisles are clamped between doubled rafters over each post and between rafters and cruck trusses embedded in the wall in the centre of each bay. Two secondary purlins to each side of the upper level are clamped between doubled rafters carried on the main cross-beams and on small truncated tie beams over the intermediate cruck trusses (upper left foreground).

2.245a

2.254b

2.255a

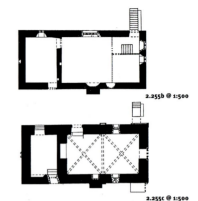

2.255b @ 1:500

2.255c @ 1:500

›**2.255 BOOTHBY PAGNALL, LINCOLNSHIRE, HALL HOUSE,** c. 1200: (a) exterior, (b, c) plans of basement and first-floor, (d) basement interior.

THE MANOR

Dominating the lightly defended village community of villeins with the adjacent church,[1.5] the simplest post-Conquest form of manor house followed the example of the seats of subject Saxon lords settled under the new regime. It was of either one or two storeys. The former was more flexible, admitting of ready extension. Intrinsically self-contained, the latter obviously offered greater security with a vaulted basement for stores – if not animals – and external stairs to the main storey where the multipurpose hall was usually partitioned to form a withdrawing room for the lord at the far end.

The one-storey hall natually offered greater freedom of access with doors opposite one another at one end and attached storerooms (pantry for bread, buttery for bottles) with a private seigneurial withdrawing room (solar) above them. At first there was no direct communication between these additional rooms and the hall. Soon, however, a window was opened in the solar to command a view of the hall below and a door in the centre of the party wall gave access to a passage, flanked by the storerooms and solar staircase, which led through to exterior kitchens.

The rare, virtually unaugmented example of the wholly

Though only for storage and, perhaps, sheltering animals, the cellar might be vaulted as a precaution against fire, as here, or simply ceilinged with the floor of the hall. The entrance stairs to the first-floor hall are more usually parallel to the wall, as in the much grander context of Castle Rising. The original doors survive on both levels and so do the solar windows (right here) but the hall window (centre) was enlarged in the 14th century: the windows would have been shuttered as glazing was beyond the reach of all but the greatest magnates. There seems already to have been a screen beyond the door, forming something of a draught lobby. The ubiquitous device of a hole in the roof for the evacuation of smoke from the hearth persisted in lofty halls built at ground level but central hearths were obviously dangerous in raised halls with wooden floors. In this context fireplaces and chimneys appear in the Norman period.

2.255d

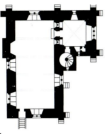

2.256b @ 1:500

›2.256 LITTLE WENHAM HALL, 1270–80:
(a, page 528) exterior, (b) first-floor plan.

Apart from the elevation of the hall over a cellar, the only defensive feature is the tower attached to the east. Providing a solar opening off the hall (now the chapel), such an addition anticipates the development of accommodation in a perpendicular wing.

›2.257 STOKESAY CASTLE, SHROPSHIRE,
c. 1285–1305: (a) plan with gatehouse (1), north tower (2), hall (3) and southern watchtower (4), (b) general view.

The site was developed with a hall and tower c. 1240. The wool merchant Laurence of Ludlow rebuilt the hall c. 1285, incorporating the north tower. Set at ground level with large windows in an area of potential trouble near the Welsh border, its defences doubtless caused concern from the outset. A new curtain wall enclosing the moated compound, a gatehouse (rebuilt in the 16th century), and the southern watchtower were built in 1291 following the issue of a licence to crenellate by Edward I.

two-storey type at Boothby Pagnall in Lincolnshire dates from c. 1200.**2.255** Little Wenham in Suffolk (c. 1275) is a variant with the projection of a small wing to the east which anticipates the development of a coherent complex in place of the random grouping of detached elements.**2.256** An example of the alternative type with ground-floor hall is still distinguishable among later buildings at Charney Bassett in Berkshire (c. 1280). There

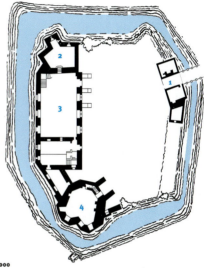

2.257a @ 1:1000

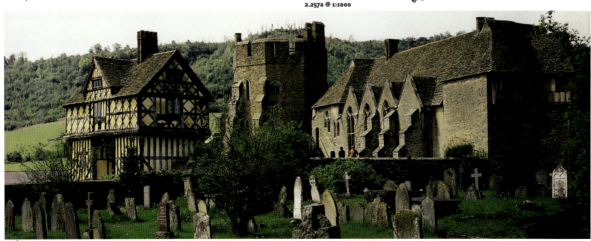

2.55b

2.258a

are many other examples with a two-storey block at each end, like Stokesay in Shropshire (c. 1290), which survives almost unchanged in its moated compound, or the nucleus of magnificent Penshurst Place in Kent (c. 1345).**2.257, 2.258**

The first concession to comfort, appearing early in the 14th century, was the screening of the entrance end of the hall to provide a draught lobby – as restored to the great

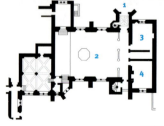

2.258b @ 1:1000

2.258c

›2.258 PENSHURST PLACE, KENT, from 1341:
(a) exterior from south, (b) plan with entrance (1), great
hall (2), buttery and pantry (3, 4), (c) great hall.

hall of Caerphilly Castle.**2.250** The raised withdrawing
room – the solar – at one end of Norman halls had been
the first concession to privacy and its repetition or expansion at the other end late in the 13th century was prophetic
of the diversification of private space which was to char-
acterize the evolution of the English country house over
the centuries to come.

2.259a

CASTLE COURT AND COURTYARD HOUSE

The blocks of additional accommodation might project at one or both ends over L-, T- or H-shaped plans. The latter was the most usual by the late-14th century and thereafter the main thrust of development from the nucleus of the hall and its projecting dependencies was in the growth of wings around increasingly rectangular courts – as at Haddon in Derbyshire in the generation after the construction of the hall c. 1300.[2.259]

The precedent for the domestic court was provided by the decentralized and regularized castles of Edward I at the end of the 13th century, as we have seen. Relatively secure at home but on the cripplingly expensive offensive in France after the truce with Philip IV was abrogated by Edward III, the crown saw little need for active patronage of military building in England during much of the 14th

›2.259 HADDON HALL, DERBYSHIRE, 1199, remodelled c. 1300 and later: (a) overview from south-west, (b) plan with (1) entrance to outer court, (2) chapel, (3) great hall, (4) kitchen, (5) dining room, (c, d) dining room and kitchen detail, (e, f) chapel interior and detail of early 15th-century fresco of S. Christopher, (g, h) great hall exterior and interior.

1070–1250	■
1300–80	■
1380–1477	■
1477–1530	■
1530–1624	■

Richard de Vernor was granted a licence to erect an uncrenellated defensive wall at Haddon in 1199. The present enclosure incorporates part of this wall, the main gate (in the north-east corner) and the chapel (south-west corner). At the beginning of the 14th century the accommodation was remodelled with the nuclear hall, entered from both sides, forming a cross-range dividing the compound into two courts.

2.259c

2.259d

2.259g

2.259b @ 1:1000

1

2

3

4

5

2.259e

2.159f

2.259h

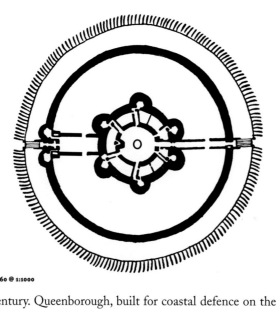

2.260 @ 1:1000

century. Queenborough, built for coastal defence on the Isle of Sheppey c. 1360 by William of Wykeham, surveyor of the king's works under Edward III, is an exception not least in its wholly concentric circular plan. It is equally symptomatic of the troubled late reign of Richard II that the near-bankrupt crown was prepared to license private builders rather than build castles itself.**2.260–2.263**

The castellated house

In 1385, following a series of French raids on the south coast, a licence to crenellate at Bodiam in East Sussex was accorded to war-enriched Sir Edward Dalyngrigge to defend the valley of the Rother. The ramparts, centred on a bombastic twin-towered gatehouse, machicolated in the French manner like many houses built with spoils from the war in France, rise from a lake-like moat and the accommodation was ranged against them around a courtyard – as at Haddon but on a regular rectangular plan without a cross-wing, as at Harlech.

Access to the complex was across causeways with drawbridges from north and south. Another causeway and drawbridge served a postern to the south. The enceinte, of Edwardian formality, has a cylindrical tower in

›**2.261 BODIAM CASTLE, SUSSEX,** 1386–89: (a) view from the north, (b) plan with hall (1), kitchen (2) and chapel (3).

2.261a

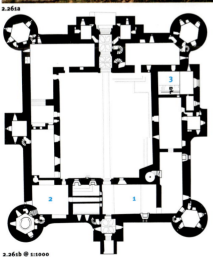

2.261b @ 1:1000

each corner and a square one in the centre of each side except for the northern entrance front where twin square towers protect the gatehouse with gunports for anti-personnel small-calibre guns. Beyond that, the accommodation was on two floors: once of considerable comfort, now ruinous, it had many fireplaces and generous fenestration was feasible without compromising defence due to the width of the moat. The great hall, buttery, pantry and kitchen formed the south range; to the east were the private chamber, guest rooms and chapel; to the west were the servants, and to the north the mercenary guard was isolated from the rest of the establishment in the gatehouse.

Bodiam had several English precedents: Raby near Durham and Bolton in Yorkshire (c. 1380), where the corner towers are rectangular, Scotney and Cooling in Kent (c. 1375), where the corner towers are cylindrical,

2.262

>**2.262 MAXSTOKE CASTLE, WARWICK-SHIRE,** 1346: view of entrance range from the south-east.

William de Clinton, Earl of Huntingdon (1337) obtained a licence to crenellate his manor house from Edward III in 1345. The licence was implemented to such an extent that, with its formidable gatehouse keep, the house had become a castle by the time it was completed within a decade: or rather it provided the very model for the English seigneurial dwelling that was not quite the one nor the other. Accommodation was ranged against the walls around the near-square court in clearly differentiated zones for the lord, his guest and servants – as later at Bodiam.

>**2.263 HERSTMONCEUX CASTLE, SUSSEX,** c. 1440: view from the south-east.

In 1441 a licence to crenellate was granted to Sir Roger Fiennes (knighted 1422, treasurer of Henry VI's

2.263

household by 1440, died 1450). The ostensible purpose, again, was coastal defence but the building was even more obviously a house dressed in military trappings. The great brick structure, hardly precedented in scale for its date, is nearly square (c. 63 by 67 metres) with octagonal towers at regular intervals to each side, including the pair framing the stone arch of the gatehouse keep. In addition to cruciform arrow slits (for vertical fire from the longbow and horizontal fire from crossbow) with oilets (circular openings at the ends for small arms) there are generous glazed windows even in the gatehouse. The accommodation ranges, framing one large court and three smaller ones, were gutted in 1777 and rebuilt in the 20th century.

Beverston in Gloucestershire (1356) and Maxstoke in Warwickshire (1346) where the corner towers are octagonal. The type reached its most ostentatious c. 1440 at Herstmonceux in Sussex.

It is ironic – but symptomatic of social mobility in an insular realm reeling from the impact of the Hundred Years' War but still relatively secure – that while the would-be-grand were assuming the constraints of military engineering – in form, at least, and often gratuitously – the already-grand preferred to emulate the lowlier lords of the manor and quit or transform their uncomfortable fortresses. The process began with the clergy towards the end of the reign of Edward I.

PALATIAL HALLS AND GREAT GATES

Always more secure than their secular peers, bishops and abbots nevertheless lived in defended compounds. Their halls and ancillary chambers set the standard for grand accommodation at least from the mid-12th century when Farnham castle was built by Henry of Blois, bishop of Winchester. Little survives there. At Wells and Lincoln there are important 13th-century remains but the most substantial survivor is the early 14th-century complex at S. David's in Wales.**2.264**

›2.264 S. DAVID'S, BISHOP'S PALACE, c. 1340: overview from cathedral.

S. David's

Developed by Henry Gower, bishop from 1328–47, on earlier foundations within the walled compound and probably incorporating the existing hall range to the west, the accommodation was ranged around three sides of a regular rectangular court – as around many abbey cloisters, as more sparsely at Harlech, and as it was soon to be at Maxstoke. The two-storey range to the east contained the bishop's hall, solar and service rooms (including the great kitchen to the south), the south range contained accommodation for distinguished guests, adjacent to the earlier great chapel (west), and a new great hall raised over existing undercrofts (unlike the original one in the western range which it superseded). The rooms in the east range were lit from both sides, the great hall mainly from the court (north) and the distinctive arcaded parapet was extended to all the main buildings to provide a measure of unity. A hall for the bishop and his ecclesiastical household and another for his secular retainers were customary by the 14th century: here the great hall would also have been used for ceremonial and the administration of justice by the bishop in his capacity as a marcher lord.

>2.265 THORNTON ABBEY, LINCOLNSHIRE, founded for Augustinian canons in 1139: gatehouse (1382).

>2.266 BATTLE ABBEY, SUSSEX, founded for Benedictines ex-voto by William the Conqueror: gatehouse, external façade (1339).

2.265

2.266

While the royal military engineers were concentrating on the perfection of the gatehouse keep, the lords of the Church began the development of the gatehouse apartment to supplement and even supplant the chambers attached to their palatial halls. Borrowing masons from the construction sites of their churches, moreover, they took the cause of aesthetics in architecture beyond the point reached by Henry III. The earliest surviving examples, more than merely defensive, are East Anglian: Peterborough from the very beginning of the reign of Edward II, Butley in Suffolk (1311) and Bury S. Edmunds (1327). By 1382 richly sculpted splendour had been achieved outside and in at Thornton in Lincolnshire. There the exterior was still blind but at Battle Abbey in Sussex half a century earlier, both fronts are fenestrated. **2.265, 2.266**

The secular magnates followed where the prelates led but for much of the 14th century, still committed to impressive defences, they were preoccupied with settling out of their keeps into more gracious halls and ancillary chambers in the baileys of their castles. In 1347, for example, the Earl of Lancaster built a great hall beside the 12th-century keep at Kenilworth which his son-in-law, John of Gaunt – one of Richard II's most powerful uncles – inherited and amplified c. 1390. Raised on an undercroft, but for

greater magnificence of approach, rather than for defence, the hall was exceptionally grand and well lit with great traceried windows to each side and a magnificent oriel to the east.**2.249, 2.267** The form was taken to its apogee in the same decade for the king himself on the site of William II's Great Hall at Westminster.**2.268**

›2.267 KENILWORTH CASTLE, WARWICK-SHIRE: remains of the great hall of John of Gaunt (see plan on page 521).

The apogee of the hall

The Great Hall of the Palace of Westminster was built in the last decade of the 14th century for Richard II by Henry Yeveley, architect of the nave of Canterbury cathedral, on William II's foundations (c. 73 by c. 21 metres). The new work was wider than the old but the original internal supports were obviated by the development of the so-called hammer-beam system of cantilevered roof construction: truncated horizontal beams project over curved braces from the wall to each side; arched braces spring from their exposed ends to span the space between; the cantilever results from embedding the rafters in the other end of the beams, where they join the wall.

›**2.268 WESTMINSTER PALACE, GREAT HALL,** from 1393: interior.

The hammer-beam system is first recorded by Villard de Honnecourt c. 1240. First known in England in the Pilgrim's Hall at Winchester c. 1325, it was approximated at Great Croxwell in the truncated tie beams over the intermediate cruck trusses.**2.254** It admitted of expansion by multiplying the number of projecting truncated beams and their braces. To span the width of Westminster's Great Hall – unsurpassed by a medieval building of the type – the principal royal carpenter, Hugh Herland, produced three levels, each with pierced tracery in the spandrels and angels bearing the arms of the king on the butt ends of the truncated beams.

The ancillary buildings at Kenilworth curved around the south of the original inner ward to form a court. Determined by defensive walls on contour lines, the complex may have been grand in scale but it was no more regular than the pragmatic arrangement at modest Stokesay – unlike Maxstoke or Bolton, let alone Bodiam, on their new sites. Free from the constraints of existing defences – or newly assumed ones, as at Bodiam – the crucial development from nuclear hall to stately country seat was the projection of regular wings.

Even after the security of the realm disintegrated in the Wars of the Roses – the course of which was primarily determined by pitched battles in the open field rather than protracted sieges – the great lords of England needed ample accommodation for their retainers more than they needed to immure themselves in forts. From the mid-14th century, at least, it was recognized that this was most efficiently done in extended ranges of similar units.

King Edward III commissioned two perpendicular ranges of cells at Windsor in the 1350s which may be traced in the foundations of the eastern and southern ranges of the upper ward.[2.237] The regularity was fortuitous, as these lodgings adhered to exceptionally straight and perpendicular bailey walls, but it was seminal in the secular field. The earliest surviving example of such a range built freestanding on an unconstrained site is generally thought to be the one added to the hall at Dartington in Devon from 1388 by John, Duke of Exeter, half-brother of Richard II.[2.269]

›2.269 DARTINGTON HALL, DEVONSHIRE, c. 1390: hall and cellular accommodation block for the retainers of the Duke of Exeter.

THE COLLEGE OF LEARNING

The direct precedent for freestanding ranges of similar cells accommodating a number of people of equal status and framing a court – as distinct from quadrangles produced by the regularization of castle design – had long been provided by the cloister of the monastery adapted to serve the purposes of teaching – in England, at least. From the late-13th century there, considerable responsibility for education was taken over by colleges of secular priests or canons established ex-voto by warriors with blood on their hands to offer intercession for their souls and schooling for their offspring. Edward III was typical of the great patrons of the period in providing for such a college in the precinct at Windsor.

As small monastic foundations had proliferated for a century or more, many affording intercession chose to endow chantry chapels associated with priestly colleges. The Augustinians had long played a prominent role in intercession and their system of life in common was taken as the model by other communities not subscribing to a defined order: they lived by the chantry chapel in hostels with uniform apartments comprising a living room with bedroom above it, associated with a dining and assembly hall served by kitchen, buttery, bakehouse and store – like the hall of the manor. Before the century progressed, chantry colleges were regularly associated with alms-houses and schools. The development culminated in the colleges of Oxford and Cambridge.

When education was centred on abbey or cathedral, lay students were accommodated at random in modest houses. The earliest hostel for scholars who were not members of a religious order was Oxford's Merton, founded c. 1264: with it was established the idea of a corporate fraternity, dedicated to learning, and the collegiate building scheme. The word 'college' actually appears in this connection in 1324 in the foundation charter of Oriel – which obliged its members to pray for the founder.

As with the manor, at Merton and in the various other foundations in England's two university towns, the various elements of the college complex cohered gradually around a court. Monumentality was achieved in the 1370s following the intervention of William of Wykeham, surveyor of the king's works at Windsor, architect of his court and college there, keeper of the privy seal, Bishop of Winchester, Chancellor of England. **2.270, 2.271**

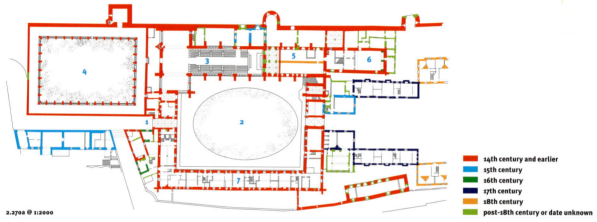

2.270a @ 1:2000

14th century and earlier
15th century
16th century
17th century
18th century
post-18th century or date unknown

The ordering of the collegiate complex

Oxford's Merton well represents the early college, with a quadrangle of cells for the fellows in place of the monastic dormitory-framed cloister sheltering under the lee of the chapel and, in place of the refectory, a great hall for assembly – not least at dinner. The inner court (known as Mob Quad) was begun c. 1288 in conjunction with the Decorated chapel. They constitute the oldest complex of college buildings at Oxford – though the quadrangle was developed over the next century and the Perpendicular tower was added to the chapel in the middle of the 15th century.

The Chancellor, William of Wyckham, conceived the idea of founding a new college at Oxford and a school to prepare boys for it at Winchester in 1369. The charter for New College, in which secular priests were to direct scholarship and pray for the soul of the founder, was granted in 1379 and

›2.270 OXFORD, NEW COLLEGE, c. 1380: (a) plan with (1) gate, (2) great quadrangle, (3) chapel with cloister (4) to its west, (5) hall, (6) kitchen, (7) cellular accommodation, (b) great quadrangle.

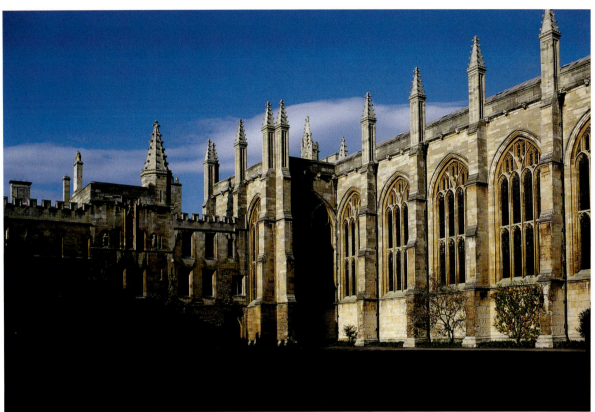

2.270b

the buildings were ready by 1386. Winchester College was realized from 1382. They were built to similar plans with chapel, hall, library, warden's lodge, service facilities, and rows of cells – extended like those at Windsor – all ranged around a single quadrangle.

Impressive in their scale and coherent Perpendicular order, Wyckham's buildings set the standard to be emulated with the expansion of university education – and, indeed, the proliferation of religious foundations constituting colleges at parish level – over the next century as court was required to succeed court beyond the great hall. Of his many emulators, Henry VI is the most eminent. Like Wyckham, he founded linked institutions, Eton and King's College at Cambridge, in 1440 and 1441 respectively. They have hardly been excelled, though it fell to his successors – Edward IV and Henry VII – to realize his ideal.

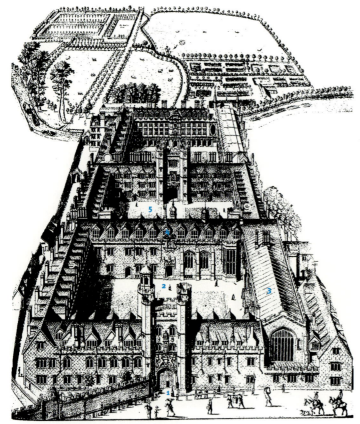

2.271a

2.271b

›**2.271 CAMBRIDGE:** (a) S. John's College (founded 1511), overview (17th-century engraving) with (1) ceremonial entrance (2) outer quadrangle (3) chapel (4) hall (5) inner quadrangle; (b) King's College, entrance range with chapel beyond.

REGULAR PLANNING

Over the same century, the regularity achieved in the college court was applied to discipline the organic growth of houses. The process may be traced from relatively modest Ightham Mote in Kent (from 1325) to the much grander South Wingfield in Derbyshire (from 1441), where there was a court for the lord and another for the servants and the carving in the masonry of the former is almost ecclesiastical in its richness, to Ockwells at Bray in Berkshire (from 1465), where window exceeds wall, and on to Oxburgh in Norfolk (from 1482) and Compton Wynyates in Warwickshire (from c. 1512).**2.272–2.274**

2.272a

2.272b

›2.272 IGHTHAM MOTE, KENT, early 14th century and later: (a) general view from west, (b) chamber.

Before the hall of c. 1320, the court developed over the following century in a variety of materials for varied masses – stone to the fore, brick and timber behind. The gatehouse was founded as part of the original defences but it was heightened when the south and west wings achieved their definitive form in the 15th century. The north wing with chapel was developed in the 16th century.

›2.273 OXBURGH HALL, NORFOLK, built from c. 1480 for Sir Edward Beddingfield: general view from north-west and north range with gatehouse.

2.273

At the apex of society, Edward IV's palace at Eltham developed the precedent set by the Duke of Exeter at Dartington a century earlier. The formula was expanded with lodging ranges framing several courts for the palaces of many secular magnates of fortune new or old, like Lord Treasurer Cromwell at South Wingfield (1439), and ecclesiastics, like Archbishop Bourchier of Canterbury's Knole (from c. 1450), or the Duke of Buckingham at Thornbury (from 1511). The culmination was in the seat of a prince of the church, Cardinal Wolsey's Hampton Court, west of London (from 1520).**2.275–2.277**

>**2.274 COMPTON WYNYATES, WARWICK-SHIRE,** from c. 1512: entrance front.

Built to a rectangular courtyard plan over earlier foundations, this beautifully sited, relatively modest manor conformed to the well-established type but required no extended wings for retainers and dispensed with the prestigious trappings of defensive gatehouses and keeps. Brick and timber are reinforced by stone at the salient points.

›2.275 THORNBURY CASTLE, GLOUCESTER-SHIRE, built from 1511 for the Duke of Buckingham but unfinished on his execution in 1522: south range.

Of two courts, the outer one with offices and service accommodation, the inner one was flanked to the east by an existing hall and to the south by the duke's accommodation.

›2.276 WEST WINGFIELD HALL, DER-BYSHIRE, built 1439–50 for the Lord Treasurer, Ralph Cromwell: (a) general view of ruins from the west, (b) main block south portal and great chamber, (c) great hall undercroft.

Of two courts, the outer one to the south was framed with cellular service accommodation, the inner one was dominated by the great chambers to the north: the substantial intermediate range was breached by the main communication passage on axis with the entrance to the main block but perpendicular to the axis of approach to the outer court.

2.275

2.276b

2.276c

2.276a

2.277a

At Compton Wynyates hall and solar are still dominant after three centuries of development. At Oxburgh – as in many colleges – the gatehouse towers over all else. At Hampton Court gatehouse and hall vie for supremacy. As the ancient symbol of sovereign power, certainly not

›2.277 HAMPTON COURT PALACE, begun by Cardinal Wolsey in 1514, extended by Henry VIII after its surrender to the crown in 1526 and extensively rebuilt in the late-17th century: (a) aerial view, (b) great hall.

Wolsey's work survives in the succession of gate-houses, the outer one (1515) rectangular in plan with octagonal turrets and generous central oriel, the three-

2.277b

storey inner one (1514) square with greater emphasis on verticality (even before the alterations to the upper storey and the insertion of the astronomical clock in 1540). The hall, planned by Wolsey, was extended by Henry VIII from 1530.

›**2.278 LAYER MARNEY TOWER, ESSEX,** c. 1520: gatehouse.

The eight-level gatehouse of exaggerated ceremonial significance, recalling Oxburgh's but greatly exceeding it, contains thirty-nine rooms and as the proposed courtyard ranges remained unexecuted after the deaths of the first two lords of Marney, it constituted the main part of the house – a tower house by default.

ignored by the contemporary French,[2.289, 2.295] the twin-towered portal was applied to religious and secular foundations alike in the 15th century: often reflected in an ornamental moat and decked with false machicolation, it was bound to be the prime badge of pseudo-seigneurial pretention. Its ostentatious development may be traced from Harlech to Bodiam and on to Herstmonceux, Oxburgh and Layer Marney in Essex.[2.278]

2.278

2.279

>2.279 WARWICK CASTLE, EAST FRONT, from 1360: with Caesar's Tower centre, Guy's Tower right, and the gatehouse between them.

The two great towers of Warwick, at the northern and eastern corners of the 11th-century bailey, were built by father and son, both Thomas Beauchamp, eleventh and twelfth Earls of Warwick (the elder died in 1369, the younger died in 1401) as part of major renovations which included the rebuilding of the great hall and augmentation of the seigneurial apartments (on the south-east side of the bailey, facing the river). Caesar's Tower (c. 1360) is trilobate and rises to c. 41 metres through six storeys. Guy's Tower (c. 1390) is dodeconal and commodious enough to stand for a keep of the Coucy type with superimposed vaulted chambers on five levels. Like most of the works of soldiers enriched by the French war (the older Thomas served with distinction at Crécy and Poitiers), both towers betray French influence: both are machicolated and the earlier work has a recessed upper storey above the wallwalk as well.

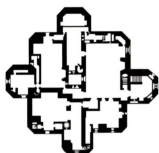

2.280a @ 1:1000
>2.280 WARKWORTH CASTLE, NORTHUM-BERLAND, founded by the Percy lords of the north in the 12th century and expanded to include a great hall by 1215: (a) plan, (b) general view.

The great cruciform keep (c. 1390) provided modern accommodation resembling a French apartment of the Vincennes type.

RESURGENT KEEPS

An alternative to the gatehouse as a badge of former feudal power, prominent in Britain but eccentric in its time, was the tower-keep. The earlier examples, such as the two great towers built by successive earls of Warwick at Warwick between 1360 and 1390, to either side of an imposing gatehouse, vary the form of Coucy.**2.279** Caister in Norfolk, built in the 1430s by the war-enriched Sir John Fastolf, is of a similar type.

At the beginning of the 15th century at Warkworth in Northumberland, a roughly square three-storey block with cruciform projections and generous windows on the upper levels replaced an earlier keep on a Norman motte at the apex of its enceinte.**2.280** Others, like the magnificent brick towers of Sir John Montgomery's Faulkbourne in Essex (from 1439), represent the multistorey development of the solar block which had been an essential element of the hall house almost from the outset.**2.282**

2.280b

›**2.281 TATTERSHALL CASTLE, LINCOLN-SHIRE, TOWER,** c. 1435: (a) exterior, (b) first-floor hall, (c) plan.

Ralph Cromwell (third Baron, Lord Treasurer to Henry VI in 1433) obtained a licence to crenellate on the site of the 13th-century castle built by Robert de Tateshale. The tower, built (to a height of 33.5 metres) beside an existing hall, is virtually independent like a traditional keep but the wide moat permitted generous windows at all five levels including the crowning wall-walk with its simulated machicolation. There is a great chamber at each level (for storage, guard, reception, private audience and sleeping in ascending order), all except the basement with fireplaces richly embellished with the Cromwell arms and other heraldic devices. The votive collegiate foundation is visible to the rear.

›**2.282 FAULKBOURNE CASTLE, ESSEX,** 1439 and later: view from north.

The licence to crenellate was issued in 1439. The core of the building, timber framed and faced in brick, seems to date from then, but the principal crenellated elements which form the north range, the hall flanked by towers (all in brick), seem to have been realized in the next generation.

›**2.283 KIRBY MUXLOE, LEICESTERSHIRE,** begun in 1480 for William, Lord Hastings, but terminated on his execution in 1483: view from the south-east.

The incompletely realized project was for a brick-built quadrangle with corner towers, accommodation blocks centred on the east, west and south sides and a gatehouse to the north: a wide moat converted the site into an island. The foundations were laid throughout but only the gatehouse and the north-west tower (with living rooms on two floors, with fireplaces) were completed.

2.281a

2.281b

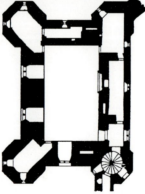

2.281c @ 1:500

Tattershall in Lincolnshire (from 1436) – the most spectacular of medieval brick buildings, other than its contemporary Herstmonceux – may be seen as a monumental variant of the solar tower type.[2.281]

Occasionally both gatehouse and tower assert the patron's pretensions. An essentially residential example is Kirby Muxloe, built by Edward IV's confidant, Lord Hasting, from 1474.[2.283] Most imposing, perhaps, Raglan commands an area of South Wales where some measure of fortification was still required. It is essentially an extravagantly defended courtyard house with a hall dividing the

2.282

2.283

bailey into two wards, as at Haddon.**2.259** Extraordinarily, however, a hexagonal keep stands beyond the polygonal towers of the monumental gatehouse like a protective barbican or bastille: designed to deflect shot, its arrow slits and gunports are aimed both in and out.**2.284**

Fortified towers dominate elsewhere in the British Isles. Edward I's success north of the Scottish border was limited and soon reversed, not least due to the impracticability of constructing a chain of castles like that to which he

›2.284 RAGLAN CASTLE: view from south-west with external keep, left, gatehouse right.

As no licence to crenellate is recorded, dating is insecure but the work was probably begun by William ap Thomas who married the heiress of the manor of Raglan, Elizabeth Bloet, in 1406, served in France under Henry V, was knighted by Henry VI in 1426 and established himself as a power in south-east Wales before he died in 1445. It is possible that a moated manor or even a motte-and-bailey castle on the site was replaced by the new work.

›2.285 EILEAN DONAN CASTLE, ROSS AND CROMARTY, from c. 1220, reconstructed from 1932: general view.

Built by King Alexander II (1214–49) as a defence against the Danes and the seat of the Macrae clan chiefs, hereditary Constables of the MacKenzies of Kintail, Eilean Donan is typical of the grander clan houses with its naturally secure island site, its walled compound with assembly hall and bleakly formidable accommodation tower.

had subjected the Welsh, and the Scots – like the Irish – sustained their tradition of defending themselves from the interminable siege warfare of clan feuding in isolated keeps rising from limited enceintes. Fulfilling the function of the manor house, with accommodation stacked vertically rather than ranged horizontally and varied in its sophistication to match the status of the incumbent, they rarely needed to withstand heavy artillery but the strength of their defences is real – at least before the 17th century.**2.285**

9 FROM CASTLE TO HOUSE IN FRANCE AND BEYOND

As elsewhere on the Continent, French *seigneurs* sought comfort within secure defences for rather longer than their English peers. However, they led in gracing the chambers contained by their stout walls with the artistic means hitherto most characteristically deployed in the palatial apartments of Benedictine abbots. Nevertheless, the re-emergence of the town as the centre of political gravity from the 12th century and changes in the nature of warfare with the eclipse of the feudal levy by the professional soldier in the 13th century and the advent of artillery in the 14th century, all led to the demise of the castle as a fortress-residence: the functions diverged – as they had begun to do with the emergence of the hall house in England.

THE IMPACT OF ARTILLERY

The re-emergence of the town was a protracted process, as we have seen. If there was a decisive event in the obsolescence of the residential castle as a military base it was the development in the late-14th century of manoeuverable cannon capable of firing metal balls.

Military building is essentially functional: it changes not on whim but of need, particularly in response to improvements in the weapons brought against it. Until the middle of the 15th century cannon were too unwieldy for the restricted space of towers or too high for effective fire if mounted on the battlements: ballistae continued to be the main weapon of attack – indeed various permutations of the catapult remained important for another century, until artillery was efficient and powerful enough seriously to threaten masonry. Until then, walls and bastions required height, thickness and solidity both to increase the range of marksmen and to withstand ballistae. Thereafter, effec-

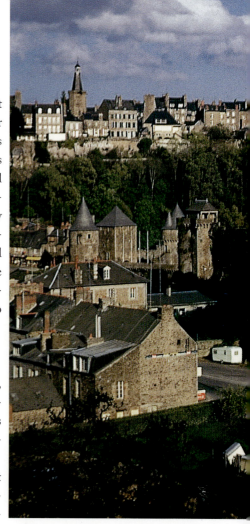

>2.286 FOUGÈRES CHÂTEAU, BRITTANY, 11th–15th century: general view from the north-west.

Founded by a vassal of the Duc de Bretagne in the 11th century on a bend in the River Nancon, the great polygonal enceinte culminates in a self-contained citadel on the highest ground to the north (centre here) with the late-12th-century remains of a massive octagonal keep (20 metres in diameter) at the apex, flanked by two later round towers. Of the other mural towers, the two enormous D-shaped bastions (20 metres in both depth and height) in the south-west sector (right) were added to mount and withstand cannon in 1480.

tively to mount cannon against outsiders, towers were brought lower and became ever more massive and restricted in habitable space. At Fougères, in addition to early 13th-century mural towers at their highest, the huge D-shaped bastions are typical of the measures taken over the next century and more to counter the battering power of shells.**2.286**

The semicircular bastion may have proved its worth on the perimeter of a fortified complex but the rectangular

2.287a

2.287b–d @ 1:500

›ARCHITECTURE IN CONTEXT »REFRACTION OF LIGHT

2.287f

2.287e

›**2.287 VINCENNES, VAL-DE-MARNE**, 1364–73: (a) inner enceinte and keep, (b–d) plans at ground-, second- and fourth-floor levels, (e) section, (f) the château in the background of a hunting scene, a detail of 'December' from *Les Très Riches Heures du Duc de Berry* by the Limbourg brothers (Chantilly, Condée Museum).

The square keep, with cylindrical corner towers and a formidable battered base, is isolated behind a moat (22 metres wide, 14 metres deep) and the square enceinte (52 metres high, 16 metres wide). The keep has five superimposed chambers, each with vaults supported in the centre of the square by a column and supplemented by smaller rooms in the corner towers: the arrangement represents the primitive constitution of an apartment suite with antechamber, bedroom and withdrawing room, whose origins have been obscured by time. Entrance is via a drawbridge at first-floor level.

form of keep was retained by conservative builders well into the 14th century. The greatest example is undoubtedly the one in the square enceinte at Vincennes founded by Philip VI in 1337 to guard the eastern approach to Paris: in whole and in part exceptional in its regular geometry, if not in its form, it accommodated the king in a series of putative apartments stacked on five storeys.**2.287**

Favouring Vincennes, Charles V (1364–80) added an enormous rectangular enceinte to house his extensive court. Punctuating the north, south and east sides were nine tall, square towers conceived as independent subsidiary keeps and the isolation of the original keep, within its own moated enceinte, was preserved to the west: the zoning was designed as much to protect the king from internal treachery, particularly of mercenary guards, as from external assault. The complex was essentially a palace like the Louvre which was developed in the same reign along similar – if larger – lines on the basis of the keep and enceinte provided by Philip Augustus.

2.288

On a rocky spur, precipitous from south-west to south-east, an irregular trapezium with cylindrical corner towers dates from the middle of the 13th century. The most massive of the towers (to the north-west, guarding the approach along the spine of the spur) is a keep of the Coucy type (left). The bailey is divided by another enormous keep, an irregular polygon developed in the mid-15th century from an earlier pentagonal structure for mounting artillery of different strengths and ranges on three floors and a roof terrace. An outer enceinte punctuated with low gun towers, semiconcentric with the original complex, was built later in the 15th century: on the vulnerable northern side the two enceintes were separated by a wide, deep moat and access to the bailey, over a drawbridge, was further protected by extensive outworks.

Completed within a generation of the introduction of cannon to French warfare, the defences of Vincennes were atypical of their time: the D-shaped bastion – like the one at Fougères – had proved its worth. However, as the striking power of artillery improved, mural towers ceded to gun platforms set low enough to level cannon fire on the plane of approach – and it was realized that broken curves or polygonal forms were better even than semicylindrical ones for deflecting shot. An alternative to lowering the walls of the castle itself was the construction of outlying dykes or bulwarks (*boulevards* or *bastilles*) of earth or stone to mount cannon and present a barrier to be crossed by an assailant under the direct fire of the marksmen on the main ramparts: the age-old principle of defence in depth, this is well represented at Bonaguil in the Auvergne.**2.288**

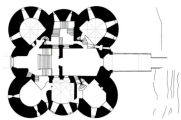

2.289a @ 1:500

›2.289 RAMBURES CHÂTEAU, SOMME, begun c. 1421: (a) plan, (b) view from the south.

A cruciform arrangement of four tangential cylindrical towers (as at Étampes) is reinforced with four great D-shaped gun emplacements on the diagonals. Built of brick, the walls are 7 metres thick at the base of the gun towers, the core cylinders are 12 metres in diameter, all rise to 20 metres from the bed of a deep dry moat. The gun slits were supplemented by windows in the 17th and 18th centuries.

2.289b

2.290a

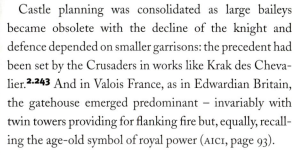

2.290b

Castle planning was consolidated as large baileys became obsolete with the decline of the knight and defence depended on smaller garrisons: the precedent had been set by the Crusaders in works like Krak des Chevalier.[2.243] And in Valois France, as in Edwardian Britain, the gatehouse emerged predominant – invariably with twin towers providing for flanking fire but, equally, recalling the age-old symbol of royal power (AICI, page 93).

›2.290 HENRICIAN COASTAL DEFENCE: (a, b) S. Mawes, Cornwall, exterior and gun embrasure; (c) Deal Castle, Kent (1539–40), aerial view.

With the resumption of authority for defence by the crown on the consolidation of the Tudor regime in England, and Henry VIII's break with Rome and the Catholic powers supporting the papal cause as a consequence of the reformation of the church in England, a series of gun emplacements was erected to protect the Channel coast from Kent to Cornwall. Many of them are noted for their circular geometry. S. Mawes worked with cylindrical Pendennis to guard the mouth of the Fal.

Deal was built as the central and largest castle of three guarding the sheltered anchorage of the Downs. To the south-west is Walmer and to the north was Sandown.

2.290c

THE DEVELOPMENT OF THE QUADRANGLE IN FRANCE

Taken to an extreme at Rambures, consolidation is also characteristic of the residential castle planning which complemented the development of the fortress from the late-14th century. The disappearance of the central keep had left a void: a court, rather than a bailey, this was usually quadrangular but varied in its regularity and around it accommodation was concentrated between parallel perimeter walls.**2.289–2.290**

Villandraut, the Girondin château of the first Avigonese pope, Clement V (1305–14), clearly acknowledges the influence of James of S. Georges and Edward I in its formality, in its court, in its habitable perimeter and in the dominance of the massive twin-towered gatehouse in the centre of the south range. To ameliorate their captivity at Avignon, Benedict XII (1334–42) and his successors contributed to the development of the type with the sumptuous double-courtyard fort-palace which still overawes the town. Surrounded by doubled walls punctuated with high towers, the largest one at the north-eastern apex protecting the original entrance and providing a keep in the manner of Coucy, it is representative of its period not least in lacking any semblance of the Edwardian formality imposed on Villandraut.**2.291, 2.292**

To facilitate circuit patrols by reduced numbers of defenders elsewhere in France, there was a continuous machicolated wallwalk and the towers were often differentiated in height only by an additional recessed storey with conical roof. Isolated behind strong partitions within this system of unified defence, the master was lodged in the imposing gatehouse so long as that remained the dominant mass, as at Chevenon. Beyond that, the *corps de logis* of great magnates expanded on the stupendous scale of the château of the dukes of Valois at Pierrefonds or the hardly

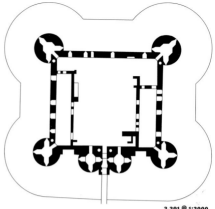

2.291 @ 1:2000

›2.291 VILLANDRAUT, CHÂTEAU, GIRONDE, c. 1305: plan.

Built by Bertrand de Goth, Archbishop of Bordeaux, Pope Clement V from 1305–14, the compound (43 by 52 metres) is strictly rectangular and dominated by the massive twin-towered gatehouse in the centre of the south range. The six towers (one to each corner, two guarding the portal) rise to 20 metres, nearly twice the height of the walls: the wallwalk seems to have been crenellated but not machicolated as provision survives for timber hoarding.

›2.292 AVIGNON, PALAIS DE PAPES, 1334–52: (a) general view, (b) model, (c) plan, (d) detail of audience chamber ceiling.

The first Avignon popes used the bishop's palace beside the Romanesque cathedral. Enlarged by John XXII (1316–34) this was demolished by his successor Benedict XII (1334–42) and replaced by the Palais Vieux. A second major campaign produced the Palais Neuf for Clement VI (1342–52). The first palace, constituting the north-eastern half of the complex round a trapezoidal court, contained the principal banqueting hall, papal chapel and private apartments. The later work, perpendicular wings forming a more regular court to the south-west, contained the main audience hall.

2.292d

2.292a

2.292c @ 1:2000

2.292b

2.293a

2.293b

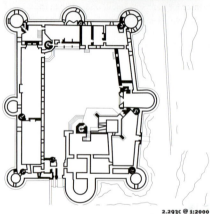

2.293c @ 1:2000

›**2.293 PIERREFONDS, OISE,** from 1392, restored from 1857: (a) restoration (after Viollet-le-Duc), (b) model, (c) plan.

Built for Louis d'Orléans, brother of Charles VI, between 1392 and 1407, slighted in 1617, the castle was imaginatively rebuilt over the original plan within substantial surviving ranges of wall by Viollet-le-Duc in the 1860s for Emperor Napoleon III. The roughly rectangular enceinte was typical of its period except in scale and the doubled walls evidently enclosed a magnificent suite of halls and chambers. Adjoining the southern tower and dominating the entrance from the south, the main residential block consists of doubled ranges of rooms forming apartments on three floors.

less modest seat of the early 15th-century Angevin kings of Provence at Tarascon. As at Pierrefonds or Tarascon and rather more in the Limbourg brothers' images of Charles V's Louvre or his brother Berry's many châteaux, the increasingly expansive chambers, secure in height, admitted light and rich ornament.**2.293–2.296**

›2.294 CHEVENON, CHÂTEAU: gatehouse keep from the west (c. 1390).

Probably built by Huguenin de Chevenon, captain of the royal château of Vincennes from 1384, the present massive building, which served as gatehouse and principal lodging, replaced the western range of a roughly rectangular 13th-century enceinte with cylindrical towers in the corners, an entrance from the east, and restricted accommodation between doubled walls. The complex was protected by a moat and a barbican further defended the new western gatehouse keep.

›2.295 TARASCON, CHÂTEAU, first half of the 15th century: view from the Rhône, with the residential block in the centre.

The so-called Château du Roi René dominates the Rhône at a strategic crossing between Provence and France, from a rocky platform which had been fortified since Roman times. A 13th-century enceinte was augmented for Louis II of Anjou, whose father, Louis I, had been adopted by Joanna I of Naples as heir to her kingdom and the county of Provence. Louis and his heirs – Louis III and his brother René – secured the latter but not the former: René (1409–80, succeeded his brother in 1434) was responsible for much of the surviving château which was complete in main part by 1450.

2.294

2.295

2.296a

2.296b

2.296c

The relaxation of the defensive character of the French castle proceeded at an irregular pace with the restoration of internal security after the end of the Hundred Years' War until the reconsolidation of central power by Louis XI. Then the not-invariable norm was a central court surrounded by an increasing number of rooms to meet the growing demand for privacy. The varied masses of *corps de logis* and *pavillons* remember the old enceinte of walls punctuated with bastions: variety is asserted in high roofs,

›2.296 SAUMUR, CHÂTEAU, 12th century and later: (a) as represented by the Limbourg brothers in the early 15th century, (b) view from the east, (c) staircase tower.

The promontory at the confluence of the Loire and Thouet Rivers was originally fortified in the 10th century by the Count of Blois as an outpost of defence

2.297a

against the Count of Anjou. Reformed in stone in the 12th century, it passed to the crown in 1207. Assigned by Jean II to his second son, Louis, with the title Duc d'Anjou, a roughly rectangular château with polygonal towers over circular bases was greatly augmented and embellished after 1367: the full panoply of dormers and chimneys, lost to us, was recorded in the context of the *Très Riches Heures* of Louis's brother, Jean, Duc de Berry.

›2.297 JOSSELIN, CHÂTEAU, WESTERN RANGE, 15th–16th centuries: (a) river front, (b) court façade.

Founded c. 1025, the château was rebuilt with the present roughly triangular enceinte over the course of several generations in the 13th century. In 1370 a huge keep of the Coucy – or Fougères – type (c. 30 metres in diameter) was erected at the southern apex and amplification of the seigneurial accommodation was begun with the reconstruction of the ramparts overlooking the river Oust. This work, with its sumptuous internal façade, was not completed until the beginning of the 16th century.

2.297b

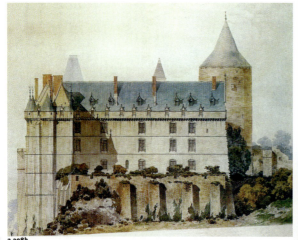

2.298b

2.298c

2.298a

conical on towers, elaborate dormers and external staircase cages. Despite the large windows lighting sumptuously decorated rooms, redundant defensive features such as wallwalks with simulated machicolation, moats and twin-towered portals are retained for prestige as badges of power.

At the grandest level, the emergence of the house from the castle may be traced through numerous splendid examples. Josselin in Brittany, Châteaudun on the Loir,

2.298d

2.298e

›**2.298 CHÂTEAUDUN, CHÂTEAU,** c. 1450–c. 1490 on the site of a keep erected c. 1170: (a) the founder, Thibaut V, Count of Blois (died 1191), (b) reconstruction after Viollet-le-Duc, (c) view of Sainte-Chapelle and Longueville Wing with open stair, (d, e) chamber in the Longueville wing and detail of incised fireplace.

Langeais and Chaumont on the Loire, and Meillant near Bourges may be taken as representative. Interiors, differentiated in scale for representation or withdrawal, were hardly less sumptuous than those of the late Duc de Berry, with tapesteries or panelling and elaborately engraved chimneybreasts under equally elaborately incised or painted ceiling beams. **2.297–2.301**

2.299a

›2.299 LANGEAIS, CHÂTEAU, 10th–15th cen-turies: (a) aerial view of town front, (b) antechamber-with crenellated fireplace, (c) hall, (d, e) bedrooms.

To the east of the motte on which Fulk Nera built his precocious stone keep in 994, skirting the bailey, the enceinte was reinforced with new stone walls c. 1100. These were repaired and rebuilt several times before the château was destroyed by the English in 1427. The ancient keep was abandoned but the enceinte was rebuilt Louis XI from 1465.

Emergence of the mansion

The enceinte rebuilt at Langeais to an enormous scale from 1465 was the first stage of an unfinished quadrilateral scheme. The walls of the main body of the building and the southern tower of the gatehouse are pierced by win-dows at a safe height, but the corner towers are unfenestrated – indeed the northern gatehouse tower, larger than the others, is virtually a keep of the Coucy type which would have formed the apex of the completed complex.

As at Pierrefonds, walls approximate the height of towers except for the recessed upper storeys and conical roofs of the latter. The relative severity of the town front – compared with other châteaux of the period in the Loire valley – was dictated by the defiance of a king determined on re-establish-ing royal authority after the chaos of the Hundred Years' War – not least by providing himself with a strong, but internally sumptuous, base from which to dominate the town of Tours. The severity of the exterior was not carried through to the interior. Tapestries usually covered the walls of grand rooms, but carved timber panelling was not uncommon in smaller with-drawing rooms and cabinets. Low-relief sculpture often provides the main ornament on major features, the chimney breasts in particular. Ceilings were not normally lined to conceal the joists and beams of the floor above.

2.299b

2.299c

2.299d

2.299e

2.300a

2.300b

>**2.300 CHAUMONT-SUR-LOIRE, LOIR-ET-CHER,** c. 1480–1510: (a) view from south-east, (b) view across river.

Dominating the Loire from its left bank, a château was first built on the site in the 10th century. It passed to the Counts of Amboise in 1039 who were dispossessed of it by Louis XI in 1465. The king demolished the original château but the site was returned to the family of Amboise on their return to royal favour in the 1470s.

›2.301 MEILLANT, CHÂTEAU, CHER, from 1490: court front.

A 14th-century château on the site passed to the family of the Counts of Amboise by marriage in 1428. Charles I d'Amboise rebuilt in sumptuous style, as at Chaumont, after regaining royal favour in the 1470s. The main campaign lasted from c. 1490 to 1510.

Presenting a much less severe countenance, the new château at Chaumont was clearly designed as a house rather than a fortress, with large windows within reach of the ground and a positively ceremonial twin-towered portal. Much of the relief is provided with emblems of past power, such as false machicolation. There were originally four wings around a square court but one was demolished c. 1740 to open the court fronts to the river.

The court fronts of all these châteaux have the flamboyant fenestration which marks the application of art to counter military science but the fashion of the period is most extravagantly represented at Josselin and Meillant. Originally an irregular polygon defined by *corps de logis*, Meillant's court was opened to the south-east in the 17th century: the elegant octagonal external stair turret represents a common feature of the period – much varied in scale and elaboration.

2.302

›2.302 INTERNATIONAL STYLE: detail of the Procession of the Medici to Bethlehem (fresco of c. 1460 by Benozzo Gózzoli in the chapel of the Palazzo Medici-Riccardi, Florence).

The style of painting represented here – dominant in the early 15th century in Italy and for longer elsewhere – is known as 'International Gothic'. It was not primarily concerned with realizing tangible volume or projecting rational space: largely at the instigation of princely patrons in sumptuous courts, like those beyond the Alps where the recording of *très riches heures* achieved the apogee of opulence in the work of the Limbourg brothers, they did not ignore the corporeal or human personality but were diverted by – or reverted to – elegant linear patterning in tapestry-like compositions, with lavish vestments, opulent trappings and, often, carpets of flora alive with fauna charmingly observed in the flamboyant late-medieval manner.

RICH HOURS IN THE GARDEN

The domestic splendour of the Duc de Berry and his most affluent contemporaries was not entirely internal: it extended to the garden. We have already encountered late-Gothic man lovingly recording his minute observation of nature in the embellishment of churches – whether to symbolize the promise of heaven in the Passion of Christ, or to celebrate the conquest of the earth in the age of maritime adventure. Another aspect of the celebration of the beauty of nature opened on the garden and it is by no means a coincidence that our earliest garden images date from the period of the so-called 'International Gothic' when the representation of plants and animals, clothes and jewels, often eclipsed the ostensible subject: the Limbourg brothers furthered the tradition for their royal French patrons. **2.302, 2.287f, 2.297a**

Hitherto medieval man had seen nature as terrible, and he had turned his back on it in the relative security of his

2.303a

2.303c

2.303b

2.303d

▸**2.303 THE MEDIEVAL GARDEN:** (a, b) the enclosed garden (*hortus conclusus*) as an allegory of the Virgin (late-medieval woodblock engraving showing the Annunciate Angel Gabriel approaching the Virgin's garden, and painting of the Virgin and Child in the inviolate garden from a work by the Puy Notre-Dame d'Amiens c. 1510); (c) the allegory violated (late-medieval woodblock engraving); (d) frontispiece to a 16th-century edition of the late-medieval *Roman de la Rose* as an allegory of sensual love showing the course of a love affair as a promenade through a lady's garden after the young man had penetrated the gate (Paris, National Library).

castle. The garden, of course, allowed him to take his first steps towards the enjoyment of his environment – though it was always to remain a place of confrontation with the mysterious forces of nature over which, at best, he exercised only limited control.

The earliest images of the garden are images of paradise, specifically the Garden of Eden. As an inviolate enclosure, the abode of Grace generated by the love of God, Eden was being used as an allegory for the immaculate Virgin Mary whose humanizing influence we have seen at the very root of medieval man's reawakening appreciation of his world. This was apparent well before the end of the 14th century but in the more secular age then developing the allegory turned against itself: the garden breached is an allegory of carnal delight. The illustration to the *Roman de la Rose* is a complex example: book and picture originated in France, but the French were certainly not alone in appreciating the delights of the garden.**2.303**

THE FRENCH MANOR

The period of reconstruction after the Hundred Years' War did not, of course, belong to the grand alone. The renewed internal security which followed the reconsolidation of royal power by Louis XI promoted the construction of numerous slightly defended, well-fenestrated houses by landowners with no pretensions to feudal power – the equivalent of the English manor house which had long proliferated in the relative security of the island kingdom. Halls and ancillary chambers are protected only by a small moat, a compound wall and a gatehouse but are otherwise innocent of the trappings of feudal defence work: colour and variety are drawn from the decorative use of local materials contrasting in tone and texture, as at S.-Germain-de-Livet in Normandy.**2.304**

>2.304 S.-GERMAIN-DE-LIVET, CHÂTEAU, late-15th century: open court.

Constructed from 1462 (and augmented with a Classicizing gatehouse c. 1584) on the site of a 12th-century château, S.-Germain-de-Livet well represents the French equivalent of the English manor which became feasible with the termination of the Hundred Years' War. It also well represents the coloristic use of materials at which Normandy excelled.

2.305

>**2.305 MONTEMASSI UNDER SIEGE** by Sienese forces led by the Condottiere Guidoriccio da Fogliano.

2.306

>**2.306 AMBROGIO LORENZETTI:** Umbrian town-scape (c. 1340).

Overlooked by the castle in its separate ward, the residential and commercial quarters are devolved organically on the flattening ground.

>**2.307 ROCCA S. LEO,** 15th century on ancient foundations: view from the south.

ITALY

The relaxation of the house was rare beyond the Rhine, even by the end of the 15th century. In Italy the Renaissance supervened and produced the villa – as we shall see (pages 730ff). As we shall also see, on the other hand (page 765), military engineering was subjected to rational revision by Renaissance masters of formal planning and there were to be many formidable gun emplacements with massive round towers – like those of the Neapolitan Castel Nuovo's outworks, built in the French style for Charles of Anjou from the mid-1440s, or the one provided in the 1470s by Giorgio Martini of Siena to defend the ancient Rocca S. Leo from the line of approach.**2.305–2.307**

2.307

2.308a

2.308b

2.308c

›**2.308 HOHENSTAUFEN RATIONALISM:** (a) Prato, Castello Imperiale (from 1242); (b) Lucera, Castello (1233, enlarged towards the end of the century), model; (c) Trani, Castello (from 1230) from the south-east; (d–f) Castel del Monte (1240), general view, plan and interior detail.

Frederick II pursued a rigorous policy of slighting the castles of rival magnates and replacing them with his own in Italy. Many were planned on rational lines, like the square work at Prato and the octagonal Castel del Monte. The latter, crowning an isolated hill, is as much an exercise in regal propaganda as Caernarvon. Recalling ecclesiastical octagons with imperial associations from Aachen to Ravenna – if not Jerusalem – it dominates the countryside with idiosyncratic Classical formality, as Frederick inherited his position from Charlemagne and based his rule on the ancient Roman imperial model – still represented in his age as much by Ravenna as by Rome itself. Suites of similar trapezoidal rooms ring the ocatagonal court on two floors.

2.308d

2.308f

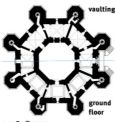

vaulting

ground
floor

2.308e @ 1:500

More than two centuries earlier, the emperor Frederick II Hohenstaufen had invested regularity with imperial authority in the last major phase of castle building throughout the peninsula: for example, at Prato, Lucera, Bari or Trani where castle and town walls are mutually supportive, and most persuasively at isolated Castel del Monte (c. 1240) – but that was a hunting lodge.**2.308** The legacy of his integrated systems of rigorously rectilinear works remained pervasive in its influence.

Within half a century of the Hohenstaufen demise, the isolated castle was eclipsed by the fortified town in the main line of Italian defensive work. There are, of course, exceptions – like Fenis in the Val d'Aosta – but typical is the projection of a bold fortress from an extensive system of mural defences – as at Carcassonne and, indeed, in several celebrated Sienese images.**2.305** The form was especially familiar in the domains of the Visconti, Scaligeri, Gonzaga and their fellow despots. The polygon

2.309a

was usually preferred to the circle in the planning of the mural bastions, as at Montagnana where the exceptionally well-preserved defences were built to the order of the Paduan tyrant Ezzelino da Romano.**2.309** Otherwise square corner towers were typically repeated at regular

›**2.309 MONTAGNANA, RAMPARTS,** c. 1250; (a) southern walls, (b) Rocca degli Alberi, (c) Porta Padova and its fort.

Unusual in their completeness, the mid-13th-century walls of Montagnana are punctuated by twenty-four towers, the majority semi-octagonal (i.e. with canted corners to the outside). Comparable in completeness, if not scale, are the defences of roughly circular Monteriggione, also near Siena, and the square outpost of the Scaliegeri at Villafranca near Verona.

2.309b

2.309C

intervals along perimeter walls. In this regard, and in general rectangularity of planning, Gradara of the Malatesta in the Marche or Sirmione on Lake Garda and the Castelvecchio of Verona, both of the Scaligeri, are typical of the despotic stronghold.[2.310]

2.310

>2.310 SIRMIONE, CASTLE, C. 1300.

Not unlike an urban tower house in its elevation, though surrounded by water, the fortress is rectangular in its compact whole and asymmetrically disposed parts. It is informally integrated with a trapezoidal naval dockyard in addition to a perpendicular mural range on the lake side of the town.

Most significantly, perhaps, Frederick II's legacy also provided the context for the distribution of palatial apartments in perpendicular wings around a quadrangular court. Mantua and Ferrara may be taken as exemplary in this, as in the projection of square towers from the corners and over the entrance where the corbels carrying the machicolated wallwalks are characteristically elongated.**2.311** Moreover, before the century was much more than half over the homogeneous mass of at least one suburban fort had been pierced by a loggia to ease transition from internal to external space – the essential feature of that quintessentially Renaissance building type, the villa.

›**2.311 FERRARA, CASTELLO OF NICCOLÒ II D'ESTE,** from 1385: view from the south-west.

The site, on a bend in the river Po, was fortified as an outpost of Ravenna by the Byzantine exarchs in the 7th century. Safer than Ravenna from seaborne depredation, it was developed into a port but was left landlocked when the river changed course in the mid-12th century: reduced to commercial impotence, but strategically placed on the road from the Veneto to central Italy, it submitted to the abrogation of its republican constitution by the Venetian Este family in 1264. Endowed with a marquisate under Venetian protection, the Este grew rich on tolls levied on travellers from the north-east and beyond, especially pilgrims on their way to Rome. At first the rulers made do with an enlarged tower – the Torre dei Leone – in the north-east corner of the town walls. After an uprising by the towns-

2.312

men against the level of imposts in the mid-1380s, Niccolò II d'Este embarked on a programme of expansion involving the construction of three new towers at the junction of wings framing a rectangular court and the excavation of a moat around the whole new complex.

›2.312 LOARRE, FORTIFIED MONASTIC COMPLEX, 11th–13th centuries: view from the south.

The complex, on a strategic site in the foothills of the Pyrenees commanding the Gallego valley, was developed from c. 1020 by Sancho III of Navarra (died 1035) to protect territory he had regained from the Muslims to the south: remains include the Homage Tower (Torre del Homenaje), the Queen's Tower (Torre de la Reina), the Chapel of S. María of Valverde and several stretches of walls. The last were developed on an impressive scale – and in an eclectic style drawn from Lombard, Poitevan and Mudéjar sources – after a community of Augustinian canons was installed by Sancho IV in 1073. On the latter's murder three years later, his cousin Sancho Ramírez of Aragón was elected to his place and projected his expansion into Huescas from Loarre. A second major campaign of development followed the accession of the Aragonese house to the throne of Navarra and continued into the 12th century. The outer range of ramparts followed a century later.

›2.313 BRAGANZA, CASTLE, 12th–16th centuries: view from the south-east.

IBERIA

The properly concentric form of castle was comparatively rare in post-conquest Iberia: in nucleus at least, Loarre in Huesca and Alarcón de las Altas Torres in Cuenca may well represent the approximation of the form with the aid of nature: at the other side of the peninsula, Braganza is a latter-day example.**2.312, 2.313**

2.313

2.314a

2.314b

›**2.314 MEDINA DEL CAMPO, CASTLE** (La Mota), 12th-15th centuries, restored in the 20th century: (a) general view from the north-west, (b) court.

Much of the restored brick complex was rebuilt from 1440 for Juan II of Castilla and expanded from 1479 for his daughter Isabella and her husband Ferdinand of Aragón.

›**2.315 PEÑAFIEL, CASTLE,** founded in the 10th century, great stone keep and ward extensions 12th century, curtain wall further extended and reformed in the first half of the 14th century.

The site, a great strategic objective of the *conquistadores* and their Muslim enemies in the early 11th century, dominates the confluence of the Duero and Duraton rivers.

2.315

2.316

›2.316 CIUDAD RODRIGO, CASTLE OF ENRIQUE II OF CASTILLA-LEÓN, 1372: (a) view from the west with section of associated city defences (mid-12th century in origin, much reformed).

›2.317 TOWER OF BELÉM, 1515: view from the north-west.

The tower, commanding the Tagus estuary below Lisbon, was built for King Manuel I by the military engineer Francesco de Arruda.

2.317

However, the massive rectangular keep was generally retained as the principal element in the complex, especially by ambitious magnates under weak kings but also by the servants of the latter against the former: the many splendid instances may be represented at Atienza in Guadalajara, Berlanga de Duero in Soria, Ponferrada in León, Peñafiel and Medina del Campo in Valladolid.**2.314, 2.315** As elsewhere, the Iberians also saw advantage in its displacement to the periphery, to concentrate strength on the most vulnerable point of entry – as at Segovia or Tomar. Occasionally they even retained an isolated four-square keep as the guardian of approach to a walled town – as at the Alcántara entrance to Toledo, at Ciudad Rodrigo near the border with Portugal or, indeed, at Belém by the approach to Lisbon from the mouth of the Tagus.**2.316, 2.317**

The influence of feudal France was at its height in the aftermath of the Hundred Years' War, following the dispatch of its English adversary – and rival for alliance with Castilla. That apart, however, the Arab legacy remained important – indeed paramount – in the development of the Iberian castle. The ranging of increasingly commodious accommodation in wings framing a central court is certainly not contrary to the current French tendency but in Iberia the courtyard plan may be seen to descend from the Moorish translation of the Syrian *qasr* at the outset of Muslim rule in the peninsula.

With its gracious courts, the alcazár had been commodious, often luxurious, long before comfort and beauty were significant considerations in the internal arrangement of feudal seats back beyond the Pyrenees. And in their superb brickwork, laid over formal plans, the Muslim builders of Spain led the way to an external aesthetic

2.318a

›2.318 COCA CASTLE, 15th century: (a) view from the west, (b) entrance over the moat.

The massive polygonal keep was built by Mudéjar masons for Alfonso de Fonseca, Archbishop of Seville. The massive battered walls of superb pink brick rise from the centre of three concentric enclosures. The two inner ones are square and would recall Harlech or

2.318a

Beaumaris but for the replacement of the gatehouse keep with a tower of the Vincennes type in the northwest corner (right here). The outer enceinte borders the moat in general response to the projection and recession of the inner ones – as at Caerphilly. The stepped pyramidal merlons, with which the ramparts and towers are crenellated, are typically Mudéjar.

which complemented highly sophisticated military engineering. To the end of the medieval era, the latter rarely admitted generous fenestration but, typically, elaborately balustraded galleries grace the court fronts of the perpendicular accommodation ranges.

The Castillo de los Mendoza at Manzanares el Real near Madrid is a splendid exercise in display masonry: atypically, an elegant gallery addresses the exterior. Coca in Castilla, built for Alfonso de Fonseca, Archbishop of Seville towards the middle of the 15th century, is an unexcelled example of the persistence of the Arab tradition both in its superb striped brickwork – which, like the masonry of Caernarvon, still reflects the prestige of Theodosian Constantinople – and in the geometry of its formal planning in whole and in symmetrically disposed part.**2.318, 2.319** As the seat of a bishop it had quasi-feudal connotations but was typical of the main stream of Iberian practice in catering for the religious community of the bishop's entourage in cloistered seclusion. Thus, if these spectacular works rival Vincennes as a latter-day expression of motte and bailey, unlike Vincennes, the nucleus was not the formidable keep but the inner ward transformed into cloister court.

2.319b

2.319a

›2.319 MANZANARES EL REAL, CASTILLO DE LOS MENDOZA, from 1435 on 13th-century foundations for the first Duke of Infantado, embellished for

the second Duke probably by Juan Guas from 1473: (a)
view from the south-east, (b) court detail.

THE EMPIRE AND BEYOND

The Hohenstaufens and their most important rivals among the magnates, such as Henry the Lion, sustained the Carolingian tradition of the *Pfalz* in works like the Burggrafenburg at Nuremberg (destroyed) and the Burg Dankwarderode at Brunswick.**2.320** Built c. 1170 by Henry the Lion over late-Carolingian foundations in a relatively lightly defended compound, the open-fronted complex of hall and ancillary chambers of the Brunswick *Pfalz* is not unlike the contemporary English palace but more coherent, more imposing. Of course, such a palace might be built in conjunction with the compound of a highly defensive site: the most spectacular example, again much restored, is the house of the Landgraves of Thuringia in the Wartburg near Eisenach, built by Ludwig III (1172–90) and his successor Herman I (died 1217).**2.321**

›**2.320 BRUNSWICK, DANKWARDERODE,** 1160, heavily restored in 1873 and again after World War II.

The name derives from Dankward, son of Ludolf of Saxony, who founded Brunswick in 860. Henry the Lion built it, supposedly on the site of Dankward's seat, 300 years later. Like the contemporary English palatial hall, it consists of one large room with small ancillary chambers raised over a basement. A defensive enceinte enclosed the hall and the neighbouring cathedral of S. Blasius.

›2.321 EISENACH, WARTBURG, founded before 1080, much new building between the late-12th and mid-16th centuries, restored between 1840 and 1890: (a–f) Landgrave's House from the southern tower, models representing the original work of Ludwig III and the addition of a third storey by Herman I, the Knight's Hall, dining hall and Elizabeth Chamber on the ground floor, (g) general view from the north-east, (h) model of complex.

The stronghold was established on an eminence commanding the road linking the imperial capital at Frankfurt am Main with the eastern outpost of Breslau (modern Polish Wroclaw) by the first Landgrave of Thuringia, Ludwig the Springer, c. 1170: the southern and northern towers and the keep adjoining the latter to its east (rebuilt after a fire in 1317 and again in 1859) were founded at that time. The two-storey residence of Landgrave Ludwig III, built c. 1180 in place of a southern adjunct to the keep, was given its third storey c. 1200: the main rooms were probably frescoed originally but early 20th-century mosaics distinguish the room named after S. Elisabeth of Hungary, who lived there from 1211–27 as the wife of Ludwig IV (succeeded 1217). The ancillary buildings framing the outer bailey, within the northern entrance portal, date mainly from the 15th and 16th century: the Governor's House in the western range accommodated Martin Luther in 1521–22.

›2.322 VESTE COBURG, from 1230, most of the existing structure dates from rebuilding after a fire in 1499 and expansion in the 17th century: 19th-century view.

2.321a

2.321b

2.321c

2.321d

2.321e

2.321f

2.321g

2.321h

Through and beyond the Empire, there is a wide range of imperial castles built to control towns, conquered territory and lines of communication. Their forms vary widely according to site, naturally, but common is the accretion of ancillary rooms around a cramped court overawed by an ancient *Burgfried* perched on top of a crag. Formal exercises, like those of Frederick II in Italy, are foreign.**2.322**

2.322

2.323a

The castles of a plethora of lesser magnates and their vassals, if not set in or by rivers to exact tolls, are invariably developed around a primitive tower. Their typically remote sites, accessible along one extremely tortuous path, obviously neither needed nor admitted the sophistications of concentric ramparts with flanking towers. There will be a regular rectilinear block of the *Pfalz* type in the most important seats but in general the accommodation is developed organically in ranges around irregular courts. And in counterpoint to the sombre practicalities of basic defence, rich decorative effect may be drawn from the display of varied materials on court fronts, or at the highest levels, as much as from the elaboration of profiles.

›2.323 BACHARACH-KAUB, MIDDLE RHINE: (a) Stahleck; (b) Pfalzgrafenstein below Gutenfels (founded c. 1200).

Stahleck and Gutenfels, strategically placed opposite one another above an island in the Rhine from which tolls could most effectively be exacted, were imperial foundations at the behest of the Counts Palatine. This dignity, first accorded to an imperial official in the mid-10th century, was granted by Conrad III to his brother-in-law Hermann von Stahleck in 1142 and by Frederick I to his half-brother Conrad in his reimposition of order in Germany in 1155: it passed to the Welfs in 1195 through the marriage of Conrad's daughter to the son of Heinrich the Lion (Duke of Saxony and Bavaria from 1142 and 1152 respectively) and was confirmed to the Welf dukes of Bavaria by Frederick II in 1214.

Stahleck was founded by Count Hermann's father c. 1135. Gutenfels was founded c. 1200 under Heinrich the

2.323b
Welf. Duke Louis III of Bavaria (Count Palatine from 1294 and Emperor from 1314 to his death in 1347) favoured the area, held court at Gutenfels in 1326 and ordered the construction of Pfalzgrafenstein c. 1328.

Riverine toll stations are nowhere better represented than by Pfalzgrafenstein on its island in the Rhine: it is dominated by Gutenfels on the right bank above Kaub.**2.323** Gutenfels apart, we have already encountered examples of complexes developed around the nucleus of a primitive *Burgfried* – not least the Marksburg on the middle Rhine. Mainly medieval, the latter is rare among Rhenish strongholds in eluding destruction by the French towards the end of the 17th century and reconstruction by industrialists in the 19th century. The plethora of spectacular survivals elsewhere may well be represented by Eltz near the Mosel and Bran far off in Transylvania.**2.324, 2.325**

2.324a

2.324b

2.324c

›**2.324 ELTZ, MOSEL,** 12th–16th centuries: (a) general view, (b) entrance, (c) court.

First recorded in the middle of the 12th century, the complex developed as a quadripartite *Ganerbenburgen* (divided seat) under the joint ownership of four families descended from multiple heirs – as the richly varied elements testify.

›2.325 BRAN, TRANSYLVANIA (ROMANIA), SO-CALLED CASTLE OF DRACULA, 12th–16th centuries: view from the south.

In lieu of the homogeneous mass and volume of the early imperial *Pfalz*, typical of its era in embracing many facets of life with limited concession to privacy, the organic hilltop complex was the natural progenitor of the late-medieval palace. The lineage may be traced in the development of Prague castle from its great hall.[2.327] The emperor Charles IV's Karlstein in Bohemia is a special case, retaining a keep for regalian security, like contemporary Vincennes or the Parisian Louvre.[2.326] The Meissen seat of the Elector of Saxony may be taken as

2.326a

2.326b

2.326c

›2.326 KARLSTEIN CASTLE: (a) general view from the south-west, (b) cut-away model of keep showing the Chapel of the Holy Cross, (c) detail of chapel interior.

Approached from the Prague road to the north, a sequence of wards preceded the royal accommodation block on the southern ramparts. That was connected by a bridge at second-floor level on its northern side with the two-storey block containing the Marian chapel where the emperor's holy relics were kept. That, in turn, was also connected by bridge to the keep on the highest, northern-most part of the site, where the imperial regalia was kept in the Chapel of the Holy Cross.

›2.327 PRAGUE CASTLE, WENCESLAS HALL, 1493–1502.

The seat of the Bohemian monarchy from the end of the 9th century, there was doubtless a hall in the earliest castle but the present one was built by the Saxon architect Benedikt Ried for King Vladislav Jagiello, who returned the court from its residence in the Old Town below in 1484. The network of willowy ribs, many with brutally pruned ends, is among the most spectacular examples of the technique developed by Reid in continuing the work of Peter Parler and his sons in the cathedral. Work on that was disrupted by the Hussites in 1421.

representative – indeed exemplary.**2.328** Consolidation of mass, typical in main part of the latter at least, is also represented by the castles of the Teutonic knights in the lands now belonging to Poland and the Baltic states,

2.327

2.368a

2.368b

2.368c

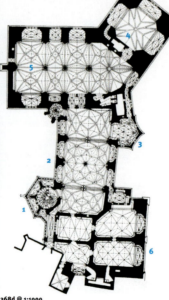

2.368d @ 1:1000

›**2.328 MEISSEN, ALBRECHTSBURG,** 1470–89
on 10th-century foundations, heavily redecorated in
the 19th century: (a) general view from the Elbe, (b)
model from the south-west, (c) chapel, (d) plan of first
floor with (1) main stairs (2) Great Hall, (3) chapel, (4)
Great Court Chamber, (5) dining hall, (6) Elector's
apartment, (e) Great Hall, (f) staircase detail, (g, h)
Heraldic Hall and Great Chamber of Appeal on second
floor.

Frederick IV of Wettin, Markgraf of Meissen, was elevated to the ranks of the Electors as Duke of Saxony-
Wittenberg in 1423. His grandsons Ernst and Albert,
who succeeded jointly in 1464, undertook the reconstruction of the Meissen seat to house themselves in
appropriate state: the work began under the direction
of Arnold von Westfalen and was completed by Konrad
Pfluger. Additions were made to the third floor for Duke
Georg in the early 1520s.

2.368e

2.368f

2.368g

2.368h

2.329a

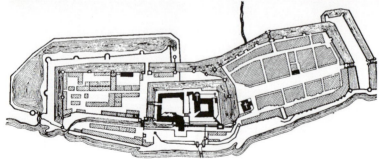

2.329b @ approximately 1:1000

most notably their headquarters at Marienburg (Malbork): there, however, the monumental scale of palatial blocks is not ameliorated by rich ornament and the site is characteristically open to facilitate widespread control of colonized territory.**2.329**

›2.329 MARIENBURG (now Polish Malbork), early 14th century: (a) view from Vistula, (b) plan.

Largely built in the second half of the 13th century, Marienburg on the Vistula was the headquarters of the Teutonic Knights from 1309 when the Grand Master Siegfried von Feuchtwagen moved there from Venice.

The Teutonic Knights of S. Mary's Hospital at Jerusalem were distinguished at the end of the 12th century from the Knights Templar and Hospitaler. After the final loss of the Holy Land they crusaded elsewhere. In particular, owing their original support to merchants from Lübeck and other Baltic trading towns which fostered the colonization of the Slav lands to the east, they took the cross and the sword through modern Poland to Lithuania and on up into north-western Russia. They based themselves on a series of riverine castles in whose quadrangular courts their original dedication to the sick was not forgotten.

›2.330 YORK, BOOTHAM BAR, 12th century and later: view from outside.

Constructed in the main under Edward III towards the middle of the 14th century, sometimes on Norman and even Roman foundations, the walls of York are among the finest and most complete survivors of medieval European town defences – though extensively restored in the 19th century. Bootham Bar was built in the early 12th century over the site of the north-west gate of the Roman rectangular camp-town: the Norman arch survived renovation in the 13th century and restoration in the 19th. The crowded complexity, but relatively modest elevation, of the housing around the cathedral within is typical of the English town.

2.330

›2.331 CAHORS, PONT VALENTRE, 1308–85: general view.

2.331

10 TOWN AND GOTHIC HOUSE

To the powers contending with one another throughout the later Middle Ages, towns were objects of envy as sources of wealth through taxation at least as important as agriculture. The techniques adopted for the defence of castles were adapted to the defence of towns. Naturally, this depended on the decentralization of mass: indeed, the essence of the urban exercise was the protection of an expansive bailey. However, only the more affluent could afford a complete circuit of walls – which doubled as customs barriers – and were often superseded to enclose new suburbs when urban growth could no longer be constrained behind the original defences. From Alnwick to Avignon, Ávila to Acre, many town walls punctuated with rectangular, polygonal or cylindrical bastions and pierced with twin-towered gates have survived in whole or in part, and there are splendid surviving defences of the main line of approach – none better than the bridge at Cahors.**2.330, 2.331**

2.332a

The complete image of a medieval town is perhaps best conveyed by Carcassonne, though it was imaginatively restored in the 19th century. Nowhere better illustrates the deployment of extensive outworks beyond concentric walls and the development of the gatehouse into a massive residential stronghold at the principal entry point – just as the modern castle builder advanced the keep to reinforce his enceinte defences at the breach. The form defined by the walls and the pattern of streets are typical of the generally pragmatic medieval approach to urban development. The earliest inhabitants followed the contours of the site for ease of movement and drainage but, when the French crown established a town in the valley below, common sense recommended regular plots for fair and convenient division.**2.332**

›**2.332 CARCASSONNE,** c. 1230-87, incorporating earlier work, restored in the 19th century: (a) general view from the north-west, (b) Porte Narbonnaise.

The site, on a rocky plateau dominating the valley of the Aude in south-western France, was fortified at least as early as the 3rd century. It was given its present form by the French kings, capitalizing on the suppression of the Albigensian heresy and the expropriation of the local viscount, to consolidate their hold on the county of Toulouse ceded to them by the Treaty of Paris (1229). There is a double enceinte, stepped for defence in depth and different ranges of fire: the higher inner one is 1100 metres long and punctuated by twenty-six towers, the exterior one is 1500 metres long with sixteen towers. The ramparts were divided into sectors for individual defence by towers which constituted independent forts with their own water supply. The citadel, integrated with the ramparts towards the north of the western range, guards the main line of approach from the river valley.

2.332b

PLANNING

Medieval urban growth began ad hoc with the expansion of villages after the settlement of the main marauders in the 10th century and was checked only by the Black Death 400 years later. It generally led from the agricultural village to the trading or manufacturing town no longer self-sufficient in food production. Reaching a climax in the late-13th century, it extended to the foundation of towns dictated by military exigency or prompted by the redevelopment of trade routes within the domain of the old Roman empire and the expansion of colonization beyond.

By its nature the seigneurial authority of manorial feudalism rarely dedicated itself to disciplining the growth of towns. The market, the focus of the local feudal economy, may have been established under the auspices of a lord, ecclesiastical or secular, but the dwellings of the merchants spread of their own accord in ribbons along the arteries of communication with the world at large. As the economy grew and specialization advanced, many streets themselves became markets and peripheral market squares devoted to specific products were usually established as and where land was available. The pattern of streets developing from these multiple hubs of commerce – paved as early as 1185 in Paris – added further complexity to the urban fabric.**2.333, 2.334**

Medieval urban growth was not invariably left to natural organic impulse even before the close of the 12th century. Much was based on Roman foundations, of whole towns and of major former elements within them: ordered plans, though blurred after centuries of neglect, were rarely entirely escapable in the age of regeneration and the remains of large structures, especially amphitheatres, provided nuclei of order. As always, moreover, the founders of new towns on fresh sites were inevitably committed to a rational plan but, as in the later districts of Carcassonne,

2.333

>**2.333 NUREMBERG, 'SCHONER BRUNNEN' IN THE MARKTPLATZ,** 1361: attributed to Heinrich Parler, restored.

The provision of water to the public in the most public of places (by tapping spring or well) was the most obvious cause for the celebration of patronage: here Emperor Charles IV is joined by the seven imperial electors and nine heroes.

>**2.334 ROTHENBURG OB DER TAUBER:** (a) general view from town hall tower, (b, c) street scenes.

2.334a

2.334b

2.334c

2.335a

2.335b

they rarely imposed a grid mechanically in total disregard of the grain of the site: pragmatism, not rationalism, was their bent.

Prominent examples of early medieval urbanism disciplined by a great Roman legacy are the quarters of Arles and Lucca developed in their amphitheatres.**2.335** One need look no further than central Arles for an excellent example of medieval growth over an inherited grid. On the other hand, Salisbury was founded on a preconceived grid plan c. 1220 after the bishop decided to move to an entirely new site from insalubrious Old Sarum: to the north of the

›2.335 AMPHITHEATRICAL URBAN DEVELOPMENT: (a) Arles (before modern clearance); (b) Lucca.

The legacy of the amphitheatre apart, one need look no further than central Arles for an excellent example of medieval growth over an inherited grid (AIC1, page 515).

›2.336 SALISBURY (1220): plan with (1) cathedral, (2) parish church, (3) market.

Water was scarce at Old Sarum and the elevated site was considered intolerably windy. The new, well-watered valley site was inhabited at least from 1180 but the planned development followed the construction of the new cathedral projected from 1212. The city's charter was granted by Henry III in 1227 and prosperity followed the diversion of the great western road from Old Sarum c. 1330.

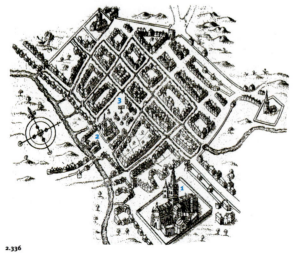

2.336

cathedral close, the residential blocks derive from a grid but their rectangularity is distorted in accordance with the contours to facilitate water reticulation and their size varies in accordance with the hierarchy of buildings accommodated, in particular the main parish church and associated market is located to the west – rather than in the centre like the typical Roman forum.[2.336]

Rigidity is uncharacteristic even when the example of the Roman camp – the origin of so many colonial towns – was remembered by medieval kings in establishing garrison settlements to defend the outlying areas of their domains. Proximity to the Roman prototype in regularity of form as well as purpose is most clearly displayed – in moderation and according to the lie of the land – by the so-called bastide towns, implanted with predetermined plans by both the French and English crowns to hold down territory under threat and as centres of commerce. The most celebrated are those built by Edward I in his Gascon dominion of south-west France, and in Aigues-Mortes, begun c. 1250 by Louis IX to guard his Mediterranean coast.[2.337, 2.338]

The bastide and medieval urban order

Rational – if not rationalist – planning is well represented by Aigues-Mortes: it is a camp on a large scale respecting the formality of the prototype, with a regular grid of streets culminating in the central town square, but with deviations dictated by topography.

After the extension of his kingdom to the Mediterranean following the suppression of the Albigensians, Louis IX began operations on his new port to defend the coast of newly acquired Provence and as an embarcation point for his ill-fated Crusades. Beyond the cylindrical Tour de Constance, built at the outset in 1246 as a citadel with a lighthouse on top, the town was protected under Philip III and Philip IV (between 1271 and 1300) with the ramparts of the Genoese engineer Boccanegra. Forming an irregular rectangle (520 by 325 by 510 by 285 metres) with round towers

2.337a

reinforcing the corners, these are pierced by ten twin-towered gates and several posterns. As usual in bastides, the royal authority was responsible for planning and defence but leased land to private proprietors who were granted the status of freemen in return for some commitment to military service and were left relatively free in the building of their premises on their standardized allotments.

2.337b

2.338a

2.338b

Even more faithful to the Roman model is Monpazier: one of the series of bastides built by Edward I while he was based in Gascony to consolidate his power, it controls the valley of the Dropt. Like the others in the series, it is a walled settlement but not a castle town like contemporary Welsh establishments. Typically, the 'tartan' grid is determined by main streets of c. 6 metres width, lanes of 2 metres and allotments of c. 7 by 22 metres. More important than in England but usual in Gascony, the market square (equal to twenty allotments in area) is central: it is surrounded by shopping arcades, which often extended to neighbouring streets, and dominated by the town hall – apart from the parish church which was often built as a defensible refuge.

Topography triumphs over regular geometry in the delineation of the perimeters of several of Edward I's Gascon bastides – Beaumont on its curved plateau, for example. In England, Libourne has a relatively regular radial plan but elsewhere the street pattern variously deviates from the grid, especially in Wales where earlier settlements were incorporated.

Comparable settlements, fortified but not always entirely predetermined in plan, were planted by rulers as diverse as the Dukes of Zahringen, south-west of the empire in territory now shared by Germany and Switzerland, by the Florentine republic to consolidate its hold on central Tuscany and by several of its neighbours responding in kind, by the kings of Bohemia as a bulwark against the expansion of Austria, and by the margraves of Brandenburg in support of Teutonic colonization beyond the Elbe.

As the name implies, Florentine Terranova was a wholly new installation, on the road to Arezzo: it conforms to the bastide type with its rectangular perimeter, regular grid and central square. Alternatively, the grid may be encapsulated in a roughly circular or elliptical perimeter. The most economical form, despite the mismatch at the edge, it is common in all areas: examples range from New Brandenburg in eastern Prussia to Český Budejovice in southern Bohemia and Sienese Monteriggioni.**2.339** On the other

2.340a

2.339

›**2.339 MONTERIGGIONI, SIENA,** 13th century: aerial view.

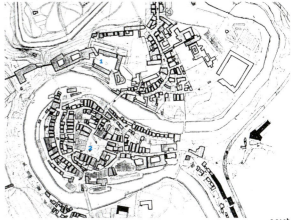

›2.340 ČESKÝ KRUMLOV, first recorded in 1235: (a) general view, (b) plan with (1) castle and the settlement of the lord's retainers (2) market square in centre of the commercial settlement.

A castle town on a peninsula site defined by three loops in the River Vltava – made insular by the cutting of a defence channel across the isthmus – depended on the castle of the Rozemberks (predating the first mention of the site in 1235, extended in the 14th century, transformed in the 16th century) who controlled traffic from Austria through south-western Bohemia to Saxony.

2.340b

hand, topography dictates the willowy spinal configuration of Berne, one of the main Zähringer towns, and a vortex cut through with arteries radiating from the central square at Český Krumlov in south-eastern Bohemia.**2.340**

SHOPS AND THE MARKET

In towns planned and unplanned, the market square was originally surrounded – even covered – by temporary stalls. As economic conditions improved and the exchange of goods occupied increasing numbers of dedicated tradesmen, first in Italy and slightly later in the commercial centres of the north, the temporary ceded to the permanent: shops reappeared. Backed by a store and usually under some form of minimal accommodation for the retailer, they hardly differed from the ancient Roman type with a counter to the open street front (AICI, pages 545f).**2.341**

In or beside the square, the civic authorities progressed to market halls with many similar shops in arcades on the

›2.341 ANCIENT ROMAN SHOP MODEL (Rome, Museum of Roman Life).

›2.342 PADUA, PIAZZA DELLE ERBE: Palazzo della Raggione (1219, renovated 1306, reroofed 1756).

2.342

›2.343 FLORENCE, PONTE VECCHIO, 1345.

Rebuilt several times until the mid-14th century, restored many times since, the oldest bridge in Florence serves traffic on the artery leading south from the centre of the Roman grid. A prime site, it has traditionally been colonized by jewellers and pawn-brokers.

›2.344 CHICHESTER, MARKET CROSS, 1501 with clock of 1724.

ground floor and a meeting room above. Beyond the square, shops spread along the neighbouring streets and even over bridges – indeed a bridge was especially prized as the location of a shop because it usually provided a unique funnel of communication. Italy showed the way but the stall survived in marketplaces everywhere, of course, and was often commemorated in stone canopies – particularly by northern benefactors when their towns were affluent in the 15th century.**2.342–2.344**

Unsavoury trades – like slaughtering or tanning – were naturally banished to suburbs but atypical was the English pattern of extended ribbon development along the main roads out of town – at least when the great age of wool-based prosperity was reached in the 14th century. Just as the relatively strong central government of a relatively secure island encouraged the early development of the country house there, so too these conditions limited the risk of building without the walls. Within, in consequence, space was not at such a high premium as in most continental towns and the English town house rarely matched the height of its continental counterpart.**2.345**

2.345a

2.345b

THE TOWNSMAN'S HOUSE

If not over shops, early town houses were usually contiguous and rarely more than two storeys high. As most were built of perishable materials, survivals are rare and as these are mainly of stone they would always have been exceptional.[2.346] Even in planned towns, terraces of identical

›2.346 LINCOLN, JEWS HOUSE, c. 1170 (the name is later).

Though stone obviously indicates affluence, decoration is limited. There was a single space on both floors, probably with movable partitions but two rooms added to the back are of uncertain date. Jews lived outside the feudal system and set new standard of domestic comfort, but the name of this house derives from a late-13th-century occupant.

2.346

houses were unusual and competition for space near the market prompted assertive individuality. Almshouses built charitably for the needy – first in Italy in the mid-14th century, elsewhere in the 15th century – were the main exceptions.

The Black Death of the mid-14th century reduced most urban populations by at least half, leaving room for the

›2.347 CLUNY, EARLY MEDIEVAL HOUSES:
(a) street fronts; (b–d) ground- and first-floor plans and elevation.

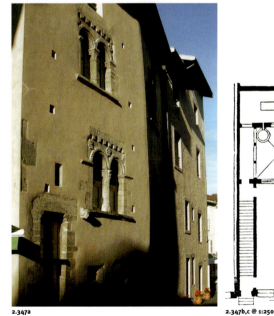

2.347a

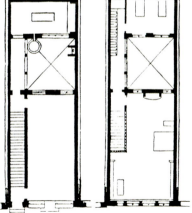

2.347b,c @ 1:250

2.347d

survivors to expand within the walls. Nevertheless, the determination to remain as close as possible to the commercial hub – as well as the need to provide for business and storage – sustained the value of central street frontages and promoted constant rebuilding there on deep, narrow plots to ever greater height and variety.

2.348

2.349

>2.348 ROUEN, medieval street scene.
Only the most affluent could afford a courtyard where land was at a premium in commercial centres: there was usually a narrow passage between buildings to stabling at the back.

>2.349 ANGERS, MAISON D'ADAM, 15th century: view from the south.

The multistorey formula was widely applied on the Continent though, of course, both height and the varied effects of mixed materials depended upon local conditions, not least the commercial significance of the building site in particular and the town in general.[2.348, 2.349] The most affluent northern merchants seem to have emulated their Italian peers and built in stone: among the gabled, half-timbered houses of many German and Netherlandish towns there are similar stone ones – especially on the most desirable sites facing a river where they are aligned with warehouses and granaries.[2.350]

›2.350 GHENT, GRASLEI EMBANKMENT, with 13th-century granary right of centre, flanked by 14th–16th century houses.

2.350

By the end of the 14th century the most affluent English merchants were imitating the houses of the nobility, particularly the manor house with its hall, solar and parlour – but there are no unaltered urban survivors to match Stokesay or the nucleus of Penshurst. In France, and Flanders too, the residences of patrons as disparate as the Bishop of Sens or the Abbot of Cluny (begun 1485) in Paris, the merchant banker Jacques Cœur in Bourges (begun 1442) and the Gruuthuis in Bruges (c. 1470) conform to type: the miniature castle with gatehouse in a low

2.351a

2.351b

>2.351 THE LATE-MEDIEVAL FRENCH TOWN MANSION: (a) Paris, Hôtel Cluny (first built by Pierre de Chalus, 21st Abbot of Cluny, rebuilt from 1485 by Jacques d'Amboise, brother of the cardinal minister of Charles VIII: street front with screen wall and carriage entrance; (b, c) Bourges, Hôtel Jacques Cœur (1442), street front and court with octagonal staircase cage. The great merchant banker was born in Bourges c. 1394: his fortune rose with the establishment of Charles VII's court at Bourges when the fortunes of France were at their lowest ebb.

2.351c

2.352a

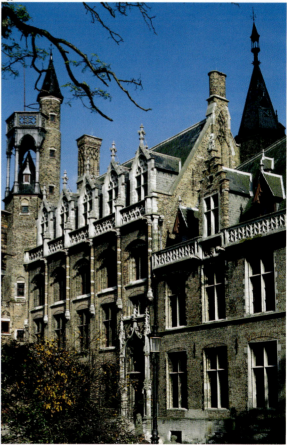

›2.352 THE LATE-MEDIEVAL TOWN MAN-
SION IN BRUGES: (a) Buersplaats with the mansions of Genoese and Florentine traders beside the
houses of local merchants; (b) Gruuthuis (c. 1470),
main courtyard façade.

2.352b

entrance range, wings well lit on the side of the court, at least, and an elegant, openwork staircase tower. In fact in France the grandest town house long remained difficult to distinguish from its country counterpart, in type if not in scale. That was relatively rare, especially in free towns of the empire: in all but the grandest patrician town houses, the main residential block faced the street and the inner courts were framed by secondary buildings.**2.351–2.353**

2.353a

2.353b

›2.353 THE LATE-MEDIEVAL TOWN MAN-SION IN GERMANY: (a, b) Nuremberg, exterior of the 15th-century house associated with Dürer and 17th-century engraving of a courtyard; (c) Bamburg, Bishop's Palace court; (d) Lübeck.

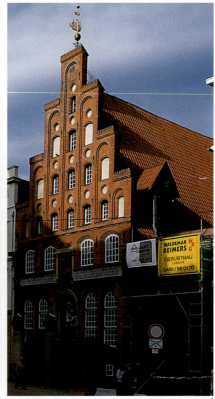

2.353c

2.353d

›2.354 POITIERS, PALAIS DE JUSTICE (ancient palace of the Dukes of Aquitaine and of Jean, Duc de Berry): (a, b) interior and exterior of the Salle des Pas-Perdus (early 13th century, substantially renovated in the late-14th century, restored 1861).

In place of the principal element of the ancient palace, the extant hall was commissioned by Berry as his seat of judgement on behalf of his brother, King Charles V. The adjoining four-towered building (exterior view right) is the truncated remnant of the Valois duke's town residence. The equivalent in the great royal palace on the Île-de-la-Cité in Paris has long been superseded.

2.354a

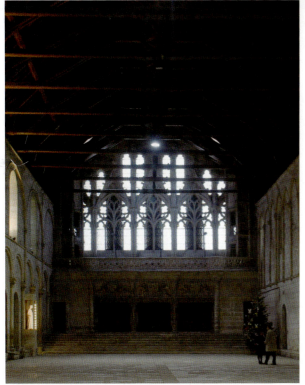

2.354b

PUBLIC PALACES IN THE NORTH

The evolution of the hall palace, which we have seen beginning in England just before the end of the 11th century, was advanced throughout Europe by the mid-14th century. Relying primarily on town defences, but within their own protective compound, the elements multiplied organically with the specialization that characterized later medieval life, political, economic and social.

The king held court in the great hall, sitting in judgement and presiding over state ceremonies, ultimately including his 'parliaments' with the representatives of the various estates of the realm. There was a lesser hall for the legislative process, which would involve consultation with legal advisers and various interested parties as well as the services of recording clerks, and yet another for the king to sit with his private councillors. Beyond the meeting halls, there were the private apartments for the various members of the royal family, accommodation for an army of administrators and barracks for the mercenary guards. The legacy is extensive from Westminster to Prague and beyond. **2.354, 2.268, 2.327,**

2.355

›2.355 **ROUEN, PALAIS DE JUSTICE** (former Treasury of Normandy), 1499 with 19th-century restoration and much rebuilding after World War II: court front with its unexcelled Flamboyant dormers.

The great hall was the essential element in all medieval public building types. The king's hall might accommodate the central parliament and judiciary of the realm but there were provincial councils, legal authorities and other organs of government to be housed. Of innumerable late-medieval structures proclaiming the majesty of the law, the Palais de Justice of Rouen and the so-called Maison du Roi in Brussels may be taken as representative. **2.355, 2.356**

Like the king's hall, too, the town hall, the focus of urban life, the seat of the independent judiciary won by the town with its freedom from the jurisdiction of feudal courts, descended from the ancient Roman basilica. Like the basilica, the earliest town halls were associated with the marketplace, indeed they usually consisted of one palatial hall with small ancillary apartments built over shopping arcades. As prosperity waxed, the town hall was naturally disposed to display the financial power and self-esteem of the mercantile community administered from it and, equally naturally, its scale and sumptuousness varied with the size of that community's economy.

2.356a

>2.356 LATE-MEDIEVAL CIVIC BUILDING IN
FLANDERS: (a) Leuven, Town Hall (1448–63); (b, c)
Brussels, Maison du Roi, Town Hall (main body
1402–44, tower from 1455); (d, e) Bruges, Market Hall
with belfry, Town Hall (from 1377), detail of exterior.

An important staging post on the road from Cologne
to Brussels, Leuven developed around the county castle from the 11th century and flourished after the count
was raised to the dukedom of Brabant in 1206, especially as a cloth-weaving centre. The town hall, due in
its final lavish form to Matthaeus de Rayens (except for
the 19th-century sculptures of eminent citizens), was
begun as the centre of Brabantine gravity shifted to
Brussels. The town hall there was built in conscious
rivalry with Bruges.

The port of Bruges, a seat of the Counts of Flanders
and the major distribution centre for Flemish cloth, was
linked to the Hanseatic ports by the mid-13th century,
to Genoa by 1277 and to Venice before the end of the
century. The belfry building dominating the market
square, with retail arcades and halls on two storeys
which served administrative and commercial purposes, was originally built by the franchised burgesses
in 1240 but was rebuilt after a fire in 1280 with a stone
tower – the octagonal upper storey was added in 1483.

Apart from the palace of king or count, dominance in
the trading towns of the north was contested between the
seats of the civic authorities and the guilds. Both needed
facilities for general assembly, private council meeting and
legislation – or regulation in the case of the guilds. Both
proclaimed the self-esteem of the merchant in confrontation with the prestige of the ecclesiastical and lay magnates in their cathedrals and castles. Given considerable

2.356b

2.356c

2.356d

diversity of form, definition of type is elusive but whether a gabled front is presented to the street framed by houses or a palatial volume is isolated on a square, the origin is clearly domestic.

With or without a bell tower, the palatial hall type of civic building is relatively consistent throughout the trading towns of Flanders and Germany – differences of scale, materials, ornament and cost apart.**2.357–2.359** At its most ostentatious, diversified in space to cater for a variety of deliberative bodies and accommodation requirements, the trappings first borrowed from the feudal defensive repertory were supplanted in the 14th century by towers, pinnacles, dormers and oriels as flamboyant as anything conceived by the Duc de Berry.

About 1300 a hall especially for marketing cloth was built to the east of the market square and the town hall was moved into space ceded by the Counts of Flanders in their neighbouring castle. There in 1377, at the height of the city's prosperity before the silting of its access to the sea, a new town hall was built (with a great hall and council room) for two burgomasters, twelve aldermen and twelve councillors. Adjacent to it is the so-called Old Chancellery of 1535.

2.356e

2.357a

2.357b

›2.357 THE LATE-MEDIEVAL TOWN HALL IN GERMANY: (a) Frankfurt, Römer on the Römerburg (c. 1405 with 19th-century embellishment); (b) Rothenburg ob der Tauber, Franconia (south front of original western block, part-rendered masonry, mid-13th century and after); (c) Brunswick, detail of south-west open aspect of north-facing stone structure with timber roofs, begun with the west wing c. 1280 and extended to the north in the first half of the 14th century, completed 1396, renovated mid-15th century, rebuilt 1984); (d) Tangermunde (south-east view of brick structure, part plastered and embellished in terracotta 1420–30).

2.357c

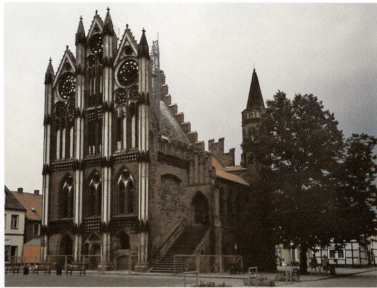

2.357d

The site of an imperial castle from the late 10th century, an imperial free town from 1274, Rothenburg owed its prosperity to its dominant position on a major tributary of the Main. Brunswick was chartered by Henry the Lion, whose base was there from 1166: it joined the Hanseatic League in 1247 as a major Lower Saxon trade centre and was independent of Henry's ducal successors from the beginning of the following century. At the confluence of the Tanger and the Elbe, Tangermunde was a staging post for eastern colonization: it was walled in the late-13th century, at least a generation earlier than the construction of the town hall.

>**2.358 PRAGUE, OLD TOWN HALL,** developed from an early 14th-century house from 1338, tower and chapel c. 1370, astronomical clock 1410.

>**2.359 TORUN (POLAND), TOWN HALL,** begun 1274, extended from 1391 and again in the late-16th century.

2.358

2.359

2.360a

Guild halls remained relatively modest in England, rare in France, but elsewhere the dominant trade was determined to display its dominance in flagrant rivalry with the town hall, especially in Flanders where the counts instituted the centralized exchange of wool in each of the major centres of production or import. This pride of self-made men in prosperity won from skill rather than inheritance was to generate the revival of humanism: concern with humanity was manifest in the secular endowment of establishments to share with the mendicant orders the care for the sick and the poor – like the magnificent Hôtel-Dieu at Beaune in Burgundy.**2.360, 2.361**

2.360b

›2.360 BEAUNE, HÔTEL-DIEU, 1443: (a) court, (b) main hall ward.

Hostels or hospices for the sick and destitute, such as the one built in Paris in 1190, were among the earliest public buildings built or endowed by secular rulers and merchants but run by religious orders. By the 15th century there were separate wards or even institutions for the sick, the mad and the poor.

The Hôtel-Dieu at Beaune was founded by Nicolas Rolin, chancellor to Philip le Bon, Duke of Burgundy, and run by the sisters of the order of the Holy Ghost based at Malines. The great ward for the sick (23.5 by 45 metres), with its spectacular keel vault, incorporated the chapel and, later, cubicles for gentlefolk: it was designed for thirty beds with two patients per bed.

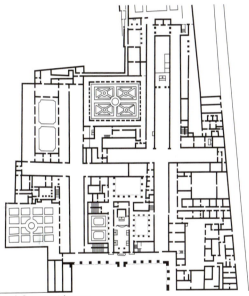

2.361 @ approxmately 1:2500

›2.361 FLORENCE, S. MARIA NUOVA: hospital plan (14th century and later).

The hospital type was well established in late-medieval Italy. In Florence c. 1334 a nucleus of order was introduced to the plan with the perpendicular intersection of two main wards in the otherwise organic complex of S. Maria Nuova (the chapel, at first in the crossing, was moved to the central position at the head of an entrance court when a second set of cruciform wards was added for women in 1657).

ITALIAN PALAZZI, PUBLIC AND PRIVATE

As we have noted, the eclipse of imperial power in Italy left a vacuum filled in part by communal authority which had been waxing at the expense of bishops – and with the mixed blessing of emperors – long before the demise of the Hohenstaufen. In opposition to the cathedral, the predominant type of its seat had emerged by the end of the 12th century when the Palazzo della Ragione of Bergamo was built. That work has been much altered, as has its successor at Cremona of 1206. The original aspect of Como's Palazzo Broletto, from c. 1215, has fared better.**2.362a**

Adjacent to the contemporary bell tower, the Torre del Comune which rose against the west front of the cathedral, Como's well-lit council chamber is supported by an open-arcaded market loggia, as the prosperity of the councillors was based on trade: reference to the imperial German *Pfalz* is probable – not without conscious irony – but the Italian prototype of the main chamber seems to have been the monastic assembly hall and the elevation was developed in the most advanced domestic architecture. Variation of the formula and its expansion are well represented respectively by Orvieto's Palazzo del Capitano of c. 1250,**2.362b** the seat of the Capitano del Popolo in Genoa

2.362a

2.362b

2.362c

›2.362 THE OPEN-ARCADED COMMUNAL
PALAZZO: (a) Como; (b) Orvieto; (c) Piacenza; (d) Perugia.

At Orvieto, where the Palazzo del Popolo was built immediately after the death of Frederick II and in response to the consolidation of bourgeois power, there is a hall on both levels: the upper one is roofed in timber on transverse arches in the manner occasionally adopted for churches, more often for refectories; the lower one was formed by enclosing the original arcaded loggia towards the end of the 13th century. When that happened, the openness which had been asserted by the loggia was reaffirmed by the introduction of the external staircase to the main floor – and with that came willful, if pragmatic, asymmetry in the extension of the landing.

At Piacenza, where a court was projected beyond the loggia but not realized, the brick structure is sheathed in pink and white marble below and embellished in terracotta above. The latter frames windows which retain the Romanesque profile of Orvieto but the lower storey is Gothic in its pointed arches and rib vaulting. Moreover, whereas the original conception at Orvieto aligned the voids vertically, here there is a syncopated relationship between the five lower arcades and six upper windows.

At Perugia, the work of the last decade of the 13th century extended ten by three bays: the ratio of solid to void is considerably greater than in our northern examples but does not reach the central Italian norm – as we are about to see. The building was widened from 1333 and given the cascade of steps serving the grand ceremonial main portal and arcaded loggia. The bays elongating the main street front beyond a secondary monumental entrance arch were added a century later, when a tower was incorporated. Between the palazzo and the cathedral – but predating the former by 20 years – is the Fontana Maggiore of Nicola Pisano.

›2.363 **GENOA, CHURCH AND PIAZZA OF S. MATTEO,** 1125 and from the late-13th century respectively: (a) general view to the north-east, (b) south-west side with Palazzo Lamba Doria (left).

The church was patronized by the powerful Doria family who developed the precinct with their various residences from the late-13th century. The Palazzo Lamba Doria was begun c. 1298 and elevated in the following decades with quadruple lancets in the arched windows (replaced on the front in the post-Renaissance era but retained on the side). The precedent for

(now Palazzo S. Giorgio), begun c. 1260, Bologna's Palazzo Comunale which was begun at much the same time, Piacenza's Palazzo del Comune of a generation later and, grandest of all, Perugia's Palazzo dei Priori, begun in 1293.**2.362c, d**

2.362d

2.363a

the buildings on this precocious square was set by the Palazzo S. Giorgio, which originated c. 1260 as the seat of the Capitano del Popolo.

2.363b

The Doria palaces on the Piazza S. Matteo in Genoa, well lit and built over open arcades like the Palazzo del Capitano, are unusual in the late-13th century – except in the most prosperous sea-trading republics. Usually the castle came to town – literally, as we have seen (pages 528ff

2.364a

2.364b

›**2.364 THE PALAZZO PRIVATO:** (a, b) Florence, cut-away perspective and Davanzati view; (c) Siena, detail of typical late-medieval exterior.

The form clearly emulates the feudal castle either in aristocratic memory of former extra-urban power or in bourgeois pretension.

and 562ff). The tower which asserted the pretensions of the contentious urban nobleman there was the fortified element in a complex of buildings housing an extensive clan: their distribution within the compound was hardly more ordered than the civic life outside. And because of the factional warfare which raged in the absence of an effective super-urban authority, the rich merchant, like the nobleman, lived in a severe, fortified house (palazzo). Typically it was a self-contained block with a central court. As there was minimal fenestration to the street, at least at the lower levels, light and air were generally to be drawn primarily from open arcades around the court, in accordance with ancient tradition.**2.364**

Open arcading and generous fenestration were not the invariable norm in the elevation of buildings for city authorities in much of the peninsula. In Tuscany, Umbria and the Marche, the *palazzo pubblico* or *del podestà* was often the most impressively fortified of all Italian city building types, except the patrician house from which it developed. The complex often had a tower designed to overawe the private ones, a grand hall for general meetings, smaller chambers for private deliberations and

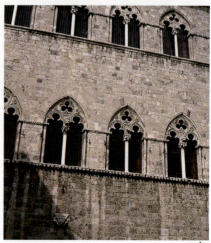

2.364c

2.365b

›**2.365** **SIENA,** **PALAZZO** **PUBBLICO,**
1297–1310: (a) overview from cathedral, (b) detail of
internal structure with transverse arches (chapel).

2.366

›**2.366** **VOLTERRA,** **PALAZZO** **PUBBLICO,**
1208, upper levels after 1257.

2.365a

accommodation for the councillors: given the factionalism of communal politics, elections aroused bitter enmities and the elected officials had to be securely lodged.

The Sienese were exceptional in providing for both the executive and judiciary in one building and like the grandest houses in the town it was relatively well lit at levels elevated above potential street violence.**2.365, 2.366** The situation in Florence was typical, if unexcelled in grandeur, with the main ceremonial square dominated by the severely rusticated, exclusive bulk of the house of the executive, the Signoria.**2.367**

The Florentine signoria

The Palazzo del Popolo (della Signoria or Vecchio) was built from 1299 possibly by Arnolfo di Cambio and was altered many times over the following century (notably in 1307, 1318, 1362, 1385). Supplanting the Bargello, the mid-century headquarters of the Capitano del Popolo whose regime was discredited by Sienese victory in 1260, it accommodated the '*signoria*' of six *priori* during their two-month tenure of office. From 1283 the city was governed by the *signoria* elected by the guilds, but as merchants could be members of several guilds their influence was paramount. As though to counter this, the *signoria* was established on the site of the ancient Roman theatre, away from the forum and the medieval market centre.

Representing amplification of the patrician town 'castle' on an unsurpassed scale, the palazzo's rusticated severity was relieved by a small balcony at the level of the main hall: that was a place of appearance which could hardly accommodate more than one dignitary with due dignity. The councillors revealed themselves to the populace and witnessed civic ceremonies in the Piazza della Signoria from the Loggia della Signoria, an exceptionally grand representative of a type which originated beside the marketplace as a covered gallery for merchants to negotiate sales and arrange the exchange of goods and money: it was built between 1376 and 1382 by Benci di Cione to a design attributed to Orcagna. The type is modelled on the ancient agora or forum colonnade where Greek or Roman citizens met to discuss politics and contract business.

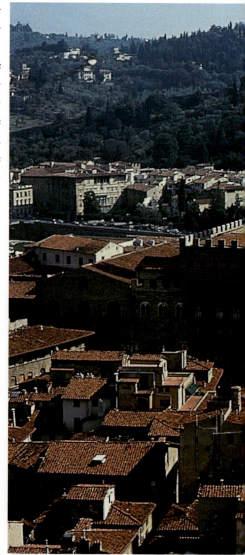

>**2.367 FLORENCE:** general view with Palazzo della Signoria (Vecchio), centre left, Piazza della Signoria and Loggia dei Lanzi, centre, Orsanmichele, right foreground.

Just off the piazza, Orsanmichele was built as a grain store in 1336 with an arcaded market below, storage above. An earlier shrine to the Madonna, tended by a religious fraternity, was incorporated in the arcade but the popular cult of its miraculous image displaced the market and the store above became a hall for the fraternity who ministered to the city guilds.

Due to its unique site, of course, Venice is exceptional in both its public and private buildings. The great palace overlooking the lagoon beside S. Marco – which served as its chapel – housed the *doge*, the head of state elected for life, but it also housed the several councils through which the aristocratic oligarchy ruled: its lightness and openness, unrivalled elsewhere in Italy, are testimony not only to the stability of the regime but also to the security of its water-logged site and its navy's command of the sea.**2.368**

2.368

The Doge's palace

A few families of hereditary nobility managed to retain supremacy over merchant and artisan alike for nearly a thousand years though their own fortunes were founded on commerce: all of them – about 2500 at the apex of their glory c. 1500 – sat as of right in the Maggior Consiglio (Great Council) which passed legislation and elected the officers of state; only the most eminent among these could provide candidates for election as *doge*, for life, or provide commanders of the armed forces and ambassadors, or sit on the various councils of state.

A 9th-century structure housing the organs of government was replaced in the 12th century. The accommodation of the Maggior Consiglio, raised over two storeys of rooms addressing the lagoon, was enlarged to accommodate its 1212 members after 1340. The ground-floor arcade, the lacy first-floor loggias and the revetment of the walls above seem to have achieved their present form later in the century and the central balcony was installed by Pierpaolo della Masegne after 1400. Six ground-floor bays deep, the palace was extended in a consistent style along the Piazzetta by another twelve from 1422 principally to house the Sala del Scrutino (used to record the votes of the Maggior Consiglio). The reversal of usual expectations in the distribution of solid and void is complemented by the floating of the upper windows directly over paired loggia roundels but in sycopated relationship with the lower arcades whose form they echo. Unusually, the building had external and internal loggias, much of the latter being renewed (like the east range, facing the Rio di Palazzo) from the 15th to the 17th centuries.

›2.368 VENICE, PALAZZO DUCALE (Doge's
Palace), from 1309: view from across the Venetian
Lagoon with the Campanile di S. Marco in the centre.

2.369a

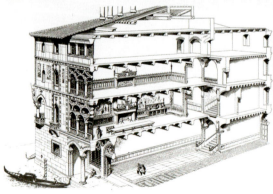

2.369b

2.369c

>**2.369 VENICE, CA' D'ORO** (Palazzo S. Sofia), built 1425–40 by Matteo Ravetti and the brothers Bon for Marino Contarini, one of the procurators of S. Marco: (a) façade from Grand Canal, (b) cut-away axonometric, (c) cortile detail.

Typically, Venetian palaces are entered primarily from the water, secondly from the network of alleys which knits the lagoon's islands together. Loggias, responding as much as to the natural security of the site as to the grid of piles on which building is invariably founded there, open at each level. The waterside one is linked by a corridor (past stores) to a cortile associated with the land entrance. The canal-front loggia of the piano nobile extends the *salone* which usually penetrates through to the cortile from which the more private rooms draw light and air and this arrangement may be repeated above.

>**2.370 THIENE, VILLA COLLEONI,** C. 1490: loggia.

2.370

In Venice, in contrast to the introverted palazzi of almost all other Italians, the houses of merchants and nobles alike, fronting canals which acted as moats instead of streets, could afford open façades with porticoes and loggias. As we have seen, these appear in an essentially Byzantine round-arch style on the upper floors of houses in the Rialto from the 11th century. By the end of the 14th century houses had changed in little more than style, the Byzantine round arch giving way to the flamboyance of deep Gothic porticoes at water level and filigree networks of ogee arches on the upper floors. The Ca'd'Oro is the most splendid example, apart from the Palazzo Ducale, but secure enough did the Venetians feel in their new estates on the *terra firma*, that they developed a rural equivalent which anticipated the Renaissance villa.**2.369. 2.370**

Introverted or extroverted, the great houses of the merchants and bankers of Florence and Venice, whose families had not been slow to rise through the ranks of society, were the cradles of humanism reborn from their pride in their achievements as the controllers of the destinies of their compatriots and the sustainers of the power of foreign kings. Though long anticipated within the Church, as we have seen, their humanism promoted the Renaissance of Classical civilization in Italy in the 15th century.

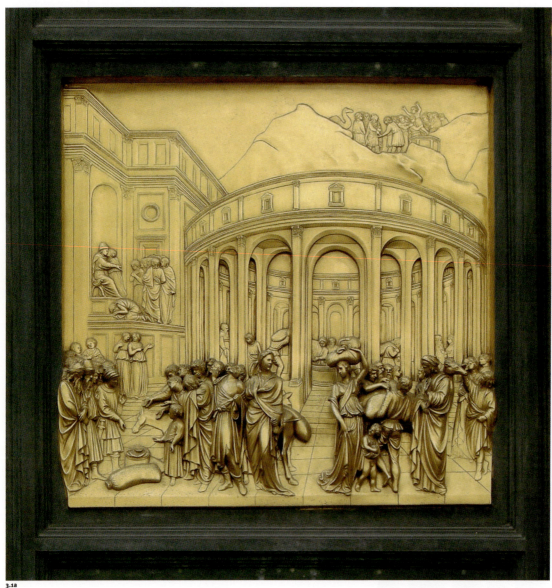

3.1a

PART 3 REVIVAL OF CLASSICISM

3.1b

3.0 INTRODUCTION

The periods into which convention divides the history of European art and architecture are usually labelled with pejorative terms applied by succeeding generations. However, the idea of a renaissance of the humanist ideals of Classical antiquity in Italy in the later 14th century, and the corollary of a 'middle age' of obscurity between that new dawn and the final drawing down of night on the Roman empire by barbarian invaders in the 5th century, belongs to the new humanists themselves – the Florentine chancellor Leonardo Bruni (c. 1370–1444) and Flavio Biondo (1392–1463) were among the most prominent.

The great Tuscan poet Petrarch (Francesco Petrarca, 1304–74) wrote of the 'slumber of forgetfulness' and predicted that 'after the darkness has been dispelled, our grandsons will be able to walk back into the pure radiance of the past'. From a similar eminence, Giovanni Boccaccio (1313–75) specifically praised Giotto for restoring art to the light of antique reason. And humanists were obsessed with the revival of antique learning, indeed the reorientation of history. The word 'rinascita' itself followed later but was certainly current by the middle of the 16th century when the Florentine artist Giorgio Vasari wrote his *Lives of the Most Eminent Painters, Sculptors and Architects*.

At the time Vasari was writing, on the other hand, humanism was rejected as pagan by church reformers. However, the Renaissance coin was reminted by the anticlerical Enlightenment of the 18th century and disseminated by 19th-century scholars – most notably, as far as the arts are concerned, by the Swiss historian Jacob Burckhardt in *The Civilization of the Renaissance in Italy* (1860). It was effectively devalued only in the later 20th century with the advancing appreciation of all the facets of 'medieval' civilization and many now would withdraw it from circulation altogether. One need not be blind to the vital development of urban man from the 12th century to see that this goes too far.

The revival of urban economies in Europe with the reopening of Mediterranean trade routes in the mid-'Middle Ages' and the consequent flowering of urban culture, were the essential conditions for the revival of Classical values.[3.1] Affluent merchants and bankers could well be moved to assert pride in their material achievements in monuments to their civic state. They were also disposed to promote a culture which celebrated their humanity – their natural sentiment as much as native reason – and the beauty of this world, as Classical culture had done.

Italy, well placed to profit from trade with the Orient, well endowed with ancient towns, the fountainhead of antique culture, led the revival of urban society in Europe – as we have seen. With huge resources of money and self-esteem, it was her merchants and bankers who endowed that society with the image of Renaissance. The Florentines were in the van but, great or small, despotic or oligarchic, the other powers too were soon vying with one another in extending lavish patronage to humanists – the writers and artists who, inspired by antique homocentric ideals, lent eternal glory to their names.

I POLITICS AND PATRONS

Apart from transitory coherence under the occasional effective German emperor, there was no unity in the medieval Italian peninsula except for the bond of the Roman legacy, especially the Latin language until regional dialects finally eclipsed it in the 13th century. The vernacular differences were relatively minor but by the opening of the 15th century they were not discordant with the geographical division of four of Italy's five great powers, Milan, Venice, Florence and Naples: the Papal States were themselves diverse (see page 239).

3.2a

ARAGONESE NAPLES AND THE PAPACY

Ladislaus of Naples had died childless in 1414, while in possession of Rome. He was succeeded by his sister, Joanna II, who promised her crown to Alfonso of Aragón, king of Sicily, but actually willed it to René of Anjou, king of Provence, on her death in 1435. Alfonso triumphed in 1442 and was invested with the kingdom by Pope Eugenius IV, then under the protection of the Florentines who had no liking for French interference. Having restored sound government to the reunited kingdom of Naples and Sicily well before he died in 1458, Alfonso was succeeded in Aragón and Sicily by his brother John, but had willed Naples to his illegitimate son Ferrante.**3.2**

Pope Eugenius had been ejected from Rome by the Colonna but parried the threat of renewed schism at Basle and returned under the protection of King Alfonso. He and his successor, Nicholas V (1447–55), furthered the renovation of Rome as a seat for their revived papacy. Calixtus III (1455–58) was preoccupied with the defence of Christendom against the Ottomans after the fall of Constantinople but his followers, especially Pius II (1458–64) and Sixtus IV (1471–84), greatly furthered the restoration of the papal monarchy and the transformation of its capital.**3.3**

›3.2 NAPLES: (a) panorama of the city with the Aragonese fleet (attributed to Francesco Rosselli c. 1466; Naples, National Museum of Capodimonte); (b) Alfonso V of Aragón, King of Naples and Sicily (bronze medal by Pisanello, 1449).

3.2b

3.3a

›3.3 PAPAL RESTORATION: (a) Rome at the end of the 15th century (from Sebastiano Munster, *Cosmographia universalis*) with the Porta del Popolo below right, the Vatican above right, Rioni centre right, and Trastevere upper left; (b) benediction loggia before the Constantinian basilica of S. Pietro in the Vatican, conceived by Nicholas V c. 1450 but begun c. 1460 by Pius II, with ancient columns, and projected from four to eleven bays by Paul II (Martin van Heemskerck, pen drawing c. 1535; Vienna, Albertina Graphics Collection); (c) Pius II enthroned in the basilica of S. Pietro (Pinturicchio, Siena Cathedral, Piccolomini Library); (d) Sixtus IV, seated like an antique emperor and attended by his nephews, Cardinals Giuliano della Rovere (Pope Julius II, 1503–13, centre) and Raffaello Riario, confirming Platina as papal librarian (Melozzo da Forli, fresco c. 1480; Rome, Vatican Museums).

The inscription on the Sistine portrait translates in main part: 'Sixtus, though you restored the churches, palaces, streets, forums, walls, bridges, and the Acqua Vergine … the city owes more to you for the library which was obscure in its decay and is now in a location of celebrity'.

Rome revived

There were c. 17,000 inhabitants when the Avignonese schism was healed and Pope Martin V (1417–31) finally installed himself in the Vatican in 1420. They mainly occupied the lower-lying Rioni district enclosed by the bend in the river opposite the Vatican. Restoration and expansion were under way by the end of the century but the area within the ancient walls was largely uninhabited – except by squatters in its overwhelmingly impressive ruins.

The lack of a centre posed a major problem to those who would order Rome's development: there were in fact several nodal points – the Capitol, the Lateran, the Vatican and the other station churches (AIC1, page 710). The most pressing need, apart from water supply and repairs to the city wall, was the improvement of communications between these and the main northern entrance, the Porta del Popolo at the end of the Via Flaminia: this meant new axial roads and bridges. Martin V revived the old communal office of Master of Buildings and Streets (popularly known as Maestri di Strada) for direction by the Curia (1425). Nicholas V (1447–55) strengthed its authority.

3.3c

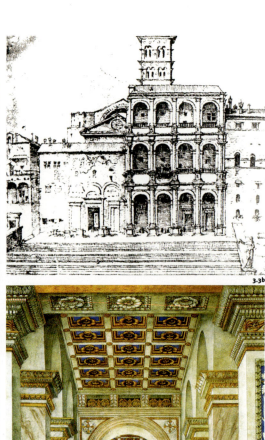

3.3b

3.3d

Restoration of the two papal basilicas, S. Giovanni in Laterano and S. Pietro in Vaticano, was begun under Martin V but little was effected before Nicholas V, who conceived a monumental extension to the latter for the accommodation of pilgrims. To improve access to the Vatican, moreover, Nicholas – and his eminent adviser, Leon Battista Alberti, of whom we shall hear considerably more – conceived a new thoroughfare linking a monumental piazza, in place of the atrium before the Constantinian basilica, with the Ponte S. Angelo (on axis with the fort of that name built on the remains of Hadrian's tomb (AIC1, page 613) which itself was to be linked with the Porta del Popolo by one of the main new axial routes. The area through which the road to the Vatican passed, known as the Borgo, was to be improved as the seat of the Curia and the Vatican palace itself extended. A benediction loggia, associated with the latter, was to address the new piazza. The restoration work on the Capitoline palaces, many churches and the Tiber island bridges was also begun in the same pontificate.

During the process of revivification, many ancient buildings succumbed to pillage. This was lamented even at the time and Pius II tried to stop the destruction in 1462. Preoccupied with Pienza, Pius continued work on his predecessor's Borgo schemes, relocating and revising the Vatican bene-diction loggia as the backdrop to the grand new piazza. He advanced work on cleansing and redecorating the Constantinian basilica – in which his coronation is splendidly depicted in his Sienese library by Pinturicchio – in preparation for its endowment with the head of S. Peter's brother, S. Andrew. That great relic had been rescued from the Turkish invasion of the Peloponnese and its enshrinement in the Vatican – as S. Peter's head was enshrined in the Lateran – was seen by the pope as a symbol of reunited Christendom's challenge to the Muslims, against whom he was promoting another Crusade.

Apart from the construction or reconstruction of several churches, Six-tus IV was responsible for extensive works designed to cater for the influx of pilgrims expected in the Holy Year 1475. The pope accorded primacy among his achievements to the Ospedale di Santo Spirito, whose architect imposed regularity in plan and articulation on the medieval model of S. Maria Nuova in Florence. His extensive arterial projects included the street linking S. Angelo with a piazza inside the Porta del Popolo and, perhaps, the one running south from S. Angelo through the most densely populated part of the medieval town towards the new Ponte Sisto which served Trastevere: the bridge was named after Sixtus IV but the route was realized by his nephew, Pope Julius II, as the Via Giulia.

By 1480 Rome had produced no native artists deemed worthy of Sixtus – for his library, let alone the great Vatican chapel he began in 1479. By the end of the century, however, the Eternal City was projected to the first rank of artistic centres, even eclipsing Florence.

>3.4 NICCOLÒ DA TOLENTINO LEADING THE FLORENTINE TROOPS AT THE BATTLE OF SAN ROMANO, 1432: by Paolo Uccello, tempera on panel c. 1445 (London, National Gallery).

In showing Tolentino in modern dress, Ucello con-formed to current ideas of historical propriety, unlike Donatello in his slightly later work on Gattamelata.

>3.5 FLORENCE AND THE MEDICI: (a) the city c. 1472 with cathedral centre, Palazzo Vecchio (Signoria) to its right (engraved by Duchet); (b) the dynasty in pro-cession, a detail from the Procession of the Magi fresco by Benozzo Gózzoli, c. 1460, in the chapel of the Palazzo Medici-Ricardi, Florence.

Cosimo to the left, beside his son Piero, with (it is generally presumed) the ten-year-old Lorenzo ideal-ized out in front as the youngest of the Magi.

3.4

CONFLICT BETWEEN THE GREAT POWERS

In the north, Giangaleazzo Visconti's son Filippo Maria had recovered most of his father's domains and led Milan to war again with Florence in 1429. By 1433 its conduct had discredited the aristocratic Albizi faction then dominant in Florentine affairs. The leader of the opposition popular faction, Cosimo de' Medici (1389–1464), had backed the *condottiero* Niccolò da Tolentino, whose forces secured victory for Florence in 1432.**3.4** In the following clash with the Albizzi, Medici won. Ostensibly he sustained the republic but a provisional assembly, reconstituted every five years by nominally popular election, acted on his advice in the appointment of officers. His son Piero took on his mantle in 1464 and passed it to his brilliant son Lorenzo in 1469.**3.5**

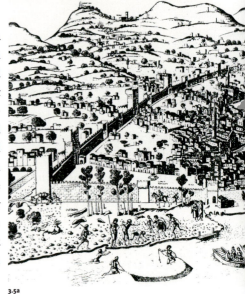

3.5a

3.5b

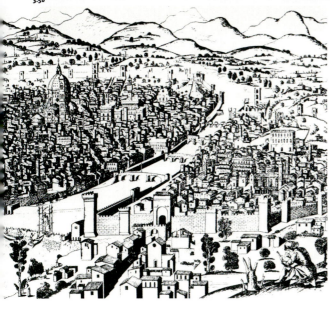

Visconti fortunes waxed and waned in contention with Florence and Venice before Filippo Maria died in 1447. After a brief republic, he was succeeded by the *condottiero* Francesco Sforza. Though usually in Visconti's service, Sforza had led the Florentines to victory against the Milanese at Anghiari in 1440. He married Visconti's daughter, Bianca Maria, the following year but maintained friendly relations with Cosimo de' Medici. Recognizing that the balance of Italian power had shifted in favour of Venice, the latter strengthened his position by embracing a revolutionary new alliance with Milan soon after Sforza's triumph in 1450. Peace between Milan and Venice followed in 1454: Sforza recognized the Venetian conquests from Verona to Bergamo and Venice recognized Sforza. Cosimo brokered the accession of Venice to the alliance.**3.6**

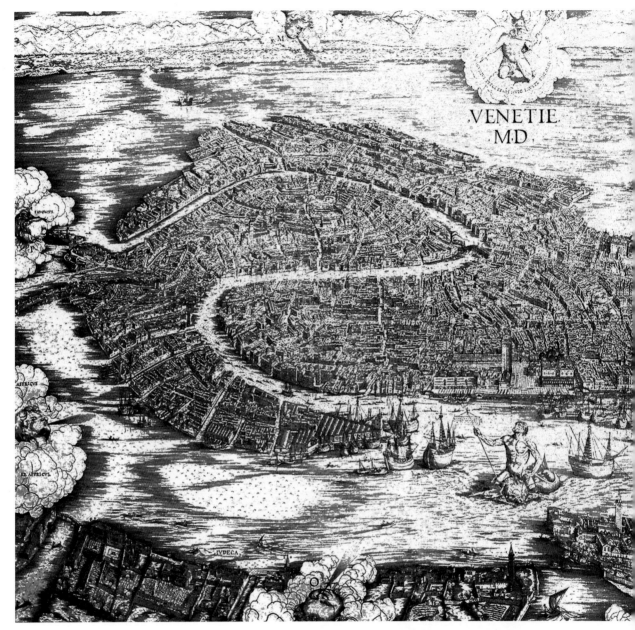

›**3.6 VENICE AT THE END OF THE 15TH CENTURY** (Jacopo de' Barbari, 1500).

Sforza furthered Visconti ambitions in the west, finally securing Genoa in 1463, and maintained close relations with France. He also furthered the great building exercises initiated by the Visconti: the completion of the cathedral (pages 450f) and reconstruction of the castle in Milan and the construction of the Certosa di Pavia in particular. His tyrannical successor Galeazzo Maria (1466–76) was assassinated by republicans but their cause failed and the infant Galeazzo Maria II ruled under the regency of his mother until his uncle, Ludovico il Moro, seized power in 1480 with the support of the pope and France. **3·7**

›3·7 MILAN, CASTELLO SFORZESCO: south front.

Galeazzo II Visconti (1355–78) built his stronghold on the site but it was destroyed by the populace after the death of Filippo Maria in 1447. Francesco Sforza began its reconstruction on taking power in 1450. The central tower (restored after an explosion of 1521) is attributed to the Florentine Antonio Averlino, called Filarete, who served the Sforza as an architect and utopian theorist.

THE LEAGUE OF THE GREAT POWERS

On the basis of the triple alliance between Florence, Milan and Venice, a league was formed dedicated to maintaining a balance between the major Italian powers and resisting foreign invasion. Nicholas V, apprehensive of Ottoman ambitions in sympathy with the Venetians, adhered the Papal States and persuaded Naples to join. The pact initially justified itself by turning back René of Anjou in his attempt to wrest Naples from the late King Alfonso's son, Ferrante, in 1458. However, it was not proof against enmity between Lorenzo de' Medici and Pope Sixtus IV (1471–84) which threatened war. Bent on the expansion of papal territory – and the power of his della Rovere clan – at Tuscan expense, the pope seemed to have blessed the abortive anti-Medici conspiracy of the Pazzi in 1478. King Ferrante came in on Rome's side but Lorenzo rushed boldly to Naples and reached an accord on the basis of which reconciliation was effected.

After his ruthless elimination of the Pazzi and his popular avoidance of full-scale war, Lorenzo was *de facto* despot of Florence until his death in 1492. And, having proved the efficacy of personal diplomacy in the resolution of the conflict with Rome, he was the mainstay of the league as an instrument for peace, particularly by preaching the danger of resurgent France and the renewal of French claims to Milan and Naples. On the other hand, Venetian enthusiasm was guaranteed by calamitous war with the Ottomans: having taken Athens and control of the Aegean three years after occupying Constantinople and in a position to control the Adriatic after taking Bosnia in 1463, the Turks won most of the Venetian holdings in the Peleponnese in hostilities lasting from 1464 to 1479 and took Otranto on the heel of Italy in 1480.

LESSER POWERS

Several smaller powers had survived the expansion of Milan, Venice, Florence and the Papal States, usually as buffers between them, often wooed by Rome. Mantua, Ferrara, Rimini and Urbino were among the most important of them.

In Mantua the Gonzaga ruler Gian Francesco I (1407–44) acquired the title of marquis from Emperor Sigismund in 1433. His son Ludovico III (1444–78) employed the greatest artists of the day – Alberti and Mantegna in particular. Thereafter, enlightened patronage was sustained by Gian Francesco II (1484–1519) and his wife, the extremely accomplished Isabella d'Este, whose family had acquired Modena, Reggio and a ducal title by 1470.**3.8**

Rimini belonged to the pope from the 8th century and was dominated by the Guelf Malatestas from the 13th century. During the papal sojourn at Avignon, they asserted virtual independence as *condottieri* and, while

›**3.8 LUDOVICO GONZAGA WITH HIS WIFE, BARBARA OF BRANDENBURG AND THEIR FAMILY:** Andrea Mantegna, fresco c. 1470 (Mantua, Camera degli Sposi in the Palazzo Ducale).

Propriety – especially the historical propriety of representing modern people in modern guise – is taken to new lengths in the representation of elevated patrons in the human mode of familial intimacy appropriate to a private room. The human dimension is enhanced, naturally, by astute observation of personality.

›**3.9 SIGISMONDO MALATESTA** (1417–68), tyrant of Rimini: bronze medal by Pisanello, 1445.

Having reunited the teritory of Rimini at the age of 14, Sigismondo's success in maintaining his independence by playing his great neighbours – Venice, Milan, Mantua, Urbino – off against one another was acknowledged in his recognition by the emperor in 1433 and Pope Nicholas V in 1450. Thereafter his ambitions conflicted with those of the Vatican: he was defeated by Pius II but reconciled with Paul II after conceding papal suzereinty.

3.10

Piero della Francesca, oil and tempera c. 1475 (Florence, Uffizi Gallery).

Count of Urbino at the age of 22, Frederico had great success – and amassed a great fortune – as a *condottiero*. Thereafter he proved an outstanding ruler and patron of the arts.

3.9

generally aligned with the papacy after its return to Rome, sustained it under the inconstant Sigismondo (1417–68).**3.9**

Urbino, an outpost of the Papal States, was the base of the Montefeltro lords. The most celebrated of these, Federico (1444–82), greatly enhanced his family's fortunes as the *condottiero* chief of the Italian League and married the daughter of Francesco Sforza. He married his son and daughter to the niece and nephew of Pope Sixtus IV. Thus connected, he was elevated to the dukedom.**3.10**

DESCENT INTO CHAOS

In 1489 the youthful Galeazzo Maria Sforza II of Milan married Isabella of Aragon, daughter of Alfonso, Duke of Calabria. In 1494 Alfonso ascended the throne of Naples on the death of his father, Ferrante, and the *de facto* Milanese ruler, Ludovico il Moro, felt threatened. He called in the aid of Charles VIII of France (1483–98) who, as Duc d'Anjou before his accession, had inherited the

Angevin claim to Naples from King René. The Italian League had collapsed and a terrible new chapter in the history of Italy had opened.**3.11**

II RENAISSANCE MAN, GOD AND ANTIQUITY

Late-medieval Italian merchants, bankers and their intellectual entourage, educated laymen with no inhibitions about enjoying pagan works but proud of their capacity for reason, were naturally inimical to the idea that their world was merely the inadequate prelude to God's Heaven. It was with limited historical perspective – and hence ignorance of the Carolingian renaissance which paved their way, let alone the humanistic implications of the Marianism elaborated in 12th-century Chartres (pages 266ff) – that the new men credited themselves with the revival of learning in the renewed study of man.

United by Latin, no less than Christianity, intellectual Europe never lost contact with the Classical past. As we have seen, the scholastics were bent on reconciling Christian and antique thought: the orthodox clerical subjection of reason to faith prevailed but provoked conflict in which the greatest of the scholastics championed the rights of reason (page 254). Of more immediate concern to society as a whole, the Roman legal tradition remained vital. From the outset, most leading humanists were lawyers used to adapting ancient precedent to modern practice. Francesco Petrarca was no exception.**3.12**

PETRARCH AND HIS FOLLOWERS

Rebelling against scholasticism, Petrarch was the most eloquent of his contemporaries in identifying the civilization of Classical antiquity as the apogee of human achievement, no less virtuous than Christianity. Rebelling against scholastic obsession with Aristotelian dialectic, rather than human well-being, he bent himself to testing his

›**3.11 THE ITALIAN WAR OF CHARLES VIII:** the king leading his forces into Florence (Francesco Granacci, 1518; Florence, Uffiizi Gallery).

›3.12 FRANCESCO PETRARCA (Petrarch, 1304–74), c. 1357 (Nardo di Cione, detail from Last Judgement fresco in the Capella Strozzi, S. Maria Novella, Florence).

The son of a legal official exiled from Florence at the papal court in Avignon, he read law at Bologna and went on to practise for the rulers of Verona. Thereafter he served, or was courted by, the rulers of Parma, Naples, Mantua, Ferrara, Rimini and Milan: in 1362 he settled in Padua (whose ruler, Francesco I Carrara and his ally, Louis I of Anjou, King of Hungary are portrayed here, centre left and centre). He died in his Eugenian retreat in 1374.

Petrarch did not ignore the flourishing vernacular tradition, which his contemporary Boccaccio was bringing to its Italian fruition, but valued his neo-Classical exercises most highly. Law apart, he was not without guidance back to the antique. Apart from Dante (died 1321), who had used Virgil as his guide, the Paduan poets Lovato (died 1309) and Mussato (died 1329) and Geri d'Arezzo (active 1320s) in Florence were already seeking to regain Classical Latin style in poetry and drama. And their contemporary, Ferrato dei Ferrati in Vicenza, was beginning the transition back from the medieval chronicle, moralizing about disasters as punishment, to Classical history.

thoughts against those of the ancients: he collected their books, sought out their manuscripts and found a world not cursed but inhabited by vital individual personalities, penetrated by reason unconstrained by church dogma. Reviving their scholarship, he devised a programme for the study of their Latin usage – as Charlemagne's servants had done (page 25) – and on the basis of the grammar thus secured he sought the revival of Classical rhetoric to promote virtue.

Though Petrarch venerated the Latins and the Greeks – for both their form and substance – he was an orthodox Christian: he admired S. Augustine's belief that the Gospel opened different minds to different truths and believed himself that its essential values were anticipated by Cicero's Stoicism. Thus he promoted the emulation, rather than reproduction, of the antique precisely because he saw its tradition of decorum as second only to the revelation of Christian grace: Christ promised the eternal welfare of the human soul but God had made the world for man's well-being. The teaching of Classical antiquity proffered the civilization of manners no less than the perfection of the intellect.

Like Aquinas, Petrarch sought the obviation of conflict between the realms of intuition and deduction. The scholastic application of Aristotelian dialectic to rationalize Christian dogma having failed (pages 254f), he turned to Plato in the quest. As we shall see, the trail was picked up by the Florentine Academy in the generation after a chair of Greek studies had been established in Florence for the Byzantine Manuel Chrysoloras in 1397.

Petrarch's followers were usually Christian but, rejecting the scholastic aim of encyclopaedic systematization of all theological thought, they focused specifically on meeting human needs. Their thought soaring free from indenture to the Church with a new faith in the dignity of man,

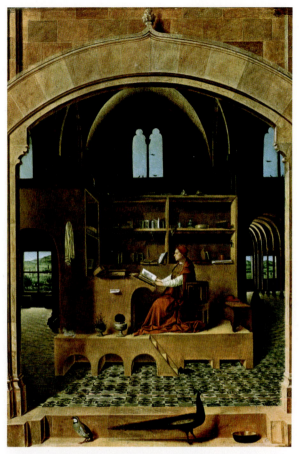

›3.13 S. JEROME IN HIS STUDY, Antonello da Messina, oil on wood (1474; London, National Gallery).

whose ancient monuments still stood witness to his worth, they were being called *umanisti* within a century of the master's death. They were assiduous quarriers of antique works from innumerable monastic libraries bent on rigorous analysis of Classical authors to penetrate the Christian veil over the Classical past.**3.13** They were also students of their fellow man through observation of his behaviour as a rational and sentient being: they stimulated enquiry into his secular circumstances and promoted his self-esteem by lauding the achievement of his terrestrial past rather than looking for apotheosis in a superterrestrial future. Private tutors and professional teachers in their independent schools or universities, they greatly increased the secular content of education. And they were didactic poets, dramatists and discoursers eloquent in asserting the freedom of man's will to shape his destiny, pragmatic in promoting an essentially secular culture in opposition to the ideal determinism of the Church, the restriction of monastic rule in education and the abstrusion characteristic of scholasticism.

Whereas the finest scholastic minds had resorted to reason for the pursuit of omniscience in the concordance of ancient philosophy and Christian theology – vainly, as it ultimately transpired, because reason still served faith – their finest Renaissance successors, like Valle in Naples or Machiavelli in Florence, showed the way to critical analysis through unprejudiced research. In particular, the critical analysis of the past was effected with the development of a sense of history as a causal process which might even be affected by men. The comprehension of historical propriety was the corollary: the Italian humanist's sense of inferiority to his ancient ancestors had been moderated and the recognition that his needs were different provided the spur to individual achievement.

The academic debate over the means to excellence would always turn on the relative weight of antique authority and native genius but, with rigorous analysis eclipsing awe, copying ceded to emulation with the implication that the moderns might even exceed the ancients. The deduction of a corpus of precept underlying practice was, of course, the key: emulation involved the fusion of antique principles with current traditions and new knowledge. Thus concern to apply the lessons of antiquity to improve modern practice led first to the recognition of the need to formulate rules – grammars for new languages of literature and the arts.

MEDICI FLORENCE

All the arts were taken to new heights in the Florence of Lorenzo de' Medici and during the twenty-three years of his pre-eminence, in the relative peace sustained by the League, the cause of humanism was furthered through the Florentine Academy. Originating with Cosimo de' Medici, it was not a teaching institute nor an official body for the codification of orthodoxy – like later Academies – but an informal group of scholars, dedicated primarily to the examination of the possibility of reconciling Platonism and Christianity, which met at Careggi. It was directed by the son of Cosimo's physician, Marsilio Ficino, under the presidency of the Medici. Its members included Leon-Battista Alberti, one of the era's greatest scholars and its foremost theorist of art and architecture.**3.14**

Alberti

Born out of wedlock in Genoa, where his patrician father had resorted in exile from Florence, he was schooled in humanist circles at Padua and studied canon and civil law, physics and mathematics, at the University of Bologna where the future Pope Nicholas V was a fellow student. At the behest of Pope Martin V, the Alberti were free to return to Florence from 1428 but Battista showed no interest in entering commerce there in the family tradition: his tertiary education directed him to the Church. By 1432, probably on return from travel north of the Alps, he was in Rome as secretary to the director of the papal chancery who appointed him to the brief-drafting branch of the secretariat in which he served until it was disbanded in 1464. The papal curia moved to Florence with Eugenius IV in 1434: Alberti moved with it and remained there until 1443.

Apart from his involvement in papal affairs, particularly the pursuit of reunion with the eastern Orthodox Church at the Council of Florence in 1438/39, he focused his attention on recent Florentine achievements in the revival of Classical discipline in the arts. In Rome from 1444, he turned his attention to the ancient monuments and was probably the principal

›3.14 LEON BATTISTA ALBERTI: self-portrait, bronze c. 1435 (Washington, National Gallery of Art).

adviser to Nicholas V on the city's restoration (1447–55). He was also architectural adviser to Sigismondo Malatesta of Rimini (from 1450), and the Florentine banker, Gian di Paolo Ruccellai (from 1452). He undertook several diplomatic missions and accompanied Pius II on excursions of state, notably to Mantua in 1459 where he attracted the patronage of Ludovico Gonzaga.

He turned to the writing of treatises to provide bases for rational analysis and criticism. The three on the visual arts, combining aesthetic principles with practical rules, were designed to elevate each metier from craft to intellectual exercise. Painting and the science of perspective came first, while he was in Florence with Pope Eugenius he wrote *De pictura* (1435) and dedicated it to Marquis Gianfrancesco Gonzaga of Mantua, patron of the pedagogue Vittorino da Feltre with whom Alberti had studied in Padua. Its Italian translation, *Della pittura* (1436), was dedicated to Filippo Brunelleschi, whose cathedral dome was consecrated by the pope that year. His works on sculpture, *De statua*, codifying ideal human proportions, and on architecture, *De re aedificatoria*, modelled on Vitruvius's *De architectura*, were begun before he left Florence but not completed until 1452. While working for the curia and advising Pope Nicholas he had also produced his *Descriptio urbis Romae* – a guide to the ancient remains – and a treatise on mathematics. His other significant works include a treatise on law (1437) and a study of the Tuscan dialect, proposing Latinized reforms, which constituted the first comprehensive Italian grammar (1450).

Lorenzo and his circle restored supreme admiration to Dante, revalued the vernacular works of Boccaccio and Petrarch and married Classical erudition with popular pragmatism. Not the least consequence was acceptance of Dante's Tuscan dialect as the vernacular standard, the common Italian language in place of Latin – and Alberti's grammar demonstrated that the dignity of the vernacular was governed by rules comparable to those of Latin. His formulation of the rules of perspective provided a similarly salutary theoretical discipline for the visual arts.

The creative energy generated by the meeting of antique precept and modern pragmatism propelled the investigation of nature, celestial and terrestrial, through experiment and invention. Exploration with improved ships over the ever-widening horizons of the globe revealed new worlds. Certainly no less crucial were the new horizons opened by the vastly enhanced dissemination of ideas which followed the introduction of paper and the inception of printing.**3.15**

BOOKS AND LIBERAL EDUCATION

At all levels the most dramatic growth in education was attendant on printing: though they were expensive, more books inevitably meant more libraries and more access to learning. And as the most assiduous producers of new books, the new humanists used the medium to counter the ecclesiastical bias of education – first in Italy. Their guides were Cicero and Quintilian, whose concern with the education of the orator was to produce a rounded individual equipped not only with fluency of expression but with wisdom and integrity, modesty and courage.

Petrarch had seen the value of Quintilian's work for leading his followers back to the light but its full text was not recovered for another two generations: then it provided the basis for the 'liberal' education developed throughout Europe until the 20th century. Starting with the medieval *trivium* (pages 253f), no one did more in furthering those 'studies worthy of a free man' than Vittorino da Feltre, called in 1423 from the chair of rhetoric at Padua to tutor the princes of the house of Gonzaga in Mantua: he provided the future Marquis Lodovico and his entourage with a stout regime of physical training to complement the fullest exposition to the classics yet available. This comprehended the analysis of all the great Latin authors for form of expression as well as content and asserted the importance of syntax, as of rule in general, no

›3.15 PRINTER'S SHOP AND PRESS, from a French ms, c. 1500.

Johann Gutenberg of Mainz is usually accounted the first European to develope printing from movable type: after some twenty years of experiment he produced his magnificent Bible in 1456. At first it promoted confidence in the security of text rather than rapid dissemination of knowledge but by 1490 there were printing presses in every country of Europe and these were responsible not only for the expansion of antique learning – especially through the production of large editions of Greek and Latin classics – but the strengthening of the vernacular. The spread of new ideas, images and music was, of course, the most vital consequence.

less than the models of rectitude provided by the lives of the great – hence the emphasis on studying history. The Este of Ferrara followed the Gonzaga example in 1429.

RELIGION AND PHILOSOPHY

Humanists were secularists by definition, attaching intrinsic value to man and his temporal aspirations. In this they reversed the medieval obsession with the immortality of the soul and consequent assessment of man's worth in virtue of his relationship with God through the Church. But they did not, in general, provoke a return to paganism nor, in fact, promote a complete break with the Christian Middle Ages. God, not man, remained in the centre of the universe. God's cosmos was ordered, like Plato's (AIC1, pages 442ff), and therefore comprehensible to man. And because he was cast in the image of God, man was free to shape his own destiny. To Petrarch and his followers that destiny was Christian but they sought to reach concordance between Christianity and Platonism and, ultimately, to distil the essence common to all religious experience.

Nicholas of Cusa (1401–64), the German associate of Pius II, maintained that 'Scripture and the philosophers have said the same thing in different terms'. The Florentine Academy pursued the ideal, in prompting Ficino's translation of Plato's dialogues and publication of his own unwieldy *Platonic Theology* (c. 1482). This attempted to assimilate Platonism and Christianity without a lucid comprehension of the median role of Neoplatonism (AIC1, pages 677ff).**3.16**

Neoplatonism recalled

Sceptical of empirical knowledge, Neoplatonism derives its name from its re-espousal of Platonic metaphysics. Yet it was syncretic: it recognized man's aspiration to salvation in union with the Supreme Being as the

universal motive and, depending on revelation for the finding of the way, it sought inspiration from all the traditional religions known to the Graeco-Roman world. A philosophy of religion rather than a theology, its abiding signifiance is, nevertheless, theological: that man's ultimate satisfaction, reunion with the Supreme Being, is beyond the sphere of reason. This was the fundamental tenet of Plotinus, the movement's prime author, whose recognition that the aspiration of the soul transcends the sensible led him to infer the suprarational nature of the Supreme Being – the Good in which everything has its purpose (AIC1, pages 677ff).

Plotinus was indebted to Philo of Alexandria, who translated Judaism into Hellenistic terms, maintained the superiority of Greek philosophy but recognized that man's spiritual needs go beyond understanding order in the universe and inferred that the suprarational God may be revealed ecstatically – like Dionysios or Orphic passage to union with the divine

›3.16 FLORENTINE HUMANISTS WITNESS-ING THE ANNUNCIATION TO ZACHARIAS in Ghirlandaio's fresco cycle of 1486–90 in the Turnabuoni Chapel, S. Maria Novella.

Antique order pervades the stage for this act of divine grace. Among the humanists dedicated to recon-ciling that order with that grace, those represented in the lower left-hand corner are (left to right) Marsilio Ficino, Cristoforo Landino, Angelo Poliziano and Demetrios Chalkondyles.

soul. The connection with Plato operates on that level somewhat subliminally but overtly fundamental to Philo is the Platonic distinction between the sensible and the intelligible – between the physical world and the ultimate principle of the cosmos, truth.

It will be recalled that, to Plato, the philosopher is a lover of the vision of Truth reflected in the universal realities (Ideas or Forms) of the cosmos, that the apprehension of Truth – the revelation of the divine – alone is knowledge and that it is gained not from experience of this world but through deductive reasoning from incontrovertible axioms like those of mathematics. The mathematical – specifically geometrical – order of Plato's cosmos was to be a prime inspiration to Renaissance architects and artists – as the rational, comprehensible, purpose of the gods had been to the Greeks. The followers of Philo were not alone in finding it difficult to disassociate Plato's vision from the mystical or his love of that vision from the ecstasy of the mystics – the rationalism notwithstanding.

Neoplatonists and Christians were bitter rivals despite community of aim, the redemption of the human soul from sensuality, and despite the shared belief that this was impossible without divine aid: Christians admitted the revelations of only one true God; Neoplatonists acknowledged many sources. After the triumph of the former, most of the latter's schools were closed but the school of Athens survived and transmitted Greek thought and Classic example to the Middle Ages.

With Petrarch virulently anti-scholastic – and many of his followers prepared to condemn Aristotle by association – the revival of antique learning not unnaturally reinvigorated interest in both Plato and Neoplatonism. Ficino identified theology and philosophy on the Platonic ground that philosophy is devoted to the study of truth and God alone is truth. To him that truth was revealed by Christ but it was Plotinus who traced for him the course of the soul's descent from truth to sensuality and pilgrimage back to the ecstatic contemplation of the Supreme Being. His friend and colleague, Pico della Mirandola (1463–94), further, recounts a Neoplatonic location of man on a median plane between the divine and the sensual, looks for his redemption in the renunciation of the lower for the higher – and ultimately in unity with God – but knows that his power to do so is charged in response to divine revelation.

The speculative mentality motivating exploration and invention, the spirit of scientific enquiry which owed its inspiration to Aristotle, may well be seen as the most pervasive characteristic of the ideal Renaissance man – Leonardo da Vinci, for example.**3.17** Yet the intellectual

orthodoxy – still essentially Platonic – was the rationalist mean, sceptical of the transitory 'realities' of this world, not lost to the mysteries of the lover of the vision of truth, but orientated to the empyrean of ideals compre-

›3.17 LEONARDO DA VINCI: self-portrait, red chalk, c. 1512 (Turin, Royal Library).

Empirical and inventive in the extreme, Leonardo may well be seen as the archetypal 'Renaissance man' – mathematician, scientist, anatomist, botanist, engineer, architect, sculptor, painter, musician and writer. Born illegitimately to a notary at Vinci, near Florence, he was trained in the studio of the painter and sculptor, Verrocchio, but received no formal Classical education – indeed his mind seems to have developed untrammelled by received ideas, humanist or scholastic, and his preoccupation was with organic development rather than finite definition.

He began his career in Florence in 1481, before he had left his master, but moved to Milan the following year without completing his first commission – from the Augustinians of S. Donato Scoperto for a panel painting of the Adoration of the Magi.**3.40a** He was in the service of Ludovico il Moro, first as a military engineer, then as much else, until the latter's fall in 1499. He returned to Florence where he was commissioned to fresco the Sala del Grand Consiglio in the Palazzo della Signoria in opposition to Michelangelo (the two were allotted the battles of Anghiari and Cascina as subjects respectively). He left this commission unfinished to return to Milan to work for the French military governor and then for the restored Sforzas: during this period he completed his work on the Madonna of the Rocks.**3.40b** He returned to Florence in 1513 on his way to Rome where he seems to have failed to convince Pope Leo X that he could bring anything to conclusion. He may have accompanied the pope to Bologna in 1515 to meet the French king François I: he entered the latter's service the following year and died at Amboise three years later.

Renowned in his time – and perhaps still – primarily as a painter, less than a score of his works were completed or survive because of his many other preoccupations and his unhappy experiments with pigment, but complemented by his illustrated notebooks on the nature of art, his legacy to practitioners, connoisseurs and historians of art is unrivalled. As an engineer, too, his legacy is inspiration rather than concrete achievement but anatomy, optics, civil engineering and hydrodynamics are greatly indebted to his scientific research.

hensible through deductive reasoning from incontrovertible axioms. Nicholas of Cusa may well be taken to represent it in satisfying himself that, unable to understand God, he could visualize him in terms of symbols like those of mathematics.

In their analytical methods as much as in the secular content of their works, the new humanists offered a challenge to a debilitated church and its corrupt establishment. Moreover, at a time when humanism was promoting the individual will to understanding and educational reform was focused on the training of the orator, and in an age of advancing literacy on a far less elevated plane, when many laymen were finding their own way directly to the sources of belief in disdain for established official dogma, it was no coincidence that even the most devout found their vocation in itinerant preaching rather than episcopal office. The Franciscan S. Bernardino of Siena (died 1444), whose passionate humanity infused field and marketplace under a banner emblazoned with the name of Jesus, was far the most popular. Ultimately the most sinister was doubtless the Dominican Girolamo Savonarola (1452–98) in his messianic quest for purification.

HUMANISM AND DISSENT ABROAD

The failings of the Conciliar Movement left a growing group of intellectuals, mainly clerical but urban in outlook and international, who had not won the initiative for reform but not lost the critical spirit of their secular environment. Beyond contempt for clerical decadence and irresponsible authority, in that environment the cost of the Roman establishment to the taxpayer was a major issue, especially as churchmen owned between a fifth and a third of all arable land – in the name of the pope – and claimed immunity from state taxation. And with moral authority no longer the unquestioned preserve of the clergy, Church doctrine was debatable, especially the dogma of apostolic succession and intermediacy between the individual devotee and God.

With rare exceptions – most eminently Duke Humphrey of Gloucester, brother of King Henry V of England and founder of Oxford's Bodleian Library – northern scholars were still clerics trained by scholastics well into the 15th century. Those with progressive pretensions were inspired by Petrarch and his followers to the rejection of Aristotelian dialectic in favour of Platonism but few approached the Italians in the appreciation of Classical texts as works of art to be emulated in style as well as drawn upon for information. No less than Greek or Latin, moreover, they valued Hebrew sources as aids to theological studies, to the progressive elucidation of the scriptures and to the reconstitution of a scriptural, non-hierarchical church in place of the corrupt Roman establishment.

›3.18 HUSSITES AND THE FIGHT FOR THE CHURCH (mid-16th-century chronicle).

Theological enquiry apart, German humanists searched in imperial Roman writing – Tacitus above all – for evidence of the antiquity and nobility of their race and then looked for vernacular sources too. The rapacity of Rome's agents propelled their endeavours into the crucial dimension of nationalism, inimical to the medieval ideal of a single empire and Catholic Church: it also ensured that the impetus for reform was boosted by the lower orders of commercial and industrial society, who felt the tax burden most onerously and who were now equipped to express themselves due to the great expansion of lay education. Not least in response to German pretension, Bohemians led.

The execution of Huss at Constance, with the connivance of the German ecclesiastical establishment in Prague, drove many of his followers to extremity.**2·35, 3·18** They claimed the right of all to communicate in wine as well as bread – *sub utraque specie*, hence their doctrine was called Utraquism and the chalice (*calix*) became the symbol of aspiration to religious reform and national freedom. In 1419 they issued the 'Four Articles of Prague' which demanded recognition of their doctrine, free preaching of the Gospel, forfeiture by the clergy of temporal possessions and punishment of offences against the Bohemian nation.

The emperor Sigismund responded to the Prague demands with German forces. This was unsuccessful but the imperial cause was furthered by internal division between the more conservative middle-class Utraquians and the radical working class – known as Taborites after their stronghold. The Taborites were defeated in pitched battle at Lipany in 1434. The victors reached an accommodation with the imperial authorities: they acknowledged the Catholic church in return for the concession of the four articles. In 1462, however, Pius II renounced the compact. Taborism revived in the Unity of Bohemian Bretheren who rejected the hierarchies of both church and state.**3.19** Conscious of national humiliation at the hands of earlier Bohemian radicals, German humanists joined the protest but it was in Germany that the cause of reformation was first to prevail, as we shall see in due course.

›3.19 THE CHURCH TURNED UPSIDE DOWN:
the peasant celebrating the Eucharist, the monk tilling the fields (*Spiegel*, J. Grünbeck; Nuremberg 1508).

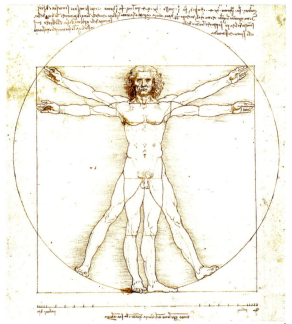

3.20b

>3.20 **VITRUVIAN MAN** as interpreted graphically by (a) Francesco di Giorgio (undated but associated with the earliest corpus of Francesco's writing begun in the 1470s, Ashburnam codex, National Library, Florence), (b) Leonardo da Vinci (c. 1485, Venice, Accademia), (c) Fra Giovanni Giocondo da Verona (Venice 1511), (d) Cesare Cesariano (Como 1521).

In place of the lost original, Renaissance theorists had Vitruvian man variously redrawn as representing the identity of microcosm and macrocosm in the ideal order of mathematics and geometry. In the version by Pietro Cataneo, that identity is explicit in the geometry and the ideal of integrated proportions derived from man for the Orders of architecture is represented by the grid. In Leonardo's celebrated version – as in Francesco's relatively primitive original – the grid is absent but the man, apparent progenitor and master of the geometry, is significantly crucified in the most persuasive synthesis of the Platonic and the Christian ever penned. From this it is but a short step to the synthesis of the centralized and longitudinal in ideal anthropomorphic terms: that step was taken by Francesco, as we shall see (page 791) and followed notably by his fellow Sienese theorist Pietro Cataneo in the 16th century.

Leonardo drew the illustrations for the treatise on proportions of the mathematician Luca Pacioli. In an appendix on architecture, recalling Vitruvius, Pacioli states: 'first we shall talk of the proportions of man because from the human body derive all measures and their denominations and in it is to be found all and every ratio and proportion by which God reveals the innermost secrets of nature ... After having considered the right arrangement of the human body, the ancients proportioned all their work, particularly the temples, in accordance with it. For in the human body they found the two main figures without which it is impossible to achieve anything, namely the perfect circle and the square' (quoted by R. Wittkower, *Architectural Principles* etc., page 15). In this light, it is hardly surprising that all Leonardo's most celebrated essays in church planning are based on the square and the circle and his colleague Bramante was similarly obsessed.[3.111] Both were fully in accord with Alberti who found divinity in the round – 'that Nature delights principally in round figures, etc.'. Representing the perfection of God, it is the circle which ideally satisfies Alberti's essential dictum of design that as 'every particular member should be exactly proportioned to all the other members and to all the rest of the body, so in a building, and especially in a temple, all the parts should be made to correspond so exactly, that ... it may bear its just proportions to all the rest' (*De re aedificatoria*, VII.4,5).

III ART IN PROPORTION AND PERSPECTIVE

Concern with human welfare may be seen as progressive, in step with the revival of towns and material prosperity, as we have seen, but the revival of humanism originated in the monastery with the theologians who promoted the early 12th-century change in Christian ideology (page 264). The re-evaluation of the significance of man had a Christian impetus in the mission of the Saviour. The new humanism, therefore, was different to the old: conditioned by generations of Neoplatonic speculation, it did not see man as the centre of all things in place of God, but it claimed that God had cast man in his own image and endowed him with an intellect capable of comprehending the order of his creation. Philosophers might distract themselves from native human experience with the quest for knowledge of God beyond ideal absolutes. However, in the flowering of the Renaissance in Italy, inspired by

3.20a

3.20c

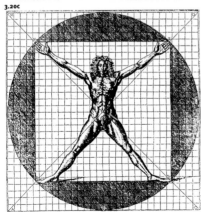

3.20d

the legacy of human achievement, it was the adaptation of the antique conception of order, the order of macrocosm and microcosm, to both Christian and secular purpose which concerned the artist – and concerns us now (see AICI, page 572).**3.20**

Vitruvian man revived

Vitruvius's manuscript disappeared with antiquity but his work survived in medieval copies – the earliest known to us dating from the 9th century. One such was reputedly 'discovered' for the Renaissance by the humanist Poggio Bracciolini, probably in the library of S. Gallen in 1416, but Petrarch, Boccaccio and their proto-humanist contemporaries already knew and used manuscript copies – not only for literary reasons. Terminological difficulties prompted translation, of course: an early attempt was left incomplete by Lorenzo Ghiberti; a complete version, with illustrations in place of the missing originals, was produced by Francesco di Giorgio in 1470 but it was not published. Inspired by the latter, Leonardo da Vinci prepared a set of illustrations for an unrealized edition. First in print was the corrupt Latin compilation of the Veronese archaeologist Sulpicius da Veroli, produced unillustrated for the Accademia Romana at the behest of Pope Innocent VIII in 1486. A sounder text, comprehensively illustrated, was published in 1511 by Fra Giocondo in the service of Pope Julius II: this provided the basis for the Italian edition published ten years later by Cesare Cesariano – a pupil of Julius's principal architect, Bramante.

If one strand in Vitruvius's work absorbed the early Renaissance above all others it was the description of man, the microcosm, as the key to macrocosmic order: Francesco produced the first known graphic version; Leonardo's iconic drawing takes the obsession to its apogee. The Vitruvian man, described by a square and circle 6 times his foot, is fully detailed in proportion defined as 'correspondence among the measures of the members of an entity, and of the whole to a certain part selected as standard': thus 'the length of the foot is one sixth of the height of the body; of the forearm one fourth, and the breadth of the breast is also one fourth', etc. (*De architectura* III.I. 1–2). From the perfect number 6 (the sum of the first three numbers or twice the sum of the first two) enshrined in man's ideal height to foot ratio, is generated the second perfect number 10 (the sum of the first four numbers) and their addition produces the most perfect 16 (the square of the first square). Defining the dimensions of buildings in these terms effected that concordance with the microcosm, and through him to the macrocosm, central to Classical objective (Vitruvius III.1).

IDEAL FORM

Gothic artists were generally bent on praising God in iconic art of convoluted symbolic significance but we detected the stirrings of a new humanism in the centre of Marianism at Chartres and the circle of Suger of S. Denis (pages 269f). The development from iconic form to personality and human space in the sculptures at Chartres – still in the service of God – is a precocious manifestation of the process which led the Italians from the iconic to the Classicizing humanism of Nicola Pisano, to the naturalistic humanism of Giotto and on to Ghiberti – in whose time the service of God was supplemented, if never supplanted, by the service of very human patrons.[3.21, 3.1]

As we know, the Greeks believed in universal Truth enshrined in number and projected in creation by the gods after their own image, and saw man (the microcosm) as manifesting the order of creation (the macrocosm), as reflecting the gods' image – imperfectly. Deducing divine perfection from natural imperfection, they idealized in ratio – as detailed by Vitruvius. Beyond representing man in his reality for Christian purposes, Renaissance artists did the same: they adopted the antique ideal of harmony in proportion, comprehensible to reason; alive to man's environment and concerned with his psychological predicament, they realized that the analysis of imperfect physical nature was the basis of the syncretic method applied by the ancients to approximate that ideal. Thus, if the pervasive Renaissance ideal was Platonic, the era's predominant artistic method was Aristotelian and, as in the exploration of man's world and body, its virtuoso excellence followed not from the mere application of antique precept but from the examination of experience with new eyes.

It is in this light that Alberti's *Della pittura* must be read in the quoting of Protagoras's dictum that 'man is the measure of all things' (AICI, page 442): man is cast in God's image and God gave man reason to fathom the mathematical order of his creation, the macrocosm reflected in the microcosm – man himself. Art follows nature but not slavishly: it does not copy nature but is inspired by the antique ideal of decorum. It is the representation of beauty in truth: truth is the ideal beyond the adventitious 'reality' of this imperfect world and comprehension of it depends on regulation and discipline; beauty is the harmony of number, deduced from the selective observation of nature to inform synthesis rather than conjured by imagination – as the ancients knew. The highest form of art is *istoria*: didactic narrative or allegory on a theme of virtue, antique or Christian, in which figures are differentiated in vitality but united in proportions integral to the order of an ideal environment. Christian and pagan are thus reconciled yet, dedicated to the emulation of antique oratorical eloquence, Alberti's stance was Ciceronian rather than specifically Christian in his promotion of virtue not solely for earning a place in heaven, but for realizing an ideal of society on earth.

FLORENTINE PIONEERS

Among the great figures of the early 15th century who led the quest for the ideal in art, Florentines predominated. The ranks of their sculptors and painters are too great for us to muster here, in an introduction to Renaissance architecture, but among them none was more important than Filippo Brunelleschi (1377–1446), Lorenzo Ghiberti (c.

1378–1455), Donato Bardi, known as Donatello (1386–1466), or Tommaso Guidi, known as Masaccio (1401–28).

The new aspiration was announced with the opening of the new century in the competition for a new set of doors for the Florentine Baptistry. Gilt doors by Andrea Pisano, relating the story of S. John the Baptist, had been installed in the south portal in 1336: their figures, in low relief, were celebrated for their Giottesque naturalism of form and personality though their context was resolutely Gothic. They were the inspiration for the response of both Ghiberti and Brunelleschi to the 1401 competition which specified Old Testament subjects in frames matching those of Pisano.**3.21**

Gates of Paradise

Both the leading contenders were trained as goldsmiths and, working in gilt bronze on a model panel of the Sacrifice of Isaac to satisfy the brief, both retain Gothic elaboration of drapery, swirling into voids to enhance the dramatic turbulence of the subject. The drapery masks a Classical prototype in at least one of Brunelleschi's figures but both artists reveal Isaac as Classically nude – and precociously Classical in conception in Ghiberti's version. Brunelleschi's composition, receding in planes like the typical antique sarcophagus frieze, is centred on Isaac over whom the human and divine forces contend from either side of the upper register. Ghiberti, apparently less concerned with defining space than generating momentum, develops a human dynamic along the diagonal and checks it with the divine.

Ghiberti prevailed. The subject was changed to the Life of Christ and the finished doors came to be known as the Gates of Paradise when they were installed in the eastern portal in 1424. Over the two decades of his work, his style evolved away from Gothic flourish towards intense Classical equipoise – often in opposing violent forces along orthogonal lines against the harmonious foil of Classical architecture. Active or passive, violent or restrained, his figures are idealized after the example detailed by Vitruvius.

Ghiberti's success at the Baptistry preoccupied him throughout his career. His triumph earned him the commission to provide a second set of

3.21a

3.21b

›**3.21 BRUNELLESCHI AND GHIBERTI:** (a) Brunelleschi (1377–1446), commemorative roundel in the south aisle of the Florentine cathedral; (b) Ghiberti (1378–1455), detail from the Florentine Baptistry 'Gates of Paradise'; (c, d) Sacrifice of Isaac, 1401 competition entry models by Brunelleschi and Ghiberti; (e) Ghiberti's definitive panel portraying the Flagellation of Christ (north door, 1403–24).

Filippo Brunelleschi's father was a notary who – typically – equipped his son with a humanistic education in expectation of a career in law. However, the boy's aspiration to art prompted apprenticeship to a goldsmith and he matriculated as a master in that profession in 1404. After losing the Florentine Baptistry competition to Ghiberti in 1401, he is reputed to have left to study architecture in Rome but certainly bent his mind to mathematics and mechanics against a background of increasing familiarity with the Floren-

3.21c

3.21d

doors dedicated to the Old Testament: progressing from the shallow ledges occupied by the frieze-like figures of his earlier work, he fused precinct and ideal architecture into completely unified perspectives, peopled with figures of the most elevated idealism. Completed in 1452, the set was installed in the eastern portal and the earlier one dedicated to Christ was moved to the north where it complemented Pisano's southern set, dedicated to the Baptist.

His protracted labour on the doors notwithstanding, Ghiberti found time to write a pioneering history of art from Classical times to its renaissance in the work of Pisano and Giotto and its culmination in his own achievement – the self-promoting autobiographical element was pioneering in its field too. Brunelleschi's failure at the Baptistry turned his attention to the cathedral, engineering and architecture.

3.21e

tine tradition of Romanesque architecture: wherever he gained his first-hand experience of Roman architecture, his synthesis of liberal and mechanical studies is central to his achievement. He continued to produce sculpture and served on municipal building advisory committees.

Lorenzo Ghiberti was the grandson of a notary. His peasant mother left his undistinguished father for the goldsmith Bartoluccio (c. 1422) to whom Lorenzo was apprenticed and with whom he collaborated in the casting of the first set of doors. Talented in all the arts, Ghiberti wrote an autobiography which stands at the head of the humanist tradition of art historiography.

Ghiberti's idealism was matched in the contemporary work of Donatello – stemming from the statue of David he provided for the exterior of the north transept of the cathedral in 1408. His later, more celebrated, David is in marked contrast – and well represents the breadth of Renaissance vision. Nude in accordance with the Classical tradition – but contrary to medieval Christian conceptions of propriety – he is a naturalistic boy standing in for one of the more mature models of Polykleitos (AIC1, page 402).**3.22** However, beyond reference to nature in the transposition of Vitruvian proportions, the equipoise of the Classical *contrapossto* formula gives repose to the God-given hero after he has slain Goliath. Yet, beyond the copying of nature – or, indeed, reproducing an antique prototype – the application of the principle of selection in accordance with an integrated set of proportions informed a supreme conception of the dignity of man and his achievement in the service of God: the result is an icon of humanism. Alberti defined the means in *De statua*.**3.23**

3.23

RATIONAL SPACE

In 1417 the Sienese called on Ghiberti to collaborate on a new font for their cathedral baptistry. As little had materialized by 1423, Donatello was also commissioned to provide a panel and the cross-fertilization of ideas between the two Florentines was crucial. Working in the medium of gilt-bronze relief for the first time, and obviously impressed with Ghiberti's achievement, Donatello saw the importance of disposing a dramatically disrupted group

3.22

›**3.22 DAVID:** bronze by Donatello (Florence, National Museum of the Bargello).

The circumstances of the commission are unrecorded. On stylistic grounds it has been dated variously to the late-1420s and mid-1440s.

›**3.23 ALBERTI'S DEVICE FOR CALCULATING THE PROPORTIONS OF THE HUMAN BODY FOR APPLICATION TO SCULPTURE** (R. du Fresne, *Trattato della pittura di Leonardo da Vinci etc con il trattato della statua di Leon Battista Alberti*, Paris 1665).

Alberti's treatise *De statua* included a table of ideal human proportions compiled from a range of examples with the aid of an apparatus (*finitorum*) designed to measure the body in three dimensions (disposition = *finitio*): a disk of 3 feet in diameter and circumference of 6 degrees, has a radial arm from measured distances along which is suspended a plumb line to determine the length and breadth of the members and to provide a perpendicular against which the height of the whole and its parts may be measured with a calibrated rod (*exempeda*). As the principal objective was to guage relative proportions, the rod was divided into six units, representing an ideal height of 6 times the foot, whatever the actual size of the body, and the divisions of the arm were likewise constant. Ancient precept was thus checked in accordance with the Classical ideal of analysis, selection and synthesis.

›3.24 SIENA, CATHEDRAL, BAPTISTRY FONT: Donatello's gilt-bronze relief panel of Herod recoiling from the head of S. John the Baptist (c. 1425).

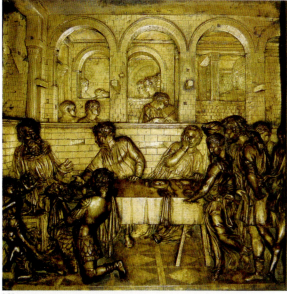

3.24

against the foil of an architectural order but he also gave it a rational space of its own – or rather, with consummate command of geometry, he constructed the illusion of such a space as a stage for his naturalistically disposed actors.**3.24**

If Ghiberti and Donatello built on the Classicizing achievement of Nicola Pisano – with the aid of early collections of antique sculpture – their contemporary painters looked back to the naturalism of Giotto in mastering the art of foreshortening, evoking three-dimensional forms on a two-dimensional plane and relating them in a realistically constructed space. As we have seen, Ghiberti credited Giotto with reinventing painting, as Pisano had returned sculpture from the iconic art of the earlier Christians (AICI, pages 681ff). For them the realities of this world paled into insignificance before the glories of the next, indeed the placing of the holy images in a realistically constructed space would have seemed paradoxical – if not blasphemous – to the orthodox medieval Christian. On the other hand, to the humanists of the Renaissance –

bent on understanding and describing this world – it was impossible to do otherwise in the belief that, real or ideal, the logic of space could be construed for Christian ends.

The crucial development in this direction was the discovery – or rediscovery – of the principles of linear perspective: that is, devising the illusion of recession on a two-dimensional plane by means of the consistent diminution of the proportional relationships between objects within a conical frame representing the apparent convergence of parallel lines to a single focus. Beyond the accomplished intuitive constructs of Ghiberti – way beyond the tentative steps of Giotto and his followers – mastery of the principles of vanishing-point perspective in painting is first apparent in work of Masaccio contemporary with Donatello's Sienese panel, c. 1425.**3.25**

Masaccio's perspective

In his Trinity fresco in S. Maria Novella, Florence, (c. 1425), Masaccio constructs a rational space to elucidate the mystical: the figure of the Godhead and the human donors occupy a chapel as ideal in conception as a Greek temple designed to reflect the perfection of the work of the gods in ordering creation. Or, rather, the artist constructs the illusion of such a chapel through the rigorous application of the laws of perspective and the perfect geometry which describes the arc of heaven as a coffered vault, Roman in its gravitas. As we know, mathematical perfection is the clearest manifestation of the divine to Platonic minds and the vision of Nicholas of Cusa. As with the Greeks, moreover, the principles underlying divine order in its totality – the macrocosm – are deduced from the study of man – the microcosm created by God after his own image: thus the columns connecting the terrestrial and celestial – the world of the donors and the arc of heaven described about the aureole of the Father – enshrine that ideal elongated after the proportions of the crucified body, median between heaven and earth, in which God became man.

To Masaccio, as to Ghiberti or Donatello, the ability to represent the 'realities' of this world is pressed into the service of the holy story and its

3.25a

›3.25 MASACCIO: (a) Expulsion of Adam and Eve from the Garden of Eden; (b) Trinity (c. 1425) (respectively Brancacci Chapel in S. Maria del Carmine and S. Maria Novella, Florence).

Masaccio's Trinity is placed opposite the south door on the wall separating the north aisle from the cloister where the extension of a real space for the chapel was not possible. The donors stand in front, the sacred actors beyond the proscenium. And it is at the eye level of the average viewer – just above the base of the cross, well below the aureole of the Father – that the orthogonal lines of the simulated architecture converge in a single-point perspective.

3.26

›3.26 PIERO DELLA FRANCESCA: Annunciation, detail from the altarpiece painted c. 1445 for S. Antonio delle Monache, Perugia (now in the Umbrian National Gallery, Perugia).

3.25b

superhuman ideal. In his depiction of Adam and Eve expelled from paradise, Eve may have Classical antecedents descending from Praxitiles but the figure of Adam is unprecedented in its anguished and painful physical realism. Moreover, the shadow-scarred space of their new-found wilderness – endlessly expansive but burdened by their naked corporeality – is in blunt distinction to the sharply delineated, strictly exclusive, portal to the Eden of God's order. The impact was the more stunning a century on from Giotto because the current 'International Style' was not primarily concerned with realizing tangible volume or projecting rational space but with elegant line and lush patterning.

The fall of man when Adam ate of the tree of knowledge at Eve's behest in Eden opened a gulf between heaven and earth only bridged in the Christian belief that the Holy Ghost penetrated the womb of a sinless woman and God became man as redeemer. The Archangel Gabriel's annunciation of that conception to the Virgin Mary, reconciling man and God, was naturally of paramount interest to artists in an age of revived humanism. And in an age committed to reconciling Christ's revelation with the absolute truth deduced by the most elevated of pagan philosophers from incontrovertible axioms, like those of mathematics, the context of the encounter was rationalized – usually in architectural terms. Fra Angelico was no stranger to the device, but Gothic charm is not lost to the new rationalism.

Piero della Francesca (c. 1416–92), master of pictorial space constructed after the ideal of cosmic order through the rigorous application of the laws of perspective, is unexcelled in the iconographic deployment of architecture. In his altarpiece now in Perugia, the Archangel Annunciate has arrived in an arcaded portico open to the sky from whence he came: the style is developed to provide the crucially enclosed chamber of the Virgin and, in between, an extended colonnade represents the caesura of central iconographic significance. And in venerating the advent of God among men – with Federico da Montefeltro – Piero della Francesca was Masaccio's worthy successor .**3.26**

PERSPECTIVE IN SCIENCE

The theoretical basis for supplanting empiricism with science in the formulation of a perspective system for representing three-dimensional form on a plane surface was elucidated by Alberti in his treatise on painting (1435). Ten years earlier, however, the achievements of Masaccio and Donatello are generally recognized to have depended on the inventive genius of their friend and colleague, Filipo Brunelleschi.**3.27**

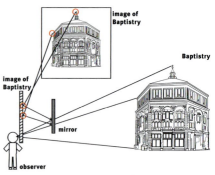

›3.27 PERSPECTIVE: Brunelleschi's demonstration with an image reflected in a mirror.

Brunelleschi left no account of his procedure and his method may only be deduced from the description of demonstration paintings in his biography of c. 1480, attributed to Antonio Manetti. The earliest and simplest of these is focused on the Florentine Baptistry from the central portal of the cathedral. Made at a distance about equal to its height (c. 56 braccia, or very approximately 34 metres, from some 1.8 metres within the cathedral portal), Brunelleschi's orthogonal image of the building and as much of its immediate vicinity as could be seen at one glance was committed to a small panel about half a braccia (c. 30.5 centimetres) square. This was to be held with its back to the viewer and its face reflected in a mirror held about 60 centimetres in front of it. The latter, needed to correct reversal, was seen through an eyehole drilled at the focal point of the composition and it is probable that the apparently converging lines of the reflected image were traced on to it for analysis. To complement this experiment in single-point orthogonal perspective he conducted another in double-point diagonal perspective, using the Piazza Signoria on a larger panel.

Prospettiva

According to Vasari, Brunelleschi was tutored by one Paolo dal Pozzo Toscanelli, a doctor who had studied optics – among much else – where Blasius of Parma had recently been professor of astrology. In his *Questiones perspectivae* (1390) – readily available in Florence – Blasius drew on Arabic

›**3.28 EUCLIDIAN VISUAL CONE AND ITS INTERSECTION BY A PICTURE PLANE.**
Euclid demonstrated that if two sides of a triangle are intersected by a straight line parallel to the third side, the resultant triangle will be identical in its proportions to the original (theorem 21). Such an incision in a visual triangle is a picture seen as a view through a window – an image impressed on its glazing or, rather, as a section cut by the glazing through the 'visual rays' transmitting it to the eye: if that incision is parallel to the perpendicular of a rectangular triangle, Euclid has it that image and object will be in precise proportion. In Brunelleschi's rectilinear isosceles visual triangle, thus cut, the ratio of the perpendicular building elevation to the viewing distance is as image size to viewing distance. His exercise was greatly simplified if his choice of viewpoint set the former at 1:1 (about 56 bracchi) and he retained the height of his panel (about half a bracchio) for its viewing distance. The same 1:1 ratio of the perpendiculars would, of course, dictate the angle of view.

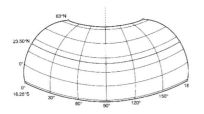

›**3.29 PTOLEMAIC PROJECTION OF THE WORLD MAP** (Ulm, 1482).

scholarship, notably the *Perspectiva* (c. 1000) in which the great Cairene scholar Alhazen had effected a synthesis between Arab science and ancient theory.

The Italian term *prospettiva*, applied to the art of delineating solids on plane surfaces in accordance with the scientific principles of optics, is derived from the Latin term *perspectiva*, applied to the study of optics in the Middle Ages. The ancient Greeks had established optics as a branch of mathematics concerned with measurable forces emitted by the eye: in his *Optica* (c. 300 BCE), Euclid delineated the rays of vision as a cone regulated by the rules of geometry – for example, that the apparent diminution of objects viewed across graduated distance responded to the diminishing size of the angle of vision.[3.28]

The *Optics* of the Alexandrine scholar Claudius Ptolemy (c.127–155 CE) graded the rays from shortest/strongest on the central axis, perpendicular to the observed surface, to longest/weakest on the peripheral inclination and, studying the angle of vision, he stressed the importance of the relative distance of objects from one another, as well as from the eye. Alhazen absorbed this and the Euclidian geometry: however, he saw that 'visual rays' were emitted not by the eye but radiated in all directions from infinite points of observation. And in this light, scholastic thinkers proffered a synthesis between Christian theology and ancient theory: as the light of the sun radiates from any physical substance and penetrates the eye attuned to its rays, so God's grace radiates from all his creation and penetrates the eye of the worthy soul; thus the Euclidian diagram of the regular visual cone was adopted as an aid to the eye of the soul in seeing the order of God.

Ptolemy applied his optics to cartography in his *Geographica* (c. 150 CE), devising a method of projecting a section of the gridded surface of the world sphere to a two-dimensional plane, with longitudinal and latitudinal coordinates converging towards the poles.[3.29] A copy was brought from Constantinople to Florence by Manuel Chrysoloras, whom we have already encountered as professor of Greek there from 1397. Its explanation of the geometric technique for constructing linear perspective was as attractive to the humanist artist, committed to the accurate representation of mundane space, as the grid it imposed on cartography was to humanists in general in an age attuned to mathematical order in the universe.

In medieval Europe objects tended to be depicted immanently in multiple facets and relationships rather than from a fixed external viewpoint: viewing was a subjective kaleidoscopic process through shifting positions, from which as much information as possible was gleaned about the individuality of forms and the complexity of their changing relationships. Following Cimabue, Giotto enhanced the corporeality of figures and furthered the realization of space for them through his observation of the apparent convergence of parallel lines but he rarely gave that convergence a single locus. A generation later – in the work of the Lorenzetti, for example – convergence was more consistently applied to the main lines of individual motifs but not yet to the space of a composition viewed as a whole.

By the opening of the 15th century, rational humanism was preferring representation that was objectively static in time and place, focused on form in unified space, as from a window. Brunelleschi opened the window to the clear comprehension of measurable space and objects relative to one another in size according to their position in that space. He showed how that space and those objects could be reduced to the two dimensions of a picture plane scientifically, rather than pragmatically in the manner of the Giotteschi who reopened the quest for a visual 'realism' beyond the kaleidoscope.

The concept of the vanishing point – the point at which parallel lines appear to converge on an infinitely remote horizon – was the basis of Brunelleschi's demonstration as described by Manetti: reflecting depth from a flat surface, the mirror of the experiment clearly revealed the reversal of the visual cone – or pyramid – with the apex in the eye opposed by the vanishing point at the level extension of the central visual line, and the geometry of the former obviously belonged to the latter. This revelation was crucial to the definition of the geometric principles for the ordering of visual space through linear perspective. And, of course, the mastery of the means for representing things as they actually appear was crucial for correcting – or creating – optical illusion in architecture.

Inveterate surveyor, empirical engineer of staggering ingenuity, architect of seminal importance, Brunelleschi doubtless pursued his graphic exercises in vanishing-point perspective primarily for the accurate recording of his archaeological surveys in scale drawings. But did he discover – or rediscover – the laws of linear perspective?

Ghiberti – whose *Commentaries* include summaries of the works of Alhazen among other medieval writers on optics – was not alone in believing, specifically, that the rules of perspective had been formulated in antiquity but lost. Apart from analyses of early imperial painting, substantiation may be found in Vitruvius. He makes it unsurprisingly clear that the concept of devising the illusion of three-dimensional space on a two-dimensional plane derived from the Greeks, particularly commentators on theatrical scene painting (*De architectura*, introduction to Book VII). Primarily, however, in defining plan (from ichnography), elevation (from orthography) and perspective (from scenography) in the first of his ten books, he specified that the last 'is the method of sketching a front with the sides withdrawing into the background, the lines all meeting in the centre of a circle' (I.2.2). Unfortunately, he did not go further and delineate the method and his Latin admits varied translation.

In the prologue to his treatise on painting Alberti speculates that the ancients knew truths – not least of art – long forgotten. Indebted to modern practitioners rather than to ancient precept in his prescription for the construction of linear perspective, however, he could well claim primacy for his theoretical treatment of the subject – though he dedicated his work to Brunelleschi.**3.30**

Alberti: decorum in perspective

With patrician background and elevated humanist education, Alberti approached the problem of defining perspective drawing primarily from an idealistic point of view but delivered his rules as a practical guide for artists. His *De pictura* (c. 1435) is comprised of three books: the first deals with geometry and optics, the second with the categories of painting, above all history painting (*istoria*), and the third with the artist. The study of perspective was introduced in the first book as a branch of optics applicable to painting – indeed, as essential to the didactic world of *istoria*. Painting pleased but in that it primarily edified at its apogee in *istoria*, it was an intellectual exercise beyond sensuality. *Istoria* edified in its proper concern with great events illustrating ethics, great personages exemplifying virtue – or its opposite. And the context for their superior existence in ideal proportions and harmonious distribution – even if the moral was stated in violent conflict – was ordered *a priori* in accordance with the immutable laws of mathematics: hence the importance to artists of comprehending the rules of linear perspective.

Describing a painting as 'the intersection of a visual pyramid at a given distance, with a fixed centre and a certain position of lights represented artistically with lines and colours on a given surface' and recalling Euclid's theorem 21, Alberti stressed the precise proportional relationship of image to object as the fundamental premise in the theory of linear perspective. The picture, analogous to an open window, was also analogous to the image impressed on the eye as, in accordance with the science of optics inherited from the Middle Ages, it was thought that the lens cut the visual cone – or pyramid – as its rays passed into consciousness. Comprehension of the science of perspective as a branch of optics, thus, meant that artists could represent what they see as their eyes see it through the linear system reflecting order in creation. One of Alberti's principal objectives in the treatise on painting was to explain this view.

In stressing the prime importance, the moral authority, of the centric line (the central ray of the visual cone), Alberti recommended that it passes through the 'centric point' in the true centre of the composition at the level of the viewer's eye. After his ideal, the usual armature for *istoria* in painting was a grid in linear perspective, transforming plane surface with the

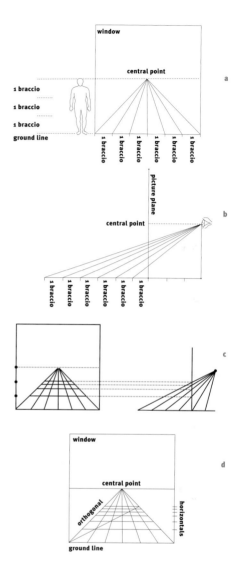

›3.30 ALBERTIAN PERSPECTIVE (after Edgerton).

Towards the delineation of perspective principles, Alberti describes two operations: to locate the vanishing point first (a) he draws a rectangle on the picture plane – 'an open window through which the subject to be painted is seen' or intersection through the visual cone – then he determines figure size, divides it in three parts proportional to the braccio (3 braccia being average for the height of a man). The same measure is adopted for the division of the rectangle's base line. Then, having established where the centric ray strikes (at the height of the viewer and of the modular figure to be depicted so that the viewer will seem to be on the same plane), he connects that point ('the centric point') with the points of division in the base line. He then draws a line parallel to the base line through the centric point ('the centric line', defining the horizon) with which the heads of figures of comparable size on the same plane are to be aligned.

The second operation (b), dependent on the first, provides a gauge for the proportional relationship of the figures. This begins with the description of a line, parallel to but evidently standing for artist or viewer in front of the 'picture window', and its division in accordance with the braccio module. From a point on this vertical corresponding to the centric point ('the distance point'), diagonals are drawn to the modular division points on a second baseline extended at 90 degrees from the base of the new vertical representing the viewer. At a distance from the viewpoint determined by the artist, the diagonals are cut by a second vertical line (representing the picture plane) – thus if the first vertical fixes the viewpoint, the second one is variable to regulate apparent depth of field.

The conjunction of the diagrams produced by the two operations (c) completes the linear matrix of the perspective system by defining the transverse lines which determine the relative height and proportions of comparable figures or objects located on the same plane, given that these transversals are divided laterally in proportion to the modular divisions of the base by the lines connecting those divisions with the centric point. Beyond that, of course, the centric point (or vanishing point) is the locus for the apparent convergence of all the parallels represented in the painter's environment. If the perspective has been constructed accurately, a diagonal will connect the corners of its projected squares (d).

›3.31 PAOLO UCELLO: the Battle of S. Romano (c. 1445; Florence, Uffizi Gallery).

plausible illusion of space at the disposition of figures proportionate to its dimensions. Naturally, it did not always provide a pavement or generate buildings and Alberti recommended the plotting of the image on a gridded veil stretched over the picture plane to intersect the visual cone.

3.31

Soon after Alberti produced his treatise, Uccello's fascination with its treatment of perspective is manifest in his splendid series of paintings on the battle of S. Romano: with the heads of all the figures contesting the same plane aligned, the vanishing point was placed centrally and the linear perspective subtended from it establishes a firm, if not entirely rational, foundation as a foil to the violent discord of the subject – the broken lances managing both to suggest reason and respond to turmoil.**3.31**

Well before Alberti, Masaccio and Donatello demonstrated that the principles of perspective were to serve, not master. Masaccio's construction of the Trinity's mansion, in accordance with God's immutable laws of mathematics, necessarily surmounted the viewer's eye level and his location of the vanishing point is below the ground penetrated by Christ's cross, well below the centre of the hieratic image. Donatello's Sienese composition centres on the meat and wine which, prefiguring Christ's Eucharist, alone occupy the caesura left by Herod's violent recoil from

3.32

Salome and her horrific offering in the centre of the lower register, below the heavenly harmony of music and architecture to which martyrdom graduates.**3.25b, 3.24**

   Donatello's figures were idealized in the way Alberti was later to codify. Piero della Francesca was studiously idealistic in the structure but naturalistic in the detail of the figures inhabiting his idealized spaces and the power of his conceptions is generated by supreme mastery of the manipulation of perspective. The vanishing point in his

›3.32 PIERO DELLA FRANCESCA: Flagellation (tempera on panel, c. 1460; Urbino, National Gallery).

   The subject is controversial. The centric point, behind the central colonnade at the level of the hand which authority washed to absolve itself of responsibility, dislocates the central event of Christ's passion, in the realm of that authority, to counter the religious authorities of whose venal disposition it was the consequence. Beyond the bifurcated perspective, the crucial dimension in Piero's Flagellation image of man's inhumanity to man derives from the irony of applying human scale to the architecture of state.

   Vasari implies that Piero was distinguished from his contemporary artists by his reputation as a mathematician. He wrote three treatises founded on mathematics of which *De prospectiva pingendi* (pre-1480?) is the most significant from the artistic point of view. It prescribes two perspective techniques which may be represented by the Annunciation and Flagellation respectively: the first is not radically different to Alberti's; the other is exhaustive in its location of elements in plan and elevation and obsessive in its geometrical calculations for their projection individually.

›3.33 IDEAL CITIES, oil on panel c. 1470: (a) Baltimore, Walters Art Gallery; (b) Urbino, National Gallery.

   The authorship and date of these panels, and a related one in Berlin, are the subjects of much debate. Their purpose is similar and each is based on an Albertian perspective grid prepared in minute detail. A dominant interest in volume has been detected in the Urbino panel, space in the others. The Urbino panel may relate

3.33a

3.33b

to an inventory record of an overdoor 'con una prospet-tiva'; it certainly relates to marquetry panels still in situ in the ducal palace – allowing for the radically different nature of the media – but otherwise only to the other two panels. The circle of Federico da Montefeltro is the most likely source and that included Piero della Francesca, Francesco di Giorgio, Luciano Laurana and Alberti. Stage-set design suggests itself as the inspiration but between them the panels are meticulous in recording the full repertory of public and private building types which Alberti discusses in his treatise on architecture: in general the settings are ideal for the elevated personages of an Albertian *istoria* and in particular the circular church stands for all that Alberti considered ideal in the genre. Thus, the panels have actually been attributed to him despite the absence of any other works from his hand to support the contention.

›**3.34 PERUGINO:** Christ Giving the Keys of His Church to S. Peter, fresco c. 1482 (Vatican, Sistine Chapel).

The Temple and the arches which flank it represent the old imperia, spiritual and temporal, which the humble recipient of authority over the new one will eclipse. The inscription panels on the arches leave no room for doubt: they convert even the grandeur of ancient Rome to Christian purpose – or to the purpose of Peter's successor – and challenge even the glory of Solomon on behalf of Sixtus IV.

Annunciation,**3.26** central to the composition but to the right of the caesura, ignores the centre of the arcade to reinforce the iconographical thrust from Angel to Virgin. In his Flagellation, where columns and naturalistic people are assimilated, the centric point is neutralized by the architecture of state authority and the nominal subject dislocated.**3.32** On the other hand, in the celebrated panels representing ideal urban space which are sometimes attributed to Piero, the Albertian ideal – perfectly centralized and admitting of neither addition nor subtraction, mathematically harmonious like the cosmos – reigns supreme.**3.33**

3.34

Erasmo da Narni of Padua, known as Gattamelata, was the most celebrated, if largely unsuccessful, *condottiero* in the service of Venice. The equestrian statue was the first work of its kind and scale cast in bronze since antiquity. Its model was the statue of Marcus Aurelius, sometime the centrepiece in Rome's Piazza Campidoglio, and the sculptor lent much of the emperor's dignity and trappings to his much less elevated subject.

ROMAN GRAVITAS REVIVED

Propriety dictated the re-evocation of the Classical forum in the ideal – as in the Urbino or Baltimore panels – to provide the setting for playing out the grand themes of *istoria*: the ideal was the divine order, of course, and the themes were antique, historical or biblical. Equally, in the increasingly precise quotation of ancient building types, temple and triumphal arch were inescapable iconographically – even when quoted ironically.**3.34**

Apart from the Greek ideal, transmitted by the Romans, the reality of antiquity was primarily the 'Eternal City' – Rome. The medieval observer was inclined to lament its fate as an object lesson in the humiliation of Godless man. On the contrary, early Renaissance man looked to its ruined buildings – as to its authors – for lessons in structure as much as style and, beyond copying with pedantic attention to detail, his followers progressed from the application of precept to emulation, to re-evocation. And the evocation of Roman gravitas was no less effective for its historical accuracy in providing the overbearing context for deploring inhuman affliction – or the resplendent context for celebrating super-human triumph.

The nobility of Donatello's conception and his technical brilliance were universally admired but, with the growing appreciation of historical propriety, his antiquarianism was criticized as inappropriate in showing Gattamalata, a very modern general, as a Roman emperor.**3.35** On the other hand, the Triumph of Julius Caesar or the Martyrdom of S. James the Great impelled Andrea Mantegna beyond the application of principle – or even the incorporation of the iconographically relevant Classical motifs – to re-evoke the mood of the imperial past. He recreated the might of its civilization in awe of the monumentality of its buildings and intimate familiarity with their ornamental detail: the glorification of imperial power is the very subject of the triumph series, of course, and the power of the state in the suppression of heterodoxy was the essence of the S. James cycle.**3.36**

›**3.36 MANTEGNA AND ROMAN GRAVITAS:** (a): S. James Led to Execution (fresco c. 1450, destroyed 1944; Padua, Church of the Eremitani); (b) The Triumph of Caesar (from the series of nine scenes painted c. 1492 for the Gonzaga court in distemper on canvas; Hampton Court, Royal Collection).

3.36a

3.36b

Mantegna's precocious accuracy of detail is worthy of the most scrupulous archaeologist, though it derived from the sculpture collections of Padua's prominent humanists rather than from the great sites of Rome. And it complements mastery of perspective worthy of Alberti – with whom he was linked for at least that part of his career spent in Mantua. And in Mantua, in the context of vaulting hardly less grave than Masaccio's – though projected as a canopy for the princely family informally disposed on the walls of a marriage chamber – Mantegna took vanishing-point perspective to new heights of illusionism: literally, in the simulated opening of the vault to a vision of the sky.**3.37**

Mantegna's role in the expansion of the renaissance of painting to northern Italy would be difficult to exaggerate: his work for the Gonzaga apart, the great cycle executed for the Paduan Eremitani measurably reinforced the lessons to be learned from Giotto in the Arena Chapel nearby. The influence was most immediately apparent in the work of his brother-in-law, the Venetian Giovanni Bellini.

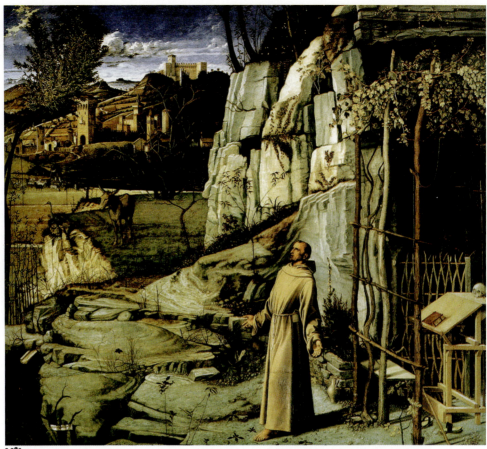

3.38a

›**3.38 GIOVANNI BELLINI:** (a) S. Francis stigma-tized in the wilderness (tempera and oil, c. 1480; New York, Frick Collection); (b) Feast of the Gods (oil, 1514; Washington, National Gallery).

Exploration of the natural world, characteristic of Italian art after its liberation from Byzantine convention, required the elimination of the chased gold ground of the typical Venetian mosaic: with Bellini, especially, it ceded to landscape in the interests of mood, emotion and the immediacy of once-hieratic figures – but in that exercise it was to be no less a humanist tool for repre-senting the world as the object of man's knowledge.

MOOD OF THE WORLD AT LARGE

On the basis of Mantegnesque draughtsmanship, Bellini projected landscape from the background to provide a vital setting of all-enveloping mood, invoked through the modulation of colour in light on clouds, fields, foliage, flood, the fabric of building and distant hills. Thus the Venetian school was launched on its brilliant career whose celebration of sensual values provided the perfect foil to Florentine rationality.**3.38**

Elevating it, Mantegna may have been elevated by the art of perspective. Penetrating through it, Bellini was

3.38b

projected beyond post-Gothic pattern to nature for the physical and emotional context of his human dramas. Leonardo da Vinci found it constraining. The window of its single-point projection plane distances the viewer from the viewed, limits his knowledge to the single aspect researched by the artist – unlike the medieval techniques which it was designed to supplant.**3.39–3.41**

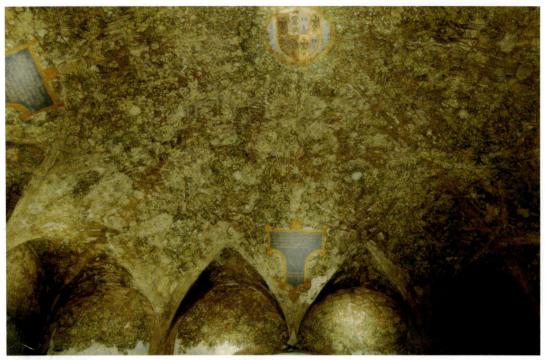

›3.39 MILAN, CASTELLO SFORZESCO: Sala della Asse (Leonardo da Vinci, completed c. 1497).

Ludovico Sforza, whom Leonardo had served primarily as a military engineer for some fifteen years, commissioned the arborial scheme of frescos for the audience chamber of his new castle. The branches of the repeated mulberry tree sustained the patron's arms, quartered with those of his wife, but as he was widowed before the scheme came to fruition the conceit was turned to the celebration of the intertwining of the Sforza and Habsburg lines on the marriage of Ludovico's niece, Bianca Maria, to Emperor Maximilian in 1493.

Leonardo's achievement

Trained in humanist Florence but empirical by nature, less interested than his colleagues there in Classical precepts than in his own experience of nature, Leonardo was revolutionary in technique and subject matter. A stunning example of the latter is his decorative scheme for a room in the Milanese Castello Sforzesco in which a forest of interlocking mulberry trees (acknowledging one of the Sforza heraldic devices) mocks the conventional use of an Order of architecture as a metaphor for load and support.

Leonardo's revolutionary technique of sculpting form on plane surface complemented the venerable interest in light with penetrating study of shadow – hence the Italian term *chiaroscuro*. He launched it, in the oil-based medium essential to it, with the Adoration of the Magi panel left incomplete in Florence when he entered the service of the Sforza in 1482. He furthered it in Milan from 1483 with the Madonna of the Rocks: defusing subtle gradations of light to create a greater illusion of plasticity – especially the soft corporeality of flesh – he endowed space with form-

3.40a

>3.40 LEONARDO DA VINCI: (a) Adoration of the
Magi (unfinished wash drawing c. 1481; Uffizi Gallery,
Florence); (b) The Madonna of the Rocks (oil on panel,
after 1495; London, National Gallery).

Beyond clear triangulation in the disposition of the
main protagonists, atmospheric interests are already
apparent in the groundwork which survives here: the
organically conceived groups, the more fully worked
ones formed of interlocking ovals and moulded with
light and shade, incompletely emerge from the obscure
depth of space evoked as the precinct of an extraordinary ruin – rather than being defined by clarity of line
and set against an ideal radiant background, as they
usually were in the mainstream of Florentine 15th-
century painting.

embracing atmosphere (*sfumato*) penetrated by strong shafts to enhance
salient features.

Leonardo's gradations of tone supplemented, but certainly did not supplant, the rational delineation of space. He promoted the restoration of the
subjective, but certainly not the kaleidoscopic, to representation: he
revived the technique of multiple exposure from varied viewpoints to
describe the complexity of objects or the evolution of events through
space and across time: the Adoration announces this; the Last Supper,
painted on the refectory wall of S. Maria della Grazie in Milan, is its most
spectacular manifestation.

Executed over the three years to 1498 – but probably not perfected in
the artist's eye before the fall of Lodovico Sforza – the Last Supper was daringly experimental in both conception and medium. As to the latter: to
obviate the problem of change in fresco, he resorted to a slow-drying tempera on dry plaster which facilitated change but proved unstable. As to the
conception, the absence of the conventional attributes of the *dramatis per-
sonae* is but the starting point for a supreme exercise in perspective complexity and psychological penetration. The real space of the room is

3.40b

extended illusionistically, in full mastery of the science of perspective, yet with wilful imprecision is bent to assert that (like Christ himself) the context of the scene was of this world and yet beyond it. Moreover, to convey the cataclysmic moment of foreseen betrayal, in which the company is broken into four distinct triads of individualistically disconcerted disciples, four subsidiary systems of formal organization are deployed as the armature of disparate emotional connections in counterpoint to the unifying perspective of the space, its furniture and the timeless triangle of Christ.

The recording of his scientific and biological studies was ultimately to eclipse Leonardo's activity as a painter: few of his commissions were to be completed and several of these suffered from his experimentation with the oil-based media essential to the realization of his atmospheric effects.

Giovanni Bellini's sensual, atmospheric cause and Leonardo da Vinci's experiments with profound variations of light and shade were both furthered through the development of oil-based paint. For that the Italians were indebted to the Flemish.

3.42a

›3.42 FLEMISH PROSPECTS: (a) Jan van Eyck (c. 1390–1441), Madonna and Child with Chancellor Rolin (c. 1434; Paris, Louvre); (b, c) Rogier van de Weyden, Madonna and Child with S. Luke, (c. 1435–40; Boston, Museum of Fine Arts), Crucifixion from the Seven Sacraments triptych (c. 1450; Antwerp, Royal Art Museum).

The sumptuously attired Nicholas Rolin, seen by van Eyck in direct communion with the Madonna and the Christ child – at the same scale and on the same plane, unlike most donors represented in devotional images – was the chancellor of Duke Philip III of Burgundy. Rather than betraying study of Classical forms and proportions the architecture of Rolin's audience chamber is perhaps best described as Byzantino-Romanesque and was apparently devised with some knowledge of Venetian indebtedness to the east to evoke the New Jerusalem.

The unified context for the diverse performances of van de Weyden's Sacraments is provided by the nave and aisles of a Rayonnant cathedral whose intuitive semidiagonal perspective is virtually flawless. Gossaert, on the other hand, is 'scientifically' flawless.

THE FLEMISH CONTRIBUTION

The Flemish were little interested in the antique for much of the 15th century and tended to be intuitive, obsessed with the observable world of nature and late-Gothic man, rather than deductive of a suprasensory ideal – empiricist rather than rationalist. The northern climate inspired no quest for an ideal in naked human form or rationally conceived perspective on space – such as moved Masaccio and his followers in the clear light of the Florentine dawn. In the recording of courtiers and merchants alike, the Flemish style developed not from mosaic under the inspiration of sculpture but from manuscript illumination. Taken to its apogee by the Limbourg brothers in the service of Burgundy's forebear, Berry, that art of lavish delight in the observation of life across the social spectrum from princely patron to peasant, must be seen as a major manifestation of the 'International Gothic' style with its meticulous detail, cursive line and ravishing colour.

Meticulous detail and ravishing colour were certainly not lost to the high art of 15th-century Flanders. However, the scale of the new endeavour, free from the page of the book on panel on easel, obviated water-based paint and the damp of the north, inimical to fresco, prompted resort to oil: quick-drying, opaque tempera ceded to translucent layers of lustrous colour floated over opaque grounds in the new slow-drying medium, removing the need for speed in execution. And the new medium furthered the revelation of minutely recorded town or landscape through atmospheric mist – and glazed window – as well as the glossy, glowing reproduction of all the facets and textures of the precious gems and rich fabrics with which the wealth of their duchy regaled Flemish patrons.**3.42a**

Van Eyck's achievement

Jan van Eyck (active c. 1422–41) was the progenitor of the Flemish school, or rather it was he who overlaid elegant line with moody atmosphere and modulated light to reveal a clearer, firmer sense of form and space – constructed intuitively rather than rationally – for his Flemish and Italian patrons, their rooms, the world beyond their windows and their individual psychology. The consummate heir to the late-Gothic mastery of representing the natural world – or its urban counterpart – he is usually credited with the revolutionary introduction of oil paint though he doubtless perfected earlier experiments. He certainly set the standard for 15th-century Flemish painting – though few of his compatriots emulated the painterly, rather than sculptural, style which his technique promoted.

Drawing on the strain of realism, physical and psychological, which we have traced back to the early 13th-century sculpture of Chartres (pages 264f) but taking it to unprecedented and unsurpassed heights, Van Eyck's portraiture is minutely descriptive of physical individuality, psychologically revelatory and wholly unidealized. Characteristically, the figures are turned towards the viewer as though to emerge from the painted to the real world. And that painted world, realized empirically through the graduation of tone as much as geometry, is a wholly plausible extension of temporal space infused with atmospheric light revealing variety of texture and defining intricate form – all of which, in religious subjects at least, retains the allegorical significance essential to medieval art.

Precocious, van Eyck's painterly achievements, particularly in evoking atmosphere, were beyond the ability – or interests – of his immediate followers to overcome the linear conventions of the 'International Gothic'. The greatest of those followers, the extraordinarily sensitive Rogier van de Weyden (c. 1399–1464), effected a transi-

3.42b

3.42c

3.42d

›3.43 **JEAN FOUQUET** (c. 1390–1441), Madonna and Child (c. 1452–55; Antwerp, Royal Art Museum).

3.43

tion to a monumental, lapidary corporeality through familiarity with the somewhat jagged sculptural tradition of his native Tournai – the angularity enhancing the pathos. And the context for his greatest representations of Christian themes is still resolutely Gothic: not for two generations were his followers to show much interest in Classical form, rational construction of space or Leonardesque *sfumato*.**3.42b,c**

In France, when peace and Valois patronage encouraged the revival of the arts, painting effected the transition from Limbourgeois illumination – and the 'International Gothic' style - to large-scale devotional work and portraiture with eyes variously focused on Flanders but not blind to Florence: the influence of van de Weyden was, of course, direct in the northern provinces bordering Flanders; in the new royal heartland of the Loire valley, on the other hand, Jean Fouquet experimented with van Eyck's coloristic gradation of space but renounced Gothic floridity for Florentine Classicism – of which he acquired first-hand familiarity in 1445.**3.43** In the royal circle Jean Clouet, from Antwerp, was the major contributor to the development of the French Renaissance style of portraiture, penetrating in its psychology.

To England, where later peace prompted similar revival, Flemish influence flowed with trade and made its mark in portraiture – especially in the reign of Henry VIII. And the Flemish style naturally asserted itself at the court of the emperor Maximilian and his Burgundian consort, as in Spain where their son was sent in marriage and where several generations of Flemish artists and architects had preceded him to satisfy the taste of prolific patrons for hybrid Gothic-Mudéjar prolixity – as we have seen (pages 466ff).

In the disunited Empire, the sculptural Flemish style met disparate influences but colonized Cologne and the northern Rhineland and prompted the development of an idiosyncratic school of engraving in the middle Rhineland.**3·44** Elsewhere in central Europe it was variously compounded with the Limbourgeois fantasy beloved of courts, the material representationalism favoured by the bourgeoisie, the mystical expressionism promoted by the devotees of fundamentalist evangelicals and Italian humanist ideals.

›3·44 MARTIN SCHONGAUER: Tempation of S. Anthony (mid-1480s?).

DÜRER

The most important northern conveyor of Italian influence to other northerners in the late-5th century was undoubtedly Albrecht Dürer (1471–1528). Trained as a goldsmith and therefore adept at engraving plates, it was as a book illustrator that he emerged as the supreme mastery of the pessimistic native expressionism. And it was with printing and engraving – wide disseminators of Renaissance ideals across the Alps – that he acquired his humanism and his impulse to visit Italy.

From 1491 he was in Venice where his native interest in the vitality of nature in landscape – and supreme facility for recording it – were enlightened with coloristic lyricism.

▸3.45 DÜRER: Madonna of the Rosary (oil on wood panel, 1506; Prague, National Gallery).

The emperor Maximilian I is shown to the right in attendance.

He also went to the Classicizing school of Mantegna where, in addition to the antique repertory of forms, he mastered the scientific construction of perspective. And his extraordinary range extend to Leonardesque atmospheric profundity – perhaps in Milan on the return home. In Nuremberg from 1495 – and Venice again from 1505–07 – his accomplishment was not lost on the emperor or, therefore, the empire.**3.45**

3.48a

1 BRUNELLESCHI AND EARLY RENAISSANCE BUILDING

Long before Mantegna, the builders contemporary with Ghiberti, Donatello and the younger Masaccio had begun the transformation of their medieval legacy by referring to the antique for lessons in construction. Like the painters, however, they soon saw that the Orders of Classical architecture reflected idealized man in their proportions and sought a new harmony in building design through the application of consistent mathematical ratios. Principle apart, moreover, they soon learned to incorporate ancient building types – particularly the triumphal arch – as iconographically relevant motifs in their designs and then to recall Roman gravitas in both mass and space. Filippo Brunelleschi was the empirical pioneer and his primary objective was the vaulting of the great octagon of the Florentine cathedral.

INNOVATION AND ANTIQUE STRUCTURE

The plague of 1348 had halted progress on the construction of the Florentine cathedral as projected c. 1290 by Arnolfo di Cambio in rivalry with the Sienese (page 408). Work was proceeding again by the early 1360s: Gothic stone vaulting had been decided upon, in place of a timber truss roof, and the incorporation of a great vaulted octagon – of the kind ultimately constructed – is first recorded soon after. Debate ensued on how to proceed: recurrent war with the Ghibelline Visconti of Milan, whose patronage encouraged an influx of Germans, aroused Guelf Florentine antipathy to Gothic intrusion which wariness of French influence over Angevin Naples did nothing to allay.

In 1367 a committee of guild members, lawyers and other professional practitioners endorsed an essentially

Romanesque approach to the future construction of the cathedral: heavy load-bearing walls rather than a Gothic skeleton with flying buttresses, and oculi instead of lancet windows. This determined the form of the clerestory and the level at which the nave vaulting was sprung. Most important, it affected the mass and dimensions of the tri-apsidal octagonal crossing now projected to overawe the nave: more than the Sienese, this Florentine synthesis of centralized and longitudinal elements was to be highly influential.**3.46**

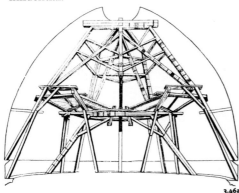

3.46a

The crowning of S. Maria de Fiori

Begun c. 1390, the great octagon of the crossing was ready for its vaulting at the beginning of the new century. Eluding Florentine builders, as yet, however, were the means for covering a centralized space of a scale unimagined since antiquity – at least outside Constantinople. The dome was not an unfamiliar feature in medieval Italy but no-one had yet con-tributed more than aesthetic preference to continuous debate on how to proceed: medieval practice – at Pisa or Siena for obvious example – offered no relevant guidance and theoretical calculations of the required magni-tude were beyond medieval mathematics – indeed, even provision of enough ground-based timberwork to support the centring usual for arcu-ate structure seemed impossible.

Brunelleschi, eliminated from work on the Baptistry in 1401, turned to the adjacent cathedral and its spectacularly pressing problem: apparently versed in Gothic building technology, as he was in late-medieval metal-

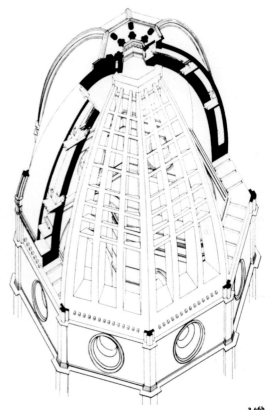

3.46b

working, he also turned to the antique – as he had done in the conception of his entry to the competition for the Baptistry doors. His first recorded intervention c. 1404 was to oppose reintroduction of Gothic elevation and lightness to the sanctuary and transeptual apses: weakening the effectiveness of these semi-octagonal masses as buttressing elements, this had been proposed to enhance the view from below of the fenestration rising over their ancillary chapel roofs. His second intervention was to recommend the raising of the dome over a drum to enhance its visibility from below: unlike the extraordinary low-slung dome of the rival Sienese scheme (pages 408ff), this recalls the Byzantine tradition exported from Constantinople to Ravenna (AIC1, page 784): an early Florentine humanist is likely to have associated the form with the antique.

The construction of a drum with oculi was approved in 1410. Eight years later, competitive tender was invited for models for the vaulting. Brunelleschi's submission developed the Gothic ribbed form of the original conception, represented by Andrea da Firenze. Double-shelled, however, his design was innovative for Europe (but not Islam; see AIC3, page 115): the shells – of sandstone for the lower courses, brick above – decrease in thickness from bottom to top and the cavity between them contains service stairs; eight tapering sandstone angle ribs, expressed with marble ridges to the exterior, transmit the load primarily to the projecting corners of the octagon; sixteen intermediate ribs, one pair concealed in each side, hold the shells. The ribs provided permanent centring for the construction of the vault in the medieval manner and corner bracing between the main ones and their neighbours is effected with segments of vaulting like small flying buttresses. However, the lateral thrust is restrained not with flying buttresses and exposed tie-beams but by incorporating stone and timber belts joined with iron clamps and secured with iron rods.

Imperial Roman engineers often incorporated horizontal and vertical fillets of masonry in their domical vaulting. As the concrete with which they worked was essentially homogeneous, hardly susceptible to the constraint of tensile devices, this was primarily to facilitate construction but Brunelleschi may well have accorded primary structural significance to the ribs and bands of such a work as the dome of the so-called Temple of Minerva Medica (AIC1, page 624). In any case, pragmatism recommended

›3.46 FLORENCE: CATHEDRAL OF S. MARIA DE FIORI: (a) 'flying' scaffolding and work platform (drawing published in a survey of the cathedral, 1755, by the then superintendent of works, Giovanni Baptista Nelli, as reproducing a Brunelleschian original), (b) structural diagram of the dome as projected by Brunelleschi, (c, d) exterior and interior of the dome with later frescoes by Giorgio Vasari and Federigo Zuccari.

The debate over whether construction should proceed in an essentially Gothic or Romanesque manner is reflected in a fresco by Andrea da Firenze, completed before the outcome: flying buttresses and Gothic windows appear in the clerestory but similar buttresses, etched on the plaster, were subsequently deleted from the main structure of the octagon.

Brunelleschi's model has disappeared but his written specifications for it survive and have been found to be in close proportionate relationship to the executed work (1:12, given 72 braccia or c. 42 metres as the diameter of the octagon constructed by 1400).

3.46c

3.46d

belting to builders faced with splaying masonry domes and Byzantine practice, most spectacularly represented by the post-1346 reconstruction of the ribbed dome of Hagia Sofia with iron clamps linking the stone cornice blocks into a chain, may well have been transmitted to Florentines by an influential Byzantine scholar such as Manuel Chrysoloras.

Brunelleschi demonstrated to the adjudicators that his conception could be realized with limited centring raised on a work platform supported at the level of the drum, obviating the traditional timber structure rising from the ground (AIC1, page 553). He was finally appointed to the task – not without the unwanted association of his rival Ghiberti – early in 1420. Developing his structure as work proceeded – and inventing machinery for hoisting the huge amount of material needed at the workface – he had overseen the completion of the dome by 1436.

The cardinal sides of the octagon, breached by major arches, were buttressed by the structures of nave and tribunes but Brunelleschi's conception of the dome entailed buttressing exedrae on the other four sides. And, of course, there was to be a crowning lantern. The design of these, perfected later, was to be in harmony with a high arcaded gallery projected above the drum: unfortunately the design of the latter was changed for execution after Brunelleschi's death and work on it terminated in condemnation by Michelangelo.

In realizing the project for his dome, Brunelleschi won his fame for heroism in confronting its gigantic problems and for ingenuity in effecting its vital synthesis between antique and Gothic practice. Most significantly perhaps, he is celebrated for the liberation of design from the constraint of medieval resource – traditional and material.

›3.47 FLORENCE, OSPEDALI DEGLI INNOCENTI, from 1419: (a) façade, (b) plan, (c) court.

Founded for the care of abandoned children, under the auspices of the Guild of Silkworkers and affiliated goldsmiths, the building was supervised by Brunelleschi until 1424 when he resigned due to pressure of work at the cathedral. The termination of the loggia under others has generally been found problematical.

The immediate precedent for ordering the plan of a hospital was S. Maria Nuova (founded 1288, enlarged in the early 15th century). Working on a much smaller scale, Brunelleschi's order extended to similar blocks containing dormitories and the chapel to either side of a square court but not to overall planning: the main line of communication is deflected from the centre by the eastern court.

Innovative in modular regularity and Classical detail – unfluted columns and fluted pilasters, Corinthianesque capitals, roundels in spandrels – the loggia is most likely to have been inspired by that of neighbouring S. Matteo (1384) but it conforms to venerable tradition: apart from the ubiquitous ecclesiastical cloister,

3.47a

loggias were common along medieval Italian streets. It was reproduced on the opposite side of the piazza (1518) and before Santissima Annunziata c. 1600 for the Servites.

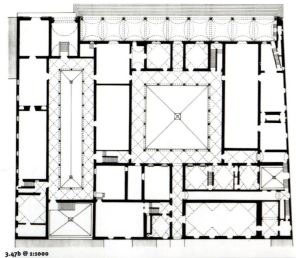

3.47b @ 1:1000

3.47c

ARTICULATION

Looked at anew with eyes reopened to the appreciation of humanist values, the physical reality of Classical building was obviously articulated for comprehension by the mind of man. Not veiled in mystical symbolism, like the archtypical Christian church (AICI, pages 822ff), essential to them was an order that sentient beings could appreciate, an order based on mathematical principles and on structural logic. In promoting the revival of these antique humanist values in architecture, Brunelleschi and his contemporaries lacked the historical perspective provided by a clear definition of chronology: they saw them as readily in the ordering of Romanesque works like S. Miniato al Monte or the Florentine Baptistry as in Roman ones like the Pantheon itself (AICI, page 616, and see above, pages 80, 90). In fact, thus, his early works were more Romanesque than Roman but his contemporaries saw him as a great innovator, returning to antiquity for the principles of truth.

We know that the arcading applied to the exteriors of S. Miniato or the Florentine Baptistry – let alone the columns taken from antique buildings and reused out of context in the nave of S. Miniato – do not constitute an Order in the Classical sense. Brunelleschi had yet to grasp that in 1419 when he initiated the Florentine Renaissance of humanist principles in architecture with the Ospedale degli Innocenti (Foundling Hospital). However, if he was yet to understand that the Classical Orders embraced both load and support in the trabeated structural tradition – post and beam, column or pilaster and entablature but not arch – he asserted the importance of regularity and conformity to a standard of dimension in plan and detail. The contrast with the Gothic tradition sustained in contemporary – and later – work in Florence and elsewhere in Italy could hardly be starker.**3.47, 2.151, 2.361**

3.48b

THE CHURCH

In several commissions, large and small, Brunelleschi established the two basic approaches to church planning which were to preoccupy architects in Italy and abroad throughout the whole course of development of revived Classicism: the centralized forms of square or circle and the Greek cross of equal arms, developed from or within them; the Latin cross of the longitudinal basilican form, overtly symbolic, hallowed by tradition, but disciplined with rational geometry and a consistent series of mathematical ratios. The latter was preferred by the Church authorities for the liturgy of congregational worship at parish or diocesan level. The former, preferred by

>3.48 FLORENCE, BRUNELLESCHI'S BASILI-CAS: (a–d) S. Lorenzo (c. 1420) overview (pages 710–711) with Medici palazzo (centre right), nave to sanctuary, plan, Old Sacristy interior; (e, f) S. Spirito (c. 1435): nave to sanctuary, plan.

The Romanesque parish church on the site descended from the 4th-century basilica of S. Zenobius which had been the cathedral until the 8th century. The commission to rebuild it on a scale to match S. Maria Novella and S. Croce was contemporary with that of the Ospedali degli Innocenti. Brunelleschi was retained at the instigation of Giovanni di Bicci de' Medici, who undertook responsibility for the east side of the north transept, including the sacristy which would provide his family with a mortuary chapel. The latter was commissioned in 1419 and the whole scheme seems to have been devised by 1421. Work was slow to progress, except on the sacristy, and stopped on Giovanni's death in 1434: it resumed again under Cosimo de' Medici's

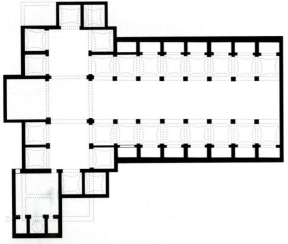

3.48c @ 1:1000

rationalist architects for the integral unity of pure geometry, was admissible for private worship, pilgrimage or commemoration: indeed the circle or the perfectly regular octagon was considered particularly relevant for shrines dedicated to the perfectly immaculate Virgin Mary – as in the crossing of S. Maria dei Fiore.

Brunelleschi was commissioned to build – or rebuild – two great Florentine basilican churches: S. Lorenzo and S. Spirito. Yet to see the illogicality in confusing the trabeated and arcuated structural system in either, he progressed from one to the other towards an understanding of the past, not only in structural procedure but also in basic planning – in the ordering of the plan and its conception as a unified entity.**3.48, 2.151**

patronage in 1442 but was furthered largely after Brunelleschi's death, with Brunelleschi's assistant and biographer, Antonio Manetti, as executive architect.

3.48d

Reordering the basilica

A comparison of S. Lorenzo with S. Maria Novella or S. Croce clearly shows the degree to which Brunelleschi was dependent on local precedent – indeed he was probably commissioned to build on existing foundations. Instead of organic growth, however, the rational generation of his plan from an accretion of squares is immediately apparent: the existing work gave the crossing square; the nave is composed of four identical squares, half the dimension of each produces eight squares in series for the aisles and these, in turn, were later halved in depth for the flanking chapels. Consistency was lost in the transepts and there is a residual organicism in the disposition of the sanctuary and sacristies despite the reiteration of the modular crossing square in each.

In S. Spirito the square of the crossing was again adopted as the module, repeated once each for sanctuary and transepts, four times for the nave and quartered for the aisle bays. The last were to extend right round the perimeter, with hemicyclical niches gauged from their sides, but the two western bays, which would have bifurcated the main entrance, were deleted in the execution of a plain provisional façade. But for this the whole exercise is a thoroughgoing synthesis of the centralized and longitudinal – of the Greek and Latin cross.

3.48e

In S. Spirito the integration of main and subsidiary elements, as in a scientifically constructed perspective, is achieved through a consistently applied module in plan and internal elevation: as an aisle bay is half the width of a nave bay, the height of the latter is twice that of the former. There is no such clear relationship at S. Lorenzo: while the width of a nave bay is double that of an aisle bay, the latter rises to five-eighths of the former (i.e. the ratio of arcade to clerestory is 5:3).

In both works functional form and aesthetic device are identified in the column. The relatively light proportions of S. Lorenzo accord with the apparent insubstantiality of its flat walls. However, the narrower intercolumniations required for the greater load in the later work enhanced monumentality and the engaged columns framing the semicircular chapels generate the undulating mass which imposes its vitality on the peripheral space.

Commissioned in 1428 by the Augustinians for a new site beside the late-13th-century church which they sought to replace, the design for S. Spirito was not constrained by existing work. Finalized only c. 1435, its execution largely followed Brunelleschi's death in 1446 and dragged on until 1482. By then, however, the main walls were in place and the colonnades begun: apart from substituting three portals for the four semicircular exedrae projected for the west end, to match the perimeter chapels, the most obvious departure from the master's ideal intention – obviously too ideal for the client – was the extension of planar walls around the exterior to mask the recurrent curves.

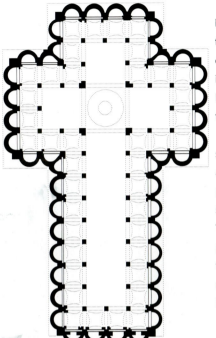

3.48f @ 1:1000

3.49a

›3.49 FLORENCE, S. CROCE, PAZZI CHAPEL,
from 1429: (a) exterior, (b) plan, (c) interior to north-east.

The project seems to have originated in the context of rebuilding after a fire of 1423. Work, begun in 1433, was unfinished on Brunelleschi's death. The portico was covered as late as 1461 with a saucer dome corresponding to the sanctuary within: its lack of accord with the interior suggests that it may have been an addition to the original scheme.

Defined by existing building, the site determined

The arcading tends to counter the monumentality of the Order but between the canonical Corinthian capitals and the arches in both works the introduction of a fragment of entablature indicates Brunelleschi's determination to assimilate the freestanding arcades with the full trabeation of the outer walls parallel to them, creating cross-vistas in perspective. It also demonstrates his awareness of the logical distinction between the trabeated and arcuate systems of building.

The Old Sacristy of S. Lorenzo is also based on a major and a minor square whose sides are in the ratio of 1:2. The main space is conceived as a cube crowned with a hemisphere. The Byzantine tradition provided the pendentives introduced to effect the transition from square to circle in support of the ribbed dome – as in the later crossing of the church itself. The purely rectangular lower half of the cube is defined by the same pilaster Order as that applied to articulate the church's outer perimeter: as the continuous entablature unites the major and minor spaces, the great arches in the centre of each side rise over it – as they would not have done in a strictly ordered antique triumphal arch.

The sacristy at S. Lorenzo and several other smaller commissions – notably the so-called Pazzi Chapel at S. Croce and S. Maria degli Angeli – allowed Brunelleschi to pursue the perfection of order in centralized planning, after the gargantuan example of the cathedral's crossing with which he was preoccupied throughout his career. And in the lantern which crowns that great work, still more in the exedrae which buttress it, he furthered the perfection of order in articulation based on the distinction between the trabeated and the arcuate.

The Pazzi Chapel at S. Croce, commissioned in 1429 as a sacristy with a burial crypt for the Pazzi family in emulation of the Medici foundation at S. Lorenzo, retains the system of articulation which distinguished the latter work though, naturally, with columns for the external portico instead of the pilasters applied to the flat planes of the interior walls. However, the expansion of the main space from a simple square through the addition of an extra half bay to each side, forming transepts, invites the introduction of segments of coffered vaulting in the antique manner announced in the portico.**3.49**

A thoroughgoing exercise in sculptural massing, anticipating S. Spirito, was evidently projected for the oratory commissioned by the Scolari for the convent of S. Maria degli Angeli in 1434: in the seminal revival of a major antique centralized planning formula, greater in weight and complexity than the accretion of squares, chapels are moulded from plastic mass to all eight sides of an octagonal space, revolving a Greek cross, and niches are gouged from the canted intermediate planes of the sixteen-sided exterior. The main arches of the octagon still rise from pilasters below the main entablature and they are repeated below a second entablature in the drum of a ribbed dome which, like that of S. Maria del Fiore, is lit through oculi.**3.50**

Within two years the system adopted for the articulation of the interior of S. Maria degli Angeli had been adapted for the exterior of the octagonal lantern with which Brunelleschi was called on to complete his cathedral work: now the arched windows, supported by the half columns of a minor Order, are framed by the pilasters and continuous entablature of the major Order – against which flying buttreses in the form of antique shell-head niches are prophetically surmounted by consoles turned into volutes. And three years later still, in the context of the perfectly clear differentiation of the trabeated and the arcuate, the gravitas expressed in space for the Scolari oratory was impressed on mass for the exedrae added to buttress the exposed sides of the cathedral's great octagon: the contrast between Brunelleschi's new Classicism and the Romanesque ordonnance from which he took his departure is particularly revealing.**3.51**

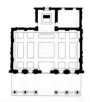

3.49b @ 1:1000

3.49c
the oblong development of S. Lorenzo's cube. Light is admitted through the lantern, oculi in the dome and windows in the façade: the frames of the last are repeated about blind panels in the minor bays opposite and to each side, below majolica roundels. This was turned inside out and applied to the traditional type of public assembly hall in a contemporary exercise for the Guelfs (Palazzo di Parte Guelf).

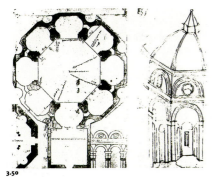

3.50

›**3.50 FLORENCE, S. MARIA DEGLI ANGELI, SCOLARI ORATORY,** from 1434: plan and interior perspective attributed to Giuliano da Sangallo, reputedly recording Brunelleschi's intentions (Florence, Laurentian Library).

Work, begun in 1434, was suspended in 1437: it was completed after 1934 on the basis of the surviving documentary evidence – which did not run to the exterior. An obvious antique precedent for the conception of space as moulded by mass rather than delineated by plane is provided by the so-called Temple of Minerva Medica, though that had ten sides (AIC1, page 624).

›**3.51 FLORENCE, CATHEDRAL DOME:** (a) lantern (after 1436), (b) south-western exedra (after 1439).

The model for the lantern was prepared – or at least revised – for a competition held after construction of the dome had been completed in 1436: winningly, it effected synthetic transition from the ribs of the essentially Gothic dome to a Classical tempietto – the scheme of S. Maria degli Angeli turned inside out with a parapet of niches in place of the arcaded drum and the revised pilasters bent uncanonically about the corners – by means of the seminal volute buttresses. Work began on the scheme just before Brunelleschi's death in 1446, and was completed over the next two decades by Michelozzo, Bernardo Rossellino and Antonio Manetti (Brunelleschi's biographer).

Necessarily massive, the semicircular tempietti of the exedrae incorporated niches framed by a Corinthian Order of engaged columns, novel in their pairing. The latter device obviously enhanced the impact of the relatively small-scale Order when viewed from the ground and to counter the distortion of foreshortening from that low viewpoint, Brunelleschi applied his expertise in perspective to the adjustment of their proportions – as in the detail of the lantern too.

Ornament was largely confined to voids – friezes, spandrels, pendentives, blind arches – in Brunelleschi's work until structural form becomes decorative in the conception of the cathedral lantern: consoles become volutes, above all the arch is extracted from a load-bearing role and spun into a sort of inverted scalloped valence of niches around the base of the conical cap. Well before this, Brunelleschi's contemporaries were less fastidious – or more lavish – especially on the relatively small scale of church furnishings.

3.51a

3.51b

›3.52 THE EARLY RENAISSANCE FLOREN-TINE AEDICULE ASSOCIATED WITH DONA-TELLO: (a) Orsanmichele, designed for a statue of S. Louis, now containing Verrocchio's Christ and S. Thomas, c. 1425; (b) S. Croce, Annunciation relief and frame.

›3.53 THE EARLY RENAISSANCE TOMB ASSOCIATED WITH DONATELLO AND MICHEL-OZZO: (a) Pope John XIII (Baldassare Coscia, died in Florence 1419) in the Florentine Baptistry, c. 1424–28; (b) Cardinal Rinaldo Brancaccio, S. Angelo a Nilo, Naples, 1426–28.

The papal tomb executed between 1424–28 was the first of Michelozzo's collaborative efforts with Dona-tello: the effigy in gilt bronze is due to Donatello but the rest is difficult to attribute individually. Essential to the formula is the aedicule as arcaded baldacchino over the deceased's effigy on a bier and sarcophagus: the earlier example was crowned by the papal device and had a medallion of the Madonna above the effigy; the later one, with fluted columns, has the Madonna medallion elevated to a convoluted pediment.

3.53a   3.53b

    Tombs, pulpits, singing galleries and the aedicular frames to statue niches or relief panels were naturally the preserve of sculptors. Leading the field, Donatello exhib-ited the virtuoso eccentricity which was to characterize the so-called Mannerist architecture of the following century, itself inspired by the licence taken by antique designers in freeing themselves from rule and convention. The aedicule which originally housed his statue of S. Louis of Toulouse at Orsanmichele (c. 1425), or the Annunciation tabernacle in S. Croce both distinguish between the arcuate and the trabeated. The former is canonical in framing one with the other but not in adopting the spiral fluting of antique Roman eccentrics for the minor Order. Uncanonical in detail too, the S. Croce tabernacle is hardly less significant in its enjoyment of a pediment rolled into a semicircle by volutes spun from consoles.**3.52**

›3.54 MONTEPULCIANO, S. AGOSTINO: façade (late-1430s).

Attribution to Michelozzo is based on style. Like the pediment medallion of the Neapolitan Brancaccio tomb, the semicircular tympanum of the main portal is framed by a blind arch which begins conventionally with quadrant curves but is cut off, as it were, the upper arc extracted and broken into two parts which are then reversed and reinserted so that the frame undulates from curve to counter-curve in a manner reminiscent of the last phase of flamboyant Gothic – but with essentially Classical architrave mouldings.

›3.55 FLORENCE, S. MARCO: library (c. 1436).

The church of S. Marco – a hall partitioned for the monks, laymen and women as usual with the Dominicans – was given a vaulted choir and a bell tower but the cloister at the heart of the medieval monastic buildings was rebuilt with Ionic arcades supporting new ranges of cells. The library is divided into three vaulted aisles by arcades carried on elegant Ionic columns like those of the cloister and the central tunnel vault is buttressed by groin vaults to the sides. Michelozzo had prior experience of renovating austere monastic buildings for the Franciscans at Bosco ai Frati (c. 1420). He applied it subsequently to the completion of Brunelleschi's scheme for the conventual buildings at S. Croce.

As Brunelleschi was preoccupied with the cathedral dome and progressing but slowly with Medicean work at S. Lorenzo, Cosimo de' Medici directed his considerable patronage to the sculptor-architect Michelozzo di Bartolomeo (1396–1472). He collaborated with Ghiberti on both sets of Baptistry doors and with Donatello on the tomb of Pope John XXIII within that building (1424–28). The aedicular formula developed there was translated to Naples for the tomb of Cardinal Rinaldo Brancaccio in S. Angelo a Nilo (1426) and was to be frequently adopted in 15th-century Florence and Rome.**3·53**

The façade of S. Agostino at Montepulciano, which displays a flamboyant mixture of Gothic and Classical elements not unrelated to the Coscia and Brancaccio tombs, has been associated with Michelozzo's early independent practice.**3·54** A little later in the 1430s, his first major religious commission from Cosimo was for extensive rebuilding in the Dominican monastery of S. Marco in Florence, including Europe's first purpose-designed public library: by then, experience of Brunelleschi's spare architectonic style had recommended simplicity but column supports arch still in the Gothic manner and regularity does not amount to Classical order.**3·55**

3·55

3.56a

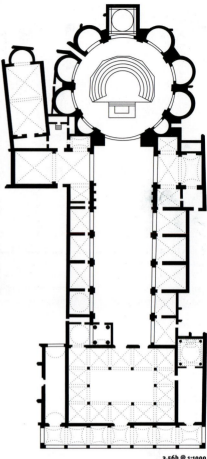

3.56b @ 1:1000

By the early 1440s Michelozzo was in charge of the Medici work at S. Lorenzo. He was appointed architect to the cathedral on Brunelleschi's death in 1446 with particular responsibility for completing the lantern. His contract for that enterprise was not renewed in 1460: he was replaced by Antonio Manetti. Meanwhile, he seems to have lost favour with the Medici perhaps because he was involved in litigation over project financing and supervision. Until then such pre-eminence had attracted many other commissions. Not least of these was from the Servite order of the Santissima Annunziata: work began on an innovative choir in the form of a rotunda there c. 1444 but was completed well after Michelozzo had left the site.**3.56a,b** His involvement ran to a ciborium for the Servites' venerable image of the Virgin which is related to the contemporary tabernacle over the Capella del Crocifisso at the head of the nave of S. Miniato al Monte (c. 1448). In these works he set the standard for elegant Classicizing detail.**3.56c**

›3.56 FLORENCE: (a, b) Santissima Annunziata: view from nave to rotunda (begun 1444, refection of nave from 1447) and plan; (c) S. Miniato al Monte, Capella del Crocifisso (1447).

Before transforming the existing Gothic basilican church into a hall with chapels in place of the aisles and projecting the atrium (Chiostrino dei Voti), Michelozzo had begun work on the polygonal choir which apparently had some financial backing from the Mantuan Gonzagas. Michelozzo left the scene c. 1455: it is unclear whether the scheme as realized is as he originally planned it or whether an enlargement, based on the walls of the original ambulatory, was effected at the behest of the patron who had designs on it as a dynastic funerary shrine: the available evidence is now more

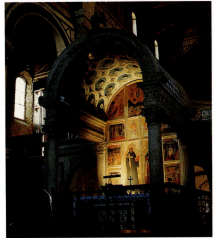

3.56c

generally interpreted as supporting the latter thesis but an author is elusive.

The Church of the Holy Sepulchre in Jerusalem (see page 184) provided the precedent, often emulated, for the attachment of a rotunda. As a prototype for the latter, the patron's purpose was well served by the so-called Temple of Minerva Medica in Rome. Brunelleschi objected to the juxtaposition of a rotunda to a longitudinal nave but Michelozzo was supported by Alberti who was involved in the completion of the project after 1470.

The nave was later overlaid with ornament, as was the ciborium sheltering the venerable image of the Madonna which was commissioned from Michelozzo by Piero de' Medici and executed c. 1448 by Pagno di Lapo. Something of the latter's original quality is conveyed by the tabernacle of S. Miniato ai Monte, with its varied capitals and rich detail recalling Michelozzo's early floridity, which was commissioned about the same time, also by Piero de' Medici.

›3.57 MONTEPULCIANO, PALAZZO COMMU-NALE: façade (c. 1440).

The type most prominently represented by the Florentine Palazzo Vecchio is revised with careful attention to symmetry in fenestration.

THE TOWN HOUSE

While Brunelleschi imposed Classical discipline on the traditional basilica, there is little evidence that he may also be credited with taming the fortified town house. He has been associated with palazzi projected for the Bardi, Lapi, Busini, Pitti and Medici but the sole concrete witness to his involvement in secular building is the fragment of the assembly hall begun for the Parte Guelfa c. 1420 and completed more than half a millennium later.

Cosimo de' Medici preferred Michelozzo to Brunelleschi for the design of his palace at least partly because the scale of the master's ideas – including a grand piazza – were evidently too grandiose for a covert autocrat. On

3·57

the other hand, Michelozzo had practical experience in revising medieval building types at Montepulciano, where he rationalized the medieval form of the Palazzo Communale.**3·57** This must have recommended itself to a banker bent on adapting the discreet block of the defensive Florentine mansion type to gracious humanist purposes without sacrificing its apparent strength. Michelozzo's response was exemplary.**3·58**

3.58a

Strength and grace for the Medici

The rustication of the exterior of the urban noble residence was common, if by no means universal, in later medieval Tuscany – as elsewhere in central and northern Italy (pages 774ff). Three storeys were the norm, but also not universal: they not only provided subsidiary accommodation for children and servants on the top floor but summer and winter apartments, at ground-

3.58b

›3.58 FLORENCE, PALAZZO MEDICI (later Riccardi), 1444: (a) cortile, (b) exterior, (c) plan.

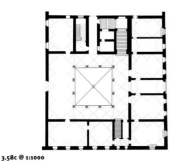

3.58c @ 1:1000

and first-floor levels respectively, for the patron and his wife. From ancient times, grand houses and apartment blocks had been fronted by shops at street level but a tax on rent discouraged this from early in the 15th century.

Persistent asymmetry in planning and alignment of voids reveals Michelozzo's difficulty in reconciling neo-Classical principle with medieval precedent. Except for the rare garden loggia, the lightest element was the cortile around which circulation revolved in superimposed galleries linked here by tunnel-vaulted staircases – Michelozzo provided two, one of parallel flights, the other L-shaped. The decoration of courtyard fronts with *sgraffito* – bands of plaster incised with florid or figural patterns showing white through a dark surface wash – had been common for at least a century: much less expensive than stone, it provided an alternative for the exteriors of more frugal builders than the Medici.

The plan of the Palazzo Medici is as rectangular as the site allows but the central courtyard is made to be square, as it was in the Ospedale degli Innocenti.**3·47** Like Brunelleschi too, Michelozzo was so obsessed with uniformity that he repeated the columns of the arcade mechanically even at the corners where the eye – if not the mind – requires greater apparent strength to cope with the thrust of perpendicular arches. The perpendicular façades, raised on a socle, crowned with a Corinthian cornice instead of battlements, uniform in fenestration, were originally open at street level with a corner loggia. Rustication was retained to accentuate dignity – and was long to do so thereafter – but the courses lose relief as they progress through three storeys graded with decreasing weight and height from bottom to top.

The impress of Michelozzo's work for the Medici was stamped on many subsequent Florentine palazzi, most immediately for the Pitti. Under construction by 1454 on its exceptional site at the edge of the town, the central seven bays of the Palazzo Pitti may be attributed to Bernardo

›3.59 FLORENCE, PALAZZO PITTI, before 1454: overview (lunette painting by Giusto Utens, 1599; Florence, Historical Museum).

The grandiose design – uncharacteristic of Florentines in its pretentiousness – is attributable to the plutocrat Luca Pitti, emulating but also self-consciously determined to overawe the Medici. If Michelozzo was not involved, it is likely that the patron was assisted by Bernardo Rossellino or Luca Fancelli.

Originally of seven bays, rather than the Medici's five, the façade closely follows the prototype in detail, except for balustrades on the upper two storeys, and it is more nearly perfect in its symmetry. Only the main range, facing the town, was begun for Luca Pitti but his scheme presumably incorporated a cortile surrounded by access loggias. The ground floor has a vast entrance vestibule and service rooms backed by loggias leading south-west to the main staircase with its parallel tunnel-vaulted flights. On the piano nobile a stupendous salone is flanked by apartments entered from the upper loggia: the main one to the north-east consisted of antechamber (closed to the salone) and rooms separated by a communication zone and a second antechamber; the other one, presumably for the lady of the house, had one antechamber.

3·59

›3.60 THE EVOLUTION OF THE VILLA UNDER COSIMO DE' MEDICI: (a) Trebbio (c. 1430), overview of converted fort and garden (lunette painting by Giusto Utens, 1599; Florence, Historical Museum); (b) Careggi (c. 1440), south front; (c) Settignano, Villa Gamberaia (c. 1450), raised loggia across enclosed platform garden; (d) Fiesole (c. 1460), overview with loggia front to garden.

Inherited from the middle ages, the chequerboard pattern of beds within the regular rectilinear garden enclosure remained typical throughout the 15th century, even after the widening of the central path to assert the main axis.

The property with farmhouse at Careggi was acquired by Cosimo in 1417 and became his preferred seat – and the centre of his literary circle – after its conversion into a villa from 1434. Cosimo and Lorenzo both died there, in 1464 and 1492 respectively.

The design of the Fiesole villa has been attributed traditionally to Michelozzo but may postdate his fall from grace: construction was supervised by Antonio Manetti. The original scheme is obscured by subsequent extension to the north.

Rossellino – of whom we shall hear more. Doubtless contemporary with the main block of the palace beside it was the enclosed garden to the left with its regular chequerboard pattern of beds – and most of the features we first detected in the formal gardens of ancient Egypt, transmitted to the Romans and recalled in the cloister of the medieval monastery (AICI, pages 142f, 541).**3.59**

VILLA AND GARDEN

The first step in transition from rural castello to villa seems to have been taken c. 1425 with the conversion of the fort at Il Trebbio, north of Florence, at the behest of Cosimo de' Medici: a regular block with asymmetrically disposed tower, its fortified aspect was not entirely compromised by the opening of windows in place of gunports.**3.60a** These remained irregular in the near-contemporary, nearby work at Cafaggiolo in the context of plastered walls flanking a central tower, and even in the next decade at Careggi,

3.60a

3.60b

where the informal suburban villa in which Cosimo attended his academy was not converted from a fort. **3.60b**

In contrast to the introverted palazzo, with its formidable outer walls and arcaded nuclear court, the villa is essentially extrovert, open of aspect: unlike Careggi, there is usually no nuclear court but, as at Careggi, at least one outer wall is breached by a loggia – as though the townhouse type had been turned inside out, as in the early days of imperial Rome (AICI, pages 540ff). At Il Trebbio – as at the Pitti on its unique suburban site – the garden was quite detached as an entity walled against a hostile environment, natural and human. It was to be several generations before humanism triumphed over medieval prejudice and encouraged man to enjoy the world around him: the elevated loggia of Careggi, breaching the security of the building to a minimum, was the first sign of change but its relationship with the garden has been obscured by time. At Gamberaia a similar loggia addresses a garden contiguous with the house but secure in the height of a gun-emplacement platform. **3.60c**

The main line of later development in the second half of the 15th century was the integration of house and garden with the extension of a dominant axis from the entrance right through the site. This depended on the low-

3.60c

ering of the loggia to ground level and its development as a portico enclosed by the house on three sides but screened from the garden on the other side only by open arcades or columns, as in the belvedere on the raised platform on high ground to the south of the Pitti, later incorporated in the Boboli garden.**3.59**

By 1460 a two-storey loggia had been incorporated in the Medici apartment of the Badia Fiesolana monastery and a grand arcaded one effected transition from house to garden in the purpose-built Villa Medici at Fiesole: both these works are attributed to Antonio Manetti who enjoyed the patronage of the Medici on Michelozzo's fall from grace. The Fiesole site overlooks Florence but the loggia addresses the enclosed garden on a terrace parallel to the view: the trappings of defence have gone but the world beyond was still held at bay.**3.60d**

3.60d

2 ALBERTI: THEORY TO PRACTICE

From mid-century, the overwhelming force behind the projection of Classical principles was Leone Battista Alberti who, as we know, was not an architect. His approach to antiquity was literary and when confronted by the concrete grandeur of the imperial past in service to the papacy bent on the restoration of Rome, his approach to antique architecture was archaeological.

Building seems to have caught Alberti's attention in Florence in 1434 when he returned there with Eugenius IV and encountered the eminently practical Brunelleschi. On his return to Rome in 1443 he embarked on the first attempt at its accurate mapping (*Descriptio Urbis Romae*, c. 1444). This was complemented by Flavio Biondo's archaeological guide to the ancient monuments categorized in a hierarchy of types ranging from temples down through public buildings to domestic ones (*Roma Instaurata*, 1446).

Enthusiastically espousing the cause of rehabilitating both his office and its seat, Nicholas V recognized the potential of buildings to proclaim power – specifically of the grand church as impressing the faithful with the authority of its builder – and pilgrimage provided the funds. The aggrandisement of the basilica of S. Pietro was entrusted to Bernardo Rossellino, who we shall encounter as a probable collaborator with Alberti. No-one was better placed than Alberti himself to direct the evolution of the urban aspect of these schemes and he translated the experience for posterity: his treatise on architecture, conceived primarily to relate antique precept to modern practice, was completed in 1452 and dedicated to the pope.

PRECEPT

A literary man, Alberti naturally approached architecture from the theoretical point of view though he was doubtless well versed in Brunelleschi's achievements in Florence before he turned to archaeology. A humanist who viewed the arts as free from their medieval subservience – from dedication to the evocation of supernatural ideals – he sought their regulation in accordance with the manifest truths of physics – and the precepts which governed antique humanist achievement. He had already expounded on optics and the scientific construction of perspective, as we have seen at some length. He had also already been in Rome and no humanist of his susceptibility could possibly have failed to be impressed with the relics of the Eternal City's stupendous past: knowing Rome – and knowing Brunelleschi – he believed that advance in modern building depended on comprehension of Roman theory. Thus, if Brunelleschi naturally proceeded *a posteriori*, the bent of Alberti's intellect was essentially – but not exclusively – *a priori*.

Familiar with Vitruvius from the mid-1430s, Alberti lamented the state in which the text of *De architectura* had descended to him – indeed the degree of obscurity with which he believed it had originally been presented. However, intrigued by the procedures it defined, he applauded its promotion of the order of perfect number and geometric purity, intrinsic to the beauty of form, over extrinsic ornament. Affirming architecture as the highest of the arts in virtue of its social purpose, he set himself to clarify its precepts and bring it up to date for his humanist peers. With reference to other commentators on antique theory – particularly Pliny the Elder – and against observation of imperial practice after the early Augustan age of Vitruvius himself, he codified the principles that were to guide the development of architecture as an intellectual discipline, rather than a craft, in his own *Ten Books on Architecture*. And he believed that in developing the tradition of the ancients, the moderns might 'acquire equal or greater praise than they did' (I.9).**3.61**

3.61a

De re aedificatoria

Alberti emulated Vitruvius in the number of his books and the organization of his material around the categories of *fermitas*, *utilitas* and *venustas* (strength, utility and beauty; AIC1, page 573)– but with more logic and consistency than his mentor. The introductory book I defines principles, outlines the history of architecture and introduces the Vitruvian categories. Books II and III deal with *fermitas* – working methods (including architectural drawing), siting, materials and construction; books IV and V deal with *utilitas* – planning, first in general in the context of the city, then in terms of individual types. Books VI to IX deal with *venustas* – intrinsic quality and ornament in the profoundest sense as the ordering of form in accordance with the concept of decorum or propriety governing the hierarchical gradation of the types from the church (or temple) down through the public domain to the house of the private citizen. Book X considers faults and their rectification.

Reborn humanism was fostered in the affluent town and humanists like Alberti elevated architecture to primacy among the arts due to its social purpose – as we have noted. Thus it is hardly surprising that in considering *utilitas* as the original concern of architects Alberti takes a broad civic view of the subject: moreover, he had provided the first comprehensive guide to the remains of the city of Rome which offered the most tangible exemplars from antiquity. He elaborates the growth of a town from the choice of its site to the interior decoration of its houses as an allegory of the harmoniously arranged universe, with all buildings disposed according to their function in hierarchical order. And, of course, function was as varied in nature as the individuality of users: Alberti distinguished mundane *necessitas*, idiosyncratic *opportunitas* and delightful *voluptas* as lending vital variety to the cityscape.

As *istoria* required nobility of conception, so too did the highest categories in the architectural hierarchy: decorum – propriety or appropriateness – raised building from a craft to a noble art. Alberti makes the point in book IX, after his exegesis on propriety: 'Architecture is a great thing which cannot be undertaken by all'. Proficient particularly in painting and mathematics, the architect 'must have intelligence and perseverance, excellent knowledge [of buildings in particular] and long practice, above all grave and severe judgement and counsel. For in matters of building the first glory is to judge well that which is fitting. To build responds to necessity; to build conveniently responds to necessity and utility; but to build so as to be praised by men of glory and not criticized by the frugal, only comes from the ability of a learned and judicious artist' (IX.10).

Vitruvius drew *venustas* from *dispositio* and symmetry: mirror-imaging across a central axis responded to the organic structure of man but congruity and modular consistency were the essentials (AIC1, page 572). In his book IX, Alberti defines beauty specifically in terms of *numerus*, *finitio* and *collocatio* – which may be translated, not without controversy, as the definition of the parts in terms of their dimensions, proportional relationships and appropriate distribution – and all three, properly considered and combined, effect an harmonious whole greater than the sum of the parts: *concinnitas* or 'congruity, that is to say the principal law of Nature' (IX.5). How this Ciceronian rhetorical ideal was to be achieved is left to the genius of the architect – except in so far as it is enshrined in the circle (pages 678f).

Intrinsic, not applied, Alberti's rationalist ideal is the beauty of Socrates: 'the harmony of all the parts ... fitted together with such proportion and connection, that nothing could be added, diminished or altered, but for the worse' (VI.2). Its 'judgement ... does not proceed from mere opinion, but from a secret argument and discourse implanted in the mind' (IX.5). Fundamental to beauty is number – the number enshrined by the immutable laws of Nature in proportions: *finitio*. In number is the truth underlying external appearances, the truth of the macrocosm reflected in the microcosm, man. A rational being, man is guided by rational precepts as is the art of building to fulfil his needs. Thus man remains the standard – in creating and inhabiting, but above all giving his proportions as the standard by which a harmonious building is judged. And the harmony of building is as the harmony of music: 'convinced of the truth of Pythagoras's saying that Nature is sure to act consistently', Alberti concluded that the 'numbers by means of which the agreement of sounds affects our ears with delight, are the very same which please our eyes and our mind' (IX.5).

Beauty is innate: imperfection might be concealed by ornament which was thus important, but auxiliary. The Orders are the highest form of ornament, elucidating *finitio* in anthropomorphic terms and associated by the Classical builder with structure. However, 'the chief and first ornament of

›3.61 ALBERTI, DE RE AEDIFICATORIA (1452, revised over thirty years and published posthumously in 1485 in Latin without illustrations): (a) title page of the 1550 vernacular edition (of the humanist C. Bartoli whose somewhat free translation was the first to include illustrations though these were far from comprehensive); (b) The Orders and the implication for their superimposition (after Giacomo Leoni, 1726): the illustration is, of course, anachronistic in style but

any thing is to be free from all improprieties ... so disposed [that] there is nothing throughout the whole fabric but what was contrived for some use or convenience, and with the handsomest compactness of all the parts ... so that you may not be so much pleased that there are such or such parts in the building, as that they are disposed and laid out in such a situation, order and connection' (VI.5).

Alberti's functionalist aesthetic did not encourage him to offer a self-contained treatise on the Orders, which might imply that *finitio* was especially their preserve: he deals with them in connection with the portico of the temple. Moreover, he is even somewhat ambiguous about the identity of the column. In several sections of his treatise (notably in books VII and IX) he draws a logical distinction between colonnade and arcade: the arch, being in principle a hole in a wall, is naturally supported by rectangular piers; the column, deriving from the post, naturally supports a beam and does not have the physical or visual strength to do otherwise. In contrast, at one point he describes a colonnade as 'nothing else but a wall open and discontinued in several parts' while elsewhere he likens columns and pilasters to bones, implying structural virility (III.6, VI.12).

In the section on the column which concludes book VI, it is certainly accounted as 'the principal ornament in all architecture ... for many of them set together embellish porticoes, walls and all manner of apertures' (VI.13). By implication they should be reserved – as and where utility requires – for the highest building types. These have their hierarchy – Alberti agrees with Vitruvius – and so too do the Orders. Logical and symbolic, that ranges from the strength and durability of the Doric – by implication, again, appropriate for ground floors and rustic buildings and the temples of warlike deities – to the grace of Corinthian (or Composite) – naturally applicable to top floors, to the palaces of the benevolent and to temples dedicated to the most refined of deities.

The decorum of the temple was one of his main concerns in defining typology in *De re aedificatoria*: book VII, with the four interpolated chapters on the Orders, extrapolates from antique precept to guide emulation by the moderns. Dedicated to a celestial deity, it should be elevated and preponderant, it should have the purity of form generated by centralized geometry – reflecting the prime elements of order in Nature. It should be

3.61b

Leoni's beautiful production was among the most faithful to Alberti's descriptions and measurements.

Alberti relates that 'the ancients ... considering that one building differed from another, upon account of the ... the purpose which it was to serve ... found it necessary to make them of various kinds. Thus from an imitation of Nature they invented three manners of adorning a building and gave them names drawn from their first inventors. One was better contrived for strength and duration: this they called Doric; another was more tapered and beautiful, this they named Corinthian; another was a kind of medium composed from the other two, and this they called Ionic ...' (IX.5).

In a passage on *finitio* more accurately according primacy to the Doric and Ionic over the Corinthian (IX.7), Alberti relates that the original Doric and Ionic Orders conformed to the perfect numbers 6 and 10, but that the Greeks resorted to arithmetical means to moderate their strength and grace: they added the two dimensions together and then divided the sum by half to establish the ideal of 8 for the Ionic; further, dividing the sum of 6 and 8, they arrived at 7 for the Doric.

The other two Orders dealt with by Vitruvius, Tuscan and Corinthian, represented the extremes from which Doric and Ionic had retreated. Alberti does not concern himself with Tuscan but was the first to identify a fifth Order, even slenderer than Corinthian, which he called Italic but which has subsequently been known as Composite in the definitive canon of five Classical Orders. The details of each are described – including the triglyphs and metopes of the canonical Doric frieze.

Alberti relates style to purpose only by implication – guided by common sense – and naturally the same applies to superimposition in his consideration of the tower: 'some architects have ... surrounded it with several porticoes like so many coronets ... The rules for these colonnades are not different from those for public edifices, only that we may be allowed to be rather more slender in all the members upon account of the weight of the building ... But whoever would erect a tower best fitted for resisting the injuries of age, etc. ... let him on a square base raise a round superstructure, etc. ... making the work less and less by degrees, according to the proportions observed in columns'. He specifies that there may be three, four or five Orders of columns (VIII.5).

vaulted for durability, have a portico to dignify its entrance and an apse for its altar. As in all the most elevated building types, all the parts must cohere as in a living organism. And just as the nature of its dedicatee determined the site and shape of the antique temple, so too it dictated the style – the Order governing its coherence: but Alberti does not elaborate.

The fundamental rule of Vitruvian propriety, indeed, is that type (style) of Order is determined by the type of building (AIC1, page 574): beyond stylistic propriety, Alberti is concerned with pervasive harmony (IX.5,6). The size and spacing of columns naturally respond to the scale of the building but the proportions of the rooms styled by them within it are determined by deriving the mean (height and hence Order or style) from the two extremes (length and breadth) in accordance with the ratios produced by the Pythagorean analysis of the musical scale. Pythagoras maintained that when four similar strings related in length to one another as 6:8:9:12 are similarly vibrated, the consonant intervals between them may be expressed as ratios: 1:2 (i.e. between the strings of 6 and 12) produce the octave; 2:3 (the strings of 6 and 9) and 3:4 (the strings of 6 and 8) respectively vary pitch by a fifth and a fourth. As Alberti points out, the ratios may be applied directly to the length and breadth of planar composition but harmonious volumetric composition derives the tertiary term for the height from the concordant interval between the extremes (which, after *Timaeus*, is defined as 'the mean exceeding one extreme and being exceeded by the other by the same fraction of the extremes') – unless recourse is had at will to arithmetic or geometric means (respectively, half the sum of the extremes and the root of the product of their multiplication).

Alberti was Platonic – and Augustinian – in seeing *venustas* as intrinsic to design, objective not subjective, dependent not on personal taste for applied ornament or the material qualities of fabric but on universal principle, above all harmony in number – *finitio*. However, in accordance with natural law and universal principle, *concinnitas* requires the union of proportion in the measure of the parts – *finitio* – with their number and distribution – *numerus* and *collocatio*. Thus Alberti clearly found no inconsistency in also seeing beauty with Aristotle in fitness for purpose, analyzing building in the biological terms of skin, bone and muscle (III.12). Fitness for purpose is essential to decorum and hence has moral overtones deriving beyond Vitruvius from Cicero – and the high plane of Platonic truth.

As in *istoria*, so in his quest for the ideal of architectural order, Alberti was Aristotelian in method. Accepting from Vitruvius that the dimensions of buildings were defined in accordance with the perfect numbers enshrined in the ideal measurements of man, resounding through the cosmos in harmony, and having defined the ideal against a wide range of samples in the table appended to *De statua*, Alberti was able to apply to the measurement of buildings – both in surveying the past and projecting the future – the standard used by the ancients themselves. However, as he was perfectly aware, the ancients had not been consistent even in the dimension of the basic unit of measurement, the foot. Therefore, just as the ideal in human proportion was deduced from a wide rage of samples, so the ideal in building was reduced to the mean established by comprehensive survey. And Alberti claims to have surveyed every ancient building of note which he encountered and to have learned more from the works than the writers.

Thus, taking the rules for the Orders from ancient theory and checking them against ancient practice, Alberti the literary humanist liberated the modern builder from subservience to ancient precept and example: 'rather, taking their lessons as points of departure, we will look for new solutions and arrive at glory equal to theirs, if not greater …'. Alberti taught too by works as well as words. But, he cautioned: 'it is enough to have offered trustworthy advice and refined drawings to the asker. If one takes it upon oneself to oversee and complete the work … all the faults and errors of others will be blamed on oneself alone'.

›3.62 PERUGIA, S. BERNADINO: façade (1457–61).

The extremely popular saint died in 1444 and was canonized in the Holy Year 1450. Many oratories were soon dedicated to him under the monogram of Jesus. The elaboration of detail furthers the early approach of Michelozzo at Montepulciano (early 1430s) and Bernardo Rossellino in the service of the fraternity of S. Maria della Misericordia at Arezzo (c. 1433).

EXAMPLE

Evolving exemplary schemes based on his ideals, Alberti restored Classical gravitas to architecture. Each of his works may be seen as a manifesto on the ordering of architecture: through the application of an appropriate antique motif as well as rationally through pure geometry and integrated proportions.

In the refection of the church of S. Francesco at Rimini as a dynastic mausoleum for Sigismondo Malatesta, he provided a Classical envelope for an undistinguished medieval building whose interior was already being transformed with the decoration of chapels for the patron and his mistress by the sculptors Agostino di Duccio and Matteo de' Pasti. Illuminating indeed is the contrast between his style and theirs, especially the extreme floridity of Agostino di Duccio which, the Malatesta chapels apart, is most prominently displayed on the façade of the small oratory of S. Bernardino in Perugia **3.62, 3.63**

Alberti chose the triumphal arch as the key to the Classicization of the church façade in general and specifically for its significance as the threshold to immortality for the triumphant ruler with imperial pretensions. And it was to the Arch of Augustus in Rimini itself that he and his patron most readily looked for the model: not only was it to hand, of course, but recalling Augustus recalled the fountainhead of legitimate imperial power and the apotheosis of the ruler. Significantly, however, he replaced the Corinthian Order of the Augustan original with the Composite which he added to the Vitruvian canon (AICI, page 561).

Beyond satisfying Malatesta's pretensions, Alberti recalled with the Augustan motif the canonical antique distinction between column and arch which his own sense of logic had led him to stress in his treatise – and which Brunelleschi had finally realized in his late work on the exedrae of the Florentine cathedral. The point was to be

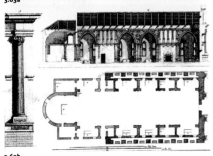

3.63a

3.63b

›3.63 RIMINI, S. FRANCESCO: (a) interior, (b) plan, section and Order, (c) west front, (d) foundation medal (Matteo de' Pasti, 1450).

Sigismondo's conception for transforming the modest friary church, in which the first lord of Rimini was buried in 1312, into a dynastic monument to his own glory was typically extravagant. Inside the existing aiseless church, the south-western pair of burial chapels, for the patron and his mistress Isotta, were

3.63c

3.63d

begun before Alberti's involvement by Agostino di Duccio and Matteo de' Pasti. The revised scheme, wrapped in a Classical envelope with niches for sarcophagi to front (closed in the event) and sides, completed the suites of chapels flanking the nave: it envisaged a tunnel vault in place of a trussed roof and projected a massive new mausoleum rotunda instead of the existing choir – apparently like Michelozzo's addition to Santissima Annunziata.

The scheme, for which Alberti produced a model as well as drawings to be followed in his absence in Rome, remained unfinished above the main cornice line: it is represented on the foundation medal with quadrants of masonry effecting transition from the lower bays of the chapel zone to the arch expressing the full height of the nave but Alberti is known to have superimposed S scrolls in pairs to either side of the central aedicule in 1454; unsatisfactorily, the outer columns carry no complementary load. Istrian stone was imported for the envelope but much of the marble, porphyry and serpentine used to clad the portal was pillaged from Ravenna. Matteo de' Pasti, who produced the foundation medal, was retained to oversee the building works.

made again in the monumental terms of the loggia built by him – or on his advice – for Pope Nicholas V in front of the Vatican basilica of S. Pietro: the motif was to be expanded across three storeys and restored to the full depth of an open arcade under the inspiration of the tabularium which had addressed the ancient Forum Romanum from the Capitoline hill (AICI, page 565).

Alberti's main concern at Rimini, perhaps, was to find an exemplary solution to a generic problem: how to devise a Classical façade for a Christian basilica. With high nave flanked by low aisles, the form was composite: in contrast, the Classical temple was an homogenous entity and Classical architecture promoted coherence. Accepting that duality was unavoidable, he unified nave and aisles horizontally by extruding the triumphal arch motif to cover the whole width, but he stressed the entity of the nave by extending the ordonnance of the central motif vertically.

Alberti's experiments with basilican façade design are generally thought to have next been furthered in Florence at S. Maria Novella, which had emerged unfinished from

>3.64 BADIA FIESOLANA, CHURCH, from c.
1461: (a) exterior, (b) nave to sanctuary.

Commissioned by Cosimo de' Medici for Lateran
canons, the architect is unknown: Manetti, in favour
with the patron c. 1460 has been suggested; Alberti's
advice is often assumed. The replacement of basilican
aisles with chapels is associated with the latter but
Michelozzo had already adopted such a scheme in the
Santissima Annunziata c. 1444.

the 13th century. Giovanni Rucellai, the richest member of
a family of wool merchants and bankers who maintained
a chapel in the great Dominican foundation, commissioned its completion in the mid-1450s. Attribution
depends largely on Vasari's assertion that Rucellai sought
Alberti's advice and received a design but as the work progressed under the supervision of others – invariably the
case with Alberti's schemes – responsibility was obscured.

The medieval Florentine tradition favoured the rich
combination of white and green marble as at S. Miniato
al Monte, where aisles and nave are distinguished in width
and height, or the Baptistry, where an attenuated Order
carrying blind arcades is framed by striped piers (page 90).
Still thought to be antique, the style was retained by an
unknown architect for the façade of the Badia Fiesolana,
where it bears no relationship to the semi-basilican interior.**3.64** It was developed at S. Maria Novella with engaged

3.64a

3.64b

3.65a

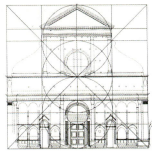

›**3.65 FLORENCE, S. MARIA NOVELLA:** (a, b) façade (c. 1458) view and analysis of geometry.

The 13th century left the façade with the base range of funerary niches continuing those of the churchyard and probably the blind arcading. The oculus is 14th century. The only evidence of Alberti's involvement is a reference to him as the designer of the marble inlay in the correspondence of the Dominican Fra Giovanni di Carlo.

Due to the rhythm imposed by the surviving medieval elements in the lower storey, the triumphal arch analogy is inexact. Pervasive is the ratio 1:2 (the octave), perfect for a Pythagorean like Alberti, who demanded consistency of proportion in building design. However, the centre of the oculus relative to the height of the whole is in the ratio of 6:10 (perfect to a Vitruvian). The circular geometry is repeated for the main ornament in the pediment and volutes which associate themselves with the portal into a cross. The application of one S scroll to each side was to be highly influential. As Alberti widened and heightened the façade beyond the actual dimensions of the church to achieve his 1:2 ratio, the relatively minor discrepancies between the physical reality and the geometrical conception (the whole within the square of 60 Florentine braccia) are doubtless to be blamed on the builders. The constraints of existing work obviously account for the lack of complete accord between the upper and lower Orders – which Alberti should have found particularly galling.

›**3.66 FLORENCE, S. PANCRAZIO, RUCELLAI CHAPEL OF THE HOLY SEPULCHRE,** c. 1458: (a, b) detail views; (c) Jerusalem, Holy Sepulchre: plan and side elevation (early 17th-century engraving).

The attribution to Alberti depends on Vasari and there is no documentary evidence for dating (other than the portal inscription registering completion in 1467).

columns on the lower storey recalling a three-bay Roman triumphal arch and a temple-front motif for the upper storey. New is the geometry: as the upper storey is virtually equal in height and half the width of the lower one over which it is centred between scroll volutes, the whole composition resolves itself into three squares within a square: extrapolation from Brunelleschi's approach to the determination of basilican plan and internal elevation is not improbable.**3.65**

Apart from the façade of S. Maria Novella, Rucellai also commissioned Alberti to provide him with a funerary chapel in his local parish church of S. Pancrazio – according to Vasari but otherwise undocumented. Claiming descent from a Knight Templar, Rucellai commissioned the remodelling of an existing chapel to encapsulate a model of the Holy Sepulchre in Jerusalem. That was supposedly conceived in the light of a survey commissioned by the patron. However, the architect imposed a regular Corinthian Order instead of blind Gothic arcading and a much smaller ciborium over the tomb chamber. The vaulting is recalled at the Badia Fiesolana.**3.66**

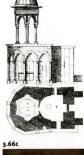

3.66c

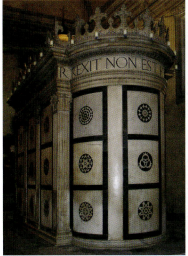

3.66a

3.66b

Alberti's other two important ecclesiastical commissions were both for Mantua. Ludovico Gonzaga instituted an extensive urban-renovation campaign there at the time of the visit of Pius II and his retinue – including Alberti – for a church council in 1459: the project was prompted no doubt in part by the pope's own recently acquired reputation as an urban reformer and partly by the presence of the now-eminent architectural theorist. The illustrious legacies of Mantegna's work on the private apartments of the castle are Alberti's work at S. Sebastiano and on S. Andrea.

S. Sebastiano is an exemplary exercise in centralized planning, combining square and Greek cross with an entrance loggia to the west and apsidal chapels at the ends of the other three arms. At S. Andrea, where he was again constrained by existing work and a dense urban site, Alberti was significantly innovative in revising the traditional basilican plan and in relating interior to exterior.**3.67**

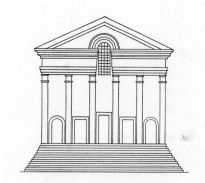

3.67b

›3.67 ALBERTI'S MANTUAN CHURCHES: (a–d), S. Sebastiano (from 1460), sketch plan and elevation (Antonio Labacco, early 16th century, ostensibly after a copy of Alberti's lost original by Luca Fancelli for Lorenzo de' Medici, 1485), reconstruction of façade after Wittkower (*Architectural Principles in the Age of Humanism*, 1962), exterior and interior; (e–j) S. Andrea (from 1470), section and plan of reconstructed hall church scheme (after Tavernor), plan of building as

3.67a

completed with domed crossing, general view and detail of west front, interior.

Alberti assured the marquis that his design for S. Sebastiano was complete in February 1460. Work began immediately and proceeded in haste, but it was never finished and its dilapidation was also rapid. Its original appearance is obscured, not least by its restoration as a war memorial in 1925 – with the addition of twin staircases to the west front, to supplement the 15th-century northern one, and rebuilt groin vault over console blocks rather than pilasters.

The peculiar rhythm of the ill-executed pilasters and voids on the façade are difficult to reconcile with Alberti's scrupulous logic – despite the antique fastigium precedent for breaking the entablature with an arch (as in the Arch of Tiberius at Orange, AIC1, page 602). Labacco's record omits a portico and the undercroft which raises the main volume above the marshy ground of a floodplain: Wittkower (*Architectural Principles*, etc., page 52) offers a reconstruction of the original project restoring the two missing pilasters and arranging steps before the basement arcades which, with their inadequate Order, he dates to the last phase of work on the building (from 1499). But for the manifest impetuosity of the patron, it is hardly plausible

3.67c

3.67d

Alberti in Mantua

Commissioned in accordance with a dream, Ludovico Gonzaga's votive oratory dedicated to S. Sebastian was sited in a marshy area of the generally unhealthy town, perhaps for the saint's protection against disease, perhaps in place of an earlier oratory. The centralized plan was considered appropriate for an exercise designed for a limited congregation, like Brunelleschi's oratory at S. Maria degli Angeli in Florence. As there – at least in the record made by Giuliano da Sangallo**3·50** – the main ratios in plan and section are as 6:8 and, though the cruciform element in the plan is more boldly expressed in Alberti's work, the conception may have included a central dome. The façade is much mutilated but the homogenous volume produced by the square in the plan seems to have been described with a temple-front motif.

In 1470 Ludovico Gonzaga determined to rebuild the Benedictine monastery church of S. Andrea so that a larger congregation could be shown the Blood of Christ, Mantua's holiest relic, which was exhibited there on Ascension Day. Alberti was consulted and responded with an 'Etruscan' scheme – by which he apparantly meant an apsidal hall with flank-

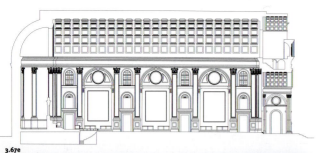

3.67e

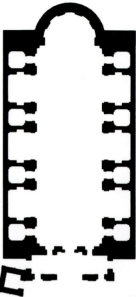

3.67f @ 1:1000

3.67h

that the need for the latter may have been realized after construction started, yet access arrangements were revised c. 1463 at the cost not least of progress. During his last visit to Mantua in 1470 Alberti reconsidered the entrance elevation and questioned whether the substructure was sound enough to support a dome.

Whether Alberti planned a cruciform termination to S. Andrea (like that later executed) instead of an apsidal end to the main hall is open to debate. It is known that the patron wanted economy and speed. More significantly, given a width of 40 Mantuan braccia and a height of 60, an apsidal termination beginning 120 braccia from the entrance (about 5 braccia more than the length of the existing nave) would have reproduced the proportions of the Temple of Solomon – the archprototype for reliquary churches, though the biblical account leaves its precise form elusive.

Stairs in the mass to either side of the portico lead to a space behind the pediment, below the so-called *ombrellone* which canopies the composition somewhat vacuously now: before the domed crossing was built, radically shifting the centre of gravity, it is possible that the Holy Blood was displayed to the congregation from its window, overlooking the nave, thus giving the portico a dual internal/external aspect. The interior articulation of end and sides doubtless included arched windows above niches between the paired

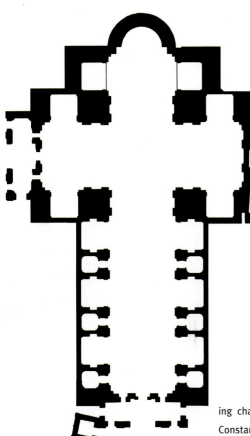

3.67g @ 1:1000

3.67i

pilasters, as on the façade: furthering concordance between exterior and interior, fenestration in the piers would not have contravened structural logic, unlike the present oculi below clerestory buttresses.

The building was executed by Luca Fancelli, largely unsupervised as Alberti died in April 1472, six months after the site had been cleared. Vaulting of the nave was nearing completion only in 1494. The cruciform east end was begun c. 1530 for Federico Gonzaga, the dynasty's most prolific builder, but the scheme was not fully realized until the 18th century.

ing chapels instead of aisles, like the Roman Basilica of Maxentius/Constantine (AIC1, page 615), the medieval church of S. Francesco at Rimini and the Badia Fiesolana.**3.63, 3.64**

For the portal Alberti overlaid a temple front on the triumphal-arch motif which centuries of church builders had found of compelling symbolic significance for the threshold to salvation. Limited by the existing tower to a width narrower than the volume of the church, it is defined by a square like the temple front which provided the upper zone of the façade of S. Maria Novella in Florence; like the lower zone there, moreover, the arched entrance is framed by a major Order – as in a three-bay triumphal arch – and supported on a minor Order in place of elementary impost piers.

Free from the standard basilican façade problem of welding nave and aisles into a unity, Alberti preferred ideal geometry to the physical reality of the main volume – like the architect of the Badia Fiesolana. He promoted the conceptual unity of the building as a whole: he imposed the intrinsically unified form of the temple-front/triumphal-arch motif and reiterated the device without its pediment to provide the internal elevation of the nave. The innate monumentality of the scheme is sadly obscured by the early 19th-century neo-Classical frescoed decoration though the vaults remain overwhelmingly impressive: it is stilted in accordance with Alberti's observation in his treatise that the purity of a semicircle is denied by a projecting cornice.

3.67j

Rucellai financial records indicate the acquisition of neighbouring properties for the expansion of his palazzo and that the process of integration had begun by 1450. Bernardo Rossellino (c. 1410–64) was then his architect and he may have retained responsibility for new work throughout. Apart from the attribution of the unifying front to Alberti by Vasari, however, it was clearly conceived independently of the amalgam of spaces behind it and follows the prescription for palazzo façade design given in *De re aedificatoria*: an odd number of doors with windows superimposed above them; void above void, solid on solid – the former twice as high as they are wide and equal in width to the latter.

Though it proved possible to develop a small piazza in front of the extended façade, the constraints of Rucellai's existing street frontage obviated the depth of the colonnade with which Alberti would ideally have distinguished a noble building. The constricted view from below, moreover, prompted an overt exercise in scenographic design with firm command of the laws of perspective: the height of the upper pilasters is extended beyond the canonical and their width sustained rather than diminished from bottom to top to obviate apparent disproportion. None of the Orders is 'correct' in antique terms and the introduction of a putative Doric was novel. Less than a decade later the Vatican Belvedere loggia belongs to another world.

The original five-bay scheme was expanded to the present seven after Rucellai bought a neighbouring property in 1458: its incompleteness betrays the intention to complete its symmetry by adding an eighth bay when further acquisitions allowed.

Alberti's conception of *concinitas* was never more clearly enunciated than in S. Andrea and, with the bold coffering of the great tunnel vault, Roman gravitas had yet to be as completely recalled. In suppressing the aisles and opening the side chapels directly from the nave, the plan was exemplary too: a century later the formula was adopted for the great church of the Counter-Reformation.

The sole essay in palace design attributed to Alberti, for Rucellai, is clearly the manifesto of a theorist.**3.68** Going beyond the abstract order of such works as the Pitti or Medici palaces in Florence, he actually applied superim-

3.68

posed Orders to achieve coherence through the articulation of the forces implicit in structure in the characteristically Roman way. No multistorey palaces survived from antiquity with superimposed Orders intact, though the type was represented by the remains of theatrical *scenae frons* and the Colosseum was the pre-eminent precedent for the procedure. Ascending from strength to grace, Doric, Ionic, Corinthian and a proto-Composite succeeded one another there and the blind storey at the top effectively seals the composition (AICI, pages 580–582).

The extent of Alberti's involvement in the realization of the project is unclear, but the façade of Palazzo Rucellai is uncanonical in its Orders and the termination of the composition is ineffective. The cornice at the top, logically proportioned to the Order of the storey which supports it, cannot relate to the whole; on the other hand, a cornice proportioned to the whole would crush the upper Order. The problem was insoluble and Florentine architects rarely again resorted to the superimposition of three Orders as a means of articulating a palace façade.

PLANNING AND THE URBAN COMPLEX

Like Vitruvius, Alberti advised on town planning and his principles are represented in the anonymous townscapes which we have already encountered.**3·33** Representing the reconciliation of the claims of the individual and the community, the buildings are harmonious in assimilation yet diversified: several are ordered in the manner of Palazzo Rucellai and the central rotunda of the Urbino panel has the hierarchical significance which Alberti required for the temple in his ideal town. Incorporating the square and circle, which define man in the Vitruvian figure and identify him with the ideal order of creation, this image of the ideal urban environment of man is obviously in general accord with Vitruvius but its rationalism stops short of Vitruvius's specific ideal (AICI, page 572).

Vitruvius's centrally planned, fully integrated entity was unrealizable in the normal course of real life, but the Albertian image was eminently practicable as a nucleus of order to be interpolated into an existing settlement. This is precisely what happened at Pienza – or rather at Corsignano which its most eminent citizen, Aenius Sivius Piccolomini, Pope Pius II, transformed into an episcopal and dynastic seat. A square flanked by palaces and dominated by a cathedral, the scheme as a whole is clearly a reduction of the ideal image in the anonymous painting: it is hard to believe that Alberti, a significant figure in the pope's entourage, was not the architect of the new order in both. Moreover, it can hardly be coincidental that Palazzo Piccolomini, built for the papal family on the northern side of the square, is virtually unique in its similarity to Palazzo Rucellai which was under construction during the papal visit to Florence of 1459. However, the work at Pienza, if not that on the Rucellai façade, seems to have been carried out by Bernardo Rossellino.**3.69**

3.69a

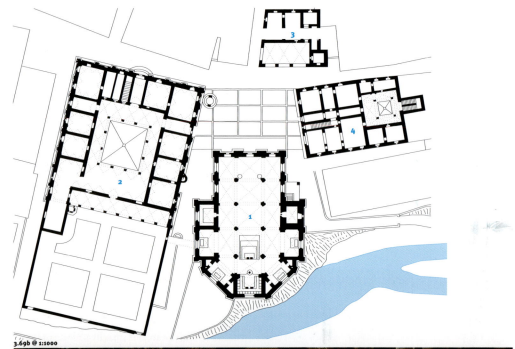

3.69b @ 1:1000

3.69c

3.69d

3.69e

›3.69 PIENZA: (a) aerial view, (b) piazza plan with (1) cathedral, (2) Palazzo Piccolomini, (3) Palazzo Comunale, (4) Palazzo Vescovile, (c) cathedral interior, (d) piazza view, (e) Palazzi Comunale and Vescovile, (f, g) Palazzo Piccolomini, side view showing loggia, cortile.

The transformation of Corsigniano was the first of its kind but remained unfinished as the palaces which members of the papal retinue were constrained to commission were not all executed. The core emerged as exemplary, however: the piazza with the cathedral (centre), whose dominance is enhanced by the trapezoidal distribution of the papal palace (right) and the episcopal palace (left). The communal palace and civic loggia complete the scheme opposite the cathedral.

Palazzo Piccolomini is less rigorous that its Florentine model in the determination of bay dimensions keyed to interior distribution rather than ideal symme-

3.69f

3.69g

try and, given a much more commodious field of view, the proportions of the Order are not adjusted to counter optical illusion but the ground-floor pilasters are rusticated and the cortile arcade is carried on columns without entablature. The entrance from the square is supplementary. The street portal, whose vestibule doubles the parallel flights of the main staircase, opens the main axis to the garden loggie and the superb view beyond: the result is a hybrid palazzo/villa. Consoles support the window sills and cornices for perhaps the first time.

In accordance with hierarchical propriety, the episcopal palace is simpler, unarticulated with Orders. The principal public building, the Palazzo Comunale, represents the ordering of the ubiquitous medieval Tuscan type but the arches of its loggia spring directly from the columns in the uncanonical manner. At the pope's specific request, the cathedral was modelled on the German hall type which he encountered as a diplomat on missions to the Empire: the elevation of the aisles required the uncanonical multiplication of entablature elements but the type obviated the problem of integrating the disparate elements of the standard basilican façade. The ordonnance of the Malatesta temple at Rimini seems to have been somewhat crudely extrapolated for the two registers framed by an elementary temple front.

ROSSELLINO

Bernardo Rossellino (c. 1407-64) was a sculptor from a family of stone masons based in Settignano. He seems to have begun his architectural career at Arezzo early in the 1430s, and gravitated to the papal court in Florence where he applied his eminence as a sculptor to the evolution of the tomb in his masterly work for Leonardo Bruni in S. Croce (c. 1446).**3.70a** He was in Rome early in the next decade, working for Nicholas V on the abortive project to extend the basilica of S. Pietro and contributed to the

3.70a   3.70b   3.70c

›**3.70 ROSSELLINO AND THE FLORENTINE TOMB:** (a) S. Croce, Chancellor Leonardo Bruni (late-1440s); (b, c) S. Miniato, Chapel of the Cardinal of Portugal (1461–69), vault and tomb.

Crowned with laurel and holding the work with which he earned it, the great historian reclines on a bier below an arch bearing his device. The epitaph, held by winged genii, sets the humanist tone in placing Bruni in the company of the great thinkers of antiquity, yet Christianity prevails in the tondo of the Madonna above.

The Portuguese chapel at S. Miniato is a square overlaid with a Greek cross, like Alberti's S. Sebastiano at Mantua: in the arm opposite the entrance is the sanctuary, in the cross-arms are the tomb and bishop's throne. After the work for Bruni, the tomb is the most distinguished early follower of the aedicular type devised by Donatello and Michelozzo for Pope John XXIII. The architecture of the chapel is attributed to Antonio Manetti. The ornament, restoring the drapery to the aedicule arch absent in the Bruni composition, is the result of collaboration between the Rossellini, Lucca della Robbia (the faience medallions in the vault), Antonio and Piero del Pollaiolo (the altarpiece, now in the Uffizi) and Alessio Baldovinetti (frescoes in the lunettes and spandrels).

restoration of ancient buildings while Alberti was engaged in his archaeological survey.

Involved in the work on Pienza in whatever capacity from 1459, he is credited with the translation of the hall type of Gothic church into contemporary Italian for the cathedral – at least in so far as the articulated piers are concerned. The hall type was admired by the pope in Germany but it had also been exported from Poitou to Spain, as we have seen, and Rossellino may have had experience of it at S. Giovanni degli Spagnoli in Rome under Pius II's predecessor, the Spanish pope Calixtus III (1455–58).

Rossellino was back in Florence executing the design for the façade of S. Maria Novella in 1457, if not that of Rucellai's palazzo. He assumed responsibility for work on the cathedral, most notably the completion of Brunelleschi's lantern, in 1461. About the same time he collaborated with his youngest brother Antonio (1427–c. 1479) on the celebrated aedicular tomb type for the Cardinal of Portugal at S. Miniato al Monte.**3.70b,c**

>3.71 MILAN, WORKS ASSOCIATED WITH
FLORENTINES: (a) S. Eustorgio, Portinari Chapel
dedicated to S. Pietro Martire (c. 1462–68), interior;
(b, c) Banco Mediceo (c. 1465), façade drawing after
Filarete and portal (preserved in the Castello
Sforzesco).

Michelozzo is credited with the bank by Vasari and
with the chapel by association – its patron was the
bank manager. However, Michelozzo was out of Medici
favour by the mid-1460s, when the bank project was
initiated. Filarete published the design for the latter's
façade and the work is clearly related to his own
Ospedale Maggiore façade. As a further complication,
it should be noted that Manetti, who replaced Michelozzo in Medici favour at home, was sent to Milan on a
mission to the Sforza in 1460.

The design for the bank is the premier essay in the
translation of early Florentine Renaissance forms into
the Milanese brick and terracotta vernacular: the prolix
effect was soon to be realized at the Ospedale Maggiore. And Milanese flamboyant sensuality subjects
Florentine rationalism to exquisitely elaborate embellishment in stucco, fresco (of the life of the saint by Vincenzo Foppa) and kaleidoscopic colour for Portinari at
S. Eustorgio (for the saint's tomb, see page 406).

3.71b

3 CENTRAL TYPES, REGIONAL VARIANTS

3.71c

In the middle decades of the 15th century, while Alberti was advising the pope in Rome, the Classical revision of the Tuscan medieval legacy promoted by Brunelleschi and Michelozzo was disseminated abroad. In the main, the lessons of the masters were translated by their associates, often the executive architects at their building sites – especially those working for Alberti. However, Michelozzo himself is reputed to have introduced Florentine principles of order to the north, working in the Milanese context on a bank for the Medici and, possibly, the chapel commissioned by the manager of the bank, Pigello Portinari, at S. Eustorgio: the attribution is disputed primarily in favour of Antonio Manetti, who emerged from the circle of Brunelleschi, and of the Florentine sculptor Antonio Averlino – known as Filarete – who emerged from the studio of Ghiberti.**3.71**

Before the Medici Milanese project was produced, Filarete was called on by Francisco Sforza to improve the fortifications of the castle. Presenting himself as the court theorist on architecture, he was commissioned to build a general hospital complex for the capital, to design the cathedral at Bergamo and to redesign an unfinished palazzo which Sforza had acquired in Venice. There is little to show for his efforts in Bergamo or Venice but he realized his synthesis between the medieval Milanese tradition and his own idiosyncratic Classicism on the grandiose scale of the hospital: his quincunx formula for church planning, the Byzantine cross-in-square with towers over the four corner chapels or sacristies, was to be particularly influential.**3.72**

The Renaissance of Classical architecture in the seats of the two great northern powers, Venice and Milan, was certainly no unified phenomenon. Each delighted in prolific ornament and the coloristic use of rich materials, masking rather than articulating structure, but their medieval traditions were disparate: the Byzantine inheritance of the one, and the continuing eastern influence on its luxurious trading elite; the great Roman inheritance of the other, and the Germanic influence exerted not least on the realization of its extraordinarily florid cathedral.**2.204** Yet the Renaissance growth, late in developing in both, was organic or, rather, it was grafted on to vigorous native plants – by Florentines in Milan and Lombards in Venice.

On the advent of the Florentines, the Milanese scene was dominated by three generations of the Solari family of Carona (Giovanni, born 1410; his son Guiniforte, 1429–81; his son Pietro, 1450–93) after Giangaleazzo Visconti had initiated the rebuilding of the cathedrals at Como and Monza and founded the Certosa of Pavia.**3.107** Also prominent was Giovanni Amadeo (1447–1522), who had married a Solari and was *capomaestro* of Milan cathedral from 1490, well after his decorative elaborations *all'antica* were eclipsed by the gravitas of Donato Bramante. Born in the orbit of Federico da Montefeltro's Urbino in 1444, the latter entered the service of Ludovico il Moro, the Sforza usurper, c. 1480.

In Venice, the Caronese sculptor Pietro Solari ('il Lombardo', 1435–1515) and the Veronese Antonio Rizzo (died 1499) first experimented with Classicizing the medieval legacy. From the 1480s Pietro was assisted by his sons Antonio (who left for Ferrara in 1506) and Tullio (died 1532) but

3.72

›3.72 MILAN, OSPEDALE MAGGIORE, begun c. 1456: entrance front.

The object of the new hospital was to bring various antiquated facilities under central control on the lines of the late-14th-century Florentine hospital of S. Maria Nuova (page 637). As the cruciform elements of that building were developed subsequently there is some controversy over the degree of Filarete's debt to it but his ventilation and drainage provisions were certainly the most advanced of the age. Problems with the Milanese builders in the attempt to effect a synthesis between the Lombard and the Tuscan and a dispute with his patron led to his resignation in 1465 and replacement by Guiniforte Solari: only the southern sector had been built.

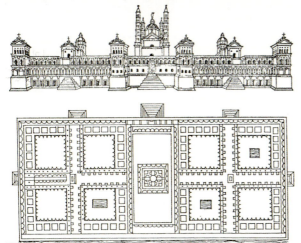

3.73a

the post-Albertian generation was dominated by the Bergamesque Mauro Codussi (c. 1440–1504), who is first recorded in Venice in 1469.

There were many others who made important contributions to regional developments elsewhere in all the Renaissance building types – whether or not they comprehended the changing attitude to antiquity manifest in Florence, Rimini, Mantua and Rome between the advent of Brunelleschi and the demise of Alberti. The most important were: Luciano Laurana (c. 1420–79), whose Dalmatian origin was far from the seminal Florentines but who emulated them at Urbino; the Sienese sculptor and engineer Francesco di Giorgio Martini (1439–1501), who was active in Umbria as well as succeeding Laurana at Urbino and who went on to Rome; the Florentine woodcarver/mason Giuliano da Maiano (1432–90), who rose to be *capomaestro* of the cathedral (1477) and ended his career in Naples as architect to the future King Alfonso II; the Florentine woodcarver Giuliano Giamberti (c. 1445–1516) from the Sangallo family, who emerged from the ambience of Alberti, worked in Rome and studied its monuments for about a decade from 1465, returned to practice in Florence under the patronage of Lorenzo the Magnificent but left again for Rome on the fall of the Medici in 1494; and the Florentine Simone del Pollaiuolo, 'Il Cronaca' (1457–1508), who left for Rome c. 1475, but returned after ten years to collaborate with Giuliano da Sangallo and ended as *capomaestro* of the cathedral.

THEORY AND PLANNING

In the age of Alberti the problem of interpreting and modernizing Vitruvius was a humanist exercise – not least philological. Alberti's work was conceived for the learned patron, rather than the practitioner: it remained inaccessible to most until it appeared in the vernacular in the mid-

16th century but by then there were wide-ranging alternatives. There were Italian editions of Vitruvius, with illustrations and commentary, of which Caesar Cesariano's not always accurate publication of 1521 was the first. There were attempts at emulating Alberti – with varying degrees of erudition – in 'modernizing' Vitruvius for both patrons and practitioners: Alberti's contemporary Filarete was first in the field in the vernacular with his extraordinary invocation to Francesco Sforza of the early 1460s. And there were compendia of more-or-less fantastic illustrations from which the genre of the pattern book was to emerge in the mid-16th century: the earliest and most bizarre of these is found in the *Hypnerotomachia Poliphili*, published anonymously in 1499.**3.73, 3.74**

Filarete's *Trattato di architettura* is presented as a 'dialogue' between architect and patron on the construction of an ideal city: the form is Platonic but the content is distinguished for imaginative invention, complementing practical information, rather than scholarly grasp of antique precept or practice. Unpublished, it was nevertheless influential in defining the stages of the design process in terms of the sketch *congetto*, the gridded *disegno proportionato* and the three-dimensional *disegno modello*. It also reconstructed the anthropomorphic basis of Classical architecture on Vitruvian lines, more obsessively than Alberti, adopting the idea of the origin of architecture in the primitive hut, crediting its creation to Adam and giving his ideal dimensions to its posts. Taking the head as the module, the Corinthian, Ionic and Doric Orders were then defined by extrapolation, bizarrely in reverse of the Vitruvian gradation from strength to grace.

Asserting the social eminence of the architect in his imaginary dialogue with his patron, Filarete was perhaps most influential in setting the precedent for ideal town-planning. The imaginary 'Sforzinda' was outlined to the

3.73b

›3.73 ANTONIO AVERLINO (alias Filarete, 'Friend of Virtue', c. 1400–65), *Trattato d' architettura*, (1461–64, revised and dedicated to Piero de' Medici after its author had lost favour in Milan, published in full facsimile in 1965): (a) ideal hospital plan and elevation transposed from the Ospedale Maggiore to Sforzinda; (b) Sforzinda, ideal city plan; (c) 'reconstruction' of the tomb of King Zogalia (Galeazzo Sforza) supposedly uncovered by excavation in the port quarter called Plusiapolis.

The work is part autobiographical – not without somewhat fantastic licence. It is marked by its anti-Gothic polemicism, contrary to the design of the Ospedale Maggiore façades. In fact, the buildings illustrated betray little of Florentine Classicism and the text is not noted for Florentine rationalism.

3.73c

duke as an octagon with radial streets on the 'Greek' model – though the diagram follows Vitruvius (AICI, page 572). As in the ancient ideal, forum and temple – piazza and cathedral – occupy the centre with markets disposed to either side and buildings are dealt with in the hierarchy of categories derived from Vitruvian precept but fully in accordance with the despotic authority of the patron.

Filarete's more fantastic individual building designs – especially the reconstructions of antique remains supposedly found in the excavation of Plusiapolis as the port for Sforzinda – clearly inspired the imagery of the *Hypnerotomachia Poliphili*, written thirty years earlier than its publication date and cryptically associated with one Brother Francesco Colonna. An allegorical 'romance', this bizarre chronicle follows the traumatic quest of a lover for the beloved through a landscape in which pseudo-Roman remains stand as witness to ancient man's achievement – but also, of course, as *memento mori*. The dream encompasses the fantastic 'restoration' of the antique architectural legacy with some knowledge of Vitruvius and Alberti as well as Filarete: the text is arcane in the extreme but the images were to inspire many generations of fantasists.

›**3.74** **HYPNEROTOMACHIA POLIPHILI,** first published in Venice in 1499, attributed to Francesco Collona and, more controversially, to Alberti: (a) the protagonist led through the ruined seaside necropolis called Polyandrion; (b) pyramidal tomb with obelisk; (c) Temple of Venus; (d) elephant with obelisk.

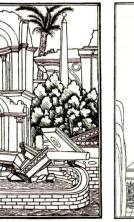

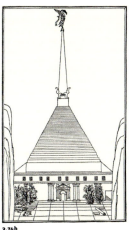

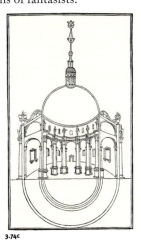

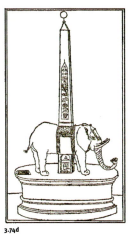

3.74a   3.74b   3.74c   3.74d

If Colonna took flight from Filarete's fantasy, the not-negligible practicality of Filarete the engineer and hospital designer was germane to the interests of Colonna's slightly younger contemporary Francesco di Giorgio Martini (1439–1501). More than Filarete, he was primarily a significant practitioner: a military engineer but also an expert in hydraulics, a sculptor, painter and architect whose major corpus of work – engineering, architecture and decoration – is in and around Urbino. Like Filarete, he wrote on the role of the architect but he was principally concerned with interpreting Vitruvian precept for post-medieval builders. Like Filarete, too, he illustrated his work but with less fantasy and he extended the medium to the translation of sections of Vitruvius – without Alberti's expertise. Like Filarete's again, his *Trattati* – actually two bodies of essays written over the last three decades of his life – remained unpublished until modern times but had considerable influence in manuscript copies – one studied even by Leonardo da Vinci. Indeed, through its influence on Baldassare Peruzzi (Francesco's

In accordance with his anthropomorphic bent in his earlier work, Francesco describes – and illustrates – the fort as the head on the body of the town. On the other

3.75a

3.75b

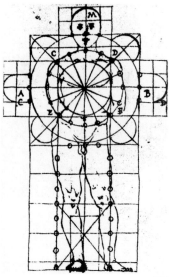

3.75c

hand, the ideal geometry of his town planning is not identified with Vitruvian man though he describes – and illustrates – the latter in square and circle and goes on to connect microcosm and macrocosm in the later version of his work.

Temple planning is governed by human proportions – ultimately enshrined in the Orders – and the ideal church is as overtly anthropomorphic in conception as the fortified town though antique prototypes are presented in the purity of centralized geometry without anthropomorphic bias. In this connection, Francesco reduces the diversity of church forms to three: round, rectangular and composite. He describes how to perfect the combination of centralized and longitudinal with the grid of his anthropomorphic diagram[3.75c] but, agreeing with Alberti that the circle represents ultimate perfection, he was exceptional for his time in his projections of the colonnaded rotunda – as was the author of the ideal cityscape in Urbino.[3.33b] Several other 'restorations' after the antique are included in an addendum to the early corpus out of concern to record endangered examples for posterity.

Francesco is credited with perfecting the bastion as a defence against artillery. He stresses the importance of setting fortresses low to mount and withstand cannon and of extending their regular geometrical perimeters with sharp projections to deflect shot and provide for maximum flanking. The lesson was not lost on Leonardo and his High-Renaissance followers.

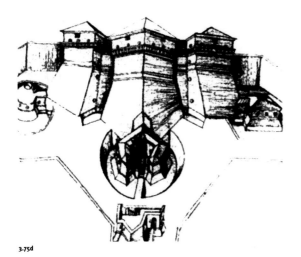

3.75d

younger compatriot) and his pupil Serlio, it prompted the compendium of artistic theory, centred on the decorum of ordonnance, and the pattern-book manual of forms which were to be of crucial importance in the widespread dissemination of neo-Classical ideals in the 16th century – and thereafter.[3.20a, 3.75]

In the first corpus, unsystematically compiled, Francesco is primarily concerned with military engineering, then with the anthropomorphic basis of order in architecture: he ultimately offers a more nearly canonical grading of the Orders than Filarete had produced and a complementary classification of religious and secular building types in accordance with the concept of decorum derived from Vitruvius. He begins the later – more systematic – corpus with the assertion of the fundamental importance of the study of the antique legacy and avows the intention to clarify Vitruvius in the light of his own comprehensive surveys. Books II and III deal with domestic architecture and the planning and defence of towns. Book IV surveys temple architecture: this extends to the consideration of the Orders as having acquired the proportions of the human body not in origin but in evolution – and Francesco is precise in relating the major constituent elements of the one to the other. Church follows temple and anthropomorphism achieves apotheosis: describing circle and square about the torso of a cruciform figure and doubling the extended grid for the legs, Francesco effects an essentially Christian synthesis between the centralized and the longitudinal in ideal church planning.

Shedding anthropomorphic trappings, he reviews ideal fortification planning in book V and other engineering exercises in his two final books. In marked contrast to Alberti's approach, the practical bent of his latest thoughts extends to the importance of drawing to communicate architectural ideas.

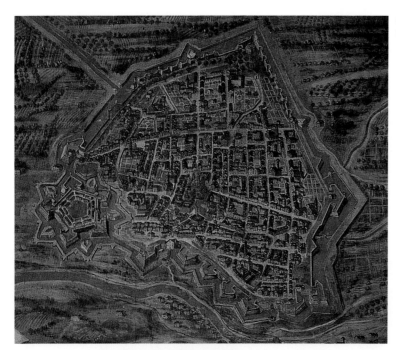

COMPLEX AND TOWN

Comprehensive urban planning on Albertian, ultimately Vitruvian, principles was rare in 15th-century Italy: it was largely confined to suburban development, as usual where non-colonial urban civilization is well established. A prime example is the Addizione Ercole of Ferrara, laid out on a grid within star-shaped fortifications at the behest of the ruling prince Ercole d'Este in the last decade of the century.**3.76** Otherwise, early Renaissance urbanism amounted to intervention in existing settlements, as at Pienza. This is effectively what happened at Urbino, though the intervention was confined to the acropolis of power and hardly touched the existing settlement. The vast palace complex, contemporary with the Gonzaga remodelling of a medieval agglomeration at Mantua but the most splendid of the era, was the seat of an enlightened ruler rather than the fortress of a tyrant.**3.77, 3.78**

›**3.77 PIERO DELLA FRANCESCA:** Madonna with Child, Saints and Federico da Montefeltro (c. 1472; Milan, Brera Library),

Montefeltro's Urbino

Federico da Montefeltro began his new palace beside an old fort on the western slope of the hill dominating Urbino c. 1450: he seems to have headed a team of architects personally. Alberti was in Urbino in 1464, doubtless advising on the project, but from c. 1466 to 1472 principal responsibility is credited to Luciano Laurana. By 1476 Laurana had ceded to Francesco di Giorgio, who seems to have entered the duke's service as a military engineer. And, with Piero della Francesco, whose influence is detected by some in the scheme's refined ordonnance, these masters are

3.78a

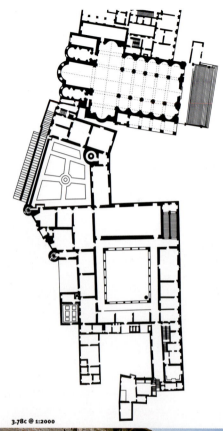

3.78c @ 1:2000

3.78b

3.78d

›3.78 URBINO: (a) general view with cathedral centre left, ducal loggia centre right, (b) cathedral section, (c) plan of complex; (d–g) palace, entrance front, cortile, Capella del Perdono, Studiolo.

Maso di Bartolomeo seems to have been in charge of the first phase but the Dalmatian master Lorenzo Laurana – who was employed by the duchess's Sforza brother at nearby Pesaro – is referred to in a document of 1466 as having prepared a plan for the palace, in another of 1467 as the duke's engineer and in another of the following year as supervisor of works on the palace. Francesco di Giorgio seems to have taken up the supervision of work c. 1476: apart from the cathedral (badly damaged in the earthquake of 1781 and transformed in rebuilding) his main contributions included the completion of the second storey of the cortile, the bathing facilities and garden terraces and service buildings to the west with an extraordinary spiral ramp for the duke to climb on horseback from the parade ground in the valley to the basement level of the palace. He may have taken over in time to revise the design of the upper storey of the loggia façade. He is also now usually credited with the wing linking the palace to the old castle (Castellare) and, therefore, with the integration of its façade with the entrance front. Change in responsibility is sometimes linked to Federico's elevation from count to duke in 1474, reflected in the change to his monogram in the decoration, but there is some two years' disparity in the dates.

Laurana may be credited with the proportions of the major rooms and the vaulting but the exquisite detail, articulating structure framing doors and windows or embellishing fireplaces, has been attributed to Domenico Rosselli and Ambrogio Barocci and linked with the intarsia work of Agostino Duccio – if not to Piero della Francesca. The artist responsible for the panels depicting ideal urban scenes[3.33] is generally associated with the similar images in marquetry installed as overdoors in the palace.

3.78e

In Piero della Francesca's panel of the Madonna and Child with saints and Duke Federico,[3.77] the assembly is enshrined in the complete illusion of antique architectural gravitas which was actually to achieve three dimensions in the palatine chapel. Perhaps the same hand was responsible for both. However, the lavish use of marble, in general, and the ubiquitous entwined medallion motifs were to be characteristic of the first Renaissance in Venice, where Laurana began his career well before the Gothic style had begun to cede to the new Classicism. However, the chapel and adjacent Tempietto delle Muse are sometimes credited to Francesco di Giorgio, who is known to have been skilled at painted and intarsia decoration – in addition to his expertise as a structural engineer.

variously given the credit for Urbino's celebrated image of the ideal town which once decorated a cabinet in the palace.[3.33]

Montefeltro's palace, imposed rather insensitively on the falling contours of the site, incorporated existing buildings in wings at right angles to one another to the east and south of a courtyard. From c. 1466 the court was closed to the north and to the west, where the range was partially doubled to accommodate a new ducal apartment opening through a grand loggia to the view. Apart from the Medici apartment in the Badia Fiesolana, the precedent for opening a palazzo to a view through superimposed loggias is to be found at Pienza. And as at Pienza the scheme was urban in scope: with the replacement of the cathedral opposite the north wing, beyond the old castle which was linked to the new one by a subsidiary range, it embraced a piazza as well as an enclosed cortile of rarely precedented scale.

To some observers, the ordonnance of the piazza façade recalls the setting of the enigmatic Flagellation commissioned by the duke from Piero della Francesca c. 1460,**3.32** and Piero may have played a role in the initial design of ornamental detail which was sustained for consistency throughout. The style pervades the adaptation of Alberti's Rucellai formula but the finely chased pilasters are restricted to the corners of the marble-clad entrance front and there are only two main storeys supporting an attic. The embellishment began with the symmetrical imposition of a pair of false doors to match the entrance portal to their right: except for part of the revetment and the aedicules which frame the main openings with their elegant smaller Order, the scheme remains incomplete and, therefore, it is not known how the cornice was to be proportioned.

In the design of the cortile, surrounded by wings with accommodation on two main storeys and a later attic, Laurana addressed the problem, inherited from Brunelleschi, unresolved by Rossellini, of apparent loss of strength in the disposition of a single column at the junction of the colonnades bordering a rectangular cortile: doubled pilasters are inserted on two levels in the corners, those of the ground floor rising to the full height of the arcade and supporting an unbroken entablature – as in Brunelleschi's major works (pages 710ff).

As at Pienza, access and view are perpendicular to one another. The entrance, off centre in the façade, is on axis with the cortile but the key to the transition is a grand staircase, with parallel flights under tunnel vaults in the Florentine manner, in the north-east corner: it opens the east–west axis of the throne room, the ducal apartment, its loggia and the view west over the town. In accordance with practice dictated by propriety recognized at least since the 14th century (see page 564), the duke's suite includes an antechamber and adjacent bedroom and cabinet (Studiolo) and a chapel (Capella del Perdono): the former is distinguished by marquetry creating the illusion of cupboards with lattice doors and shelves supporting a variety of objects: the jewelbox-like chapel is sumptuously revetted in coloured marble below a tunnel vault of virtuoso stucco work. The patron's humanism required a Tempietto delle Muse, beside the chapel on the ground floor, and his standard of comfort – novel for his day but antique in inspiration – demanded cold, tepid and hot baths in the lower storey of the loggia.

3.78f

3.78g

›3.79 NAPLES: (a) Castelnuovo, Arch of Alfonso of Aragón (1452); (b) Porta Capuana (Giuliano da Maiano, c. 1485).

Francesco da Laurana seems to have been associated on the Castelnuovo project with one Pietro di Martino da Milano who came to Naples at the behest of King Alfonso in 1452 – but for the embellishment rather than the design. The form of the entrance arch, with its coupled columns, is derived from the Arch of Sergius, Pola (Pula in Istria, c. 15 BCE). The attic was enhanced to receive a relief panel of the king's triumph. Originally designed to be freestanding, when incorporated into the castle portal extra height was gained by repeating the motif to frame his equestrian statue as the main arch would frame him actually mounted in procession.

PALAZZO AND VILLA

The precedent for Urbino's loggias, evidently by Laurana but inconsistent in style with the cortile, was set at Naples for Alfonso of Aragón on which Luciano's fellow Dalmatian Francesco Laurana worked as a sculptor. The superimposed loggias there mark an important advance in Renaissance architecture, not only because they open to the world at large: rather than merely observing Classical precepts, they reproduce an antique prototype. This is, of course, the triumphal arch and given the ruler's pretensions to divine right the context is absolutely relevant, especially in Naples where the motif is actually reinstated as the king's portal – the place of epiphany in the Mesopotamian palace from which the Romans extracted it (AICI, pages 561f). Applied to the twin-towered portal as a single great arch, as in the Porta Capuana, the motif proved of extremely wide relevance for the symbolic Classicizing of the late-medieval noble seat.**3.79**

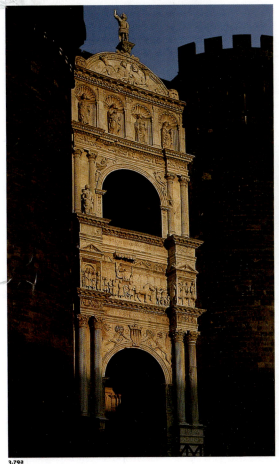

3.79a

3.79b

As at Pienza, the loggia at Urbino gave the palace something of the aspect of a villa, belied by the thoroughly urban piazza front. In post-Albertian Florence, the typical palazzo façade followed the Medici example rather than the Rucellai alternative observed in part at Urbino and wholly at Pienza. Giuliano da Sangallo's Palazzo Cocchi façade, addressing the Piazza S. Croce, is a rare exercise in superimposing Orders on two floors above a partly rusticated basement. Rusticated masonry was sometimes extended to all floors, sometimes confined to the basement and to the voussoirs of the upper-floor windows where it offset ashlar walls. Alternatively the upper window frames might be chased with Classicizing ornament instead and the upper floors painted and incised in the manner known as *sgraffito*, expanding 14th-century practice after the example of the cortile of the Medici palace.**3.80**

3.80b

3.80a

3.80c

3.80d

3.80f

3.80e

›**3.80 FLORENTINE PALAZZO VARIANTS:** (a) Lenzi (c. 1470); (b) Pazzi-Quaratesi (from c. 1462); (c) Guadagni (c. 1500); (d) Cocchi (1470s); (e, f) Scala, cortile and vault detail (from c. 1473); (g–i) Strozzi, cortile, plan, exterior.

With rustication confined to the ground floor and elegantly chased window frames, the Palazzo Pazzi-Quaratesi is attributed to Giuliano da Maiano (who had previously worked on the completion of Michelozzo's Palazzo Strozzino in a similar mode) and in the Palazzo

The cortile was the main field for decoration, though colonnaded arcades remained the norm. Giuliano's work for Palazzo Scala c. 1472, one of his earliest commissions on return from Rome where he had assiduously studied the antique, was exceptional in its combination of Roman gravitas and Florentine grace, not least due to the precocious adoption of Doric pilasters. Roman gravitas and

Florentine rusticated strength are matched on the exterior of Palazzo Strozzi. Exceptional in its scale and regularity, rusticated throughout and crowned with a cornice of antique monumentality, that work is due to Giuliano in collaboration with Cronaca: the uncanonical articulation of the cortile elevations may be due to the latter but the derivation of the massive cornice from the forum of Emperor Nerva in Rome is highly characteristic of the student returned from the antique fountainhead.

3.80g

Guadagni attributed to Cronaca. The near-contemporary Palazzo Lanzi, unattributed, offers a prominent example of *sgraffito* embellishment (much restored).

Working for the chancellor, Bartolomeo Scala, on a suburban site, Sangallo reflected current ideas of the antique villa with the main apartment on the ground floor and a loggia opening to a garden east. Symmetry in planning within a square perimeter involved four identical staircases opening off each of the corners of the square nuclear court. The combination of an Order framing the cortile arcades, in accordance with Albertian precept, and an upper Order of pilasters framing windows with frescoed embellishment over a richly sculpted socle was unprecedented; the reliefs, moralizing allegories from poems by the patron, have also been attributed to Sangallo. The system of articulation is developed, without lavish relief, on the upper two floors of the Palazzo Cocchi.

Sangallo was paid for a model of the Palazzo Strozzi in 1490 but Cronaca seems to have had considerable responsibility for the execution. The regularity of the conception and the monumentality of the mass are attributable to Sangallo: it is difficult to credit the same master with the relatively unsophisticated interior elevations.

Florentines were to match the monumentality of the Strozzi's vast rectangular block – the perfection of the medieval tradition – only with the expansion of the Pitti. There is an imposing portal centred on all three fronts, a regular sequence of arcaded windows on the two main floors above smaller rectangular ones in the basement in the context of graded rustication – a system which reappears with even more refinement in Sangallo's contemporary Palazzo Gondi. The cornice remained unfinished.

The cortile is the nucleus of a plan which is among the most regular of any produced in the 15th century but aberrant at this stage is the arcaded colonnade, from which even fragments of entablature have been omitted, and the lack of reinforcement in the corners. Uncanonical, too, the proportions of the unfluted Corinthian columns are squat but much lighter than the piers which carry the piano-nobile arcade above. Columns reappear on the top level on pedestals with balustrades between them. The two main staircases, in the south range where the neighbouring property inhibited fenestration, lead to loggia antechambers for the main reception rooms in the north range and the two main apartments east and west.

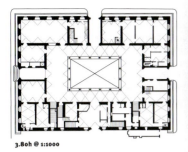

3.8oh @ 1:1000

3.8oi

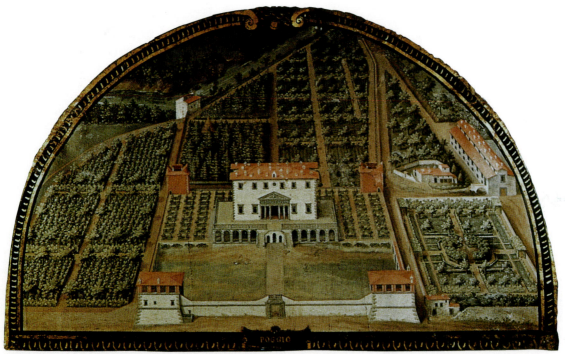

3.81a

Giuliano da Sangallo's mature rationalism is apparent in the Medici Villa at Poggio a Caiano – and, as we shall see, in the nearby church of S. Maria della Carcerie at Prato. The former was produced in response to a competition held by Lorenzo de' Medici before 1485. The patron reputedly wanted to emulate Pliny's Villa Tusculum but Giuliano developed the symmetrical mode of his Scala palazzo/villa. On a podium sited, in accordance with Alberti, on a slight eminence where it commands a view of its estate, and symmetrically planned in a square with an apartment in each corner framing a salone of monumental gravitas, the villa is distinguished by the temple front which forms its entrance portico. If the superimposition of Orders had failed as a means of Classicizing the palazzo façade, the introduction of the temple-front motif was resoundingly successful in the Classicizing of the villa.**3.81**

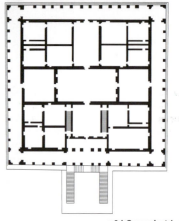

3.81b @ approximately 1:1000

3.81c

›3.81 POGGIO A CAIANO, VILLA MEDICI
(from c. 1485): (a) overview (lunette painting by Giusto
Utens, 1599; Florence, Historical Museum), (b) plan, (c)
entrance front, (d) detail of side recession, (e) hall.

The antique motifs of the podium and temple front
are characteristic of Sangallo's inventive use of the
Roman legacy: the external staircase, with its twin
curved flights to a projecting terrace, is an amplification of the original. The temple-front motif, markedly
novel in the secular context, opens a grand vestibule: it
was translated with Florentine refinement but the coffered tunnel vault behind it is Roman in its gravitas. The
tunnel-vaulted central salone, lit through the deep
recessions in the side façades, has few secular precedents either but the form was, of course, common in
ecclesiastical architecture and Sangallo reiterated it to
reduced scale at about the same time at S. Spirito:**3.95**
the novel terracotta coffers, cast in curved moulds,
were later embellished in stucco. Beyond the transverse salone, an axial one addresses the garden but the
podium seems to have denied the need for a loggia.

The axial salone separates two pairs of secondary
apartments, the inner ones ill-lit from the side reces-

3.81d

3.81e

sions. Doubled to fill squares in the outer corners to either side of the entrance 'atrium', the principal apartments are comprised of the conventional private reception room, bedroom and cabinet: the patroness, on the left, was also provided with a service room.

The Florentine palazzo type proliferated throughout Italy in several permutations. With minimal relief beyond the graded rustication of the two main floors, the Strozzi type appeared in Naples in the Palazzo Cuomo which seems to have been begun in the mid-1460s and may be associated with Giuliano da Maiano. His main contribution to the architecture of the southern kingdom, however, was the palatial villa which he built at Poggio Reale for the future king, Alfonso II, c. 1487: its covered nuclear court had projecting blocks to all four corners containing apartments, in the manner recently established by Giuliano da Sangallo at Poggio a Caiano, and space flowed between interior and exterior through intermediate loggias. This may have been a reduced version of an expansive Vitru-

›3.82 NAPLES, POGGIO REALE VILLA-
PALACE: (a) scheme of Giuliano da Maiano (and others, executed from 1487, destroyed); (b) related contemporary unexecuted scheme by Giuliano da Sangallo for a palace for King Ferrante with central court and apartments in four identical corner blocks.

Sangallo credits the scheme to the Medici ruler who dispatched him to deliver it in Naples. Emulating the Vitruvian *domus* on the grandest scale yet attempted in Renaissance planning, it incorporates a central peristylium in addition to the vestibulum and atrium which may be distinguished at Poggio a Caiano. The latter's transverse *salone*, displaced by the peristyle, is relocated at the head of the main axis as the principal audience hall with attached chapel – or amplified triclinium and tabularium.

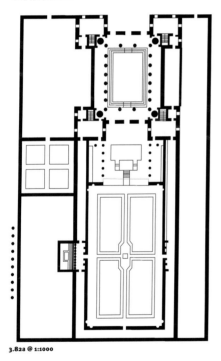

3.82b @ 1:1000

3.82a @ 1:1000

vian exercise produced by Sangallo under the direction of Lorenzo the Magnificent.**3.82**

Sangallo is sometimes identified with one Giuliano di Francesco da Firenze who is recorded as having worked on the cortile of Palazzo S. Marco (Venezia) in Rome, begun in the year he arrived there from Florence (1465). Dedicated to recording his observation of the antique remains there, as his drawing of the ruins of the Roman Basilica Aemilia serves to demonstrate,**3.125a** the young Sangallo would have been well equipped to assist the advance of the new Classicism towards Roman monumentality of the Colosseum type. With its superimposed Tuscan and Ionic Orders of attached columns framing arches, like the Albertian Benediction Loggia begun five years earlier for Pius II, the great cortile was preceded, also c. 1461, by the loggia façade of the titular church – in which only the lower Order is three-dimensional. The principal architect of the extensive scheme is identified as Francesco

3.83a

3.83C

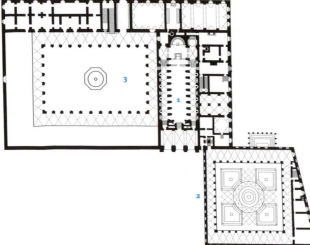

3.83b @ 1:2000

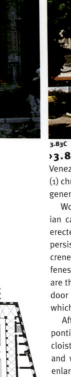

>3.83 ROME, PALAZZO S. MARCO (now called Venezia), 1455, 1464–71: (a) great court, (b) plan with (1) church of S. Marco, (2) Palazetto, (3) great court, (c) general view.

Work on the palace was begun c. 1455 for the Venetian cardinal, Pietro Barbo. As in the Vatican palace erected for Nicholas V over the previous decade, the persistence of medieval attitudes is apparent in the crenellated and machicolated parapet, the irregular fenestration and the residential tower. Traditional too are the high basement and the travertine window and door frames offsetting the red-brown plaster with which the walls are rendered.

After 1464, when the patron was elevated to the pontificate as Paul II, the complex was extended with a cloistered garden to the south (the so-called Palazetto) and wings around a grand court to the west of the enlarged chapel. Francesco del Borgo is named as the architect in a document of 1466: he died in 1468; the grand court was begun after the pope's death in 1471.

In the Palazzetto cortile, Ionic columns are superimposed over Composite, both carrying arches directly. The main cortile ranks with the Vatican belvedere scheme as among the first to approximate Roman Doric: the advance in monumentality over the pilasters of the lower storey of the Palazzo Rucellai is palpable.

del Borgo who had graduated from superintending building works for Nicholas V and who, indeed, may have assumed responsibility for executing the Vatican Benediction Loggia.**3.83**

Like the Vatican palace of Nicholas V, the Palazzo Venezia is a rare survival from a series of new residences for newly promoted prelates, built in the era of reconstruction after the return of the papal court from exile. Grand in scale but usually conforming to the irregular configuration of streets defining the site, like an antique *insula*, such complexes usually incorporated a titular church, a residential tower, and reception rooms in wings with loggias addressing a partially open garden and/or wholly enclosed court.

3.84a

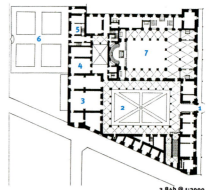
3.84b @ 1:2000

›**3.84 ROME, CANCELLERIA,** begun c. 1489: (a) exterior, (b) plan with (1) main entrance, (2) main cortile, (3) reception hall and antechambers, (4, 5) bedroom and private suite, (6) garden court, (7) titular church, (c) cortile.

Unusually, the site was cleared and a new start was made: the ancient basilica of S. Lorenzo in Damaso was to be the principal victim and had first to be superseded by the new palatine chapel. Shops incorporated at street level – following the antique tradition of the insula (AIC1, page 545)– were let in 1492; the church was in use by 1495 and an inscription of that year marks the completion of the entrance front; extensions were carried out between 1503 and 1511.

The most likely author of the project is Baccio Pontelli who had been appointed military engineer to the Vatican by Pope Innocent VIII (1484–92) but he disappeared from Rome soon after his pontifical patron's demise, well before the completion of the first phase of construction – the chapel and the adjoining entrance wing. His most likely successor was Giuliano da Sangallo's brother Antonio, who was at the start of his official career with the papal establishment in the closing years of the century: if so, he was soon to move on from the conservatism of the cortile to the sturdy piers of the cortile arcades in the Rocca of Civitas Castellana (c. 1499).

In the evolution from urban castle to palace, projections subsist to the corners but the tower was reduced to a block addressing the garden and, apart from the Orders applied to the façade, novel in the Roman context was the shallow rustication and the arched windows instead of rectangles divided by cruciform transoms. The problem of the proportions of the cornice relative to the ordonnance, encountered by those who would follow the Rucellai example, was modified

The Vatican palace apart, by far the most resplendent early Renaissance Roman palazzo is the Cancelleria built for Cardinal Raffaello Riario from c. 1490. The complex is as cohesive in massing as the site allowed and, despite the pragmatism of the perimeter, the anonymous architect bound his composition together with the superim-

by the confining of the Orders to the two upper floors – as in Giuliano da Sangallo's Palazzo Cocchi in Florence: the pilasters, doubled only at the sides there, are doubled throughout here. After the example set by Laurana at Urbino, the corner columns of the typical Florentine cortile are replaced by piers to lend strength where weakness was apparent. An inscription on the façade is dated to 1495.

The main entrance, deflected off-centre in the entrance front by the chapel, is on axis with the colonnaded cortile: the transverse cloister range leads left to the staircase. Doubling back on itself in the usual early Renaissance way, the latter arrives at the upper cortile gallery which leads left again to the patron's apartment overlooking a garden to the north.

>3.85 FERRARA, PALAZZO DEI DIAMANTI, c. 1493: entrance front.

The architect was Biagio Rosetti, who designed the Addizione Ercole.**3.76** The facets, recalling the diamond device of the Este, are graded in depth of projection on each storey.

3.84c

3.85

position of Orders on the upper two storeys of its rusticated exterior: the pilasters are paired to either side of the windows in what was subsequently to be identified as the rhythmic bay.**3.84**

Milan retains no significant unaltered palazzi from the period of the Banco Mediceo,**3.71** but the Palazzo Ghisalberti at Lodi closely follows the formula represented there. Late in the century the Albertian type with pilasters appears in various Lombard cities, notably in Amadeo's Palazzo Bottigella at Pavia and the Raimondi palazzo at Cremona. Further east along the Po, at Ferrara, one of the most spectacular of all provincial examples, with corner pilasters as in Urbino, is known as the Palazzo dei Diamanti after the prominent pyramidal cutting of the rustication on both its main storeys – a mark of the ruling Este (c. 1493).**3.85**

In Mantua, two buildings of different purpose are distinguished by their novelty. The house of Mantegna is a cube in conception with a circular courtyard.**3.86** The ducal Nova Domus has two superimposed pilaster Orders which foreshadow the colossal as they each embrace two storeys: moreover, projecting corner bays mark a rare departure from the typical Italian homogeneous block refined by the Renaissance Florentines.

With its long tradition of deep plans, entered from water gates, and open façades – indeed of villa-like loggias addressing canals**2.369** – Venice was bound to apply the new Classicism idiosyncratically. The Gothic still flourished at mid-century in the lush naturalism of the late-Flamboyant style. This first cedes to a permutation of Renaissance Classicism in the Ca' del Duca attributed to Bartolomeo Bon: only a rusticated corner with an inset columnar pier was executed. The new style first appears on a significant scale in the rebuilding of the east wing of the Doge's palace by Antonio Rizzo after a fire in 1483.**3.87**

Well before the end of the 1480s, Pietro Lombardo had introduced Venice to his native taste for elaborate marble revetment with which to supplement the deep contrasts of light and shade provided by the typical loggia. He also brought Classical ornament of a refinement he would have acquired working on the palace at Urbino under Laurana – or under the influence of Piero della Francesco. The Palazzo Dario (1487) with its asymmetrically disposed loggias over a centrally placed entrance and entwined medallions in varicoloured marble well represents his style in the secular field – and the late flowering of the first Renaissance in the security of the lagoons at the head of the Adriatic.**3.88a** We shall encounter his ecclesiastical contribution in due course.

The Classicizing of the open Venetian tradition – relatively unconstrained by the normal urban need for pro-

3.86

›3.86 MANTUA, MANTEGNA'S HOUSE: cortile.

Mantegna settled in Mantua in 1460 but does not seem to have began work on his house for at least a decade: the near biaxial symmetry of planning, within a square, about a circular cortile, probably responded to advice from Alberti on his last visit in 1470. Work, begun c. 1473, continued until c. 1494 on what was as much an exhibition gallery as a residence.

›3.87 VENICE, PALAZZO DUCALE: east wing of court and Scala dei Gigante (after 1493).

The remodelling of the east wing of the great complex, built or rebuilt in various stages from the 12th century, embraced the storeys above the surviving Gothic arcade. Pietro Lombardo replaced Antonio Rizzo in charge from 1498. To counter the extended horizontals with assertive verticals, the aedicular windows with their chased pilasters were paired (irregularly) between paired relief panels. In accordance with Venetian practice in grand locations, a monumental external Scala dei Gigante was added on axis with the Porta della Carta, the main ceremonial entrance from the piazza added in Gothic style by Giovanni and Bartolommeo Bon in 1438. At the head of the staircase, the Gothic arcade was superseded with a rich, if uncanonical, neo-Classical one. The varigated marble with which the façade and stairs were covered enhanced the decorative quality of the spectacular exercise.

›3.88 VENICE, PRIVATE PALACES: (a) Dario, canal front (begun 1487); (b) Corner-Spinelli (originally Lando, c. 1490), canal front; (c) Loredan Vendramin-Calergi (c. 1504), canal front.

The Palazzo Corner-Spinelli is attributed to Codussi on the insecure basis of the style of the bifurcated arched windows (which, adapted from the models provided by Alberti/Rossellino, match his known later work): a counter-claim may be staked for Antonio Rizzo

3.87

3.88a

tection from streets or square – was furthered in the 1490s
by Mauro Codussi – or Antonio Rizzo. Advance in symmetry is marked at the Palazzo Corner-Spinelli though
the main pilaster Order is uncanonical in scale, disposition and detail in stark contrast with the intellectual order
of the Palazzo Rucellai. Early in the new century, this is
corrected in a comprehensive ordonnance of pilasters and
superimposed columns on the façade of Codussi's masterpiece, the Palazzo Loredan Vendramin-Calergi: problems of proportion remain but the way to the High
Renaissance in the Venetian mode is clear.**3.88b,c**

3.88b

3.188c

in virtue of his earlier work on the Doge's palace. Istrian stone is used throughout for the first time: it provides a firm rusticated base, in the Florentine manner, for two similar loggia storeys in the Venetian tradition. As at Urbino, pier-pilasters are superimposed only at the corners.

The piano nobile of the Palazzo Loredan Vendramin-Calergi is distinguished in height – by the interpolation of a socle – and by the fluting of its columns. The uncanonical pairing of the supports to frame the side bays provides effective closure to the composition: fully in accord with the Venetian tradition, this is novel in the broad context of Renaissance palace façade design except for the occasional resort of Giuliano da Sangallo and in the Roman Cancelleria. The problem of proportioning the upper entablature – to the whole or to the Order of which it is actually a part – remains unresolved but the generosity of the intermediate horizontals tends to obviate it.

›3.89 THE VENETIAN SCUOLA: (a, b) S. Marco, exterior (from 1487) and detail; (c) S. Giovanni Evangelist, staircase (1498).

Pietro Lombardo and Mauro Codussi were among several architects involved in the rebuilding of the S. Marco scuola after a fire in 1485 – Pietro was already at work on the ground floor by 1487, Codussi was in charge from 1490–95. In the context of rich materials, asymmetry, multiplication of forms like the segmental pediments and profuse relief, nothing better illustrates the Venetian scenographic approach to architecture than the embellishment of the main front with illusionistic perspeclves on the ground floor (attributed to Tullio Lombardo by Francesco Sansovino in 1581); the rest of the confection is probably due to Codussi under direction from the scuola authorities. Codussi's staircase, with twin flights rising to a central domed landing, was destroyed in the early 19th century and re-erected in 1952. Similarly, his staircase connecting the halls of the Scuola di S. Giovanni Evangeslista runs the whole length of the building in two straight flights to the lavish domed landing which leads through an anteroom to the sumptuous main hall.

3.89a

3.89b

3.89c

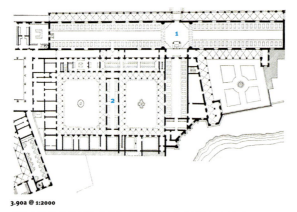

3.90a @ 1:2000

3.90b

›**3.90 ROME, OSPEDALE DI S. SPIRITO:** (a) plan with (1) original cruciform ward with chapel at junction, (2) later additional ward, (b) general view from the south-east.

CHARITABLE AND PUBLIC BUILDING

Charitable building, already endowed in significant numbers by the rich in the 14th century, continued to proliferate in the 15th century. Several hospitals with a cruciform arrangement of wards derive from the Florentine Ospedale di S. Maria Nuova and Filarete's Ospedale Maggiore in Milan: the Ospedale di S. Spirito in Rome conforms notably to type.**3.90, 2.361, 3.72**

There were of course numerous other charitable building types, dedicated to caring for body and mind. A specifically Venetian type, dating from the 13th century, was the *scuola*. Typical is an ostentatious façade, great halls on two floors, and a monumental staircase conceived scenographically: two outstanding 15th-century examples are dedicated to S. Marco and S. Giovanni Evangelista.**3.89**

The most costly public works of the era were undoubtedly fortifications and Italian engineers were in the forefront of their improvement, as we have seen. Defence works apart, the public building effort was primarily devoted to communal halls and charitable facilities. The major cities of Italy had been well equipped with assembly halls for governmental and social purposes – secular basilicas – well before the advent of the Renaissance. The two 15th-century examples which we have encountered –

3.91a

3.91b

3.91c

›3.91 THE RENAISSANCE COMMUNAL BUILDING: (a) Pesaro, Palazzo Comunale (ground floor from c. 1450, upper floor c. 1470); (b) Verona, Palazzo del Consiglio (from 1474); (c) Bologna, Palazzo del Podestà (from 1483).

at Montepulciano and Pienza**3.54, 3.69** – conform to the traditional Tuscan type with added discipline in the relationship of solid and void. The one at Pienza is significant for the incorporation of a loggia: the public loggia was a feature of the late-medieval Italian town (pages 637ff), and the proliferation of the type, integrated with a civic hall and addressing a piazza, was the 15th century's most characteristic contribution to the Italian urban scene.

The Palazzo Comunale at Pesaro established the main line of Renaissance development from the medieval civic building type, with the ground-floor market arcade replaced by a loggia after the example of Brunelleschi's scheme for the Florentine Ospedale degli Innocenti – itself derived from the late-medieval loggia façade of the Ospedale S. Matteo. Novel at Pesaro, however, are the rusticated piers of the arcade. The type is represented at its most refined by the Palazzo del Consiglio in Verona, at its most robust by the Palazzo del Podestà in Bologna.**3.91**

3.92a

3.92b @ 1:1000

CHURCHES

Despite the predisposition of the Classical architect for the geometric integrity of centralized forms, Christian liturgical requirements ensured that the Latin-cross basilica remained the dominant type for congregational churches – though regular polygons were readily admitted for sacristies and chapels and the Greek cross was allowed for oratories and commemorative works.

›**3.92 FAENZA, CATHEDRAL OF S. PIETRO APOSTOLO:** (a) nave to sanctuary (from 1474), (b) plan.

Contrary to Brunelleschi's early Christian continuity of arcading, but conforming to his square geometry, the bays are doubled in the more monumental Romanesque manner to support a domical vault over each compartment. The differentiation of column and wall remains incompletely resolved: pilasters carry the main entablature but pilasters and columns alike carry the fragmented subsidiary entablature. However, the differentiation in the expression of the Order – pilasters articulating the piers, columns carrying the arcades between them – is Albertian in its logic. The Order is unexpectedly uncanonical and the antique shell motif somewhat overscaled to fit the apse semidome. Despite its shortcomings, the building was influential: Biaggio Rosetti, for example, recalled it for S. Cristoforo in Ferrara c. 1495.

The Poitevan – or German – type of hall church with aisles rising to the height of the nave, as at Pienza, was extremely rare in Italy, unlike the universal mendicant type with a single large volume flanked by chapels. After the example of S. Francesco at Rimini, reinforced by Michelozzo in Florence at Santissima Annunziata and by Manetti or an unknown Albertian at the Badia Fiesolana, Alberti's design for S. Andrea in Mantua was to be seminal in replacing aisles with chapels. The pattern of Brunelleschi's two great Florentine basilicas with aisles and chapels was most persistent, however, often with varied rhythm in the combination of colonnade and arcade.

Of many possible representative examples, representing increasing maturity in ordonnance too, Giuliano da Maiano's cathedral at Faenza (c. 1474) is of the standard basilica type enriched with an alternating rhythm of piers defining doubled bays subdivided by arches carried on columns in the Romanesque manner.[3.92] It may instructively be compared with Cronaca's S. Salvatore al Monte in Florence, with its unvaried Order of pilasters framing a regular sequence of arcaded chapels.[3.93]

›3.93 FLORENCE, S. SALVATORE AL MONTE, from c. 1490, consecrated 1504: (a) plan, (b) nave to sanctuary.

A hall church in the Franciscan tradition – with side chapels on the Albertian model – the work relies essentially on the contrast of the arcades and the framing Tuscan Order in pietra serena with the rendered wall. Alternating triangular and segmental pediments to the aedicular windows of the clerestory, inside and out, established an important method of varying rhythm in ordonnance. The great proscenium arch approximates the so-called Serliana form which derives from Alberti's S. Andrea portal. The monumental simplicity fittingly marks the climax of the Florentine 15th century in architectural development.

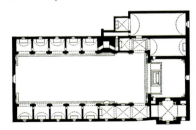

3.93a @ 1:1000

3.93b

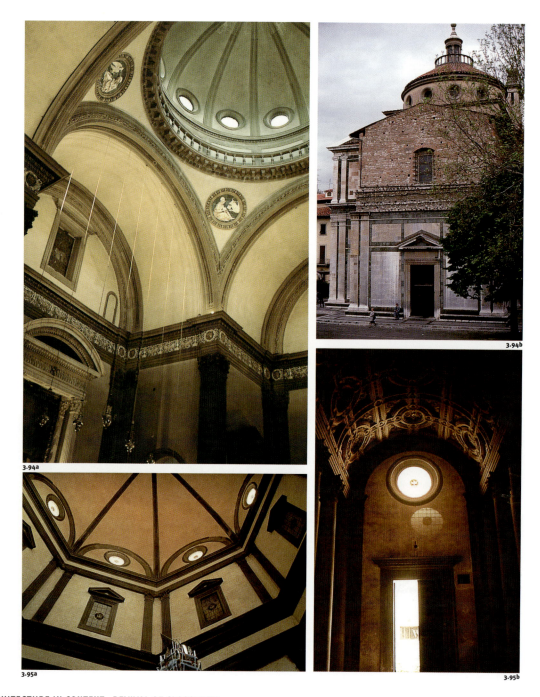

3.94b

3.94a

3.95a

3.95b

›3.94 **PRATO, S. MARIA DELLA CARCERI,** from 1485: (a) interior, (b) exterior.

A competition to erect a shrine for a miraculous image of the Madonna – on a prison wall in the castle – was won by Giuliano da Maiano but Lorenzo de' Medici chose Sangallo. The latter's Greek cross in a square follows S. Sebastiano in Mantua – drawn for Lorenzo in 1485 – and may be seen as perfecting the development begun by Brunelleschi in the Old Sacristy of S. Lorenzo and furthered in the Portuguese Chapel of S. Miniato.

The Order is strictly trabeated inside and out. Apart from the wholly architectonic door and niche aedicules, extraneous internal relief is confined to the majolica roundels in the pendentives: the zoomorphic variation of Corinthian, after the example of the Augustan forum in Rome but in reference to the Evangelists, demonstrates Giuliano's observation of the antique. On the other hand, the proportions of the Doric and Ionic on the exterior reverse antique convention and the former lacks triglyphs in its frieze: the pilasters are reinforced by the tectonic pattern which varies traditional two-tone marble revetment. The relationship of the latter to the church of the ideal town in the panel painting at Urbino[3.33] has not escaped notice (by G.L. Frommel in particular, who attributes both to Sangallo).

›3.95 **FLORENCE, S. SPIRITO,** c. 1489: (a) sacristy, (b) vestibule.

Sangallo was commissioned to provide the sacristy in collaboration with Cronaca. Relying on the strong contrast between the splendid articulating Composite Order in stone and rendered wall, the octagonal form pays homage to the Florentine Baptistry and, more immediately, to Brunelleschi's S. Maria degli Angeli. The colonnaded vestibule, related to the loggia at Poggio ai Caiano in its coffered vaulting, is due to Sangallo but was executed with the collaboration of Cronaca.

›3.96 **FLORENCE, S. MARIA MADDALENA DE' PAZZI:** atrium (c. 1491).

The medieval Cistercian hall church was refurbished from c. 1480. Revising the ubiquitous early Christian type of atrium with an eye to Brunelleschi, Sangallo reinforces the Pazzi chapel façade formula with a pier in each corner – instead of the column retained, for instance, in the Strozzi cortile.

3.96

Cronaca's great contemporary, Giuliano da Sangallo, has hardly been surpassed in the purity of his excursion into centralized planning for S. Maria della Carceri at Prato and the octagonal sacristy of S. Spirito. He linked the latter to Brunelleschi's church with a corridor in which his care for the integrity of column and wall is exemplary of the powerful effect to be generated from conceiving enclosure as layered membrane rather than solid mass. At the same site, having failed in his defence of Brunelleschi's four-bay façade scheme against the demand for the traditional central entrance, he opted to retain an unarticulated wall. No less in homage to Brunelleschi, he masked the refurbished S. Maria Maddelena de' Pazzi (c. 1490) with an atrium developing the system adopted for the façade of the Pazzi chapel at S. Croce.**3.94–3.96**

3·97

›3.97 LODI, INCORONATA, from 1488: detail of octagonal interior.

Giovanni Battaggio da Lodi occupied an official position as an engineer in Milan from 1479 but was overlooked in favour of G.A. Amadeo as architect to the cathedral in succession to G. Solari in 1481. Amadeo's collaborator, the Milanese sculptor-architect G.G. Dolcebuono, displaced Battaggio at the Lodi site from 1489. Battaggio had previously adopted the octagon for another notable Marian shrine, S. Maria della Passione in Milan (1486), and subsequently encapsulated an octagon in a circle for his most celebrated work, S. Maria della Croce at Crema (1490).

3.98 URBINO, S. BERNARDINO, from c. 1482: interior, nave to tribune.

The corner columns which dignify the chancel in support of pendentives derive from the great halls of the antique thermae (AIC1, page 640) but, somewhat surprisingly, they are not distinguished from the flat plastered walls in material or tone – as are the stringcourse, the entablature and the rim of the dome. The windows of the nave are novel in the alternation of their triangular and segmental pediments.

The synthesis of centralized and longitudinal planning represented so stupendously by the Florentine cathedral was projected, but unexecuted, for S. Petronio at Bologna (c. 1400) and often later: the circle or octagon proved particularly suitable for the distribution of pilgrims around shrines, as in the mortuary church of S. Bernardino at L'Aquila (1454) or the sanctuary at Loreto built from the late-1460s by Giuliano da Maiano and others for the extremely popular veneration of the house of the Madonna – which had miraculously arrived there from the Holy Land. Spectacular later regional examples include the Marian shrines at Crema and Lodi (c. 1490).**3·97**

Alternatively, the synthesis of the Greek and Latin cross with which Brunelleschi had first experimented (pages 719ff), was furthered towards reconciliation between liturgical requirements and Classical aspiration in the churches of Francesco di Giorgio: the Ossavanza in Siena (c. 1467), S. Bernardino at Urbino (1482) and S. Maria del Calcinaio at Cortona (c. 1485). In the first of these, he reiterated the domed square of the crossing twice for the nave: the former was distinguished in height by a low drum; the nave compartments, separated by a pair of pier-pilasters under a continuous entablature, extend laterally into chapels through their paired arcades. In S. Bernardino, a sepulchral chapel for the Montefeltro dynasty, the square

3.98

3.99a

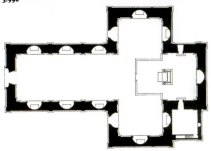
3.99b @ approximately 1:1000

3.99 CORTONA, S. MARIA DEL CALCINAIO,
1484: (a) exterior, (b) plan, (c) interior.

Cruciform, aisleless, the monumentality of the work derives not from weighty mass – though the semicircular chapels are gouged from thick walls – but from scale articulated by the relentless planar geometry of superimposed pier-pilasters, stringcourse and entablature in dark-grey pietra serena against white plaster. Uncanonical in proportions and detail – notably the composite capitals – the pilasters are confined to the corners where the transverse arches of tunnel vaulting rise over the weighty entablature: as in Francesco di Giorgio's work for the Osservanza in Siena, there is no confusion of columns and arches. Lucidity is illuminated through aedicular windows in the upper level, oculi at all four ends and the dome. And consistency is taken to the extreme of imposing the internal articulation on the exterior despite asymmetry resulting from the disparity of bay dimensions introduced by the thickness of the façade and transept walls.

domed chancel prevails over the rectangular nave but, in character with the approach of a military engineer, their volumes are clearly distinguished entities. In S. Maria del Calcinaio (c. 1484), on the other hand, the Greek cross of transepts and sanctuary is extended into a Latin one to produce the nave without compromising clarity of volume: in accordance with theory, practice was rationalized in neo-Platonic terms to identify the church plan with the figure of ideal man as Christ on the cross. A more graphic attempt at reconciling Christian and humanist ideals is hard to imagine.**3.98, 3.99**

3.99c

3.100a

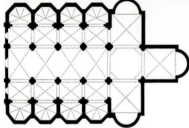

3.100b @ 1:1000

3.100c

(a–c) S. Maria del Popolo (from 1472), nave to sanctuary, plan, façade; (c–e) S. Agostino (from 1479), façade, nave to sanctuary, plan.

Rebuilt for a Lombard order of Augustinians over a late-11th-century foundation at the gate through which pilgrims entered Rome after their journey south along the Via Flaminia, the church of S. Maria del Popolo is a traditional basilica but with the polygonal form of chapel familiar in Lombardy. The arcades are carried on piers with attached columns of a debased Corinthian Order, still somewhat Romanesque in detail and inconsistent proportion, which both frames and supports the arches. The groin vaulting follows the antique thermae model. The pontifical patron retained the modestly talented Giovanni dei Dolci as architect.

S. Agostino was commissioned by Guillaume d'Estoutville, a French cleric in the service of Sixtus IV. The nave arcade is carried on piers but the doubling of the bays is effected by attached columns and an attic Order of pilasters carrying the transverse arches of the groin-vaulted compartments. Beyond the aisles, the chapels are semicircular, like those of S. Spirito, rather than semi-octagonal, as at S. Maria del Popolo, and the apse is flanked by rectangular chapels in perpetuation of the old Romanesque échelon form. An inscription on the syncretic façade, with its off-centre side doors and awkward volutes hiding the buttresses, records completion in 1483 under the direction of Jacopo da Pietrasanta.

3.100d

3.100e

If not in Florence, homage to the basilican façade formula developed by Alberti for Rimini is displayed often in Rome, first in the reign of Sixtus IV, who fostered enhanced activity in the ecclesiastical field, as in urban renewal. The prime example – if somewhat less than triumphant – was given to the renovated basilica of S. Maria del Popolo (1472). The pressing need for restoration of the plentiful existing stock of churches absorbed most of the available resources and few new works were undertaken. Most prominent among these, still essentially medieval in the ratio of height to width in volume, is S. Agostino (c. 1480), whose anonymous architect had to enhance the podium, elongate the pilaster Order and add a truncated pediment to the façade formula to achieve sufficient elevation.**3.100**

3.100f @ 1:1000

3.101a

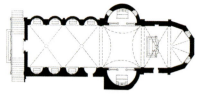

3.101c @ 1:1000

›3.101 ROME, SISTINE HALL CHURCHES,
c. 1480: (a–c) S. Pietro in Montorio, nave to sanctuary,
façade, plan; (d, e) S. Maria della Pace, plan and
interior.

S. Pietro has semicircular chapels gouged from massive walls like Francesco di Giorgio's S. Maria del Calcinaio and the façade follows the same model: an
anonymous project was evidently inherited c. 1488 by
Baccio Pontelli, Francesco's assistant at Urbino until
they both left in 1482 and subsequently recorded in the
service of Sixtus IV's della Rovere clan. In place of a timber truss roof, he vaulted the hall with groins over the
doubled bays of the nave and choir, a canopy dome (rising from the base of the pendentive zone) over the
crossing and half an umbrella dome in the apse. The
pilaster Order of the nave, framing the chapel arches, is
repeated beyond the crossing but not continued into
the sanctuary: the raising of the clerestory (or lunette)
zone over a socle dictates the corresponding elevation
of the crossing arches and the uncomfortable insertion
of a truncated attic Order.

S. Maria della Pace, attributed to Giovanni di Dolce
in the absence of evidence that his papal patron had
found a more accomplished alternative, has a truncated nave and octagonal sanctuary recalling in miniature Michelozzo's Santissima Annunziata – if not
Alberti's unrealized Rimini scheme. It has subsequently been much embellished – not least by Raphael
inside – given a cloister by Bramante and a new front by
Pietro da Cortona. The original façade – like that of S.
Pietro in Montorio but less elevated – was related in
type to the contemporary S. Maria del Calcinaio. The
embellishment to the chapels is later (that shown here
is by Antonio da Sangallo the Younger and Simone
Mosca in marble pillaged from the temple of Jupiter
Capitolinus).

3.101b

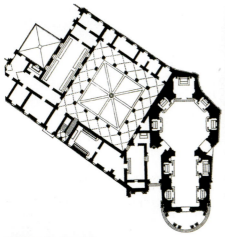

3.101d @ 1:1000

3.101e

3.102a

3.102b

›**3.102 VATICAN, TOMB OF POPE INNOCENT VIII,** by Antonio and Piero Pollaiuolo, c. 1492: (a) as re-erected in the south aisle of the new S. Pietro and (b) restored to its original form (after Seymore).

Like John XXIII and Pius II – but unlike Sixtus IV in Pollaiuolo's own precedent exercise – the pope on his bier is raised well above eye level on a Classical structure of niches containing virtues. A second, living, image is new to the Donatello-Michelozzo formula and there is no canopy: both were essential elements of the late-medieval Neapolitan type but the pose is more assertively antique here. Imperial enthronement, already adopted for Sixtus IV in his library,**3.3d** was henceforth a norm of papal iconography.

Apart from the eponymous Vatican chapel, the most notable works of the Sistine reign are S. Pietro in Montorio and S. Maria della Pace (both c. 1480). The former, on the supposed site of S. Peter's crucifixion, where there had long been a church, is a hall with semicircular chapels gouged from massive walls. S. Maria della Pace, with its truncated nave and octagonal sanctuary, was a new foundation recalling in miniature Michelozzo's Santissima Annunziata or even the Florentine cathedral – if not Alberti's unrealized Rimini scheme.**3.101**

Sixtus IV's Vatican tomb was a sumptuous interpretation of the traditional bier type, with the recumbent effigy raised over virtues to the viewer's eye level. However, his predecessors and successors varied the formula evolved by Donatello and Michelozzo for John XXIII. Most significantly, an additional living image of antique imperial origin was introduced to represent Innocent VIII.**3.102**

Venetian church planning remained eclectic: the early Christian basilica was the dominant type but there were aisleless halls too and the Byzantine tradition of the quincunx was certainly not forgotten. For both the composite forms – basilica and quincunx – homage was paid to

3.103a

3.103d @ 1:1000

Alberti's Rimini church façade formula.**3.63** Mauro Codussi is credited with the closest reproduction of the scheme shown on Mateo de' Pasti's foundation medal for S. Michele in Isola (from 1469): the triumphal arch is lost but the attic with its semicircular pediment and match-

›3.103 VENICE, MAURO CODUSSI AND THE CHURCH: (a) S. Michele in Isola (1468), façade; (b, c) S. Zaccaria (1444–1500), façade and interior; (d, e) S. Giovanni Crisostomo (from 1497), plan, interior.

Codussi is first recorded in Venice as architect of S. Michele in 1469: the church was consecrated in 1477. There are many medieval precedents for curved gables – most notably the lunettes of S. Marco – but the Albertian derivation is also clear. With an ordonnance of pilasters rather than engaged columns, as in the original, the junction of the quadrant volutes with the attic is awkward. In the first Venetian façade to be revetted with Istrian stone, simplification of the formula extends to continuing the rustication over the pilasters, as on the Palazzo Piccolomini at Pienza.

Work was begun on S. Zaccaria by an unknown builder on a basilican plan in the Gothic style of the surviving apse in 1444 and his Gothic proportions subsisted. By 1458, Antonio Gambello was in charge but the extent of his contribution by 1483, when Codussi took over, is undetermined. The lowest zone had certainly been completed and perhaps the accumulation of small-scale elements in the second zone, at variance with the size of the façade, had been begun before Codussi terminated the exercise with the curved pediment and matching volutes related to his work on S. Michele. Like S. Michele, S. Zaccaria is a traditional aisled basilica and, to achieve the un-Classical height,

3.103e

3.103C

the arcade is carried on an uncanonical Order of columns raised over high pedestals.

After experimenting with the Classicization of the Byzantine church type in the rebuilding of S. Maria Formosa (from 1492) over existing foundations, Codussi turned to the building of a new version of the quincunx. The problem of integrating the Greek cross with the square corner units through the application of a Classical Order was not entirely resolved. The main entablature is sustained over all the corner arcades by pilasters which become piers at the crossing – as in Francesco di Giorgio's S. Maria in Calcinaio, but less robust. The transverse arches which carry the ceiling rise over the capitals of this elevated Order but a smaller Order is required to carry the arches of the corner bays: these spring from the level of a stringcourse which is carried over to the corner piers to provide the arches with their imposts and double as proto capitals – ingeniously but quite uncanonically. The clerestory lighting seems to date from the 17th century. The façade follows the lines of S. Michele but with still greater simplicity in plastered brick.

3.103b

ing volutes is gained. Codussi simplified the form for his quincunx schemes – S. Giovanni Crisostomo (1497), for example – and extruded it to accommodate Gothic proportions for the partially Gothic S. Zaccaria. The style echoed down the Dalmatian coast.**3.103, 3.104**

3.104a

3.104b

›3.104 ŠIBENIK (SEBENICO), CATHEDRAL
OF S. JACOB, begun 1431: (a) interior, (b) west front.

The original project was expanded from 1441 by Giorgio di Matteo (Giorgio da Sebenico), who was born at Zadar and apprenticed to the Buon in Venice. His work is Renaissance in some detail but largely Gothic in essence. Diverted from completing the exercise by work elsewhere in Dalmatia and Italy, he was succeeded in 1475 by the obscure Niccolò di Giovanni Fiorentino: he completed the work to the west in the style developed by Codussi but was novel in expressing the tunnel vault on the roof.

›3.105 VENICE, S. MARIA DEI MIRACOLI, 1481–89, (a) exterior front, (b) interior.

A votive chapel commissioned to house a miraculous image of the Madonna was enlarged into a church as donations exceeded expectation. The original plan was for a simple hall: the chancel raised over a sacristy responded to the new brief. The coloured marble revetment seems to have come from S. Marco but the formal and stylistic similarity with Montefeltro's Capella del Perdono at Urbino may not be fortuitous as the decoration includes Duke Federigo's device of a flaming cannonball – yet connection through the obvious bond of patronage has remained elusive and a common prototype known to Laurana would not necessarily explain the shared cannonball motif.

›3.106 VENICE, SS. GIOVANNI E PAOLO: doges' tombs, (a) Pietro Mocenigo (died 1476); (b) Andrea Vendramin (died 1478) by Pietro and Tullio Lombardo.

The tent-like canopy of the type derived from Tino di Camaino and his predecessors for Doge Francesco Foscari in S. Maria dei Frari (attributed to Antonio Bregno c. 1457) or Pasquale Malipiero in SS. Giovanni e Paolo (Pietro Lombardo c. 1463), symbolizing resurrection, may be seen as prospective. Its replacement for

The most notable early Renaissance Venetian hall church is the jewelbox-like S. Maria dei Miracoli, whose single tunnel-vaulted volume is devoid of satellite spaces, except for the raised domed sanctuary at its head. The exterior is stunning with its array of coloured marbles and intricately incised Orders, whose superimposition bears no relationship to the hall's essentially homogeneous volume.**3.105** The work is the ecclesiastical masterpiece of Pietro Lombardo who first made his mark in Venice with the design and execution of ducal tombs in SS. Giovanni e Paolo. His earliest such exercise, for Doge Pasquale Malipiero c. 1463, retains the medieval tent-like canopy familiar elsewhere in Venice but for Doge Pietro Mocenigo c. 1476 he adopted the triumphal arch instead. There he was assisted by his son Tullio who went on to develop the form for Doge Andrea Vendramin c. 1490.**3.106**

3.105a

3.105b

Mocenigo with a triumphal arch framing a standing image of the doge on his sarcophagus, flanked by soldiers and based on a plinth representing temporal victories, is a clear manifestation of Renaissance humanism: though characteristically surmounted by an image of Christian resurrection, it must be seen as a retrospective celebration of human achievement, of the triumph of fame over death, as of faith in salvation.

The triumphal-arch tomb-design formula was developed from the Florentine aedicule wall-tomb type.[3.52] Pietro may well have seen such works at the outset of his career – when he was based in Bologna – and he had applied the formula most notably c. 1465 for the tomb of Doge Antonio Rosselli in S. Antonio, Padua – from where he went to Venice c. 1474. Of the work's many followers in Venice, Tullio Lombardo's tomb for Doge Andrea Vendramin (c. 1490) is an outstanding variant on the triumphal arch theme: the arch is far closer than Mocenigo's version to the Classical canon (well represented in the Venetian realm by the Arco dei Gavi of Verona) and the guardian soldiers stand free of niches but the effigy is traditionally recumbent.

3.106a

3.106b

3.107a

In Pietro's homeland, the advent of Francesco Sforza to power in 1450 was soon followed by the reinauguration of the great Visconti building projects in Milan, Como, Monza and at the Certosa of Pavia. As we have reiterated, the traditional Lombard materials – brick and terracotta – lend themselves to prolixity in the modelling of ornament – as on the façade of the Ospedale Maggiore.**3.72** However, the grandiose Visconti and their still more ostentatious Sforza successors were not to be content with brick and terracotta for their major works: the latter is at its finest in the several cloisters of the Pavia Certosa but

›3.107 PAVIA, CERTOSA: (a) basilica façade, (b) small cloister, (c) tomb of Giangaleazzo Visconti.

Having lapsed on the death of Giangaleazzo Visconti in 1402, work was taken up again in the third decade of the century by Giovanni Solari (born c. 1410) – the first of a dynasty of master-mason/architects to rise to prominence. As the fortunes of the patron, Filippo Maria, waned, progress was slow and it ceased altogether during the republican period which followed his death in 1447. When it was taken up again by Sforza in the late-1450s, Giovanni Solari was assisted by his son, Guiniforte (1429–81). The structure of the church – but not its façade or tower or internal embellishment – was finished in 1472.

Work on the small cloister (as distinct from the large cloister surrounded by the monks' apartments) seems to have been concluded by 1473: the colonnaded arcade, with splendid terracotta ornament to which G.A. Amadeo contributed in collaboration with the Solari, is echoed for the mural galleries which relieve the church exterior in the Lombard – and German – Romanesque manner (pages 62ff).

Work on the façade, which responded to the nave section, was begun c. 1474 by G.A. Amadeo in collaboration with A. and C. Montegazza but continued well into the new century: responsibility for the base level is due to the Solari but their conception seems to have been eclipsed by the richer confection of Amadeo (who seems to have been predominant from 1492 when he was also playing a leading role in the completion of Milan cathedral).

The tomb of Giangaleazzo, in the form of a miniature shrine sheltering the recumbent effigies and surmounted by an attic with their statues, was to find favour with the French invader early in the next century. The prototype is the Arca di S. Agostino of S. Pietro in Ciel d'Oro, Pavia, executed c. 1362 by Campionese sculptors in amplification of the tabernacle element of the Arca di S. Pietro Martire in S. Eustorgio, Milan (page 406).

3.107b

3.107c

Classical motifs in exceptional array, not least pinnacles modelled on antique candelabra, jostle with one another to supplant the luscious naturalistic detail of the flamboyant in variegated marble on the basilica's façade and the later additions to the interior.**3.107**

3.108a

3.108b

3.108c

›3.108 COMO, CATHEDRAL, 1396, remodelled
1426–1596: (a) interior (b) apse, (c) detail of exterior
revetment.

3.109b

›3.109 BERGAMO, S. MARIA MAGGIORE:
Colleoni Chapel, (a) exterior, (b) tomb (from 1470).

Like Brunelleschi's Old Sacristy, the mortuary
chapel was to double as a sacristy. To the formula
imported from Florence for Portinari, elaborated in
accordance with Milanese taste for coloristic patterning and retaining the traditional Lombard gallery, Giovanni Amadeo added lavish decoration *all' antica*: he
was to prove particularly influential in drawing inspiration from Roman coins to perpetuate his master's memory. The tomb too was to be influential in translating the
medieval Lombard type surmounted by an equestrian
statue (represented by the work of Bonino da Campione in Verona and Bergamo) into Classical terms – as
the architect of the Triumph of Alfonso of Aragón had
done with the related Neopolitan tradition.

Giovanni Amadeo (1447–1522) played a leading role in
the embellishment of the Certosa and he achieved something of the same effect entirely in pink marble at Como,
where the Renaissance realization of the late-medieval
basilica overshadows all else. Working on a mortuary
chapel for the celebrated *condottiero* Bartolomeo Colleoni
in Bergamo, Amadeo took decorative elaboration to an
extreme to further the pretensions of the patron: Alberti
could hardly be more remote from this Lombard
realm.**3.108, 3.109**

3.109a

In Milan, while Amadeo was waxing prolix in Bergamo, discipline was imposed by two new immigrants from the south: Donato Bramante (c. 1444–1514), whose career began as a painter in the outpost of Florentine culture at Urbino, and Leonardo da Vinci, whose career had developed in Florence itself. The maturity of High-Renaissance Classicism is their achievement above all others.

BRAMANTE IN MILAN

Bramante's first documented work in Lombardy was the painted façade of the Palazzo del Podestà in Bergamo. His first important work in Milan was on the rebuilding of the church of S. Maria presso S. Satiro. If the sacristy there is richly embellished to the Milanese taste, the main body of the church is a model of correctness in the purity of its geometry and articulation but it is also radical: there was not enough room on the site for the sanctuary to match the arms of the cross so Bramante – the scenographer – evoked it in low-relief sculpture and painting.**3.110a–d**

Restrictions of site were not a constraint on the other major Milanese commission associated with Bramante, the addition of a domed crossing and sanctuary to the church of S. Maria della Grazie as a mortuary chapel for Ludovico il Moro. Enigmatically related to sketches of a great centralized church by Leonardo, the scheme set a standard of spatial monumentality which was to be emulated for centuries to come.**3.110e–i, 3.111**

Illusionism and monumentality

The original architect of S. Maria presso S. Satiro is unknown but on the completion of his work, Bramante witnessed the purchase of new land to the west, signed the building contract for a sacristy there and was engaged to add a basilican nave. The richly relieved octagonal sacristy, still clearly cast in the local mould, is in stark contrast with the broad, short nave covered by a weighty tunnel vault over a fluted pilaster Order: the uncanonical detailing

3.110a

>**3.110 MILAN, ECCLESIASTICAL WORKS ASSOCIATED WITH BRAMANTE**: (a) a temple transformed into a church – or the triumph of Christian faith over pagan substance (engraving by Prevedari of 1481 after a drawing attributed to Bramante); (b–d) S. Maria presso S. Satiro, nave to sanctuary, detail of sanctuary wall, plan; (e) S. Ambrogio, cloister, (f–i) S. Maria della Grazia, section and plan, interior and exterior of domed choir.

The sources of inspiration identified in the Prevedari engraving include Brunelleschi – or whoever took his style to Milan (for the ribbed 'melon' dome in particular,**3.46** Piero della Francesca's Pala di Montefeltro (for the scallop-shell niche, page 722), Francesco di Giorgio (for the succession of centralized bays and the stocky astylar pier),**3.75** the ancient Milanese shrine of S. Satiro in whose precinct he was currently working – if not Venice – (for the quincunx) and Amadeo at Bergamo (for the oculus with hub and spokes like a wheel, indeed for prolixity in general).**3.109** As in Leonardo's Last Supper, there is a primary and secondary perspective system: the perspective of the main space is constructed on Albertian lines; the perspective of the secondary space is purposefully divergent.

The construction of an oratory in honour of the miraculous image of the Virgin, enshrined in the pre-Romanesque centralized church dedicated to S. Satiro, was built over four years from 1478: it had a central

3.110b

3.110c

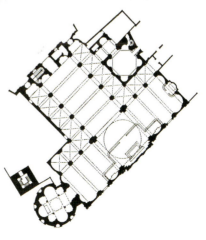

3.110d @ approximately 1:1000

in terracotta is Lombard but the gravitas of the vaulted space is Albertian. A precedent for the illusionistic extension of space had been provided by Mantegna in the painted oculus of the Camera degli Sposi at Mantua, but it was Bramante who first used the device to redress a real spatial problem: rather than vertical and celestial it was horizontal and wholly architectonic.

Wilfully unarchitectonic – but flattering to the Sforza in allusion to their arborial heraldic device – is the representation of tree trunks in the central bays of the cloister of S. Ambrogio. Otherwise the composition is conservative. The dominant central bay rises through the full height of the façade over pilasters which themselves rise through the full height of the ground-floor arcade: in this and in the combination of Order and arch, the approach recalls the internal elevations of Brunelleschi's two Florentine basilicas.

3.110e

domed space with three aisleless bays to each side – the scheme recalled Brunelleschi's Pazzi Chapel to a larger scale but incorporated niches instead of aisles, like Alberti's S. Andrea.

The monastic church of S. Maria della Grazia was built by Guiniforte Solari from 1463 on the basilican formula with columns supporting pointed arches. Within twenty years, Ludovico il Moro conceived the idea of replacing it with a monumental modern structure culminating in a vast choir dedicated to his immortality. A competition was held in 1497: construction was advanced when Ludovico fell in 1499 but dragged on until well into the next century. The nave was never rebuilt.

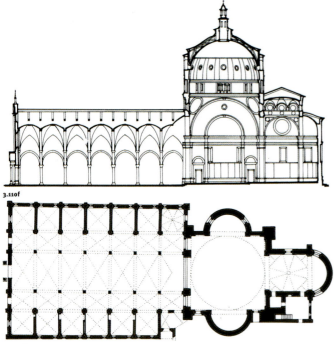
3.110f

3.110g @ 1:1000

The winner of Ludovico il Moro's competition for the design of a Sforza funerary chapel at S. Maria della Grazie emulated the Portinari Chapel which itself followed the funerary precedent of Brunelleschi's Medici Chapel at S. Lorenzo. Bramante's responsibility for the conception is trad-

3.110h

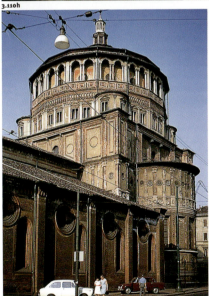

3.110i

itionally accepted but not documented. Whatever his involvement might have been, he seems to have left the construction to others, primarily Amadeo – perhaps guided by Albertian prudence, perhaps preoccupied with finding a more secure position after Ludovico's fall – and the embellishment of the space was effected long after he had left Milan for Rome. In execution the work lost some of its symmetry and was stamped with decorative patterns which ill-accord with its essential monumentality. In detail the exterior in particular betrays the hand of the local craftsman but its form is a masterly realization of the ideal tantalizingly sketched by Leonardo.

Bramante is associated with a contemporary project of even greater proportions than the new choir of S. Maria della Grazie, indeed comparable in scale to the work progressing at Como: the cathedral at Pavia.[3.112] An unknown architect had designed a basilica with an octagonal

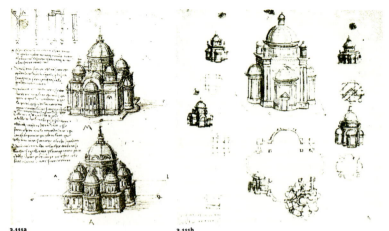

3.111a   3.111b   3.111c

crossing which emulated Brunelleschi's phenomenal achievement at Florence but translated it into the Lombard dialect with reference to the nearby Certosa. The scheme was submitted to Bramante and Leonardo and the initial campaign of work – on the crypt and the piers of the crossing – was Bramantesque but complex changes to the original conception followed Amadeo's appointment as engineer in charge in 1497. **3.112**

›3.111 LEONARDO DA VINCI: (a–c) sketch design variations for centralized domed church.

Leonardo's starting point – if a starting point is in fact represented here – was clearly the domed crossing of the Florentine cathedral but idiosyncratic is the plasticity – not so much sculptural as painterly in his chiaroscuro manner. In the isolated drawing of a domed cubicle building with apses to all sides, he seems also to have been interested in il Moro's requirements at S. Maria della Grazia.

›3.112 PAVIA, CATHEDRAL, conceived c. 1488: (a) exterior, (b–d) model, (e) plan.

Commissioned by Cardinal Ascanio Sforza, brother of Duke Ludovico, the initial plan was submitted to Bramante late in 1488 and the magnificent surviving model, by Cristoforo Rocchi, was discussed with Leonardo da Vinci in 1490. The ideal aspect of the synthesis between basilican and centralized planning accords well with the interests of these advisers – and the contemporary practice of Bramante. However, it is difficult to reconcile the latter with the profusion of forms outside and the confusion of articulation inside – where elements expressive of structure double one another meaninglessly.

3.112a

3.112b

3.112c

3.112d

The masters of the early Renaissance had felt their way towards an understanding of Classical architecture, especially of the intellectual nature of its order and the substantive role of the Orders as articulating agents rather than mere decorative appendages. With Bramante, at the time of his transition from Milan to Rome at the beginning of the 16th century, comprehension of the full dignity of Roman form was based on total command of Roman syntax and the antique language of architecture was spoken with complete fluency.

3.112e @ 1:2000

3.113

3.2 CATACLYSM AND CLASSICISM AT LARGE

INTRODUCTION I
VALOIS, HAPSBURGS AND ITALIANS

On his way to assert his Angevin claim to Naples in the autumn of 1494 Charles VIII of France swept through Lombardy unopposed: the Milanese usurper Ludovico il Moro, who had looked to France for help, had declared himself duke on the opportune death of Galeazzo Maria Sforza. In Florence Lorenzo de' Medici's son and successor, Piero, had sided with the Aragonese regime in Naples but sued for peace with the invaders as they took Pisa and Florence's hard-won coastal territory. The French were hailed by the messianic Dominican friar Savanarola as the well-earned instrument of God's chastisement for the impiety of the humanist Medici regime and provoked reaction: Lorenzo the Magnificent's heir, atypical of the Medici in his incompetence, was dismissed in favour of a pro-French republic. However, Charles's extortionate demands and Savanarola's demented extremism soon disillusioned the Florentines.

Charles and his troops entered Rome at the end of the year and temporarily overawed Pope Alexander VI (1492–1502), the particularly venal Spanish Borgia reviled by Savanarola. They swept on to Naples and took the crown from Alfonso II in early spring 1495. However, the formation of the 'Holy League' against Charles by the pope, the emperor, the Spanish monarchs and Venice forced him to turn immediately for home. His return journey degenerated into retreat as he narrowly escaped defeat at Fornovo by Italian forces and a Spanish army sent by King Ferdinand, who had inherited Sicily with Aragón in 1479. The Aragonese claimant, Alfonso II's son Ferdinand, was restored to the Neapolitan throne in 1495 but died within a year: his brother Frederick proved unable to master the forces of contention unleashed among the kingdom's notoriously unruly feudal baronage by the French intervention.

›3.113 LEONARDO DA VINCI, The Deluge, c. 1514 (Windsor Castle, Royal Collection).

›3.114 AMBOISE, CHÂTEAU: river front.
The site of a Merovingian stronghold, a royal residence was developed here by Charles VII. Charles VIII, born here in 1470, began a complete transformation in the fashionable Italianate style in 1491 but left it incomplete on his death (caused by hitting his head on a low lintel in the old building) in 1498. François I continued the work but was more fully engaged elsewhere: he received Emperor Charles V here in 1539.

›3.115 BLOIS, CHÂTEAU: entrance front (from 1498) with equestrian statue of Louis XII (replaced in the mid-19th century).
Louis XII began the transformation of the medieval castle, seat of his father as Duke of Orléans, with the eastern entance range adjoining the 13th-century Salle des États to the north. At the same time he rebuilt the Chapelle S. Calais which flanked the southern side of the court.

3.114

3.115

In 1498 Charles VIII died unexpectedly from a fall in his château of Amboise, to which he had introduced the first signs of the Renaissance in France.**3.114** His successor, Louis XII, immediately prepared to re-enter the Italian fray to wrest Milan from its usurper.**3.115** As Duke of Orléans, grandson of Charles VI's brother Louis d'Orléans, he claimed the duchy by right of descent from his grandmother Valentina Visconti, daughter of Gian Galeazzo. The Holy League did not survive his intervention: he acquired the support of the pope and the Venetians; Ludovico was backed by the emperor.

The French won at Novara in 1500 and Ludovico died their captive in 1508. With Louis installed as Duke of Milan, powerfully supported, it suited Ferdinand of Spain to come to terms in 1500: Louis gained the crown of Naples, but not all its territory, and King Frederick also went to France. However, when Ferdinand had reconsolidated his forces he repudiated the treaty and defeated the French at Garigliano at the end of 1502. The old Norman kingdom was again reunited and, thereafter, the Spanish king wore the crowns of both Sicily and Naples until the early 18th century.

Meanwhile, the forces of the Holy League had been turned on Florence in 1496 at the instigation of the pope, Alexander VI Borgia, but two years expired before Savonarola was deposed, tried for heresy and burned. The pope, notorious for promoting the interests of his rapacious family, hoped to restore the Medici while preparing to consign Tuscany to one of his illegitimate sons. However, the republic was reformed and launched a campaign to recover Pisa. Rapid gains had been expected when Cesare Borgia was appointed captain general of the Florentine forces in 1501 but, assisted by the French, he was preoccupied with asserting his personal rule over the Papal States when he fell with his father's death in 1503. He had extended his power in the Romagna and most of his gains went to Rome but Venice exacted part as the price of acquiescence. The Venetians had also gained part of Lombardy from their association with Louis XII.

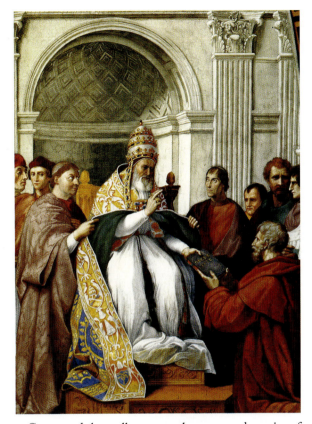

The image is modelled on Melozzo da Forli's group portrait of Sixtus IV with his nephews – the future Julius II is in the centre.

As a major part of his determination to restore the prestige of the Church in an age of corruption and humiliating foreign invasion, Julius II instituted the grandest and most costly works in the Vatican since the age of Constantine: the total replacement of the venerable basilica of S. Pietro centred on an enormous tomb for himself, the painting of the Sistine vault, the augmentation of the papal apartments, incorporating a suite of rooms which knows no peer, and the vast extension of the palace. As we are about to see, to execute these works he had at his disposal three of the greatest talents in the history of European art: Bramante, Raphael and Michelangelo.

Concerned above all to restore the power and prestige of the Church after the depradations of the Borgia, the new pope, Julius II della Rovere (1503–13), first turned his attention to Venice. After seeking support from the emperor, Maximilian, he persuaded the other powers interested in Italy that the republic was growing too powerful. France, Spain and the Empire sank their rivalries in the League of Cambrai in 1508 and the pope adhered. The following year, after defeat largely by the French at Agnadello, the Venetians relinquished their gains in Romagna and Lombardy to the Holy See. Pope Julius then turned to reassert pontifical sovereignty over Ferrara but Duke Alphonso I d'Este eluded him with French support.**3.116, 3.117**

3.117

God creating the heavenly bodies, the firma-
ment and Adam (from bottom to top, fresco, 1508–
c. 1510, Vatican).

Early in the pontificate of Julius II extensive repairs
were needed to the structure of the chapel and its cycle
of frescoes – dedicated to the unfolding of Old and New
Testament law and hence the history of church and
papacy. By 1506 the work had prompted the idea of a
great vault fresco dedicated to the prophets, sibyls,
ancestors of Christ and key moments from Genesis:
these are variously set in, supported by or viewed
through illusionistic architecture on the main verticals
of which idealized images of nude youths effect the
transition from the world of stone to the supernatural.
Observers have not generally failed to note the similarity in motif and motive between Creator and Pontif.

›3.118 LORENZO AND GIULIANO DE'
MEDICI: marble sculptures by Michelangelo, after
1520 (Florence, S. Lorenzo, Medici Chapel).

Repudiating Cambrai, the pope formed a new Holy
League with Venice and Spain to drive out the French.
After initial reverses this was accomplished with the help
of the Swiss in 1512 and the Sforza were restored to power
in Milan. In the same year a Spanish force entered Florence and engineered the restitution of the Medici. Piero,
Lorenzo the Magnificent's oldest son, had died in 1503 but
his brother Giuliano was preferred to Piero's son Lorenzo
as *de facto* head of state. Lorenzo succeeded on Giuliano's
death in 1514.**3.118**

3.118

Pope Julius II died in 1513, having exhausted himself in
destroying the power of France in Italy and rebuilding that
of the Church in a mere decade – a decade during which
his patronage restored Rome to cultural pre-eminence and
took the arts to a level of achievement never surpassed for
the union of strength with serenity, harmony and balance
– despite the extreme political turmoil. Giovanni de'
Medici – Lorenzo the Magnificent's second son – was
elected to his place as Leo X (1513–21). The new pope was

Such a group portrait in oil on panel was unprecedented – though obviously inspired by the frescoes representing Sixtus IV by Melozzo and Julius II by Raphael himself. Novel too is the frankness with which the pope is represented in indolent luxury examining a manuscript among select treasures.

If Julius II was the grandest of papal patrons, Leo X was the most luxurious. In his unexpectedly short pontificate, in particular he availed himself of Raphael's unrivalled talents to continue the work on the basilica of S. Pietro but also commissioned him to design tapestries for the Sistine Chapel, which were to be woven with thread of gold and silver, and to build the grandest villa since imperial antiquity on the outskirts of Rome ostensibly for his cousin Giulio. And he engaged the genius of Michelangelo to produce a Medici family mortuary chapel and library attached to S. Lorenzo in Florence. All these works were of such radical moment that they initiated a new era in the history of Italian neo-Classicism.

conciliatory, unlike his predecessor, but no less determined to preserve the power of the Holy See, and he was certainly no less disposed to employ the arts at which Italians then excelled to glorify it.**3.119**

Louis XII died in 1515 and was succeeded by his nephew, François I.**3.120** Ferdinand of Aragón died in 1517 and was succeeded in Spain and Naples by his grandson, Charles of Hapsburg, who had succeeded his father, Philip the Fair, as Duke of Burgundy in 1506. He was elected emperor in 1519 on the death of Maximilian I, his other grandfather. With the failure of Maximilian's attempt to forge an effective imperial monarchy the abstract concept of universal sovereignty had ceded to the reality of territorial power and of that Charles had plenty – little of it in Germany.

›3.120 FRANÇOIS I: by Jean Clouet, oil on panel, c. 1525 (Paris, Louvre).

The new French king launched a new invasion and retook Milan in the year of his accession. The pope met the conqueror at Bologna, acknowledged his claims to Milan and concluded a concordat conceding the French king's pre-eminence over the Gallican church. That earned the enmity of the emperor. The latter's Spanish and Burgundian realms straddled France and he proceeded to drive the French from Italy during the brief pontificate of the Netherlandish pope Adrian VI (1522–23) (who tried unsuccessfully to deflect the energies of the contestants against Ottomans in the east).

The new pope, Leo X's cousin Giulio de' Medici, who reigned as Clement VII (1523–34), reaffirmed support for François in fear of Habsburg power in Italy. In 1525, however, the emperor defeated and captured the French king at Pavia, sent him prisoner to Madrid and exacted a treaty renouncing all French claims to disputed territory in Italy and the old duchy of Burgundy. François repudiated the agreement on his release and at Cambrai in 1527 it was agreed that he would keep his holdings in Burgundy but renounce his claim to Milan in favour of the Sforza. Bent on chastising the Medici papacy, Charles descended on Rome with Spanish and German troops, who sacked the city with appalling barbarity in May 1527.

The sack of Rome, at the height of the Italian High Renaissance, marked the end of Italian independence. Spain was the principal political beneficiary and, from 1527, the main concern of the increasingly centralized Spanish administration was to overawe the pope, distance those parts of Italy under its rule or protection – Milan, Naples and Sicily, Genoa and Sardinia – from the other Italian powers – Venice and Florence above all – and suppress political and religious disturbance. But the conquerors – German and French as well as Spanish – were open to the cultural dominion of the conquered.

3.121

II HIGH RENAISSANCE SENSE AND SENSIBILITY

His Milanese activities having been disrupted by Sforza reverse, Bramante set off for the ancient imperial seat at the behest of the new pope, Julius II, and there completed his mastery of the Classical language of architecture – Latin, of course, as the Roman legacy was overwhelming and the seminal achievements of the Greeks were known to the Renaissance only by repute. And thus, ironically, his pupil Raphael projects the High-Renaissance ideal of spatial architecture for his School of Athens in the image of an imperial Roman hall, as the master was to do at S. Pietro.

The qualities most pronounced at the peak of civilization reached in Italy at the beginning of the 16th century – the High Renaissance – are nowhere better represented than in the fresco cycle of which the School of Athens is a major part. With it Raphael elevated Pope Julius II's Vatican library, later the court of the supreme ecclesiastical council known as the Segnatura, to pre-eminence among all the rooms of Christendom.**3.121**

The Stanza della Segnatura

The schema of the square room embraced the four faculties of humanist scholarship: theology, philosophy, poetry and jurisprudence. Each of these disciplines is personified in a mosaic ceiling roundel above a fresco assembling its major exponents or their allegories. On the window walls allegories of civil and canon law face writers, antique and modern, assembled on Parnassus with Apollo and his muses. Faith and reason, the complementary ways to truth, are represented in the unbroken lunettes to either side: by the communion of saints and doctors of Catholicism expounding the mystery of the Eucharist below the Trinity and the encircling heavenly host and, opposite, by the muster of the philosophers who informed the development of humanism from that other peak of civilization achieved by the Greeks two thousand years earlier in the School of Athens.

Under the great basilican vault of ancient philosophy, principal players have been identified – not incontrovertibly – with supreme modern masters: Leonardo appearing as Plato engaged with Aristotle in the centre, Michelangelo as the brooding Heracleitus sprawled on the steps below Aristotle, Bramante as Euclid dominating the group to Aristotle's right – and Raphael himself as a modest observer by the pier to the extreme right. Painters, all these except Leonardo were to be practising architects whose seminal importance it would be difficult to overestimate, and all except Leonardo gravitated to Rome where they were enrolled by Julius II to work on the Vatican palace or the great basilica to which it is dependent.

›3.121 THE SCHOOL OF ATHENS, c. 1510–11: fresco by Raphael in the Stanza della Segnatura in the Vatican Palace.

In the Stanza della Segnatura – perhaps in his School of Athens above all – Raphael distils the essence of his era's achievement: the supreme harmony of the Classical ideal in a world of unedifying chaos, equilibrium in the disposition of vigorously diversified forms in an age of turbulently contending forces, homogeneity of unprecedented grandeur in the Julian era of aspiration to the mighty unity of Catholicism. And, in the School of Athens, Raphael's mastery of asymmetry in the distribution of his figures in diversified groups, infused with energy but integrated into an organic whole with a consummate sense of balance, is complemented by the grand symmetry of the ideal church as its context. If inspired by Bramante's scheme for S. Pietro – which, as we shall see, lacked none of the gravitas of imperial Rome at its height – it is built around a congregation whose inner logic itself determines space.

The vital organicism of Raphael's School of Athens, especially that of its central group, has been compared with Leonardo's Last Supper – the masterpiece which announced the High Renaissance in Milan more than a decade earlier. And the silhouetting of the central figures clearly reveals the indebtedness of the younger genius to the older – though how the debt was actually incurred may only be conjectured.

Leonardo was certainly not the first to complement the asymmetry of a figure composition with the symmetry of building – the device is essential to Alberti's prescription for *istoria* (page 736) – but no one had more convincingly inhabited a static space with a vital organism. However, it is the operation of light on the actors in the obscurity of their theatre, drawing them together but stressing the diversity of their reactions to supreme drama, which represents Leonardo's most influential innovation. That was crucial to the older master's evocation of the sombre atmosphere in which the sin of betrayal was canvased and the mystery of the Eucharist invoked as the key to absolution but it was of little use to Raphael's glorification of reason and faith.

Leonardo's younger contemporary, Michelangelo (1475–1564), was to be no less revolutionary though his moody temperament was to take Italian art in a very different direction – as those who persevere with this series

›3.122 DONI TONDO, c. 1504: by Michelangelo, oil and tempera on panel (Florence, Uffizzi Gallery).

Fusion is effected through the extraordinary passing of Jesus to S. Joseph backwards from S. Mary: the momentum arising from the torsion of the latter, transmitted to the former, meets resistance in the breadth of S. Joseph's shoulders with locking force. And the force of the integration is enhanced by the looseness of the youths disporting in their bizarre middle ground. Before and beyond that, moreover, colour is invoked to establish the Saviour's transition from heaven to earth and back again. In that no less than in mastery over contorted form, the prime purpose of the exercise seems to have been the demonstration of virtuosity in the extreme.

will see in due course.**3.122** Primarily a sculptor, he produced the most celebrated of all fresco schemes for Julius II on the vault of the Sistine Chapel.**3.117** Both this stupendous work and Leonardo's Last Supper inspired Raphael's achievement in the School of Athens – the one for compositional and psychological vivacity, the other for physical power and grandeur. And in the context of Bramantesque architecture, the work admirably demonstrates Raphael's supreme synthesizing genius. In his extended series of panels representing the Madonna and Child, Raphael drew on Leonardo – specifically the Adoration of the Magi – for the organic constitution, psychological fusion and geometric ordering of grouped figures: indeed these exercises may be seen as variations on an essentially asymmetrical theme played in counterpoint over a regular ground base to reconcile physical and psychological vitality with the Albertian conception of *concinnitas*.**3.123** However, until his late years he preferred not to lose the clarity of his forms in Leonardesque *sfumato*: on the contrary, after entering the service of Julius II he played a leading part in translating the linear clarity of the Florentine style – consequently known as *disegno* – into the grander, graver idiom of Rome.

In Venice meanwhile, Leonardo's achievement of atmospheric integrity was paralleled by the heirs of Giovanni Bellini: his probable pupils Giorgione (Zorzi da Castelfranco, c. 1476–1510) and Titian (Tiziano Vecellio, c. 1485–1576), whose collaboration was so close that distinguishing the latest work of the one from the earliest of the other is sometimes problematical. This is especially the case in the genre of the so-called poesie, devloped from Bellini's introduction of the atmospheric landscape which might establish the mood for a religious icon or even assert its own pre-eminence over the ostensible subject. Among the most celebrated examples of the type, variously attrib-

›**3.123 MADONNA OF THE MEADOWS,** 1505 : by Raphael, oil on panel (Vienna, Art History Museum).

Strict triangular geometry disciplines the three-dimensional massing, idealizing the group as its constituents are idealized in the standard Classical way: classification of a range of observations, determination of means between the extremes in part and whole and recombination (AIC1, page 380). And the Classical principles of contrapassto affect balance of form and force across the body, across the group and across the environment (AIC1, page 403). For example: within the ideal symmetry of the pose, the Virgin's head is deflected to the left to link her by gaze with S. John who is engaged with the Christ child – as is his theological purpose – and all this psychological activity is balanced by a distant – infinite – river view of seductive haziness; on the other hand, the right side of the composition is relatively static and the large and clearly delineated object of secondary interest in the foreground, the Virgin's foot, is counterbalanced by a middle distance view in which a clearly delineated bluff dominates.

›3.124 **VENETIAN COLORE:** (a) Sleeping Venus, Giorgione, c. 1510, possibly completed by Titian, oil on canvas (Dresden, Gemaldegalerie); (b) Noli me Tangere, Titian, 1411–12, oil on canvas (London, National Gallery).

Forms are built with colours graded in tone and merged through the operation of colour-enhancing light or repressive shadow: atmosphere is evoked and, through its chromatic tones, mood. The opening of Alberti's rationally constructed perspective box to admit the glow of real Venetian sunlight, or the menace of the storm, was made possible by oil painting. After Bellini oil was mixed with flexible resin and the timber panel ceded to canvas. promoting a new freedom of brushwork in thick and rich, but also thin and opaque, pigment. Supreme examples of early 16th-century Venetian achievement range from Venus's luscious flesh textures and the languid mood of her sultry afternoon, to the mortal richness of the Magdalen's vestments and the melancholy glow of her mystical evening.

3.124a

3.124b

uted to both Giorgione and Titian, are the enigmatic Concert Champêtre and the languid, sensuous Sleeping Venus whose contours are those of mother nature writ large in the world beyond her resting place. Much of the same landscape recurs in Titian's Noli me Tangere but the golden summer afternoon becomes a disturbing autumnal dawn, redolent of death and resurrection, at the poignant moment in which the mortal Magdalen finds her immortal beloved beyond reach.**3.124**

The intellectual Florentines were given to no such sensuality or moodiness: nowhere is their *disegno* better contrasted with Venetian *colore* than in Raphael's Madonna of the Meadows and Titian's Noli me Tangere. The relative merits of the two schools would be the subject of debate in artistic academies for centuries to come, their parts being taken respectively by those identified as 'Ancients' and 'Moderns' – that is, of course, those whose artistic impulse was governed by reason drawn from antique models and those whose genius had freer range. Naturally, the combination of the two would be seen as the greatest objective.

3.125a

›**3.125 GIULIANO DA SANGALLO AND THE TRIUMPHAL ARCH:** (a) Portico of Gaius and Lucius, sometimes called 'Arco di Gallo' or Basilica Aemilia (1470s); (b) Capella Gondi in S. Maria Novella, Florence (c.1501); (c) Vatican, Loggia dei Trombettieri (project, 1505).

The three-bay model was the Arch of Septimius Severus (AIC1, page 562), even to the attic Order framing the inscription, but Sangallo demonstrates a refined understanding of the Vitruvian – or Albertian – concept of decorum in modifying it. The site demanded considerable éclat and Sangallo provided it with the sculptural relief. However, the status of the commission recommended not the grand display of an attached Corinthian columnar Order – fit for an imperial hero – but relatively utilitarian Doric – or Tuscan – pilasters without the canonical triglyph frieze.

3.125c

4 THE HIGH RENAISSANCE: BRAMANTE AND HIS ASSOCIATES

In Rome after the fall of his Sforza patron, Bramante was quickly favoured with patronage at the highest level. The new pope, Julius II, would inaugurate the new century with the most important Roman ecclesiastical building campaign since the era of Constantine: the replacement of the ancient basilica which enshrined the burial place of S. Peter in the Vatican. Moreover, the spot where the apostle was martyred, venerated at S. Pietro in Montorio, would be endowed with a new shrine.

While Bramante was establishing himself in Rome, Giuliano da Sangallo presented his own credentials as a master neo-Classicist with a project for a Loggia dei Trombettieri in the Vatican piazza.**3.125** Highly accomplished though it was as an exercise in adapting the antique

3.125b

In place of arches springing uncanonically from columns, as in his Ambrosian cloister in Milan – and as in the typical works of his contemporaries in Lombardy – Bramante adopts the canonical formula derived by Alberti from the Arch of Augustus at Rimini – or by the architect of the Palazzo Venezia from the Roman Colosseum. The arches are unmoulded and the Order, which virtually disappears in the corner where it might have been doubled for visual strength, attains full relief only in the upper storey. There the columns are inserted between piers with pilasters to help support the cornice: uncanonically, the columns are Corinthian but the pier capitals and entablature are Composite.

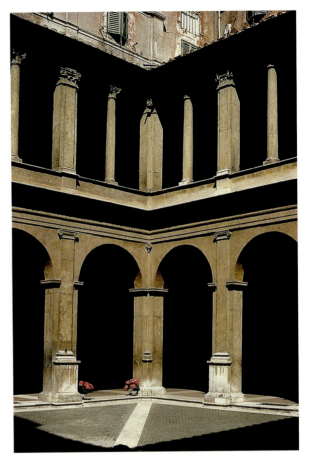

motif of the triumphal arch to contemporary purpose, that scheme was never to be realized and Sangallo was accorded only the secondary role to Bramante in the greatest project of the age.

First Bramante provided S. Maria della Pace with a cloister at the behest of Cardinal Oliviero Caraffa and demonstrated that the influence of his new environment had supplanted that of Milan.**3.126** However, it was with the tiny Tempietto in the Montorio cloister that he first demonstrated his mastery of the antique in the mode of the ancient tholos as adapted by the Romans to

3.127a

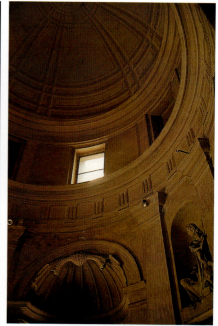

3.127b

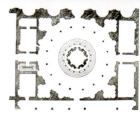

3.127c @ 1:1000

accommodate the rites of the Vestal Virgins (AICI, pages 520f, 566f). Pure in its geometry, the whole depends solely on circle, cylinder and hemisphere. Beyond that, the Doric Order ringing the main volume with a frieze of metopes and triglyphs (with guttae) and conforming in its proportions to Vitruvian prescription, is absolutely canonical for perhaps the first time – as we have seen, early Renaissance architects realized that several architrave mouldings bent up under the impost of an arch did not constitute an entablature but they were slower in grasping that each Order had its own distinct frieze and cornice.**3.127**

›**3.127 ROME, S. PIETRO IN MONTORIO, TEMPIETTO,** from 1502: (a, b) exterior and detail of interior, (c) plan in the context of a circular court after Serlio.

The circular peripteral form was known to Alberti and projected, with variations, by Francesco di Giorgio who departed from the Roman precedent in incorporating a drum as the base for a saucer dome.**3.75ª** The proportions of Bramante's Doric (1:8.5) are slenderer than the canon but Vitruvius specifically requires this in circular temples. As the scale did not admit the precise concordance of external and internal articulation, the regular repetition of the Order cedes to pairing in the rhythm of the triumphal arch – the so-called 'rhythmic bay' – inside. This may be seen as appropriate in the commemoration of one of the principal resurrected martyrs of the church. The scallop-shell motif of the niches recalls the Prevedari drawing and Piero della Francesca's Montefeltro Madonna and Child – Bramante's most likely source.**3.77**

As in Raphael's School of Athens, Bramante's replacement for the dilapidated Constantinian basilica of S. Pietro was ideally to be a Greek cross crowned by a vast dome. Except for the apses which terminate each arm of the cross, the whole is described by a square and smaller squares fit into the corners. A kit of discrete parts assembled to form a whole greater than their sum, it accords with Alberti's dictum that beauty depends on such a conception that nothing could be added or subtracted but for the worse. Nevertheless, crucial additions were to be made even by Bramante at the outset of the project's protracted development.**3.128**

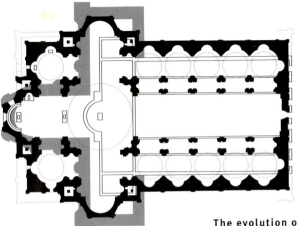

3.128a @ 1:2000

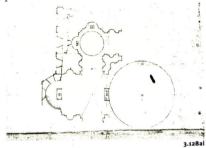

3.128ai

The evolution of S. Pietro's new sanctuary

Julius II's ambitions for his church and its premier basilica far exceeded those of his predecessors. As to the basilica: inspired by Brunelleschi's work on Florence cathedral, Nicholas V had commissioned Rossellino to project a new choir and transept from the Constantinian nave – as we have noted. Bramante began with Rossellino's foundations but incorporated a huge dome at the crossing by cutting Rosselino's corners, added apsidal ends to the arms of the cross and inserted domed 'sacristies' in the re-entrant angles to buttress the dome: there are sketches of a basilican nave on the back of the only surviving drawing for this initial scheme.**3.128a,ai**

›**3.128 ROME, VATICAN, BASILICA OF S. PIETRO:** (a) Rossellino's scheme overlaid with Bramante's first thoughts which are taken to have been recorded by an assistant in sketches dated to March 1505 (ai); (b, c) part plan of Bramante's ideal central-

To accommodate the vast and complex monument projected by Michelangelo for Julius II in 1505, the sanctuary was to be widened: the transept arms inherited from Rossellino were reformed to match and the

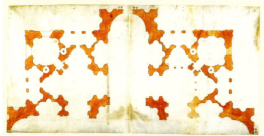

3.128b

satellite spaces in the corners were correspondingly enlarged and diversified. Though no more is projected on the so-called 'parchment plan', it has generally been assumed that the basilican nave was to be replaced with the similar fourth arm of an ideal Greek cross.**3.128b**

The Constantinian basilica provided Bramante's central dimensions: the width of its nave and inner aisles was spanned by the diameter of the dome projected over the octagonal crossing and that was commensurate with Brunelleschi's Florentine exemplar. Rather than the latter, however, the Pantheon provided the model for the single-shell concrete dome but, crucially, instead of setting it on a cylinder based firmly on the ground, Bramante raises it over a colonnaded drum on the chamfered central piers – as at Pavia, if not Florence. The great imperial thermae provided the precedent for the scenographic planning of ambulatory vistas through the columns screening the varied main and secondary spaces of the 'parchment plan'. Directly expressing the complexity of the spatial forms, the exterior massing illustrated on the foundation medal is clearly the expansion of the ideal evolved in collaboration with Leonardo in Milan: domes, towers and exedrae elevated over major and minor Greek crosses and their dependencies cede nothing of their individuality even to the Orders which assert the distinction between the storeys.**3.128c**

Consulted by the pope, Giuliano da Sangallo condemned the central piers of the 'parchment plan' as too weak. His revisions, weighted to mass at the expense of space, were to a Greek-cross plan which is presumed to have echoed Bramante. However, the latter responded by thickening his piers and reducing the subsidiary spaces in a double-aisled basilican scheme sketched in red chalk over Rossellino's plan.**3.128d** Worked up in reference to S. Lorenzo in Milan for justification of his estimate of the weight of mass required, the design proved too expensive even for Julius II.

3.128c

ized scheme (mid-1505) and foundation medal based on it; (d) sketched basilican revisions with sketch of crossing showing huge piers with twin pilasters separated by niches (red chalk, late-1505); (e) part plan attributed to Bernardino della Volpaia (who recorded great antique and modern buildings probably at Leo X's instigation); (f, g) details of front and choir elevation of revised basilican scheme (which may be associated with a model of the 1506 scheme made for Julius II or even Leo X, though none is recorded in payments); (h) structure at crossing c. 1524 (sketch attributed to Jan van Scorel); (i, j) structure at crossing recorded by M. van Heemskirk (c. 1535); (k, l) Giuliano da Sangallo's projects of early and late-1514, adding ambulatories to the transepts and ultimately the choir; (m, n) Raphael's second project, probably of 1518, for restoring subsidiary crossings to either side of the choir, reforming the latter with an ambulatory to echo the transepts and integrating the major and minor Orders of the new parts on the exterior; (o) structure at crossing c. 1560 showing the arch of the western-most nave bay and its pier with paired giant pilasters (drawing attributed to Battista Naldini).

(ai, b, d, f, g, k, are 3a, 1a, 20a, 4a, 5a, 7a are in the collection of the Uffizi Gallery, Florence; e is in Sir John Soane's Museum, London; h and l are in the Vatican; the Heemskirk drawings are in the National Museum, Berlin; o is in the Hamburg Art Museum.)

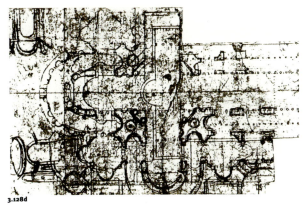

3.128d

Giuliano produced a regular double-aisled basilican scheme without circular subsidiary spaces. Bramante's response is undocumented but later
evidence suggests that Rossellino's foundation prevailed in basilican revisions of late-1505 and the ambulatory spaces in the corners of the ideal
centralized concept were deleted. The scheme was developed early in
1506: in April the pope laid the foundation stone and incarcerated the
foundation medals though these were prepared in connection with the
original ideal scheme. Giuliano returned disappointed to Florence.

Internal elevation sketches of the choir arm, with typically Bramantesque fenestration, are not inconsistent with the red-chalk drawing.**3.128e,f** These differ in measurement, but not in disposition, from a
plan of the crossing of a partial basilican scheme:**3.128g** presumed to represent the position approached under Bramante's direction by the end of
Julius II's pontificate, when the crossing arches had been completed. This
accords in general with the external perspective drawn by Jan van Scorel in

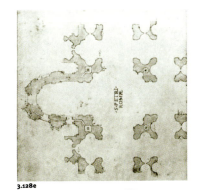

3.128e

3.128f   3.128g   3.128h

3.128i

the early 1520s[3.128h] and with the more celebrated records of Maerten van Heemskirk of a decade later.[3.128i,j]

An unencumbered entity housing Michelangelo's projected monument, the revised choir was lit through vast windows set within great arches screened with columns below concentric semicircles framing circular oculi – as in the rather clumsy embellishment of the crossing of S. Maria delle Grazie or the rather more accomplished transept elevations of S. Maria presso S. Satiro in Milan.[3.110b] The fenestration drawings[3.128e,f] and Heemskirk[3.128i] agree that the scallop-shell motif of the Tempietto niches – and of Piero della Francesca[3.77] – was to be redeployed on a grand scale in the choir, above a giant pilaster Order. The latter's articulating agency is asserted, the weight of the mass denied, by the penetration of voids between the shafts – as in the contemporary scheme for enshrining the Santa Casa at Loreto.[3.130]

3.128j

Framed by giant pilasters inside and out – rather than the superimposed Orders of the medal design – the fenestration of the choir may well have been repeated to light the outer aisles of the basilica's main body – though those shown on the red-chalk sketch are not represented on the partial drawing. On the other hand, it is clear from the latter that the nave eleva-

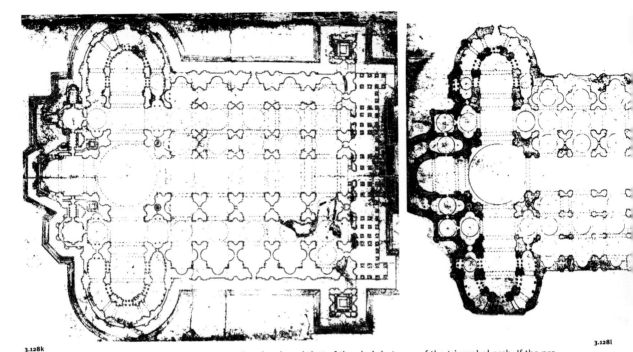

3.128k

3.128l

tion developed that of the choir in terms of the triumphal arch. If the project was still based on the red-chalk sketch, there would have been three interlinked triumphal arches as in S. Andrea in Mantua, though Alberti's side chapels had given way to the doubled aisles: that apart, the resemblance went further if it is to be believed that Alberti had projected a domed crossing on the scale ultimately realized at Mantua.

Pope Leo X called for a revised scheme in 1513, partly because of the lack of sufficient chapels, partly because of doubts about the structure of the dome. Fra Giocondo was called to Rome as technical adviser: apart from editing Vitruvius (see above, page 679), he was engaged in extensive engineering projects in the Veneto and was considered the leading engineer of his day. After Bramante's death in the late spring of 1514, he was appointed architect to S. Pietro in collaboration with Raphael and Giuliano da Sangallo – but died within the year. Giuliano had returned to Rome looking for preferment from the Medici pope: he projected apsidal side chapels in several variants on Bramante's latest scheme but no ambulatories obscured the articulation of the extended sanctuary until early in 1515.**3.128k,l**

3.128m

3.128n

3.128o

To Giuliano's disappointment, Raphael succeeded as principal architect to S. Pietro in August 1514. As reproduced later in the century, his scheme of 1515 follows his master's red-chalk project in extending a basilican nave with generous side chapels from a revision of the ideal 'parchment' scheme with ambulatories around choir and transepts. He revised the internal and external elevations in 1518, incorporating the precious columns of the Constantinian basilica in a minor Order proportioned to the subsidiary spaces in contrast to the colossal pilasters of Bramante's main volume.[3.128m,n] The continuation of the small Order behind the large is contrary to the latest indication of Bramante's intentions for the elevation but consistent with work attributed to him elsewhere.

On Bramante's death only the great piers and arches of the crossing and part of the choir had been built to the extent shown in Scorel's drawing of 1524 and little more had been realized by the 1560s.[3.128o] However, the clarity and lucidity of the conception, which emulated the grandest scale of antique monumentality, had been realized on the minute scale of the Tempietto and projected for the S. Biagio chapel of the Palazzo dei Tribunali in the new Via Giulia.[3.129a] The essence of that monumentality is distilled on a median scale in the coffer-vaulted choir and scalloped apse with which Bramante completed S Maria del Popolo c. 1508.[3.129b]

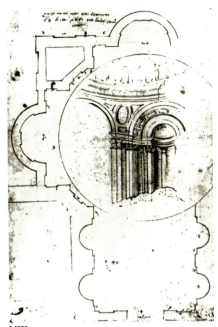

3.129a

3.129b

›3.129 BRAMANTE AND THE APSE: (a) sketch scheme for the church of S. Biagio in the Palazzo dei Tribunali (c. 1507); (b) S. Maria del Popolo, choir (1508).

The coffering and the concentric arches of the Popolo apse, but not the scallop shell, are combined with pilasters for the S. Biagio chapel in the abortive scheme to rehouse the various arms of papal justice in a massive Palazzo dei Tribunale on the new Via Giulia. The S. Biagio plan is a reduced version of S. Maria della Pace, where Bramante had worked on the cloister. The articulation of the apse is highly unorthodox in the disposition of the central pilaster.

›3.130 LORETO CATHEDRAL, SANTA CASA, begun 1509.

Paired columns were to reach a new apotheosis in Bramante's scheme for enshrining the Casa Santa, the house of the Virgin Mary which the faithful believed had been miraculously transported to Loreto.

3.130

3.131a

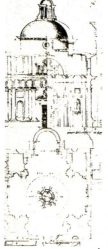

3.131b

BRAMANTE'S HEIRS AND THE CHURCH

Apart from the project for S. Biagio, Bramante made several excursions into small-scale church planning. In Rome the lost quincunx of SS. Celso e Giuliano is notable as a minute reduction of the ideal scheme for S. Pietro. A similar design, solicited by a papal official for S. Maria Annunziata in Roccaverano (Piedmont), offered a new solution to the problem of Classicizing the composite façade: a giant Order and pediment in the centre, representing the nave, is overlaid on a minor Order supporting fragments of a pediment on the flanking spaces. This follows the projection of the colossal and regular Orders of the nave and subsidiary spaces on to the exterior of S. Pietro – which Raphael elaborated after the master's demise.**3.128c, n**

Well before Bramante died, Rome was endowed with several centralized churches inspired by him. Most notable are S. Eligio degli Orefici, S. Maria di Loreto, S. Giovanni dei Fiorentini and the hospital chapel of S. Giacomo degli Incurabili. All were finished later and none now appears as its architect originally intended. S. Eligio

›3.131 ROME, S. ELIGIO: (a) interior, (b) plan and elevation drawings attributed to Raphael.

Unlike Bramante's most monumental schemes, but like the major works of Brunelleschi and his followers, the dome is supported on pendentives.

›3.132 TODI, S. MARIA DELLA CONCILIAZIONE, begun 1508, finally domed nearly a century later: (a) plan, (b) interior, (c) overview.

The church was built to enshrine a miraculous image of the Madonna, attractive to pilgrims from early in 1508: foundations were laid within months and work on the fabric began to a triapsidal scheme in the spring of 1509 but the fourth apse had been approved by May. The definitive project seems to have been adopted only in spring 1512.

A semicircular, rather than polygonal, perimeter distinguishes the apse containing the image: initially none of the apses was to have been polygonal. The purity of the geometry and the consequent monumentality inevitably associate the conception with a master – but a late-Quattrocento figure uninspired by Bramante's Petrine complexities.

Cola da Caprarola was paid as *capomaestro* in autumn 1508 and reappears in the accounts until late in 1515. Inference has been drawn from the fact that he was a master builder who had worked late in the 1490s under the direction of Antonio da Sangallo the Elder at the Rocca of Città Castellana. However, the latter's ordonnance of pilasters framing arcades is much more monumental than the Orders superimposed on the exterior and interior here, except for the colossal pilasters of an uncanonical Doric at the crossing – but their interpolation recalls an earlier era. Specifically, the window aedicules and the incessant projection of the entablatures recall Francesco di Giorgio.**3.75**

As foreman of works, Cola may have had some say in the design of the building. However, a more likely candidate as architect is Giovanni di Taddeo da Cione who was working at the cathedral of Orvieto at the time and was paid for work on the new Todi project from mid-1508. it is known that over the protracted course of construction several eminent architects were consulted: among the first were Peruzzi and Antonio da Sangallo the Younger but work was well advanced by 1532 when the latter was called upon.

is closest to that intention: an admirably austere little Greek-cross building with only an abstract pilaster Order within, it is now usually assigned to Raphael.**3.131**

Among others, Bramante's name has traditionally been associated with the design of the church of S. Maria della Conciliazione at Todi which was built by the master mason Cola da Caprarola: the relationship to S. Maria della Grazie in Milan is close, but even more closely it follows the

3.132a @ 1:1000

3.132b

3.132c

3.133a

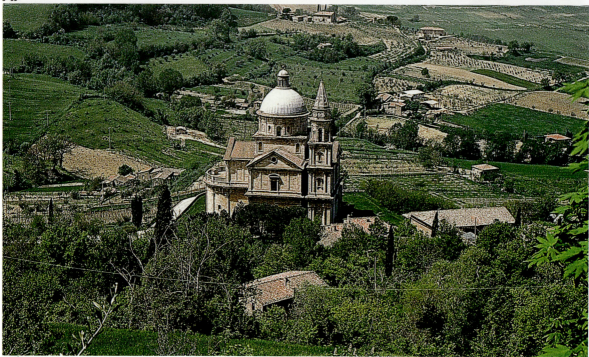

3.133b

›3.133 MONTEPULCIANO, MADONNA DI S. BIAGIO, 1518–29: (a, b) exterior from west and south, (c) plan, (d) interior.

The simplicity of the geometry recalls Antonio's brother Giuliano's S. Maria della Carceri at Prato**3.94** and the stocky proportions of the Order recall his record of the antique Arco di Gallo (Portico of Gaius and Lucius, page 832) – though contrary to the antique norm represented there, the corner pier pilasters bear axial triglyphs at the expense of corner strength in the frieze. Rather than brick revetted in marble, stone is used throughout, prompting the gravitas of a three-dimensional expression of the internal Order: otherwise *concinnitas* is respected in the articulation of the lower storey outside and in. Moreover, the pure centralization of the model cedes to axiality with the extension of the sanctuary arm into an apse enclosing a sacristy. Unlike the model, on the other hand, the pure geometry of cylinder and hemisphere distinguishes the dome: articulated in the current Roman manner, the latter was finished after Sangallo's death in 1534 and so too was the multistorey tower.

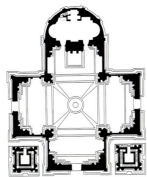

3.133c @ 1:1000

3.133d

ideal of Leonardo – or, rather, one of the stages through which he passed in pursuit of that ideal.**3.132** Exemplary as an essay in emulating these models, it is matched by Antonio da Sangallo the Elder's Madonna di S. Biagio at Montepulciano of 1518. Indeed, with its superimposed Doric and Ionic Orders outside and its grand Doric attached columns inside, Sangallo's work is the supreme example of High-Renaissance monumentality. It is also an exemplary exercise in asserting the Classical discretion of building in a natural setting of outstanding beauty (see also AICI, page 433).**3.133**

3.134b

3.134c

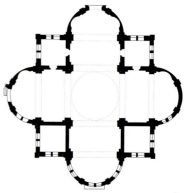

3.134a @ 1:1000

›**3.134 PARMA, MADONNA DELLA STECCATA,**
1521: (a) plan, (b) exterior detail, (c) interior.

Unlike S. Maria della Conciliazione at Todi, but like Bramante's ideal scheme for S. Pietro, the apses are distanced from the crossing by interpolated rectangular bays which, in turn, are backed by subsidiary spaces – here square sacristies rather than secondary crossings in an ambulatory system – to buttress the thrust of the dome. Unlike the Petrine scheme, the latter has a shallow curve and the arcaded drum fails to raise it to full view from below. The interior articulation with pilasters framing generous tracts of wall throughout is conservative, as is the fenestration, and the decorative elaboration – taken to superlative extremes later by Parmigianino – fully accords with Quattrocento Lombard taste for concealing brickwork.

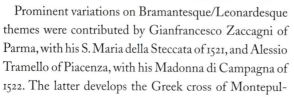

Prominent variations on Bramantesque/Leonardesque themes were contributed by Gianfrancesco Zaccagni of Parma, with his S. Maria della Steccata of 1521, and Alessio Tramello of Piacenza, with his Madonna di Campagna of 1522. The latter develops the Greek cross of Montepul-

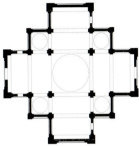

3.135a @ 1:1000

›3.135 PIACENZA, MADONNA DI CAMPAGNA,
1522: (a) plan, (b) exterior detail, (c) interior.

Smaller than the Parmesan Steccata, Tramello's
work is still more elementary in plan but the spatial
conception is enriched by the opening of the domed
corner spaces to the arms of the cross – though the
result may hardly be expected to approximate the
ambulatory of Bramante's great Petrine ideal. Rather
than that indeed, the conception relates to the Byzantine quincunx as most recently interpreted by Codussi
in Venice. However, the octagonal drum carries an
upper storey which conceals the dome in the Lombard
manner – as on Bramante's S. Maria della Grazia.

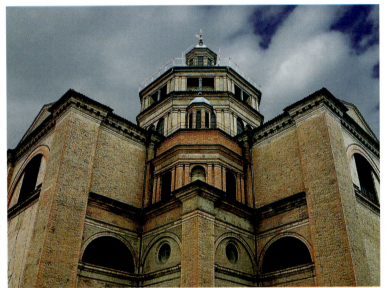

3.135b

3.135c

ciano, the former develops the quatrefoil geometry of
Todi, but both may also be seen as extreme simplifications
in centralized terms of Bramante's ideal 'parchment'
scheme for the rebuilding of S. Pietro.**3.134, 3.135**

›**3.136 NAPLES, S. GIOVANNI A CAR-
BONARA:** Capella Caracciolo (from c. 1515)

The articulation clearly recalls Giuliano's Loggia dei
Trombettiere, even to the details of the Doric capitals
and the swags between them – though pilasters are
replaced by columns, as in the related triumphal-arch
motif which dominates the contemporary design for S.
Lorenzo in Florence. Unlike the latter, the pedestals of
the former are retained and the shafts are fluted. Unlike
the loggia, on the other hand, both the Florentine and
the Neapolitan schemes incorporate the canonical
Doric entablature.

In 1515, Giuliano da Sangallo may have provided inspiration for the anonymous designer of the Caracciolo
chapel in the ancient Neapolitan church of S. Giovanni a
Carbonara: it will be recalled that he had worked for
Neapolitan patrons before he sought promotion to the top
of his profession from Pope Julius II in Rome. Be that as
it may, towards the end of the year he returned to Florence
to work on the façade of S. Lorenzo – as did others, including Raphael, to no avail.**3.136, 3.137**

Back in Rome there were others who's work approximated the ideal, at least in plan and space if not in monumental plasticity of mass. Ultimately most significant was
Antonio da Sangallo (1484–1546), nephew of Giuliano and
his brother Antonio, who had begun as a carpenter and
trained under his uncle in Florence and Rome (from 1503).
In 1506 he entered service with Bramante as a technician.
Thus different from the leading architects of the day, all of
whom were artists rather than craftsmen, he was nearly

3.137a

3.137b

›3.137 FLORENCE, SCHEMES FOR THE FAÇADE OF S. LORENZO: (a, b) Giuliano da Sangallo (1515); (c) Raphael (1516).

Alberti was able to impose a temple front/triumphal-arch hybrid on the non-basilican volume of S. Andrea at Mantua – with scant regard to the physical reality of the latter – but failed entirely to resolve the problem of adapting an intrinsically unified form to the composite basilican section at Rimini. Sangallo first attempts this by superimposing a hybrid temple-front/triumphal-arch motif over an Albertian series of triumphal-arch motifs. Raphael anchors his composition with a pair of 'rhythmic bays' – developed from his master's Belvedere scheme – and also superimposes a hybrid temple-front/triumphal-arch motif over the extruded centre to match the elevation of the nave. Perhaps in response to this, Sangallo revises the rhythm of the bays in his most elaborate scheme which incorporates a terrace-topped narthex: the Order, without pedestals, is removed from the corners, the main intercolumniations are contracted and in conformity the superstructure approximates a temple front rather than a triumphal arch.

3.137c

3.138b

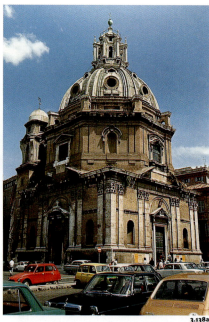

3.138a

›3.138 ROME, S. MARIA DI LORETO, begun 1507, vaulted later: (a) exterior, (b) interior.

thirty before he was entrusted with the small pilgrimage church of S. Edigio in Cellere (1513): he responded systematically with a square containing an octagon and Greek cross opened by pilastered porticoes except for the eastern apse. He went on to complete the similar S. Maria di Loreto which had been founded in 1507, possibly by his uncle Antonio.**3.138** That was beside the remains of the Forum of Trajan, north of the Forum Romanum (AICI, pages 564ff), where he followed his uncle Giuliano in the assiduous study of the Eternal City's antique legacy. Meanwhile, he had distinguished himself in extensive work on fortifications in and beyond Rome for Pope Leo X and for Cardinal Alessandro Farnese (later Pope Paul III).

Because of his technical expertise the younger Sangallo was appointed to secondary responsibility in Raphael's studio at S. Pietro on the death of his disappointed uncle in 1516. Two years later he proposed alternative basilican and centralized schemes for S. Maria in Monserrato in Rome: the former, Albertian in its replacement of aisles with linked chapels, was executed. At much the same time, similarly, he entered alternative centralized and basilican schemes in the competition for the design of S. Giovanni dei Fiorentini. Initially unsuccessful, he was ultimately employed on the basilican project but, clearly preferring elementary geometry, had his unexecuted rotunda scheme

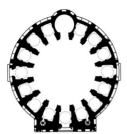

3.139b @ 1:1000

›3.139 ROME, S. GIOVANNI DEI FIOREN-
TINI: (a) Antonio da Sangallo's competition entry,
1518, section (engraved by his pupil Labacco), (b) plan.

The development of the Via Giulia eliminated the
chapel of the Florentine community by the Tiber at the
end of the Via del Consolato. Bramante provided plans
for its replacement but only a temporary chapel eventu-
ated as the sandy site proved problematical. The Florentine Leo X encouraged the idea of a grand new
church and ordered the community to proceed in 1518.
An expensive base was begun and a competition
announced early in 1519: Raphael, Antonio da Sangallo, Baldassare Peruzzi and the Florentine sculptor
Jacopo da Sansovino responded. Probably because of
the nature of the site as much as aesthetic predisposition, all the schemes seem to have been centralized but
Sangallo provided a truncated basilica as an alternative to a magnificent rotunda inspired by the Pantheon.
Sansovino won – reputedly with an octagon in a square.

Within a year Sansovino – whose architectural
endeavours had so far extended mainly to festive temporary structures – was replaced by Antonio da Sangallo who had been working on the difficult site as
structural engineer from the outset. Evidently he had
already submitted a revised scheme in which he developed the basilican alternative to his rotunda. The nave
was begun, never roofed and finally abandoned in
favour of a centralized scheme by Michelangelo forty
years later.

3.139a

published in engravings. That was crucial in advertising
how the cavernous volume of the Pantheon could be transformed with light: rather than enclosed by a cylindrical
mass with exedrae, the circular space was ringed with
chapels between radial spur walls; these bore the weight
of the fenestrated drum but the thrust of the dome was
transmitted to the perimeter fabric by console brackets
acting as flying buttresses.**3.139**

Antonio was promoted to the position of principal
architect to S. Pietro on Raphael's death in April 1520.
Assisted by the Sienese painter and architect Baldassare
Peruzzi (1481–1536), probably from the outset, he spent the
next quarter-century elaborating various projects for
extending Bramante's scheme. Practical considerations –
ranging from the support of the dome to the integration
of the basilica with the adjacent papal palace – seem to
have been uppermost in his mind – but that takes us well
beyond the temporal confines of this volume.

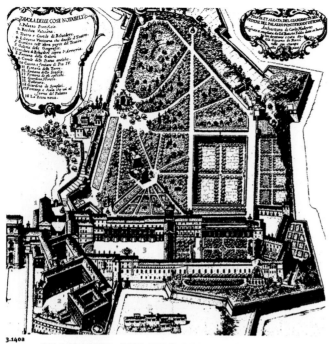

3.140a

BRAMANTE AND THE PALAZZO

While working on his great basilica, Bramante was commissioned by Pope Julius to extend the Vatican palace. He was to abandon the apartment contaminated in his eyes by his Borgia predecessor and resort to the level above – where Raphael was to execute his marvellous didactic frescoes. There were to be new facilities for the conclave and for the reception of foreign rulers – the Sala Regia gained from the basilica's precinct by the extended Scala Regia in the narrow gap between the Sistine Chapel and the basilica. At the heart of the scheme, the Cortile di S. Damaso was to be surrounded by colonnaded loggias on three levels: Heemskirk shows the east range as virtually complete on Bramante's death.**3.140**

The extensive Cortile del Belvedere was commissioned by the pope to link the Vatican palace with a villa built by Innocent VIII on the compound's highest eminence,

3.140b

>**3.140 ROME, VATICAN PALACE:** (a) overview (17th-century engraving) with (1) Sistine Chapel, (2) Cortile di S. Damaso, (3) Cortile del Belvedere, (4) Cortile della Pigna, (5) Palazzo Belvedere, (b, c) Cortile di S. Damaso (west range logge c. 1504, extended to form court c. 1580), Heemskirk's drawing and detail of northern corner, (d) Cortile del Belvedere (probably initiated c. 1504, extended to a third corridor level c. 1506, a fourth level was added c. 1580 for Gregory XIII by Ottaviano Mascarino, the library of Sixtus V was inserted over the original lateral stairs from 1587 by Domenico Fontana); drawing by Giovanni Antonio Dosio (1533–1609; Florence, Uffizi), (e–h) Palazzo Belvedere, Bramante's spiral staircase, drawing and view to top, exedra (drawing after Serlio showing circular staircase with concentric steps flanked by niched piers), façade to the Cortile della Pigna.

The logge of S. Damaso – arcades framed by Doric and Ionic pilasters on the middle levels, Corinthian colonnade on top – expand on the precedent set in the Piccolomini palace at Pienza but, instead of addressing the countryside over a walled garden, they face the town over a walled precinct. Their novel role as an open façade was lost c. 1580 when they were repeated around the precinct to form an enclosed court with fenestrated façades to the town and the piazza of S. Pietro.

Its variety of articulating systems apart, the Belvedere project is distinguished by the variety of its stair forms. Most notable outside, on the top level, is

3.140c

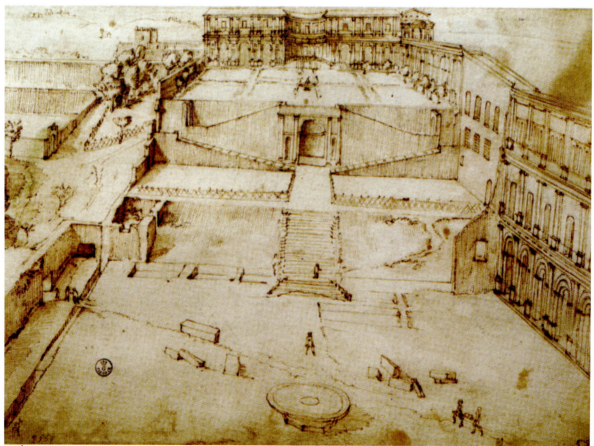

3.140d

where a sculpture court was under construction. A vast ground plane and two garden terraces were framed by extended corridors – on three levels after the pope moved into his elevated new apartment c. 1506. Preceded by a broad flight of steps, the two terraces were linked with a pair of staircases doubling back on themselves. The scheme was unprecedented in the scope of its formal ordering since antiquity: fully in accord with the antiquarianism which its architect had developed in his Roman environment, its inspiration was the Temple of Fortuna at Palestrina (AIC1, page 522).

the opposition of concave and convex steps about a circular landing: inside the eastern tower of the expanded villa, communicating with the northern entrance, is a spiral staircase of four revolutions, through four storeys, distinguished by four Orders: in accordance with the example of the Colosseum, these ascend from the virile Tuscan through decreasingly weighty Doric and Ionic to elegant Composite (AIC1, page 582).

3.140e

3.140f

In the arcading of his extensive reworking and expansion of Innocent VIII's villa on the Belvedere terrace, Bramante referred to the typical triumphal arch: he departed from the simple repetition of identical bays, as in the colonnades of S. Damaso or the lower level of the corridor wings, and varied the rhythm of the articulation by adding the minor term of a niched pier between the pilasters which frame each arch. As we have seen, that motif distinguished his contemporary basilican scheme for S. Pietro where it derived from Alberti's S. Andrea in Mantua. As we have also seen, columns are paired to

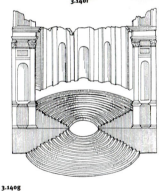

3.140g

3.140h

support the concentric arches and oculi inserted in the windows of that scheme as it had in the transept elevations of S. Maria presso S. Satiro in Milan. That motif reappears within the thermal complex, or nymphaeum, at Genazzano where paired pilasters frame the triple-arched loggia.**3.141**

The so-called rhythmic bay, or triumphal-arch motif, provided the key to the immeasurable enrichment of the Classical tradition. The pilasters frame the arches but as they also frame the piers, the autonomy of the parts is compromised. So too are the rules based on the logic of structural necessity – which does not run to pairing the posts of a regular peripteral structure. Giuliano da Sangallo, for one, had ignored this in providing a resolute closing motif to an extended series of pilasters.**3.80d, 3.137** Alfonso of Aragón's architects in Naples, for instance again, had used the motif in its natural context of entry and its supernatural one of apotheosis – which, of course, had recommended it to Romanesque church builders (pages 27, 29). Alberti transposed it from that context to the interior of S. Andrea at Mantua in the interest of *concinnitas*.**3.67d** Bramante seems to have been bent on following that precedent at S. Pietro but in the Vatican Belvedere he licensed the general use of the motif out of context.

Paired half-columns had appeared prominently at the outset of Bramante's Roman career in a work of seminal importance, the Palazzo Caprini (or House of Raphael, after its owner from 1517). Setting himself to solve the problem of applying the Orders to the articulation of a multistorey palace façade, Bramante distinguished two zones architecturally and in accordance with the hierarchical order of society: the base block of shops and service quarters, addressing the world of the street, and the plane of the patron elevated over it – the piano nobile. The arcades of

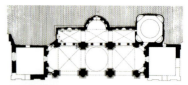

3.141a @ 1:1000

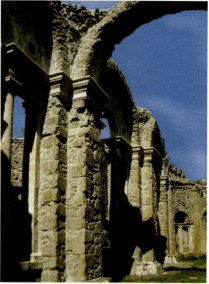

3.141b

›**3.141 GENAZZANO, NYMPHAEUM**, c. 1509: (a) plan, (b) reconstructed elevation.

The loggia, now ruined, is reconstructed with a central domical bay flanked by groin-vaulted ones extended into scallop-shell niches: the inspiration was the great hall of a Roman thermal complex. Beyond it the nymphaeum – conceived as a tepidarium? – is groin vaulted. Accessible from the inner corners of each of these longitudinal spaces is the domed octagonal caldarium which completes the complex.

The projection of a minor Order as support for an arch in a framed bay is a natural development from Alberti's transformation of the impost piers in the portal of S. Andrea at Mantua: misleadingly, therefore, this motif is usually called 'Serliana' after its 16th-century publicist.

the former were rusticated in staunch support of the Order, which was confined to the latter, and the elevated cornice – properly proportioned to the attached Doric columns, of course – accommodated the windows of a low attic. Thus an object lesson in Vitruvian decorum provided the solution to the Albertian problem of adapting the Vitruvian conception of order to modern buildings.**3.142**

3.142

BRAMANTE'S HEIRS AND THE PALAZZO

Raphael has traditionally been credited with the Palazzo Vidoni-Caffarelli – the closest surviving Roman follower of Bramante's palazzo prototype, the house acquired by Raphael himself.**3.143** However, work began on the site four years after the death of the young genius: he had been quick to realize the full implications of his master's achievement but, equally quickly, he and his circle – in parallel with Michelangelo – had set out in a new direction.

Raphael had taken a radical departure from his master's palazzo formula by 1518 in the design for the Palazzo Branconio dell'Aquila – which shall be reviewed in due course. His first subtle moves in reordering the face of living quarters above a commercial basement were made in the Palazzo Alberini-Cicciaporci and the Palazzo da Brescia. The latter is nearer to the model except for the mezzanine,

›3.142 ROME, PALAZZO CAPRINI (HOUSE OF RAPHAEL), 1501, demolished: engraving by Lafrieri (1549).

›3.143 ROME, PALAZZO VIDONI-CAFFA-RELLI: detail of façade.
Vasari attributes the original seven bays to Raphael's pupil Lorenzetto: subsequent augmentation produced a toltal of seventeen bays and an enlarged attic.

3.143

3.144a   3.144b

the attic, the type of rustication and the pilaster Order: most significantly, the prominent but awkward trapezoidal site invited the incorporation of a triumphal-arch motif at the truncated apex. For Alberini the master deployed an astylar, wholly tectonic system of articulation derived from a radical reduction of Doric which assimilated capital and architrave.**3.144**

Peruzzi was to follow late Raphael, rather than Sangallo, with a daring inversion of Bramante's formula in the last decade of his life – as those who persevere with this exercise will see in due course – but at the outset of his Roman career he was the heir of Francesco di Giorgio. Commissioned by a scion of the Sienese Chigi family of bankers to produce a villa in Trastevere, which came to be known as the Farnesina, he revived the problematic idea of superimposed Orders. What the result lacks in grace or strength is obliterated by the work's two supreme masterpieces of interior decoration: Raphael's loggia, which we shall also revisit in a later context, and Peruzzi's own Sala delle Colonne with its illusionistic revelation of Rome beyond the sumptuous feigned architecture.**3.145**

›3.144 ROMAN PALACES ASSOCIATED WITH RAPHAEL: (a) Brescia, exterior detail (1515, rebuilt on the corner of Via Rusticucci and Via dei Corridori after the construction of Via Conciliazione in the 1930s); (b) Alberini (Cicciaporci), exterior detail (from 1512).

The original site at the confluence of Via Sistena and Via Alessandrina was allocated to the papal doctor, Jacopo da Brescia, and it is probable that the pope ensured that the building was entrusted to a master. Contrary to the usual rustication, imitating stonework as on the Caprini, the revetment of the basement is entirely horizontal in line. In stark contrast, the verticals of the piano nobile are enhanced by projecting the Doric pilasters in triads and breaking the entablature out over them. Horizontals and verticals are reconciled in the attic storey which replaces Bramante's mezzanine and obviates any confusion about the role of the Doric entablature: it clearly relates solely to the piano nobile of whose Order it is an integral part.

Giulio Alberini embarked on his speculative apartment-building exercise in 1512 and work was advanced enough by 1515 for the letting of the shops and an apartment on the piano nobile. There is no proof that Raphael was involved from the outset – or, indeed, at all – but the treatment of the rusticated basement, with thin incisions in stucco which mock the metaphor of protean load-bearing masonry, is usually seen as characteristic of his wayward approach to convention. So too is the merging of capital and frieze in the reduced – cardboard-thin – Tuscan Order of the piano nobile: the attic storey, with its novel blind panels continuing the verticals, and the overweening entablature may have been executed with or without the intervention of the master's pupil, Giulio Romano.

›3.145 ROME, VILLA FARNESINA, 1509–11: (a) garden front with loggia, (b) Sala delle Colonne, (c) plan.

Francesco di Giorgio's heir – as yet – Peruzzi had designed a villa near Siena for Sigismondo Chigi: with a pair of wings projecting from a rectangular block and two storeys articulated with pilasters, it was followed closely for Sigismondo's brother Agostino in Rome. The superimposition of slender Tuscan pilasters was hardly innovative but it was difficult otherwise to accommodate a ground-floor loggia and a full second storey.

A master of theatrical scenography, Peruzzi was revolutionary in his evocation of the real world of a turbulent city – rather than the Arcadian or celestial ideal – in the embellishment of the major room of a suburban retreat. The psychological perspective of the achievement is grasped in the recognition that it took much of the previous century for Renaissance man to embrace the view of his own estate beyond his garden wall.

3.145a

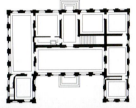

3.145c @ 1:1000

3.145b

3.146

The alternative approach to palazzo façade design, without a major Order but with a minor one confined to aedicular window frames, was developed for the Florentine Pandolfini: though unsatisfactory in its present massing, which wants completion as a nine-bay composition,

3.147a

›3.146 FLORENCE, PALAZZO PANDOLFINI: detail of incomplete principal elevation.

Giannozzo Pandolfini sought enlargement of a palazzetto on a semi-suburban site: Raphael probably sent the design in the year of his death – the year of the foundation inscription. Pandolfini died in 1525 but work continued until Gianfrancesco died in 1530.

Despite the Roman provenance of the design, not even the cornice would have seemed out of place in the Florence of Giuliano da Sangallo: the rustication of the portal recalls that of the Palazzo Strozzi and the aedicules descend from Cronaca's S. Salvatore al Monte. Characteristic of Raphael's attitudes to convention are the merging of pedestals into a continuous dado and the continuation of the aedicular frieze and architrave as an elaborated stringcourse which, of course, has an entirely different morphological function.

›3.147 MONTEPULCIANO, HIGH-RENAISSANCE PALAZZO FAÇADES: (a) Contucci-del Monte begun by Antonio da Sangallo the Elder for the future Pope Julius III in 1519 and completed with its attic probably by Baldassare Peruzzi c. 1534; (b) Cervini begun c. 1518 for Cardinal Marcello Cervini, later Pope Marcellus II, but unfinished.

3.147b

›**3.148 FLORENCE, PALAZZO BARTOLINI SALIMBENI,** 1520–23: façade on Piazza S. Trinità with the Column of Justice right.

Baccio d'Agnolo (1462–1543) is the most prominent member of the dynasty of Florentine artists who first made their name as woodworkers. Architect to the Duomo from 1506, his work on the gallery of the dome was halted by Michelangelo's ridicule.

Though Raphael's design for Pandolfini predates its construction, the palazzo marks the introduction of the style 'alla romana' to Florence: novel is the amplification of the aedicules for the main portal; the insertion of niches between the piano nobile aedicules derives from Raphael's late-Roman Palazzo Branconio dell'Aquila (an innovative scheme which must be considered in the context of the origin of the Mannerist style).

The Column of Justice was extracted from the main hall of the Roman Baths of Caracalla and presented to Grand Duke Cosimo I by Pope Pius IV in 1560.

3.148

it may be seen as the ultimate refinement of the formula developed in opposition to the Rucellai exercise. It was begun by Antonio da Sangallo the Younger's cousin Gianfrancesco to a design sent from Rome by Raphael.**3.146** The two Antonio da Sangallos and their contemporaries worked in the mode in Tuscany, and the younger Antonio embarked on notable exercises in Rome, above all for the Farnese, but the complex history of their project takes us well beyond the confines of this volume.**3.147, 3.148**

3.149a

3.149b

3.149e

3.149c

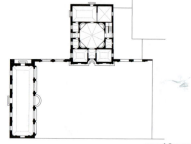

3.149d @ 1:1000

›**3.149 PADUA**: (a–d) Cornaro palace garden complex (1524), theatre pavilion, northern pavilion, reconstruction and plan; (e) Porta S. Giovanni (1528).

Falconetto worked to the patron's conception of a 'forum' for theatrical and musical performances to be inserted in the garden of the Cornaro palace: the open loggia of the larger pavilion, emulating an antique scenae frons, served the former; the enclosed octagon of the northern building, recalling the antique Odeon to the patron's mind, was the concert hall. The articulation of the larger pavilion – the theatre – with engaged columns below and pilasters above, recalls that of the loggia front of S. Marco beside the Palazzo Venezia in

Rome though the bays of the upper storey have alternating windows and niches with the segmental or triangular pediments favoured by Cronaca.

Like Giuliano in his design for the Loggia dei Trombettieri, Falconetto reproduces the antique triumphal arch for his Paduan gates: his Corinthian Order is closer to their common model, the Arch of Septimius Severus, but elaborate relief was deemed inappropriate to the essentially defensive – rather than commemorative – purpose of his exercise.

›3.150 LUVIGLIANO, VILLA DEI VESCOVI,
c. 1535: (a) general view, (b) façade detail.
The Villa dei Vescovi's regular repetition of arcaded bays, with pilasters applied to the piers, is also typical of Florence in the late-1490s. Its setting on a podium recalls Poggio a Caiano and conforms to Albertian precept at the instigation of its humanist patron.

Roman variants and alternative developments notwithstanding, Bramante's example continued to be followed closely by architects throughout Italy – some of them among the greatest of the era – for at least two generations. Most notable, perhaps, are the early works of Giovanni Maria Falconetto, whose major works are in and around Padua, of the Florentine Jacopo Sansovino, who left his major mark on Venice, and the Veronese master Michele Sanmichele, who also presided over the Venetian profession.**3.149, 3.150**

Falconetto (1468–1535) introduced the High Renaissance to the north primarily under the influence of Cronaca and Giuliano da Sangallo, well within a decade of the latter's demise. However, at least a decade separates the first Bramantesque achievements of Sanmichele and Sansovino from the 1527 Sack of Rome – which prompted them to turn north – and they may best be viewed in the context of subsequent stylistic developments, not least because they led to the apotheosis of Venetian architecture in the second half of the century.

3.150b

3.150a

EPILOGUE: FROM MEDIEVAL TOWARDS NEO-CLASSICAL ABROAD

Outside Italy the first phase of Renaissance was invariably characterized by the grafting of Classical motifs on to medieval forms and it was usually announced in funerary works or church furniture. Isabella of Castile and Ferdinand of Aragón led the way at Toledo, Ávila and Granada.[3.151]

SPAIN

In addition to their exceptionally florid Gothic legacy, the joint Catholic Monarchs were heirs to an equally lavish Muslim tradition. Ruling in Italy while the Renaissance was expanding there, moreover, King Ferdinand's Aragonese cousins were used to the homogeneity of the

3.151a

›**3.151 MORTUARY OF THE REYES CATÓLICOS:** (a) Toledo, S. Juan de los Reyes (completed 1492 under the direction of the Flemish-trained Breton Juan Guas), chapel retable; (b) Granada, Capilla Reale (1506–21), interior with monument to Ferdinand and Isabella (died 1516 and 1504 respectively) right, left Phillip the Fair and Joanna la Loca (died 1506 and 1555 respectively).

The Granada project was to supersede the chapel under construction at S. Juan de los Reyes in Toledo: the building is attributed to Enrique Egas, the screen (completed 1520) to a French artist known in Spain as Maestro Hilario, the effigies on their bier are by the Florentine sculptor Domenico Fancelli (completed 1517), the retable by Felipe de Vigarni (1522).

3.151b

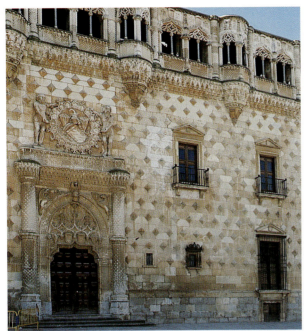

**›3.152 GUADALAJARA, PALACIO DEL DUQUE
DEL INFANTANDO,** from 1461–92: façade.

This eclectic work, setting Plateresque portal and
window frames into a late-Gothic-Mudéjar context, is
attributed to Juan Guas whose main royal commission
was for S. Juan de los Reyes at Toledo (c. 1480).

**›3.153 COGOLLUDO, PALACIO DE DON
ANTONIO DE MENDOZA:** façade (from c. 1495).

Distantly recalling the Milanese Banco Mediceo or
Ospedale Maggiore confection of Gothic and Renaissance detail – and Michelozzo or Donatello in the style
of the portal – this work is attributed to the Segovian
Lorenzo Vazquez. His most important commission was
for the Colegio de S. Cruz at Valadolid where he had
already inserted an Italianate portal with a semicircular pediment into a rusticated wall.

typical Italian palazzo – which was certainly not alien to
the climatic conditions of much of Iberia – as well as to
early Renaissance decorative motifs, and he was their heir
after protracted struggle with the French. Usurprisingly,
therefore, the application of Classical detail to flamboyant forms at the inception of the Spanish Renaissance was
of exceptional prolixity – indeed, it is called Plateresque
after stone-carving of such elaborate intricacy that it
resembles beaten metalwork. And the authors of extreme
floridity in Spanish retable façade design, the Flemish
were no less fecund in substituting Classical motifs for
stylized vegetation: indeed they rivalled even the most
prolix of the Lombards.**3.152, 3.158**

The initial hybrid phase may be represented by works
ranging from those commissioned by grandees in the
provinces **3.153** to charitable foundations in the royal capitals:**3.154, 3.155** it persisted well beyond the first quarter of
the century.**3.156, 3.157** Meanwhile, however, the new king

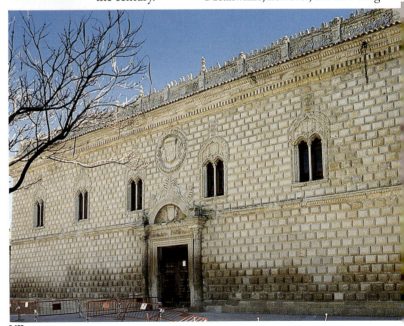

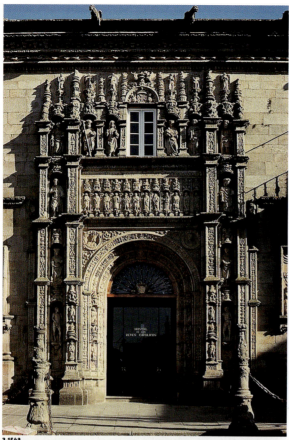

3.154a

3.154b

The complex, commissioned in 1499 by the joint
monarchs to provide accommodation for pilgrims, was
designed on the cruciform Italian hospital model by
Enrique Egas. The portal is attributed to Martin de Blas.

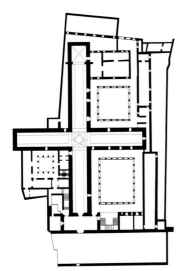

3.155a @ 1:2000

›**3.155 TOLEDO, HOSPITAL DE S. CRUZ,**
1504–14: (a) plan, (b) portal (Coverrubias, after 1515),
(c) open-cage staircase (Egas and Covarubbias).

The general scheme, related to the one at Santiago,
is attributed to Enrique de Egas: Alonso de Covarubbias was responsible for much of the embellishment.
The precedent for opening the staircase cage to expose
rectangular returns to view (rather than confining parallel flights to tunnels as elsewhere) was set at S. Juan
de los Reyes in Toledo (1504): unlike the latter, the S.
Cruz composition is unscreened from the court – like
the central staircase of the castle of Calahorra (1509,
attributed to the Genoese Michele Carlone and more
Italianate in its Classicizing detail than its contemporaries in Spain).

3.155b

3.155c

3.156a

3.156b

3.156c

›3.156 SALAMANCA: (a) University (founded by King Alfonso of León in 1230), portal (commissioned by the Catholic Monarchs, whose portrait medallion is the centrepiece, but not completed for at least a decade after Ferdinand's death in 1516); (b, c) S. Esteban (from 1524), retable façade and cloister.

S. Esteban is the major surviving work of Juan de Álava (active for some thirty years until c. 1537). Álava, noted for articulating Gothic structure with elements of debased Classical Orders, may also have been responsible for the incorporation of Classicizing detail into a thoroughly late-Gothic context on the retable-like University portal.

3.157

›3.157 SEVILLE, CASA DE AYUNTAMIENTO,
1527 and later: exterior from the south-east.
    Lombard influence is apparent in the lush articula-
tion, especially the incorporation of candelabra-like
pilasters: the architect was Diego de Riano who had
been called from Valladolid in 1517 to produce designs
for the chapter of the cathedral.

›3.158 COLOGNE, S. MARIA-IM-KAPITOL,
SCREEN, 1523: by the Flemish artist Jan van Roome.

Charles I (Duke of Burgundy and Emperor) imported
Italians to regulate a new departure in Spain – but that
must be viewed in the light of developments in contemporary Italy.

3.158

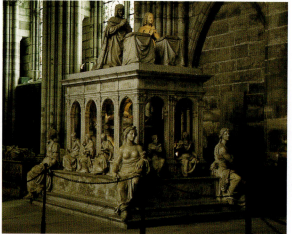

›3.159 S. DENIS, ABBEY CHURCH: tomb of
Louis XII (Antonio and Giovanni Giusti, c. 1515).

The deceased are shown living, in prayer above, and
laid out in death on the sarcophagus surrounded by the
Apostles and attended by the Virtues below (after
Andrea Sansovino in Genoa cathedral and S. Maria del
Popolo, Rome, respectively). The introduction of a
miniature freestanding chapel recalls the Visconti
tomb in the Certosa at Pavia – as does the application
of low-relief ornament to the panelled shafts of the
pilasters. However, the tombs of Louis XI and Charles
VIII (lost) provided the French precedents for the superimposition of an image of the deceased in prayer and
the representation of the corpse perpetuates the late-
Gothic norm. Charles VIII, at least, was accompanied by
Classicizing images of the Virtues but in roundels
rather than in the round, as here.

The motif of the deceased in living prayer is promi-

FRANCE

Gothic diversity of mass, especially the verticality of the
major elements, set a problem for the Classical designer
bound to effect an harmonious relationship between all
the parts of his building: providing the solution, the
French developed an alternative Renaissance. As we have
seen, they oscillated between an architectonic and an anti-
architectonic approach to the embellishment of form –
between articulating structural forces with the elements of
a structural system and masking them irrationally with a
web of essentially insubordinate ornament. It took them
half a century to effect the transition from the one to the
other in Renaissance terms.

Launched on its brilliant course about the turn of the
16th century, the French Renaissance began with the fashionable adaptation of imperfectly understood Classical
detail, drawn from the Italian Renaissance repertory, to
the essentially un-Classical forms of the Flamboyant. Not
until mid-century did it fully comprehend the intellectual
essence of Florentine Classicism – order and unity based
on symmetry, the harmony of proportions enshrined in
the Orders.

3.163a

nent in the contemporary tomb of the Amboise Cardinal in Rouen cathedral – a lavish confection of the Classical and the Flamboyant.

›**3.160 CAEN, S. PIERRE:** chevet (from 1528).

Attributed to Hector Sohier, the work is Flamboyant in form but ogival arches cede to semicircles on the exterior and fashionably Lombard Classicizing detail – notably the candelabra motif standing for the pinnacle – is preferred to stylized naturalism. Perhaps as much as a decade earlier, a similar approach to interior embellishment had produced the choir screen at Fécamp: the work was commissioned by the abbot, Antoine Bohier, who imported Genoese sculptors to provide him with a tomb in his abbey church.

3.160

The Valois establishment and its entourage succumbed to the fashion for Renaissance decorative motifs through the importation of books and engravings but above all through the exportation of their dynastic ambitions to Naples and Milan. The *seigneurs* who reached Naples saw Alfonso of Aragón's juxtaposition of the antique triumphal arch with the medieval twin-towered portal. Many more would have had first-hand experience of the prolix Lombard synthesis of Gothic and Classical represented most spectacularly at the Certosa of Pavia: there the king was clearly impressed by the tomb of Gian Galeazzo Visconti and his wife, Isabelle de Valois – Louis XII's great-grandmother.**3.159** The lesson of the Certosa were applied to the occasional French church, sometimes with great exuberance,**3.160** but the main interest of the returning lords was in building fashionable new houses and for that the Neapolitan lesson was of greatest import.

As we have seen, the relaxation of the defensive character of the French château responded to the reconsolidation of the power of the central monarchy under the late-15th-century Valois. Then the military mode was retained only for prestige in the context of the courtyard

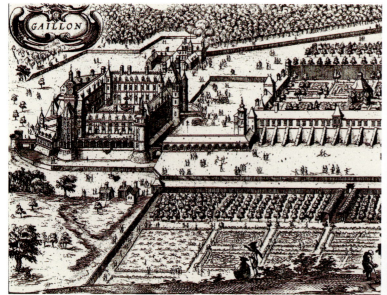

3.161a

3.161b

house. Derived from the old enceinte of walls punctuated with bastions, the ranges (*corps de logis*) which framed the court met in massive towers (*pavillons*): the former normally had rooms aligned in single file (*enfilade*); in the towers stacked rooms were grouped into putative apartments. The varied masses – juxtaposed rather than coherent in their massing – retained the traditional high and flamboyant roofline, open and elaborate staircases, large windows, elegant tracery and naturalistic decorative detail.**2.297, 2.298** The last, of course, was most vulnerable to the fickleness of fashion. Beyond that, most significantly, Aragonese Naples demonstrated how prestige was to be served by the motif of the triumphal arch.**3.79**

In the sumptuous palace built by both French and Italian craftsmen for Cardinal Georges d'Amboise, Archbishop of Rouen, at Gaillon (1502–10), a precocious attempt was made at unifying the disparate elements of the symbolic twin-towered postern by subjecting it to elements of an Order, recalling the pattern of the Roman tri-

›3.161 GAILLON, CHÂTEAU, 1502–10: (a) overview (engraving), (b) entrance portal.

The patron, Cardinal Georges d'Amboise, was Louis XII's Viceroy of Milan. In addition to French builders from Tours entrusted with the bulk of the work on his irregular quadrangular Flamboyant château, he imported Genoese sculptors to furnish the garden and other Lombards to advise on the embellishment of the last phase of building, the entrance range begun in 1508. The uncanonical orders – delicately incised in the Lombard manner – are superimposed to link the mullioned fenestration vertically in the Flamboyant manner but pursuit of Classical coherence extrudes the cornice mouldings round the octagonal towers as stringcourses to bind together the disparate masses of the traditional twin-towered portal.

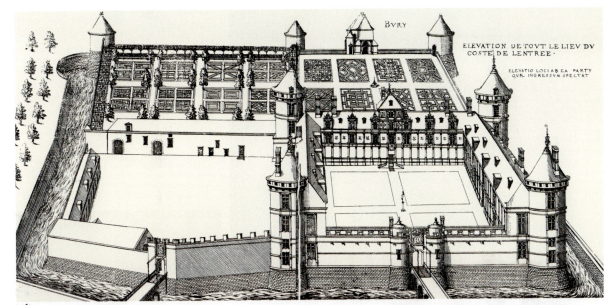

BURY

ELEVATION DE TOVT LE LIEV DV
COSTE DE LENTREE ·

ELEVATIO LOCI AB EA PARTE
QVÆ INGRESSVM SPECTAT

3.162

>3.162 BURY, CHÂTEAU, from 1511, destroyed:
bird's-eye perspective (J.A. du Cerceau).

The patron was Louis XII's courtier, Florimond
Robertet. Classical regularity is brought to the late-
medieval quadrangle but prestige claimed the retention of the once-defensive moat, twin-towered
gatehouse and cylindrical bastions. The court framed
by three ranges of living accommodation (*corps de
logis*) and an entrance screen, with towers (*pavillons*)
at all four corners and in the centre of the main block
opposite the entrance, was to remain standard for well
over a century.

>3.163 CHENONCEAU, CHÂTEAU, from 1515: (a,
pages 870–871) general view from the south with original building right, later 16th century addition left, (b)
entrance front.

The first phase of construction produced a square
block, turreted at the corners, with a longitudinal central corridor (from the entrance in the east front) and a
lateral central staircase between the two rooms of the
northern range: the staircase is of the Italian type, with
parallel flights in a double tunnel, rather than the usual
French spiral. The patron was the financier Thomas
Bohier, brother of Abbot Antoine of Fécamp.

umphal arch.**3.161** Further, the château of Bury (1511, lost)
marked a prophetic regularization of the medieval courtyard and symmetry was imposed on its principal façades,
as in the entrance front at Chenonceau or the garden
façade at Azay-le-Rideau (1518).**3.162–3.164** Azay-le-
Rideau is also precocious in using a three-dimensional, if
uncanonical, Order to imply distinction of vertical mass

3.163b

3.164a

3.164b

›**3.164 AZAY-LE-RIDEAU, CHÂTEAU,** from 1518: (a) general view from south, (b, c) detail of staircase vault and court front and staircase.

The patron was the financier Gilles Berthelot, related to the Bohiers by marriage, who fell from grace with François I before the work was completed. The arrangement of two perpendicular wings represents half the late-medieval norm but the traditional round towers are reduced to turrets between which each front is symmetrical. As at Gaillon, superimposed uncanonical Orders link the windows vertically but their sill and cornice mouldings are extruded laterally to provide a unifying grid. The Orders are of little substance except where they grasp the attenuated colonettes which alone lend projection to the once-open staircase. The latter is of the Flamboyant type, like the dormers, but Pavian in Classicizing detail.

›**3.165 ANGERS, HÔTEL PINCE,** from 1523: the perpendicular fronts of the fore-court.

The Hôtel d'Alluye at Blois and Hôtel Lallemant at Bourges are prominent quadrangular examples from 1508 and 1518 respectively.

for the staircase pavilion which is Flamboyant in all but the decorative detail. Though deprived of a fully enclosed court, the Hôtel Pince at Angers is an unexcelled example of the comparable 'Classicization' of the late-medieval town house – most sumptuously represented by the hôtel of Jacques Cœur at Bourges.**3.165**

Naturally, the main line of development in the first phase of the French Renaissance may be followed in the

3.164c

3.165

great series of works commissioned by François I, first from 1515 at Blois in the heart of the Touraine where his predecessors had established themselves. Before the decade was out he had embarked on the enormous hunting lodge at Chambord.**3.166, 3.167**

3.166c

Royal spectacle

At Blois, where Louis XII had rebuilt the entrance range of the 13th-century comptal castle, François I began the transformation of the forecourt with the north wing closing obliquely and aligned with the 13th-century Salle des États. Irregular medieval foundations influenced the massing of the building and the fenestration is governed by the internal disposition inherited from the past: while the pilasters might not have been out of place in

3.166a

from 1515: (a) court front with open-cage staircase, (b) town front with 'loggias', (c) guard chamber chimneypiece, (d) cabinet with panelling of c. 1520 adapted for Henri II.

3.166d

early Renaissance Lombardy, the conception in plan and elevation is still essentially non-Classical despite the Classicizing grid extended over the plain surfaces of the court façade. That is insubstantial in the manner of its day but in stark contrast is the monumental translation of the Flamboyant open-cage spiral staircase on which the wing was originally centred. Contrast again is presented by the outer façade overlooking the town from its embanked cliff: superimposed loggia-like window arcades emulate the garden front of the Palazzo Piccalomini at Pienza or, more immediately, the Vatican cortile of S. Damaso, but the buttressing dictated the doubling of the pilasters in the outer bays in approximation of the rhythm of the triumphal arch as applied by Bramante to the Belvedere.

Chambord is a rigorously symmetrical transformation of the feudal donjon and bailey but the original Italianate scheme was not fully realized:

3.166b

superimposed arcades – blind on the upper levels – ceded to the insubstantial grid of uncanonical orders which is the hallmark of early French Renaissance articulation; a tunnel staircase was replaced by a double spiral of native inspiration. The latter's lantern provides the centrepiece of a roofscape unimaginable in Italy, despite its Classical motifs, but highly characteristic of *Flamboyante* France. Indeed, Chambord descends directly from the fantasies illustrated by the Limbourg brothers for the Duc de Berry and the precedent for the habilitation of donjon and bailey was set for that magnate's brother, King Charles V, at Vincennes. There the rooms of the king's suite in the keep were superimposed on two storeys; here, served by the spectacular staircase in the centre, they were ordered horizontally like the apartments of Giuliano da Sangallo's Medici villa at Poggio a Caiano.

›**3.167 CHAMBORD, CHÂTEAU,** from 1519: (a) plan, (b) general view from west, (c) roof and chimney detail, (d) staircase.

Work began in 1519 but was interrupted by the Italian campaign of 1524 and the patron's imprisonment at Madrid after the disastrous battle of Pavia two years later. A decade after the site was reactivated, the main block was being roofed (1537): the wings followed between 1539 and the mid-1550s. Once attributed to Leonardo da Vinci, the design is now generally credited to Domenico da Cortona, an associate of Giuliano da Sangallo: known through 17th-century drawings of the original model, it was evidently interpreted by French master-masons.

3.167b

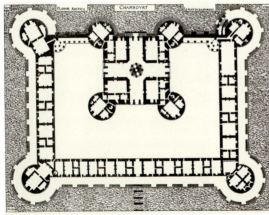

3.167a @ 1:2500

3.167c

3.167d

Work on the great royal projects was halted during the war of 1524–26 and the king's captivity in Madrid. It began again immediately after peace was settled but the royal attention turned to the Île-de-France where his architects laid the foundations for the alternative to the homogeneous Italian tradition of revived Classicism which would largely prevail in the post-Gothic north.

ACROSS THE CHANNEL AND BEYOND THE RHINE

Two years before Louis XII was interred in Milanese style at S. Denis, Henry VII of England joined his queen in the tomb prepared for him by the Florentine Pietro Torrigiani at Westminster. Henry VIII commissioned a larger work which was not to be realized but Torrigiani satisfied considerable demand from non-royal patrons: applied to the wall of Rolls Chapel in Chancery Lane, his monument to Dr John Young of c. 1516 first transformed a prolific genre. Similarly interpolated out of context in the gatehouse towers of Hampton Court, commemorative medallions of Roman emperors introduced the Renaissance to the exterior of secular building: formerly attributed to Torrigiani, they are now credited to his follower, Giovanni da Maiano.**3.168, 3.169**

The Renaissance in England was confined to the insertion of monuments or furniture for at least a generation. The plain brick surfaces of Hampton Court were not unaccommodating to the exercise but Torrigiani's work is highly incongruous in the extraordinarily flamboyant Perpendicular context of Henry VII's chapel at Westminster. On the other hand, the rather more austere Perpendicular environment of King's College Chapel in Cambridge is not uncomplemented by England's most extensive surviving early Renaissance confection: the screen in the lush French Renaissance style of Gaillon

3.168a

›3.168 PIETRO TORRIGIANI AND THE EARLY ENGLISH RENAISSANCE FUNERARY MONUMENT: (a) for Henry VII and Elizabeth of York (gilt-bronze effigies on marble bier after 1512; London, Westminster Abbey); (b) for Dr John Young (marble and terracotta, after 1516; London, Chancery Lane, Rolls Chapel).

Apparently impressed by Torrigiani's work on the tomb of his grandmother, Lady Margaret Beaufort (commissioned at the end of 1511), Henry VIII commissioned his father's tomb in October 1512. Torrigiani was further commissioned in 1516 to create the altar of Henry VII's chapel (destroyed in the mid-17th century, partially reconstructed from 1932).

3.168b

3.170

inserted from 1533 to the order of Henry VIII, probably under the direction of Maiano.**3.170**

A decade before Torrigiani began his work for Henry VII of England, Emperor Maximilian I embarked on his funerary monument in the Hofkirche at Innsbruck. Near to the Veneto, it incorporates an Italianate bier but the superb figure sculpture for which the ensemble is celebrated is due to artists from Nuremberg.**3.171**

3.169

›3.169 HAMPTON COURT, GATEHOUSE TOWER: Classical medallion (terracotta, 1521).

Giovanni da Maiano, to whom the work is now generally attributed, seems to have been brought to England from Florence by Pietro Torrigiani to work on the altar of Henry VII's chapel and the tomb of Henry VIII at Westminster.

›3.170 CAMBRIDGE, KING'S COLLEGE CHAPEL: choir screen (1533–36).

›3.171 INNSBRUCK, HOFKIRCHE: monument to Emperor Maximilian I (begun 1502, completed 1584).

3.171

Despite the contribution of many Italians, a thorough-going transformation of style in the empire and its sphere of influence lagged behind the Florentine achievement by a century or more, behind France by a generation. Beyond that, as ever more modern ideas were crossing the Alps to affect building with varying degrees of concision in the second quarter of the century, no clear line of development is discernible and any attempt to trace the strands must comprehend those 'modern' ideas. Inevitably, the first phase of Germanic Renaissance was generally hybrid: it may be defined in terms of Flamboyant misunderstanding of the true import of Classicism well into the 1540s.**3.172–3.175**

3.172a

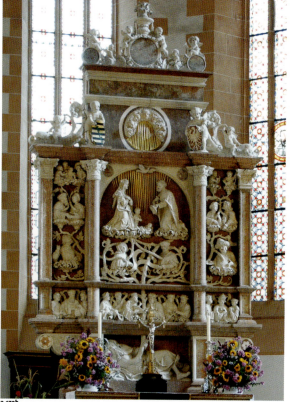

3.172b

›**3.172 PROTO-RENAISSANCE CHURCH FUR-NISHING IN GERMAN-SPEAKING LANDS:** (a) Augsburg, Fuggerkapelle (c. 1510, attributed to Sebastian Lochner in virtue of the initials on the drawing); (b) Annaberg, Annakirche high altar (1519–22); (c) Vienna, Salvatorekapelle (c. 1525, attributable on stylistic grounds to a Comesque artist), portal.

The Fuggerkapelle, at the west end of the church below the later organ, replaces the west choir: except for the late-Gothic vaulting, it is generally recognized as the first manifestation of Italian Renaissance design in the Empire, though a much more Brunelleschian exercise preceded it at Estergom in Hungary for Archbishop Bakocz (1506). In the work for Fugger, the influence of Francesco di Giorgio may be seen in the superimposed square pilaster-piers supporting the semicircular arch which define the entrance from the nave in contrast to the lower aisle arcades, and in the oculus of the western lunette. Within the decade at S. Katherine's church in Augsburg – and elsewhere, the Regensburg of Augsburgian Hans Hieber for example, or the tomb of Frederick the Wise in the Schlosskirche at Wittenberg – piers are replaced by attenuated columns or pilasters with pseudo-Corinthian capitals.

3.172c
More usually Gothic height is achieved with superimposed colonettes of varied uncanonical form – as, for
example, in S. Maria-im-Kapitol, Cologne.³·¹⁵⁸

›3.173   DRESDEN,   RESIDENZSCHLOSS:
Georgbau, court front (Bastien Kramer, from 1530,
destroyed).

Facing the Elbe, the Georgbau was the gate-tower
added to the medieval complex as extended in the
1470: its attribution to Kramer is not undisputed and a
Comesque architect was clearly referred to – or
employed – in the design of the portal. The dressing in
pseudo-Classical guise of medieval forms – especially
stepped gables and turrets – persisted for generations
in German lands.

3.173

3.174a

3.175

›ARCHITECTURE IN CONTEXT »REVIVAL OF CLASSICISM

›3.174 TORGAU, SCHLOSS HERTENFELS: Johann-Freidrichsbau (from c. 1535, by the Hessian master-builder Konrad Krebs): (a) court front, (b, c) east wing portal and oriel detail (d) detail of open-cage staircase.

Krebs's building is exceptional in scale for an early German Renaissance exercise in whole and in part – especially the astonishing open-cage stair tower. Embellished with arabesques in the early French–late-Milanese Renaissance manner, the latter is late-Gothic in its proportions. Symmetry is missed in the spacing of the windows whose scalloped valences echo the cusping of the Meissen Albrechtsburg.[2.328] The window type is carried over to the oriel, heavily charged with Classicizing reliefs and candelabra-like colonnettes, in the centre of north-east wing .

›3.175 BERLIN, JOACHIMSBAU, built from 1538 by the Saxon master Kaspar Theiss with Konrad Krebs as consultant, destroyed: court front.

As here, the Johann-Freidrichsbau at Torgau originally had multitiered gables flanking the staircase cage. As there, similar gables were applied to the early medieval burgfried.

3.174b   3.174c

3.174d

By 1520 the sophistication of Bramante's Lombard contemporaries had reached Poland. The funerary chapel of the Polish King Zygmunt and his Sforza queen in the Wawel cathedral, Krakow, is attributed to Florentine sculptors and recalls the form of Brunelleschi's Old Sacristy at S. Lorenzo – imported into Milan for Portinari - but in its embellishment it recalls Amadeo's Colleoni Chapel at Bergamo.**3.176, 3.48, 3.109** Such sophistication would long remain foreign to Russia.

›3.176 KRAKOW, WAWEL CATHEDRAL: (a, b) Zygmuntowska Chapel (Bartholomeo Berecci, after 1519 and later), exterior and interior with royal tombs.

King Sigismund (Zygmunt) the Old and his son Augustus – the last of the Jagiellonian dynasty – are both interred here: the latter above the former within the red Hungarian marble triumphal arch.

3.176a

3.176b

THE EAST

The ruthless line of Muscovite dukes was descended from a younger son of the northern prince, Alexander Nevski. After the destruction of Vladimir and its principality by the Tatars, Mikhail Khorobrit asserted his independence under the protection of the khans and his heirs steadily absorbed their neighbours, including both Suzdal and

**›3.177 THE SANCTIFIED EMPEROR CON-
STANTINE** with Russian rulers (top left, centre and right respectively) and patron saints (undated icon; Vologda Museum).

Vladimir. Dominance, marked by the removal of the head of the church from Vladimir to the Moscow citadel (kremlin), was secured by Ivan I (1328–41). Prince Dmitri Donskoy (1359–89) successfully championed the nationalist cause against the Tatars at Kulikovo in 1380. Thereafter, success was intermittent but with the absorption of Novgorod, Ivan III (the Great, 1462–1505) was powerful enough to refuse to pay the Tatars any longer and could truly claim to be the Grand Prince, ruler of 'all the Russias'.

Meanwhile the Constantinopolitan Church had achieved accord with Rome at Florence in 1439 but the Russians refused to comply and had asserted the independence of their metropolitan by 1448 – five years before the fall of the eastern capital to the Turks. Ivan III, triumphant over the Tatars, presented himself as the defender of Orthodox Christianity, heir to Byzantium, and major buildings were conceived to satisfy the new pretentions of church and state. To bolster the latter, the grand prince married the niece of the last emperor, Constantine Paleologus. And as on the conception of imperial power, Constantinople remained the dominant influence on architecture.**3.177**

The impact of the Gothic style on Russia had been at best superficial: massive load-bearing walls were not to cede to the counter-opposition of arcuate force. However, the eclecticism richly arrayed for the Monomakhs on the façades of S. Dmitri at Vladimir was furthered with the occasional pointed arch and multilobed gable.**3.178** Ultimately, there were ogee profiles – as on the Dormition cathedral at Zvenigorod which has been dated to the very end of the 14th century, the Trinity cathedral in the great monastery at Zagorsk of 1422, and the contemporary Transfiguration cathedral in the Andronikov Monastery, Moscow.**3.179, 3.180**

The origin of the ogival profile is obscure. An obvious source is Venice, directly or indirectly – the west front of

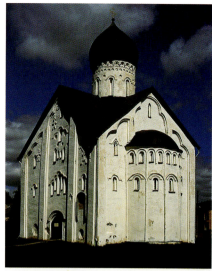

›**3.178 NOVGOROD, CHURCH OF S. THEO-DORE STRATILATES,** 1360: view from south-east.

›**3.179 MOSCOW, ANDRONIKOV MON-ASTERY** (Spas-Androniikov), cathedral of the Saviour (Spasski sobor, 1422).

The earliest of Moscow's churches to survive in any degree of completeness, the foundation may date from as early as 1410. The traditional symmetry of the quincunx, ceded at Zagorsk, is restored as the basis for multiple zakomari and their purely decorative blind progeny (kokoshniki). These diminish in size as they ascend to the single dome as the external expression of corbelled structure. The resulting richly articulated pyramidal profile was to be highly influential – not least as the inception of the tower form of the 16th-century Muscovite church.

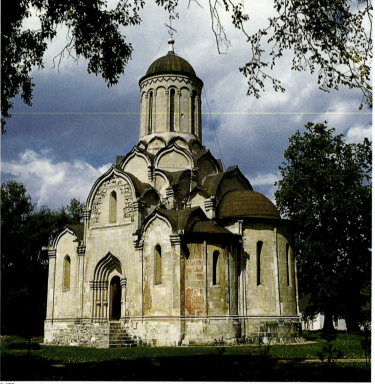

3.179

3.180a

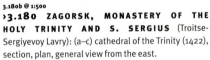

3.180b @ 1:500

3.180c

›3.180 ZAGORSK, MONASTERY OF THE HOLY TRINITY AND S. SERGIUS (Troitse-Sergiyevoy Lavry): (a–c) cathedral of the Trinity (1422), section, plan, general view from the east.

The hermitage of S. Sergius of Radonezh, established c. 1340, developed into the pre-eminent Muscovite monastery dedicated to spiritual reform – but also to support the nationalist cause of the Muscovite princes – from which missionary colonists set out for northern Russia. The Trinity cathedral was built by the Grand Prince Vasili I in collaboration with S. Sergius's godson, Prince Yuri of Zvenigorod, whose domain owed allegiance to the Muscovite ruler: the type descends from mid-12th-century Polotsk and is represented as far away as Serbian Gracanica (AIC1, page 835) but the model was the Assumption cathedral in the Zvenigorod palace compound – but with marked austerity and uncanonical asymmetry resulting from the amalgamation of the eastern quincunx range with the sanctuary.

S. Marco introduced the motif to spectacular prominence and there are echoes in 14th-century Constantinople (AIC1, pages 835ff). Less obviously, the Tatars may have found it in late-Ilkhanid or Timurid works (AIC3, pages 378, 399). It was echoed by the finial of domes and the return of the curves at base, effecting the characteristic onion-shape, which was supposedly transmitted from Timurid domains.

Ivan III began rebuilding the Moscow Kremlin on an imperial scale worthy of the 'Third Rome' – as his seat aimed to be. Within its impressive walls, around the central ceremonial square, he called for emulation of the cathedrals of Vladimir, Kiev and ultimately Constantinople to provide for the coronation, marriage and burial of his descendants in grand structures. In consequence, the first two of these are essentially Byzantine in form and Romanesque in detail. The third marks a new departure initiated by Italian architects imported towards the end of the reign but the first product is characteristic of early Renaissance works elsewhere beyond Italy in the application of debased Classical motifs to the traditional medieval forms.**3.181**

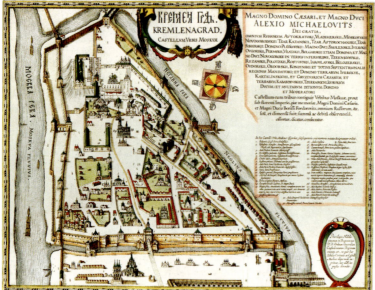

3.181a

The Kremlin of Ivan the Great

Founded in the 10th century, the citadel on the Borovitski hill at the confluence of the Moscow and Neglinnaya rivers was developed in the mid-12th century as an outpost of the principality of Vladimir. The wooden ramparts were burned by the Tatars but their replacements were enlarged by Ivan I and transformed in stone under Dmitri Donskoy. By the end of the 15th century, Ivan III had thickened the walls massively in brick with the help of imported Italians familiar with the regular geometry of fortification promoted by Francesco di Giorgio but constrained by the existing irregular triangle. First in the field was Aristotele Fioravanti from Bologna who had worked for the Sforza with Filarete in Milan from 1458. He was followed by Pietro Antonio Solario, also from Milan, and several other northern Italians

3.181b

3.181c

›3.181 MOSCOW, KREMLIN: (a) general view from the east with the bell tower of Ivan the Great (as extended laterally in the 1530s and vertically in 1600; (b, c) plan (1601), and diagrammatic perspective (c.

1520) with (1) Assumption, (2) Annunciation, (3) Virgin's Veil, (4) Faceted Palace, (5) bell tower, (6) Archangel Mikhail, (7) Apostle Philip; (d–h) Faceted Palace and cathedral of the Assumption (Upenski), plan of cathedral, interior details of cathedral and palace; (i–k) cathedral of the Annunciation (Blagoveshchenski), plan, section and exterior from the north-east; (l–n) cathedral of the Archangel Mikhail (Arkhangelski), section, plan and exterior from the north-west; (o) bell tower.

As built from 1505 by Marco Bono, S. Ivan's bell-tower (subsequently called Kolokolnya 'Ivan Veliki' in honour of Ivan the Great) had two tiers: the upper storey and dome were added after 1600. The adjoining belfry was begun by Petrok Mali in 1532: the articulation of the substructure remains bizarre, in the main, but aedicules set into scallop-shell niches announce the next stage of the Renaissance in Moscow.

surnamed Friazin ('Frank' or foreigner) by their hosts. Assisted by Mark Friazin (Marco Ruffo), Solario transformed the palace in stone: of their work the main surviving element is the 'Faceted Palace' (Granovitaya Palata) of c. 1490: the rustication resembles that of the unfinished Venetian Ca' del Duca begun c. 1460 for Francesco Sforza. The contemporary elaboration of the gate towers was clearly designed to assert the prestige of the regime – and the process was furthered over the following century.

Stone had been used for the first time in the construction of the cathedrals of the Dormition (Upenski), the Archangel Mikhail (Arkhangelski) and the bell-tower church of S. Ivan Klimakos (Ivan Lestvichnik) under Ivan I. The Annunciation (Blagoveshchenski) and Birth of the Virgin (Bogoroditsa) followed under Donskoy. Ivan III ordered the reconstruction of the first four of these on a grander scale: the Upenski by Aristotele Fioravanti, the Arkhangelski by Alvise Lambertini da Montagnana (an

3.181d

3.181f

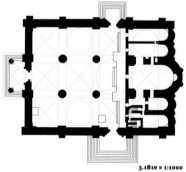

3.181e ▪ 1:1000

3.181g

3.181h

associate of Codussi in Venice, known in Russia as Aleviz Friazin Novi), the bell tower by Marco Bono (Bon Friazin) and the Blagoveshchenski by masons from Pskov. On site in the late-1480s, the last simultaneously built the new cathedral of the Deposition of the Robe (or Miracle of the Virgin's Veil, Tserkov Rizpolozheniya) on the model of the Zagorsk Trinity but with symmetry restored. Limestone was supplemented by more versatile brick at the instigation of the Italians, especially in the vaulting of large space.

The Upenski, the seat of the patriarch in life and death, the theatre of the imperial coronation, owes its form not to Italian precedent but to emulation of the Vladimir Uspenski.[1.105] As in the nucleus of the model, the quincunx is separated from multiple apses by the iconostasis but it bears all five domes as there are no surrounding galleries or narthex. Ivan I's church was replaced on those lines by local Muscovite architects in 1472 but the new work was destroyed on completion in 1474 by an earthquake. As a noted engineer, Aristotele Fioravanti was called in for the rebuilding and managed to transform the traditional quincunx – with its dominant crossing – into a hall of twelve commensurate bays defined by four relatively slender columns: the substitution of brick groin vaults for stone tunnels in the undomed bays lightened the load and enhanced the lighting, oak beams lent resilience to the deep foundations and iron tie-rods braced the stone walls in the absence of galleries. Later modifications include the introduction of onion domes in the mid-1560s and of groin vaulting c. 1625. The interior was redecorated from c. 1670. From its consecration it was to be the model for the most important official civic and monastic commissions throughout Russia.

The Blagoveshchenski, the royal chapel connected with the Granovitaya Palata, was first built in stone in the late-14th century, replaced on the quincunx formula with three relatively shallow eastern apses in 1416 and rebuilt again from 1483: to enhance the impact of the church on the cathedral square to its east, the corner bays are domed and the apses are embellished with the miniature blind arcading of the latest works at Vladimir and Bogoliubovo – or the lower façades of the nearby Upenski; the zakomari are ogival in profile and surmounted by one range of kokoshniki. The south gallery was enclosed and reworked in 1562 after the style of the Arkhangelski.

3.181i

3.181j

3.181k @ 1:1000

3.181l

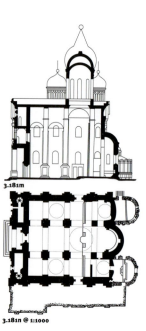

3.181m

3.181n @ 1:1000

The Arkhangelski, built over foundations of 1333, was the royal necropolis: Novo, who seems to have come from the Veneto, reproduced a traditional quincunx, extended east into a tripartite sanctuary with central apse, and introduced a narrow narthex with private chambers for the royal women. The exterior, five bays by three, was the first in Russia to be articulated with pilasters – uncanonical Corinthian superimposed in two tiers with similar stringcourse and cornice – and crowned with segmental zakomari framing scallop shells in the manner of Carducci – and Bramante.

3.1810

CONCLUSION

Ivan the Great's son Vasili III (1505–33) completed his father's work on the Kremlin, the nucleus of the Third Rome. He also completed the annexation of Great Russian domains and began to expand beyond them: when his son, Ivan IV, came of age he was crowned with the title of Tsar. Thus a new territorial empire, the ultimate heir to Rome in the east, was established just as the major provinces of the western empire were asserting themselves as nation states – not least those which provided the power base of the titular Holy Roman Emperor himself.

The death of Leo X towards the end of 1521 completed the change of cast in the tragedy played out on the stage of western European history in the second half of the second decade of the 16th century. And there were more remote – if no less significant – deaths in the subplot recently opened with the revelation of a New World: Montezuma, the last effective Aztec emperor, and Atahuallpa, the last effective Inca of Peru, succumbed to the Spanish *conquistadores* in 1520 and 1533 respectively.

Towards the end of the second decade of the century the act changed too. If the main theme was the eclipse of empire by nation states – or, rather, autocratic monarchies forged from the territories of Europe's main linguistic groups – the plot turned on the protest of a German priest against the corruption of S. Peter's see and the curtain came down on the old, unreformed church – indeed on the reality of a truly catholic church. The new play would open to the confusion of national aspiration and ecclesiastical reform – and colonial rivalry as the main subplot.

The compilation of Martin Luther's list of 95 theses on the failings of the ecclesiastical establishment in 1517 – occasioned immediately by the means and morality bent to the account of Pope Leo X's extravagance – must be seen against the background of a century of stifled reform.

Beyond an end to specific venalities, freedom of conscience was the overarching demand. Freedom of the spirit – from dogma and superstition and imposed orthodoxy – was to be the essential aspiration of modern man, citizen of the nation state. And the aspiration of the modern artist was to freedom of personal genius – liberation to surmount the constraints of inherited convention or precept to expressionistic purpose. Ironically enough, if the first of these is at last clearly articulated in opposition to all that Leo X represented, the second was precociously promoted by the architects who served that luxurious pope with works which ushered in a new era – and, therefore, with which the last volume of this series will begin.

Aspirations to freedom of the individual heart and mind are humanist, of course, familiar to the Hellenistic past recalled by a wide range of late-medieval thinkers, formative of the future. In terms of effecting those aspirations, thus, if a date is sought for departure from the 'Middle Ages' to 'modernity' under the inspiration of 'antiquity', one might well look to the end of the second decade of the 16th century.

GLOSSARY

ABACUS flat slab forming the top of a capital.

ADDORSED 'back to back' (of, for example, columns).

AEDICULE ornamental niche housing a sacred image, for example.

AISLE side passage of a church or temple, running parallel to the nave and separated from it by columns or piers.

ALCÁZAR any of a series of palaces built by the Moors in Spain. From Arabic *al qasr*.

ALTAR focus of attention in religious ritual; the communion table in a Christian church.

AMBULATORY semicircular or polygonal arcade or walkway surrounding, for example, a sanctuary.

AMPHITHEATRE more or less circular theatre, with banks of seats surrounding the performance space.

APSE semicircular domed or vaulted space, especially at one end of a basilica, hence **APSIDAL**, in the shape of an apse.

ARCADE series of arches supported by columns, sometimes paired and covered so as to form a walkway. Hence **BLIND ARCADE**, a series of arches applied to a wall as decoration.

ARCH curved load-bearing masonry structure spanning an opening. Formed of wedge-shaped bricks or blocks of stone held together by their mutual pressure.

    CUSPED composed of two or more arcs with a cusp at their intersection.

    DIAPHRAGM in which the area from springing line to apex is made blind with an infill.

    OGEE composed of two cyma reversa mouldings meeting head to head at the apex.

    STILTED in which an interpolated pier raises the springing line above the impost.

ARCHITRAVE one of the three principal elements of an entablature, positioned immediately above the capital of a column, and supporting the frieze and cornice.

ARCUATE shaped like an arch. Hence (of a building) **ARCUATED**, deploying arch structures (as opposed to trabeated).

ARTESONADO coffered ceiling formed of decorative wood panels and interlaced beams.

ASHLAR masonry cut and laid to present a smooth finished surface (as opposed to, for example, Cyclopean or rubble construction).

ATRIUM entrance-hall or courtyard, often open to the sky.

ATTIC shallow storey above the main Orders of a façade, or a wall at the top of the entablature concealing the roof.

AULA REGIA public audience chamber or throne room in a royal or imperial court.

BAILEY castle courtyard protected by outer defensive wall.

BALDACHINO canopy raised on columns over an altar or tomb.

BALUSTER short column or pillar, usually bulbous towards the base, supporting a rail.

BALUSTRADE a row of balusters supporting a rail.

BAPTISTRY building, adjunct to a church, dedicated to baptism.

BARBICAN a fortified gate or tower projecting from a castle's outer wall and defending its entrance.

BARTIZAN corner turret overhanging the walls of a castle.

BASILICA church, temple or other public building, consisting principally of a colonnaded rectangular space with an apse at one end, generally enclosed by an ambulatory, or having a central nave and side aisles, and lit by a clerestory.

BASTIDE one of a series of towns built as centres of colonization and defence in Languedoc, Gascony and Aquitaine in the 13th and 14th centuries. Most are planned on a grid on the Roman *castrum* model.

BASTILLE fortified tower, originally an outlying bulwark protecting a castle.

BASTION structure projecting from the angle of a defensive wall enabling enhanced vision and mobility for a garrison.

BATTERING reinforcement of walls and column bases by building sloping supporting structure.

BAY one of a series of compartments of the interior of a building, the divisions being created by piers or columns, for example.

BELFRY bell tower or the particular room in a bell tower where the bells are hung.

BELVEDERE open-sided roofed structure, freestanding or situated on the roof of a building, placed so as to command a view.

BOSS ornamental projection at the apices where the ribs of a vault meet.

BURGFRIED German castle keep; also, the productive area administered from a castle.

BUTTRESS support, usually stone, built against or adjacent to a wall to reinforce or take a load.

CAMPANILE bell tower, usually freestanding.

CANOPY roof for a niche or statue, often supported by slender poles.

CANOPY VAULT, *see* **VAULT, CANOPY**.

CAPITAL top part of a column, supporting the entablature, wider than the body of the shaft, usually formed and decorated more or less elaborately.

CATHEDRAL large church, the focal point for a bishop in his diocese.

CAVETTO concave moulding with a quarter-circular cross-section.

CENTRALIZED PLAN building design in which the structure is symmetrical in plan around the centre, allowing for reflection about both 90- and 180-degree axes.

CHANCEL part of a church where the clergy and choir are ranged, separated by screen or railing from the main body of the building.

CHANTRY CHAPEL chapel dedicated to the chanting of masses to save the soul of the sponsor.

CHAPEL subsidiary space having its own altar, situated within a larger church or cathedral.

CHAPTER assembly of canons in a cathedral or abbot and senior monks in a monastery, responsible for managing institutional affairs.

CHAPTERHOUSE room or building within or adjacent to a monastery or cathedral, in which the chapter meets.

CHARTERHOUSE (French *chartreuse*) Carthusian monastery.

CHEVET apse at the east end of a church wherein there is an ambulatory with chapels or miniature apses radiating off it.

CHEVRON decorative moulding composed of a zigzag pattern.

CHIAROSCURO the use of light and shadow in a painting, creating the illusions of depth and volume, often to dramatic effect.

CHOIR area of a church near the altar, in which the choir (singers) sit.

CIBORIUM canopy raised on columns so as to form a covering above an altar or tomb, for example.

CLERESTORY windowed upper level, providing light from above for a double-storey interior.

CLOISTER covered arcade, often running around the perimeter of an open courtyard.

COFFERING decoration of a ceiling or vault, for example, with sunken rectangular or other polygonal panels.

COLONNADE line of regularly spaced columns.

COLONNETTE small column, decorative and/or functional.

COLUMN vertical member, usually circular in cross-section, functionally structural or ornamental or both, comprising (usually) a base, shaft, and capital.

COLUMN, ENGAGED column which does not stand completely proud of a wall, either having stone ties or being partially sunk into the wall, though not so much as a pilaster.

CONTRAPOSSTO Italian for 'counterpoise': in figure sculpture, a pose in which the body is balanced and gracefully curved and weight appears to be taken by one leg.

CORBEL support bracket, usually stone, for a beam or other horizontal member. Hence **CORBELLED**, forming a stepped roof by deploying progressively overlapping corbels.

CORINTHIAN ORDER *see* Order, Corinthian.

CORNICE projecting moulding forming the top part of an entablature. More generally, a horizontal ornamental moulding projecting at the top of a wall or other structure.

CORTILE arcaded courtyard in an Italian palazzo.

COSMATESQUE geometric ornamental inlaid mosaic work named after the 12th-century Roman Cosmati family – principally Lorenzo and Jacopo Cosmati – who developed but did not invent the style.

COVE/COVING curved concave moulding forming or covering the junction between wall and ceiling.

CRENELLATION indentation in a parapet.

CROCKET carved ornament usually in the form of a curled leaf.

CROSSING the area where the transept of a church crosses the nave and chancel, often surmounted by a tower.

CRYPT underground chamber, often beneath the chancel of a church.

CURTAIN WALL defensive wall of a castle.

CUSP projection formed between two arcs, especially in stone tracery, hence **CUSPED**.

CYCLOPEAN masonry made up of massive irregular blocks of undressed stone.

CYMA RECTA wave-shaped moulding, usually forming all or part of a cornice, the upper part being convex and the lower concave.

CYMA REVERSA wave-shaped moulding, usually forming all or part of a cornice, the upper part being concave and the lower convex.

DADO the middle part, between base and cornice, of, for instance, a pedestal, or the lower part of a wall treated as a continuous pedestal.

DECORATED an English version of the High Gothic Rayonnant style characterized by the decorative use of tracery compounded by lavish painted and carved embellishment.

DIAPERWORK repeated pattern in brick or tile, for example, often involving diamond shapes.

DIAPHRAGM ARCH, *see* **ARCH, DIAPHRAGM**.

DOGE Venice's chief magistrate.

DOME more or less hemispherical roof or vault, hence domical.

DONJON French term denoting the keep or main tower protected by the walls of a castle.

DORIC ORDER *see* Order, Doric.

DORMITORY building or chamber in which monks slept.

EAVES the part of a roof which overhangs the outer face of a wall.

ENCEINTE the whole fortified area of a castle.

EN ECHELON disposed in parallel, like the rungs of a ladder.

ENGAGED COLUMN, *see* **COLUMN, ENGAGED**.

ENTABLATURE that part of the façade of a church, etc., which is immediately above the columns, and is generally composed of architrave, frieze and cornice.

EXEDRA recess, usually apsidal, containing seats.

EXONARTHEX extension to the narthex of a church, formed by the aisles.

FAN VAULT, *see* **VAULT, FAN**.

FASTIGIUM pediment or other structure in the shape more or less of the gable end of a house, especially when dignifying the entrance to a temple precinct or palace, hence a place of epiphany.

FILIGREE decorative work formed of a mesh or by piercing material to give the impression of a mesh.

FINIAL ornament at the top of a gable or roof, for example.

FLAMBOYANT highly decorative late-Gothic style of architecture developed in France in the late-14th and 15th centuries.

FLYING BUTTRESS an arch and more or less freestanding buttress which together take the load of a roof, for example.

FONT freestanding basin, usually of stone, sited in a church for use in the Christian baptism ritual.

FRESCO method of painting done on plaster which is not yet dry, hence also the resultant artefact.

FRIEZE the middle part of an entablature, above the architrave and below the cornice. More generally, any horizontal strip decorated in relief.

FRONTISPIECE principal entrance and its surround, usually distinguished by decoration and often standing proud of the façade in which it sits.

GABLE more or less triangular vertical area formed by the ends of the inclined planes of a pitched roof.

GALLERY upper storey projecting from the interior of a building, and overlooking the main interior space.

GLACIS slope or ramp in front of a defensive wall.

GOLDEN SECTION architectural proportions thought to produce an effect particularly pleasing to the eye, whereby, for example, the ratio of width to length equals the ratio of length to (width plus length).

GOTHIC ARCHITECTURE style featuring pointed arches, rib vaults and flying buttresses, which prevailed in Western Europe roughly from the 12th to the 16th century.

GREEK CROSS cross with four arms of equal length.

GROIN rib formed at the intersection of two vaults.

GROIN VAULT, *see* **VAULT, GROIN.**

GUTTAE projections, more or less conical in form, carved beneath the triglyphs of a Doric entablature.

HALL CHURCH church in which nave and aisles are of equal height, or nearly so, often under a single roof.

ICON image of a sacred subject, often acquiring sacred significance in its own right. Hence **ICONIC**, possessing sacred significance.

ICONOSTASIS screen separating the nave from the sanctuary in a Byzantine church, latterly used for placing icons.

IMPOST structural member – usually in the form of a moulding or block – at the top of a pillar, for example, on which an arch rests.

INFIRMARY building dedicated to the care of the sick within a religious institution.

IONIC ORDER *see* Order, Ionic.

IWAN vaulted hall or recess opening off a court.

JAMB side of a doorway or window frame.

JOISTS horizontal timbers typically supporting a floor.

KEEP main tower of a castle, providing living accommodation.

KOKOSHNIKI style of Russian architecture employing layers of blind pointed corbelled arches.

KREMLIN Russian term for a fortress or castle.

LADY CHAPEL chapel dedicated to the Virgin Mary.

LANCET arch or window rising to a point at its apex.

LANTERN TOWER windowed structure lighting an interior, situated on a roof, often at the apex of a dome.

LATIN CROSS cross with one arm longer than the other three.

LIERNE short intermediate rib, often decorative rather than structural.

LINTEL horizontal member over a window or doorway, or bridging the gap between two columns or piers.

LOGGIA gallery open to the elements on one side.

LUNETTE semicircular window or recess, usually at the base of a dome or vault.

MACHICOLATION gallery or parapet projecting on corbels from the outside of defensive walls, with holes from which missiles might be dropped or thrown.

MANOR feudal estate, usually with a demesne farmed directly for the benefit of the lord of the manor and other land granted to tenants in return for rents, labour or goods.

MANUELINE ARCHITECTURE late-Gothic style developed in Portugal (and named after King Manuel I, 1495–1521) in which maritime imagery and Spanish, Italian and Flemish influences were brought together with singularly lavish results.

MAUSOLEUM building providing a monumental carapace for a tomb.

MERLON solid part of a battlement providing protection to defenders sheltering behind it.

METOPE originally the space between the triglyphs in a Doric frieze, and subsequently the panel, often carved in relief, occupying that space.

MINSTER cathedral or major church attached to a monastery.

MONASTERY buildings providing accommodation for a community of monks or nuns.

MOSAIC decoration formed by embedding small coloured tiles (tesserae) in cement.

MOTTE AND BAILEY defence structure composed of a steep mound (motte) usually surmounted by a tower, the whole being situated within a walled courtyard (bailey).

MUDÉJAR architecture based on the use of brick and with a geometrical approach to decoration profoundly influenced by Moorish practice. It was developed from the 12th century by Arabs who remained in Spain after the Christian reconquest.

MULLION vertical element forming subdivisions of a window.

MULTIFOIL much subdivided basically arcuate or circular form of ornament.

MUQARNAS miniature squinch forms used in combination functionally in effecting transition from, for instance, polygonal chamber to domed roof; and/or used decoratively to produce a honeycomb effect.

NARTHEX chamber adjunct to the nave of a church.

NAVE central body of principal interior of, for example, a church.

OCULUS circular window in a church, for example.

OGEE ARCH, *see* **ARCH, OGEE**.

ORATORY small room for prayer; in a Benedictine monastery, a communal prayer room.

ORDER defining feature of Classical architecture, comprising a column – itself usually composed of base, shaft, and capital – together with its entablature.

  CORINTHIAN an evolution from the Ionic Order, characterized by the replacement of the capital volutes with a more elaborate and deeper decorative arrangement. Later Corinthian columns evolved so as to be even taller relative to their base diameters than the Ionic. The entablature retained the comparatively light characteristics of the Ionic.

  DORIC the oldest and most simply functional of the Greek Orders of architecture, characterized by a fluted and tapered column without a base, topped by a usually plain capital, surmounted by a relatively high entablature made up of architrave, frieze, and cornice.

  IONIC slightly later and more elaborate order than the Doric, featuring fluted columns with bases and characteristically topped by a capital with scrolled volutes. The columns typically are taller relative to their base diameters than are the Doric, and are correspondingly less acutely tapered. The entablature is less tall than that of the Ionic, being originally composed of architrave and cornice only, though a frieze became usual later.

PALATINATE area ruled by a count palatine.

PALAZZO in Italy, a mansion or other large and imposing building.

PALISADE defensive structure of wooden stakes driven into the ground.

PARAPET low wall, often protecting a walkway at the top of an outer wall, originally for defensive purposes.

PAREKKLESION funerary chapel built next to a church.

PARISH the smallest ecclesiastical administrative unit, the area under the spiritual eye of one priest.

PASTOPHERIA in the Byzantine church, areas to the sides of the rear of the sanctuary, used by the priests for preparations for ritual.

PAVONAZZETTO type of variegated marble.

PEDESTAL base supporting, for example, a column or statue.

PEDIMENT triangular area of wall, usually a gable, above the entablature, enclosed above by raking cornices.

PENDENTIVE curved concave triangular member used at the corners of a square or polygonal structure so as to enable reconciliation with a domed roof.

PERPENDICULAR late English Gothic architectural style emphasizing verticality and the development of very large windows and fan vaulting.

PFALZ palatinate in south-west Germany.

PIANO NOBILE main, usually the first, floor of a large house or palazzo, location of the important reception rooms.

PIER supporting pillar for wall or roof, often of rectangular cross-section and sometimes formed from a composite mass of masonry columns.

PILASTER pier of rectangular cross-section, more or less integral with and only slightly projecting from the wall it supports.

PINNACLE slender ornamental termination at the top of a gable or buttress, for example, often in the shape of a miniature turret.

PLATERESQUE intricate and decorative stonework, from the Spanish *plata* (silver).

PLINTH rectangular base or base of, for example, a column or wall.

PODIUM continuous base or pedestal consisting of plinth, dado and cornice, to support a series of columns.

PORCH covered entranceway to a building.

PORTA COELI entrance to a sacred building, literally 'gate of heaven'.

PORTAL doorway, usually on the grand scale..

PORTICO entrance to or vestibule of a building, often featuring a colonnade.

POST vertical element in, for example, a trabeated structure.

POSTERN small, cunningly insignificant door or gate to a castle.

PRESBYTERY area reserved for clergy, at the eastern end of a church, in which the main altar is situated.

PULPIT raised structure in church, from which the preacher addresses the congregation.

QASR Arabic term for a castle.

QUADRATBAU choir which is square in plan.

QUATRALOBE area composed of four interlocking circular segments.

QUATREFOIL having a curved shape composed of four subsidiary curves.

QUINCUNX structure composed of an agglomeration of five elements, four being identical and disposed so as to form more or less a hollow square, its centre being filled by the fifth.

QUOIN external corner of a building, where the stones are arranged to form a key pattern.

RAMPART defensive earthwork, usually surrounding a fortress or citadel, often with a stone parapet.

RAYONNANT style of tracery in which the pattern radiates from a central point; the name derives from the characteristic pattern of rose windows.

REFECTORY communal dining hall in a monastery or convent.

RELIEF carving typically of figures, raised from a flat background usually by cutting away more (high relief) or less (low relief) of the material from which they are carved.

RELIQUARY vessel or chamber holding relics of the saints, often in the form of bones or mummified body parts.

REREDOS carved or painted screen in wood or stone, rising from behind an altar.

RETABLE carved screen or reredos rising above and behind the altar, especially in the Spanish tradition.

RETROCHOIR the area behind the high altar in a large church.

REVETMENT decorative reinforced facing for retaining wall.

RIB raised band on a vault or ceiling.

RIB VAULT, *see* **VAULT, RIB**.

ROMANESQUE ARCHITECTURE style featuring massive masonry constructions with groin vaults and round arches, which prevailed in Western Europe roughly from the 8th century to the 12th, when it was superseded by the Gothic.

ROSE WINDOW large circular window, often situated at the west end of a church, with tracery radiating from the centre.

ROTUNDA circular room or building, usually with a domed roof.

SACRISTY room in a church for storing valuable ritual objects.

SANCTUARY the most sacred part of a church, usually where the altar is situated.

SARCOPHAGUS coffin or outer container for a coffin, usually of stone and decorated with carvings.

SCOTIA concave moulding on the base of a column, often between two convex torus mouldings, thus providing an apparently deep channel between them.

SCREEN partition separating one part of an interior from another.

SCREEN WALL false (i.e. non-structural) wall to the front of a building, masking the façade proper.

SCUOLA in Venice, a co-operative institution bringing together citizens from various professions with, originally, religious or charitable goals. Hence a building type to house such an institution.

SFUMATO in painting, a modelling technique using thin glazes to blur outlines and suggest distance.

SGRAFFITO Italian term meaning 'to scratch', a decorative technique in which a layer of plaster is scored to reveal a contrasting colour beneath.

SHAFT more or less cylindrical element of a column rising from the base to the capital.

SOCLE shallow plinth supporting, for example, a piece of sculpture.

SOFFIT the underside of an architectural element in, for example, a cornice or architrave.

SOLAR a chamber, often elevated, providing private accommodation for the household head in a hall dwelling.

SPANDREL triangular space formed by the outer curve of an arch and the horizontal and vertical elements of the (often virtual) rectangle within which the arch sits.

SPIRE elongated conical or pyramidal shape forming the apex of a tower.

SPRINGING the point at which an arch springs from its support.

SQUINCH arch placed across the corner of a square structure so as to form a polygon capable of being roofed with a dome.

STAVE CHURCH timber-framed church with a trabeated structure and plank infill. Once common in north-west Europe.

STELE upright stone marker in shape of column or panel, usually with decorative carving and/or inscription.

STILTED ARCH, *see* **ARCH, STILTED**.

STRINGCOURSE projecting horizontal course of structural elements or moulding.

STUCCO plaster, especially used where decoration is to be applied.

TABERNACLE niche or cupboard, usually housing the consecrated host or sacred relic.

TEMPIETTO small temple or a building in the form of a small temple.

TESSERA small tile made of marble or glass, for example, used in conjunction with others to form a mosaic.

TETRACTYS a set of four components, especially the first tetractys, composed of the numbers 1, 2, 3, 4.

THOLOS dome, either freestanding or forming the centre of a circular building.

TIE-BEAM horizontal beam preventing two other structural components from separating.

TIERCERON third rib interpolated between the main members of a rib vault.

TITHE BARN a barn, usually close to a church, dedicated to storing tithes, the tenth of produce that had to be donated to the church by independent farmers.

TORUS large moulding, typically at base of a column, of more or less semicircular cross-section.

TRABEATED structurally dependent on rectilinear post and beam supports.

TRACERY pattern of ribs or bars inset to ornamental effect into a window or on to a panel.

TRANSEPT that part of the interior of a large church or cathedral which crosses the nave or principal interior space at right angles.

TRANSOM cross-bar or lintel, especially of a window.

TREFOIL having a curved shape composed of three subsidiary curves.

TRIBUNE vaulted apse, often the site of an altar or throne, or a semicircular recess behind the choir of a church, or a vaulted gallery over an aisle and commanding the nave.

TRIFORIUM arcaded corridor facing on to the nave or chancel of a church, situated immediately below the clerestory.

TRIGLYPH block carved with vertical channels, used in a Doric frieze.

TRIUMPHAL ARCH originally a monument commemorating a victory, often taking the form of a massive rectangle penetrated by an arch.

TURRET small tower, often at the angle of a building.

TYMPANUM an area, usually recessed, formed by a lintel below and an arch above.

VAULT structure forming an arched roof over a space.
  BARREL enclosing a more or less hemicylindrical space.
  CANOPY creating a roof for a niche or tomb.

DOMICAL enclosing a more or less hemispherical space.

FAN in which ribs of equal length, spaced equidistantly, are disposed around cones whose closest point of approach creates the apex of the vault.

GROIN enclosing a space composed of two intersecting more or less hemicylindrical shapes.

RIB composed of load-bearing ribs, carrying the material which fills the spaces between them.

TUNNEL enclosing a more or less hemicylindrical space.

VESTIBULE originally the courtyard in front of the entrance to a Greek or Roman house; hallway to a building; space adjunct to a larger room.

VILLA freestanding house, originally a Roman country house.

VOLUTE scroll or spiral ornamental and/or support member, characteristic of Ionic capitals.

VOUSSOIR wedge-shaped stone deployed in building an arch. Hence **VOUSSOIR ARCH**, where such stones are used.

WALLWALK platform around the top of a castle's curtain wall from which defenders might fight.

WARD castle courtyard, bailey.

WESTWORK entrance hall and superstructure at the west end of a Romanesque or Carolingian church.

ZAKOMARI in Russian architecture, semicircular gables.

FURTHER READING

This set of volumes, *Architecture in Context*, is based on a survey series of lectures covering the whole spectrum of architectural history developed over a quarter of a century at the Canterbury School of Architecture. It is therefore impossible, even if it were desirable, to enumerate all the books that I have consulted and, in one way or another, depended on, over that period. Beyond students of architecture, for whom this whole process was initiated, I hope that the present work will provide the general reader with a broad but also reasonably deep introduction to the way our environment has been moulded over the past five thousand years. With this in mind, rather than a bibliography, I hope it will be useful if I provide a rough guide to how I would go about developing a course in further reading, were I starting now.

First, I would consult the *Macmillan Dictionary of Architecture*, as much for the bibliographies attached to each section of each subject as for the individual articles – inevitably some are better than others as different authors naturally bring different standards of scholarship to bear on their products. Second, for greater depth and breadth, I would consult the relevant volumes of *The Pelican History of Art*: now published by Yale University Press, many of these have been updated or, where the text is an historical document in itself, edited with minimal corrections. The quality in these works is in general much more even as each self-contained subject is usually given to one scholar of outstanding academic record. Again, the bibliographies appended to each volume will be an invaluable guide to even broader and deeper reading.

Taschen (under the indefatigable editorship of Henri Stierlin) and Könemann have both published lavishly illustrated multivolume series that have perhaps been over-ambitious and therefore incomplete: the Könemann volumes on Romanesque, Gothic and Renaissance, edited by Rolf Toman (Cologne 1997, 2004, 1995 respectively) offer particularly sumptuous, comprehensively illustrated coverage of both art and architecture.

Third: specific histories of architecture. As any student of the subject knows, the inescapable primer is the work first published in 1896 by Sir Banister Fletcher as *A History of Architecture on the Comparative Method*: that was essentially a catalogue arranged roughly chronologically by area – starting with ancient Egypt and Mesopotamia – but as the method was gradually superseded more room was found in the later-20th-century editions for essential analysis. Focused more specifically on the period covered by this volume (and the next), is David Watkin's enduring *A History of Western Architecture* (London 1986, revised edition 2005). Beyond that, from my view in the 1970s the most useful general survey of architectural history was the multivolume series initiated by Electa in Milan, edited by Pier Luigi Nervi and published in English by Abrams (and later by others): it had its flaws, not least in the relationship of text to illustrations, and much was lost in translation from the authors' native languages into English: that affected the Gothic volume in particular, but obviously not the fine account of Renaissance architecture by Professor Peter Murray. The range of scholars involved was impressive (notwithstanding some flagrant political bias) and, despite their age, some of the material not otherwise easily available is still essential reading.

In particular I would recommend the following monographs and their bibliographies: George Zarnecki, Janet Holt and Tristram Holland (eds.), *English Romanesque Art 1066–1200* (London 1984); Paul Binski, *Becket's Crown: Art and Imagination in Gothic England 1170–1300* (New Haven 2004); Otto von Simson, *The Gothic Cathedral: Origins of Gothic Architecture and the Medieval Concept of Order* (Princeton 1974); Erwin Panofsky, *Gothic Architecture and Scholasticism* (New York 1957); Jean Bony, *French Gothic Architecture of the 12th & 13th Centuries* (Berkeley 1983); Nicola Coldstream, *The Decorated Style: Architecture and Ornament 1240–1360* (Toronto 1994); Norbert Nussbaum, *German Gothic Church Architecture*

(New Haven and London 2000); Wolfgang Müller-Wiener, *Castles of the Crusaders* (New York 1966); William Anderson, *Castles of Europe: From Charlemagne to the Renaissance* (London 1970), M.W. Thompson, *The Decline of the Castle* (Cambridge 1987); Charles-Laurent Salch, *Dictionnaire des Châteaux et des Fortifications du Moyen Âge en France* (Strasbourg 1979); José Ortiz Echagüe, *España: Castillos y Alcazáres* (Madrid 1960); Jonathan Alexander and Paul Binski (eds.), *Age of Chivalry: Art in Plantagenet England 1200–1400* (London 1987); Xavier Barral i Altet (ed.), *Art and Architecture of Spain* (Boston 1998); Peter Kidson and Peter Murray, *A History of English Architecture* (New York 1962); William Craft Brumfield, *A History of Russian Architecture* (Cambridge 1993); Rudolf Wittkower, *Architectural Principles in the Age of Humanism* (New York 1965); Christoph Luitpold Frommel, *The Architecture of the Italian Renaissance* (New York 2007); Henry A. Millon and Vittorio Magnago Lampugnani (eds.), *The Renaissance from Brunelleschi to Michelangelo: The Representation of Architecture* (Milan 1994); Hanno-Walter Kruft, *A History of Architectural Theory* (London 1994); Robert Tavenor, *On Alberti and the Art of Building* (New Haven 1998); Isabelle Hyman (ed.). *Brunelleschi in Perspective* (Englewood Cliffs, N.J. 1974); Samuel Y. Edgerton, Jr, *The Renaissance Rediscovery of Linear Perspective* (New York 1975); Michael Levey, *Early Renaissance and High Renaissance* (Harmondsworth 1967 and 1975).

My own dependence on the contributors to the series cited above will be apparent to even the most cursory reader, and I apologize that it is far too wide-ranging individually to acknowledge here.

FRANKISH KINGDOMS FROM THE 5TH CENTURY TO CHARLEMAGNE

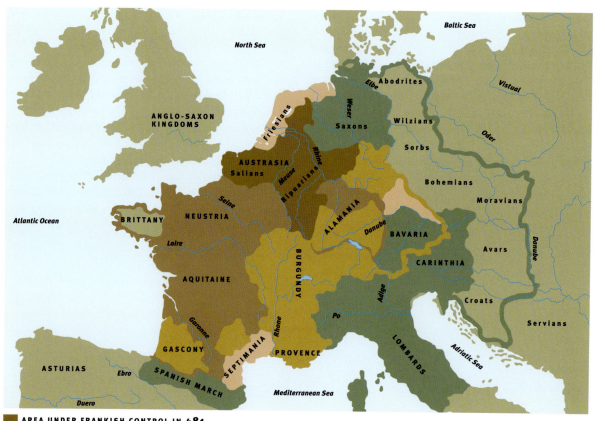

- ■ AREA UNDER FRANKISH CONTROL IN 481
- ■ AREA CONQUERED BY CLOVIS, 486–511
- ■ AREA CONQUERED BETWEEN 531 AND 614
- ■ AREA CONQUERED BETWEEN 714 AND 768
- ■ AREA CONQUERED BY CHARLEMAGNE, 768–814
- — AREAS TRIBUTARY TO CHARLEMAGNE

THE HOLY ROMAN EMPIRE
C. 1100

North Sea

Duchy of Pomerania

KINGDOM OF ENGLAND

Duchy of Saxony

North March

March of Lusatia

KINGDOM OF POLAND

KINGDOM OF THE GERMANS

March of Meissen

County of Flanders

Duchy of Lower Lorraine

Duchy of Franconia

Duchy of Bohemia

Duchy of Normandy

HOLY ROMAN EMPIRE

Blois Champagne

Duchy of Upper Lorraine

Duchy of Swabia

Duchy of Bavaria

Anjou

East March

KINGDOM OF THE FRANKS

Duchy of Burgundy

County of Burgundy

KINGDOM OF HUNGARY

KINGDOM OF BURGUNDY

KINGDOM OF ITALY

KINGDOM OF CROATIA

Duchy of Guyenne

County of Provence

ROMAN EMPIRE

County of Toulouse

Church states

Duchy of Apulia and Calabria

Mediterranean Sea

County of Sicily

―――― EXTENT OF EMPIRE UNDER OTTO I

·········· EXTENT OF EMPIRE UNDER KONRAD II

PRINCIPALITIES OF KIEVAN RUS
C. 1100

CRUSADES

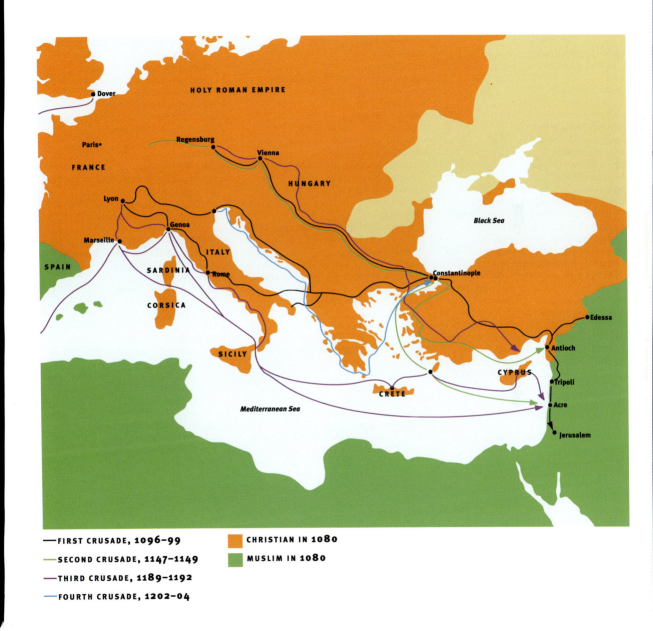

Dover

HOLY ROMAN EMPIRE

Paris•

Regensburg

Vienna

FRANCE

HUNGARY

Lyon

Genoa

Black Sea

Marseille

ITALY

SPAIN

SARDINIA

Rome

CORSICA

Constantinople

Edessa

SICILY

Antioch

CYPRUS

Tripoli

CRETE

Acre

Mediterranean Sea

Jerusalem

—— FIRST CRUSADE, 1096–99   CHRISTIAN IN 1080
—— SECOND CRUSADE, 1147–1149   MUSLIM IN 1080
—— THIRD CRUSADE, 1189–1192
—— FOURTH CRUSADE, 1202–04

INDEX

Page numbers in *italics* denote an illustration or illustration caption.

manors, medieval 7, *7*
mansions, France 576–9
al-Mansur 36
Mantegna, Andrea 697–8, *697*, 786
Mantua 662; Castello di S. Giorgio 698, *698*; Mantegna's house 786, *786*; S. Andrea 746, 747, *748–9*, 749, *750*, 751, 793, 856; S. Sebastiano 746, *746*, 747, *747*
Manuel I, King 471, *472*, 476
Manueline style 471–2, 474
Manzanares el Real: Castillo de Los Mendoza 592, *595*
maps *251*
Marburg: S. Elisabeth 305, 307, *307*, 367
Margat Castle 512–13, *512*, 514–15, *516*
Maria del Mur, S. 51, *51*, *53*
Maria Laach: abbey of 75, *76–7*, *78*
Marianism 264, 664, 680
Marienburg 608, *608*
market squares 612, 617, 620–1
Marksburg *153*, 601
Marmoutier abbey church 67, *67*
Marmoutier-les-Tours: monastery of 10
Marsilius of Padua 252
Martel, Charles 22
Martin, S. 10
Martin V, Pope 260, 653, 654
Masaccio 686–7, *686*, 688, 693
masonry: German late-Gothic virtuoso *448*, *449*; and Lombards 42, 85
mathematics *253*
Matilda of Canossa 97
Matilda, Queen 196, 202, 226
Maximilian I, Emperor 246–7, 248, *248*, 824, 881
Maxstoke Castle 540, *541*
measurement of buildings: and Alberti 740
Medici, Cosimo de' 656, 657, *657*, 668, 725, 727, 731
Medici, Giovanni, *see* Leo X, Pope
Medici, Giuliano 823, *823*
Medici, Giulio, *see* Clement VII, Pope
Medici, Lorenzo de' 656, 657, 661, 668, 778, 818, 823, *823*
Medici, Piero 656, *657*, 818, 823
Medina del Campo: castle 590, *591*
Meillant château (Cher) 579, *579*
Meissen 603–4; Albrechtsburg *606–7*; cathedral 366, *445*, 446
Melle: S. Hilaire 179, *179*
mendicants 351–2, 367, 376–7, 398, 401, 407
merchant houses: Venice 108
Merovingians 11–15, 22
Michael of Canterbury *383*, 387
Michael I, Emperor 25

Michelangelo 829–30, *829*; *Doni Tondo* 829; Sistine chapel *822*
Michelozzo di Bartolomeo 724, 725–6, 727–8, 729, 730, *758*, 759
Milan 238, 656, 657, 760, 785, 823; basilica of S. Vincenzo *43*, 43, 44, *44*; Bramante in 810–15; Castello Sforzesco 660, *701*; cathedral 450, *450–1*; church of S. Satiro 43, *43*; Medici Bank *758*, 759; Ospedale Maggiore 760, *760–1*, 790; S. Ambrogio 43, *83*, 85, *85*, *86*, 87, 98, 812; S. Eustorgio 406–7, *758*; S. Maria della Grazie 812–13, *812*, *813*, 843; S. Maria presso S. Satiro 810, *811*, 812, *812*; S. Nazarro Maggiore 87
Modena cathedral 95, *97*, 226
Moissac priory church 161, *162*
Molfeta cathedral 107
monarchy, *see* kings
monastic cathedrals: Russia 130, *130–1*
monastic plan 37–8, *37*
monasticism 10–11, 36
money 482–4
Mongols 141
Monpazier 617, *617*
Monreale: cathedral of S. Maria Nuova 104, *106*
Mont S. Michel 201, *201*
Montagnana 586, *586*
Monte Cassino (Italy) 10, *10*
Montealegre *150*
Montecassino: abbey of 84
Montefeltro, Federico de 663, *663*, 767
Montepulciano: Madonna di S. Biagio 844, *845*; Palazzo Communale 727, *728*; Palazzo Contucci-dei Monte *860*; Palazzo Cervini *861*; S. Agostino 724–5, *725*
Monteriggioni (Siena) 618, *618*
Montreuil, Pierre de 341, *341*
Moors 23, 144, 249, 250
Moravia 119
mosaics 83, 107, 108, 109, *109*, *110*, 111
Moscow 141; Andronikov Monastery *888*; Kremlin 889–95, *890–1*, *892*, *893*, *894*, 896
motte-and-bailey castles 196–7, *197*, 501
Mozarabacists 49, *50*, 185
Mstislav 130, *132*
Munich: Frauenkirche 440, *441*, 442
music 4, 166
Muslims 22, 23, 592
mysticism 257

Nantes cathedral 428
Naples 237, 239, 485, *652*, 661, 773, 818; Castelnuovo *773*; Palazzo Cuomo 780; papacy

and Araganese 652–5; Poggio Reale villa-palace 780, *781*; Porta Capuana 773, *773*; S. Chiara 405, *407*; S. Giovanni a Carbonnara 848, *848*; S. Maria donna Regina 405, 407
Naranco 46, *48*
Narbonne: cathedral of S. Just 347
Naumburg cathedral 361–2, *361*, *362*, 436
Navarra 36, 144, 223
Neoplatonism/Neoplatonists 267, 671–3
Nera, Fulk 147, *148*, 198, 502, *576*
Neri: church of Intercession on the 137, 138–9, *139*
net vaulting 442
Neustria/Neustrians 13
Nevers: S. Étienne 161, *161*
Newcastle castle 506
Nicholas of Cusa 671, 675, 686
Nicholas II, Pope 98
Nicholas V, Pope 652, 654, 661, 734, 835
Nicholas VI, Pope 260
Nicolo Pisano 406–7, *407*, 409
Niort *502*, 503
nodding ogee arches *397*, *416*, 396
Noier, Geoffrey de 326
Normandy 33, 35, 195, 209, 228
Normans 98, 102, 143, 194–213; castles 17–19, *194*, 195, *195*, 196–7, *197–9*, *198*, *199*, 501; churches (France) 199–213; churches (England) 205–13
Norsemen, *see* Vikings
Norwich cathedral *418*
Novgorod 119, 131, 133–4, 135, 141, 887; cathedral of S. Nikolai 131–2, *132*, 133; cathedral of S. Sofia 128–9, *129*; cathedral of the Yuriev monastery 132, *132*, 133; church of S. Paraskeva Piatnitsa 134, 135; church of S. Theodore Stratilates *888*; church of SS. Pyotr i Pavel 134
Noyon: cathedral of Notre-Dame 277, *277–8*, 279, 290
numerus 737, *739*
Nuremberg 486–7; Frauenkirche *437*; S. Sebaldus 436, *437*; 'Schoner Brunnen' in the Marktplatz *612*; townhouse *628*

Oakham Castle 529, *529*
Ockwells (Bray) 550
Oderisi, Pietro 404, *406*
ogee arch 386, 388, 396, 647
Old Sarum cathedral 206
Oleg of Novgorod 119
Oporto 144
optics 689
Orcival: S. Austremoine 175, *175*